Lecture Notes in Artificial Intelligence 11743

Subseries of Lecture Notes in Computer Science

Series Editors

Randy Goebel
University of Alberta, Edmonton, Canada
Yuzuru Tanaka
Hokkaido University, Sapporo, Japan
Wolfgang Wahlster
DFKI and Saarland University, Saarbrücken, Germany

Founding Editor

Jörg Siekmann
DFKI and Saarland University, Saarbrücken, Germany

More information about this series at http://www.springer.com/series/1244

Haibin Yu · Jinguo Liu ·
Lianqing Liu · Zhaojie Ju ·
Yuwang Liu · Dalin Zhou (Eds.)

Intelligent Robotics and Applications

12th International Conference, ICIRA 2019
Shenyang, China, August 8–11, 2019
Proceedings, Part IV

 Springer

Editors
Haibin Yu
Shenyang Institute of Automation
Shenyang, China

Jinguo Liu
Shenyang Institute of Automation
Shenyang, China

Lianqing Liu
Shenyang Institute of Automation
Shenyang, China

Zhaojie Ju
University of Portsmouth
Portsmouth, UK

Yuwang Liu
Shenyang Institute of Automation
Shenyang, China

Dalin Zhou
University of Portsmouth
Portsmouth, UK

ISSN 0302-9743   ISSN 1611-3349   (electronic)
Lecture Notes in Artificial Intelligence
ISBN 978-3-030-27537-2   ISBN 978-3-030-27538-9   (eBook)
https://doi.org/10.1007/978-3-030-27538-9

LNCS Sublibrary: SL7 – Artificial Intelligence

This Springer imprint is published by the registered company Springer Nature Switzerland AG
The registered company address is: Gewerbestrasse 11, 6330 Cham, Switzerland

Preface

On behalf of the Organizing Committee, we welcome you to the proceedings of the 12th International Conference on Intelligent Robotics and Applications (ICIRA 2019), organized by Shenyang Institute of Automation, Chinese Academy of Sciences, co-organized by Huazhong University of Science and Technology, Shanghai Jiao Tong University, and the University of Portsmouth, technically co-sponsored by the National Natural Science Foundation of China and Springer, and financially sponsored by Shenyang Association for Science and Technology. ICIRA 2019 with the theme of "Robot Era" offered a unique and constructive platform for scientists and engineers throughout the world to present and share their recent research and innovative ideas in the areas of robotics, automation, mechatronics, and applications.

ICIRA 2019 was most successful this year in attracting more than 500 submissions regarding the state-of-the-art development in robotics, automation, and mechatronics. The Program Committee undertook a rigorous review process for selecting the most deserving research for publication. Despite the high quality of most of the submissions, a total of 378 papers were selected for publication in six volumes of Springer's *Lecture Notes in Artificial Intelligence* a subseries of *Lecture Notes in Computer Science*. We sincerely hope that the published papers of ICIRA 2019 will prove to be technically beneficial and constructive to both the academic and industrial community in robotics, automation, and mechatronics. We would like to express our sincere appreciation to all the authors, participants, and the distinguished plenary and keynote speakers.

The success of the conference is also attributed to the Program Committee members and invited peer reviewers for their thorough review of all the submissions, as well as to the Organizing Committee and volunteers for their diligent work. Special thanks are extended to Alfred Hofmann, Anna Kramer, and Volha Shaparava from Springer for their consistent support.

August 2019

Haibin Yu
Jinguo Liu
Lianqing Liu
Zhaojie Ju
Yuwang Liu
Dalin Zhou

Organization

Honorary Chairs

Youlun Xiong   Huazhong University of Science and Technology, China

Nanning Zheng   Xi'an Jiaotong University, China

General Chair

Haibin Yu   Shenyang Institute of Automation, Chinese Academy of Sciences, China

General Co-chairs

Kok-Meng Lee   Georgia Institute of Technology, USA

Zhouping Yin   Huazhong University of Science and Technology, China

Xiangyang Zhu   Shanghai Jiao Tong University, China

Program Chair

Jinguo Liu   Shenyang Institute of Automation, Chinese Academy of Sciences, China

Program Co-chairs

Zhaojie Ju   The University of Portsmouth, UK

Lianqing Liu   Shenyang Institute of Automation, Chinese Academy of Sciences, China

Bram Vanderborght   Vrije Universiteit Brussel, Belgium

Advisory Committee

Jorge Angeles   McGill University, Canada

Tamio Arai   University of Tokyo, Japan

Hegao Cai   Harbin Institute of Technology, China

Tianyou Chai   Northeastern University, China

Jie Chen   Tongji University, China

Jiansheng Dai   King's College London, UK

Zongquan Deng   Harbin Institute of Technology, China

Han Ding   Huazhong University of Science and Technology, China

Xilun Ding	Beihang University, China
Baoyan Duan	Xidian University, China
Xisheng Feng	Shenyang Institute of Automation, Chinese Academy of Sciences, China
Toshio Fukuda	Nagoya University, Japan
Jianda Han	Shenyang Institute of Automation, Chinese Academy of Sciences, China
Qiang Huang	Beijing Institute of Technology, China
Oussama Khatib	Stanford University, USA
Yinan Lai	National Natural Science Foundation of China, China
Jangmyung Lee	Pusan National University, South Korea
Zhongqin Lin	Shanghai Jiao Tong University, China
Hong Liu	Harbin Institute of Technology, China
Honghai Liu	The University of Portsmouth, UK
Shugen Ma	Ritsumeikan University, Japan
Daokui Qu	SIASUN, China
Min Tan	Institute of Automation, Chinese Academy of Sciences, China
Kevin Warwick	Coventry University, UK
Guobiao Wang	National Natural Science Foundation of China, China
Tianmiao Wang	Beihang University, China
Tianran Wang	Shenyang Institute of Automation, Chinese Academy of Sciences, China
Yuechao Wang	Shenyang Institute of Automation, Chinese Academy of Sciences, China
Bogdan M. Wilamowski	Auburn University, USA
Ming Xie	Nanyang Technological University, Singapore
Yangsheng Xu	The Chinese University of Hong Kong, SAR China
Huayong Yang	Zhejiang University, China
Jie Zhao	Harbin Institute of Technology, China
Nanning Zheng	Xi'an Jiaotong University, China
Weijia Zhou	Shenyang Institute of Automation, Chinese Academy of Sciences, China
Xiangyang Zhu	Shanghai Jiao Tong University, China

Publicity Chairs

Shuo Li	Shenyang Institute of Automation, Chinese Academy of Sciences, China
Minghui Wang	Shenyang Institute of Automation, Chinese Academy of Sciences, China
Chuan Zhou	Shenyang Institute of Automation, Chinese Academy of Sciences, China

Publication Chairs

Yuwang Liu   Shenyang Institute of Automation, Chinese Academy
of Sciences, China

Dalin Zhou   The University of Portsmouth, UK

Award Chairs

Kaspar Althoefer   Queen Mary University of London, UK

Naoyuki Kubota   Tokyo Metropolitan University, Japan

Xingang Zhao   Shenyang Institute of Automation, Chinese Academy
of Sciences, China

Special Session Chairs

Guimin Chen   Xi'an Jiaotong University, China

Hak Keung Lam   King's College London, UK

Organized Session Co-chairs

Guangbo Hao   University College Cork, Ireland

Yongan Huang   Huazhong University of Science and Technology,
China

Qiang Li   Bielefeld University, Germany

Yuichiro Toda   Okayama University, Japan

Fei Zhao   Xi'an Jiaotong University, China

International Organizing Committee Chairs

Zhiyong Chen   The University of Newcastle, Australia

Yutaka Hata   University of Hyogo, Japan

Sabina Jesehke   RWTH Aachen University, Germany

Xuesong Mei   Xi'an Jiaotong University, China

Robert Riener   ETH Zurich, Switzerland

Chunyi Su   Concordia University, Canada

Shengquan Xie   The University of Auckland, New Zealand

Chenguang Yang   UWE Bristol, UK

Tom Ziemke   University of Skövde, Sweden

Yahya Zweiri   Kingston University, UK

Local Arrangements Chairs

Hualiang Zhang   Shenyang Institute of Automation, Chinese Academy
of Sciences, China

Xin Zhang   Shenyang Institute of Automation, Chinese Academy
of Sciences, China

Contents – Part IV

Fuzzy Modelling for Automation, Control, and Robotics

Development of Ultra-Thin-Film, Flexible Sensors, and Tactile Sensation

Robotic Technology for Deep Space Exploration

Navigation/Localization

Swarm Intelligence Unmanned System

User Association and Power Allocation in UAV-Based SWIPT System

Mei Yang[(⋈)], Fei Huang, Yongling Zeng, Yunzhen Wu,
and Chuanshuo Zhang

College of Communications Engineering, Army Engineering University of PLA,
Nanjing 210014, China
iamymei@163.com, huangfeicjh@sina.com,
yuanmuyaocen@163.com, yunzhenwu@163.com,
LYun1208@163.com

Abstract. In recent years, the wireless communication network supported by unmanned aerial vehicles (UAVs) has attracted extensive attention due to its high channel gain. At the same time, simultaneous wireless information and power transfer (SWIPT) is used in many scenarios because of its efficient information transmission capability. In this paper, we investigate SWIPT in UAV-based network, where each UAV equipped with a transmitter transfers energy and transmits information simultaneously to the ground node. The objective is to maximize the sum of information rate obtained by all nodes under the condition of ensuring the minimum energy requirement of each node and UAV energy constraint. In order to solve the complex multiple variable optimization problem, we first transform the problem into two sub-problems, and then solve the problem above through the multi-variable alternative optimization algorithm. Simulation results show that the efficiency of power transferring and information transmitting of UAVs to ground nodes is improved through optimization.

Keywords: Unmanned aerial vehicles ·
Simultaneous wireless information and power transfer · Power allocation ·
User association

1 Introduction

UAVs attract more and more attention in every aspects of life due to its wide application prospect [1–3]. Specifically, the UAVs own better communication channels between the nodes on the ground. As we know, the communication network constituted by UAVs is playing an important role in many aspects, such as emergency rescue, information collection and so on. In recent years, the SWIPT supported by UAVs is widely concerned because it is a promising new technology which provides convenience and continuous energy supply for wireless network.

In the current application scenarios of UAVs, there have been studies on the UAVs which only transfer energy to the nodes on the ground [4–6]. At the same time, there also have been researches on the UAVs which only transmit information to ground

H. Yu et al. (Eds.): ICIRA 2019, LNAI 11743, pp. 3–13, 2019.
https://doi.org/10.1007/978-3-030-27538-9_1

nodes [7]. The research on simultaneous wireless information and power transmission is in an infancy stage [8–12], but there are few studies on the application of UAV in SWIPT [13]. Different from most existing researches, this paper investigates that multiple UAVs transfer energy and transmit information simultaneously with power splitting to ground nodes.

In some special cases, UAVs need to be deployed to transfer energy and transmit information to ground nodes. For example, the real-time detection of some marine organisms requires the deployment of nodes on the sea surface, as the movement of nodes requires energy consumption. However, the traditional cable charging method is difficult to be carried out in this case, the deployment of UAVs can effectively solve this problem. At the same time, the sensor node needs to receive information to complete the detection instruction, so the UAVs also need to transmit information to the sensor nodes. As a result, the SWIPT supported by the UAVs is extremely important. In this paper, we formulate a multiple variable optimization problem with the target to maximize the sum of information rate collected by all nodes on the ground during a finite charging period time, subject to the power limit and energy requirement. In order to solve the problem effectively, we put forward an effective algorithm by jointing optimizing user association, transmission power, and power splitting ratios.

2   System Model and Problem Formulation

As shown in Fig. 1, we consider a UAV-based communication system where multiple UAVs transfer energy and transmit information to the nodes on the ground simultaneously. Denote $\mathcal{M} = \{1, \cdots, M\}$ as the set of UAVs. Each UAV $(m \in \mathcal{M})$ is deployed at the fixed height H. Then the 3D coordinate of the m-th UAV is given as $(x_{U,m}, y_{U,m}, H)$, the 2D coordinate of the m-th UAV projected to the horizontal plane can be expressed by $q_m = (x_{U,m}, y_{U,m})$, $m \in \mathcal{M}$. There are K static nodes deployed on the ground and denote $\mathcal{K} = \{1, \ldots, K\}$ as the set of ground nodes. The position of the

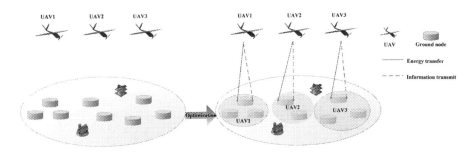

Fig. 1. The UAV-based SWIPT system

k-th node is denoted as $w_k = (x_k, y_k)$, $k \in \mathcal{K}$. The distance from m-th UAV to k-th node is given by:

$$d_{m,k} = \sqrt{\|q_m - w_k\|^2 + H^2} . \tag{1}$$

It is assumed that each UAV has a maximum instantaneous transmitting power P, and the power splitting ratio of each node is denoted as ρ_k. The finite operating time of UAVs is denoted as T, and noise power is denoted as σ^2. The user association coefficient between the UAV and the node is expressed by $b_{m,k}$, where $b_{m,k} = 1$ represents the link between the m-th UAV and the k-th node, and $b_{m,k} = 0$ represents the m-th UAV and the k-th node is irrespective. The transmit power of the m-th UAV to the k-th node is given by $p_{m,k}$. As the wireless channel between the UAVs and nodes on the ground is normally LOS-dominated, we adopt the free-space path loss model similarly as in [14–16]. The channel gain of the m-th UAV to the k-th node is modeled as:

$$h_{m,k} = \beta_0 d_{m,k}^{-\alpha} = \frac{\beta_0}{\left(\sqrt{\|q_m - w_k\|^2 + H^2}\right)^\alpha}, \tag{2}$$

where β_0 denotes the channel power gain and α denotes the environmental factor. Due to the UAV's power amplifier limitation, this constraint can be denoted by:

$$\sum_{k=1}^{K} p_{m,k} b_{m,k} \leq P, \ \forall m \in \mathcal{M}, \forall k \in \mathcal{K}, \tag{3}$$

in order to ensure the minimum energy requirement of each node, we have the following constraint:

$$E_k = T \sum_{m=1}^{M} \frac{\eta(1 - \rho_k) p_{m,k} b_{m,k} \beta_0}{\left(\sqrt{\|q_m - w_k\|^2 + H^2}\right)^\alpha} \geq \psi, \ \forall m \in \mathcal{M}, \forall k \in \mathcal{K}. \tag{4}$$

From (1) and (2), the total amount of information rate (bits/Hz) collected by all nodes is denoted as:

$$R = T \sum_{m=1}^{M} \sum_{k=1}^{K} \log_2 \left(1 + \frac{\rho_k p_{m,k} b_{m,k} \beta_0}{\sigma^2 \left(\sqrt{\|q_m - w_k\|^2 + H^2}\right)^\alpha}\right)^2. \tag{5}$$

In this paper, we solve the maximum amount of information by optimizing the user association, transmission power, and power splitting ratio. In order to deal with the objective function more conveniently, we maximize the minimum of the energy harvested by all nodes during a given charging period. Auxiliary variable S is introduced, which represents the minimum value of energy collected by K nodes in the charging duration T, denoted by $S = \min R$, the above problems studied in mathematics can be expressed as follows:

$$
\max_{\{b_{m,k}, \rho_k, p_{m,k}, S\}} S
$$

$$
s.t. \quad C1 : T \sum_{m=1}^{M} \sum_{k=1}^{K} \log_2 \left(1 + \frac{\rho_k p_{m,k} b_{m,k} \beta_0}{\sigma^2 \left(\sqrt{\|q_m - w_k\|^2 + H^2} \right)^\alpha} \right) \geq S
$$

$$
C2 : \sum_{k=1}^{K} p_{m,k} b_{m,k} \leq P, \forall m \in \mathcal{M}, \forall k \in \mathcal{K}
$$

$$
C3 : E_k = T \sum_{m=1}^{M} \frac{(1 - \rho_k) p_{m,k} b_{m,k} \beta_0}{\left(\sqrt{\|q_m - w_k\|^2 + H^2} \right)^\alpha} \geq \psi, \forall m \in \mathcal{M}, \forall k \in \mathcal{K}
$$

(6)

This paper studied the user association and power allocation optimization problem in UAV-based SWIPT system. The constraint C1 and C3 of problem (6) are all non-convex, which is difficult to be solved by standard convex optimization because it involves the optimization of transmission power and power splitting ratio.

3   The Design and Analysis of Algorithm

In order to effectively solve the above problem, two sub-problems are firstly proposed: the optimization of the user association with the given transmit power and power splitting ratio, the joint optimization of the transmission power and power splitting ratio with the given user association. Through observation, the optimization problem aforementioned is convex about the user association with given transmission power and power splitting ratio, but non-convex about the joint transmission power and power splitting with given user association.

3.1   User Association Optimization

With the given transmission power and power splitting ratio, in this section, the transmission power and power splitting ratio are constant, then the user association optimization can be expressed as follows:

$$\max_{\{b_{m,k},S\}} \quad S$$

$$s.t. \quad C1 : R = T\sum_{m=1}^{M}\sum_{k=1}^{K}\log_2\left(1 + \frac{\rho_k p_{m,k} b_{m,k}\beta_0}{\sigma^2\left(\sqrt{\|q_m - w_k\|^2 + H^2}\right)^{\alpha}}\right) \geq S$$

$$C2 : \sum_{k=1}^{K} p_{m,k} b_{m,k} \leq P, \forall m \in \mathcal{M}, \forall k \in \mathcal{K}$$

$$C3 : E_k = T\sum_{m=1}^{M}\frac{\eta(1-\rho_k)p_{m,k}b_{m,k}\beta_0}{\left(\sqrt{\|q_m - w_k\|^2 + H^2}\right)^{\alpha}} \geq \psi, \forall m \in \mathcal{M}, \forall k \in \mathcal{K}$$

(7)

In order to maximize the target function with the fixed transmission power and the fixed power splitting ratio, it can be seen from C1 of problem (7), the distance between the UAV and the node determines the value of the objective function. The shorter the distance, the greater the value of the target function. The UAV closest to k-th node is denoted as $m^* = \min_k d_{m,k}$, and the user association between the m-th UAV and the k-th node is denoted by:

$$b_{m,k} = \begin{cases} 1 & m = m^* \\ 0 & m \neq m^* \end{cases}$$

Obviously, problem (7) is a standard convex problem and can be solved by using standard convex optimization techniques.

3.2 Joint Transmit Power and Power Splitting Ratio Optimization

For the given user association, the joint optimization problem of transmission power and power splitting ratio can be expressed as follows:

$$\max_{\{p_{m,k}\rho_k,S\}} \quad S$$

$$s.t. \quad C1 : R = T\sum_{m=1}^{M}\sum_{k=1}^{K}\log_2\left(1 + \frac{\rho_k p_{m,k} b_{m,k}\beta_0}{\sigma^2\left(\sqrt{\|q_m - w_k\|^2 + H^2}\right)^{\alpha}}\right) \geq S$$

$$C2 : \sum_{k=1}^{K} p_{m,k} b_{m,k} \leq P, \forall m \in \mathcal{M}, \forall k \in \mathcal{K}$$

$$C3 : E_k = T\sum_{m=1}^{M}\frac{\eta(1-\rho_k)p_{m,k}b_{m,k}\beta_0}{\left(\sqrt{\|q_m - w_k\|^2 + H^2}\right)^{\alpha}} \geq \psi, \forall m \in \mathcal{M}, \forall k \in \mathcal{K}$$

(8)

Now, in order to analyzing the concavity and convexity of the problem, we denote the power splitting ratio of each node as $x = \rho_k$ and the power of each node as $y = p_{m,k}$. Then we assume that constraint C1 in problem (8) as $f_1(x,y) = \log_2(1+xy)$ and the constraint C3 in problem (8) as $f_2(x,y) = (1-x)y$. By using the first-order Taylor expansion, we obtain that

$$f_1(x,y) = \log_2(1+xy) \geq \log_2\left(1 - \frac{1}{2}\left(x^2 + y^2\right) + \frac{1}{2}(x_0 + y_0)^2 + (x_0 + y_0)(x + y - x_0 - y_0)\right), \quad (9)$$

$$f_2(x,y) = (1-x)y \geq y - \frac{1}{2}\left(x_0^2 + y_0^2\right) + x_0(x - x_0) + y_0(y - y_0) - \frac{1}{2}(x+y)^2. \quad (10)$$

Because (9) and (10) are all concave function, then the convex function $R_{k,lb}^{i+1}$ and $E_{k,lb}^{i+1}$ can be obtained on the basis of the known values of ρ_k^i, $p_{m,k}^i$ in the i-th iteration:

$$R_{k,lb}^{i+1} = T\sum_{m=1}^{M}\sum_{k=1}^{K}\log_2\left(1 + \frac{\beta_0 b_{m,k}}{\sigma^2\left(\sqrt{\|q_m - w_k\|^2 + H^2}\right)}\left(-\frac{1}{2}(\rho_k^{i+1})^2 + \left(p_{m,k}^{i+1}\right)^2 + \frac{1}{2}\left(\rho_k^i + p_{m,k}^i\right)^2 + \left(\rho_k^i + p_{m,k}^i\right)\left(\rho_k^{i+1} + p_{m,k}^{i+1} - \rho_k^i - p_{m,k}^i\right)\right)\right)$$

$$(11)$$

$$E_{k,lb}^{i+1} = T\sum_{m=1}^{M}\frac{\eta b_{m,k}\beta_0}{\left(\sqrt{\|q_m - w_k\|^2 + H^2}\right)^2}\left(p_{m,k}^{i+1} - \frac{1}{2}\left(\rho_k^{i+1} + p_{m,k}^{i+1}\right)^2 + \frac{1}{2}\left((\rho_k^i)^2 + \left(p_{m,k}^i\right)^2\right) + \rho_k^i(\rho_k^{i+1} - \rho_k^i) + p_{m,k}^i\left(p_{m,k}^{i+1} - p_{m,k}^i\right)\right)$$

$$(12)$$

Then the constraint C1 in problem (8) is converted to $R_{k,lb}^{i+1}$ and the constraint C3 in problem (8) is converted to $E_{k,lb}^{i+1}$, the above problem is converted to

$$\begin{aligned}
&\max_{\{\rho_k, p_{m,k}, S\}} \quad S \\
&\text{s.t.} \quad \text{C1: } R_{k,lb}^{i+1} \geq S, \forall k \in \mathcal{K} \\
&\qquad \text{C2: } E_{k,lb}^{i+1} \geq \psi, \forall k \in \mathcal{K} \\
&\qquad \text{C3: } \sum_{k=1}^{K} p_{m,k} b_{m,k} \leq P, \forall k \in \mathcal{K}, \forall m \in \mathcal{M}
\end{aligned} \quad (13)$$

Algorithm 1.	Joint optimization of transmission power and power splitting ratio

1:Intialize the UAV's transmit power $\{p_{m,k}\}^l$,power splitting ratio $\{\rho_k\}^l$ and iteration

number $l = 0$

2:**Repeat**

3:Solve the problem(13)with given user association by standard convex optimization techniques.

4:Update the transmit power $\{p_{m,k}\}^l$, power splitting ratio $\{\rho_k\}^l$ and minimum information

rate quantum S^{l+1}

5: **Repeat**

6:Get the optimal solution at the i-th iteration

7:**Until** $S^{i+1} - S^i \leq \varepsilon$

8:Update the transmit power $\{p_{m,k}\}^{l+1} = {p_{m,k}}^i$,and power splitting ratio $\{\rho_k\}^{l+1} = {\rho_k}^i$

9:**Until** $S^{l+1} - S^l \leq \varepsilon$

10:Return the transmit power $p_{m,k}$ * and power splitting ratio ${\rho_k}^*$

After the above analysis and discussion, problem (13) is a convex optimization problem and can be solved by using standard convex optimization techniques. Since the optimization variables are the increments at the each iteration, a series of non-decreasing values can be obtained. On the other hand, these values must be the optimal solution of the upper bounded, so the convergence is guaranteed.

4 Simulations and Discussions

This paper studied the user association and power allocation optimization problem in UAV-based SWIPT system. In this section, simulations are implemented to demonstrate the superiority of the proposed algorithm. We considered 100×100 m^2 area where three UAVs transfer energy and transmit information simultaneously to eight nodes on the ground. Two different positions of UAVs and nodes are given in case I and case II. The nodes are distributed on the ground randomly. All UAVs are deployed at a fixed height of 10 m. The channel power gain is $\beta_0 = 10^{-3}$. Other system parameters are as follows $T = 50$ s, $P = 1000$ mW. In both cases, the UAVs are in the same position. In case I, ground nodes are evenly distributed, but in case II, the nodes distribution is relatively concentrated. Firstly, the node establishes a connection with the nearest UAV. The simulation results are as follows:

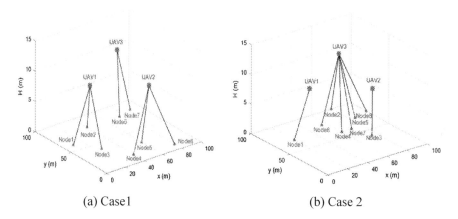

(a) Case 1   (b) Case 2

Fig. 2. User association

Figure 2(a) and (b) depict the optimized user association under the different location of nodes in case I and case II. We observe that the ground nodes firstly choose the nearest UAV.

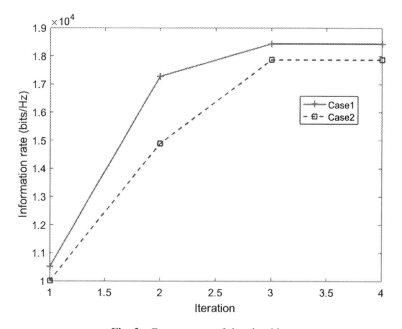

Fig. 3. Convergence of the algorithm

It is observed in Fig. 3, as the iteration number increases, the sum of information rates tends to a constant, which verifies the convergence of this algorithm.

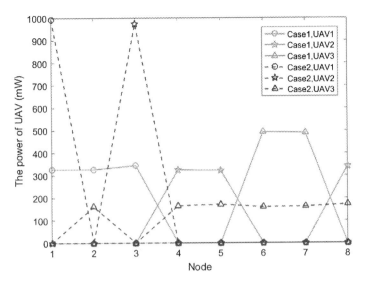

Fig. 4. Power allocation of UAVs

As shown in the Fig. 4, each UAV allocates power to the associated ground nodes. Meanwhile, the better the channel between the UAV and the node, the more power the node will get.

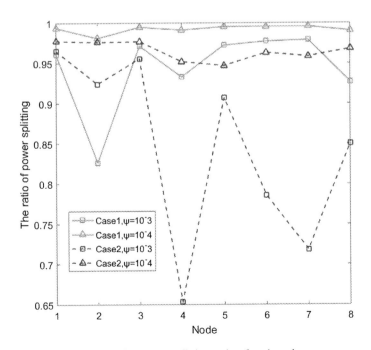

Fig. 5. The power splitting ratio of each node

Figure 5 shows the power splitting ratio of each node in two cases under two different minimum energy thresholds, the ratio of the splitting power of each node in two cases is different, which is related to the minimum energy requirement of ground node, the higher the threshold value, the smaller the node segmentation ratio.

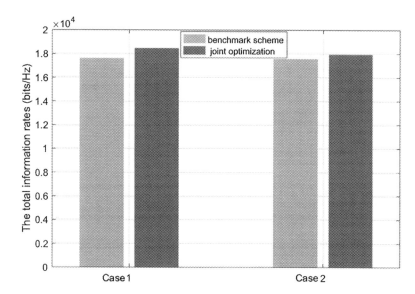

Fig. 6. The comparison in two cases

To evaluate the performance of the proposed algorithm, the final optimization results in two cases as shown in Fig. 6. Simulation results show that the UAV with optimized user association, transmission power and power splitting can improve the sum bits. It is observed that the proposed algorithm outperforms the benchmark, the results show the effectiveness of the proposed algorithm.

5   Conclusion

In this paper, user association and power allocation optimization problem for UAV-based SWIPT system was investigated. We formulate a multiple variable optimization problem with the target to maximize the sum of information rate collected by all nodes on the ground during a finite charging period time, subject to the power limit and energy requirement. In order to solve the problem effectively, we put forward an effective algorithm by jointing optimizing user association, transmission power, and power splitting ratios. Simulation results demonstrate the effectiveness of the proposed algorithm.

References

1. Zeng, Y., Zhang, R., Lim, T.J.: Wireless communications with unmanned aerial vehicles: opportunities and challenges. IEEE Commun. Mag. **54**(5), 36–42 (2016)
2. Valavanis, K.P., Vachtsevanos, G.J.: Handbook of Unmanned Aerial Vehicles. Springer, Netherlands (2015). https://doi.org/10.1007/978-90-481-9707-1
3. Ding, G., Qihui, W., Zhang, L., Lin, Y., Tsiftsis, T.A., Yao, Y.-D.: An amateur drone surveillance system based on cognitive internet of things. IEEE Commun. Mag. **56**(1), 29–35 (2018)
4. Xu, J., Zeng, Y., Zhang, R.: UAV-enabled multiuser wireless power transfer: trajectory design and energy optimization. In: 2017 23rd Asia-Pacific Conference on Communications, pp. 1–6 (2017)
5. Xu, J., Zeng, Y., Zhang, R.: UAV-enabled wireless power transfer: trajectory design and energy region characterization. In: 2017 IEEE GLOBECOM Workshops, pp. 1–7 (2017)
6. Wang, H., Ding, G., Gao, F., Chen, J., Wang, J., Wang, L.: Power control in UAV-supported ultra dense networks: communications, caching, and energy transfer. IEEE Commun. Mag. **56**(6), 28–34 (2018)
7. Xue, Z., Wang, J., Ding, G., Zhou, H., Qihui, W.: Maximization of data dissemination in UAV-supported internet of thing. IEEE Wirel. Commun. Lett. **8**, 185–188 (2019)
8. Zhou, X., Zhang, R., Ho, C.K.: Wireless information and power transfer: architecture design and rate-energy tradeoff. IEEE Trans. Commun. **61**, 4754–4767 (2013)
9. Bi, S., Ho, C.K., Zhang, R.: Recent advances in joint wireless energy and information transfer. In: 2014 IEEE Information Theory Workshop, pp. 341–345 (2014)
10. Zhang, R., Ho, C.K.: MIMO broadcasting for simultaneous wireless information and power transfer. IEEE Trans. Wirel. Commun. **12**, 1989–2001 (2013)
11. Shi, Q., Liu, L., Xu, W., Zhang, R.: Joint transmit beamforming and receive power splitting for MISO SWIPT systems. IEEE Trans. Wirel. Commun. **13**, 3269–3280 (2014)
12. Zhou, X., Zhang, R., Ho, C.K.: Wireless information and power transfer in multiuser OFDM systems. IEEE Trans. Wirel. Commun. **13**, 2282–2294 (2014)
13. Yin, S., Zhao, Y., Li, L.: UAV-assisted cooperative communications with time-sharing SWIPT. In: 2018 IEEE International Conference on Communications, pp. 1–6 (2018)
14. Xie, L., Xu, J., Zhang, R.: Throughput maximization for UAV-enabled wireless powered communication networks. IEEE Internet Things J. **1** (2019)
15. Zeng, Y., Zhang, R., Lim, T.J.: Throughput maximization for UAV-enabled mobile relaying systems. IEEE Trans. Commun. **64**, 4983–4996 (2016)
16. Xu, J., Zeng, Y., Zhang, R.: UAV-enabled wireless power transfer: trajectory design and energy optimization. IEEE Trans. Wirel. Commun. **17**, 5092–5106 (2018)

Joint Location Selection and Supply Allocation for UAV Aided Disaster Response System

Nanxin Wang[1]([⊠]), Jingheng Zheng[2]([⊠]), Jihong Tong[3]([⊠]), and Kai Zhang[4]([⊠])

[1] International School, Beijing University of Posts and Telecommunications,
Beijing 100876, China
2016213131@bupt.edu.cn
[2] School of Information and Communication Engineering,
Beijing University of Posts and Telecommunications, Beijing 100876, China
zhengjh@bupt.edu.cn
[3] School of Information Engineering, Eastern Liaoning University,
Dandong 118003, Liaoning, China
sysam0902@163.com
[4] Department of Electronic Engineering, Tsinghua University, Beijing 100084, China
kaizhangee@gmail.com

Abstract. Unmanned aerial vehicles (UAVs) attract public attention because of its mobility, transportability and agility. UAVs can be assistants in disaster relief operation, and such a transportable disaster response UAV system is supposed to take responsibility for both reconnaissance and delivery of supplies. There are many researches about UAV system used when disasters occur. Nevertheless, how to identify the deployment locations where UAVs take off is seldom considered. Furthermore, the space for deployment is limited because of the adverse condition of the ground, but there will be a large requirement of disaster relief supplies. There is an urgent need for utilizing limited space to store as many as possible required supplies delivered to destinations. Aiming to solve the first problem, we identify the best locations for deployment, which makes the disaster response system reconnoiter as many as possible main roads when promising to delivery supplies to as many as possible destinations in some areas. For the second one, we propose an algorithm to maximize the space utilization, which allows the system to store more supplies in a given space.

Keywords: Location selection · Supply allocation · UAV · Disaster response system

1 Introduction

Unmanned aerial vehicles (UAVs), also commonly known as drones, have attracted significant attention due to high mobility and transportability [1].

© Springer Nature Switzerland AG 2019
H. Yu et al. (Eds.): ICIRA 2019, LNAI 11743, pp. 14–26, 2019.
https://doi.org/10.1007/978-3-030-27538-9_2

Up till now, there are various applications, such as assisting communication in space-air-ground networks [2], investigating and remedying ecosystem [9] and maintenance [8], which shows that UAV has been used in many places. Typically for the disaster relief, the areas that encounter disaster are isolated from the outside because arterial traffic may be cut off and base stations for communication may be damaged. In this condition, both delivery of supplies for disaster relief and information about the areas are quite important. Instead of ground vehicles, UAVs can not only approach the areas easily, but can also load essential supplies, showing that UAVs are capable of providing disaster relief.

In practice, UAVs have been considered as assistants when some areas encounter natural disaster. Lin [3] and Erdelj [4] proposed that UAVs with certain equipment can carry out remote sensing and disaster management, facilitating rescuer teams to save humans' life quickly and precisely.

Many scholars study the operation of UAV system. Wu performs continuous convex optimization to determine the iteration coordinate of UAVs [5]. Hu proposes two contracts for spectrum trade, which makes either basic station optimal or society optimal [7]. As for spectrum which is important for communication, Jiang integrates the design of spectrum sensing and access algorithms together [14], and proposes a dynamic spectrum access protocol for secondary users confronting with unknown primary behavior [15], which probably solves the communication between UAVs. Additionally, Wang studies both power control [6] and reliability of cloud controlled UAV system [13], which saves resources and increases computational performance for the system. Shah proposes a nonlinear guidance schime of UAVs using a sliding model approach and manages to control the lateral track error of the vehicle during flight [10]. However, there are few people taking how to identify deployment locations where UAVs take off for UAV systems into account. It is worth mentioning that how to deploy such a system is a precondition of which UAV system can execute its task. Furthermore, the space of deployment location is limited, and it is difficult to store many supplies in the place where UAVs take off. But there will be a great demand for disaster relief supplies when disaster occurs. Inspired by the problems, in this article, we not only analyze how to identify the best locations for aided disaster response UAV system, and we also solve the problem how to maximize the amount of required supplies in a given space. Our work can be summarized as follows:

– Identify the best location of UAV deployment: We introduce a model to identify the best locations for UAV system, which makes it possible for the system to reconnoiter as many as possible main roads when promising to deliver required supplies to as many as possible destinations in some area.

– Maximize amount of supplies: We recognize supplies as many kinds of packets and the limited space as a container and propose an algorithm called Space-segmenting and Recursion Bin-packing (SSR-BP) based on improved bottom-left algorithm [12], which allows us to place as many as possible packets into the container.

– Apply to a practical scenario: We select a country called Puerto Rico that encounters natural disaster frequently. According to the main hospitals and main traffic routes located in this country, we identify the best places for deployment of UAV system and make the aided disaster response UAV system offer sufficient supplies for local hospitals.

The remainder of this paper is organized as follows. In system model, identification of the best deployment location where UAVs take off is displayed in Sect. 2.1. As for supply allocation, the optimization objective is shown in Sect. 2.2, while SSR-BP algorithm is given in Sect. 2.3. In Sect. 3, we provide both our result and analysis of simulation, which is followed by the conclusion we draw in Sect. 4.

2   System Model

The system model has been illustrated in Fig. 1. In this part, we first find the best deployment locations where UAV system can reconnoiter as many as possible roads when promising deliver supplies to as many as possible destinations in the area encountering a disaster. Then we propose an algorithm to carry out space optimization to deal with a large requirement for supplies.

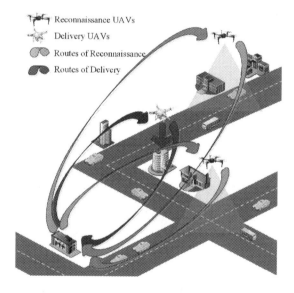

Fig. 1. System model

2.1   Identification of the Best Deployment Location

There is a map in a two-dimensional plane represented by a coordinate system whose horizontal and vertical axis is x and y respectively. The map contains a topological structure of α sides, indicating α main roads in the map. Furthermore, the map contains β points which represent β delivery destinations. There are l deployment locations in the map, and every UAV fleet deployed at these locations is supposed to reconnoiter as many as possible roads when promising the delivery of supplies to as many as possible destinations, because of conserving resources.

For each deployment location, suppose that the location of deploying UAV system where UAVs take off is represented as (x_0, y_0). Define that UAVs complete their reconnaissance mission if the UAVs arrive the middle point of roads, and each UAV is just responsible for one road. Considering timely completion is critical, all UAVs including those who are responsible for reconnaissance and those for delivery fly straightly to their destinations before they fly back in the same manner. Assume all the time spent on both taking off and landing is ignored and the supplies carried by UAVs will not outstrip the load capacity. Suppose the average flying speed of UAV is $\bar{v}$ and the maximum flying time is t_{max}, we have the maximum flying distance as follows:

$$d_{max} = \bar{v} \times t_{max}. \tag{1}$$

Identification of Deployment Locations

1. Every middle point of road is represented by (x_i, y_i) where $i = 1, 2, ..., \alpha$, indicating there are α roads in the map. According to the assumption, points located in each circle whose center is (x_i, y_i) and radius is d_{max} represent the possible places of cargo container in order to complete the reconnaissance of the road. Therefore, for the side whose middle point is (x_i, y_i), the condition where the side can be reconnoitered is following:

$$\sqrt{(x_0 - x_i)^2 + (y_0 - y_i)^2} \le d_{max}. \tag{2}$$

Recalling that (x_0, y_0) is the location of deployment, define the set of points that satisfies the above-mentioned in equation as A_i.

2. Every delivery destination is represented by (x_j, y_j) where $j = 1, 2, ..., \beta$, indicating there are β destinations in the map. We find the set of points using the same method. Therefore, for the destination whose coordinate is (x_j, y_j), the condition where UAV can accomplish its delivery task is following:

$$\sqrt{(x_0 - x_j)^2 + (y_0 - y_j)^2} \le d_{max}. \tag{3}$$

Define the set of points that satisfies the above-mentioned inequation as B_j.

3. For an arbitrary point z whose coordinate is (x, y) and a set of arbitrary points P, define that $T(z, P) = 1$ as the situation where point z is belong to

set P, and define $T(z, P) = 0$ as the opposite. We define (4) as the number of overlapped circles whose centers are destinations of delivery.

$$f(z) = \sum_{j=1}^{\beta} T(z, B_j) \tag{4}$$

Therefore, the set of points K should satisfy the following equation:

$$K = \{z \,|\max f(z)\} . \tag{5}$$

It represents the points where the number of overlapped circles whose centers are β delivery destination is maximum. For $z \in K$, we define (6) as the number of overlapped circles whose centers are the middle points of main roads.

$$f(z) = \sum_{i=1}^{\alpha} T(z, A_i) \tag{6}$$

Therefore, the set of points E should satisfy (7).

$$E = \{z \,|\max f(z)\} \tag{7}$$

Consequentially, all the points in set E are the best locations of deployment locations where UAVs take off, which make it possible for the system to reconnoiter as many as possible roads when promising to deliver supplies to as many as possible destinations. The number of such sets in the map is tantamount to l.

2.2   Maximization of Supplies

Because the condition on the ground will probably be so adverse that the space for deployment is limited when natural disasters occur, the space optimization should be carried out in order to meet a great demand for disaster relief supplies. For each deployment location, suppose that there are m kinds of supplies the delivery destinations require. And for each kind of supplies, the number of supplies is denoted as $\mu_i, i \in \{1, 2, ..., m\}$ and the volume of supplies is denoted as $V_i, i \in \{1, 2, ..., m\}$. As a result, the total volume of supplies, denoted as V_{total}, is displayed in the following equation.

$$V_{total} = \sum_{i=1}^{m} \mu_i V_i \tag{8}$$

Assuming there is a limited space whose shape is a cuboid for piling up supplies, and length, width and height of such a limited space is L_0, W_0 and H_0 respectively. Namely, the capability of volume is denoted as $V_c = L_0 W_0 H_0$. In order to make the system carry as many as possible supplies, we have the optimization objective.

$$\max \; V_t$$
$$s.t. \quad V_t \leq V_c \tag{9}$$

In order to achieve such a objective, we propose a algorithm called Space-segmenting and Recursion Bin-packing (SSR-BP) algorithm.

2.3   Space-Segmenting Recursion Bin-Packing Algorithm

We recognize m kinds of supplies as m kinds of packets whose length, width and height is L_i, W_i and H_i ($i \in \{1, 2, ..., m\}$). Also, the limited space whose volume is V_c is recognized as a cargo container. Equivalently, we study a three-dimensional online bin-packing problem (3D-OBPP), which makes as many as possible packets be placed into a container. In order to solve 3D-OBPP, we propose a algorithm called SSR-BP based on a floor programming algorithm called improved Bottom-left (IBL) [12] which is an improved version of BL [11] algorithm. The schematic diagram of both BL and IBL is shown in Fig. 2. IBL is different from BL algorithm when moving: the packet is capable of moving downward as soon as it can when it is moving toward left, which decreases the wasted planes. The newly arriving packet enters the container from the top right corner of planform of the container and moves downward before it begins moving toward left.

SSR-BP divides the 3D space into plenty of planes with corresponding heights when iterating and performs floor programming on each plane.

Free rotation of both packet and container is not allowed. We define a parameter called priority to describe the relationship among different sorts of packets. We represent the priority as p, where $1 \leq p \leq m$, and m is the maximum value of p. Noting that the packet whose priority is higher has larger bottom area, the relationship among packets satisfies (10).

$$\begin{cases} L_i > L_{i-1} \\ W_i > W_{i-1} \ j \in \{2, 3, ..., m\} \\ H_i > H_{i-1} \end{cases} \tag{10}$$

For packets arriving online, packets are constructed as a heap before such a heap is placed into the container according to the floor of the heap based on IBL algorithm. We call the operation that performs IBL algorithm according to the floor, briefly, as two-dimensional floor planning (2D-FP). In the procedure of constructing a heap, we name the packet whose surface is a place on which there will be a 2D-FP as reference packet. If the newly arriving packet have lower p compared with reference packet, we perform 2D-FP for such a relatively lower-priority packet on the surface of reference packet. If the newly arriving packet has the same or larger p, we place the packet just beneath the reference packet. After the heap is constructed completely, and if the heap satisfies restrictions, we perform 2D-FP for the heap on the floor of container.

Optimization Objective. Initially, we denote $num_i, i \in \{1, 2, ..., m\}$ as the number of each kind of already planned packets with different priority on the surface (the surface of packet or the floor of container) where there is a 2D-FP. Furthermore, let $num_{ij}, i \in \{1, 2, ..., m\}, j \in \{1, 2, 3, 4\}$ denote the number of packets with priority i in the first row when we look at the container from the direction j. Each direction is vertical to one of 4 sides of the container's bottom surfaces. For each heap, we have the optimization objective shown in (11) where $rank\_now$ denote the priority p of the packet whose surface is a place where there is a 2D-FP currently.

$$\max \sum_{i=1}^{m} num_i$$

$$s.t. \quad \sum_{i=1}^{m} num_{i1} \le W_{rank\_now}, \quad \sum_{i=1}^{m} num_{i2} \le L_{rank\_now}, \tag{11}$$

$$\sum_{i=1}^{m} num_{i3} \le W_{rank\_now}, \quad \sum_{i=1}^{m} num_{i4} \le L_{rank\_now},$$

$$H_{heap} \le H_0.$$

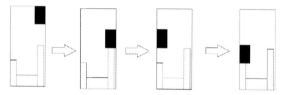

(a) Schematic diagram of BL algorithm

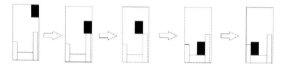

(b) Schematic diagram of IBL algorithm

Fig. 2. Comparison between two algorithm

We make every heap be as high as possible, and make the number of packets consisting of the heap be as large as possible, which indicates that we make every heap fill the cuboid which is a part space of container as much as possible. For the floor of container, we have the optimization objective shown in (12).

$$\max \sum_{i=1}^{m} num_i$$

$$s.t. \quad \sum_{i=1}^{m} num_{i1} \le W_0, \quad \sum_{i=1}^{m} num_{i2} \le L_0, \tag{12}$$

$$\sum_{i=1}^{m} num_{i3} \le W_0, \quad \sum_{i=1}^{m} num_{i4} \le L_0.$$

The formula shown above makes the number of heaps be as large as possible, which indicates that we make all heaps fill the container as much as possible to maximize the space utilization.

SSR-BP Algorithm. The algorithm has been already shown in Algorithm 1. We denote a packet whose surface will be programmed as a reference packet and *temp* as a list used for recording packets. For every heap, there are three probable situations.

If priority of the newly arriving packet is larger than that of the packet whose surface is a place where there is a 2D-FP currently, the arriving packet will be placed under such the reference packet. If the height of the heap is smaller than that of container, we push current reference packet into *temp* which allows rollback in the future. Now, the reference packet become the newly arriving packet so that we perform 2D-FP on the surface of X later. If the height of updated heap is larger than that of container, we place the arriving packet in the next heap, which means the newly arriving packet will be the first one in the next heap.

If priority of the new packet is equal to that of reference packet, the situation is similar to the situation mentioned above. However, the reference packet will not change.

If smaller, we first perform 2D-FP on the reference packet, and if the operation is successful, the height of heap should be considered because IBL algorithm is a two-dimensional planning, which does not take into account the height. If both two conditions are satisfied, we place the new packet and the reference packet will not change. Noting that if 2D-FP is failed, there is a probable situation where the new packet is unable to be placed on the current reference packet but is able to be placed on formerly placed packets. The algorithm begins rollback, therefore, information of each packet reserved in temporary list will be drawn with descending order according to its priority. Each packet will be compared with the new packet until the new one is placed properly. Then, we continue programming on the reference packet before drawing from *temp*. Particularly, if priority of the packet reserved in list is equal to that of the new one, the new one will be placed just under the packet with the same priority. After the new packet has been placed, which indicates the rollback has stopped, all packets drawn from list in this turn will be discarded. Once the new packet is not placed eventually, we clean *temp* and place the arriving packet into the next heap.

For the successfully constructed heap, we perform 2D-FP on floor of the container to try to place the heap. If succeed, the algorithm will start a new cycle. If not, it means there is no place for a new heap and the algorithm comes to the end.

By making larger packets move towards the bottom, it is possible to make the layout of the floor of container regular and tight, because there will be less fragmentary planes. In the process of iteration, rollback operation is implemented, which avoids local optimum when constructing a heap. Such rollbacks can reserve the arriving packet and can search if there is sufficient space on larger packets programmed, which is different from best-fit (BF) algorithm.

3   Simulation

Puerto Rico is a country that frequently encounters hurricane. When such a disaster occurs in this country, hurricane not only destroys main roads, hindering rescue teams from carrying disaster relief operation, but it also causes casualties. In such case, there is an urgent need of reconnoitering main roads and of delivering medical packets to local medical stations. Employing a fleet of UAVs is the best choice. We have looked up relative reference materials. The map of Puerto Rico is shown in Fig. 3. Noting that 5 medical stations and 43 main roads have been marked, UAV system should reconnoiter as many as possible main roads when promising to deliver packets to these stations.

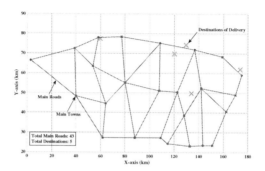

Fig. 3. The map of Puerto Rico

For UAV, the average speed $\bar{v}$, which marked in 2.1, is 79 km/h and the maximum flying time t_{max} is 40 min. According to the system model, the best locations for deployment of transportable disaster response UAV system are identified. All the best locations and all the trajectories are shown in Fig. 4, where green line are the trajectories for reconnaissance and the red ones are that for delivery.

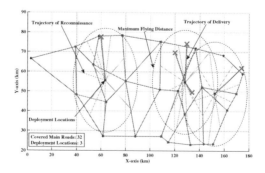

Fig. 4. Locations and trajectories

The covering rate of reconnaissance when promising delivery is calculated.

$$\eta_{\text{cover}} = \frac{n_{cv}}{n_{total}} = 72.42\% \tag{13}$$

Only having just 3 locations of deployment is capable of covering 32 main roads out of 43, proving the high serving efficiency. Furthermore, each location is responsible for both two missions of the UAV system, which allows the system to achieve both multi-functional and high-efficiency goals.

Assuming there are two types of supplies to be stored, the length, width and height of Type-A supplies are 24, 20 and 20 inches respectively, and those of Type-B are 8, 10 and 14 inches. The length, width and height of the limited space whose shape is a cuboid is 220, 82 and 94 inches correspondingly. By setting the arriving probability of Type-A to be 0.6 and that of Type-B to be 0.4, we perform SSR-BP algorithm to work out the packing configuration. The planform of the limited space is shown in Figs. 5 and 6. Note the former one illustrates the layout of supplies placed at the bottom, and the latter one illustrates that of supplies placed at the top of limited space.

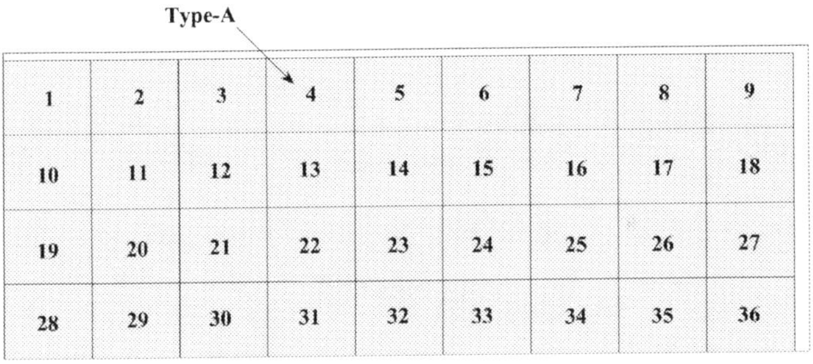

Type-A
1
2
3
4
5
6
7
8
9
10
11
12
13
14
15
16
17
18
19
20
21
22
23
24
25
26
27
28
29
30
31
32
33
34
35
36

Fig. 5. Layout at the bottom

Type-A
Type-B
The second tier of Type-B
1
6
7
13
20
25
29
32
33
36

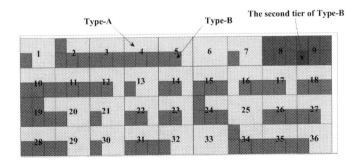

Fig. 6. Layout at the top

There are 143 Type-A supplies and 85 Type-B supplies encapsulated in the limited space, and the space utilization is shown in (14).

$$\eta = \frac{143 \times V_A + 85 \times V_B}{V_{space}} = 86.57\% \tag{14}$$

The limited space is called as container. With the arrival of Type-A supplies which is larger than Type-B, Type-A supplies move forward the bottom of the container according to SSR-BP algorithm. This leads to the following phenomena. The bottom plane of container will be segmented more regularly, which makes it possible to reduce fragmentary planes. Therefore, the layout can be more tight, which is shown in Fig. 5. Type-As can offer planes for placing Type-Bs, which allows the smaller packets to utilize the fragmentary space located at the top of container. Each heap is programmed according to the floor of larger packets, so larger floor causes that the whole floor of container will be filled more quickly, which reduces the number of iteration.

As for rollbacks, there is only one situation where rollbacks occur. There was a Type-B supply arriving last in the previous heap, and the supply was unable to be placed, which is displayed in No. 8 heap in Fig. 6. So it would be the first one in the next heap, which ensures that this Type-B would be pushed into the list, *temp*. When Type-B can not be placed on the surface of Type-A anymore, rollbacks make a newly arriving Type-B be placed on another Type-B located at the top of container, which is shown in No. 9 heap. There are two tiers of Type-B. Such rollbacks allow us to place more Type-B supplies, which increases the space utilization.

For the distribution of arriving supplies, the space utilization will be higher if the probability of one kind of supplies is larger than that of other kind of supplies. This is because the overall shape of every heap can be more regular, which makes fragmentary space smaller and enlarge space utilization. And the performance will be better if the number of kinds of supplies is smaller. There is more fragmentary space and the situation is more complex if there are many kinds of packets arriving, which degrades the performance. In this simulation, we suppose there are two kinds of supplies whose probabilities are 0.6 and 0.4, and the space utilization is so high that reach 86.57%.

4   Conclusion

In a nutshell, we study how to deploy an aided disaster response UAV system used for both delivering required supplies and reconnoitering main roads in some areas, which is a precondition of which UAV system can execute its tasks. We introduce out model to identify the best deployment location where UAVs take off, making the system achieve both multi-functional and high-efficiency goals. Considering there will be limited space in deployment locations for the system to store supplies that are delivered to destinations, we propose an algorithm called Space-segmenting Recursion Bin-packing (SSR-BP) based on IBL algorithm to solve the allocation of supplies–a three dimension online bin-packing problem

(3D-OBPP), which allows the UAV system to store as many as possible supplies. These problems we solve are critical in practice, and we apply our model to a country called Puerto Rico, which is proved that there is a meaning for practice.

Algorithm 1. *SSR-BP Algorithm*

1: Initialization: Assuming that the first arriving packet's priority is p, and the surface of the packet will be programmed.

2: A packet whose priority is x arrives and such a packet is denoted as X. The reference packet whose priority is y, similarly, is denoted as Y.

3: **if** x is larger **then**

4:    X will be placed beneath the reference packet. If height of the updated heap is smaller than H_0, record the reference packet into *temp* before update all packets in the list. The arriving packet becomes reference packet and go back to step 2. Otherwise, jump to step 18.

5: **end if**

6: **if** equal **then**

7:    If height is allowed, X will be placed beneath the reference packet but reference packet will not change. Update the whole list before go back to step 2. Otherwise jump to step 18.

8: **end if**

9: **if** smaller **then**

10:    Try to place X on Y using IBL. If succeed and then if height is allowed, reference packet will not change and go back to step 2. If height is not allowed, jump to step 18. If fail, begin rollback. Draw packets from the list with descending order and compare with X until *temp* is empty.

11:    **if** x is larger than y **then**

12:       Try to place X on Y. IF succeed and height is allowed, stop drawing. Reference packet will not change. Namely, continue programming on the packet before rollback. Go back to step 2. IF fail, delete the drawn packet and draw the next packet.

13:    **end if**

14:    **if** equal **then**

15:       Determine the height. IF height is allowed, place X beneath Y. Reference packet will not change, either. Then for all packets whose priority are smaller than x, update them. Stop drawing and go back to step 2; otherwise, delete the drawn packet and draw the next packet.

16:    **end if**

17: **end if**

18: The packet that is not placed successfully will be the first one in next heap. For the heap constructed successfully, try to place it on floor of container using IBL. IF succeed, go back to step 2; otherwise, discard the heap and finish the algorithm.

References

1. Wang, J., Jiang, C., Han, Z., Ren, Y., Maunder, R.G., Hanzo, L.: Taking drones to the next level: cooperative distributed unmanned-aerial-vehicular networks for small and mini drones. IEEE Veh. Technol. Mag. **12**(3), 73–82 (2017)
2. Wang, J., Jiang, C., Wei, Z., Bai, T., Zhang, H., Ren, Y.: UAV aided network association in space-air-ground communication networks. In: 2018 IEEE Global Communications Conference (GLOBECOM), Abu Dhabi, United Arab Emirates, pp. 1–6 (2018)
3. Lin, Y., Hyyppa, J., Rosnell, T., Jaakkola, A., Honkavaara, E.: Development of a UAV-MMS-collaborative aerial-to-ground remote sensing system – a preparatory field validation. IEEE J. Sel. Top. Appl. Earth Obs. Remote Sens. **6**(4), 1893–1898 (2013)
4. Erdelj, M., Natalizio, E., Chowdhury, K.R., Akyildiz, I.F.: Help from the sky: leveraging UAVs for disaster management. IEEE Pervasive Comput. **16**(1), 24–32 (2017)
5. Wu, Q., Zeng, Y., Zhang, R.: Joint trajectory and communication design for multi-UAV enabled wireless networks. IEEE Trans. Wirel. Commun. **17**(3), 2109–2121 (2018)
6. Wang, J., Jiang, C., Wei, Z., Pan, C., Zhang, H., Ren, Y.: Joint UAV hovering altitude and power control for space-air-ground IoT networks. IEEE Internet Things J. **6**(2), 1741–1753 (2019)
7. Hu, Z., Zheng, Z., Song, L., Wang, T., Li, X.: UAV offloading: spectrum trading contract design for UAV-assisted cellular networks. IEEE Trans. Wirel. Commun. **17**(9), 6093–6107 (2018)
8. Rahnama, E., Asaadi, M., Parto, K.: PRE-flight checks of navigation systems and PAPI lights using a UAV. In: 2018 Integrated Communications, Navigation, Surveillance Conference (ICNS), Herndon, VA, pp. 2B4-1–2B4-7, April 2018
9. Keyworth, S., Wolfe, S.: UAVS for land use applications: UAVs in the civilian airspace institution of engineering and technology. In: IET Seminar on UAVs in the Civilian Airspace, London, pp. 1–13, March 2013
10. Shah, M.Z., Samar, R., Bhatti, A.I.: Guidance of air vehicles: a sliding mode approach. IEEE Trans. Control Syst. Technol. **23**(1), 231–244 (2015)
11. Chazelle, B.: The bottomn-left bin-packing heuristic: an efficient implementation. IEEE Trans. Comput. **C-32**(8), 697–707 (1983)
12. Liu, D., Teng, H.: An improved BL-algorithm for genetic algorithm of the orthogonal packing of rectangles. Eur. J. Oper. Res. **112**(2), 413–420 (2007)
13. Wang, J., Jiang, C., Ni, Z., Guan, S., Yu, S., Ren, Y.: Reliability of cloud controlled multi-UAV systems for on-demand services. In: IEEE Global Communications Conference (GLOBECOM), Singapore, pp. 1–6, December 2017
14. Jiang, C., Chen, Y., Gao, Y., Liu, K.J.R.: Joint spectrum sensing and access evolutionary game in cognitive radio networks. IEEE Trans. Wirel. Commun. **12**(5), 2470–2483 (2013)
15. Jiang, C., Chen, Y., Liu, K.J.R., Ren, Y.: Renewal-theoretical dynamic spectrum access in cognitive radio network with unknown primary behavior. IEEE J. Sel. Areas Commun. **31**(3), 406–416 (2013)

Energy Minimization for Rotary-Wing UAV Enabled WPCN

Fahui Wu[1], Dingcheng Yang[2(✉)], and Lin Xiao[2]

[1] Jiangxi Province Key Laboratory of Intelligent Information Systems,
Nanchang University, Nanchang 330031, China
[2] Information Engineering School, Nanchang University, Nanchang 330031, China
yangdingcheng@ncu.edu.cn

Abstract. In this paper, we consider an unmanned aerial vehicle (UAV) enabled wireless-powered communication network (WPCN), where a rotary-wing UAV is employed as a hybrid access point (AP) to serve multiple ground users (GUs). Specifically, the GUs harvest radio frequency (RF) energy from the signal sent by the UAV, which is then used by the GUs to power their uplink information transmission to the UAV. We aim to minimize the energy consumption of the UAV while scarifying the communication requirement of each GUs. The UAV trajectory, user scheduling as well as time allocation need be jointly optimized. Because of the nonconvexity of the problem, we propose an algorithm to obtain a locally optimal solution based on the successive convex approximation (SCA) technique for the proposed path discretization design. Finally, simulation results are provided to validate the effectiveness of our study.

Keywords: UAV communication · Rotary-wing UAV ·
Energy consumption · Wireless powered communication networks

1 Introduction

Unmanned aerial vehicles (UAVs) have been around for several decades and have significantly influenced our lives. Originally designed for military purposes, UAVs are not limited to military missions, but it is only recently that civilian and commercial uses have become feasible with the development of electronic technology and materials science. Of late, UAVs (also known as drones) are being used for a wide range of applications, such as surveillance, cargo delivery and aerial imaging. The research community is now actively working towards exploiting UAVs to improve the performance of wireless communications as UAVs can bring numerous new opportunities including on-demand, ultra-flexibility, 3D-controllable movement, cost-effective technology and inherent ability for line-of-sight (LoS) communications. This is highly relevant for future networks with requirements for ubiquitous, temporary and high-capacity communications. Recent research advocates that, in the future, wireless networking should go beyond conventional 2D cellular architecture. Moreover, according to a recent report from the

© Springer Nature Switzerland AG 2019
H. Yu et al. (Eds.): ICIRA 2019, LNAI 11743, pp. 27–40, 2019.
https://doi.org/10.1007/978-3-030-27538-9_3

US Federal Aviation Administration (FAA), the world will see the emergence of 7 million UAVs in 2020 [1]. A novel communications framework and the explosion of high-mobility UAVs brings new challenges and opportunities: it calls for a re-think of wireless network design.

One of the main scenarios in next generation communication networks is what is called "low-power massive-connections" with a very large number of ubiquitous and autonomous low-power and energy limited IoT devices. RF-based wireless power transfer (WPT) can provide a solution with no wires and no contacts, that is available on-demand and gives a predictable energy supply; with these attributes it is regarded as a promising solution for energizing low-power devices. However, as energy signals suffer from path loss, the harvested energy can be significantly degraded in a far-field WPT scenario. UAVs have an inherent ability to give LoS communications and in [3–6,8] UAV enabled WPT architectures were proposed to improve the energy harvesting efficiency. It was shown that the harvested energy can be significantly increased by optimizing the UAV trajectory. Specifically, in [6], the UAV trajectory in a UAV-enabled wireless power transfer system was optimized to maximize the sum harvested energy and minimum harvested energy, respectively. In [3], the UAV was deployed to power the ground device-to-device users, where the time resource allocation was optimized to maximize the average throughput of all device-to-device pairs. In [5] a UAV-enabled wireless-powered communication network was considered where a UAV was deployed to power ground users in the downlink, and collect data in the uplink, sent by the users using their received energy. In [4], the minimum throughput maximization problem was studied for two UAV based WPCN network; the minimum throughput was maximized by jointly optimizing the UAV trajectory and resource allocation. A UAV-assisted mobile-edge computing system with one UAV and multiple-users was studied in [8], where the UAV acted to give wireless power transfer in the downlink and as a mobile edge computing server in the uplink. Summarizing, the UAV is acting as a special aerial base station that can transfer energy and transmit/receive information.

In this paper, we consider a scenario where the UAV is deployed as a flying hybrid AP to charge multiple ground users in the downlink via RF based WPT, and the users use their harvested energy to send its information in uplink. Furthermore, compared to fixed-wing UAVs, rotary-wing UAVs have the ability to take off and land vertically as well as being able to hover. Much remains to be done in considering rotary UAVs in different systems. Thus, we try to minimize the energy consumption for a rotary wing based WPCN network.

2   System Model and Problem Formulation

In this paper, we consider a UAV-enabled WPCN system, where a rotary-wing UAV is employed to collect data from the K ground users (GUs), which are denoted by $\mathcal{K} = \{1, \ldots, K\}$. The GUs contain a rechargeable battery and each user can harvest energy from the wireless energy signal transmitted by the UAV. Afterwards, they utilize the stored energy to communicate with the UAV in

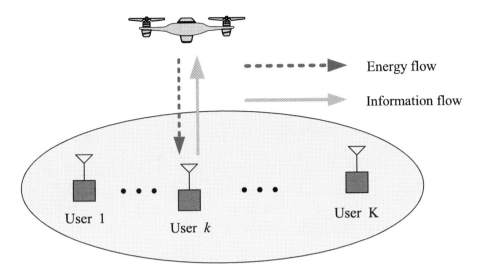

Fig. 1. System model

the uplink. All the users are fixed at the given locations; these are denoted by $\mathbf{w}_k \in \mathbb{R}^{2 \times 1}$ for user $k, k \in \mathcal{K}, \mathcal{K} = \{1, \ldots, K\}$ (Fig. 1).

We consider the path discretization (PD) approach to the UAV-enabled WPCN. The main idea of this approach is to model the continuous trajectory as a finite point (i.e., to divide the UAV trajectory into a finite number of line segments), and the duration of the hovering above each location is uncertain. The traditional time discretization method tries to equally divide the time scope into a finite number of slots, each time slot being sufficiently small so the channel gain is regarded as unchanged in each slot. However, different from the traditional time discretization approach where only the location in a certain time needs to be optimized, both the location and the duration of each line segment needs to be optimized in path discretization. Thus, this approach is more practical when the UAV completion time is a variable to be optimized.

It is assumed that the UAV flies (hovering) at a constant altitude H with the maximum speed V_{max} and the trajectory when projected onto the horizontal plane is denoted by $\mathbf{q}[n] \in \mathbb{R}^{2 \times 1}$. Now we explain the deals of the path discretion: the path is divided into N line segments that are represented by $N + 1$ way-points $\{\mathbf{q}[n]\}_{n=1}^{N+1}$, with $\mathbf{q}[1] = \mathbf{q}_I$ and $\mathbf{q}[N + 1] = \mathbf{q}_F$. To obtain a practicable channel gain model, it is assumed that the distance between two successively accessed points is sufficiently small:

$$\|\mathbf{q}[n + 1] - \mathbf{q}[n]\| \leq \Delta_{\mathrm{max}}, \forall n, \tag{1}$$

thus the distance between the UAV and GUs is approximately unchanged within each line segment. The Δ_{max} is usually chosen as $\Delta_{\mathrm{max}} \ll H$. With a given Δ_{max}, to ensure the trajectory can be optimized within appropriate accuracy, N should be chosen such that $N\Delta_{\mathrm{max}} \geq \hat{D}$, where $\hat{D}$ represent the upper bound of the required total UAV flying distance. The distance from the UAV to each GU k can be expressed as

$$d_k[n] = \sqrt{\|\mathbf{q}[n] - \mathbf{w}_k\|^2 + H^2}, \forall k, n \tag{2}$$

It is assumed the communication channels from the UAV to the GUs are dominated by LoS channels. The channel between the UAV and GU k can be modeled by the free-space path loss model as

$$h_k[n] = \frac{\gamma_0}{\|\mathbf{q}[n] - \mathbf{w}_k\|^2 + H^2}, 1 \le n \le N, k \in \mathcal{K}, \tag{3}$$

where γ_0 denotes the reference channel power gain at distance of 1 meter (m).

Within each line segment n, the UAV adopts the TDMA protocol, each duration $T[n]$ is divided into $K + 1$ subsets. $t_k[n], k \in \mathcal{K}$ denotes the time allocated to GU k for uploading information to the UAV, and $t_{K+1}[n]$ denotes the time allocated for the UAV for WPT. Then the time allocation should follow following constraint

$$\sum_{k=1}^{k=K+1} t_k[n] = T[n], \forall n. \tag{4}$$

The total time taken to complete the mission is

$$T_t = \sum_{n=1}^{N} T[n]. \tag{5}$$

The instantaneous achievable rate of GU k when the UAV is at the nth line segment can be written as

$$R_k[n] = B \log_2 \left(1 + \frac{P_k \gamma_0 / \sigma^2}{\|\mathbf{q}[n] - \mathbf{w}_k\|^2 + H^2} \right). \tag{6}$$

where P_k represents transit power of user k, B stands for the channel bandwidth, σ^2 is the receiver noise power. In this paper, all ground users employ a constant power transmission, and we assume $P_k = P, k \in \mathcal{K}$.

Therefore, the total information bits transmitted from GU k over N line segments can be denoted as

$$\bar{R}_k(\{\mathbf{q}[n]\}, \{t_k[n]\}) = B \sum_{n=1}^{n=N} t_k[n] \log_2 \left(1 + \frac{P_k \gamma_0 / \sigma^2}{\|\mathbf{q}[n] - \mathbf{w}_k\|^2 + H^2} \right), k \in \mathcal{K}. \tag{7}$$

Suppose the capacity of the battery is sufficient large, the UAV broadcasts energy signals with constant transmit power P_{UAV}, the harvested energy at GU k when the UAV is at the nth line segment is given by

$$E_k[n](\{t_{K+1}[n]\}, \{\mathbf{q}[n]\}) = t_{K+1}[n] \frac{\zeta_k \gamma_0 P_{\mathrm{UAV}}}{\|\mathbf{q}[n] - \mathbf{w}_k\|^2 + H^2}, k \in \mathcal{K}, \forall n. \tag{8}$$

where $\zeta_k \in (0,1]$ denotes the energy converting efficiency of user k (all users share the same ratio in this paper, i.e., $\zeta_k = \zeta \,, \forall\, k \in \mathcal{K}$).

It is reasonable to assume that the battery is not empty otherwise the users may be completely dead. Suppose that the initial energy of all users is sufficient to power their forthcoming data transmission, and their harvested energy will exceed that consumed in the duration T_t. More specifically, at the end of the UAV flight, the energy stored in the battery should no less than initially. As a result, the energy non-causality constraints should be maintained for each of the K users

$$\sum_{n=1}^{N} t_k[n]P_k \le \sum_{n=1}^{N} E_k[n], k \in \mathcal{K}. \tag{9}$$

The energy consumption model for the rotary-wing UAV in this paper uses the model proposed in [7], the main idea of this model being that the rotary-wing UAV is following a straight flight and the acceleration energy consumption can be ignored, thus the propulsion power consumption is a function of speed V, which can be formulated as

$$P(V) = \underbrace{P_0 \left(1 + \frac{3V^2}{U_{\text{tip}}^2}\right)}_{\text{blade profile}} + \underbrace{P_i \left(\sqrt{1 + \frac{V^4}{4v_0^2}} - \frac{V^2}{2v_0^2}\right)^{1/2}}_{\text{induced}} + \underbrace{\frac{1}{2}d_0\rho s A V^3}_{\text{parasite}}, \tag{10}$$

where the first and third component is blade profile power and parasite power, which increase quadratically and cubically with V, respectively. The second part is the induced power to overcome induced drag, which decreases with V, more details about parameters setting in (10) can be obtained from [7].

Suppose that the UAV flies with a constant velocity and denote the velocity that the UAV remains in the nth line segment as $T[n]$, then the UAV velocity along the nth segment is $\mathbf{v}[n] = \frac{\mathbf{q}[n]-\mathbf{q}[n+1]}{T[n]}, \forall n$. Then the UAV energy consumption can be expressed as

$$Q(\{T[n]\}, \{\mathbf{q}[n]\}, \{t_k[n]\}) = \sum_{n=1}^{n=N} T[n]P\left(\frac{\Delta[n]}{T[n]}\right) + \sum_{n=1}^{n=N} P_{\text{UAV}}t_{K+1}[n]$$

$$= P_0 \sum_{n=1}^{n=N}\left(T[n] + \frac{3\Delta[n]^2}{U_{\text{tip}}^2 T[n]}\right) + P_i \sum_{n=1}^{n=N}\left(\sqrt{T[n]^4 + \frac{\Delta[n]^4}{4v_0^4}} - \frac{\Delta[n]^2}{2v_0^2}\right)^{1/2} \tag{11}$$

$$+ \frac{1}{2}d_0\rho s A \sum_{n=1}^{n=N} \frac{\Delta[n]^3}{T[n]^2} + \sum_{n=1}^{n=N} P_{\text{UAV}}t_{K+1}[n]$$

where $\Delta[n] \triangleq \|\mathbf{q}[n] - \mathbf{q}[n+1]\|$ is the length of the nth line segment.

The focus of this paper is to minimize the energy consumption and the corresponding UAV trajectory. Mathematically, we can write:

$$(\text{P1}): \min_{\{T[n], \mathbf{q}[n], t_k[n]\}} Q(\{T[n]\}, \{\mathbf{q}[n]\}, \{t_k[n]\})$$

$$\bar{R}_k(\{\mathbf{q}[n]\}, \{t_k[n]\}) \geq R_{\min}^k, k \in \mathcal{K}, \tag{12a}$$

$$\|\mathbf{q}[n] - \mathbf{q}[n+1]\| \leq \min(\Delta_{\max}, T[n]V_{\max}), n \in \mathcal{N}, \tag{12b}$$

$$\mathbf{q}[1] = \mathbf{q}_I, \mathbf{q}[N+1] = \mathbf{q}_F, \tag{12c}$$

$$\sum_{k=1}^{k=K+1} t_k[n] \leq T[n], n \in \mathcal{N}, \tag{12d}$$

$$0 \leq t_k[n] \leq T[n], n \in \mathcal{N}, k \in \hat{\mathcal{K}} \tag{12e}$$

$$\tag{9}$$

where the minimum required throughput of user k is denoted as $R_{\min}^k$, the $V_{\max}$ represents the maximum UAV speed, $\mathbf{q}_I, \mathbf{q}_F \in \mathbb{R}^{2 \times 1}$ denote the UAV's initial and final locations projected onto the ground, respectively.

3   Problem Solution

Notice that (P1) is a non-convex optimization problem due to the cost objective function, the throughput constraints as well as the energy usage constraints are being non-convex. To tackle this difficulty, we provide an algorithm to give a locally optimal solution to (1) based on the SCA technique. First, introduce slack variables to the rate function

$$\Phi_k[n]^2 = Bt_k[n] \log_2 \left(1 + \frac{P_k[n]\gamma_0/\sigma^2}{\|\mathbf{q}[n] - \mathbf{w}_k\|^2 + H^2} \right), \tag{13}$$

where $k \in \mathcal{K}, n \in \mathcal{N}$. In the same time, the throughput requirement constraints become

$$\sum_{n=1}^{n=N} \Phi_k[n]^2 \geq R_{\min}^k, k \in \mathcal{K}. \tag{14}$$

Next, introduce slack variables $\Psi_k[n]$ such that

$$\Psi_k[n]^2 = t_{K+1}[n] \frac{\zeta_k \gamma_0 P_{\text{UAV}}}{\|\mathbf{q}[n] - \mathbf{w}_k\|^2 + H^2}, k \in \mathcal{K}, \tag{15}$$

then the energy usage constraints are reformulated as

$$\sum_{n=1}^{N} t_k[n]P_k \leq \sum_{n=1}^{N} \Psi_k[n]^2, k \in \mathcal{K}. \tag{16}$$

Furthermore, let us introduce slack variables $y[n]$ to the UAV energy consumption function such that

$$y[n]^2 = \sqrt{T[n]^4 + \frac{\Delta[n]^4}{4v_0^4}} - \frac{\Delta[n]^2}{2v_0^2}, n \in \mathcal{N} \tag{17}$$

which is equivalent to

$$\frac{T[n]^4}{y[n]^2} = y[n]^2 + \frac{\Delta[n]^2}{v_0^2}, n \in \mathcal{N} \tag{18}$$

As a result, the UAV energy consumption is expressed as

$$Q(\{T[n]\}, \{\mathbf{q}[n]\}, \{t_k[n]\}, \{y[n]\}) = P_0 \sum_{n=1}^{n=N} \left(T[n] + \frac{3\Delta[n]^2}{U_{\text{tip}}^2 T[n]} \right)$$
$$+ P_i \sum_{n=1}^{n=N} y[n] + \frac{1}{2} d_0 \rho s A \sum_{n=1}^{n=N} \frac{\Delta[n]^3}{T[n]^2} + \sum_{n=1}^{n=N} P_{\text{UAV}} t_{K+1}[n] \tag{19}$$

with the additional constraints (18). Finally, with the above manipulations, (P1) can be reformulated as

$$(\text{P1-1}): \min_{\substack{\{T[n]\},\{\mathbf{q}[n]\},\{t_k[n]\} \\ \{y[n]\},\{\Phi_k[n]\},\{\Psi_k[n]\}}} Q(\{T[n]\}, \{\mathbf{q}[n]\}, \{t_k[n]\}, \{y[n]\})$$

$$\text{s.t.} \sum_{n=1}^{n=N} \Phi_k[n]^2 \geq R_{\min}^k, k \in \mathcal{K}, \tag{20a}$$

$$\frac{\Phi_k[n]^2}{t_k[n]} \leq B \log_2 \left(1 + \frac{P_k[n]\gamma_0/\sigma^2}{\|\mathbf{q}[n] - \mathbf{w}_k\|^2 + H^2} \right), k \in \mathcal{K}, \tag{20b}$$

$$\frac{\Psi_k[n]^2}{t_{K+1}[n]} \leq \frac{\zeta_k \gamma_0 P_{\text{UAV}}}{\|\mathbf{q}[n] - \mathbf{w}_k\|^2 + H^2}, k \in \mathcal{K}, \tag{20c}$$

$$\frac{T[n]^4}{y[n]^2} \leq y[n]^2 + \frac{\Delta[n]^2}{v_0^2}, \tag{20d}$$

$$y[n] \geq 0, \forall n, \tag{20e}$$

$$(16), (12d) - (12e); n \in \mathcal{N}.$$

It can easily be checked that at the optimal point of (P1-1), the newly introduced inequality constraints (20b), (20c) and (20d) holds with equality, this can be shown by contradiction, thus (P1-1) is equivalent to (P1). Still, (P1-1) is a non-convex problem due to the non-convex constraints and cost function. Using the fact that the first-order Taylor expansion is a global lower bound of convex function, for $\Phi_k[n]^2$, we have

$$\Phi_k[n]^2 \geq \Phi_k[n]^{(l)2} + 2\Phi_k[n]^{(l)}(\Phi_k[n] - \Phi_k[n]^{(l)}) \tag{21}$$

where $\Phi_k[n]^{(l)}$ represents the value of $\Phi_k[n]$ at the lth iteration. Similarly, $\Psi_k[n]^2$ is lower bounded by

$$\Psi_k[n]^2 \geq \Psi_k[n]^{(l)2} + 2\Psi_k[n]^{(l)}(\Psi_k[n] - \Psi_k[n]^{(l)}) \tag{22}$$

The global concave lower bound of the RHS in constraints (20d) can be written as

$$
\begin{aligned}
y[n]^2 + \frac{\Delta[n]^2}{v_0^2} &\geq y[n]^{(l)2} + 2y[n]^{(l)}(y[n] - y[n]^{(l)}) - \frac{\left\| \mathbf{q}[n]^{(l)} - \mathbf{q}[n+1]^{(l)} \right\|^2}{v_0^2} \\
&+ \frac{2}{v_0^2}(\mathbf{q}[n]^{(l)} - \mathbf{q}[n+1]^{(l)})^T(\mathbf{q}[n] - \mathbf{q}[n+1]) \\
&\triangleq Y_n^{(l)}(\mathbf{q}[n])
\end{aligned}
\tag{23}
$$

where $\mathbf{q}[n]^{(l)}$ and $y[n]^{(l)}$ are the value of the corresponding variables at the lth iteration. The global concave lower bound can be obtained for the RHS of (20b) as

$$
\begin{aligned}
B \log_2\left(1 + \frac{P_k\gamma_0/\sigma^2}{\|\mathbf{q}[n] - \mathbf{w}_k\|^2 + H^2}\right) &\geq B \log_2\left(1 + \frac{P_k\gamma_0/\sigma^2}{\|\mathbf{q}[n] - \mathbf{w}_k\|^2 + H^2}\right) \\
&- \alpha_k[n]\left(\|\mathbf{q}[n] - \mathbf{w}_k\|^2 - \left\|\mathbf{q}[n]^{(l)} - \mathbf{w}_k\right\|^2\right) \\
&\triangleq R_{nk}^{(l)}(\mathbf{q}[n])
\end{aligned}
\tag{24}
$$

where $\alpha_k[n] = \frac{(\log_2 e)P_k\gamma_0/\sigma^2}{(\|\mathbf{q}[n]-\mathbf{w}_k\|^2+H^2)(\|\mathbf{q}[n]^{(l)}-\mathbf{w}_k\|^2+H^2+P_k\gamma_0/\sigma^2)}$. Furthermore, applying the first-order Taylor expansion of the RHS of (20c), the lower bound is given by

$$
\begin{aligned}
\frac{\zeta_k\gamma_0 P_{\mathrm{UAV}}}{\|\mathbf{q}[n] - \mathbf{w}_k\|^2 + H^2} &\geq \frac{\zeta_k\gamma_0 P_{\mathrm{UAV}}}{\left\|\mathbf{q}[n]^{(l)} - \mathbf{w}_k\right\|^2 + H^2}\left(2 - \frac{\|\mathbf{q}[n] - \mathbf{w}_k\|^2 + H^2}{\left\|\mathbf{q}[n]^{(l)} - \mathbf{w}_k\right\|^2 + H^2}\right) \\
&\triangleq E_{nk}^{(l)}(\mathbf{q}[n])
\end{aligned}
\tag{25}
$$

Now the problem (P1-1) with the above manipulations can be expressed as

$$(P1\text{--}2) \quad \min_{\substack{\{T[n]\},\{\mathbf{q}[n]\},\{t_k[n]\} \\ \{y[n]\},\{\Phi_k[n]\},\{\Psi_k[n]\}}} Q(\{T[n]\},\{\mathbf{q}[n]\},\{t_k[n]\},\{y[n]\})$$

$$\text{s.t.} \sum_{n=1}^{n=N} \left[\Phi_k[n]^{(l)2} + 2\Phi_k[n]^{(l)}(\Phi_k[n] - \Phi_k[n]^{(l)}) \right] \geq R_{\min}^k, \tag{26}$$

$$\frac{\Phi_k[n]^2}{t_k[n]} \leq R_{nk}^{(l)}(\mathbf{q}[n]), \tag{27}$$

$$\sum_{i=1}^{N} t_k[i] P_k[i] \leq \sum_{i=1}^{N} \left[\Psi_k[i]^{(l)2} + 2\Psi_k[i]^{(l)}(\Psi_k[i] - \Psi_k[i]^{(l)}) \right], \tag{28}$$

$$\frac{\Psi_k[n]^2}{t_{K+1}[n]} \leq E_{nk}^{(l)}(\mathbf{q}[n]), \tag{29}$$

$$\frac{T[n]^4}{y[n]^2} \leq Y_n^{(l)}(\mathbf{q}[n]), \tag{30}$$

$$y[n] \geq 0, \forall n,$$

$$(12b) - (12e); k \in \mathcal{K}, n \in \mathcal{N}. \tag{31}$$

It can easily be checked that (P1-2) is a convex optimization problem, which can be solved efficiently by an existing software solver e.g., CVX. Note that (P1-2) is an approximated convex problem of (P1-1), the feasible region of (P1-2) is a subset of that of the original problem (P1-1), thus an upper bound solution of problem (P1-1) can be obtained by solving its approximation (P1-2). As a result, a solution for (P1-1) can be obtained by successively updating the local point at each iterative solve (P1-2), which is summarized as Algorithm 1. The convergence and local optimality of Algorithm 2 can be proved by the similar conclusion as in [7].

Algorithm 1. SCA-based algorithm for (P1)

1: Initialization: Find a feasible $\left\{ T^{(0)}[n] \right\}, \left\{ \mathbf{q}^{(0)}[n] \right\}$, and $\left\{ t_k^{(0)}[n] \right\}$, set $l = 0$.

2: **repeat**

3:    Based on (13), (15) and (17), calculate $\left\{ \Psi_k[n]^{(l)} \right\}, \left\{ \Phi_k[n]^{(l)} \right\}$ and $\left\{ y[n]^{(l)} \right\}$, respectively.

4:    Solve problem (P1-2) for the given local point $\left\{ \Psi_k[n]^{(l)}, \Phi_k[n]^{(l)}, y[n]^{(l)} \right\}$, and denote the optimal solution as $\{T^*[n]\}, \{\mathbf{q}^*[n]\}$, and $\{t_k^*[n]\}$.

5:    Update the local point: $T^{(l+1)}[n] \leftarrow T^*[n]$, $\mathbf{q}^{(l)}[n] \leftarrow q^*[n]$, and $t_k^{(l)}[n] \leftarrow t_k^*[n]\Psi_{ki}^*$.

6:    Update: $l = l + 1$

7: **until** convergence or maximum a number of iterations.

---

4   Numerical Results

In this section, we provide the numerical results to validate the performance of our proposed approach. In the simulation, we set the UAV altitude as $H = 10$ m, the maximum UAV flying speed as $V_{\max} = 25$ m/s, the transmit power at the UAV as $P_{\mathrm{UAV}} = 15$ W, and the noise power at the UAV as $\sigma^2 = -90$ dBm. The channel power gain at the distance of 1 m is $\gamma_0 = -30$ dB, available communication bandwidth is $B = 10$ MHz, and the energy harvesting efficiency of all users is $\zeta_k = 55\%$. The uplink transmission power at all users is $p_k = p = -10$ dBm. We consider that the initial and final positions of the UAV are $\mathbf{q}_{\mathrm{I}} = [0, 0]^T$, and $\mathbf{q}_{\mathrm{F}} = [100\,\mathrm{m}, 100\,\mathrm{m}]^T$, there are $K = 6$ ground users with their locations marked by the blue stars in Fig. 2. It is assumed that all users have an identical throughput requirement $R_{\min}^k = R_{\min}, \forall k \in \mathcal{K}$. For comparison, we also plot the performance of the fly-hovering-communication (FHC) scheme wherein the UAV communicate with users only when hovering.

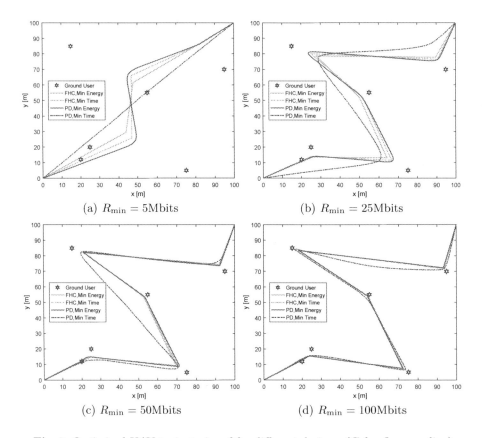

(a) $R_{\min} = 5$Mbits

(b) $R_{\min} = 25$Mbits

(c) $R_{\min} = 50$Mbits

(d) $R_{\min} = 100$Mbits

Fig. 2. Optimized UAV trajectories of for different designs. (Color figure online)

The trajectories of two schemes in the case of energy non-causality (for minimum energy and minimum time) are shown in Fig. 2; the corresponding UAV speed is shown in Fig. 3. For the PD scheme, it is firstly observed from Fig. 2(a), (b) and (c) that the total traveling distance of the trajectories that minimize the time is shorter than that of the trajectories that minimize the energy; however, when $R_{min} = 100$ Mbits, the total traveling distance of the trajectories that minimize the time is longer than that of the trajectories that minimize the time. This is expected due to the following trade-off: while UAVs fly close to the users to minimize the communication time, they must travel longer distances and hence more time is needed for flight. When the communication requirement is sufficient large ($R_{min} = 100$ Mbits), although the longer distance increases the flight time, the reduced communication time is more significant for achieving energy minimization.

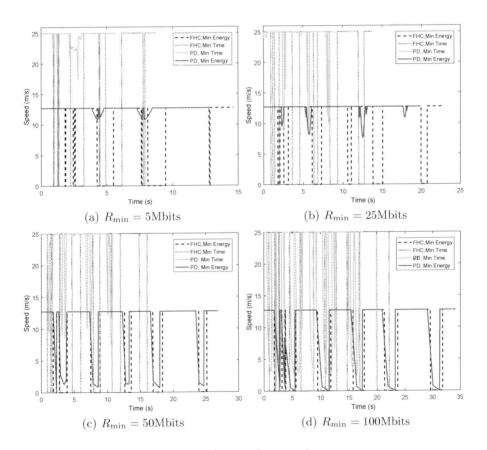

(a) $R_{min} = 5$Mbits

(b) $R_{min} = 25$Mbits

(c) $R_{min} = 50$Mbits

(d) $R_{min} = 100$Mbits

Fig. 3. UAV speed versus time.

It is also found that the distance between each user to its nearest UAV hovering points when $R_{min} = 10$ Mbits is smaller than that when $R_{min} = 2.5$ Mbits, what's more, the total traveling distance when $R_{\min} = 10$ Mbits is longer than that when $R_{\min} = 2.5$ Mbits. This can be explained as follows: the total energy consumption of UAV in FHC scheme contains two parts: one is the consumption when UAV moving another is that when UAV hovering, the optimization procedure is to balance the tradeoff between UAV's moving energy consumption and UAV's hovering consumption via optimizing the hovering location. Note that while hovering position closer to each GU, both the WPT and DG links channel gain becomes more considerable hence reduces the hovering time, the minimum hovering time for DG achieved when UAV hovering exactly above each GUs. However, as the hovering time decreases, the UAV's traveling distance increased hence more energy consumption is needed for UAV flying. Thus, the higher the throughput requirement is, the closer the optimized hovering locations will be from the GUs.

Figure 3 shows that in PD scheme, for the case with relatively low throughput requirement of $R_{\min} = 2.5$ Mbits, the resulting UAV is almost flying with V_{MR} to minimize energy. To minimize the completion time without considering the energy consumption, the UAV within PD scheme always fly at maximum speed in order to visit the GU as soon as possible. Interestingly, by comparing Figs. 2 and 3, it is observed that with relatively high throughput requirement $R_{\min} = 10$ Mbits, as the UAV approaches the GU, it tends to slow its speed and detour its path towards the GU, instead of hovering somewhere. This clearly shows that hovering is not the most energy-conserving UAV status, and slow down the speed makes UAV can enjoy the favorable communication channel for a longer time.

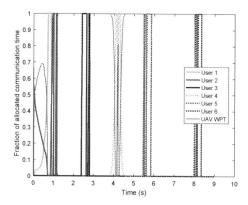

Fig. 4. Fraction of allocate communicate time for PD-based completion time minimization

Next, Fig. 4 shows the fraction of allocated time of UAV at each time instant for proposed PD, namely the values of $t_k[n]/T[n]$. It is observed that communication (WPT or data gather) happens during all the flying period, moreover, the UAV is tends to allocating more time to communicate with the nearer GU.

Finally, Fig. 5 shows the energy consumption and mission completion time versus the communication requirement R_{min}, respectively. For comparison, we also consider the performance of the benchmark scheme, namely hovering at geometric center. It is firstly observed that the proposed schemes can significantly reduce the energy consumption and completion time when compare with that of benchmark scheme. Moreover, it found that completion time minimization and energy minimization are not two conflicting goals, minimize the mission completion time can to some extent reduce the energy consumption and vice versa.

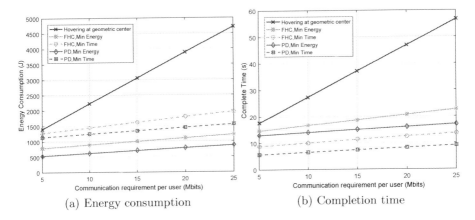

(a) Energy consumption   (b) Completion time

Fig. 5. Energy consumption and mission completion time versus throughput requirement

5   Conslusion

In this paper, we studied the energy minimization for the rotary-wing UAV enabled WPCN. We proposed a SCA technique based algorithm for the path discretion protocol, the trajectory and time allocation are jointly optimized while satisfying the communication throughput requirement for each GUs. Numerical results revealed that our proposed algorithms can achieve a better communication performance.

References

1. Federal aviation administration reports. https://www.faa.gov/about/plans-reports
2. Grant, M., Boyd, S.: CVX: MATLAB software for disciplined convex programming, version 2.1, March 2014. http://cvxr.com/cvx

3. Wang, H., Wang, J., Ding, G., Wang, L., Tsiftsis, T.A., Sharma, P.K.: Resource allocation for energy harvesting-powered D2D communication underlaying UAV-assisted networks. IEEE Trans. Green Commun. Netw. **2**(1), 14–24 (2018). https://doi.org/10.1109/TGCN.2017.2767203

4. Wu, F., Yang, D., Xiao, L., Cuthbert, L.: Minimum-throughput maximization for multi-UAV-enabled wireless-powered communication networks. Sensors **19**(7) (2019). https://doi.org/10.3390/s19071491

5. Xie, L., Xu, J., Zhang, R.: Throughput maximization for UAV-enabled wireless powered communication networks. IEEE Internet Things J. **6**(2), 1690–1703 (2019). https://doi.org/10.1109/JIOT.2018.2875446

6. Xu, J., Zeng, Y., Zhang, R.: UAV-enabled wireless power transfer: trajectory design and energy optimization. IEEE Trans. Wirel. Commun. **17**(8), 5092–5106 (2018). https://doi.org/10.1109/TWC.2018.2838134

7. Zeng, Y., Xu, J., Zhang, R.: Energy minimization for wireless communication with rotary-wing UAV. IEEE Trans. Wirel. Commun. **18**(4), 2329–2345 (2019). https://doi.org/10.1109/TWC.2019.2902559

8. Zhou, F., Wu, Y., Hu, R.Q., Qian, Y.: Computation rate maximization in UAV-enabled wireless-powered mobile-edge computing systems. IEEE J. Sel. Areas Commun. **36**(9), 1927–1941 (2018). https://doi.org/10.1109/JSAC.2018.2864426

Secrecy Energy Efficiency Maximization for UAV-Aided Communication Systems

Meng Hua, Chunguo Li, and Luxi Yang[(⊠)]

School of Information Science and Engineering, Southeast University,
Nanjing 210096, China
{mhua,chunguoli,lxyang}@seu.edu.cn

Abstract. This paper investigates unmanned aerial vehicle (UAV) enabled secure transmission systems, where a source UAV (SUAV) intends to send confidential signals to the legitimate user in the presence of a potential eavesdropper. To improve the system's secrecy rate, a jamming UAV (JUAV) is leveraged to cooperatively send interference signals to the potential eavesdropper. By taking into account the limited energy budget of UAV, our goal is to maximize the system secrecy energy efficiency (SEE), namely the achievable secrecy rate per energy consumption unit, by jointly optimizing UAV trajectory and transmit power under the constraints of UAV mobility as well as the maximum transmit power. The formulated problem is shown to be a non-convex fractional optimization problem, which is challenging to solve. To this end, we decompose the original problem into two sub-problems, and then an efficient iterative algorithm is proposed by leveraging block coordinate descent and Dinkelbach method in combination with successive convex approximation techniques. Simulation results show that the proposed scheme outperforms other benchmarks significantly in terms of the system SEE.

Keywords: Secure transmission · UAV · Trajectory optimization · Cooperative jamming

1 Introduction

The unmanned aerial vehicles (UAVs) have already received significant attention both from academia and industry for various applications such as energy transmission, data collection, hot spot offloading and wireless communication [1–6]. The UAV's flexible mobility provides a potential line-of-sight (LoS) in air-to-ground channels with great probability, which means that a higher throughput can be achieved.

Although the UAVs leveraged in wireless communication bring many benefits, e.g., higher throughput, better QoS, lower delay and etc., the UAV-aided wireless communication systems are not safe and are more vulnerable to be

© Springer Nature Switzerland AG 2019
H. Yu et al. (Eds.): ICIRA 2019, LNAI 11743, pp. 41–51, 2019.
https://doi.org/10.1007/978-3-030-27538-9_4

wiretapped by malicious eavesdroppers due to the high probability of LoS channel obtained by eavesdroppers. Unfortunately, the sustainability and performance of UAV-enabled communication systems are fundamentally limited by the onboard energy of UAVs [7,8]. Therefore, the secrecy energy efficiency (SEE) of UAV-enabled communication systems, which defined as the ratio of the total secrecy rate of the systems to the total UAVs energy consumption measured by bits/Joule, is of paramount importance in practice. In fact, there have been a large number of works studied the SEE in traditional physical layer system [9–12]. Different from the literatures for the traditional cellular network, the UAV-aided secure transmission considers not only the system secrecy rate but also the UAV propulsion energy consumed by its movement. It is worth pointing out that the UAV communication energy is several orders of magnitude lower than the UAV propulsion energy consumption [8]. Therefore, the SEE of UAV-enabled transmission design still remains a new open issue.

In this paper, we consider a secure transmission system where a SUAV is leveraged to help data transmission to the legitimate user in the presence of a potential eavesdropper. For improving the secrecy rate, a JUAV is also used for transmitting the jamming signals to the potential eavesdropper. As a result, our goal is to maximize the system SEE by jointly optimizing the UAV trajectory and transmit power under constraints of UAV mobility as well as maximum transmit power.

The rest of this paper is organized as follows. In Sect. 2, we introduce the multi-UAV enabled cooperative secure communication systems and formulate the SEE problem. Section 3 proposes an efficient iterative algorithm to solve formulated problem by using block coordinate descent and Dinkelbach method, as well as SCA techniques. In Sect. 4, the numerical results are presented to illustrate our scheme, and compare the proposed scheme with other benchmarks. Finally, we conclude the paper in Sect. 5.

2   System Model and Problem Formulation

We consider a UAV-aided secure transmission network, which consists of one JUAV, one SUAV, one legitimate user and one eavesdropper. Denote the horizontal coordinates of the legitimate user and eavesdropper respectively as $\mathbf{w}_2$ and $\mathbf{w}_1$. We assume that both UAVs fly at a fixed altitude H, the collision between UAVs is ignored here since it can be readily extended by adding the minimum security distance constraints as in [13]. The horizontal coordinates of JUAV and SUAV are respectively denoted as $\mathbf{q}_1(t)$ and $\mathbf{q}_2(t)$, $t \in T$. To make the problem more tractable, the period time T is equally divided into N time slots with duration δ. As such, the horizontal coordinate of the i-th UAV trajectory, velocity and acceleration over horizon time T can be approximately denoted by N-length sequences as $\{\mathbf{q}_i[n]\}$, $\{\mathbf{v}_i[n]\}$ and $\{\mathbf{a}_i[n]\}$, $i \in \{1, 2\}$.

Channel Model: The air-to-ground channel (A2G) is dominated by line-of-sight (LoS) propagation as the altitude of UAV is above 100 m [1,13,14].

Therefore, the A2G channel power gain from SUAV to any ground user k, $\mathbf{w}_k \in \{\mathbf{w}_1, \mathbf{w}_2\}$, at time slot n can be modeled as

$$h_k[n] = \frac{\beta_0}{d_k^2[n]} = \frac{\beta_0}{\|\mathbf{q}_2[n] - \mathbf{w}_k\|^2 + H^2}, \tag{1}$$

where $d_k[n]$ denotes the distance between SUAV and ground user k within time slot n, β_0 represents the reference channel gain at $d = 1\,\mathrm{m}$. Similarly, the A2G channel gain from JUAV to ground user k at time slot n, is denoted as $g_k[n]$, $\mathbf{w}_k \in \{\mathbf{w}_1, \mathbf{w}_2\}$.

Problem Formulation: At any time slot n, the achievable rate of legitimate user in bps is given by

$$R_2[n] = B\log_2\left(1 + \frac{p_2[n] h_2[n]}{p_1[n] g_2[n] + \sigma^2}\right), \tag{2}$$

where B denotes the system bandwidth, $p_1[n]$ and $p_2[n]$ are JUAV transmit power and SUAV transmit power at time slot n, respectively, and σ^2 is the additive Gaussian white noise power.

Similarly, the achievable rate of eavesdropper at time slot n is given by

$$R_1[n] = B\log_2\left(1 + \frac{p_2[n] h_1[n]}{p_1[n] g_1[n] + \sigma^2}\right). \tag{3}$$

Therefore, the system's secrecy rate over horizon time T is given by [15],

$$R = \sum_{n=1}^{N} [R_2[n] - R_1[n]]^+, \tag{4}$$

where $[b]^+ = \max\{b, 0\}$.

The total energy consumption of UAV consists of two parts: UAV communication energy and UAV propulsion energy. However, [8] shows that the UAV communication energy consumption is several orders of magnitude lower than the UAV propulsion energy consumption. Thus, the UAV communication energy consumption can be ignored compared with UAV propulsion energy consumption. Based on [8], the total propulsion energy consumption of UAV i over T is given by

$$E_i = \sum_{n=1}^{N} \left(c_1 \|\mathbf{v}_i[n]\|^3 + \frac{c_2}{\|\mathbf{v}_i[n]\|}\left(1 + \frac{\|\mathbf{a}_i[n]\|^2}{g^2}\right)\right), \tag{5}$$

where g is the gravitational acceleration with nominal value $9.8\,\mathrm{m/s^2}$, c_1 and c_2 are the constant parameters related to the UAV wing area, air density and UAV's weight [8].

Let us define $P = \{p_i[n], \forall i, n\}$, $Q = \{\mathbf{q}_i[n], \mathbf{v}_i[n], \mathbf{a}_i[n], \forall i, n\}$ and $\mathcal{N}_1 = \{0, 1, ..., N\}$. As a result, the problem can be formulated as follow

$$\text{(P)} \max_{P,Q} \frac{\sum\limits_{n=1}^{N} [R_2[n] - R_1[n]]^+}{\sum\limits_{i=1}^{2} \sum\limits_{n=1}^{N} \left(c_1 \|\mathbf{v}_i[n]\|^3 + \frac{c_2}{\|\mathbf{v}_i[n]\|} \left(1 + \frac{\|\mathbf{a}_i[n]\|^2}{g^2} \right) \right)}$$

$$\text{s.t.} \quad 0 \le p_i[n] \le P_{\max}, n \in \{1, 2, ..., N\}, i \in \{1, 2\}, \tag{6}$$

$$\mathbf{q}_i[n+1] = \mathbf{q}_i[n+1] + \mathbf{v}_i[n]\delta + \frac{1}{2}\mathbf{a}_i[n]\delta^2, n \in \mathcal{N}_1, i \in \{1, 2\}, \tag{7}$$

$$\mathbf{v}_i[n] = \mathbf{v}_i[n] + \mathbf{a}_i[n]\delta, n \in \mathcal{N}_1, i \in \{1, 2\}, \tag{8}$$

$$\mathbf{q}_i[0] = \mathbf{q}_i[N+1], i \in \{1, 2\}, \tag{9}$$

$$\mathbf{v}_i[0] = \mathbf{v}_i[N+1], i \in \{1, 2\}, \tag{10}$$

$$\|\mathbf{v}_i[n]\| \le v_{\max}, n \in \mathcal{N}_1, i \in \{1, 2\}, \tag{11}$$

$$\|\mathbf{a}_i[n]\| \le a_{\max}, n \in \mathcal{N}_1, i \in \{1, 2\}, \tag{12}$$

where $P_{\max}$ in (6) denotes the UAV's maximum transmit power, (7)–(12) denote the UAV trajectory constraints; $\mathbf{q}_i[0]$ and $\mathbf{q}_i[N+1]$ denote the initial location and final location of UAV i, $\mathbf{v}_i[0]$ and $\mathbf{v}_i[N+1]$ denote the initial velocity and final velocity of UAV i.

Problem (P) is a non-convex fractional optimization problem, which is challenging to solve. Because both numerator and denominator in objective function are non-convex, which lead to a non-convex fractional objective function.

3 Proposed Solution

We decompose the original problem into two sub-problems, namely UAV transmit power optimization and UAV trajectory optimization. Then, an efficient iterative algorithm is proposed via alternately optimizing these two sub-problems.

3.1 UAV Transmit Power Optimization

For any given UAV trajectory Q, the UAV transmit power can be optimized by solving the following problem

$$\text{(P1)} \max_{P} \sum_{n=1}^{N} [R_2[n] - R_1[n]]^+$$

$$\text{s.t.} \ (6) \tag{13}$$

Problem (P1) is also non-convex. To proceed, define $p_1^r[n]$ as the given JUAV transmit power at time slot n in the r-th iteration, the lower bound for $R_2[n]$ is given by

$$R_2[n] \ge B\log_2 \left(p_2[n]h_2[n] + p_1[n]g_2[n] + \sigma^2 \right) -$$
$$\left(B\log_2 \left(p_1^r[n]g_2[n] + \sigma^2 \right) + \frac{B}{\ln 2} \frac{g_2[n]}{p_1^r[n]g_2[n] + \sigma^2} (p_1[n] - p_1^r[n]) \right) \triangleq R_2^{lb}[n].$$

$$\tag{14}$$

Similarly, define $p_2^r[n]$ as the given SUAV transmit power at time slot n in the r-th iteration, the upper bound for $R_1[n]$ is given by

$$R_1[n] \leq \left(\frac{B}{\ln 2} \frac{h_1[n](p_2[n] - p_2^r[n]) + g_1[n](p_1[n] - p_1^r[n])}{p_2^r[n]h_1[n] + p_1^r[n]g_1[n] + \sigma^2} + \right.$$
$$\left. B\log_2\left(p_2^r[n]h_1[n] + p_1^r[n]g_1[n] + \sigma^2\right) \right) - B\log_2\left(p_1[n]g_1[n] + \sigma^2\right) \triangleq R_1^{up}[n].$$

(15)

Therefore, with the given local point $\{p_i^r[n]\}$, lower bound R_2^{lb} and upper bound R_1^{up}, we have

$$(P1.1) \max_P \sum_{n=1}^{N} \left[R_2^{lb}[n] - R_1^{up}[n] \right]$$

s.t. (6)

(P1.1) is a convex optimization problem, which can be efficiently solved by standard convex techniques. Consequently, problem (P1) can be approximately solved by successively updating the UAV transmit power based on the results obtained from (P1.1).

3.2 UAV Trajectory Optimization

For any given UAV transmit power P, the problem (P) can be simplified as

$$(P2) \max_Q \frac{\sum_{n=1}^{N} [R_2[n] - R_1[n]]^+}{\sum_{i=1}^{2} \sum_{n=1}^{N} \left(c_1 \|\mathbf{v}_i[n]\|^3 + \frac{c_2}{\|\mathbf{v}_i[n]\|} \left(1 + \frac{\|\mathbf{a}_i[n]\|^2}{g^2} \right) \right)}$$

s.t. (7)–(12).

To tackle this non-convex fractional problem, we first transform the fractional objective function into subtraction form, we have

$$(P2.1) \max_Q \sum_{n=1}^{N} [R_2[n] - R_1[n]] - \eta \sum_{i=1}^{2} \sum_{n=1}^{N} \left(c_1 \|\mathbf{v}_i[n]\|^3 + \frac{c_2}{\|\mathbf{v}_i[n]\|} \left(1 + \frac{\|\mathbf{a}_i[n]\|^2}{g^2} \right) \right)$$

s.t. (7)–(12),

where η denotes the positive update factor. By introducing slack variables $\{\mu_i[n]\}$, we have

$$(P2.2) \max_Q \sum_{n=1}^{N} [R_2[n] - R_1[n]] - \eta \sum_{i=1}^{2} \sum_{n=1}^{N} \left(c_1 \|\mathbf{v}_i[n]\|^3 + \frac{c_2}{\mu_i[n]} \left(1 + \frac{\|\mathbf{a}_i[n]\|^2}{g^2} \right) \right)$$

s.t. (7)–(12),

$$\mu_i[n], \geq 0, \forall n, i \in \{1,2\}, \tag{16}$$
$$\|\mathbf{v}_i[n]\|^2 \geq \mu_i[n], \forall n, i \in \{1,2\}. \tag{17}$$

Obviously, (17) is a non-convex constraint. By applying the first-order Taylor expansion at local point $v_i^r[n]$, we have

$$\|\mathbf{v}_i[n]\|^2 \geq \|\mathbf{v}_i^r[n]\|^2 + 2(\mathbf{v}_i^r[n])^T (\mathbf{v}_i[n] - \mathbf{v}_i^r[n]) = \Upsilon^{lb}(\mathbf{v}_i[n]), \forall n, i \in \{1,2\}. \tag{18}$$

As such, the constraint (17) can be rewritten as

$$\Upsilon^{lb}(v_i[n]) \geq \mu_i[n], \forall n, i \in \{1,2\}, \tag{19}$$

which is convex since $\Upsilon^{lb}(\mathbf{v}_i[n])$ is linear w.r.t. $\mathbf{v}_i[n]$. Substituting (1) into (2), we have

$$R_2[n] = \bar{R}_2[n] - B \log \left(1 + \frac{p_1[n]\gamma}{H^2 + \|\mathbf{q}_1[n] - \mathbf{w}_2\|^2}\right), \tag{20}$$

where $\bar{R}_2[n] = B \log \left(\frac{p_2[n]\gamma}{H^2 + \|\mathbf{q}_2[n] - \mathbf{w}_2\|^2} + \frac{p_1[n]\gamma}{H^2 + \|\mathbf{q}_1[n] - \mathbf{w}_2\|^2} + 1\right)$, and $\gamma = \beta_0/\sigma^2$. Taking the first order derivative of $\bar{R}_2$, we have

$$\begin{aligned}
\bar{R}_2[n] \geq &B \log \left(\frac{p_2[n]\gamma}{H^2 + \|\mathbf{q}_2^r[n] - \mathbf{w}_2\|^2} + \frac{p_1[n]\gamma}{H^2 + \|\mathbf{q}_1^r[n] - \mathbf{w}_2\|^2} + 1\right) \\
&- \frac{B}{\ln 2} \frac{\frac{p_2[n]\gamma(\|\mathbf{q}_2[n] - \mathbf{w}_2\|^2 - \|\mathbf{q}_2^r[n] - \mathbf{w}_2\|^2)}{(H^2 + \|\mathbf{q}_2^r[n] - \mathbf{w}_2\|^2)^2} + \frac{p_1[n]\gamma(\|\mathbf{q}_1[n] - \mathbf{w}_2\|^2 - \|\mathbf{q}_1^r[n] - \mathbf{w}_2\|^2)}{(H^2 + \|\mathbf{q}_1^r[n] - \mathbf{w}_2\|^2)^2}}{\left(\frac{p_2[n]\gamma}{H^2 + \|\mathbf{q}_2^r[n] - \mathbf{w}_2\|^2} + \frac{p_1[n]\gamma}{H^2 + \|\mathbf{q}_1^r[n] - \mathbf{w}_2\|^2} + 1\right)} \\
&\triangleq \bar{R}_2^{lb}[n].
\end{aligned} \tag{21}$$

By introducing slack variables $\{S_1[n]\}$, $R_2[n]$ can be reformulated as

$$R_2^{new}[n] = \bar{R}_2^{lb}[n] - B \log \left(1 + \frac{p_1[n]\gamma}{H^2 + S_1[n]}\right), \tag{22}$$

with additional constraint

$$\|\mathbf{q}_1[n] - \mathbf{w}_2\|^2 \geq S_1[n], \forall n. \tag{23}$$

Since the constraint (28) is non-convex. Similarly, by taking the first-order Taylor expansion of $\|\mathbf{q}_1[n] - \mathbf{w}_2\|^2$ at the given $\{\mathbf{q}_1^r[n]\}$, we have

$$\|\mathbf{q}_1^r[n] - \mathbf{w}_2\|^2 + 2(\mathbf{q}_1^r[n] - \mathbf{w}_2)^T (\mathbf{q}_1[n] - \mathbf{q}_1^r[n]) \geq S_1[n], \forall n. \tag{24}$$

Substituting (1) into (3), we have

$$R_1[n] = B\log_2 \left(\frac{p_2[n]\gamma}{H^2 + \|\mathbf{q}_2[n] - \mathbf{w}_1\|^2} + \frac{p_1[n]\gamma}{H^2 + \|\mathbf{q}_1[n] - \mathbf{w}_1\|^2} + 1\right) - \bar{R}_1[n], \tag{25}$$

where $\bar{R}_1[n] = B\log_2\left(\frac{p_1[n]\gamma}{H^2+\|\mathbf{q}_1[n]-\mathbf{w}_1\|^2}+1\right)$. Taking the first order derivative of $\bar{R}_1$, we have

$$\bar{R}_1[n] \geq -\frac{B}{\ln 2}\frac{\frac{p_1[n]\gamma}{\left(H^2+\|\mathbf{q}_1^r[n]-\mathbf{w}_1\|^2\right)^2}}{\left(\frac{p_1[n]\gamma}{H^2+\|\mathbf{q}_1^r[n]-\mathbf{w}_1\|^2}+1\right)}\left(\|\mathbf{q}_1[n]-\mathbf{w}_1\|^2-\|\mathbf{q}_1^r[n]-\mathbf{w}_1\|^2\right).$$

(26)

By introducing slack variables $\{e^{x_2[n]}\}$ and $\{e^{x_1[n]}\}$, $R_1[n]$ can be reformulated as

$$R_1{}^{new}[n] = B\log_2\left(e^{x_2[n]}+e^{x_1[n]}+1\right)-\bar{R}_1[n],$$

(27)

with additional constraints

$$\begin{cases}\frac{H^2+\|\mathbf{q}_2[n]-\mathbf{w}_1\|^2}{p_2[n]\gamma} \geq e^{-x_2[n]}, \forall n, \\ \frac{H^2+\|\mathbf{q}_1[n]-\mathbf{w}_1\|^2}{p_1[n]\gamma} \geq e^{-x_1[n]}, \forall n\end{cases}$$

(28)

With the introduced slack variables $\{Z_2[n]\}$ and $\{Z_1[n]\}$, the (28) can be recast into

$$\begin{cases}\frac{H^2+Z_2[n]}{p_2[n]\gamma} \geq e^{-x_2[n]}, \forall n, \\ \frac{H^2+Z_1[n]}{p_1[n]\gamma} \geq e^{-x_1[n]}, \forall n,\end{cases}$$

(29)

with additional constraints

$$\begin{cases}Z_2[n] \leq \|\mathbf{q}_2[n]-\mathbf{w}_1\|^2, \forall n, \\ Z_1[n] \leq \|\mathbf{q}_1[n]-\mathbf{w}_1\|^2, \forall n.\end{cases}$$

(30)

similarly to (24), the constraint (30) can be recast into

$$\begin{cases}Z_2[n] \leq \|\mathbf{q}_2^r[n]-\mathbf{w}_1\|^2 + 2(\mathbf{q}_2^r[n]-\mathbf{w}_1)^T(\mathbf{q}_2[n]-\mathbf{q}_2^r[n]), \forall n, \\ Z_1[n] \leq \|\mathbf{q}_1^r[n]-\mathbf{w}_1\|^2 + 2(\mathbf{q}_1^r[n]-\mathbf{w}_1)^T(\mathbf{q}_1[n]-\mathbf{q}_1^r[n]), \forall n.\end{cases}$$

(31)

It can be readily verified that both constraints (29) and (31) are convex. Then, the problem (P2.2) can be transferred into

$$(\text{P2.3}) \quad \max_{Q,\mu_i[n],Z_i[n],S_1[n],x_i[n]} \sum_{n=1}^{N}[R_2{}^{new}[n]-R_1{}^{new}[n]]-$$

$$\eta\sum_{i=1}^{2}\sum_{n=1}^{N}\left(c_1\|\mathbf{v}_i[n]\|^3+\frac{c_2}{\mu_i[n]}\left(1+\frac{\|\mathbf{a}_i[n]\|^2}{g^2}\right)\right)$$

s.t. (7)–$(12), (16), (19), (22), (24), (29), (31).$

Based on previous discussion, the problem (P2.3) can be efficiently solved by standard convex techniques. Then, with given η, the problem (P2.1) can be approximately solved by successively updating the UAV trajectory based on the optimal solution to problem (P2.3). Finally, an iterative algorithm, namely Dinkelbach method [16], is proposed for solving problem (P2). Based on the two sub-problems, we can alternately optimize these two sub-problems until reach convergence.

4   Simulation Results

In this section, numerical simulations are provided to evaluate the performance of our proposed scheme. The channel gain of the system is set to $\beta_0 = -60\,\text{dB}$, and the noise power is $\sigma^2 = -110\,\text{dB}$. The system bandwidth is $B = 1\,\text{MHz}$. The

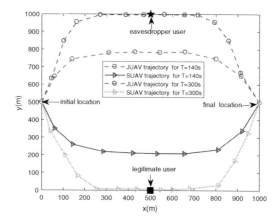

Fig. 1. Optimized UAV trajectories for different period T.

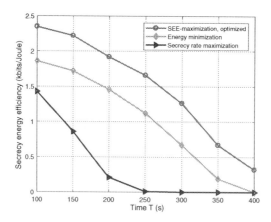

Fig. 2. The SEE comparison of different schemes.

UAV altitude is fixed at $H = 100\,\text{m}$ with maximum transmit power $P_{\max} = 1\,\text{W}$, maximum speed $v_{\max} = 10\,\text{m/s}$, and maximum acceleration $a_{\max} = 5\,\text{m/s}^2$. The duration of each time slot is $\delta = 0.5\,\text{s}$. The horizontal locations of the legitimate user and eavesdropper user are respectively set to $\mathbf{w}_2 = (500\,\text{m}, 0\,\text{m})$ and $\mathbf{w}_1 = (500\,\text{m}, 1000\,\text{m})$. In addition, the UAV energy consumption coefficients are set to $c_1 = 9.26 \times 10^{-4}$ and $c_2 = 2250$ [8].

Figure 1 shows the optimized UAV trajectories projected onto the horizontal plane for the different period T. As expected, the SUAV prefers moving close to the legitimate users to improve its achievable rate, while the JUAV prefers moving close to the eavesdropper to jamming its received signals. Meanwhile, we can also see that the UAV trajectories are smooth since it is in general less power-consuming [8]. In addition, both JUAV and SUAV tends to fly in a straight line, which is energy efficiency trajectory for saving UAV propulsion energy.

To show the superiority of our proposed scheme in terms of SEE of UAV systems, we consider the following benchmark schemes:

- **Optimized SEE maximization scheme:** This is our proposed scheme obtained by jointly optimizing the UAV transmit power and UAV trajectory.
- **UAV energy consumption minimization scheme:** For this scheme, we first obtain the optimized UAV trajectory via minimizing the UAV propulsion energy consumption. Then, with the obtained UAV trajectory, the secrecy rate is optimized by jointly optimizing the UAV transmit power.
- **Secrecy rate maximization scheme:** The UAV energy consumption is not optimized in this scheme. Our aim is to maximize the secrecy rate by jointly optimizing the UAV transmit power and UAV trajectory.

It is observed from Fig. 2 that for our proposed scheme, the SEE monotonically decreases with period T. This is because that the incremental of UAV energy consumption is dramatically increased compared with the incremental of secrecy rate as period T becomes larger, thus decreases the system SEE. In addition, we can see that our proposed scheme achieves significantly higher SEE as compared with the benchmarks, which demonstrates the superiority of our proposed scheme.

5   Conclusion

This paper investigates the energy-efficient UAV enabled secure transmission system. We aim at maximizing the SEE of UAV systems by jointly optimizing the user scheduling, transmit power and UAV trajectory. Numerical results show that the UAV mobility is beneficial for achieving higher secure rate than other benchmarks without considering trajectory optimization. Moreover, three useful insights are extracted from the numerical results. First, our proposed JUAVs-aided secrecy rate maximization scheme achieves significantly higher secrecy rate compared with no JUAVs-aided secure scheme. Second, the SEE of UAV systems does not monotonically increase or decrease with period time T, in contrast, the

SEE of UAV systems is firstly increasing with period T and then decreasing with period time T. Third, our proposed SEE scheme gains significantly higher energy efficiency than that of the energy-minimization and secrecy rate maximization schemes.

Acknowledgments. This work was supported by National High Technology Project of China 2015AA-01A703, Scientific and Technological Key Project of Henan Province under Grant 182102210449 and China Postdoctoral Science Foundation under Grant 2018M63- 3733, Scientific Research Foundation of Graduate School of Southeast University under Grand YBPY1859, National Natural Science Foundation of China under Grant 61801435, Grant 61671144, Grant 61372101, Grant 61720106003, in part by the Scientific Key Research Project of Henan Province for Colleges and Universities under Grand 19A510024.

References

1. Zeng, Y., Zhang, R., Lim, T.J.: Throughput maximization for UAV-enabled mobile relaying systems. IEEE Trans. Commun. **64**(12), 4983–4996 (2016)
2. Hua, M., Wang, Y., Zhang, Z., Li, C., Huang, Y., Yang, L.: Outage probability minimization for low-altitude UAV-enabled full-duplex mobile relaying systems. China Commun. **15**(5), 9–24 (2018)
3. Alzenad, M., El-Keyi, A., Lagum, F., Yanikomeroglu, H.: 3-D placement of an unmanned aerial vehicle base station (UAV-BS) for energy-efficient maximal coverage. IEEE Wirel. Commun. Lett. **6**(4), 434–437 (2017)
4. Mozaffari, M., Saad, W., Bennis, M., Debbah, M.: Efficient deployment of multiple unmanned aerial vehicles for optimal wireless coverage. IEEE Commun. Lett. **20**(8), 1647–1650 (2016)
5. Bor-Yaliniz, R.I., El-Keyi, A., Yanikomeroglu, H.: Efficient 3-D placement of an aerial base station in next generation cellular networks. In: 2016 IEEE International Conference on Communications (ICC), pp. 1–5 (2016)
6. Wu, Q., Zhang, R.: Common throughput maximization in UAV-enabled OFDMA systems with delay consideration. IEEE Trans. Commun. **66**(12), 6614–6627 (2018)
7. Hua, M., Wang, Y., Zhang, Z., Li, C., Huang, Y., Yang, L.: Power-efficient communication in UAV-aided wireless sensor networks. IEEE Commun. Lett. **22**(6), 1264–1267 (2018)
8. Zeng, Y., Zhang, R.: Energy-efficient UAV communication with trajectory optimization. IEEE Trans. Wirel. Commun. **16**(6), 3747–3760 (2017)
9. Sheng, Z., Tuan, H.D., Nasir, A.A., Duong, T.Q., Poor, H.V.: Power allocation for energy efficiency and secrecy of wireless interference networks. IEEE Trans. Wirel. Commun. **17**(6), 3737–3751 (2018)
10. Wang, D., Bai, B., Chen, W., Han, Z.: Energy efficient secure communication over decode-and-forward relay channels. IEEE Trans. Commun. **63**(3), 892–905 (2015)
11. Xu, X., Yang, W., Cai, Y., Jin, S.: On the secure spectral-energy efficiency tradeoff in random cognitive radio networks. IEEE J. Sel. Areas Commun. **34**(10), 2706–2722 (2016)
12. Nghia, N.T., Tuan, H.D., Duong, T.Q., Poor, H.V.: MIMO beamforming for secure and energy-efficient wireless communication. IEEE Sig. Process. Lett. **24**(2), 236–239 (2017)

13. Wu, Q., Zeng, Y., Zhang, R.: Joint trajectory and communication design for multi-UAV enabled wireless networks. IEEE Trans. Wirel. Commun. **17**(3), 2109–2121 (2018)
14. Matolak, D.W., Sun, R.: AirCground channel characterization for unmanned aircraft systems Part III: the suburban and near-urban environments. IEEE Trans. Veh. Technol. **66**(8), 6607–6618 (2017)
15. Zhu, Z., Chu, Z., Wang, N., Huang, S., Wang, Z., Lee, I.: Beamforming and power splitting designs for AN-aided secure multi-user MIMO SWIPT systems. IEEE Trans. Inf. Forensics Secur. **12**(12), 2861–2874 (2017)
16. Dinkelbach, W.: On nonlinear fractional programming. Manag. Sci. **13**(7), 492–498 (1967)

An Efficient Image Quality Assessment Guidance Method for Unmanned Aerial Vehicle

Xin Guo[1]([⊠]), Xu Li[2], Lixin Li[2], and Qi Dong[3]

[1] School of Life Sciences, Northwestern Polytechnical University,
Xi'an 710072, Shaanxi, China
`guox@nwpu.edu.cn`
[2] School of Electronics and Information, Northwestern Polytechnical University,
Xi'an 710072, Shaanxi, China
[3] China Academy of Electronics and Information Technology,
Beijing 100041, China

Abstract. More and more advanced unmanned aerial vehicles (UAVs) equipped with different kinds of sensors can acquire images of various scenes from tasks. Some of them have to assess the obtained images first and then decide the subsequent actions like humans. Accurate and fast image quality assessing capability is critical to UAV. One or more objective quality indexes are usually selected by UAV to assess all the whole image, which may lead to inefficient evaluation performance. In order to further link human cognition pattern with intelligent vision system and provide useful guidance to shorten the image quality assessment time for UAV, a new experimental method of subjective image assessment based on local image is proposed in this paper. 60 participants are invited to conduct subjective image quality assessment experiment, in which 15 original images including people, scenery and animals are distorted by four methods, i.e., Gaussian additive white noise, Gaussian blur, jpeg compression and jp2k compression. Moreover, a new local image segmentation method is designed to segment each image into 6 local areas. For the subjective scores, global-local correlation is analyzed by Spearman Rank Order Correlation Coefficient (SROCC). The experimental results show that the global subjective assessment has the strongest correlation with the local subjective assessment having the best image quality. Further analysis shows that the local images with the best quality often have sufficient color information and rich texture details. Assessing the local images instead of the global ones provides a shortcut to design objective evaluation algorithms, which is a practical guidance for UAV to perform efficient images quality assessment.

Keywords: UAV · Image quality ·
Spearman Rank Order Correlation Coefficient · Subjective assessment

1 Introduction

With the rise of future unmanned combat mode and the development of automation level, unmanned aerial vehicle (UAV) will play an irreplaceable role. It can be predicted that UAVs, in the near future, will have the ability to learn independently and

© Springer Nature Switzerland AG 2019
H. Yu et al. (Eds.): ICIRA 2019, LNAI 11743, pp. 52–62, 2019.
https://doi.org/10.1007/978-3-030-27538-9_5

adapt to the environment like humans. The formation of these abilities largely depends on the support of UAV's "vision" system. Acquiring and assessing images by "vision" system is one of the key issues which will define UAV's subsequent tasks. In flight mission, UAV will be affected by attitude change, relative motion, lens defocusing, mechanical vibration, coding and decoding errors and channel transmission interference. The acquired images may produce blurring, block effect and other distortions. At the same time, the aberration of imaging equipment and the change of motion speed will also cause color loss and drift distortion, which will cause the captured images with drift distortion. How to make UAV to efficiently evaluate the acquired images to meet the real-time requirement is a key technology of intelligent vision system. In order to link human subjective cognition pattern with intelligent vision system and provide useful guidance to objective image quality assessment algorithms for UAV, this paper tries to find and analyze the relationship between global and local image subjective assessments and presents a new experimental method of subjective image assessment based on local image.

Image quality assessment methods can be divided into two categories: subjective image quality assessment method and objective image quality assessment algorithm. The subjective assessment method of image quality is to perform the evaluation by human visual system (HVS) through psychological testing [1]. The objective assessment algorithm is to simulate the perception mechanism of HSV by establishing a mathematical model to evaluate image quality. In practical research, the subjective assessment results from the participants can effectively guide the design of objective evaluation algorithms.

At present, the research on subjective image quality assessment at home and abroad mainly includes organizing subjective experiments, establishing subjective image quality assessment database, and judging the performance of objective image quality assessment algorithm by the consistency of subjective and objective assessment. There are mature subjective assessment technologies and international standards in the world. The ITU-R_BT.500-11 [2] protocol of the International Telecommunication Union (ITU) stipulates subjective assessment methods of television image quality. The setting of test environment, the preparation of test images, the selection of participants, the compilation of test instructions, the selection of test methods and test data are described in detail. During the process of database construction, researchers can refer to the relevant provisions of ITU-R_BT.500-11 [2]. Firstly, prepare the test images and design the experimental process, then recruit participants to evaluate the image quality, finally collect and process the subjective assessment results, and establish the subjective database of image quality. Up to now there are more than 20 subjective image quality assessment databases published internationally. Typical databases are TID2008 database [3, 4], TID2013 database [5, 6], CSIQ database [7, 8], LIVE database [9, 10], IRCCyN/IVC database [11, 12], A57 database [13, 14], MICT database [15], etc.

Subjective image quality assessment plays a significant guidance role in measuring and improving the objective algorithms for UAV. This paper innovatively proposes an experimental method of subjective image assessment based on local image. A new local image segmentation method is also proposed to segment each image into 6 local areas. SROCC is adopted to analyze the correlation between global and local image quality subjective assessment. The feature of local image is also described and analyzed in detail, so as to make further understanding of human cognition pattern and provide guidance to improve the efficiency of the objective image quality assessment algorithm for UAV.

2   Construction of Subjective Image Quality Assessment Experiment Based on Local Image

2.1   Participants of the Experiment

According to the international standard ITU-R_BT.500-11 [2], the number of participants should be at least 15. In order to make subjective assessment have statistical significance, this experiment designed a subjective assessment experiment of 60 participants (25 females and 35 males aged between 20 and 31), with an average age of 25. Before the beginning of the experiment, the color vision and visual acuity of the participants were tested to ensure that all of them had normal color vision and normal visual acuity, and ensure that the experiment method was clearly understood by all the participants.

2.2   Test Images of the Experiment

The test images come from 15 original images, including characters, scenery, animals, food and so on. In addition, 15 original images were distorted by four types of distortion, namely, Gaussian additive white noise, Gaussian blur, JPEG compression and jp2k compression. Each type of distortion is divided into four levels. The total number of test images is 15 * 4 * 4 = 240.

2.3   Segmentation Method

Image segmentation is to divide a certain image into several non-overlapping regions according to its gray level, color, texture and shape. It is an important method in the field of image processing and image analysis to make these features similar in the same region and show differences among different regions [16]. Because traditional segmentation methods divide too many local areas which make the participant hardly able to evaluate the local image quality accurately, a new local segmentation method for subjective image quality assessment is designed for the experiment. According to experimental experience, the proposed segmentation method divides each image into six parts and the segmenting steps are as follows:

Step 1: Image Selection. 15 original images were selected to have different contents such as natural scenery, architecture, animals and characters. In order to make the local segmentation operable, ensure the scientificity of the subsequent local image quality assessment experiment and analysis and meet the above requirements of local segmentation, the contents of each local areas should have certain differences. Select images with rich content and significant edge information, and avoid selecting images with single subject and background.

Step 2: Determine the Order of Segmentation. The local parts 1 to 6 are obtained according to the order from the top left to the bottom right. Due to the difference of each image's content and layout, the order of division is slightly different, but it follows this rule as a whole.

Step 3: Step-by-step Segmentation. Firstly, the image is roughly divided into two or three parts according to its content. Then, the local structure, texture, content and other characteristics are considered, the previously segmented areas are further subdivided into four or five parts. Finally, according to the local color, brightness, contrast and other characteristics, the final segmentation results are fine-tuned and six parts are obtained. The segmentation procedure is illustrated as Fig. 1.

(a) Preliminary Segmentation   (b) Fine Segmentation   (c) Fine-tuning Result

Fig. 1. Step-by-step segmentation

Step 4: Discuss the Rationality of Segmentation. After the step-by-step segmentation, it is necessary to judge whether the segmentation results meet the requirements of subjective experiment and to revise the unreasonable segmentation results. Figure 1(c) is the final result after revision. The unreasonable segmentation, such as too fine division area and unreasonable background division, has been revised.

Step 5: Realize local Segmentation. First, the boundary closure curves of each local region are divided. The mouse position on the edge of the current segmentation area are recorded, and the current position is linked with the previous position by straight line. A small section of tangent is used to fit the edge curve of the area. Click along the contour of the current segmentation area, and make sure that the distance between each click is as small as possible, then the closed boundary curve of a local area can be obtained. Repeat this step until all six local areas are divided distinctly. Then use brush object to fill the local region, the color and transparency are set accordingly. When displaying the current assessment area, adjust the color and transparency of brush to cover the rest parts of the image, so that the current assessment area can be clearly indicated to the participant. The local segmentation settings are adjusted by viewing the local segmentation effect map. According to the above segmentation method, 15 original images were segmented respectively.

2.4   Experiment Method

For the experiment, no reference method was used. There was no reference image in the test process and only the test image is displayed. The participants are asked to make subjective assessment and give their opinion scores according to the quality of the whole image and its local areas. The five-point system is adopted in the assessment. The five grades are very good (5 points), good (4 points), general (3 points), poor (2 points) and very poor (1 point), respectively. Figure 2 shows the interactive interface in the experiment.

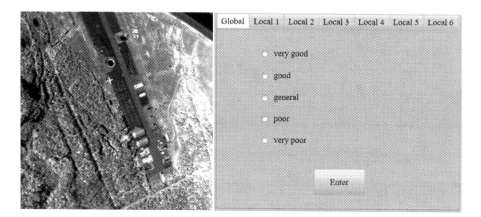

Fig. 2.   Interactive interface

3   Subjective Assessment Experiment Results and Data Analysis

The subjective image quality assessment experiment lasted 12 days. 240 test images and their six local areas were traversed 30 times. Finally, 30 global subjective scores (global scores) and 30 local subjective scores (local scores) corresponding to six local areas of each test image were obtained.

The mean opinion score (MOS) of the global image and the local image is calculated and noted as the global MOS and the local MOS, which is defined as

$$\bar{u}_{jk} = \frac{1}{N}\sum_{i=1}^{N} u_{ijk} \tag{1}$$

in which u_{ijk} is the *i-th* participant's subjective score of the original image k distorted by the *j-th* distortion type. N is the number of participants. The global MOS and local MOS of each test image are obtained using (1).

Note that the six local MOS of each test image is $LMOS_r$ ($r = 1,\dots,6$). The maximum, minimum, mean and median values of local MOS are defined as

$$MOS_1 = max\{LMOS_r | r = 1, \ldots, 6\} \tag{2}$$

$$MOS_2 = min\{LMOS_r | r = 1, \ldots, 6\} \tag{3}$$

$$MOS_3 = mean\{LMOS_r | r = 1, \ldots, 6\} \tag{4}$$

$$MOS_4 = medium\{LMOS_r | r = 1, \ldots, 6\} \tag{5}$$

The local MOS_1–MOS_4 of each test image are obtained by using (2)–(5).

Spearman Rank Order Correlation Coefficient (SROCC) is a statistical analysis index reflecting the degree of rank correlation obtained by ranking the sample values of two elements according to the size of data and replacing the actual data with the sample values of each element.

$$SROCC = 1 - \frac{6 \sum_{i=1}^{n} (RX_i - RY_i)^2}{n(n^2 - 1)} \tag{6}$$

In this performance index, the global subjective score and the local subjective score are sorted descendingly or ascendingly. n represents the total number of test sequences. RX_i and RY_i represent the serial numbers of the first global MOS and the local MOS in their respective sequences, respectively. Generally, the SROCC value is between 0 and 1. The larger the SROCC value, the more relevant of the global MOS and the local MOS.

The SROCC values between global MOS and local MOS_1, local MOS_2, local MOS_3 and local MOS_4 are calculated by (6), and the correlation between global and local image perception is further analyzed based on SROCC.

3.1 Analysis of the Correlation Between Global and Local Image

According to the experimental data, the SROCC between the global MOS and the mean values of local MOS is 0.95, which means that there is a strong correlation between the global MOS and local MOS. Furthermore, the SROCC between the global MOS and the maximum, minimum, average and median values of the local MOS is calculated and the results are listed in Table 1.

Table 1. Global-local SROCC

	Maximum value	Minimum value	Mean value	Median value
SROCC	0.96	0.854	0.958	0.943

It can be seen that the SROCC value between the global MOS and the local maximum MOS is the highest. Since the maximum value of local MOS can be regarded as the local assessment with the best image quality, it can be concluded that the correlation between the global quality assessment and the local assessment with the best image quality is the strongest.

In order to further verify this conclusion, random grouping SROCC calculation method is used to demonstrate. Firstly, SROCC between 240 global MOS and local MOS is calculated. Then global MOS and local MOS are randomly grouped. From the random grouping results, a group of SROCC between the maximum, minimum, mean and median of global MOS and local MOS is calculated, and the SROCC average value is obtained by repeating the calculation process of random grouping 10,000 times. This paper divides the original data into two groups, four groups and eight groups accordingly. Figure 3 shows the SROCC calculation results derived from 1/2, 1/4 and 1/8 of all the data. It can be seen that the random grouping SROCC between the global MOS and the local MOS maximum of is still the highest, which further verifies that the correlation between the global quality assessment and the local assessment with the best image quality is the strongest.

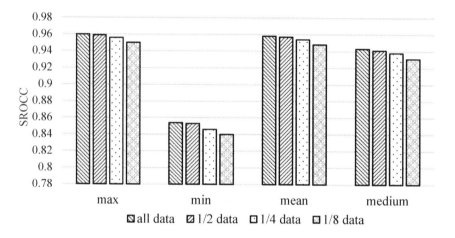

Fig. 3. Random grouping global-local SROCC

3.2   Analysis of Local Image Feature

Further analysis of image features is conducted based on the local areas with the best image quality and the local areas with the worst image quality. Among 240 images, the local 4 of more than 60 images obtains the highest local MOS, and the local 1 of more than 70 images obtains the lowest local MOS. Therefore, the local 4 is used to represent the local areas with best quality and the local 1 is used to represent the local with worst quality. The image features of local 1 and local 4 are analyzed respectively.

Image features mainly include color features, texture features and shape features [17]. This paper focuses on the color feature and texture feature of local 1 and local 4. The basic representation of color features is color histogram, which reflects the composition and distribution of color in the image, i.e. the kinds of colors appearing in the image and the probability of various colors appearing in the image. The function expression is as follows:

$$H(k) = \frac{m_k}{M} (k = 0, 1, \ldots, L - 1) \tag{7}$$

Where L is the number of available feature values, m_k is the number of pixels with the feature value k in the image, M is the total number of pixels in the image. As can be seen from the above formula, the color histogram can well describe the proportion of different colors in the whole image. Use ipc012 as an example, Figs. 4(a) and (b) show the color histograms corresponding to the local 1 and the local 4 of ipc012. It can be seen that the color information of local 4 is relatively richer than local 1.

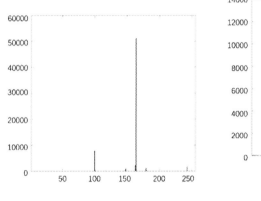
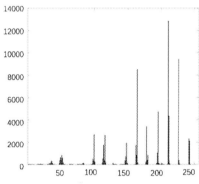

(a) ipc012 color histogram of local 1   (b) ipc012 color histogram of local

Fig. 4. ipc012 color histogram

Gray level co-occurrence matrix is one common method for texture feature analysis. The method gets its co-occurrence matrix by calculating gray level image, and then calculates the co-occurrence matrix to get part of the eigenvalues of the matrix to describe some texture features of the image. Gray level co-occurrence matrix can derive many texture features. Let P represent gray level co-occurrence matrix.

$$P(g_1, g_2) = \frac{\#\{[(x_1, y_1), (x_2, y_2)] \in S | f(x_1, y_1) = g_1 \& f(x_2, y_2) = g_2\}}{\#S} \tag{8}$$

where # represents number, the molecule is the number of pairs of pixels with specific spatial connections and the gray values are g_1 and g_2 respectively, and the denominator is the sum of the number of pairs of pixels.

Based on the co-occurrence matrix, the texture descriptor of an image can be defined, if the following data are defined:

$$P_x(i) = \sum_{j=1}^{M} P(i,j) \ (i = 1, 2, \ldots, M) \tag{9}$$

$$P_y(j) = \sum_{i=1}^{M} P(i,j) \ (j = 1, 2, \ldots, M) \tag{10}$$

From these data, the following texture descriptor can be derived. Energy is a measure of the stability of gray level change of image texture. It reflects the uniformity of gray level distribution and texture roughness. The larger the value of W_1 is, the more uniform and regular the texture changes.

$$W_1 = \sum_i \sum_j P(i,j)^2 \tag{11}$$

Entropy is a measure of the randomness of the information contained in an image, which indicates the complexity of the gray distribution of the image. The larger the value of W_2 is, the more complex the image is.

$$W_2 = -\sum_i \sum_j P(i,j) \log P(i,j) \tag{12}$$

Contrast is a measure of the distribution of matrix values and local changes in images. It reflects the clarity of images and the depth of texture trenches. The larger the value of W_3 is, the deeper the texture grooves and the clearer the image.

$$W_3 = \sum_i \sum_j (i-j)^2 P(i,j) \tag{13}$$

Relevance, also known as homogeneity, is a measure of similarity of gray levels in row or column directions, which reflects local gray correlation. The larger the value of W_4 is, the stronger the texture consistency.

$$W_4 = \frac{1}{\sigma_x \sigma_y} \left[\sum_i \sum_j ijP(i,j) - \mu_x \mu_y \right] \tag{14}$$

$\mu_x, \sigma_x, \mu_y, \sigma_y$ are the mean and mean variance of $P_x(i)$ and $P_y(j)$.

The co-occurrence matrices corresponding to the local 1 and the local 4 of different test graphs are calculated, and four texture eigenvalues, such as energy, entropy, contrast and correlation, are derived from the co-occurrence matrix. Figure 5 shows the mean distribution of energy, entropy, contrast and correlation of local 1 and local 4 of all images. It can be seen that the energy value and relevance of the local 1 are much larger than that of the local 4, which means that the texture complexity of the local 4 is higher than that of local 1. To sum up, the local areas with the best image quality often have sufficient color and texture complexity.

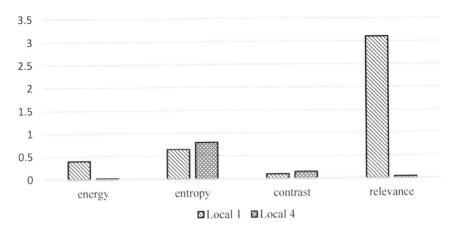

Fig. 5. Distributions of energy, entropy, contrast and relevance of local 1 and local 4

4 Conclusion

The capability of accurate and efficient image quality assessment is a key point to the intelligent visual system of UAV. In order to make UAV to evaluate images quickly like humans, this paper designs a novel subjective assessment experiment trying to link UAV with human cognition pattern from the perspective of bionics. A new local segmentation method is proposed and SROCC is used in analysis of the subjective assessing results. The experimental results show that the strongest correlation exists between the global image assessment and the local image assessment having the best quality. In other words, the quality assessment of the local area in the image can replace the assessment of the whole image. This is a practical guidance for UAV to perform image quality assessment with lower computational cost. Moreover, more efficient objective assessment methods can be designed for the intelligent vision system of UAV. In this paper, there are still some abnormal cases in the experimental statistics, which affects the final statistical results. Since the subjective assessment experiment is uncertain, increasing the number of participants can effectively reduce the statistical bias, which is one of the future research work.

References

1. Zhou, J.C., Dai, R.W., Xiao, B.H., et al.: Review of image quality assessment. Comput. Sci. **35**(7), 1–4 (2008)
2. Recommendation ITU-R BT.500-11, Methodology for the Subjective Assessment of the Quality of Television Pictures. International Telecommunication Union (2002)
3. Ponomarenko, N., Lukin, V., Zelensky, A., et al.: TID2008-a database for assessment of full-reference visual quality assessment metrics. Adv. Mod. Radioelectron. **10**(4), 30–45 (2009)
4. Tampere Image Database 2008 (TID2008). http://www.ponomarenko.info/tid2008.htm. Accessed 10 May 2018

5. Ponomarenko, N., Ieremeiev, O., Lukin, V., et al.: Color image database TID2013: peculiarities and preliminary results. In: European Workshop on Visual Information Processing (EUVIP), pp. 106–111. IEEE, France (2013)
6. Ponomarenko, N., et al.: A new color image database TID2013: innovations and results. In: Blanc-Talon, J., Kasinski, A., Philips, W., Popescu, D., Scheunders, P. (eds.) ACIVS 2013. LNCS, vol. 8192, pp. 402–413. Springer, Cham (2013). https://doi.org/10.1007/978-3-319-02895-8_36
7. Larson, E.C., Chandler, D.M.: Most apparent distortion: full-reference image quality assessment and the role of strategy. J. Electron. Imaging **19**(1), 011006 (2010)
8. Categorical image quality (CSIQ) database. http://vision.okstate.edu/csiq. Accessed 15 Aug 2018
9. Sheikh, H.R., Sabir, M.F., Bovik, A.C.: A statistical assessment of recent full reference image quality assessment methods. IEEE Trans. Image Process. **15**(11), 3440–3451 (2006)
10. LIVE image quality assessment database. http://live.ece.utexas.edu/index.php. Accessed 25 Apr 2019
11. Ninassi, A., Autrusseau, F., Callet, P.L.: Pseudo no reference image quality metric using perceptual data hiding. Hum. Vis. Electron. Imaging XI 60570G–60570G-12 (2010)
12. Subjective quality assessment-IVC database. http://www2.irccyn.ec-nanates.fr/ivcdb. Accessed 30 Oct 2016
13. Chandler, D.M., Lim, K.H., Hemami, S.S.: Effects of spatial correlations and global precedence on the visual fidelity of distorted images. Hum. Vis. Electron. Imaging XI (2010)
14. A57 database. http://foulard.ece.cornell.edu/dmc27/vsnr/vsnr.html. Accessed 30 Nov 2018
15. MICT image quality assessment database. http://mict.Eng.u-toyama.AC.jp/mictdb.html. Accessed 03 June 2017
16. Gu, K., Zhai, G., Lin, W., Liu, M.: the analysis of image control: from quality assessment to automatic enhancement. IEEE Trans. Cybern. **46**(1), 284–297 (2016)
17. Cao, F.M., Tian, H.J., Fu, J., Liu, J.: Image semantics segmentation based on feature map segmentation. Chin. J. Image Graph. **24**(03), 464–473 (2019)

Equal Gain Combining Based Sub-optimum Posterior Noncoherent Fusion Rule for Wireless Sensor Networks

Fucheng Yang[1(✉)], Jie Song[1], Yilin Si[2], and Lixin Li[3]

[1] Research Institute of Information Fusion, Naval Aviation University,
Yantai, China
fucheng85@sina.com
[2] Yantai Engineering and Technology College, Yantai, China
[3] School of Electronics and Information, Northwestern Polytechnical University,
Xi'an, China

Abstract. The maximum *a-posteriori* (MAP) noncoherent fusion rule has been introduced for the best noncoherent detection performance, however, which is prohibitively complex for widely practical applications. In this contribution, a novel noncoherent detector named equal gain combining aided sub-optimum MAP (EGC-SMAP) is employed for the fusion detection in wireless sensor networks (WSNs). Explicate, our proposed EGC-SMAP fusion rule starts the detecting via EGC principle which shrinks the searching range. Then, the final decision is made by MAP fusion rule within the searching range. The novel EGC-SMAP fusion rule has two major advantages compared with the previous work. (1) It allows noncoherent detection, hence, the phase information of carrier is no longer required. As such, it is particularly suitable for WSNs applications with severe resource constraints. (2) This EGC-SMAP fusion rule can be viewed as a combination of EGC and MAP fusion rules, which is capable of achieving various required detection performance as well as computation complexity via justifying the searching range.

Keywords: Wireless sensor network · Frequency-hopping ·
M-ary frequency-shift keying · Fusion rules · Noncoherent detection ·
Rayleigh · Equal-gain combining · Maximum *a-posteriori* principle

1 Introduction

The pervasive advent of wireless sensor networks (WSNs) is leading to a prevalent trend toward employed the concentrate of massive low-cost and possibly unreliable sensor nodes as opposed to single "super-sensor-node" [1–3]. A wide variety of applications are being envisioned for WSNs, including disaster relief, border monitoring, traffic management, condition-based machine monitoring, and surveillance in battlefield scenarios [4–6]. In WSNs tasked with a distributed or fusion detection problem, geographical dispersed sensor nodes make peripheral

© Springer Nature Switzerland AG 2019
H. Yu et al. (Eds.): ICIRA 2019, LNAI 11743, pp. 63–72, 2019.
https://doi.org/10.1007/978-3-030-27538-9_6

decisions based on their own local observations. These decisions are transmitted through wireless channels to the fusion center (FC) where a final decision regarding the state of the monitored event is made. Many challenges must be overcome before the concept of WSNs become a wide reality involving unattended sensor nodes operating on irreplaceable power source, power resource constrains as well as the time-sensitive nature of many detection problems require prudent use of bandwidth. Orthogonal multi-pulse modulation (OMM) is considered for distributed WSNs [4,7]. In such a scheme, each sensor node transmits m bits of information at a time by sending one of M possible orthogonal signals. M-ary Frequency shift keying (MFSK) modulation is therefore a common example of OMM. In contrast to quadrature phase shift keying (QPSK) modulation and coherent detection [4,7], where instantaneous channel information (ISI) must be performed, the problem of signal reception for MFSK can be accomplished noncoherently, and hence, without explicate channel estimation. MFSK modulation with noncoherent detection is, therefore, the modulation detection method of choice for WSNs that must be designed to operate in moving scenario where the wireless channels to quickly to reliably estimated, and/or in WSNs where the extra cost and complexity of channel estimation is infeasible.

In this paper, we consider the triple-layer WSN monitoring single event with various number of local sensors and one fusion center (FC). To achieve low-complexity and reliable fusion detections, a novel posterior fusion rule based on the equal gain combining (EGC) fusion rule and maximum *a-posteriori* (MAP) fusion rule is employed, which is referred as EGC aided sub-optimum MAP (EGC-SMAP) fusion rule. Generally, in the principle of EGC-SMAP fusion rule, EGC fusion is introduced for sketchy search, then, the optimum posterior fusion rule is employed for the final decision. Our studies and simulation results show that the proposed EGC-SMAP fusion rule can be viewed as a combination of the EGC and the optimum posterior fusion rule. The trade-off between the computation complexity and detection performance is satisfied by setting reasonable search space's size.

The reminder of this paper is organized as follows. In Sect. 2, we provide the operations at the proposed WSNs, which including the sensor processing and fusion processing. The characteristics of the EGC-SMAP assisted FH/MFSK WSN is analysed in Sect. 3. Then, Sect. 4 provides the simulation performance results and corresponding discussions. Finally, in Sect. 5, our conclusions are derived.

2   System Description

As shown in Fig. 1, the objective is to determine the true state of the observed source event (SE) from M hypotheses. In the triple-layer WSN, partial information from L observations about the state of SE is available for local decisions. At the FC, square-law operations are implemented on received signal ignoring the carrier phases. A novel posterior fusion rule based on the equal gain combining (EGC) fusion rule and maximum *a-posteriori* (MAP) fusion rule is employed,

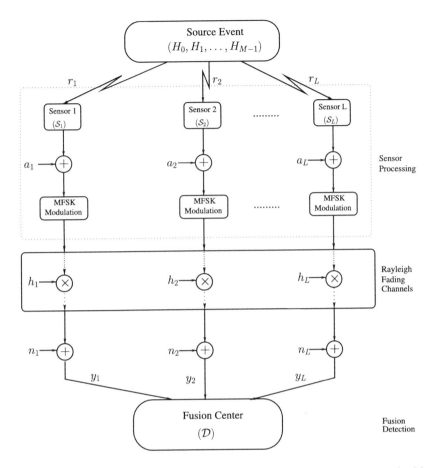

Fig. 1. Triple-layer system model for the FH/MFSK WSN monitoring single M-ary source event.

which is referred as EGC aided sub-optimum MAP (EGC-SMAP) fusion rule. Below, details about the signal processing is shown as follows.

2.1 Local Sensing

In this particular WSN model, the local sensors have no means of exchanging their local estimations, except to the FC, and the FC does not acquire independent measurements. Conditioned on the mth state H_m, the corresponding measurement signal at the l sensor node can be expressed as

$$r_l = H_m + n_l, \ l = 1, 2, \dots, L,$$

where n_l is the observation noise at each sensor, which is assumed to be Gaussian distributed with zero mean and a variance σ^2.

Each sensor employs a likelihood ratio (LR) decision rule γ, which can be considered as mappings for the continuous observation space S. Explicitly, the local decision of the lth sensor node is

$$s_l = m, \; if \; state \; H_m \; isdeclared$$

2.2   Signal Transmission

After processing the observations locally, the elements of decisions vector **s** are transmitted to the FC. To achieve low-complexity overall detection, noncoherent MFSK modulation is employed for signal transmission. Let $s_l \in [0, M-1]$ be an M-ary local decision transmitted by the lth sensor node and $a_l \in GF(M)$ be the corresponding frequency hopping (FH) address.

The vector of complex baseband signalling waveforms corresponding to L sensor nodes is defined as

$$\boldsymbol{m} = [m_1, m_2, \cdots, m_L] = \boldsymbol{s} \oplus \boldsymbol{a} \tag{1}$$

where $\oplus$ represents the addition operation in the Galois field $GF(M)$.

The observation sample of the received signals at the FC can be expressed as considered, the elements of $\boldsymbol{R}$ have the values

$$R_{ml} = \left| \frac{1}{\sqrt{\Omega P T_h}} \int_{iT_s + (l-1)T_h}^{iT_s + lT_h} r_l(t) \psi_{T_h}^* (t - iT_s - [l-1]T_h) \right.$$
$$\left. \times \exp(-j2\pi[f_c + f_m]t)dt \right|^2, \tag{2}$$

where $m = 0, 1, \ldots, M-1$ and $l = 1, 2, \ldots, L$, and $\Omega = E[|h_l|^2]$ denotes the average channel power.

3   Signal Detection at Fusion Center

When the FC received the signals in the form of (2), the SE's state is estimated using noncoherent approach detailed as follows.

The FC starts the detection by forming a time-frequency matrix $\boldsymbol{R}$ of $(M \times L)$-dimensional based on the observations extracted from the signals received from the L number of LSNs. Specifically, when the square-law noncoherent detection is considered, the elements of $\boldsymbol{R}$ have the values

$$R_{ml} = \left| \frac{1}{\sqrt{\Omega P T_h}} \int_{iT_s + (l-1)T_h}^{iT_s + lT_h} r_l(t) \psi_{T_h}^* (t - iT_s - [l-1]T_h) \right.$$
$$\left. \times \exp(-j2\pi[f_c + f_m]t)dt \right|^2, \tag{3}$$

where $m = 0, 1, \ldots, M - 1$ and $l = 1, 2, \ldots, L$, and $\Omega = E[|h_l|^2]$ denotes the average channel power. Since it has been assumed that the M number of frequency bands invoked are completely orthogonal to each other, hence there is no interference between any two frequency bands. Consequently, upon substituting (2) into (3) and absorbing the carrier phase ϕ_l into h_l, we obtain

$$R_{ml} = \left| \frac{\mu_{mm_l} h_l}{\sqrt{\Omega}} + N_{ml} \right|^2, \quad m = 0, 1, \ldots, M - 1;$$
$$l = 1, 2, \ldots, L \tag{4}$$

where, by definition, $\mu_{mm_l} = 1$, if $m = m_l$ while $\mu_{mm_l} = 0$, if $m \neq m_l$. In (4), N_{ml} represents a complex Gaussian noise sample in terms of the mth frequency band and the lth time-slot, which is given by

$$N_{ml} = \frac{1}{\sqrt{\Omega P T_h}} \int_{iT_s + (l-1)T_h}^{iT_s + lT_h} n_l(t) \psi_{T_h}^*(t - iT_s - [l-1]T_h)$$
$$\times \exp(-j2\pi[f_c + f_m]t)dt \tag{5}$$

which can be shown that has mean zero and a variance of $LN_0/(\Omega E_s) = L/\bar{\gamma}_s$, where $E_s = PT_s$ represents the total energy for transmitting one M-ary symbol with each LSN's transmitted energy per symbol being $E_h = E_s/L$, while $\bar{\gamma}_s = \Omega E_s/N_0$ denotes the average SNR per symbol.

Based on the time-frequency matrix $\boldsymbol{R}$ for $m = 0, 1, \ldots, M - 1$ and $l = 1, 2, \ldots, L$, the FC makes final decision using optimum fusion rule and EGC-SMAP fusion rule respectively, detailed as follows.

3.1 Optimum Fusion Rule

Let us now consider the optimum fusion rule which is based on MAP and ML principles. The optimum fusion rule is derived based on the observations provided by the square-law devices. Let us assume that the observed SE is at state H_m, where $m = 0, \ldots, M - 1$. For a given state value X of the SE and a FH address of $\boldsymbol{a}$, the probability density function (PDF) of the received matrix $\boldsymbol{R}$ can be expressed as $p(\boldsymbol{R}|X, \boldsymbol{a})$. Then, based on the MAP principles, the SE's state can be estimated according to the optimization problem

$$\widehat{X} = \max_{X \in \mathcal{X}} p(X|\boldsymbol{R}, \boldsymbol{a})$$
$$\overset{\triangle}{=} \max_{X \in \mathcal{X}} \{P(X)p(\boldsymbol{R}|X, \boldsymbol{a})\} \tag{6}$$

where $\mathcal{X} = \{0, 1, \cdots, M - 1\}$ is a set containing the M possible states. When all the hypotheses for the states of the SE are equal-probability, the influence of $P(X)$ can be ignored in (6). Furthermore, using the fact that the ML entries in the received matrix $\boldsymbol{R}$ are independent, $p(\boldsymbol{R}|X, \boldsymbol{a})$ can be then rewritten as

$$p(\boldsymbol{R}|X, \boldsymbol{a}) = \prod_{m=0}^{M-1} \prod_{l=1}^{L} p(R_{ml}|X, \boldsymbol{a}) \tag{7}$$

Upon substituting (7) into (6) and considering the equal-probability of the hypotheses, the MAP-assisted optimization can be modified to

$$\widehat{X} = \max_{X \in \mathcal{X}} \{ \prod_{m=0}^{M-1} \prod_{l=1}^{L} p(R_{ml}|X, \boldsymbol{a}) \} \tag{8}$$

Let the local estimations made by the L LSNs be collected to $\boldsymbol{s} = [s_1, s_2, \ldots, s_L]$. Then, one given SE's state corresponds to M^L possible local estimation vectors $\boldsymbol{s}_n$. Hence, (8) can be rewritten as

$$\widehat{X} = \max_{X \in \mathcal{X}} \{ \sum_{n=0}^{M^L} P(\boldsymbol{s}_n|X) \prod_{m=0}^{M-1} \prod_{l=1}^{L} p(R_{ml}|\boldsymbol{s}, \boldsymbol{a}) \} \tag{9}$$

when assuming that the channels from LSNs to the FC are Rayleigh fading channels, the PDF of R_{ml} can be expressed as

$$p(R_{ml}|\boldsymbol{s}, \boldsymbol{a}) = \frac{1}{K_{ml} + \sigma^2} \exp \left(-\frac{R_{ml}}{K_{ml} + \sigma^2} \right) \tag{10}$$

where σ^2 denotes the normalized noise variance, $K_{ml} = 1$, if the lth LSN actives the (m, l)th element in the received matrix $\boldsymbol{R}$, otherwise, $K_{ml} = 0$. Finally, when substituting (10) into (9), the optimization problem can be described as

$$\widehat{X} = \max_{X \in \mathcal{X}} \left\{ \sum_{n=0}^{M^L} P(\boldsymbol{s}_n|X) \prod_{m=0}^{M-1} \prod_{l=1}^{L} \frac{1}{K_{ml} + \sigma^2} \right. \\ \left. \times \exp \left(-\frac{R_{ml}}{K_{ml} + \sigma^2} \right) \right\} \tag{11}$$

3.2   EGC-SMAP Fusion Rule

From the above discussion, it can be seen that, when communicating over Rayleigh fading channels with Gaussian noise, the FC needs to carry out $M \times M^L = M^{L+1}$ tests to find the final decision. Therefore, the complexity of the optimum detection increases exponentially with the value of M, which is prohibitive for practical application. Following, a sub-optimum fusion rule is considered, when the MAP is operated after using the EGC to find some desirable candidates. In brief, when the FC forms the received matrix $\boldsymbol{R}$, EGC fusion rule is first employed to get several possible estimations (candidates) of the SE's state. Then the FC makes further decision among the possible states using the MAP principles. In detail, this sub-optimum fusion rule is stated as follows.

1. **Frequency De-hopping:**

$$D_{(m \ominus a_l)l} = R_{ml} \tag{12}$$

where $m = 0, 1, \ldots, M-1$ and $l = 1, 2, \ldots, L$.

2. **EGC Estimation:** After the frequency de-hopping, M decision variables are formed in EGC principles [8] as

$$D_m = \sum_{l=1}^{L} D_{ml}, \quad m = 0, 1, \ldots, M-1 \tag{13}$$

3. **Identification of candidates:** $W = 1, 2, \cdots, M$, largest elements of $\{D_0, D_1, \cdots, D_{M-1}\}$ are selected and their indexes represent the W possible states of the SE. The set of the possible states is defined as $\mathcal{X}_W$.
4. **Detection:** Final decision is made according to the optimization:

$$\widehat{X} = \max_{X \in \mathcal{X}_W} \left\{ \sum_{n=0}^{M^L} P(\boldsymbol{s}_n | X) \prod_{m=0}^{M-1} \prod_{l=1}^{L} \frac{1}{K_{ml} + \sigma^2} \right.$$
$$\left. \times \exp\left(-\frac{R_{ml}}{K_{ml} + \sigma^2}\right) \right\} \tag{14}$$

From (14), it can be seen that the EGC-SMAP fusion rule needs $W \times M^L$ tests, in order to make the final decision, which is W/M lower complexity than the optimum fusion rule. Furthermore, when $W = M$, the EGC-SMAP fusion rule is the same as the optimum fusion rule. By contrast, in the case of $W = 1$, EGC-SMAP fusion rule is the same as the conventional EGC fusion rule, as optimization of (14) is unnecessary.

4   Performance Results

In this section, the symbol error rate (SER) performance of the FH/MFSK WSN employing novel EGC-SMAP fusion rule is investigated, when assuming that the wireless channels from the LSNs to the FC experience Rayleigh fading. Note that, as mentioned in Sect. 3, our proposed EGC-SMAP fusion rule becomes conventional EGC fusion rule when $W = 1$, meanwhile, EGC-SMAP fusion rule equals to the optimum fusion rule, when $W = M$.

Figure 2 shows the SER performance of the FH/MFSK WSN employing $L = 10$ LSNs monitoring an SE with $M = 32$ states (hypotheses). From the simulation results, we can explicitly observe that both the LSNs' reliability and the channel SNR have strong impact on the overall achievable detection performance of the FH/MFSK WSN. As shown in Fig. 2, the SER performance of the FH/MFSK WSN degrades, as the correct detection probability P_d decreases from $P_d = 0.95$ to $P_d = 0.8$. As seen in Fig. 2, increasing the value of channel SNR improves the overall detection performance whenever the value of M is chosen. For a given value of channel SNR, enlarging the searching area enhances the overall detection performance, however, this also increases the computation complexity. Our proposed EGC-SMAP fusion rule can be viewed as a trade-off between EGC fusion rule and the optimum fusion rule, which is flexible for different purpose.

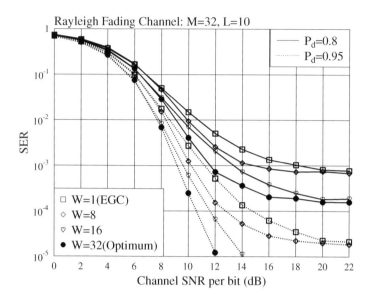

Fig. 2. SER versus channel SNR per bit performance of the FH/MFSK WSN monitoring 32-ary SE using $L = 10$ LSNs, when communicating over Rayleigh channels.

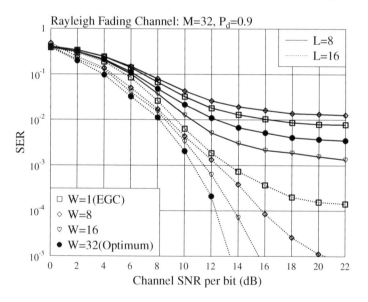

Fig. 3. SER versus channel SNR per bit performance of the FH/MFSK WSN supporting 32-ary SE employing various number of LSNs with $P_d = 0.9$, when communicating over Rayleigh channels.

Figure 3 illustrates the impact of the number of LSNs used on the SER performance of the FH/MFSK WSN supporting a 32-ary SE, when all the LSNs have the same correct detection probability of $P_d = 0.9$. As shown in Fig. 3, when the channel SNR is sufficiently high, the SER performance of the FH/MFSK WSN improves significantly, as the WSN employs more LSNs for attaining the space diversity. However, this detection performance improvement costs the higher system complexity and computation delay. From Fig. 3, again, we can find the detection performance of our proposed EGC-SMAP fusion rule impoves, as the value of M increases. Corresponding, our EGC-SMAP achieves the best detection performance when $W = 32$ and $L = 16$. In this case, the FC needs to carry out $M^{L+1} = 32^{17}$ times computations for final decision, which is prohibitive complex for practical applications. Thus, for some implements need quick responds, our EGC-SMAP fusion rule is capable of reducing the computation complexity with smaller value of W.

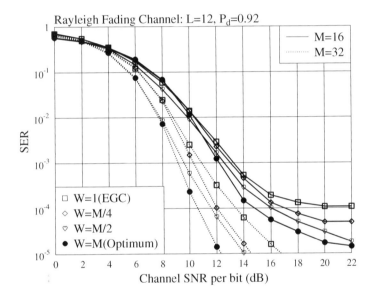

Fig. 4. SER versus channel SNR per bit performance of the FH/MFSK WSN supporting single SE using $L = 12$ LSNs with $P_d = 0.92$, when communicating over Rayleigh channels.

In Fig. 4, we illustrate the effect of the value of M on the SER performance of the FH/MFSK WSN supporting single SE using $L = 12$ LSNs with $P_d = 0.92$, when communicating over Rayleigh fading channels. In context of the EGC-SMAP fusion rule, the number of possible states W, based on EGC fusion rule, is increasing from 1 to M. Explicitly, increasing the value of W, which means enlarging the possible estimations by EGC fusion rule, is capable of improving the overall detection performance. We can observe that the EGC-SMAP fusion rule achieves better detection performance with higher value of W, provided that the channel SNR is sufficiently high. However, if the channel SNR is not sufficient, the EGC-SMAP fusion rule may have similar detection performance with different value of M. This observation becomes very explicit for the case of $M = 16$. Furthermore, the results of Fig. 4 show that the SER performance of the FH/MFSK WSN improves significantly, as the number of states of M increases.

5   Conclusions

Our studies and simulation results show that the proposed FH/MFSK WSN with the flexible EGC-SMAP fusion rule is capable of achieving different detection performance via setting reasonable searching range of W, given practically reasonable values for the LSNs' reliability, channel SNR, etc. In general, under the principle of our proposed EGC-SMAP fusion rule, the MAP is operated after using the EGC to find some desirable candidates. Given proper value of W, EGC-SMAP fusion rule is capable of achieving better detection performance than that of EGC fusion rule, meanwhile, it works with lower computation complexity compared with the optimum fusion rule. Explicitly, when $W = 1$, EGC-SMAP fusion rule is the same as the conventional EGC fusion rule. Furthermore, when $W = M$, EGC-SMAP fusion rule turns out to be the optimum fusion rule. In fact, our proposed EGC-SMAP fusion rule can be viewed as a trade-off between the EGC fusion rule and the optimum fusion rule, which is flexible for different weights.

References

1. Chamberland, J.-F., Veeravalli, V.V.: Decentralized detection in sensor networks. IEEE Trans. Signal Process. **51**, 407–416 (2003)
2. Lin, Y., Chen, B., Varshney, P.K.: Decision fusion rules in multi-hop wireless sensor networks. IEEE Trans. Aerosp. Electron. Syst. **41**, 475–488 (2005)
3. Wang, T.-Y., Han, Y.S., Chen, B., Varshney, P.K.: A combined decision fusion and channel coding scheme for distributed fault-tolerant classification in wireless sensor networks. IEEE Trans. Wirel. Commun. **5**, 1695–1705 (2006)
4. Iwaza, L., Kieffer, M., Al-Agha, K.: MAP estimation of network-coded correlated sources. In: International Conference on Advanced Technologies for Communications (ATC 2012), pp. 199–202 (2012)
5. Plata-Chaves, J., Lazaro, M., Artes-Rodriguez, A.: Optimal Neyman-Pearson fusion in two-dimensional sensor networks with serial architecture and dependent observations. In: Proceedings of the 14th International Conference on Information Fusion (FUSION 2011), pp. 1–6, July 2011
6. Zhang, J., Teh, K.C., Li, K.H.: Maximum-likelihood FFH/MFSK receiver over Rayleigh-fading channels with composite effects of MTJ and PBNJ. IEEE Trans. Commun. **59**, 675–679 (2011)
7. Lampe, L., Schober, R., Pauli, V., Windpassinger, C.: Multiple-symbol differential sphere decoding. IEEE Trans. Commun. **53**(12), 1981–1985 (2005)
8. Yang, L.-L., Yen, K., Hanzo, L.: A Reed-Solomon coded DS-CDMA system using noncoherent M-ary orthogonal modulation over multipath fading channels. IEEE J. Sel. Areas Commun. **18**, 2240–2251 (2000)

Secure Transmission Design for UAV-Based SWIPT Networks

Shidang Li[1,2], Chunguo Li[2(✉)], and Hui Zhong[1]

[1] School of Physics and Electronic Engineering, Jiangsu Normal University,
Xuzhou 221116, China
shidangli@jsnu.edu.cn, 253957419@qq.com
[2] National Communications Research Laboratory, Southeast University,
Nanjing 210096, China
chunguoli@seu.edu.cn

Abstract. Due to the higher probability of the existence of LoS links between the transmitter and the UAVs and the broadcast nature of simultaneous wireless and information power transfer. To overcome it, we consider a secure UAV-enabled communication system with SWIPT under a non-linear EH model where the UAVs are able to collect energy from the radio frequency signals as they are idle. We formulate the secure transmit signal design as an optimization problem which aims to maximize the minimum fairness energy power at the UAVs. In addition, the considered optimization problem also considers different quality of service requirements: a maximum tolerable capacity at UAVs and a minimum needed signal-to-interference-ratio at ground information receivers. To obtain a manageable solution, we reexpress the referred problem by variable substitutions and replacing a non-convex constraint with a convex form. Then, we adopt the semidefinite relaxation (SDR) technique to obtain the optimal solution of the original problem. Simulation results indicate that the developed secure transmit signal algorithm can obtain better performance gains than other algorithms.

Keywords: Secure communication · SWIPT · Energy harvesting · UAV

1 Introduction

The development of IoT enables mobile users to enjoy communication services with higher quality of service, such as virtual reality [1]. However, because the battery capacities installed in those devices are finite, the lifetime of these network is limit which importantly decreases the users' QoE. Fortunately, energy harvesting technique is envisioned to be the promising to solve this problem. It enables users to collect energy from the RF signals. In the past few years, energy harvesting technique has gained great attention from both industry and academic [2–5]. As one category of the energy harvesting, SWIPT is attractive due to the fact that it can simultaneously convey energy and information to

© Springer Nature Switzerland AG 2019
H. Yu et al. (Eds.): ICIRA 2019, LNAI 11743, pp. 73–83, 2019.
https://doi.org/10.1007/978-3-030-27538-9_7

mobile users. In a typical SWIPT network, some mobile users act as information receivers to decode the desired information and the others act as energy receivers to collect energy from RF signals.

Compared to the traditional energy harvesting techniques, such as wind or solar charging, SWIPT can supply controllable energy to battery-limited devices. However, the energy collecting efficiency is limited owing to the channel fading. To improve the energy collecting efficiency, many approaches has been investigated, such as multiple antenna techniques [6], energy waveform optimization [7]. Recently, the technique of UAV-enabled SWIPT has been studied. Due to the small size, the low cost and easy deployment, UAVs have been widely applied in various fields, such as transportation, searching and aerial photography. Also, the UAVs have been used in cellular communication systems [8,9].

Several works have been investigated to exploit the physical layer security to improve the performance of security for UAV-based mobile communication network. Zhang et al. [10] investigated the secrecy rate maximization optimization problem of both downlink and uplink UAV communications with a desired receiver. Recently, UAV-based jamming approaches were exploited to imptobr the achieved secrecy rate in UAV-based communications. Moreover, [11] considered the UAV as a jammer to improve the secrecy performance between a basestation and a user fixed at the ground with a eavesdropper. Different from [11], two UAVs are considered in [12]. To extend into a general scenario, Lee et al. [13] considered a similar communication system with several legitimate users and TDMA was exploited to ensure that confidential messages are intended to one scheduled receiver at each time slot. However, the authors assumed that the locations of multiple eavesdroppers is perfect known in the above related works. Cui et al. [14] studied the worst-case secrecy rate optimization problem by jointly designing the transmit power and trajectory of the UAV system. However, these works have not considered SWIPT.

In this paper, we consider the optimal secure transmit signal for a MISO UAV-SWIPT network with multiple UAVs deployed with multiple antenna under a non-linear EH model. We aim to, under the constraints of the maximum transmit power threshold at base station and secure communication requirement, maximize the minimum fairness collected energy by jointly optimizing the energy beamforming vectors, the transmit beamforming vectors and artificial noise covariance. For getting a manageable solution of the referred non-convex problem, the considering problem can be reexpressed as equivalent problem via variable substitutions and replacing a non-convex security capacity constraint with a convex form. Then, the recast non-convex problem could be solved by a semi-definite programming based transmit signal design algorithm.

2 System Model and Problem Formulation

Considered a UAV-SWIPT downlink communication system, which includes a transmitter and two types of receivers, that is K_I information ground-receivers and K_E energy UAVs with a fixed position. The transmitter has N_T transmit antennas while the K_I information receivers have one receive antenna.

Besides, the K_E energy UAVs (potential eavesdroppers) have N_R antennas. The energy UAVs perform dual functions of collecting energy and decoding information. In this system, the energy UAVs can potentially wiretap the confidential message of the information receiver by changing its working mode to decode information. $\boldsymbol{h}_k \in \mathbb{C}^{N_T \times 1}$ is denoted as the channel between the transmitter and the k-th information ground-receiver, $\forall k \in \{1, 2, \cdots, K_I\}$, and $\boldsymbol{G}_i \in \mathbb{C}^{N_T \times N_R}$ is called the channel between the transmitter and the i-th energy UAV, $\forall i \in \{1, 2, \cdots, K_E\}$. To restrain the K_E energy UAVs (act as potential eavesdroppers) from intercepting the message for K_I desired information receivers and to facilitate energy collecting at the intended information receivers, energy signals and artificial noise signals can be also introduced at the transmitter. Therefore, the conveyed signal, $\boldsymbol{x} \in \mathbb{C}^{N_T \times 1}$, comprises of the K_I intended information signals, the K_E energy signals and artificial noise, and could be represented mathematically as

$$\boldsymbol{x} = \sum_{k=1}^{K_I} \boldsymbol{w}_k s_{I,k} + \sum_{i=1}^{K_E} \boldsymbol{v}_{E,i} s_{E,i} + \boldsymbol{v}_0 \tag{1}$$

where $s_{I,k} \in \mathbb{C}$ and $\boldsymbol{w}_k \in \mathbb{C}^{N_T \times 1}$ are the baseband signal and the referred beamforming vector of the k-th information receiver, respectively. $s_{E,i} \in \mathbb{C}$ and $\boldsymbol{v}_{E,i} \in \mathbb{C}^{N_T \times 1}$ are the energy-bearing signal with $\mathcal{E}\{|s_E|^2\} = 1$ and the corresponding energy beamforming vector for the i-th energy UAV, respectively. $\boldsymbol{v}_0 \in \mathbb{C}^{N_T \times 1}$ denotes the artificial noise introduced by the transmitter to combat potential eavesdroppers, and it can be modelled as $\boldsymbol{v}_0 \sim \mathcal{CN}(\boldsymbol{0}, \boldsymbol{V}_0)$. Then, the received signals at the k-th information receiver and the i-th energy UAV can be written as

$$\begin{aligned} y_{I,k} &= \boldsymbol{h}_k^H \boldsymbol{x} + n_{I,k}, \forall k \in \{1, \cdots, K_I\} \ and \\ \boldsymbol{y}_{E,i} &= \boldsymbol{G}_i^H \boldsymbol{x} + \boldsymbol{n}_{E,i}, \forall i \in \{1, \cdots, K_E\}, \end{aligned} \tag{2}$$

respectively. where $n_{I,k} \sim \mathcal{CN}(0, \sigma_I^2)$ and $\boldsymbol{\sigma}_{E,i} \sim \mathcal{CN}(\boldsymbol{0}, \sigma_E^2 \boldsymbol{I}_{N_R})$ denote the additional Gaussian white noise at the k-th information user and the i-th energy user, respectively. σ_I^2 and σ_E^2 is the noise power of the k-th information receiver and the i-th energy UAV, respectively. In this work, we utilize a practical nonlinear EH model. According to [6], we can model the collected energy of the energy UAV i as:

$$E_{E,i}^{\mathrm{Non-Linear}} = \frac{\Psi_{E,i}}{X_{E,i}} - Y_{E,i} \tag{3}$$

with

$$\Psi_{E,i} = \frac{M_{E,i}}{1 + \exp\left(-a_{E,i}\left(P_{E,i}\left(\{\boldsymbol{W}_k\}, \boldsymbol{V}, \boldsymbol{V}_0\right) - b_{E,i}\right)\right)} \tag{4}$$

$$P_{E,i}\left(\{W_k\}, V, V_0\right) = \sum_{k=1}^{K_I} \|G_i^H w_k\|^2 + \sum_{j=1}^{K_E} \|G_i^H v_{E,j}\|^2 + \|G_i^H v_0\|^2$$

$$= Tr\left[G_i^H \left(\sum_{k=1}^{K_I} W_k + V + V_0\right)G_i\right], \forall i$$

(5)

where $X_{E,i} = \dfrac{\exp\left(a_{E,i} b_{E,i}\right)}{1 + \exp\left(a_{E,i} b_{E,i}\right)}$, $Y_{E,i} = \dfrac{M_{E,i}}{\exp\left(a_{E,i} b_{E,i}\right)}$, $W_k = w_k w_k^H$ and $V = \sum_{j=1}^{K_E} v_j v_j^H$. $P_{E,i}\left(\{W_k\}, V, V_0\right)$ denotes the received RF power at the i-th energy UAV. Three parameters, namely, $M_{E,i}$, $a_{E,i}$ and $b_{E,i}$ in (4) are introduced to exploit the influence of numbers of non-linear phenomena with respect to hardware limitations in EH circuits. Moreover, $M_{E,i}$ is the maximum power which could be harvested by the energy acquiring circuit unit while $a_{E,i}$ and $b_{E,i}$ depend on the leakage currents and the resistance.

Assuming that the perfect channel state information (CSI) is available at the information receivers, the channel capacity between the transmitter and the k-th information receiver could be expressed as

$$C_k = \log_2\left(1 + \Gamma_k\right)$$

(6)

where

$$\Gamma_k = \frac{|h_k^H w_k|^2}{\sum_{m \neq k}^{K_I} |h_k^H w_m|^2 + \sum_{j=1}^{K_E} |h_k^H v_{E,j}|^2 + Tr(H_k V_0) + \sigma_I^2}$$

$$= \frac{Tr(H_k W_k)}{Tr\left[H_k\left(\sum_{m \neq k}^{K_I} W_m + V + V_0\right)\right] + \sigma_I^2}$$

(7)

denotes the received signal-to-interference-plus-noise ratio (SINR) at the k-th information receiver and $H_k = h_k h_k^H$.

Generally, the energy UAVs could be also considered as a wiretapper to eavesdrop the confidential messages for the information receivers. Besides, it is assumed that the energy UAV i applies the interference cancellation technology to eliminate all cochannel interference and only intercepts the information intended for the k-th information receiver. As a result, the channel capacity from the transmitter to the i-th energy UAV for decoding the message of the information receiver k is

$$C_{E,i}^k = \log_2 \det\left(I_{N_R} + Q_i^{-1} G_i^H w_k w_k^H G_i\right)$$
$$Q_i = G_i^H V_0 G_i + \sigma_E^2 I_{N_R} \succ 0$$

(8)

where Q_i denotes the covariance matrix of interference plus noise for the i-th energy UAV supposing the worse case for secure communication. Therefore, the achieved secrecy rate is given by

$$C_{s,k} = \left[C_k - \max_{i \in \{1,2,\cdots,K_E\}} C_{E,i}^k \right]^+ \tag{9}$$

The optimal secure beamformer design strategy, $\{\{W_k^*\}, V^*, V_0^*\}$, for maximizing the minimum fairness collected energy power over K_E multiple antennas energy UAVs, could be got by resolving

$$\max_{w_k, V, V_0} \min_{i \in \{1,2,\cdots,K_E\}} E_{E,i}^{\mathrm{Non-Linear}}$$

$$s.t. \quad C1: \Gamma_k \geq r_k, \forall k$$

$$C2: C_{E,i}^k \leq R_{E,i}^k, \forall k, i \tag{10}$$

$$C3: \sum_{k=1}^{K_I} \|w_k\|^2 + Tr(V) + Tr(V_0) \leq P$$

$$C4: V \succeq 0, \quad C5: V_0 \succeq 0,$$

Constraint C1 denotes the received SINR at the k-th information receiver is needed to be larger than a preset value, $r_k > 0$, for ensuring reliable data transmission. The upper bound $R_{E,i}^k$ in constraint C2 is introduced to restrict the channel capacity of the i-th energy UAV if it tries to eavesdrop the message of the k-th information receiver. Constraint C3 represents the maximum allowed transmit power at the transmitter. Constraint C4 and constraint C5 indicates that the covariance matrix V and V_0 are the positive semidefinite Hermitian matrices.

3 Solution of the Considering Optimization Problem

To get the solution of the problem (10), a optimized variable $t \geq 0$ is firstly introduced. With t, we can equivalently formulate the problem (10) as:

$$\max_{W_k, V, V_0, t} t$$

$$s.t. \quad C1: \frac{Tr(H_k W_k)}{r_k} - Tr\left[H_k\left(\sum_{m \neq k}^{K_I} W_m + V + V_0\right)\right] \geq \sigma_I^2, \forall k$$

$$C2: C_{E,i}^k \leq R_{E,i}^k, \forall k, i \tag{11}$$

$$C3: Tr\left(\sum_{k=1}^{K_I} W_k + V + V_0\right) \leq P$$

$$C4: V \succeq 0, \quad C5: V_0 \succeq 0,$$

$$C6: E_{E,i}^{\mathrm{Non-Linear}} \leq t, \forall i$$

$$C7: W_k \succeq 0, \forall k, \quad C8: rank(W_k) = 1, \forall k$$

where constraint C7 and constraint C8 in (11) are introduced to ensure that $W_k = w_k w_k^H$ holds after optimizing W_k, $\forall k$. To facilitate the problem (11), we introduce another slack variable τ_i, $\forall i \in \{1, \cdots, K_E\}$, the problem (10) can be rewritten as

$$
\max_{\boldsymbol{W}_k, \boldsymbol{V}, \boldsymbol{V}_0, t, \tau_{E,i}} t
$$

$$
s.t. \quad C1: \frac{Tr(\boldsymbol{H}_k \boldsymbol{W}_k)}{r_k} - Tr\left[\boldsymbol{H}_k\left(\sum_{m \neq k}^{K_I} \boldsymbol{W}_m + \boldsymbol{V} + \boldsymbol{V}_0\right)\right] \geq \sigma_I^2, \forall k
$$

$$
C2: C_{E,i}^k \leq R_{E,i}^k, \forall k, i
$$

$$
C3: Tr\left(\sum_{k=1}^{K_I} \boldsymbol{W}_k + \boldsymbol{V} + \boldsymbol{V}_0\right) \leq P \tag{12}
$$

$$
C4: \boldsymbol{V} \succeq \boldsymbol{0}, \quad C5: \boldsymbol{V}_0 \succeq \boldsymbol{0},
$$

$$
C6: \frac{M_{E,i}}{1 + \exp\left(-a_{E,i}(\tau_{E,i} - b_{E,i})\right)} \geq X_{E,i}(Y_{E,i} + t), \forall i
$$

$$
C7: \boldsymbol{W}_k \succeq \boldsymbol{0}, \forall k, \quad C8: rank(\boldsymbol{W}_k) = 1, \forall k
$$

$$
C9: Tr\left(\boldsymbol{G}_i^H\left(\sum_{k=1}^{K_I} \boldsymbol{W}_k + \boldsymbol{V} + \boldsymbol{V}_0\right)\boldsymbol{G}_i\right) \geq \tau_{E,i}
$$

From (12), we can easily know that constraints C1, C3 and C9 are jointly concave over the information beamforming matrix $\boldsymbol{W}_k$, the energy beamforming matrix $\boldsymbol{V}$ and the artificial noise matrix $\boldsymbol{V}_0$. Next, we deal with constraint C2. Though constraints C1, C3 and C9 are jointly concave with respect to $\boldsymbol{W}_k$, $\boldsymbol{V}$ and $\boldsymbol{V}_0$, the optimization problem (12) is still challenging to solve owing to the existence of determinant function in constraint C2. To overcome the non-convexity, the constraint C2 in optimization problem (12) can be rewritten as

$$
\det\left(\boldsymbol{I}_{N_R} + \boldsymbol{Q}_i^{-1}\boldsymbol{G}_i^H \boldsymbol{W}_k \boldsymbol{G}_i\right) \leq 2^{R_{E,i}^k}, \ \forall k, i \tag{13}
$$

To proceed further, we introduce the following lemma.

Lemma 1. *Let $\boldsymbol{A} \succeq \boldsymbol{0}$, the following inequality holds true that*

$$
\det(\boldsymbol{I} + \boldsymbol{A}) \geq 1 + Tr(\boldsymbol{A}) \tag{14}
$$

and the equality in (14) holds if and only if $rank(\boldsymbol{A}) \leq 1$.

By exploiting the Lemma 1 and $\det(\boldsymbol{I} + \boldsymbol{AB}) = \det(\boldsymbol{I} + \boldsymbol{BA})$ to the left hand side of (13), we have

$$
\det\left(\boldsymbol{I}_{N_R} + \boldsymbol{Q}_i^{-\frac{1}{2}}\boldsymbol{G}_i^H \boldsymbol{W}_k \boldsymbol{G}_i \boldsymbol{Q}_i^{-\frac{1}{2}}\right) \geq 1 + Tr\left(\boldsymbol{Q}_i^{-\frac{1}{2}}\boldsymbol{G}_i^H \boldsymbol{W}_k \boldsymbol{G}_i \boldsymbol{Q}_i^{-\frac{1}{2}}\right) \tag{15}
$$

Therefore, combining with (13) and (15), it follows that

$$Tr\left(\boldsymbol{Q}_i^{-\frac{1}{2}}\boldsymbol{G}_i^H\boldsymbol{W}_k\boldsymbol{G}_i\boldsymbol{Q}_i^{-\frac{1}{2}}\right) \leq 2^{R_{E,i}^k} - 1 \tag{16}$$

Owing to the fact that $Tr(\boldsymbol{A}) = \lambda_{\max}(\boldsymbol{A})$ holds for any matrix $\boldsymbol{A} \succeq \boldsymbol{0}$ and $\boldsymbol{Q}_i^{-\frac{1}{2}}\boldsymbol{G}_i^H\boldsymbol{W}_k\boldsymbol{G}_i\boldsymbol{Q}_i^{-\frac{1}{2}} \succeq \boldsymbol{0}$, we have:

$$(16) \Longrightarrow \lambda_{\max}\left(\boldsymbol{Q}_i^{-\frac{1}{2}}\boldsymbol{G}_i^H\boldsymbol{W}_k\boldsymbol{G}_i\boldsymbol{Q}_i^{-\frac{1}{2}}\right) \leq 2^{R_{E,i}^k} - 1$$

$$\Longleftrightarrow \boldsymbol{Q}_i^{-\frac{1}{2}}\boldsymbol{G}_i^H\boldsymbol{W}_k\boldsymbol{G}_i\boldsymbol{Q}_i^{-\frac{1}{2}} \preceq \left(2^{R_{E,i}^k} - 1\right)\boldsymbol{I}_{N_R} \tag{17}$$

$$\Longleftrightarrow \boldsymbol{G}_i^H\boldsymbol{W}_k\boldsymbol{G}_i \preceq \left(2^{R_{E,i}^k} - 1\right)\boldsymbol{Q}_i$$

Therefore, we can get from (17) that

$$\left(2^{R_{E,i}^k} - 1\right)\boldsymbol{Q}_i - \boldsymbol{G}_i^H\boldsymbol{W}_k\boldsymbol{G}_i \succeq \boldsymbol{0} \tag{18}$$

Now, we replace the constraint C2 in optimization problem (12) with (18). The optimization problem (18) can be reexpressed as

$$\max_{\boldsymbol{W}_k, \boldsymbol{V}, \boldsymbol{V}_0, t, \tau_{E,i}} t$$

$$s.t. \ \ C1: \frac{Tr(\boldsymbol{H}_k\boldsymbol{W}_k)}{r_k} - Tr\left[\boldsymbol{H}_k\left(\sum_{m\neq k}^{K_I}\boldsymbol{W}_m + \boldsymbol{V} + \boldsymbol{V}_0\right)\right] \geq \sigma_I^2, \forall k$$

$$\bar{C}2: \left(2^{R_{E,i}^k} - 1\right)\boldsymbol{Q}_i - \boldsymbol{G}_i^H\boldsymbol{W}_k\boldsymbol{G}_i \succeq \boldsymbol{0}, \forall k, i$$

$$C3: Tr\left(\sum_{k=1}^{K_I}\boldsymbol{W}_k + \boldsymbol{V} + \boldsymbol{V}_0\right) \leq P$$

$$C4: \boldsymbol{V} \succeq \boldsymbol{0}, \ C5: \boldsymbol{V}_0 \succeq \boldsymbol{0}, \tag{19}$$

$$C6: \frac{M_{E,i}}{1 + \exp\left(-a_{E,i}\left(\tau_{E,i} - b_{E,i}\right)\right)} \geq X_{E,i}\left(Y_{E,i} + t\right), \forall i$$

$$C7: \boldsymbol{W}_k \succeq \boldsymbol{0}, \forall k, \ C8: rank(\boldsymbol{W}_k) = 1, \forall k$$

$$C9: Tr\left(\boldsymbol{G}_i^H\left(\sum_{k=1}^{K_I}\boldsymbol{W}_k + \boldsymbol{V} + \boldsymbol{V}_0\right)\boldsymbol{G}_i\right) \geq \tau_{E,i}$$

From (19), constraint (C8): $rank(\boldsymbol{W}) = 1$ is the key difficult in getting the solution of the problem (19). By dropping the rank-one constraint (C8), the optimization problem (19) becomes:

$$\max_{\boldsymbol{W}_k, \boldsymbol{V}, \boldsymbol{V}_0, t, \tau_{E,i}} t \tag{20}$$

$$s.t. \ \ C1, \bar{C}2, C3, C4, C5, C6, C7, C9$$

It is noteworthy that the relaxed problem (20) falls into a standard convex SDP problem that could be solved by well-known numerical solvers, i.e. $SDPT3$

and $SeDuMi$. If the rank of the acquired solution $\boldsymbol{W}_k$ of the relaxed problem (20) is one, then we can conclude that the obtain $\boldsymbol{W}_k$ is the corresponding optimal solution of the referred problem (19). Then, the optimal k-th information vector $\boldsymbol{w}_k$ can be obtained via eigenvalue decomposition on $\boldsymbol{W}_k$. But, if the rank of $\boldsymbol{W}_k$ is not one, we can conclude that the obtained solution can not achieve the optimal result of the problem (20). Next, we will develop a theorem to bring insight into the tightness of the problem (20). In the end, a approach for forming an optimal solution for the problem (20) with rank$(\boldsymbol{W}_k) = 1$.

Theorem 1. *Assume the optimal solution of the relaxed optimization problem (20) is expressed as $\left\{\boldsymbol{W}_k^*, \boldsymbol{V}^*, \boldsymbol{V}_0^*, t^*, \tau_{E,i}^*\right\}$, $r_k > 0$, and rank$(\boldsymbol{W}^*) > 1$. Then, we can find a feasible solution of (20), expressed as $\left\{\bar{\boldsymbol{W}}^*, \bar{\boldsymbol{V}}^*, \bar{\boldsymbol{V}}_0^*, \bar{t}^*, \tau_{\bar{E},i}^*\right\}$, which not only permits a rank-one matrix $\bar{\boldsymbol{W}}_k$, i.e, rank$(\bar{\boldsymbol{W}}_K) = 1$, but also gets the same objective value as $\left\{\boldsymbol{W}_k^*, \boldsymbol{V}^*, \boldsymbol{V}_0^*, t^*, \tau_{E,i}^*\right\}$.*

Proof. Due to space limitation, the proof of the theorem is omitted.

4   Simulation Results

In this section, we show the efficiency of the proposed secure transmit signal schemes through some simulation results. We assume that the all the channel of the UAV-SWIPT communication system is Rayleigh flat-fading channel. Unless otherwise indicated, we suppose that our considered system includes $K_I = 3$ information ground-receiver and $K_E = 2$ energy UAVs. Indeed, some other system configurations could be performed with difference number of transmit antennas, receiver antennas and energy UAVs, however, we can obtain the similar numerical results, the only difference is the calculation complexity. In the numerical simulations, we set $N_T = 6$, $N_R = 3$, $r_k = r = 10\,\mathrm{dB}$, $R_{E,i}^k = 1\,\mathrm{bit/s/Hz}$, $P = 15\,\mathrm{dBW}$, $\sigma_I^2 = \sigma_E^2 = \sigma^2 = -23\,\mathrm{dBm}$. We set the parameters referred to the non-linear EH model as: $M_{E,i} = M = 24\,\mathrm{mW}$, $a_{E,i} = \bar{a} = 1500$, $b_{E,i} = \bar{b} = 0.014$.

In Fig. 1, we investigate the max-min collected energy power with respect to the minimum needed SINR of information ground-receiver, r, for different secure beamformer design algorithms. We can see that the average minimum collected energy per energy UAV for the proposed optimal and suboptimal secure beamforming algorithms decreases when the minimum required SINR, r, increases from 0 dB to 20 dB. This is due to the fact that our secure transmit signal design schemes can obtain a tradeoff between the guarantee of physical layer security of information ground-receivers and the power harvesting of energy UAVs. Particularly, to meet a more rigorous SINR requirement of information receiver, the base station is constrained to assigning a higher transmit power to the demand information at the cost of distinctly low power harvesting of energy UAVs, and the converse is also true. To illuminate the superior performance of our developed secure transmit signal design schemes, we also provide the performance of two baseline secure transmit signal algorithms for $N_T > K_I$. For baseline algorithm 1, the secure beamforming algorithm is designed for the conventional linear EH model. Then, we optimize the beamforming vectors $\boldsymbol{W}_k$, $\forall k$, $\boldsymbol{V}$ and $\boldsymbol{V}_0$

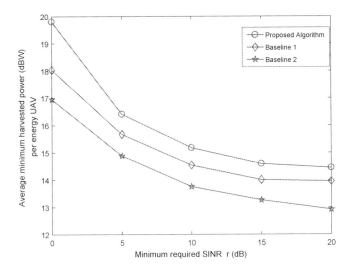

Fig. 1. Max-Min collected power against the required minimum SINR at the information receiver, r

with regard to the constraints in (10). We can observe that the proposed optimal algorithm still show a better performance than the baseline scheme 1. For baseline scheme 2, the energy signals and the artificial noise are conveyed into the null space which is spanned by the wireless communication channel of the K_I information receivers. Then, we maximize the minimum fairness energy power at the energy UAVs by optimizing W_k, $\forall k$, subject to the same constraints in (10). From Fig. 1, we can also see that for the developed optimal secure transmit signal algorithm, the energy UAVs can collect more energy than other baseline secure transmission schemes, owing to the joint optimization of W_k, $\forall k$, V and V_0.

In Fig. 2, we compare our proposed optimal scheme with two baseline schemes in terms of the average minimum collected energy per energy UAV for different number of transmit antennas, N_T, with fixed $P = 15$ dBW and $r = 10$ dB. It is quiet evident from the figure that greater requirement of maximize the minimum fairness energy power at the energy UAVs could be fulfilled by increasing the number of the transmit antennas. Indeed, increasing the number of transmit antennas at the transmitter will increase the degrees-of-freedom for the secure beamformer design which provides a more power efficient wireless energy transfer to the energy UAVs. It is also observed that the gap of the harvested energy performance between the developed optimal secure transmit signal scheme decreases with the number of the transmit antennas.

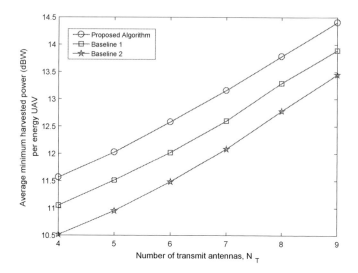

Fig. 2. Max-Min collected power against the required minimum SINR at the information ground-receiver, r

5   Conclusions

In this paper, we considered the secure transmit signal design for UAV-SWIPT communication network as a non-convex optimization problem which took into account of the non-linearity of practical EH circuit unit. The formulation of the referred optimization problem supports the double use of energy signal and artificial noise for ensuring efficient wireless energy transfer and secure transmission in presence of the potential eavesdroppers. Due to the intractability of the resulting fairness enabled collected energy among all the multiple antennas energy UAVs, the referred problem was recast and solved with variable substitutions and a SDR method. Numerical results indicated the favorable performance gain in collected energy of our developed secure transmit signal algorithms compared to the baseline secure transmit signal schemes.

Acknowledgments. This work was supported in part by the Natural Science Foundation of Jiangsu Higher Education Institutions of China under Grants 17KJB510016, by the Research Fund for the Doctoral Program of New Teachers of Jiangsu Normal University under Grant 17XLR029, 17XLR003, and 17XLR046, by the National Natural Science Foundation of China under Grants 61372101, 61422105, 61671144, and U1404615, by the 863 Program of China under Grant 2015AA01A703.

References

1. Zhou, F., Wu, Y., Hu, R.Q., Wang, Y., Wong, K.K.: Energy-efficient NOMA enabled heterogeneous cloud radio access networks. IEEE Netw. **32**(2), 152–160 (2018)
2. Huang, K., Larsson, E.: Simultaneous information and power transfer for broadband wireless systems. IEEE Trans. Signal Process. **61**(23), 5972–5986 (2013)
3. Wu, W., Wang, B.: Robust secrecy beamforming for wireless information and power transfer in multiuser MISO communication system. EURASIP J. Wirel. Commun. Netw. **161**, 1–11 (2015)
4. Wu, W., Wang, B.: Efficient transmission solutions for MIMO wiretap channels with SWIPT. IEEE Commun. Lett. **19**(9), 1548–1551 (2015)
5. Zhang, R., Ho, C.: MIMO broadcasting for simultaneous wireless information and power transfer. IEEE Trans. Wirel. Commun. **12**(5), 1989–2001 (2013)
6. Boshkovska, E., Koelpin, A., Ng, D.W.K., Zlatanov, N., Schober, R.: Robust beamforming for SWIPT systems with non-linear energy harvesting model. In: Proceedings IEEE SPAWC, Edinburgh, U.K., pp. 1–5 (2016)
7. Clerckx, B., et al.: Waveform design for wireless power transfer. IEEE Trans. Sign. Process. **64**(23), 6313–6328 (2016)
8. Zeng, Y., Zhang, R., Lim, T.J.: Wireless communications with unmanned aerial vehicles: opportunities and challenges. IEEE Commun. Mag. **54**(5), 36–42 (2016)
9. Wu, Q., Zhang, R.: Common throughput maximization in UAV-enabled OFDMA systems with delay consideration. IEEE Trans. Wirel. Commun. **66**(12), 6614–6627 (2018)
10. Zhang, G., Wu, Q., Cui, M., Zhang, R.: Securing UAV communications via joint trajectory and power control. IEEE Trans. Wirel. Commun. **18**(2), 1376–1389 (2019)
11. Li, A., Wu, Q., Zhang, R.: UAV-enabled cooperative jamming for improving secrecy of ground wiretap channel. IEEE Wirel. Commun. Lett. **8**(1), 181–184 (2019)
12. Li, A., Zhang, W.: Mobile jammer-aided secure UAV communications via trajectory design and power control. China Commun. **15**(8), 141–151 (2018)
13. Lee, H., Eom, S., Park, J., Lee, I.: UAV-aided secure communications with cooperative jamming. IEEE Trans. Veh. Commun. **67**(10), 9385–9392 (2018)
14. Cui, M., Zhang, G., Wu, Q., Ng, D.W.K.: Robust trajectory and transmit power design for secure UAV communications. IEEE Trans. Veh. Commun. **67**(9), 9046–9052 (2018)

Spectrum Sharing Scheme for Multi-UAVs Relay Network Based on Matching Theory

Jingmin Zhang[1,2], Xiaomin Liu[3], Lixin Li[3(✉)], Fucheng Yang[4], Qi Dong[5], and Xiaokui Yue[1]

[1] School of Astronautics, Northwestern Polytechnical University, Xi'an 710072, China
[2] No.208 Research Institute of China Ordnance Industries, Beijing 102202, China
[3] School of Electronics and Information, Northwestern Polytechnical University, Xi'an, China
lilixin@nwpu.edu.cn
[4] Research Institute of Information Fusion, Naval Aviation University, Yantai 264001, China
[5] China Academy of Electronics and Information Technology, Beijing 100041, China

Abstract. In this paper, we study the multi-UAVs network which acts as the relays to assist ground mobile devices (MDs) to communicate. In this scenario, the MDs are outside the coverage of cellular networks, therefore, the UAVs need to share the spectrum resources with the cellular users (CUs). In order to solve the problem of spectrum sharing between the UAVs and the CUs, we model the spectrum sharing problem as a marriage problem, and propose a one-to-one matching method to get a one-to-one stable matching between the UAVs and the CUs. The simulation results show that the proposed scheme is obviously superior to the random matching scheme and can improve the throughput of the system. Meanwhile, the UAV can achieve higher utility as the number of the CUs increases.

Keywords: UAV · Relay · Cellular network · Matching theory

1 Introduction

Recently, the UAVs have been widely used in various communication scenarios due to mobility, small size, and flexible deployment [1–3]. Especially the UAV can be used as a relay to assist the communication between the source node and the destination node, which can make the communication among many source nodes and destination nodes possible, also improve the quality of communication. Compared with the traditional ground relay, the UAV has better mobility, which is convenient for deployment and position adjustment to improve communication quality. Meanwhile, the UAV is deployed in the air, and acts as the relay which is less affected by the shadows and channel fading than the ground relay [4,5].

H. Yu et al. (Eds.): ICIRA 2019, LNAI 11743, pp. 84–92, 2019.
https://doi.org/10.1007/978-3-030-27538-9_8

There are a variety of devices in the wireless network, and they all tend to pursue their own interests, regardless of the interests of other devices [6,7]. As a economic theory, game theory can also be applied to the field of wireless communication to model the interaction among various devices. However, the traditional game theory methods can only solve the problems in which of the devices with the same properties. For the network of the devices with different characteristics and requirements, the traditional game theory is out of capability. As a branch of game theory, matching theory is an useful tool to deal with the interaction among devices with different characteristics and requirements [8].

At present, many works have been done on UAV communication networks. In [9], a UAV network to assist the mobile device (MD) and the base stations (BSs) to communicate was studied. The authors minimized the system's outage probability by optimizing the UAV's transmit power and trajectory. The authors studied the UAV as a relay of network and shared spectrum with the D2D, and optimized the throughput of the system with jointly optimizing the transmit power and trajectory of the UAV [10]. The network in which the UAV and the cellular user (CU) coexist was studied in [11], and the author improved the rate of the system uplink by the channel allocation and power optimization.

However, the network based on multi-UAVs assisting multiple MDs to communicate has not been studied. In this paper, we study the problem of spectrum sharing in multi-UAVs network.

The main contributions of this paper are as follows:

– To solve the spectrum allocation problem between the UAVs and the CUs, we model the interaction between the UAVs and the CUs as a traditional marriage problem, and propose a one-to-one matching method to solve it.
– In order to improve the throughput of the system, we model the achievable rate at the BS as a utility function for the UAVs and establish a list of preferences to obtain a stable matching scheme between the UAVs and the CUs.

The rest of the paper is organized as follows. In Sect. 2, we describe the system model. In Sect. 3, we model the spectrum sharing problem and solve the problem using matching theory. Simulation results are shown in Sect. 4, and finally, we conclude this paper in Sect. 5.

2   System Model

We consider a network based on multi-UAVs which act as the relays to assist the ground MDs to communicate. As shown in Fig. 1, in a single cellular network, there are M CUs, which means that each CU has its own licensed spectrum, the set of the CUs can be denoted as $\mathcal{M} = \{1, 2, ..., M\}$. At the same time, there are still N MDs outside the coverage of the cellular network, and the set of the MDs is expressed as $\mathcal{N} = \{1, 2, ..., N\}$. Therefore, there are K UAVs that act as relays to help these MDs which outside the coverage of BS to communicate with the BS. The set of UAVs is expressed as $\mathcal{K} = \{1, 2, ..., K\}$. In addition, since the

UAVs don't have their own licensed spectrum, the UAV can rent the spectrum resources of the CUs to forward the information of the MDs. In the transmission process, it is assumed that the system contains T time slots. In two consecutive time slots, the MDs transmit information to the UAVs that serve themselves in the first time slot, and in the second time slot, the UAVs forward the received information to the BS.

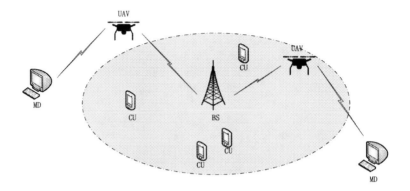

Fig. 1. System model

The distance between the BS and each MD is represented as L. The transmission power of the UAV and MD are expressed as P_U and P_M, respectively. It is assumed that average distance that the UAV can fly in each time slot is v, and $v \ll L$. The position of the ith UAV in the time slot t is denoted as $(x_i(t), y_i(t), h_i(t))$. Then the flight distance of the UAV from the time slot t to the time slot $(t+1)$ is

$$d_i(t, t+1) = \sqrt{(x_i(t+1) - x_i(t))^2 + (y_i(t+1) - y_i(t))^2 + (h_i(t+1) - h_i(t))^2}. \quad (1)$$

In this paper, we assume that the location of the MD is constant and does not change in each time slot. The location of the BS is expressed as $(0, 0, 0)$, and the location of the ith MD is represented as $\left(x_i^M(t), y_i^M(t), 0\right)$. Therefore, in time slot t, the distance between the ith MD and the jth UAV can be expressed as

$$d_{i,j}^M(t) = \sqrt{\left(x_i(t) - x_i^M(t)\right)^2 + \left(y_i(t) - y_i^M(t)\right)^2 + (h_i(t))^2}. \quad (2)$$

The distance from the ith UAV to the BS can be denoted as

$$d_i^B(t) = \sqrt{(x_i(t))^2 + (y_i(t))^2 + (h_i(t))^2}. \quad (3)$$

In time slot t, the ground MD transmits information to the UAV, and in time slot $(t+1)$, the UAV forwards the received information to the BS. In both processes, the line-of-sight (LOS) link and the non-line-of-sight (NLOS) communication are both exist. Therefore, in the time slot t, when the ith MD transmits information to the jth UAV, the path loss of the LOS and NLOS can be expressed as

$$PL^M_{LOS,ij}(t) = L^M_{FS,ij}(t) + 20\log\left(d^M_{i,j}(t)\right) + \eta_{LOS}, \tag{4}$$

$$PL^M_{NLOS,ij}(t) = L^M_{FS,ij}(t) + 20\log\left(d^M_{i,j}(t)\right) + \eta_{NLOS}, \tag{5}$$

where $L^M_{FS,ij}(t) = 20\log(f) + 20\log\left(\frac{4\pi}{c}\right)$, it represents the free space path loss, f is the channel frequency, and c represents the speed of light. η_{LOS} and η_{NLOS} represent additional losses that caused by LOS and NLOS connections, respectively.

In addition, the possibility of LOS connection is expressed as follows

$$\lambda^M_{LOS,ij}(t) = \frac{1}{1 + a\exp\left(-b\left(\theta^M_{ij}(t) - a\right)\right)}, \tag{6}$$

where a and b are the constants that determined by the environment, and $\theta^M_{ij}(t) = \sin^{-1}\left(h_i(t)/d^M_{i,j}(t)\right)$, it represents the elevation angle of the ith MD when the ith MD sending information to the jth UAV. Therefore, the average path loss in dB when the ith MD sending information to the jth UAV is expressed as

$$PL^M_{arg,ij}(t) = PL^M_{LOS,ij}(t) \times \lambda^M_{LOS,ij}(t) + PL^M_{NLOS,ij}(t) \times \lambda^M_{NLOS,ij}(t), \tag{7}$$

where $\lambda^M_{NLOS,ij}(t) = 1 - \lambda^M_{LOS,ij}(t)$, which indicates the possibility of NLOS connection during the process when the ith MD sending information to the jth UAV.

3 Optimization Scheme Based on Matching Theory

Since the UAVs don't have their own licensed spectrum resources, the UAVs can lease the licensed spectrum resources of the CUs for forwarding the information. There are many CUs in the cellular network, when a UAV is renting spectrum resources of the CUs, it is necessary to select one that is most suitable for itself. Therefore, we can use the matching theory to solve the problem of the selection of the spectrum resources of the UAVs.

In this paper, it is assumed that each CU allows only one UAV to lease its own channel in each time slot. At the same time, each UAV will only lease one CU's channel in each time slot. Therefore, the problem can be modeled as a traditional marriage problem. In the optimization scheme, the channels of the CUs and the UAVs are regarded as the sets of men and women in the marriage problem, that is, the two parties need to be matched. Therefore, a one-to-one matching method can be modeled to obtain the set of the final stable matching.

3.1   Utility Function of the UAV

In the time slot t, when the ith UAV rents the channel of the jth CU, the channel can be used by the mobile device served by the ith UAV and itself to use, that is, the MD served by the ith UAV sends the information to the ith UAV also through the channel rented by the ith UAV. Then, in the time slot $(t+1)$, the ith UAV forwards the received information to the BS on the leased channel. Therefore, when the MD that served by the ith UAV transmits information to the ith UAV on the channel of the jth CU, the achieved rate of the ith UAV is

$$R_{ij,UAV}^{j} = \lambda_C^j \log_2\left(1 + \frac{P_{ij}^U}{\sigma^2}\right) + \left(1 - \lambda_C^j\right)\log_2\left(1 + \frac{P_{ij}^U}{\sigma^2 + \underline{P}_{ij}^U}\right), \tag{8}$$

where λ_C^j is the probability that the licensed channel of the jth CU is idle. And $P_{ij}^U = \frac{P_M}{10^{PL_{\text{arg},ij}^M(t)/10}}$, is the power that received by the ith UAV. $\underline{P}_{ij}^U = \frac{P_C}{10^{PL_{\text{arg},ij}^C(t)/10}}$, which is the interference caused by the jth CU to the ith UAV, and P_C is the power of the CU. In addition, $PL_{\text{arg},ij}^C(t)$ denotes the average path loss between the jth CU and the ith UAV. σ^2 represents the variance of additive white Gaussian noise.

When the ith UAV receives the information sent by the MD, then it forwards the information to the BS in the next time slot. In this process, the amplification factor of the UAV acting as a relay can be expressed as follows

$$G_i = \sqrt{P_U / \left(P_{ij}^U + \sigma^2 + \left(1 - \lambda_C^j\right)\underline{P}_{ij}^U\right)}. \tag{9}$$

In the time slot $(t+1)$, when the ith UAV forwards the information received from the MD to the BS on the licensed channel of the jth CU, the achievable rate at the BS is

$$R_{ij,BS}^{j} = \lambda_C^j \log_2\left(1 + \frac{G_i{}^2 P_{ij}^U / 10^{PL_{\text{arg},ij}^B(t+1)/10}}{\sigma^2 / 10^{PL_{\text{arg},ij}^B(t+1)/10} + \sigma^2}\right) + $$
$$\left(1 - \lambda_C^j\right)\log_2\left(1 + \frac{G_i{}^2 P_{ij}^U / 10^{PL_{\text{arg},ij}^B(t+1)/10}}{\left(\sigma^2 + \underline{{}^U_{ij}}\right)/10^{PL_{\text{arg},ij}^B(t+1)/10} + \sigma^2 + \underline{P}_{ij}^B}\right), \tag{10}$$

where $PL_{\text{arg},ij}^B(t+1)$ is the average path loss when the ith UAV forwards the information to the BS on the licensed channel of the jth CU in the time slot $(t+1)$. It is denoted by $\underline{P}_{ij}^B = \frac{P_C}{10^{PL_{\text{arg},ij}^{CB}(t+1)/10}}$ that the interference caused by the jth CU to the BS, where $PL_{\text{arg},ij}^{CB}(t+1)$ is the path loss when the jth CU sends information to the BS, which can be expressed as

$$PL_{\text{arg},ij}^{CB}(t+1) = L_{FS,ij}^C(t+1) + 20\log\left(d_j^{CB}(t+1)\right) + \eta_{NLOS}, \tag{11}$$

where $d_j^{CB}(t+1)$ is the distance from the jth CU to the BS in the time slot $(t+1)$.

Therefore, in this process, we define the utility function of the ith UAV when the ith UAV rents the channel of the jth CU as follows

$$U_{ij}^U = R_{ij,BS}^j. \tag{12}$$

3.2   The Utility Function of CU

The CU prefers the UAV that pays a higher price and has less interference with it when renting its channel. Therefore, when the jth CU leases the channel to the ith UAV, we define the utility function of the jth CU as

$$U_{ij}^{C} = \rho_j \log_2 \left(1 + \frac{P_C/10^{PL_{\text{arg}.ij}^{CB}(t+1)/10}}{\sigma^2 + P_U/10^{PL_{\text{arg}.ij}^{B}(t+1)/10}} \right), \tag{13}$$

where ρ_i is the fee paid by the ith UAV when the ith UAV rents the channel of the jth CU.

Algorithm 1. The stable matching algorithm for UAV network

Input: Set of UAVs $\mathcal{K}$; Set of CUs $\mathcal{M}$; location and power of all users and BS.
Iitialization:
Set matrices of path loss for UAVs and BS; Set matching set $Matched(m_j)$ for each CU.
Step 1: Forming the list of preferences
for i=1:K **do**
    Obtain a list of preference PL_k for each UAV.
end for
Step 2: The UAV applies to the CU
Each $k_i \in \mathcal{K}$ applies to the first CU in PL_k.
Construct the application set $AU(m_j)$ for every CU.
Step 3: CUs make decisions
for j=1:N **do**
    if $|AU(m_j)| + |Matched(m_j)| \leq 1$ **then**
        CU accepts UAV in $AU(m_j)$ and adds it to $Matched(m_j), \forall m \in \mathcal{M}$.
    else
        CU selects one UAV that it prefers most in the set $AU(m_j) \cup Matched(m_j)$ according to its own list of preference.
    end if
end for
Step 4:
Each CU m_j updates its matching set $Matched(m_j)$, and each UAV deletes the first element in PL_k.
If $PL_k (\forall k \in \mathcal{K})$ is empty, end the algorithm, otherwise go to step 1.
Output: the optimal matching set.

When the UAVs matches with the CUs, as shown in Algorithm 1, first, establish a list of preferences based on the utility functions of the UAVs and of the CUs.

The ith UAV prefers the jth CU to the j'th CU, if $U_{ij}^{U} > U_{ij'}^{U}$, where U_{ij}^{U} is the utility function of the ith UAV when the ith UAV matches with the jth CU, $U_{ij'}^{U}$ is the utility function of the ith UAV when the ith UAV matches with the j'th CU, and $j \neq j'$.

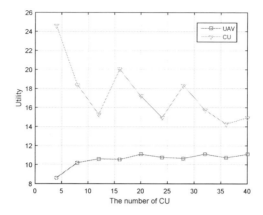

Fig. 2. The total utility of the UAV and CU

The jth CU prefers the ith UAV to the i'th UAV, if $U_{ij}^C > U_{i'j}^C$, where U_{ij}^C is the utility function of the jth CU when the jth CU matches with the ith UAV, $U_{ij'}^U$ is the utility function of the jth CU when the jth CU matches with the i'th UAV, and $i \neq i'$.

After establishing the list of preferences for both UAVs and CUs, each UAV makes a request to the first CU in its preference list. If the CU receives only a request from the UAV, then the CU temporarily chooses to accept the request from the UAV, and the UAV that accepted no longer makes a request to the CUs in the preference list. When receiving one or more requests from another UAV again, the CU will select one UAV that it most preferred one to accept among the requesting UAVs and the accepted UAVs, and reject the requests from other UAVs. The UAVs rejected by CU will make a request to the next UAV in the preference list. Repeat the process until the final stable matching set is obtained, where there are no motivations for all UAVs and CUs to deviate from the current state.

4   Simulation and Discussion

In this section, the performance analysis of the proposed matching optimization scheme are shown. Consider a single cellular network based on multiple UAVs as the relays. There are three UAVs and three MDs that need UAVs to serve. The distance between the BS and the MD is 520 m, and it is assumed that the locations of MDs and CUs are constant in each time slot, and the other simulation parameters are set as shown in Table 1.

Table 1. The parameter of the system

Parameter	Value
Center frequency f	1 GHz
Constant a	12
Constant b	0.135
The variance of noise σ^2	−96 dBm
Probability of channel idle λ_C	0.6
Loss η_{LOS}	1
Loss η_{NLOS}	20
The transmission power of UAV P_U	23 dBm
The transmission power of CU P_C	23 dBm
The transmission power of MD P_M	23 dBm
Average speed of UAV	10 m/time slot

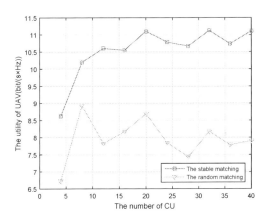

Fig. 3. The total utility of the UAV

In Fig. 2, we show the utility of UAVs and CUs. As the number of CUs increases, it can be seen that the utility of UAVs gradually increases. This is because that the number of licensed channels that the UAV can select increases as the number of CU grows, so the utility of UAVS is gradually increasing. Since the locations of CUs and UAVs are randomly generated, the location of the CUs that ultimately match with the UAVs is mutative, and thus the utility of the CUs is changing as shown in Fig. 2.

As shown in Fig. 3, we compare the optimization scheme based on stable matching with the random matching scheme. In the random matching scheme, the UAV and CUs are randomly matched. It can be seen from the Fig. 3 that the rate at the BS of the proposed stable matching scheme is obviously better than the random matching scheme.

5   Conclusions

In this paper, we study the network based on the multi-UAVs who act as the relays to assist the ground MD to communicate with BS. By using one-to-one matching to solve the spectrum sharing problem of UAVs and CUs, we obtain the set of the stable matching between UAVs and CUs. The simulation results show that the proposed optimization scheme based on stable matching can improve the achievable rate at the BS, and the UAV can achieve higher utility as the number of the CUs increases.

References

1. Merwaday, A., Tuncer, A., Kumbhar, A., Guvenc, I.: Improved throughput coverage in natural disasters: unmanned aerial base stations for public-safety communications. IEEE Veh. Technol. Mag. **11**(4), 53–60 (2016)
2. Zeng, Y., Zhang, R., Kumbhar, A., Lim, T.J.: Throughput maximization for UAV-enabled mobile relaying systems. IEEE Trans. Commun. **64**(12), 4983–4996 (2016)
3. Chen, J., Gesbert, D.: Optimal positioning of flying relays for wireless networks: a LOS map approach. In: 2017 IEEE International Conference on Communications (ICC), Paris, May 2017
4. Li, L., Xu, Y., Zhang, Z., Yin, J., Chen, W., Han, Z.: A prediction-based charging policy and interference mitigation approach in the wireless powered Internet of Things. IEEE J. Sel. Areas Commun. **37**(2), 439–451 (2019)
5. Xue, K., Zhang, Z., Li, L., Zhang, H., Li, X., Gao, A.: Adaptive coverage solution in multi-UAVs emergency communication system: a discrete-time mean-field game. In: 2018 14th International Wireless Communications Mobile Computing Conference (IWCMC) Limassol, pp. 1059–1064, June 2018
6. Xu, Y., Li, L., Zhang, Z., Xue, K., Han, Z.: A discrete-time mean field game in multi-UAV wireless communication systems. In: 2018 IEEE/CIC International Conference on Communications in China (ICCC), Beijing, China, pp. 714–718, August 2018
7. Han, Z., Niyato, D., Saad, W., Basar, T., Hjørungnes, A.: Game Theory in Wireless and Communication Networks: Theory, Models, and Applications, January 2001
8. Bayat, S., Li, Y., Song, L., Han, Z.: Matching theory: applications in wireless communications. IEEE Signal Process. Mag. **33**, 103–122 (2016)
9. Zhang, S., Zhang, H., He, Q., Bian, K., Song, L.: Joint trajectory and power optimization for UAV relay networks. IEEE Commun. Lett. **22**(1), 161–164 (2018)
10. Wang, H., Wang, J., Ding, G., Chen, J., Li, Y., Han, Z.: Spectrum sharing planning for full-duplex UAV relaying systems with underlaid D2D communications. IEEE J. Sel. Areas Commun. **36**(9), 1986–1999 (2018)
11. Zhang, S., Zhang, H., Di, B., Song, L.: Cellular UAV-to-X communications: design and optimization for multi-UAV networks. IEEE Trans. Wireless Commun. **18**(2), 1276–1536 (2019)

A Hybrid Multiagent Collision Avoidance Method for Formation Control

Zezhi Sui[1,2], Zhiqiang Pu[1,2(✉)], Jianqiang Yi[1,2], and Tianyi Xiong[1,2]

[1] Institute of Automation, Chinese Academy of Sciences, Beijing 100190, China
zhiqiang.pu@ia.ac.cn
[2] University of Chinese Academy of Sciences, Beijing 100049, China

Abstract. Collision avoidance in formation control is an essential and challenging problem in multiagent filed. Specifically, the agents have to consider both formation maintenance and collision avoidance. However, this problem is not fully considered in existing works. This paper presents a hybrid collision avoidance method for formation control. The formation control is designed based on consensus theory while the collision avoidance is achieved by utilizing optimal reciprocal collision avoidance (ORCA). Furthermore, the stability of the multiagent systems is proved. Finally, a simulation demonstrates the effectiveness of the proposed method.

Keywords: Collision avoidance · Formation control · Multiagent

1 Introduction

In recent years, swarm of agents is applied in various areas, including surveillance, disaster rescue and so on. More and more researchers have been attracted in this field. As a typical scenario of swarm intelligence, formation control has also received increasing attention from researchers. In order to improve the performance of the swarm, it is essential to investigate the formation control. In fact, three typical frameworks have been widely investigated for formation control, including leader-follower based approach [1], behavior based method [2], and virtual structure based strategy [3]. Although significant progress has been made in the formation control, collision avoidance in formation control is not fully investigated. In a leader follower formation architecture, one agent is chosen as the leader which decides the whole movement of the formation, while the others are followers which need to follow the leader. Actually, the formation shape will change due to different mission requirement, which may lead to collisions in the formation. Thus, collision avoidance in formation is a representative crucial issue during the mission process.

Traditional collision avoidance algorithms mainly include off-line methods [4], force-field methods [5], and sense-and-avoid methods [6]. Off-line methods is aimed at computing the collision free trajectory in advance with many constraints, but this method is computationally expensive and time consuming. The force-field methods solve the problem of collision by introducing virtual fields around obstacles and agents. However, they may encounter the problems of local minima and unreachable targets.

© Springer Nature Switzerland AG 2019
H. Yu et al. (Eds.): ICIRA 2019, LNAI 11743, pp. 93–102, 2019.
https://doi.org/10.1007/978-3-030-27538-9_9

The sense-and-avoid methods prevent collisions by sensing the around information and changing the immediate action accordingly, which are widely used.

Existing works on formation control with collision avoidance usually take the collision factor as an input in controller design procedure. By combining artificial potential field (APF) [7] method, an adaptive leader-following formation control with collision avoidance strategy is developed in [8]. APF is also utilized in [9] to solve obstacle avoidance problem. In [10], the collision avoidance constraint is imposed by the 2-norm of a relative position vector at each discrete time step. However, with the number of the agents increasing, those methods with collision avoidance constraints may increase the complexity and reduce the robustness of the multiagent system.

This paper presents a hybrid collision avoidance method in formation control to achieve an arbitrary transformation of formation shape based on optimal reciprocal collision avoidance (ORCA) [11] and formation control. In our proposed method, each agent only obtains information from its neighbors, and the formation controller generates the desire velocity for each agent. Afterwards, the collision avoidance module takes the preferred velocities as inputs and outputs the collision-free velocities at next step. To confirm the effectiveness of the proposed method, a numerical simulation is conducted.

The rest of the paper is organized as follows. In the next section, the preliminaries are presented. In Sect. 3, the basic ORCA method and formation control design are provided. And the hybrid method is presented. In Sect. 4, numerical simulation is provided.

2 Preliminaries

2.1 Modeling an Agent

Generally, the dynamics of an agent can be treated as a second-order system as follows,

$$\begin{cases} \dot{\mathbf{P}}(t) = \mathbf{V}(t) \\ \dot{\mathbf{V}}(t) = \mathbf{u}(t) \end{cases},$$

where $\mathbf{P}(t)$ represents the position, $\mathbf{V}(t)$ represents the velocity, and $\mathbf{u}(t)$ is the input of the system.

2.2 Graph Theory

In this paper, we define a multiagent system consisting of N agents is a system where each agent shares information with other agents via certain communication architecture. Generally, a graph denoted by $G = (V, E, A)$ is used to describe the information topology among agents. We define a single agent as node v_i, then $V = \{v_1, v_2, \ldots, v_n\}$ is the set of agents, and $E \subseteq V \times V$ represents the set of edges, where E is defined such that if $(v_j, v_i) \in E, j \neq i$, there is an edge from agent j to agent i, which means that agent j can send information to agent i. In addition, $A = [a_{ij}] \in R^{N \times N}$ is the associated adjacency matrix with $a_{ij} \geq 0$. We set $a_{ij} > 0, j \neq i$ if and only if $(v_j, v_i) \in E$; otherwise

$a_{ij} = 0$. Agent j is said to be the neighbor of agent i if and only if $a_{ij} > 0$, and $N_i = \{v_j \in V : (v_j, v_i) \in E\}$ represents the neighbor set of agent i. An undirected graph is called connected if there is a path between any two agents of graph G. Define $D = \text{diag}\{d_1, d_2, \ldots, d_N\} \in R^{N \times N}$ as the in-degree matrix, where $d_i = \sum_{v_j \in N_i} a_{ij}$. Then, the Laplacian matrix of graph G is defined as $L = D - A$.

3 Hybrid Collison Avoidance Method

3.1 Formation Control

Considering the following second-order dynamics of the ith follower

$$
\begin{cases}
\dot{P}_i^F(t) = V_i^F(t) \\
\dot{V}_i^F(t) = u_i^F(t),
\end{cases}
\tag{1}
$$

where $P_i^F = [P_{i,x}^F, P_{i,y}^F]^T$, $V_i^F = [V_{i,x}^F, V_{i,y}^F]^T$ and $u_i^F = [u_{i,x}^F, u_{i,y}^F]^T$ represent position, velocity and control input vector of the ith follower respectively.

Let $P^L = [P_x^L, P_y^L]^T$ and $V^L = [V_x^L, V_y^L]^T$ represent position and velocity vector of the leader. In addition, the follower is supposed to track the trajectory of the leader while keeping a certain distance, and $H_{i,P} = [H_{i,x}, H_{i,y}]^T$ stands for the expected relative offset vector of P_i^F with respect to P^L.

Let $e_{i,P} = P_i^F - P^L - H_{i,P}$, $e_{i,V} = V_i^F - V^L$. The followers and leader are said to achieve formation tracking if for any given bounded initial states

$$
\begin{aligned}
\lim_{t \to \infty} e_{i,P} = 0 \\
\lim_{t \to \infty} e_{i,V} = 0
\end{aligned}
\tag{2}
$$

Design the following control protocol for the ith follower:

$$
\begin{aligned}
u_i^F(t) = -\sum_{i=1}^{N} a_{ij} \Big[k_1 \Big(P_i^F(t) - H_{i,P} - \big(P_j^F(t) - H_{j,P} \big) \Big) + k_2 \Big(P_i^F(t) - H_{i,P} - \big(P_j^F(t) - H_{j,P} \big) \Big) \Big] \\
- b_i \big[k_1 \big((P_i^F(t) - P^L(t) - H_{i,P}) + k_2 (V_i^F(t) - V^L(t)) \big) \big] + \dot{V}^L(t),
\end{aligned}
\tag{3}
$$

where $k_1, k_2 > 0$ are control gains. a_{ij} is the elements of the adjacent matrix A among the followers, $b_i > 0$ if and only if the ith follower can receive the states information from the leader; otherwise $b_i = 0$.

Lemma 1 [12]: Matrix $L + B$ is a positive stable matrix if and only if the communication topology G has a spanning tree with the leader being the root node, where matrix L is the corresponding Laplacian matrix among the followers, $B = \text{diag}(b_1, b_2, \ldots, b_N)$.

Lemma 2 [13]: Matrix M is Hurwitz, if matrix $L+B$ is positive stable, where

$$M = \begin{bmatrix} 0 & I_N \\ -k_1(L+B) & -k_2(L+B) \end{bmatrix} \otimes I_2,$$

and $\otimes$ represents Kronecker product and I_2 is a two-dimensional identity matrix.

Theorem: If the communication topology G has spanning tree with the leader being the root node, then under the control protocol (3), formation tracking for the followers and leader can be achieved.

Proof: Let $e_{i,P} = P_i^F - P^L - H_{i,P}$ and $e_{i,V} = V_i^F - V^L$ be the formation tracking position and velocity error, respectively. Then system (1) can be rewritten as

$$\begin{cases} \dot{e}_{i,P} = e_{i,V} \\ \dot{e}_{i,V} = u_i^F - \dot{V}_i^F. \end{cases} \tag{4}$$

Let $e_P = \left[e_{1,P}^T, e_{2,P}^T, \ldots, e_{N,P}^T\right]^T$, $e_V = \left[e_{1,V}^T, e_{2,V}^T, \ldots, e_{N,V}^T\right]^T$ and $e = \left[e_P^T, e_V^T\right]^T$. Submitting (3) into (1), then system (1) can be further rewritten as

$$\dot{e} = \left(\begin{bmatrix} 0 & I_N \\ -k_1(L+B) & -k_2(L+B) \end{bmatrix} \otimes I_2\right)e = Me. \tag{5}$$

According to Lemmas 1 and 2, the matrix M is Hurwitz. Therefore, there exists a positive definite matrix P such that

$$M^T P + PA = -Q, \tag{6}$$

where matrix Q is an arbitrary positive definite matrix.

Construct the following Lyapunov function:

$$V = \frac{1}{2}e^T Pe. \tag{7}$$

Taking the derivative of (7) with respect to t, we obtain

$$\begin{aligned} V &= e^T P\dot{e} \\ &= e^T PMe \\ &= -\frac{1}{2}e^T Qe \leq 0 \end{aligned} \tag{8}$$

Then system (5) is asymptotic stable, that is, $e \to 0$, as $t \to 0$. Thus, the followers and the leader can achieve formation tracking under the control protocol (3).

3.2 Collision Avoidance Method

In this part, the collision avoidance module is presented. In the process of performing missions, the agents in the formation need to change their positional relationship due to the mission requirements. Thus, collision avoidance between agents need to be taken in consideration. In order to comprehensively consider the factors of the velocity information and the interactions among agents, the ORCA method is adopted here.

For two agents A and B, we define an open disc of radius r centered at $\mathbf{p}$ as follows,

$$D(\mathbf{p}, r) = \{\mathbf{q} | \|\mathbf{q} - \mathbf{p}\| < r\}.$$

Then the velocity obstacle is $VO^{\tau}_{A|B}$,

$$VO^{\tau}_{A|B} = \{\mathbf{v} | \exists t \in [0, \tau] :: t\mathbf{v} \in D(\mathbf{p}_B - \mathbf{p}_A, r_A + r_B)\},$$

where $\mathbf{p}_A$ and $\mathbf{p}_B$ are the position of agents A and B; r_A and r_B represent the radius of their safe zone. τ is the time windows in which agent A and B will not collide. $VO^{\tau}_{A|B}$ means the set of all relative velocities of A with respect to B that may collide at some moment before τ.

Let $\mathbf{v}^{now}_A$ and $\mathbf{v}^{now}_B$ be the current velocities of agent A and B. and let $\mathbf{u}$ be the vector from $\mathbf{v}^{now}_A - \mathbf{v}^{now}_B$ to the closet point on the boundary of $VO^{\tau}_{A|B}$.

$$\mathbf{u} = \left(\underset{\mathbf{v} \in \partial VO^{\tau}_{A|B}}{\arg\min} \|\mathbf{v} - (\mathbf{v}^{now}_A - \mathbf{v}^{now}_B)\| \right) - (\mathbf{v}^{now}_A - \mathbf{v}^{now}_B).$$

$ORCA^{\tau}_{A|B}$ is defines as follows,

$$ORCA^{\tau}_{A|B} = \left\{ \mathbf{v} | \left(\mathbf{v} - \left(\mathbf{v}^{now}_A + \frac{1}{2}\mathbf{u} \right) \right) \cdot \mathbf{n} \geq 0 \right\},$$

where $\mathbf{n}$ is the normal vector of $\mathbf{u}$. By choosing the velocities for agent A and B using $ORCA^{\tau}_{A|B}$ and $ORCA^{\tau}_{B|A}$ respectively, both agents will take half of the responsibility to avoid collision with each other, which ensures the generation of a collision-free trajectory.

When more than one other agent exists around agent A, collision avoidance among multiagent need to be considered. The n-body collision avoidance is introduced here. By calculating $ORCA^{\tau}_{A|B}$ for each agent around agent A, $ORCA^{\tau}_A$ is defined as follows,

$$ORCA^{\tau}_A = D(0, \mathbf{v}^{max}_A) \cap \bigcap_{B \neq A} ORCA^{\tau}_{A|B}.$$

It is clear that the set $ORCA_A^\tau$ contains the interaction effect among agents. Next, the agent selects a new velocity $\mathbf{v}_A^{new}$ which is closest to its preferred velocity $\mathbf{v}_A^{pref}$ as follows

$$\mathbf{v}_A^{new} = \arg\min_{\mathbf{v} \in ORCA_A^\tau} \left\| \mathbf{v} - \mathbf{v}_A^{pref} \right\|,$$

where $\mathbf{v}_A^{pref}$ is the preferred velocity given by global planning strategy, which mainly guide the global movement of the agent. In addition, the selection procedure can be efficiently solved by linear programming.

3.3 Hybrid Strategy

In order to deal with the formation control and collision avoidance comprehensively, a hybrid method based on formation control law and collision avoidance method ORCA is presented in this paper. We take the output of the formation controller as the preferred velocity in the ORCA module. Then the ORCA algorithm generates the collision avoidance velocity for each agent in formation. In this way, the formation will eventually be stable when there is no possibility of collision in a certain range. The formation controller is designed based on consensus theory and the stability analysis is given as above. The diagram of this method is shown as Fig. 1.

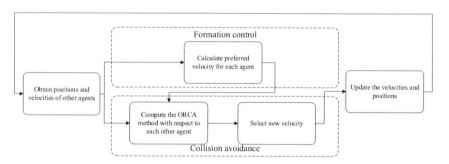

Fig. 1. The diagram of our hybrid method.

4   Simulation

In this part, we chose two typical scenarios to demonstrate the effectiveness of our method. In the first scenario, four agents are supposed to keep a square formation in the horizontal X-Y plane. In addition, the virtual leader is set as the formation center. At the beginning, the positions of agents 1–4 are $(-10, -10)$, $(10, -10)$, $(-10, 10)$, $(10, 10)$ respectively. The side length of the square is 20, which is supposed to be 10 in our formation control design. Besides, the interaction graph is shown in Fig. 2, and the control and collision avoidance parameters are set as Table 1. For a better demonstration of the proposed method, two potential collision are set in this simulation.

Firstly, during the forming process, agent 3 and 4 may get collide. Secondly, the desired formation shape will change at 100 s. Specifically, agent 1 and 4 will exchange their position, as well as agent 2 and 3. In this scene, the middle area will form a particularly crowded state. In the second scenario, four agents are supposed to keep a square formation as well, but the leader' movement is a sinusoid. Besides, four agents' initial positions and target positions are set to generate collisions among them.

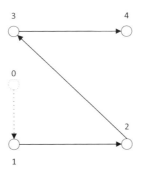

Fig. 2. The interaction graph.

Table 1. Parameters

Parameters of control		Parameters of ORCA	
k_1	1.5	Neighbor disc	5
k_2	3.5	Max neighbors	5
		Time horizon	5
		Time horizon obstacle	5
		Radius	0.3
		Max speed	10

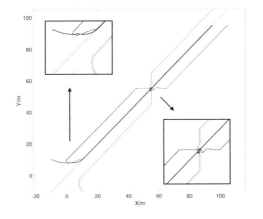

Fig. 3. The trajectories of the four agents in scenario1.

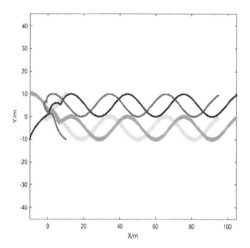

Fig. 4. The trajectories of the four agents in scenario2.

As shown in Figs. 3 and 4, the following phenomena can be observed: (i) the four agents successfully formed a square formation at the beginning; (ii) the virtual leader agent 0 moves along a straight line, the other followers also moves along the leader; (iii) during the two potential collision zones, the agents are able to adjust their velocities to avoid the potential collisions; (iv) After the collision avoidance movement, the formation is able to reform the formation shape.

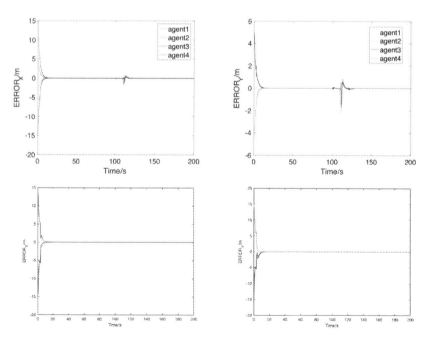

Fig. 5. The formation position tracking error on X-axis and Y-axis.

As shown in Fig. 5, the position error in both X-axis and Y-axis are small enough such that the formation will not be broken. And it implies that all agents can follow the reference position after finishing the collision avoidance. Therefore, the simulation results demonstrate that the proposed method performs well in the process of collision avoidance as well as formation control.

5 Conclusion

This paper presents a hybrid collision avoidance method in formation control to achieve arbitrary transformation of positions in formation based on optimal reciprocal collision avoidance and consensus theory. Specifically, the output of the formation control is treated as the input of the collision avoidance module, which guarantees the generation of collision free velocities. The simulation demonstrates the effectiveness of the presented method. In the further, we are looking forward to applying our method in multi ground-robot system.

Funding. This work is supported by National Natural Science Foundation of China (NNSFC) No. 61603383, No. 61421004 and Beijing Advanced Innovation Center of Intelligent Robots and Systems under Grant 2016IRS23.

References

1. Das, A.K., Fierro, R., Kumar, V., Ostrowski, J.P., Spletzer, J., Taylor, C.J.: A vision-based formation control framework. IEEE Trans. Robot. Autom. **18**(5), 813–825 (2002)
2. Balch, T., Arkin, R.C.: Behavior-based formation control for multirobot teams. IEEE Trans. Robot. Autom. **14**(6), 926–939 (1998)
3. Lewis, M.A., Tan, K.H.: High precision formation control of mobile robots using virtual structures. Auton. Robots **4**(4), 387–403 (1997)
4. Richards, A., How, J.P.: Aircraft trajectory planning with collision avoidance using mixed integer linear programming. In: Proceedings of the 2002 American Control Conference, pp. 1936–1941. IEEE, Anchorage, USA (2002)
5. Kuriki, Y., Namerikawa, T.: Consensus-based cooperative formation control with collision avoidance for a multi-UAV system. In: 2014 American Control Conference, pp. 2077–2082. IEEE, Portland, USA (2014)
6. Mastellone, S., Stipanović, D.M., Graunke, C.R., Intlekofer, K.A., Spong, M.W.: Formation control and collision avoidance for multi-agent non-holonomic systems: theory and experiments. Int. J. Robot. Res. **27**(1), 107–126 (2008)
7. Khatib, O.: Real-time obstacle avoidance for manipulators and mobile robots. In: Proceedings. 1985 IEEE International Conference on Robotics and Automation, pp. 500–505. IEEE. St. Louis, USA (1985)
8. Shi, Q., Li, T., Li, J., Chen, C.P., Xiao, Y., Shan, Q.: Adaptive leader-following formation control with collision avoidance for a class of second-order nonlinear multi-agent systems. Neurocomputing **350**, 282–290 (2019)
9. Wen, G., Chen, C.P., Liu, Y.J.: Formation control with obstacle avoidance for a class of stochastic multiagent systems. IEEE Trans. Ind. Electron. **65**(7), 5847–5855 (2018)

10. Lee, S.M., Myung, H.: Receding horizon particle swarm optimisation-based formation control with collision avoidance for non-holonomic mobile robots. IET Control Theory Appl. **9**(14), 2075–2083 (2015)
11. Van Den Berg, J., Guy, S.J., Lin, M., Manocha, D.: Reciprocal n-body collision avoidance. In: Pradalier, C., Siegwart, R., Hirzinger, G. (eds.) Robotics Research, vol. 70, pp. 3–19. Springer, Heidelberg (2011). https://doi.org/10.1007/978-3-642-19457-3_1
12. Hu, J., Hong, Y.: Leader-following coordination of multi-agent systems with coupling time delays. Physica A: Stat. Mech. Appl. **374**(2), 853–863 (2007)
13. Ren, W., Atkins, E.: Distributed multi-vehicle coordinated control via local information exchange. Int. J. Robust Nonlinear Control **17**(10–11), 1002–1033 (2007)

Computational Intelligence Inspired Robot Navigation and SLAM

Improved Neural Network 3D Space Obstacle Avoidance Algorithm for Mobile Robot

Yuchuang Tong[1,2,3], Jinguo Liu[1,2(✉)], Yuwang Liu[1,2],
and Zhaojie Ju[4]

[1] State Key Laboratory of Robotics, Shenyang Institute of Automation,
Chinese Academy of Sciences, Shenyang 110016, China
liujinguo@sia.cn
[2] Institutes for Robotics and Intelligent Manufacturing,
Chinese Academy of Sciences, Shenyang 110016, China
[3] University of the Chinese Academy of Science, Beijing 100049, China
[4] School of Computing, University of Portsmouth, Portsmouth PO1 3HE, UK

Abstract. Path planning problems are classical optimization problems in many fields, such as computers, mathematics, transportation, robots, etc., which can be described as an optimization problem in mathematics. In this paper, the mathematical model of obstacle environment is established. The characteristics of neural network algorithm, simulated annealing algorithm and adaptive variable stepsize via linear reinforcement are studied respectively. A new neural network 3D space obstacle avoidance algorithm for mobile robot is proposed, which solves the problem of the computational duration and minimum distance of the traditional neural network obstacle avoidance algorithm in solving the optimal path. According to the characteristics of the improved neural network algorithm, it is fused with a variety of algorithms to obtain the optimal path algorithm that achieves the shortest path distance and meets the requirements of obstacle avoidance security. The simulation experiment of the algorithm is simulated by Matlab. The results show that the improved neural network spatial obstacle avoidance algorithm based on the multiple algorithms proposed in this paper can effectively accelerate the convergence speed of path planning, realize the minimum path distance, and achieve very good path planning effect.

Keywords: Global path planning · Obstacle avoidance algorithm · Improved neural network algorithm · Adaptive variable stepsize · Simulated annealing

1 Introduction

Path planning has a wide range of applications in many areas, such as traffic, logistics, routing search for communication systems, robot walking route planning, etc. [1, 2]. Demand for drones and underwater vehicles is growing, the 3D path planning issues involved are complex, so the use at civil and commercial areas is still very limited [3, 4]. The path planning problem can be expressed as a mathematical multi-objective optimization problem, so the path planning problem is transformed into solving the corresponding mathematical optimization problem [5, 6]. At present, in the study of

© Springer Nature Switzerland AG 2019
H. Yu et al. (Eds.): ICIRA 2019, LNAI 11743, pp. 105–117, 2019.
https://doi.org/10.1007/978-3-030-27538-9_10

global path planning problems based on environmental prior information, the typical methods proposed in [7–9] are visibility graph, artificial potential field method and so on. The advantage of the visibility graph is that the shortest path can be obtained, but there is a drawback of the combined explosion problem. The artificial potential field method overcomes the combinatorial explosion problem by finding the minimum value point of the path point energy function, avoiding the combined explosion problem, but has the problem of local minimum value and is not suitable for finding the shortest path. Since the computational time of deterministic algorithms and complexity increases exponentially with the dimensions of the configuration space, these algorithms cannot provide a reliable solution for real-time applications [10, 11].

In order to solve the problem of mobile robot movement in 3D environment, it is an effective method to apply neural network to mobile robot motion trajectory automatic generation and mobile robot path planning in literature. Neural network path planning algorithm introduces the network structure method according to the basic idea of the artificial potential field method. The calculation is simple and can avoid some local extreme values [12, 13]. In this paper, the simulated annealing algorithm is used to optimize the collision penalty function of the neural network algorithm. The adaptive variable step size algorithm is used to optimize the iterative step size parameters of the neural network algorithm. The two algorithms complement each other to further achieve the optimization effect. Therefore, based on the algorithm, an improved algorithm for neural network path planning based on adaptive variable stepsize via linear reinforcement and simulated annealing algorithm is proposed. It not only has the advantages of the original algorithm, but also runs faster than the original algorithm. In particular, the planned collision-free path can quickly reach the shortest path of the destination, basically meeting the needs of real-time path planning.

The rest of this paper is structured as follows: Sect. 2 is the main part of this paper. It will briefly introduce the principles and specific steps of traditional neural network obstacle avoidance algorithms, and show the description of obstacles and obstacle modeling. Section 3 improved neural network 3D obstacle avoidance path planning algorithm is proposed, which solves the problem of the computational duration and minimum distance when the traditional algorithm solving the optimal path. And in Sect. 4 the problem of the improved neural network in solving the nonconvex optimization problem is obtained, and the algorithm is combined with the continuous simulated annealing algorithm. Section 5 based on the previous algorithm, the adaptive selection of the step size is realized by the linear reexcitation learning method. Its future development trends are studied in Sect. 6.

2 Related Work

2.1 Principle of Neural Network Obstacle Avoidance Algorithm

As a highly parallel distributed system, neural network provides a great possibility to solve the problem of high real-time requirements of robot systems, and is applied to intelligent autonomous mobile robot navigation and path planning. In this section, the idea of solving the path planning problem is using neural network to describe the environmental constraints and calculate the collision energy function. The sum of the collision energy function and the distance function of the iterative path point set is used as the optimization objective function, and the optimization objective function is obtained. The extremum determines the equation of motion for the point set and eventually makes the set of iterative path points tend to the optimal planning path.

2.2 Neural Network Modeling of Obstacles

The collision penalty function of a path is defined as the sum of the collision penalty functions of each path point, and the collision penalty function of one point is obtained through its neural network representation of each obstacle. The obstacle is assumed to be a polygon, which can be represented by a set of linear inequalities, so that the points in the obstacle must satisfy the limits of all inequalities. Figure 1(a) shows neural network from a penalty function to an obstacle. The bottom two nodes represent the coordinates x and y of the given path point respectively. Each node of the middle layer corresponds to an inequality constraint of the obstacle. The connection weight coefficients of the bottom layer and the middle layer are equal to the x and y front of the inequality. The coefficient of each node in the middle layer is equal to the constant term in the corresponding inequality. The connection weight from the middle layer to the top layer is 1, and the threshold of the top node is taken as the number of inequalities minus the negative number after 0.5.

The operational relationships in the neural network model are:

$$C = f(I_0) \tag{1}$$

$$I_0 = \sum_{m=1}^{M} O_{Hm} + \theta_T \tag{2}$$

$$O_{Hm} = f(I_{Hm}) \tag{3}$$

$$I_{Hm} = w_{xm} + x_i + w_{ym}y_i + w_{zm}z_i + q_{Hm} \tag{4}$$

Where x_i, y_i are the horizontal and vertical coordinates of the path point, C is the top node output, I_0 is the top node input, θ_T is the top node threshold, O_{Hm} is the output of the m-th node middle layer, I_{Hm} is the m-th node the middle layer input, θ_{Hm} is the threshold of the m-th node of the middle layer, w_{xm}, w_{ym} is the coefficient of the m-th inequality constraint. The sigmoid function is selected as the excitation function shown in Eq. (5).

$$f(x) = \frac{1}{1 + e^{-x/T}} \tag{5}$$

Figure 1(c) shows the shape of the single obstacle collision penalty function in the two-dimensional obstacle environment of the mobile robot obtained by the simulation of the collision penalty function, which corresponds to the environment shown in Fig. 1(b).

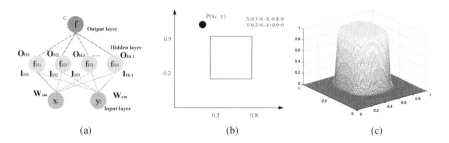

(a)   (b)   (c)

Fig. 1. (a) Neural network model of a single obstacle. (b) Single obstacle model. (c) Single obstacle collision penalty function shape in two-dimensional obstacle environment.

The working environment of mobile robots often has multiple obstacles, and one path is also composed of multiple path points, so the collision penalty function of one path point is defined as the sum of the collision penalty functions of all intermediate path points on the path. The collision penalty function of a point is obtained through its neural network representation of each obstacle. Figure 2(a) shows a neural network model of multiple obstacle environments. In this way, as long as the x coordinate and the y coordinate of each intermediate point of the path are sequentially input to each layer, the model output is the total energy of the collision penalty function corresponding to the entire path to be adjusted.

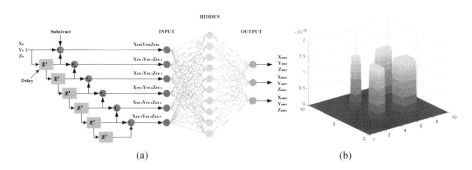

(a)   (b)

Fig. 2. (a) Multiple obstacle model. (b) Multi-obstacle collision penalty function shape in 2D obstacle environment.

Based on the simulation results of Figs. 2(b) and 1(c), it can be concluded that the collision energy function of the iterative path point set can accurately describe the obstacle environment of the mobile robot. Combined with the distance function of another factor that path planning should consider, the obstacle environments can successfully realize the static environment path planning task of mobile robot.

2.3 Path Point Motion Equation

The entire path corresponds to the energy of the collision function as follow,

$$E_c = \sum_{i=1}^{N} \sum_{k=1}^{K} C_i^k \tag{6}$$

Where K is the number of obstacles, N is the number of path points, C_i^k represents the collision function of the i-th path point $P(x_i, y_i, z_i)$ against the k-th obstacle.

The energy corresponding to the length of the path is defined as the sum of the squares of the lengths of all the line segments, for all path points $P(x_i, y_i, z_i)$, that is

$$E_l = \sum_{i=1}^{N-1} \left| (x_{i+1} - x_i)^2 + (y_{i+1} - y_i)^2 + (z_{i+1} - z_i)^2 \right| \tag{7}$$

The total energy function of the entire path is defined as

$$E = w_l E_l + w_c E_c \tag{8}$$

Where w_l and w_c respectively represent the weighting of each part.

The above analysis shows that the shorter the path, the smaller the energy function E and the smaller the collision penalty function value, and the farther the path is from the center of the obstacle, the smaller the energy function E is.

If E is used to derive the derivative of time

$$\dot{E} = \sum_{i} (\nabla_{pi} E)^T p_i'$$

$$\sum_{i} \{ [w_l(\frac{\partial L_i^2}{\partial x_i} + \frac{\partial L_{i-1}^2}{\partial x_i})] + w_c \sum_{k} \frac{\partial C_i^k}{\partial x_i} \} \dot{x}_i + [w_l(\frac{\partial L_i^2}{\partial y_i} + \frac{\partial L_{i-1}^2}{\partial y_i})]$$

$$+ w_c \sum_{k} \frac{\partial C_i^k}{\partial y_i} \} \dot{y}_i + [w_l(\frac{\partial L_i^2}{\partial z_i} + \frac{\partial L_{i-1}^2}{\partial z_i})] + w_c \sum_{k} \frac{\partial C_i^k}{\partial z_i} \} \dot{z}_i \} \tag{9}$$

And the dynamic equation of motion about the point $P(x_i, y_i, z_i)$ is

$$\dot{x}_i = -\eta_1 \{ 2w_l(2x_i - x_{i-1} - x_{i+1}) + w_c \sum_{k=1}^{K} f'[(T_I)_i^k][\sum_{m=1}^{M} f'[(I_{Hm})_i^k] w_{xm}^k] \} \tag{10}$$

$$\dot{y}_i = -\eta_1 \{ 2w_l(2y_i - y_{i-1} - y_{i+1}) + w_c \sum_{k=1}^{K} f'[(T_I)_i^k][\sum_{m=1}^{M} f'[(I_{Hm})_i^k] w_{ym}^k] \} \tag{11}$$

$$\dot{z}_i = -\eta_1 \{ 2w_l(2z_i - z_{i-1} - z_{i+1}) + w_c \sum_{k=1}^{K} f'[(T_I)_i^k][\sum_{m=1}^{M} f'[(I_{Hm})_i^k] w_{zm}^k] \} \tag{12}$$

Where

$$f'(g) = \frac{1}{T}(g)(1 - f(g)) \tag{13}$$

And

$$\dot{x}_i = -\eta_2(2x_i - x_{i-1} - x_{i+1}) \tag{14}$$

$$\dot{y}_i = -\eta_2(2y_i - y_{i-1} - y_{i+1}) \tag{15}$$

$$\dot{z}_i = -\eta_2(2z_i - z_{i-1} - z_{i+1}) \tag{16}$$

2.4   Traditional Neural Network Obstacle Avoidance Algorithm Steps

The initial path point sequence selects a uniformly distributed point sequence on the line connected from the start point to the end point. The entire energy is a function of the various path points, moving each path point in a direction that reduces energy. In the traditional path planning algorithm, different dynamic equations of motion are selected according to different locations of the path points located inside and outside the obstacle.

First, three assumptions are made here: (1) The obstacle is a plane figure enclosed by polygons. (2) The robot is a circular point robot, and the size of the obstacle has been appropriately expanded according to the radius of the robot. (3) The obstacle is static.

The traditional neural network obstacle avoidance algorithm steps are as follows:

Step 1. Enter the coordinates of the starting point $P(x_1, y_1, z_1)$ and the target point (x_N, y_N, z_N). For $t = 0$, the initial path is generally taken as a point array uniformly distributed on the straight line from the starting point to the target point.

$$x_i = x_1 + i(x_N - x_1)/(N - 1) \tag{17}$$

$$y_i = y_1 + i(y_N - y_1)/(N - 1) \tag{18}$$

$$z_i = z_1 + i(z_N - z_1)/(N - 1) \tag{19}$$

Step 2. For the path point $P(x_i, y_i, z_i)$, $i = 2, 3,..., N - 1$, the parameters are $w_1 = w_c = 0.5$, $\eta_1 = 0.1$, $\eta_2 = 2.5$,
If $P(x_i, y_i, z_i)$ is in the obstacle, move according to Eqs. (10)–(12),
If $P(x_i, y_i, z_i)$ is outside the obstacle, move according to Eqs. (14)–(16).
Step 3. Repeat step 2 until the path converges.

3   Improved Neural Network Obstacle Avoidance Algorithm

3.1   Principle of Improved Neural Network Obstacle Avoidance Algorithm

In each iteration of the improved algorithm, if the line connecting any one of the path points and the target point does not collide with the obstacle, the coordinates of all the path points following the path point take the same value as the coordinates of the path point. This method allows the path to converge quickly to the shortest path without collision. The improved algorithm avoids the modeling of space by collision detection of sampling points in the state space, and can effectively solve the path planning problem of high dimensional space and complex constraints.

3.2   Steps of Improved Neural Network Obstacle Avoidance Algorithm

The improved fast neural network path planning algorithm is given below:

Step 1. After determining the starting point and the target point, connect the starting point and the target point and evenly take n intermediate path points, same as the traditional algorithm.

Step 2. Connect the target point to the first, second, and n-th path points, and determine whether the two points are in collision with the obstacle.

Step 3. If the connecting line of the two points does not collide with the obstacle, then all the path point coordinates after the path point are taken to be the same as the path point.

Step 4. If the two-point connection line collides with the obstacle, return to step 1, recalculate the target point according to the path planning method of the neural network, and connect with the target point again until the target point and the intermediate path point connection does not collide with the obstacle. Here, in order to solve the safety problem of the path planning of the mobile robot, the obstacle can be subjected to a series of puffing treatment.

The execution result of the path planning algorithm is shown in Fig. 3.

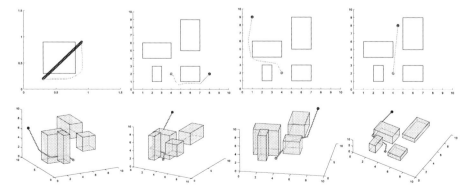

Fig. 3. Above: Single obstacle and multi-obstacle obstacle avoidance planning in two-dimensional space. Below: Multi-obstacle obstacle avoidance in three-dimensional space.

3.3 Comparison of Algorithm Performance

The following Fig. 4 shows the trajectory comparison of the traditional neural network obstacle avoidance algorithm and the improved neural network obstacle avoidance algorithm. The red line is the traditional algorithm and the green line is the improved algorithm.

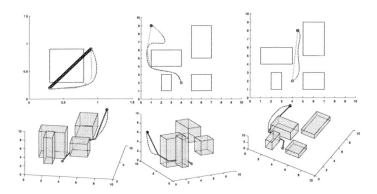

Fig. 4. Obstacle avoidance path planning algorithm based on traditional neural network method and improved neural network obstacle avoidance algorithm (Color figure online)

Since the traditional neural network will judge whether each path point is outside the obstacle in each iteration step, the improved algorithm only needs to judge whether the connection line between each path point and the target point collides with the obstacle. If the line do not collide, only other path points need to be judged to be related to obstacles, which saves running time and iteration times. By comparison, the path planned by the traditional neural network obstacle avoidance algorithm is not the optimal path, the path is long, the number of iterations is large, and the running time is long. The improved neural network obstacle avoidance algorithm can ensure the path is smooth and shortest, and can also reduce unnecessary iterative and obstacle collision detection steps, save path planning time.

4 Simulated Annealing Algorithm

4.1 Principle of Simulated Annealing Algorithm

Simulated annealing is a random search method that is inspired by the annealing process. The basic idea is to first set the temperature to a level high enough that most of the random motion directions are feasible, and a relatively low target area can be found in a relatively large space. As the temperature slowly decreases according to certain rules, the probability that each direction is selected will become different, and of course the accuracy of the search will continue to increase.

4.2   Parameter Setting

When using the simulated annealing algorithm to solve the optimization problem, whether the parameter setting is reasonable or not greatly affects the performance of the algorithm. However, in practical applications, the algorithm is only required to give a solution that satisfies the accuracy in a reasonable time. In order to meet the requirements of accuracy and efficiency, it is necessary to analyze and design several main parameters of the simulated annealing algorithm and set the size reasonably.

- **Initial temperature T_0 selection**

  When the value of the parameter T is different, the model diagram of the obstacle is as shown in Fig. 5. It can be obtained through simulation that when the parameter T taken in (5) is appropriate, the collision penalty function can accurately reflect the distribution of obstacles in the environment where the mobile robot is located.

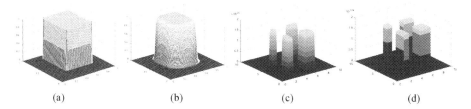

(a)   (b)   (c)   (d)

Fig. 5.   (a) 3D model of single obstacle at T = 0.01. (b) 3D model of single obstacle at T = 0.05. (c) 3D model of multiple obstacles at T = 0.01. (d) 3D model of multiple obstacles at T = 0.05.

- **Selection of Temperature Drop Function**

  Using the relationship between the parameter T and the penalty function energy surface, by starting with a higher "temperature" T, the path point is coarsely adjusted, then gradually decreasing T, and fine-tuning the path point to achieve simulated annealing effect.

  It can be shown that when the "temperature" T changes according to the following rules:

$$\frac{T_a(t)}{T_0} = \frac{1}{log(1+t)} \tag{20}$$

Since the convergence speed is slower according to the above formula, the following simulated annealing law can be adopted:

$$T(t) = \frac{T_a}{1+t} \tag{21}$$

Adopting this rule greatly accelerates the convergence speed and shortens the calculation time of path planning.

4.3   Steps of Simulated Annealing and Improved Algorithm Combined

In this algorithm, the simulated annealing algorithm is combined with the improved neural network obstacle avoidance algorithm obtained in Sect. 3. The main steps can be described as follow:

Step 1. According to the method in Sect. 3 to generate uniform track points. And determine the initial temperature T_0.
Step 2. For the path points $P(x_i, y_i, z_i)$, the derivatives of the points in the x, y, z direction are calculated according to the improve algorithm, thereby performing iterative operations and moving.
Step 3. Repeat step 2 until the temperature is reached at the internal circulation stop condition (sampling stability condition), then go to step 4;
Step 4. Decrease the temperature T according to Eq. (21) and proceed to step 2. The search is terminated when the temperature T drops enough to converge the entire path to the global minimum.

4.4   Comparison of Algorithm Performance

In this paper, the simulation platform is used as the Matlab program, and the comparison of the results is shown in Table 1. In the table, the improved algorithm refers to the improved neural network algorithm in Sect. 3, and the optimization algorithm is combination of the simulated annealing method and the improved algorithm in Sect. 3.

Table 1. Comparison of results of different algorithms

Algorithm	Number of iterations	Time consuming /s
Improved algorithm	310	1.319
Optimized algorithm	140	0.688

In the case where the results are same, the latter is nearly 1/2 faster than the former. The results in the above table show that the neural network is combined with the continuous simulated annealing algorithm to solve the non-convex optimization problem by using the local optimization ability. The results show that the combination of neural network and annealing algorithm overcomes the limitation of neural network for solving nonconvex optimization problems, and it is more efficient.

5   Adaptive Variable Step Size via Linear Reinforcement

5.1   Principle of Adaptive Variable Step Size via Linear Reinforcement

In the improved NA algorithm in Sect. 3, the step rolling η_1, η_2 is constant. When the selection of η_1, η_2 is too large, the path planning will be divergent. When the selection of η_1, η_2 is too small, the convergence speed is slow, especially for different planning path, there is no universal fixed step size, and sometimes it has to be re-selected.

In this paper, we combine this algorithm with the improved algorithm obtained in the previous chapter, use the idea of re-energized learning to find an adaptive variable step size algorithm to realize the automatic selection of step size, accelerate the convergence speed of NA algorithm, and reduce the number of iterations of path planning. The basic idea of the adaptive variable step size algorithm is: if two iterations are repeated, the gradient direction foot is opposite to the sign, which means "falling too much", the step size is too large, the step size should be reduced, conversely, if it is consecutive iteration, the sign of the gradient direction is the same, which means that the decline is slow and has not reached a minimum, the step size should be increased. This paper adopts the following method in the combined algorithm, as the Eqs. (22)–(23).

$$\eta_1(\eta+1) = \eta_1(n) + \lambda \times sgn((E(n) - E(n-1)) \times (E(n-1) - E(n-2))) \quad (22)$$

$$\eta_2(\eta+1) = \eta_2(n) + \lambda \times sgn((E(n) - E(n-1)) \times (E(n-1) - E(n-2))) \quad (23)$$

Where λ is a constant ranging from 0.001 to 0.003. The above algorithm actually utilizes and memorizes the symbol change information in the gradient direction.

5.2 Comparison of Algorithm Performance

The comparison of the results is shown in Table 2. In the table, the optimization algorithm is combination of the adaptive variable step size algorithm and the Sect. 4 optimization algorithm.

Table 2. Comparison of results of different algorithms

Algorithm	Number of iterations	Time consuming /s
Improved algorithm	310	1.319
Optimized algorithm	30	0.0109

Using this combined algorithm for path planning, the same shortest obstacle avoidance path as in Fig. 3 is obtained, and the convergence speed of path planning is nearly 10 times faster. The results in the above Table 2 show that the adaptive selection of the step size is realized by the linear re-excitation learning method, the path planning of the adaptive variable-step neural network path planning algorithm using adaptive variable stepsize via linear reinforcement algorithm is faster than the improved NA algorithm in the previous sections.

6 Conclusion

This paper mainly introduces an improved neural network obstacle avoidance method that combines multiple algorithm. which saves the planning time, effectively speeds up the convergence of path planning, and achieves the minimum path distance, achieving very good path planning results. The innovations of this paper includes: (a) A new neural network 3D space obstacle avoidance algorithm for mobile robot is proposed, which solves the problem of the computational duration and minimum distance of the traditional neural network obstacle avoidance algorithm in solving the optimal path. (b) The characteristic of the algorithm is combined with a variety of algorithms to obtain an optimal path algorithm that achieves the shortest path distance and meets the requirements of obstacle avoidance security. The improved neural network spatial obstacle avoidance algorithm based on the proposed algorithm can combine the advantages of each algorithm to achieve the path obstacle avoidance planning. (c) The characteristics of neural network algorithm, simulated annealing algorithm and linear re-energized adaptive variable step size algorithm are studied respectively, and their advantages are combined to form a new algorithm.

The future work mainly includes: (a) Adding fuzzy control algorithm to neural network path planning algorithm to solve obstacle avoidance problems in dynamic environments. (b) Combining powerful visual directions to solve the problem of obstacle avoidance in unknown 3D space.

References

1. Foux, G., Heymann, M., Bruckstein, A.: Two-dimensional robot navigation among unknown stationary polygonal obstacles. IEEE Trans. Robot. Autom. **9**(1), 96–102 (1993)
2. Luo, Y.F., Liu, J.G., Gao, Y., Lu, Z.L.: Smartphone-controlled robot snake for urban search and rescue. In: The 7th International Conference on Intelligent Robotics and Application (ICIRA), pp. 352–363 (2014)
3. Khosla, P., Volpe R.: Superquadric artificial potentials for obstacle avoidance and approach. In: IEEE International Conference on Robotics & Automation, pp. 1778–1784. IEEE (2002)
4. Lee, M., Park, M.: Artificial potential field based path planning for mobile robots using a virtual obstacle concept. In: IEEE/ASME International Conference on Advanced Intelligent Mechatronics, pp. 735–740. IEEE (2003)
5. Zhang, X., Liu, J.G.: Effective motion planning strategy for space robot capturing targets under consideration of the berth position. Acta Astronaut. **148**, 403–416 (2018)
6. Fei, K., YaoNan, W.: Robot path planning based on hybrid artificial potential field/genetic algorithm. J. Syst. Simul. **18**(3), 774–777 (2006)
7. Yun, S.C., Ganapathy, V., Chong, L.O.: Improved genetic algorithms based optimum path planning for mobile robot. In: International Conference on Control Automation Robotics & Vision, pp. 1565–1570. IEEE (2011)
8. Wzorek, M., Doherty, P.: Reconfigurable path planning for an autonomous unmanned areal vehicle. In: International Conference on Hybrid Information Technology (ICHIT 2006), pp. 438–441. IEEE (2006)
9. Liu, T.L., Wu, C.D., Li, B., Liu, J.G.: The adaptive path planning research for a shape-shifting robot using particle swarm optimization. In: 5th International Conference on Natural Computation, pp. 324–328. IEEE (2009)
10. Ge, S.S., Cu, Y.J.: New potential functions for mobile robot path planning. IEEE Trans. Robot Autom. **16**(5), 615–620 (2000)
11. Yang, S., Meng, M.: Real-time collision-free path planning of robot manipulators using neural network approaches. Auton. Robots **9**(1), 27–39 (2000)

12. Xu, X., Xie, J., Xie, K.: Path planning and obstacle-avoidance for soccer robot based on artificial potential field and genetic algorithm. In: World Congress on Intelligent Control & Automation, pp. 3494–3498. IEEE (2006)
13. Li, Q., Zhang, W., Yin, Y., Wang, Z., Liu, G.: An improved genetic algorithm of optimum path planning for mobile robots. In: 6th International Conference on Intelligent Systems Design and Applications, pp. 637–642. IEEE (2006)

An Improved A* Algorithm Based on Loop Iterative Optimization in Mobile Robot Path Planning

Gang Peng[1,2], Lu Hu[1,2(✉)], Wei Zheng[1,2], and Shan Liang Chen[1,2]

[1] School of Artificial Intelligence and Automation,
Huazhong University of Science and Technology, Wuhan 430074, China
hulu525@foxmail.com
[2] Key Laboratory of Image Processing and Intelligent Control
of Education Ministry, Wuhan, China

Abstract. In the mobile robot system, point-to-point path solving is one of the research hotspots in the field of robotics. Due to the many inflection points in the path planned by the traditional A* algorithm, the number of robot turns and the moving distance increases. Therefore, an improved A* algorithm is proposed. Based on the path of the traditional A* algorithm, a loop iterative optimization process is added. The path solved by the traditional A* algorithm is taken as the initial path of the loop iterative optimization process, from rough to fine layered iterative optimization until the total number of path nodes is minimized, and the optimal path solution is obtained. Compared with the traditional A* algorithm, the improved A* algorithm proposed in this paper effectively reduces the total number of path nodes and the number of inflection points, which can significantly improve the mobility of the robot in the actual environment. Experimental comparison results verify the feasibility and effectiveness of the proposed method.

Keywords: Loop iterative optimization · A* algorithm · Path inflection point · Path planning · Mobile robot

1 Introduction

With the development of robot technology and the continuous expansion of the application range, and the working environment of robots is becoming more and more complicated, one of the biggest technical challenges for intelligent mobile robots is efficient and smooth movement in the scene. Therefore, in the robot system, point-to-point path solving is one of the research hotspots in the field of robotics. The purpose of path solving is to find an optimal collision-free path from the starting point to the target point according to an evaluation index in an obstacle environment [1]. A lot of researches have been done on robot path solving, including sampling-based Voronoi diagram method, fast search random tree method etc. [2], node-based Dijkstra, A* algorithm, D* algorithm etc. [3, 4], based on biological heuristics Neural networks, genetic algorithms, ant colony algorithms etc. [5]. Among them, the A* algorithm is widely used in mobile robot path solving [6]. Because there are many inflection points

© Springer Nature Switzerland AG 2019
H. Yu et al. (Eds.): ICIRA 2019, LNAI 11743, pp. 118–130, 2019.
https://doi.org/10.1007/978-3-030-27538-9_11

in the path solved by the A* algorithm, there are many redundant nodes in the path. Such a path is neither optimal nor conducive to control the movement of the robot, causing the robot to move less efficiently.

Therefore, aiming at the problem of traditional A* algorithm path solving, an improved A* algorithm is proposed. Based on the traditional A* algorithm solution path, one loop iterative optimization process is added. The path solved by the traditional A* algorithm is used as the initial path of the loop iterative optimization process, and the loop iterative optimization is continuously performed until the total number of path nodes reaches the minimum, and the global optimal path is obtained.

2   Improved A* Algorithm

The A* algorithm is a classic method based on heuristic information search optimal path, which maintains a cost function and evaluates the current feasible path according to the cost function [7]. The cost function is composed of the current existing cost value and the estimated cost value. The estimated cost value, that is, the heuristic information, is the core of the whole A* algorithm [8]. The cost function has a different design depending on the application backgrounds. For the field of ground mobile robots, the 2D grid map is used to represent the robot motion space. Therefore, the A* algorithm is applied to the 2D grid map to realize the point-to-point path solution of the mobile robot. At the same time, an improved A* algorithm is proposed aiming at the deficiency of traditional A* algorithm in path solving.

2.1   A* Algorithm Principle

Using the heuristic information from the starting point of the robot to the target point, as well as selecting the appropriate cost function [9], the optimal solution is obtained by dynamically adjusting the search strategy according to the value of the cost function. Therefore, the key to the A* algorithm is to find the cost function, as in Eq. (1).

$$f(n) = g(n) + h(n) \tag{1}$$

In Eq. (1), $g(n)$ is the cost that has been paid from the starting node *Start* to the current node n, and $h(n)$ is the cost estimation function from the current node n to the target node *Goal*. The A* algorithm starts from the starting node s and searches for the node with the smallest $f(n)$ value until the target point is searched to determine the shortest path.

The A* algorithm solution path is divided into the following steps:

(1)   Create two tables: Open list and Close list, Open list records the nodes to be detected, and Close list records the nodes that have been detected;
(2)   Add the starting node to the Open list;
(3)   Repeat the following steps:
  (a)   Find the node with the smallest $f(n)$ value in the Open list, use it as the current node, and transfer it to the Close list table;

(b) Consider the eight neighbor nodes of the current node:

   (b.1) If the neighbor node is unreachable or already in the Close list, ignore the neighbor node, otherwise continue with the following steps:

   (b.2) If it is not in the Open list table, add it, calculate the $f(n)$ of the neighbor node, and then use the current node as its parent node;

   (b.3) If it already exists in the Open list table, it is necessary to judge whether the path from the current node to the neighbor node is better, the method is to use the cost $g(n)$ to judge, if the $g(n)$ from the current node to the neighbor node is smaller than the neighbor node The original $g(n)$, then change the original parent node of the neighbor node to the current node, and recalculate its $f(n)$, and reorder the Open list table;

(c) When the target node has been added to the Open list, it means that a path has been successfully searched; or if the target node is not found when the Open list is empty, it means that the path cannot be found.

(4) Starting from the target node, based on the direction of its parent node, back to the state of the starting node, an optimal path is generated.

In the above algorithm, the proportion of $h(n)$ in the whole cost function $f(n)$ determines the efficiency of the path solution [10]. If the $h(n)$ ratio is too small, that is, the heuristic information of the current node n to the target node g is too small, the search rate of the algorithm becomes slow, increases the solution time, but can get a better path. Conversely, the A* algorithm can have a faster search rate, and you can find a passable path if you search for fewer nodes, but it may not be the optimal path.

Therefore, considering the rate and quality of the solution, this paper uses the D-Euclidean distance to design the heuristic function $h(n)$, as shown in Eq. (2). First, a better path is solved in advance in a short time, and then optimized based on the solution path to obtain the optimal path.

$$h(n) = D * \sqrt{(n.x - Goal.x)^2 + (n.y - Goal.y)^2} \tag{2}$$

In Eq. (2), n is the current node, *Goal* is the target node, and D is the cost to move one step from the current node along the Euclidean distance, Eq. (2) represents the pre-estimated cost that needs to be paid to move from the current node n along the Euclidean distance to the target point *Goal*.

2.2 Loop Iterative Optimization Process

In the grid map, no matter how the heuristic function $h(n)$ is designed when using the traditional A* algorithm, there are always many inflection points in the path of the solution, resulting in many redundant nodes in the obtained path, as shown by the black solid line in Fig. 1. The path is not optimal and is not conducive to controlling the motion of the robot. Therefore, the path to be solved needs to be optimized to reduce the number of redundant nodes in the path and improve the efficiency of robot movement.

The black square in Fig. 1 represents the obstacle, the white square represents the passable area, the solid black line represents the unoptimized path, and n1 to n5 are the

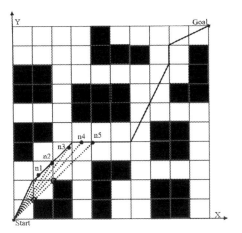

Fig. 1. Path optimization principle

nodes on the unoptimized path. Connect to subsequent nodes from the starting point of the path, such as In Fig. 1, the starting node *Start* is connected to the dotted line between n1 and n5 respectively. If there is an obstacle on the dotted line between the starting node *Start* and the current node, then the dotted line between the starting node *Start* and the previous node will be as the optimal path. Looking at Fig. 1, it can be seen that the point on the dotted line between *Start* and n5 contact with the obstacle area. As shown by the circle in Fig. 1, the line between *Start* and n5 is impassable and cannot be optimized. Therefore, the dotted line between *Start* and n4 is selected as the current optimal path.

From the above analysis, the idea of improving the A* algorithm is as follows, on the basis of the path solved by the traditional A* algorithm, a path loop iterative optimization process is added until the total number of path nodes from the starting node to the target node is minimized, and the optimal path solution is found.

It should be noted that in order to obtain the global optimal path solution, the idea of hierarchical iterative optimization is adopted, that is, the path optimized by each layer is used as the initial path of the next layer of iterative optimization, and the hierarchical iteration from coarse to fine. Until the total number of path nodes reaches the minimum or the number of loop iterations is reached, the optimal path solution is obtained. The detailed process is shown in Fig. 2.

Define a local start node Local_start, local target node Local_goal, last local target node Last_local_goal, and assign the global start node *Start* to Local_start, Local_goal, Last_local_goal.

Firstly, the path solved by the traditional A* algorithm is taken as the initial path of the optimization process, and then each path node is considered from the Local_goal, and it is judged whether there is an obstacle on the line of Local_goal to Local_start, and the optimal path is found by the method until the global The target node *Goal* is Local_goal, backtracks to the global starting node *Start*, generates an optimal path, completes an iterative optimization, calculates the total number of path nodes obtained by the current optimization, and determines whether the current iteration number

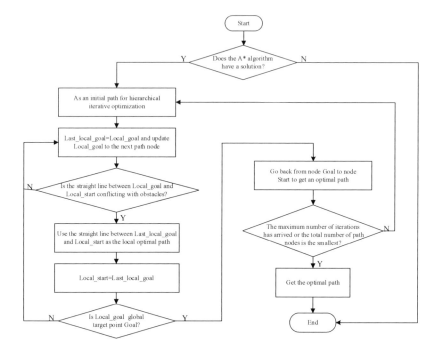

Fig. 2. Flow chart of the loop iterative optimization process

reaches the set maximum number of iterations, or current Whether the number of path nodes reaches the minimum, otherwise the path obtained this time is used as the initial path for the next iteration optimization, and the layered iteration is continued until the optimal path is obtained.

In the hierarchical iterative optimization process, it is the most time-consuming step in the whole optimization process to determine whether there are obstacles on the line between the two nodes, which determines the rate of path optimization. Considering the real-time motion of the robot, the optimal path needs to be solved quickly. Therefore, in order to accelerate the path optimization process, the Bresenham [11] line algorithm is used to quickly determine whether there are obstacles on the line of the two-pixel node. The algorithm is as follows.

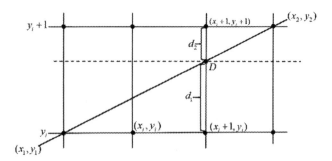

Fig. 3. Bresenham line algorithm principle

As shown in Fig. 3, the intersection of the horizontal line and the vertical line is regarded as a pixel node, and if there is an obstacle on the line between the two pixel nodes (x_1, y_1) and (x_2, y_2), it is necessary to calculate the coordinates of each pixel node between the two pixel nodes. The calculation is stopped until a pixel node whose coordinates are obstacles is encountered.

Suppose the line equation is $y = k * x + b$, and its slope k is between 0 and 1, if $x_2 > x_1$, then $\Delta x = (x_2 - x_1)$, $\Delta y = (y_2 - y_1)$. The principle of the algorithm is to find the pixel node closest to the point D on the straight line. The judgment of the distance is determined by comparing the sizes of d1 and d2. It is assumed that the i-th step has determined that the coordinates of the i-th pixel node is (x_i, y_i), then the i+1th pixel coordinate:

$$\begin{cases} d_1 \geq d_2 & (x_i + 1, y_i + 1) \\ d_1 < d_2 & (x_i + 1, y_i) \end{cases} \tag{3}$$

As can be seen from Fig. 3, $d_1 = (y - y_i)$, $d_2 = (y_i + 1 - y)$ in the formula (3). Multiply both sides of the equal sign of d_1 and d_2 by Δx, and bring the line equation $y = k * x + b$ into d_1 and d_2, as shown in Eq. (4):

$$\begin{cases} \Delta x \cdot d_1 = \Delta x \cdot (y - y_i) = \Delta y \cdot (x_i + 1) + \Delta x \cdot b - \Delta x \cdot y_i \\ \Delta x \cdot d_2 = \Delta x \cdot (y_i + 1 - y) = \Delta y \cdot (y_i + 1) - \Delta x \cdot (x_i + 1) - \Delta x \cdot b \end{cases} \tag{4}$$

Among them, the size of d_1 and d_2 can be compared by difference, so it can be derived from Eq. (4).

$$\Delta x \cdot (d_1 - d_2) = 2\Delta y \cdot x_i - 2\Delta x \cdot y_i + c \tag{5}$$

In Eq. (5), c is a constant. Since $\Delta x = (x_2 - x_1)$ and $x_2 > x_1$, therefore Δx is greater than 0, then the sign of $d_1 - d_2$ does not change. Let $p_i = \Delta x * (d_1 - d_2)$, then the final point-finding equation is:

$$\begin{cases} p_i \geq 0, & (x_i + 1, y_i + 1), & p_{i+1} = p_i + 2(\Delta y - \Delta x) \\ p_i < 0, & (x_i + 1, y_i), & p_{i+1} = p_i + 2\Delta y \end{cases} \tag{6}$$

The pixel coordinates of the next node are selected by the positive and negative of p_i, and it is judged whether the pixel node is an obstacle. If yes, the judgment is stopped. Otherwise, the value of p_{i+1} is calculated by Eq. (6), and then the coordinates of the next pixel are selected by the positive and negative of p_{i+1}, and the relationship between p_{i+1} and p_{i+2} is calculated, thereby continuously recursively calculating. Finally, it is determined whether the line between the two pixels (x_1, y_1) and (x_2, y_2) conflicts with the obstacle.

The algorithm can effectively reduce the amount of computation in the iterative optimization process and greatly accelerate the solution process of path loop iterative optimization.

3 Experimental Analysis

In order to verify the application effect of the improved A* algorithm in the actual complex environment. The original A* algorithm and the improved A* algorithm is integrated into the ROS system environment, and a comparative experiment was carried out on a mobile robot equipped with a single-line lidar. Figure 4 shows the mobile robot system used in this experiment. Figure 5 shows an experimental environment with a length of 10 m and a width of 7 m. Set the maximum linear speed of the robot to 0.5 m/s and the maximum angular velocity to 1 rad/s.

Fig. 4. Mobile robot system   **Fig. 5.** Experimental environment

3.1 Improved A* Algorithm Experiment

In order to verify the path optimization performance of the improved A* algorithm, this paper pre-uses the laser mapping algorithm to build a grid map with a resolution of 0.025 m in a laboratory scene with a length of 10 m and a width of 7 m, as shown in Fig. 6. And the occupied grid map is binarized and corroded. In the figure, white is a passable area, black is an obstacle area, S is a starting node, and G is a target node.

Under the premise of the same starting node S and target node G, the traditional A* algorithm and the improved A* algorithm is used to solve the path separately. Figure 7 shows the path solution of the traditional A* algorithm, there are many inflection points in the path in the Fig. 7. As shown in the blue circle in Fig. 7, there are many redundant nodes in the path. Such a path will reduce the motion efficiency of the robot. Therefore, the path can be further optimized. Under the premise of ensuring effective obstacle avoidance, the path is used as the initial value of hierarchical iterative optimization, and the path is optimized. Figure 8a is the result of iterative optimization once. Compared with the path before optimization, the number of inflection points is significantly reduced, but the total number of path nodes does not reach the minimum at this time. Therefore, the path is used as the initial value of hierarchical iterative optimization, and the second optimization is continued, as shown in Fig. 8b, at this time, the path is optimal. The number of inflection points is the smallest and the total number of path nodes is minimized.

The experimental results show that, based on the initial value, the improved A* algorithm only needs to be iterated several times to make the path optimal. Table 1 compares the performance of the algorithm. The final optimization result is compared with the path of the traditional A* algorithm. The path length is reduced by 13.9%, and the cumulative number of inflection points is reduced by 62.5%. Using the optimized path to control robot movement can effectively reduce the number of turns and improve the robot's moving efficiency.

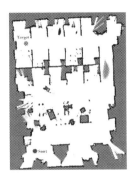

Fig. 6. Occupy the grid map

Fig. 7. A* algorithm solution results

(a) Iterative optimization 1 time

(b) Iterative optimization 2 times

Fig. 8. Improved A* algorithm solution results

Table 1. Comparison of algorithm performance

Algorithm	Traditional A* algorithm	Improved A* algorithm	
		Iterative optimization 1 time	Iterative optimization 2 times
Number of inflection points	16	10	6
Path length	17.302 m	15.515 m	14.895 m

3.2   Comparison of Original A* Algorithm and Improved A* Algorithm

In order to verify the improvement effect of the loop iterative optimization process on the original A* algorithm, a comparative experiment was conducted in a laboratory environment with dense obstacles and a narrow space. As shown in Fig. 5, a Cartographer mapping algorithm was used in advance to establish a high-precision global occupied grid map in this environment. the current position of the robot taken as the global starting point, the global target point is randomly selected in the blank area occupying the grid map, as shown by the blue and red dots in Figs. 9 and 10. On the map, the point-to-point path solving experiment is performed using the original A* algorithm and the improved A* algorithm, respectively, and the robot is controlled to move along the pre-planned path at the same linear velocity and angular velocity. Figure 9 shows the path solved by the original A* algorithm, among which the blue circle is the path inflection point. Figure 10 is the path after the improved A* algorithm is optimized twice in the loop iteration.

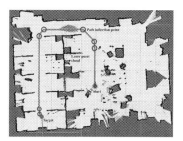   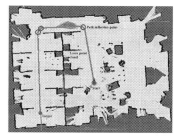

Fig. 9. Original A* algorithm results (Color figure online)   **Fig. 10.** Improved A* algorithm results (Color figure online)

In order to effectively evaluate the performance of the improved A* algorithm, multiple sets of different global starting points and target points were used to perform multiple sets of comparison experiments using the original A* algorithm and the improved A* algorithm. Among them, the total length of the path solved by the two algorithms, the total time of the robot moving to the target point, the number of turns along the path movement are used as performance evaluation indicators, and the robot is controlled to complete the motion experiment at the same linear velocity and angular velocity, the experimental results are shown in Table 2.

It can be seen from the analysis in Table 2 that, compared with the original A* algorithm, no matter where the global starting point and the target point are set, the total length of the solved path is the shortest, and the number of path turns is the least, the time to move to the global target point is minimal. Therefore, using the improved A* algorithm to solve the path can effectively reduce the number of turns, shorten the movement time, and improve the robot movement efficiency.

Table 2. Multi-group path solving comparison experiment

Number of experiments		1	2	3	4	5
Start(X, Y)m		1.17, 0.34	1.43, 0.06	0.08, −2.97	2.72, 3.82	−0.28, −2.86
Target(X, Y)m		0.05, −2.88	0.08, −2.79	2.72, 3.82	1.50, 0.19	−0.48, 3.78
Original A* algorithm	Path length	9.22 m	8.99 m	12.25 m	8.23 m	15.78 m
	Number of turns	8 Times	9 Times	7 Times	6 Times	8 Times
	Time of movement	61.1 s	62.3 s	69.25 s	53.32 s	80.21 s
Improved A* algorithm	Path length	8.42 m	8.33 m	11.42 m	7.85 m	14.52 m
	Number of turns	4 Times	3 Times	3 Times	3 Times	3 Times
	Time of movement	49.39 s	47.26 s	59.03 s	45.41 s	66.21 s
	Iterative times	3 Times	2 Times	2 Times	2 Times	3 Times
Path length reduction (%)		8.67%	7.34%	6.77%	4.61%	7.98%
Reduced number of turns (%)		50%	66.6%	57.1%	50%	62.5%

3.3 Experimental Comparison of Obstacle Avoidance Path Planning Methods

In order to verify the actual effect of the improved A* algorithm in obstacle avoidance path planning, in the same experimental environment, the same obstacle environment, the same linear velocity and angular velocity, the improved A* algorithm and the artificial potential field method were compared in multiple groups.

Obstacle Avoidance Path Planning Experiment with Improved A* Algorithm
In the experimental environment shown in Fig. 5, the improved A* algorithm is used to perform the obstacle avoidance path planning experiment for the special obstacle of the human body. The experimental verification process is shown in Fig. 11.

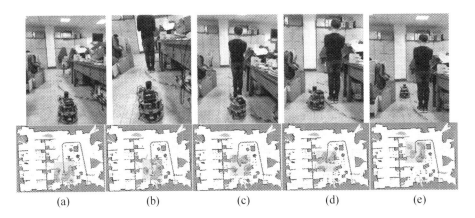

(a)   (b)   (c)   (d)   (e)

Fig. 11. Robot avoids the human body

The obstacle avoidance process in Fig. 11 shows that, after the robot detects the obstacle, in order to bypass the obstacle, an improved A* algorithm is used to plan an optimal path from the current position to the global target point. The robot is controlled to move along the path to avoid obstacles. At the same time, in the obstacle avoidance process, the obstacle avoidance method can adjust the obstacle avoidance path in real time according to the safety distance between the robot and the obstacle. Therefore, the improved A* algorithm is used for obstacle avoidance path planning, which having the advantages of short moving distance and stable motion, which can effectively shorten the motion time of the robot and improve the motion efficiency.

Multiple Sets of Comparison Experiments
In order to effectively compare the obstacle avoidance path planning performance of the improved A* algorithm, five different global starting points and target points, five different obstacle environments are shown in Fig. 12. A comparative experiment was conducted on two obstacle avoidance path planning methods. Among them, the minimum safe distance between the robot and the obstacle, the time to complete the obstacle avoidance, the moving distance of the robot to bypass the obstacle is the performance evaluation index, and the control robot completes the motion experiment under the same expected linear velocity and angular velocity. The results are shown in Table 3.

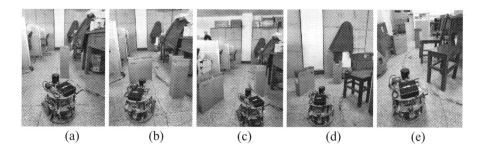

| (a) | (b) | (c) | (d) | (e) |

Fig. 12. Five obstacle environments

Table 3. Multiple sets of contrast experiments for two obstacle avoidance path planning methods

Number of experiments		1	2	3	4	5	Average
Artificial potential field algorithm	Minimum safe distance	28 cm	30 cm	26 cm	27 cm	20 cm	26.2 cm
	Distance to bypass obstacles	2.95 m	3.39 m	3.78 m	3.99 m	4.41 m	3.704 m
	Complete an obstacle avoidance time	25.32 s	28.13 s	32.5 s	34.1 s	42.3 s	32.47 s
Improved A* algorithm	Minimum safe distance	20 cm	14 cm	10 cm	13 cm	8 cm	13 cm
	Distance to bypass obstacles	1.62 m	1.56 m	2.56 m	2.32 m	2.96 m	2.204 m
	Complete an obstacle avoidance time	9.93 s	8.76 s	15.2 s	13.4 s	17.2 s	12.898 s
Avoid obstacle distance reduction %		45.08%	53.98%	32.27%	41.85%	32.87%	4.49%
Reduced timed for obstacle reduction %		60.7%	68.85%	53.23%	60.70%	59.33%	60.27%

It can be seen from Table 3 that in the five experiments, the improved A* algorithm compared with the artificial potential field method. In order to avoid obstacles, the distance of movement is reduced by an average of 40.49%, and the time to complete an obstacle avoidance is reduced by an average of 60.27%. Therefore, the obstacle avoidance method of this paper can effectively shorten the obstacle avoidance time and reduce the moving distance. However, in Table 3, the minimum safe distance performance of the obstacle avoidance method of this paper is not as good as the artificial potential field method. The reason is that the closer the artificial potential field method is to the obstacle, the greater the repulsive force generated, which makes the safe distance of the robot from the obstacle larger. The obstacle avoidance method in this paper is based on the principle of solving the optimal path to avoid obstacles, so that the safety distance between the robot and the obstacle is small. At the same time, due to the error of the localization accuracy of the robot, the estimated distance between the robot and the obstacle is deviated from the actual distance.

4 Conclusion

Aiming at the problem of the original A* algorithm having many inflection points in the field of robot path planning which leads to many redundant nodes in the path, this paper proposes an improved A* algorithm. That is, adding a loop iterative optimization process based on the original A* algorithm, using the path solution solved by the original A* algorithm as the initial value of the loop iterative optimization process, and minimizing the total number of path nodes through continuous loop iteration, so as to obtain the optimal path. The experimental results show that the improved A* algorithm only needs a simple iteration several times to optimize the path, which makes the algorithm feasible in engineering applications. At the same time, the improved A* algorithm is applied to the obstacle-intensive and complex experimental environment for multi-group comparison experiments. The results show that the improved A* algorithm proposed in this paper can effectively reduce the number of path inflection points and shorten the path length. The moving efficiency of the mobile robot in the actual environment is improved. The experimental comparison results fully verify the feasibility and effectiveness of the improved A* algorithm proposed in this paper.

When the mobile robot turns around the obstacle, due to the localization error and the noise of the laser sensor, there is a certain error between the estimated distance between the robot and the obstacle and the actual distance. Therefore, the optimal obstacle avoidance path solved by the improved A* algorithm is close to the obstacle, which causes the risk of the robot to increase along the obstacle avoidance path. This problem can be solved by increasing the range of obstacles in the grid map, or by improving the accuracy of the lidar and localization.

References

1. Eele, A.J., Richards, A.: Path-planning with avoidance using nonlinear branch-and-bound optimization. J. Guid. Control Dyn. **32**(2), 384–394 (2015)
2. Kothari, M., Postlethwaite, I.: A probabilistically robust path planning algorithm for UAVs using rapidly-exploring random trees. J. Intell. Rob. Syst. **71**(2), 231–253 (2013)
3. Zhang, B., Cao, Q.X., Wang, W.S.: Path planning of mobile robot using 3D grid map. J. Xi'an Jiaotong Univ. **47**(10), 57–61 (2013)
4. Montiel, O., Sepúlveda, R., Orozco-Rosas, U.: Optimal path planning generation for mobile robots using parallel evolutionary artificial potential field. J. Intell. Robot. Syst. **79**(2), 237–257 (2015)
5. Zhu, D.Q., Sun, B., Li, L.I.: Algorithm for AUV's 3-D path planning and safe obstacle avoidance based on biological inspired model. Control Decis. **30**(5), 798–806 (2015)
6. Wei, W., Dong, P., Zhang, F.: The shortest path planning for mobile robots using improved A* algorithm. J. Comput. Appl. (2018)
7. Fu, B., Chen, L., Zhou, Y., et al.: An improved A* algorithm for the industrial robot path planning with high success rate and short length. Robot. Auton. Syst. **106**, 26–37 (2018)
8. Jing, X., Yang, X.: Application and improvement of heuristic function in A ∼ * algorithm. In: The 37th China Control Conference (2018)
9. Wang, Y., Liu, Z., Zuo, Z., et al.: Local path planning of autonomous vehicles based on A ∼ * algorithm with equal-step sampling. In: The 37th China Control Conference (2018)
10. Wei, W., Dong, P., Zhang, F.: The shortest path planning for mobile robots using improved A ∼ * algorithm. J. Comput. Appl. (2018)
11. Li, X., Shao, X.: Fast line drawing algorithm by circular subtraction based on Bresenham. In: Proceedings of SPIE - The International Society for Optical Engineering, vol. 8349, p. 20 (2012)

Indoor Environment RGB-DT Mapping for Security Mobile Robots

Lijun Zhao[1]([✉]), Yu Liu[1], Xinkai Jiang[1], Ke Wang[1], and Zigeng Zhou[2]

[1] State Key Laboratory of Robotics and System, Harbin Institute of Technology, Harbin, China
zhaolj@hit.edu.cn, 13091863132@163.com
[2] Kunming Power Supply Bureau, Kunming, China

Abstract. Many robot applications, such as environmental monitoring, security and surveillance help people to do tasks in day-to-day scenarios. However, the growing security demand for environment perception is a key issue of mapping or frequent updating in the long term, such as fire detection in early stage. A hybrid mapping method is proposed based on fusing RGB, depth and thermal (DT) information from Kinect and infrared sensors equipped in the mobile robot. Firstly, the proposed pipeline will estimate the robot's pose by extracting and matching ORB features in RGB images successively. Then Poses corresponding to each depth and thermal- Infrared image are estimated through a combination of timestamp synchronization and the result of the extrinsic calibration of the system, and the map with both appearance and the temperature of environment is generated by the combination of The RGB and temperature information. Finally, the depth information is used to project the pixel points to the world coordinate system to generate the RGB-DT map. Extensive results verify the effectiveness of the proposed RGB-DT mapping for environments perception

Keywords: SLAM · Environment mapping · ORB-SLAM · Multi-sensor fusing

1 Introduction

In recent years, with the development of the robot industry, more and more robots come into our live, such as sweeping and companion robots which can provide cleaning or voice communication services, and bring us much convenience. However, with the extensive usage of household appliances, electrical safety has become an important safety hazard, so people expect to replace themselves for the robots to detect environmental safety in everyday life.

The premise of a security mobile for human service is to be able to fully perceive the environment. Environmental awareness includes "feeling" and "knowing and understanding" [1], which acquires and utilizes the surrounding environment information from sensors. The robot feeling environment mainly relies on visual sensors including range sensors and image sensors, and locating and mapping simultaneously by the obtained appearance and depth information to explore the unknown

H. Yu et al. (Eds.): ICIRA 2019, LNAI 11743, pp. 131–141, 2019.
https://doi.org/10.1007/978-3-030-27538-9_12

environment. However, it is necessary to know the temperature information in the environment for the security mobile robot to judge the dangerous areas caused by fire and realize safety inspection.

This paper proposes a system combining a RGB-D camera and a thermal-infrared camera for the security mobile robot to solve the above issues. The RGB camera can provide rich color and texture information, while the thermal-infrared camera receives the temperature of the objects, but the imaging is blurred. Therefore, the robot can build a 3D temperature map with both appearance and temperature information, and divide hazardous areas, which can provide a basis for locating and grabbing objects on target objects.

Our major contributions are as follows:

- Synchronization of Heterogeneous Sensors: Infrared and Kinect cameras.
- RGB-DT framework and data synchronization method.

Section 2 reviews related work in the resent research topics. Section 3 explains the fusion method between the RGB-D camera and the thermal imager. Section 4 introduces the RGB-DT mapping system. The experimental results are shown in Sect. 5, and Sect. 6 concludes the paper.

2   Related Work

At present, there are many methods for mapping 3D models based on visual sensors. However, since RGB-D cameras can directly acquire the pixel's depth, it's convenient to build a SLAM (Simultaneous Localization and Mapping) system. In [2], a RGB-D SLAM algorithm for building dense 3D models was proposed, which used the ICP algorithm to estimate camera motion, combined RGB images to generate point clouds, and represented the models using voxels, but it needed to use GPU to accelerate calculations. In [3], a local-to-global optimization strategy was raised to reduce the number of optimizations and speed up the optimization process by running on the GPU, which requires high hardware facilities. The [4] utilized the features that extracted from the RGB images to obtain pose estimation, which greatly reduced the requirements for hardware. In addition, the locating accuracy of the robot has also been improved. However, these methods are not combined with temperature sensors and can't be used for safe inspection of mobile robots.

The [5] was the first to combine a RGB-D camera with a thermal imager for energy auditing of buildings. They designed a handheld 3D temperature mapping system, which only captured data and then processed the data offline. The processing process requires GPU acceleration, which demands high processing equipment and the device cannot move autonomously. The Thermal Mapper project [6] involved a mobile robot with a laser scanner and a thermal-infrared camera, which can project temperature onto a 3D model as it explores an environment. This project is mainly used to audit indoor environmental energy. In [7], they also used a 3D LiDAR laser and a thermal imager to build a 3D thermography map for rescue missions. However, the 3D LiDAR is expensive, and the details of the generated model are blurred because of lacking appearance information.

3   Multi-sensor Fusion

Multidimensional external information is obtained through different types of sensors, which need to fuse. The fusion process requires four steps, which we will introduce in this section.

3.1   Intrinsic Calibration of RGB and Thermal Cameras

The pinhole model is used to represent the geometric model of the camera from the 3D world to the 2D image. In this model, P is the point in the world coordinate system, p is the perspective projection point from P to image that can be calculated by the camera intrinsic matrix K and the translation matrix T, the rotation matrix R of the camera coordinate system relative to the world coordinate system.

A common method for estimating intrinsic matrix K is the Zhang's [8], which uses a checkerboard. However, for the low resolution thermal cameras a normal checkerboard is not clearly visible. So the calibration plate is improved to make the checkerboard clearly visible in both the RGB-D and the thermal cameras.

First we attach the printed regular checkerboard to the black cardboard, then hollow the white part of the checkerboard and fix it on a transparent plastic plate so that the entire checkerboard is on a flat surface and is transparent to heat radiation. In the experiment, the improved checkerboard is attached to the surface of the external heating source, so that the hollow portion and the non-hollow portion transmit different heat radiation. In order to complete the calibration of the thermal and the RGB camera simultaneously, we covered the calibration plate on a white heating electric blanket. Figure 1 demonstrates the effectiveness of the method.

Fig. 1. Improved calibration template extracts corner points using calibration tools

3.2   Extrinsic Calibration of RGB and Thermal Cameras

In order to make the acquired images have a uniform virtual focus, the thermal Camera coordinate system with the RGB-D camera needs to be aligned, after obtaining the intrinsic parameters of the camera.

The common method was used to get the extrinsic matrix is that each sensor observes the same pair of checkerboard [9]. Experiments show that the errors are large. In [10], a line-to-line method for extrinsic calibration of range and image sensors was proposed. Inspired by this method, this paper used the line features in the image to realize the extrinsic calibration of the thermal and RGB-D cameras, which is easy to operate.

This method mainly comprises three steps. First we extract a 2D line l on the thermal infrared image. Next, a corresponding 3D line L is extracted in the RGB-D image. Finally the 3D line L is projected onto the thermal-infrared image coordinate system using the initial extrinsic parameters, and the optimal solution can be obtained by minimizing the distance between the corresponding 3D-2D lines.

In order to get better calibration results, one 3D calibration template is made, as shown in Fig. 2. When solving the nonlinear least squares problem, it is necessary to compare the initial values close to the optimal solution to avoid local optimum. The initial extrinsic parameters is obtained by the intrinsic calibration process. Finally the optimal solution is obtained by L-M algorithm.

Fig. 2. Thermal infrared image of 3D calibration plate

3.3 Synchronization Between the RGB-D and Thermal Cameras

Since the sampling frequencies of the cameras are different, it is necessary to time-registered the acquired images to ensure the consistency of the shooting scene. In [11], master-slave synchronization technology was applied to synchronize RGB camera and thermal imager. A beam splitter was used in [12] to synchronize the camera. The synchronization result is ideal with hardware, but most cameras do not have a beam splitter, and the hardware increases the cost and requires extra installation space.

The timestamp mechanism is used to achieve images synchronization of heterogeneous sensors. The timestamps of different source images are separately recorded and compared. The image is considered to be matched if the time difference is less than 20 ms (half of the camera sampling time), and may be ignored if it is larger than the difference value. In this way, the mechanism guarantees the time synchronization between sensors.

The thermal camera will perform regular intensity calibrations to ensure the accuracy of temperature measurement because of two factors. Firstly, the mechanical shutter will close and the output thermal-infrared images will be unchanged during the calibration process which will last approximately 1 s. Secondly, the camera's calibration period is every 10 min as the camera is in a steady state. This process will have a large impact on the map construction. So the captured thermal-infrared images need to be compared when the robot is running for 9 to 11 min. If the thermal-infrared images are found to be the same, they will be discarded along with time-registered RGB and depth images.

3.4   RGB and Thermal Information Fusion

The thermal-infrared image can be known as a 2D color image with colored bars that are associated with temperature estimates in order to help human observation. The thermal camera has a variety of color modes according to different applications. For clarity, the dark-blue mode is adopted, with red indicating hot and blue indicating cold.

Thermal-infrared images are susceptible to the influence of electronic heat source noise during the acquisition process, so the Gaussian noise will appear in the images commonly [13]. Therefore, guided filter is selected to remove the noise before the data fusion.

Compared with thermal-infrared images, RGB images can provide richer color and texture information. Therefore, the appearance information in the RGB image needs to be preserved during the process of merging the images. We use the pixel-level fusion to make each point cloud in the 3D model contain both appearance and temperature estimates. In response to those requirements, the method of transforming color space is used to complete images fusion. The specific operation is shown in Fig. 3.

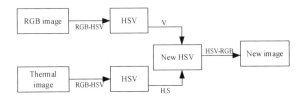

Fig. 3. RGB and thermal-infrared images fusion scheme

HSV model consists of three components [14], where H represents the range of colors, S determines the shade of the color. V indicates the degree of light and darkness of the color. According to the meaning of the components, we extract the H and S components from the thermal-infrared image which represent the color information, and the V component that represents the luminance from the RGB image to merge into a new image.

4   RGB-DT Mapping

Inspired by the ORB-SLAM2 algorithm framework, the proposed algorithm improves the framework with RGB-DT Module to map depth and thermos information simultaneously. The proposed framework system (shown in Fig. 4) is divided into four parts: Tracking, Local Mapping, Loop Closing and RGB-DT Mapping, which complete pose estimation, pose optimization, loop detection and RGB-DT mapping respectively.

4.1   Tracking

Firstly, the ORB features are extracted from RGB image and calculate their descriptors, then they are matched according to the Euclidean and the angle distance between the

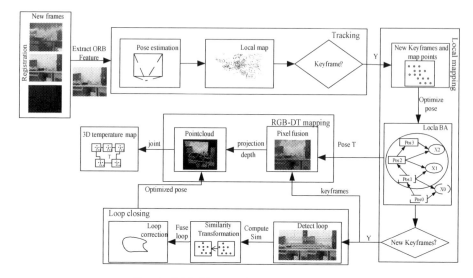

Fig. 4. RGB-DT mapping system overview

descriptors. The EPnP algorithm [15] is then used to estimate the pose of the camera between adjacent frames. Since the camera sampling frequency is high, many repetitive scenes will be generated, so the current frame won't be inserted as the keyframe into the local mapping thread if the 90% points of the current frames appear in other frames.

4.2 Local Mapping

When a new keyframe K_i generated by the tracking thread, the covisibility graph will be updated, and the local BA is used to perform pose optimization on the current keyframe K_i and the keyframe K_C having a common view relationship in the graph. It is known that the 2D keypoints in K_i is $x_{i,j} \in \mathbb{R}^2$, that the matching 3D keypoints is $X_{C,j} \in \mathbb{R}^3$ in K_C whose pose is $T_C \in SE(3)$, so the error for the keypoint j in the keyframe i is

$$e_{i,j} = x_{i,j} - \lambda_{i,j}(T_C, X_{C,j}) \tag{1}$$

Where $\lambda_{i,j}$ is the projection function

$$\lambda_{i,j}(T_C, X_{C,j}) = \begin{bmatrix} f_x \frac{x_{c,j}}{z_{c,j}} + c_x \\ f_y \frac{y_{c,j}}{z_{c,j}} + c_y \end{bmatrix} \tag{2}$$

$$[x_{c,j} \quad y_{c,j} \quad z_{c,j}] = R_c X_{C,j} + T_c \tag{3}$$

Where $R_c \in SO(3)$ and $T_c \in \mathbb{R}^3$ are respectively the rotation and translation parts of T_C, while (f_x, f_y) and (c_x, c_y) are the focal length and principle point associated to camera. The cost function to be minimized is:

$$E = \sum_n h_c \left(e_{i,j}^{\mathrm{T}} \Omega_{i,j}^{-1} e_{i,j} \right) \tag{4}$$

Where h_c is the Huber robust cost function and $\Omega_{i,j}$ is the covariance matrix.

Therefore, the pose of the keyframe is optimized by minimizing the formula (4). Since the number of keyframes will increase as the image is added, we will remove the keyframes which are closer to adjacent frames in order to maintain succinct and effective map.

4.3 Loop Closing

When the new keyframe K_i inserts the system, the similarity between K_i and other keyframes are calculated, and the search process is accelerated by the DBoW2 [16]. After detecting the loop, we calculate the similarity transformation matrix S_{iCa} of the keyframe K_i and the candidate keyframe K_{Ca}, and the pose of K_i is optimized by using S_{iCa}. Then the optimization process is passed to the neighbors of the keyframe K_i to perform the multi-frame Loop correction. In order to effectively close the loop, the pose map optimization is performed on the Essential Graph, which can distribute the loop closing error.

Assume n matches $i \Rightarrow j$ between the two keyframes K_i and K_{Caj}. We use the minimized reprojection error to find the similarity transformation matrix S_{iCa} between the two frames:

$$
\begin{aligned}
e_i &= x_{i,i} - \lambda_{i,j} \left(S_{iCa}, X_{Ca,j} \right) \\
e_{Ca} &= x_{Ca,j} - \lambda_{Ca,i} \left(S_{iCa}^{-1}, X_{i,i} \right)
\end{aligned}
\tag{5}
$$

the cost function to minimize is:

$$E = \sum_n \left(h_c \left(e_i^{\mathrm{T}} \Omega_{i,i}^{-1} e_i \right) + h_c \left(e_{Ca}^{\mathrm{T}} \Omega_{Ca,j}^{-1} e_{Ca} \right) \right) \tag{6}$$

4.4 RGB-DT Mapping

We get the keyframe K_i with less redundancy of scene information whose pose relative to the world coordinate system is T_i. The pose is optimized through the local mapping thread. The keyframe is a 2D RGB image, whose pixel points $p_{i,j} \in \mathbb{R}^2$ projecting to the world coordinate system are the 3D points $P_{i,j} \in \mathbb{R}^3$. The conversion relationship is as follows:

$$P_{i,j} = T_i * z_{i,j} K^{-1} p_{i,j} \tag{7}$$

Where K represents the intrinsic matrix of the camera, $z_{i,j}$ represents the depth value of the pixel, and all the keyframes are jointed to obtain a dense 3D models.

The thermal-infrared image corresponding to each keyframe obtained by time synchronization is fused before the pixel point projection, and the fusion method is shown in Sect. 3.4, which can improve the registration accuracy of temperature and appearance information in the motion scene effectively, and avoid the fusion of point clouds in space. All keyframes are projected using Eq. (7) to obtain the final RGB-DT map.

5   Evaluation

The camera model for obtaining thermal-infrared images is DS-2TD2636T-10, and the camera for obtaining RGB-D images is Kinect2. The specifications of the camera are shown in Table 1.

Table 1. Camera specifications

Sensor	Thermal camera	RGB-D cameras
Model	DS-2TD2636T-10	Kinect2
FOV	37.7° × 28.7°	84.1° × 53.8°
Resolution	388 * 284	1920 * 1080
Framerate	25FPS	30 FPS
Wavelength	8–14 μm	
Range	−20 °C–150 °C	

The experimental platform for capturing data is shown in Fig. 5. The experimental platform includes thermal camera, Kinect2 and wheeled motion system. In order to have the same vision of the thermal imager and Kinect2, two cameras are installed horizontally and the results of the extrinsic calibration is used to unify the size of RGB, depth and thermal images to make the information fusion process go smoothly.

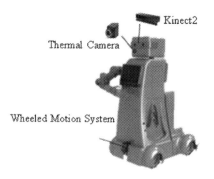

Fig. 5. Security Mobile Robot system

We acquired 3 image sequences from different indoor scenes, the scene 1 is relatively simple, and the temperature difference is small (see Fig. 6); the scene 2 has more objects, the offset of the temperature is larger (see Fig. 7); scene 3 is a large hall (see Fig. 8).

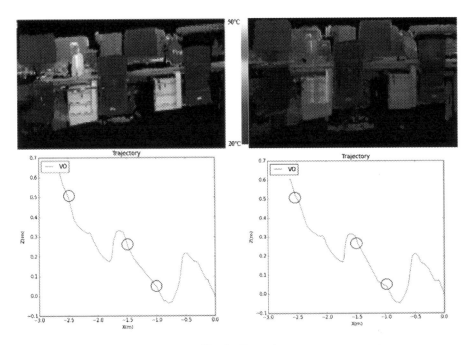

Fig. 6. Scene 1

For the scene 1, the running area of the robot is marked in advance, and the robot passes these marks which are shown by the circle in the Fig. 6 during the motion. We use the initial position of the robot as the origin of the world coordinate system. The trajectory map indicates that the system is positioned accurately. The error is small.

For the scene 2, an office area is explored with more objects, and the temperature difference is large in the scene. We can clearly see the temperature estimate of each object in the RGB-DT map, while retaining the appearance of the object. The outline of the computer, chair and box is very clear, even the patterns on the box can be seen.

For the scene 3, the hall of our lab building is selected, which has a large area. There are some cleaning cars. The texture and temperature information of the car can be clearly seen from the RGB-DT map.

When constructing the 3D models, the tracking time is recorded for the RGB-DT mapping algorithm to process a single frame, as shown in Table 2. The result shows that the algorithm can constructing 3D models in real time.

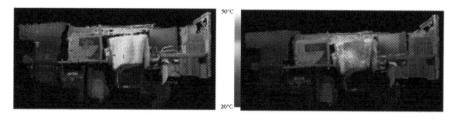

Fig. 7. Scene 2

Fig. 8. Scene 3

Table 2. Time record for RGB-DT mapping

Scene	Median time/ms	Mean time/ms
Scene 1	18.43	18.51
Scene 2	19.07	19.46
Scene 3	15.23	17.20

6 Conclusion

In this paper a framework of RGB-DT mapping for security robots is designed, which have improved ORB-SLAM algorithm, so that thermal map is synchronized to fuse 3D matric map of indoor environment. Experiments show that the RGB-DT map registration error is small and the real-time performance is less than 20 ms, which can meet the needs of robot environment exploration and comprehensive inspection. If potential fire hazards are detected by thermal field information, accurate location can be easily achieved, and the safety problem of environmental perception can be further solved. The research focus on security perception based on stable infrared and RGB-D information during the robot exploring or mapping stage, and its effectiveness and practicability have been verified. Therefore, the proposed system can be used not only for security robots, but also for rescue or fire-fighting robots, as well as electrical and structural building inspections in the future.

References

1. Tan, Y.: A survey on visual perception for firefighting robots. J. Mianyang Teach. Coll. **2**, 40–45 (2018)
2. Newcombe, R.A., Izadi, S., et al.: KinectFusion: real-time dense surface mapping and tracking. In: IEEE International Symposium on Mixed and Augmented Reality. pp. 127–136. IEEE, Basel (2011)
3. Dai, A., Izadi, S., Theobalt, C.: BundleFusion: real-time globally consistent 3D reconstruction using on-the-fly surface re-integration. ACM Trans. Graph. **36**(4), 76a (2017)
4. Mur-Artal, R., Tardós, J.D.: ORB-SLAM2: an open-source SLAM system for monocular, stereo, and RGB-D cameras. IEEE Trans. Robot. **33**(5), 1255–1262 (2017)
5. Vidas, S., Moghadam, P., Bosse, M.: 3D thermal mapping of building interiors using an RGB-D and thermal camera. In: IEEE International Conference on Robotics and Automation, pp. 2311–2318. IEEE, Karlsruhe (2013)
6. Borrmann, D., Nüchter, A., Djakulovi'C, M., et al.: The project thermal mapper-thermal 3D mapping of indoor environments for saving energy. In: International IFAC Symposium on Robot Control, pp. 31–38 (2012)
7. Nagatani, K., Otake, K., Yoshida, K.: Three-dimensional thermography mapping for mobile rescue robots. In: Yoshida, K., Tadokoro, S. (eds.) Field and Service Robotics, pp. 49–63. Springer, Heidelberg (2014). https://doi.org/10.1007/978-3-642-40686-7_4
8. Zhang, Z.: A flexible new technique for camera calibration. IEEE Trans. Pattern Anal. Mach. Intell. **22**(11), 1330–1334 (2000)
9. Zhang, Q., Pless, R.: Extrinsic calibration of a camera and laser range finder (improves camera calibration). In: IEEE/RSJ International Conference on Intelligent Robots & Systems. IEEE, Sendai (2005)
10. Moghadam, P., Bosse, M., Zlot, R.: Line-based extrinsic calibration of range and image sensors. In: 2013 IEEE International Conference on Robotics and Automation. IEEE, Karlsruhe (2013)
11. Hwang, S., Choi, Y., Kim, N., et al.: Low-cost synchronization for multispectral cameras. In: International Conference on Ubiquitous Robots & Ambient Intelligence. IEEE, Goyang (2015)
12. Baar, J.V., Beardsley, P., Pollefeys, M., et al.: Sensor fusion for depth estimation, including TOF and thermal sensors. In: 2012 Second International Conference on 3D Imaging, Modeling, Processing, Visualization & Transmission, pp. 472–478. IEEE Computer Society, Zurich (2012)
13. Ge, P., Yang, B., Han, Q., et al.: Infrared image detail enhancement algorithm based on hierarchical processing by guided image filter. Infrared Technol. **40**(12), 45–53 (2018)
14. Chang, H., Chen, C.: Image fusion based on HSV color space model and wavelet transform. Comput. Eng. Des. **28**(23), 5682–5684 (2007)
15. Lepetit, V., Moreno-Noguer, F., Fua, P.: EPnP: an accurate O (n) solution to the PnP problem. Int. J. Comput. Vis. **81**(2), 155–166 (2009)
16. Galvez-Lo, P.D., Tardos, J.D.: Bags of binary words for fast place recognition in image sequences. IEEE Trans. Robot. **28**(5), 1188–1197 (2012)

Navigate to Remember: A Declarative Memory Model for Incremental Semantic Mapping

Wei Hong Chin[1(✉)], Naoyuki Kubota[1], Zhaojie Ju[2], and Honghai Liu[2]

[1] Faculty of Systems Design, Tokyo Metropolitan University, Hino, Japan
chin-weihong@ed.tmu.ac.jp, kubota@tmu.ac.jp
[2] University of Portsmouth, Portsmouth, UK
{zhaojie.ju,honghai.liu}@port.ac.uk

Abstract. Biologically inspired computational techniques play a crucial role in robotic cognition. Artificial learning agents and robots that interact in complex environments must constantly acquire and refine knowledge over long periods of time. In this paper, we propose a novel recurrent neural architecture that mimics humans' declarative memory system for continuously generating a cognitive map during robot navigation. The proposed method termed as Declarative Memory Adaptive Recurrent Model (DM-ARM), and consists of three hierarchical memory courses: (i) Working Memory, (ii) Episodic Memory and (iii) Semantic Memory layer. Each memory layer comprises a self-organizing adaptive recurrent incremental network (SOARIN) with a different learning task respectively. The Working Memory layer quickly clusters sensory information while the Episodic Memory layer learns fine-grained spatiotemporal relationships of clusters (temporal encoding). Both the memory layer learning is in an unsupervised manner. The Semantic Memory layer utilizes task-relevant cues to adjust the level of architectural flexibility and generate a semantic map that contains more compact episodic representations. The effectiveness of the proposed recurrent neural architecture is evaluated through a series of experiments. We implemented and validated our proposed work on the tasks of robot navigation.

Keywords: Cognitive map · Navigation · Mobile robot · Episodic memory

1 Introduction

Spatial cognition is the basic ability of mammals to map, locate and navigate in different environments [1]. However, up-to-date intelligence computational models are still far from creating an artificial agent that can accomplish daily chores in an unstructured environment. This is a common task which requires semantic information and episodic memory [2].

© Springer Nature Switzerland AG 2019
H. Yu et al. (Eds.): ICIRA 2019, LNAI 11743, pp. 142–153, 2019.
https://doi.org/10.1007/978-3-030-27538-9_13

The semantic memory is known as the brain mechanism for acquiring and constructing the internal spatial representation. In the meantime, episodic memory allows people to learn higher-level tasks through self-experience and to plan actions respectively. In order to perform spatiotemporal tasks, both elements play crucial roles for humans. In both cognitive science and neuroscience, extensive research has been carried out to reveal the semantic memory and episodic memory's fundamental principles and neural bases [3–5].

The cognitive map is a kind of intelligence description of the external environment since animal cognition of the environment is an expression of the external environment. It represents the relative geometric relationship of the external space features. At present, cognitive map-based robot navigation has drawn the attention of many researchers. Tian et al. [6] proposed a brain-inspired SLAM to build a cognitive map of the office environment by combining odometry information with RGB-D sensors data. The cognitive map consists of a set of space coordinates that the robot has experienced and these nodes used to generate a global path. Chin et al. [8] proposed an unsupervised learning model of episodic memory to categorize and encode experiences of a robot to the environment and generates a cognitive map.

Recently, the Complementary Learning System (CLS) theory has been updated to consolidate additional findings of neuroscience [9, 10]. The first set of findings considers the role of memory replay stored in the hippocampus as a mechanism that supports the goal-oriented manipulation of experience statistics as well as the integration of new information. The hippocampus promptly encodes episodic events that can be reactivated during resting and intentional or unintentional memory recall. In this way, the information in the neocortex is consolidated by reactivating encoded experiences in terms of multiple internal replays. The combination of working memory, episodic memory, and semantic memory are known as declarative memory.

In this paper, we propose a novel recurrent neural architecture that mimics humans' declarative memory system to build a semantic map incrementally for robot navigation. The proposed architecture consists of three hierarchical memory layers: (i) Working Memory, (ii) Episodic Memory and (iii) Semantic Memory layer. Each memory layer comprises a self-organizing adaptive recurrent incremental network (SOARIN) with a different learning task respectively. The Working Memory layer quickly learns feature vectors from sensors (clustering); while the Episodic Memory layer learns fine-grained spatiotemporal relationships of feature vectors (temporal encoding). Both the memory layer learning is in an unsupervised manner. The Semantic Memory layer utilizes task-relevant cues to adjust the level of architectural flexibility and generate a semantic topological map (categorization). For the navigation task, we used text-to-speech to pass information to the robot for space labeling in Semantic Memory layer. All networks in the respective layer can grow or shrink for adapting incoming sensory information. In order to alleviate the catastrophic forgetting, the Episodic Memory layer regularly reactivates previously learned temporal neurons activations and replays to itself and to the Semantic Memory layer (memory replay) during robot rest time. The memory replay is accomplished without the needs of external sensory information. The memory replay mechanism allows the robot to continually learn incoming novel sensory input while retaining knowledge that has been learned previously.

Contributions of this paper are (i) the proposed method, DM-ARM enables a robot to build a semantic topological map from scratch and continually update the map for global path planning and navigation; (ii) DM-ARM overcomes the catastrophic forgetting which helps the robot *remembers* previously explored environment while moving to new environments; and (iii) the robot utilizes the generated semantic topological map to switch its moving behaviors according to environmental conditions such as fall-following, obstacle avoidance, and fast-speed moving.

2   Proposed Method: DM-ARM

DM-ARM architecture consists of three hierarchical Self-organizing Adaptive Recurrent Incremental Network (SOARIN) as shown in Figure. SOARIN is the evolved version of the Gamma-GWR [11] that adaptively and dynamically generate new neurons and topology connections according to novel consecutive sensory input. The Working Memory layer (WML) instantly clusters incoming input vectors in an unsupervised manner. Next, the episodic memory layer (EML) receives firing neuron weights from WML and encodes the spatiotemporal neurons activation patterns. Next, the Semantic Memory layer (SML) receives neural activation trajectories from EML and task-relevant signals (labels) from users to update the network and generate more compact representations of episodic experience with semantic meaning. Therefore, WML, EML, and SML mitigate catastrophic forgetting through continually generate neurons if novel input is encountered, update neurons weights if received input is similar with previously learned knowledge. In addition, neurons that are inactive for a long time will be eliminated automatically for maintaining the storage capacity.

In robot navigation, WML works as a novelty detector where each neuron in the network represents a group of similar input vectors and generate new neurons if incoming input vectors do not fit into the network. In EML, the network encodes the sequence of the robot's movement and each neuron in the network stores the robot's location for local localization. In SML, the network encodes a set of neurons in EML to define a place of the explored environment. Each neuron in SML represents an area of the environment and the robot utilizes the information for switching its moving behaviors such as wall following, obstacle avoidance or fast-speed moving. The overall architecture as shown as Fig. 1.

2.1   Working Memory Layer

Each memory layer contains a Self-Organizing Adaptive Recurrent Incremental Network (SOARIN) which is an adaptive recurrent extension of the Gamma-Grow-When-Required-Network (Gamma-GWR) [11] self-organizing network.

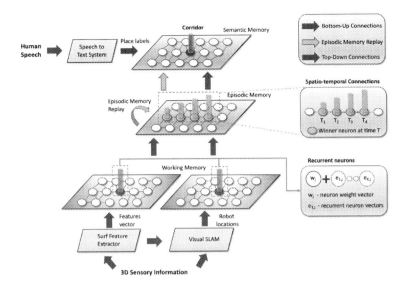

Fig. 1. DM-ARM overall architecture

The SOARIN embeds a self-adaptive learning threshold that allows the network to dynamically grow or shrink according to input vectors. SOARIN serves as the short-term memory buffer in which new neurons will be generated to represent incoming inputs and connections will be generated to link neurons that activated subsequently via competitive Hebbian learning. The notations of the SOARIN is tabulated in Table 1.

Initially, the network generates 2 recurrent neurons based on received sensory inputs. Each neuron of the layer consists of a weight vector w_j and a number K of temporal attributes e_j^k. For subsequent learning, the network computes the neuron that best matches with the current sensory $x(t)$ using Eqs. 1, 2 and 3.

$$b = \arg\min(T_j), \tag{1}$$

$$T_j = \alpha_0 \parallel x(t) - w_j \parallel^2 + \sum_{k=1}^{K} \alpha_k \parallel E_k(t) - e_{j,k} \parallel^2, \tag{2}$$

$$E_k(t) = \beta \cdot w_b(t-1) + (1-\beta) \cdot e_{b,k-1}(t-1) \tag{3}$$

Next, the activation value of the best matching neuron b is computed as follows:

$$a_b(t) = \exp(-T_b) \tag{4}$$

If the activation value $a_b(t)$ less than a preset threshold a_T. A new neuron N is added to the network with the new weights as below:

$$w_N = 0.5 \cdot (x(t) + w_b) \tag{5}$$

Table 1. The SOARIN notations

Notation	Definition
k	Number of temporal attribute
T_j	Activation value of neuron j
$w_b(t-1)$	Best matching neuron weights $t-1$
$E_k(t)$	Global attribute of the network at t, $E_k(t=0)=0$
$e_{j,k}(t)$	Temporal elements of neuron j
$\alpha_i, \beta \in [0,1]$	Contributing factors
r_j	Regularity counter of neuron j
τ_j, λ	Decay factors for regularity counter
ρ	Learning threshold
$P_{(m,n)}$	Temporal connection between neuron m and n
V	Associative matrix for labeling
b	Index of best matching neuron

$$e_{k,N} = 0.5 \cdot (E_k(t) + e_{k,b}) \qquad (6)$$

A new connection is created to connect the neuron b and the second best matching neuron. If the $a_b(t)$ larger than a_T, it means that the neuron b can represents the input $x(t)$. Thus, the neuron b and its neighbor neurons n is updated according to input $x(t)$ as follows:

$$w_{j(\text{new})} = \gamma_j \cdot r_j \cdot (x(t) - w_{j(\text{old})}) \qquad (7)$$

$$e_{j,k(\text{new})} = \gamma_j \cdot r_j \cdot (E_k(t) - e_{j,k(\text{old})}) \qquad (8)$$

If there is no connection between best matching neuron $a_b(t)$ and second best matching neuron, a new connection will be created to connect them. Each edge has an age counter that increases by one at each iteration. The age of the connection between between best matching neuron and second best matching neuron is reset to zero. Connections with an age larger than a preset threshold will be removed, and neurons without connections are deleted from the network.

We introduce a self-update threshold that allows the threshold to adjust its value adaptively in response to sensory input. The self-adjust equation as follows:

$$\rho_{(\text{new})} = (1 - r_b) \cdot a_b(t) + r_b \cdot \rho_{(\text{old})} \qquad (9)$$

The self-update equation adjusts the threshold value that closes to the best matching neuron activation value. This means that the threshold value is changing dynamically. This is because the robot observes the environment sequentially, based on the nature of SOARIN learning, it is able to recognize the sequential sensory data and lower the threshold allows the network to update itself without adding new neurons. Thus, it helps to overcome the node proliferation issue. However, the threshold is reset to the baseline if a mismatch occurs in the network. The best matching neuron's weight are feed forward to the episodic memory layer as input vector.

2.2 Episodic Memory Layer

In episodic memory layer, the network learning is similar to WML with additional conditions. First, in each iteration, the input of the network is WML best matching neuron's weight. Next, each episodic neuron contains a regularity counter $r_j \in [0,1]$ indicating its firing strength over time. Newly generated episodic neuron has value of $r_j = 1$. In each iteration, the regularity value of best matching neuron and its neighbor neurons decrease using equation as follows:

$$\Delta r_j = \tau_j \cdot \lambda \cdot (1 - r_j) - \tau_j \tag{10}$$

In addition, a new episodic neuron will only be added to the network if $a_b^{em}(t) < \rho_a^{em}$ and $r_b^{em} < \rho_r^{em}$. Thus, the episodic network resets its threshold value and sends a feedback signal back to WML to reset its threshold ρ_a^{wm} is send. If the activation and regularity value are fulfilled the threshold, the episodic neurons update using Eqs. 7 and 8.

In episodic memory structure, a sequence of events forms an episode to store specific past experiences and episodes are correlating to each other. We implement temporal connections that learn activation patterns of recurrent neurons in the network.

The temporal connections encode the sequence of neurons that have been activated during the learning stage. For each learning iteration, a temporal link will be increased by 1 between two neurons that are sequentially stimulated. Specifically, when best matching neuron b that triggered at time t and $t-1$ subsequently, the temporal link between them is reinforced as follow:

$$P_{(b(t),b(t-1))}^{new} = P_{(b(t),b(t-1))}^{old} + 1, \tag{11}$$

In this way, for each recurrent neuron m, the next neuron g can be retrieved from the encoded temporal sequence by choosing the largest value of P as below:

$$g = \arg \max P_{(m,n)} \tag{12}$$

where n are the neighbors of m. As a result, the activation sequence of recurrent neurons can be restored without requiring any input data.

In order to generate meaningful sequential data for the playback purpose, we utilize the spatiotemporal relationship of neurons that encoded in the episodic memory layer. The sequential data playback can be generated in episodic memory layer for each episodic neuron whenever the network receives incoming sensory data. For example, if the winner episodic neuron b is triggered by input data, we can determine the next temporal neuron by choosing the neuron that has the largest activation value of P. A set of neurons playback with length $K^{\mathrm{sm}} + K^{\mathrm{em}} + 1$ for each neuron j is computed as follows:

$$U_j = \langle w^{\mathrm{em}}_{u(0)}, w^{\mathrm{em}}_{u(1)}, \cdots, w^{\mathrm{em}}_{u(K^s)}, \rangle \tag{13}$$

$$u(i) = \arg\max P_{(j,u(i-1))} \tag{14}$$

where $P(i,j)$ is the episodic temporal connection matrix and $s(0) = j$.

2.3   Semantic Memory Layer

The semantic memory layer is hierarchically connecting with episodic memory layer. It consists of an ar-GWR network which receives bottom-up inputs from the episodic memory layer, top-down inputs such as labels or tags for developing representations that contain semantic knowledge across a wider temporal scale. The semantic knowledge can be retrieved by providing cues from the top-down signals.

The neural activities mechanism in the semantic memory layer is similar to the episodic memory layer with an additional condition for generating a new neuron. In this layer, neuron learning happens if the network accurately predicts the class label of a labeled input sequence from the episodic memory layer through the learning process. A new neuron will be created if the predicted class label from the network is incorrect. Thus, this is the additional factor that modulates the neurons update rate. In addition, each semantic neuron encodes information over higher temporal sequences than episodic neurons due to the hierarchical learning of input data.

Episodic memory is formed by a sequence of activation events. In previous work, authors only calculate the distance difference of the semantic best matching neuron's weight and bottom-up episodic inputs for semantic learning without measuring the inter-relationship of events between them. The inter-relationship of episode neurons is important for recognition and retrieval purpose. Therefore, we introduce a new equation to measure the inter-relationship between the best matching neuron's weight and bottom-up inputs for improving the semantic learning performance. Thus, Eqs. 1–3 becomes:

$$b_s = \arg\min(T^{\mathrm{sm}}_j), \tag{15}$$

$$T_j^{\text{sm}} = \alpha_1 \parallel w_b^{\text{em}} - w_j^{\text{sm}} \parallel^2 +$$

$$\sum_{k=1}^{K} \alpha_k^{\text{sm}} \parallel E_k^{\text{sm}}(t) - e_{k,j}^{\text{sm}}(t) \parallel^2 \cdot$$

$$\exp\left(-\left(1 - \frac{w_b^{\text{em}} \cdot w_j^{\text{sm}}}{\parallel w_j^{\text{sm}} \parallel \cdot \parallel w_b^{\text{em}} \parallel} + \right.\right.$$

$$\left.\left.\sum_{k=1}^{K} \left(\frac{E_k^{\text{sm}}(t) \cdot e_{k,j}^{\text{sm}}(t)}{\parallel e_{k,j}^{\text{sm}} \parallel \cdot \parallel E_k^{\text{sm}(t)} \parallel}\right)\right)\right),$$

$$\tag{16}$$

$$E_k^{\text{sm}}(t) = \beta \cdot w_{J-1}^{\text{sm}} + (1 - \beta) \cdot e_{k-1,J-1}^{\text{sm}} \tag{17}$$

With these equations, the selected neuron either is expected to be the correct semantic neuron for the particular sequence of episodic inputs or it is more notable than other semantic neurons or both.

The semantic memory layer receives input neural data from the episodic memory layer which means the BMNs of the episodic memory layer with respect to $x(t)$. Hence, BMNs in this layer are calculated using Eqs. 15–17. Note that, the input is from bottom-up neural episodic weights, therefore $x(t)$ is substituted by w_b^{em} for the network learning. The labeling method is similar to episodic memory layer where each neuron in semantic memory layer is assigned to a label that obtains from $x(t)$ using Eq. 12 and ??.

As a result, a new semantic neuron is generated only if the BMN b does not fulfill 3 conditions: (1) $a_b^{\text{sm}}(t) < \rho_a$; (2); $r_b^{\text{sm}} < \rho_r$; and (3) BMN's label ζ_b^{sm} is not identical with the data input's label ζ (equation ??). Note that, this label matching condition in semantic memory layer is not taken into account if the data input is not labeled. If the winner semantic neuron b predicts the label ζ_b that same with the class label ζ of input $x(t)$, then the neuron learning process is triggered with an additional learning factor $\psi = 0.001$. Therefore, Eqs. 7 and 8 become:

$$w_{j(\text{new})}^{\text{sm}} = \psi \cdot \gamma_j \cdot r_j \cdot (w_b^{\text{em}} - w_{j(\text{old})}^{\text{sm}}), \tag{18}$$

$$e_{k(\text{new})}^{\text{sm}} = \psi \cdot \gamma_j \cdot r_j \cdot (E_k^{\text{sm}}(t) - e_{k,j(\text{old})}^{\text{sm}}) \tag{19}$$

As such, the semantic memory layer learns more compact representations with respect to data input labels. The data labels control the layer stability and plasticity where new semantic neurons are generated only if the network is unable to predict the correct class label of data input. In addition, the network learning rate of bottom-up measurements is decreasing if the class prediction is correct. Since semantic neurons learn from episodic neurons' weight, it means that each semantic neuron encodes episodic events in a larger temporal size. Since episodic neurons will activate for a number $K^{\text{em}} + 1$ of incoming data, whereas each of semantic neurons will activate for a number $K^{\text{sm}} + 1$ of neurons activated in episodic memory layer. Therefore, the total input size that encoded in semantic neurons is $K^{\text{sm}} + K^{\text{em}} + 1$.

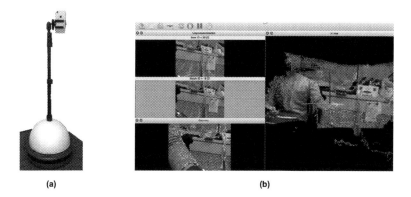

(a)   (b)

Fig. 2. (a) Robot attached with various sensors (b) Visual SLAM with surf features

3   Experimental Setup And Results

We validate our proposed method using a iRobot Roomba robot that attached with a Hokuyo Laser scanner, Intel RealSense stereo camera, and Intel i5 processor computer as shown in Fig. 2. The laser scanner signal was sampled at 10 Hz. Since the robot has to traverse the environment autonomously, we developed a Fuzzy motion movement behavior that allows the robot for obstacle avoiding and wall-following. The moving speed of the robot varies from 0.05 m/s to 0.5 m/s. The episodic memory layer receives a surf features vector with a temporal resolution of 3 scans ($K^{em} = 2$). As mentioned in Sect. 2.3, the semantic memory layer will encode for a total of 5 scans in the experiment. For the semantic topological map building, classification and retrieval, we determine the predicted label of a new input data using the Eq. 15 from semantic layer's best matching neuron. A place label is predicted for each incoming sensory information.

The experiments were conducted in the 7th floor of university corridor, study area, and rest area that connecting with each other. The grid map of the experimental place as shown in Fig. 3(a). We conduct the experiment in such environmental conditions is to validate our proposed method is able to work in natural environment with moderate changing of environmental conditions.

We commanded the robot to traverse the experimental place starting from the study area and travel to the rest area through the corridor then back to the start point again. During the traverse, DM-ARM continually learns incoming sensory information and generates the semantic map for representing the environment. After each traverse, the robot will go for charging and then memory replay is triggered for semantic map memory consolidation. Once the robot is fully charged, memory replay is deactivated and the robot starts traversing and continuously learns and updates the semantic map again. For space labeling, we developed a speech-to-text iOS application to obtain the space labels for labeling the semantic map. As shown in Fig. 3, the semantic map is segmented into 2 regions, the study area is colored in black and the corridor is colored in blue respectively.

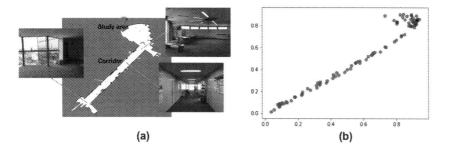

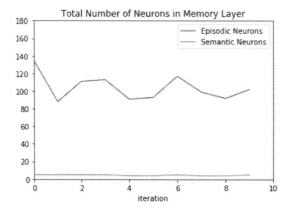

(a)   (b)

Fig. 3. (a) Experimental environment (b) Built Semantic Map (Color figure online)

Fig. 4. Total number of generated neurons for each traverse

After the first traverse, with the semantic information, the robot navigates the environment with different moving behaviors according to the region. For example, the robot is switched to obstacle avoidance mode in the study area where the place populated with moving people and furniture. When it traversed to the corridor, the moving behavior is then switched to the wall following mode and fast-speed mode since the corridor is a straight path.

We repeated the experiment for ten times and the generated spatial map quality was measured by Total Quantization Error (TQE) and localization rate. Figure 4 illustrates the total number of neurons in the map that generated by SOARIN and [11] for each traverse. TQE measures the similarity between sensory information and weights of episodic neurons in the spatial map. Figure 5 shows the TQE of the learning approach for each traverse. Next, the localization rate is measured by computing the euclidean distance between the winner neuron's encoded location and robot current location that obtained from the SLAM algorithm. The robot is localized successfully if the euclidean radius is within a threshold value (0.01 m). The localization rate result is shown in Fig. 6. Results showed that the proposed method able to generate a semantic topological map that can be used for path planning and robot moving behavior switching.

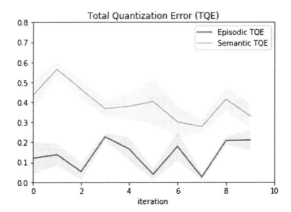

Fig. 5. Total Quantization Error of the learning method for each traverse

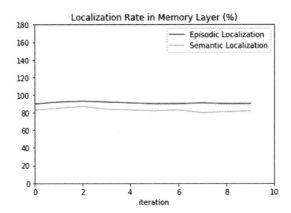

Fig. 6. Localization rate of the learning method for each traverse

4   Conclusion

In this paper, we proposed a model termed as DM-ARM that models human declarative memory which can continually learn the spatiotemporal relationship of sensory data from both active sensors and proprioceptive indications to generate a semantic map incrementally. DM-ARM updates the semantic map by expanding or shrinking its memory structure autonomously. In addition, DM-ARM consolidates the episodic semantic map through its self episodic memory playback without the needs of external sensory cues. DM-ARM has been validated through real robot implementation. In the future, we will integrate DM-ARM with path planning algorithm to utilize the topological structure of the spatial map for goal-directed navigation. Lastly, we will further improve and validate the performance of DM-ARM in more challenging and larger environments.

References

1. Rebai, K., Azouaoui, O. Achour, N.: Bio-inspired visual memory for robot cognitive map building and scene recognition. In: 2012 IEEE/RSJ International Conference on Intelligent Robots and Systems, Vilamoura, 2012, pp. 2985–2990 (2012). https://doi.org/10.1109/IROS.2012.6385493

2. Buzsáki, G., Moser, E.I.: Memory, navigation and theta rhythm in the hippocampal-entorhinal system. In: Nature Neuroscience 2013, vol. 16, pp. 130–138. Nature Publishing Group (2013). https://doi.org/10.1038/nn.3304

3. O'keefe, J., Nadel, L.: The Hippocampus As a Cognitive Map, vol. 3. Clarendon Press, Oxford (1978)

4. McNaughton, B.L., Battaglia, F.P., Jensen, O., Moser, E.I., Moser, M.-B.: Path integration and the neural basis of the cognitive map. Nat. Rev. Neurosci. **7**(8), 663–678 (2006). https://doi.org/10.1038/nrn1932

5. Tulving, E.: Episodic and semantic memory1. In: Organization of Memory, pp. 381–402 (1972)

6. Tian, B., Shim, V.A., Yuan, M., Srinivasan, C., Tang, H., Li, H.: RGB-D based cognitive map building and navigation. In: 2013 IEEE/RSJ International Conference on Intelligent Robots and Systems, Tokyo, pp. 1562–1567 (2013). https://doi.org/10.1109/IROS.2013.6696557

7. Yan, W., Weber, C., Wermter, S.: A neural approach for robot navigation based on cognitive map learning. In: 2012 International Joint Conference on Neural Networks (IJCNN), Brisbane, QLD, pp. 1–8 (2012)

8. Chin, W.H., Toda, Y., Kubota, N., Loo, C.K., Seera, M.: Episodic memory multimodal learning for robot sensorimotor map building and navigation. IEEE Trans. Cogn. Dev. Syst. https://doi.org/10.1109/TCDS.2018.2875309

9. Kumaran, D., Hassabis, D., McClelland, J.L.: What learning systems do intelligent agents need? complementary learning systems theory updated. Trends Cogn. Sci. **20**(7), 512–534 (2016)

10. McClelland, J.L., McNaughton, B.L., O'Reilly, R.C.: Why there are complementary learning systems in the hippocampus and neocortex: insights from the successes and failures of connectionist models of learning and memory. Psychol. Rev. **102**(3), 419–457 (1995). https://doi.org/10.1037/0033-295X.102.3.419

11. Parisi, G.I., Tani, J., Weber, C., Wermter, S.: Lifelong learning of humans actions with deep neural network self-organization. Neural Netw. **96**, 137–149 (2017). https://doi.org/10.1016/j.neunet.2017.09.001

Fuzzy Modelling for Automation, Control, and Robotics

Variable Universe Fuzzy Control for Direct Yaw Moment of Distributed Drive Electric Vehicle

Sen Cao[1], Yaping Wang[2], Haoran Jia[1], and Zheng Zhang[1(✉)]

[1] Institute of Robotics and Intelligent Systems,
School of Mechanical Engineering, Xi'an Jiaotong University,
Xi'an 710049, China
2889221067@qq.com, zhangzh@mail.xjtu.edu.cn
[2] Institute of Automotive Engineering,
Shaanxi Communications Technical College, Xianyang 710018, China

Abstract. A direct yaw moment control (DYC) system based on variable universe fuzzy logic is proposed to improve the stability of distributed drive electric vehicle in this paper. The upper layer of controller is a two-stage variable universe fuzzy controller, and the deviation between actual value and reference of yaw rate and side slip angle is used to calculate the required yaw moment. The lower layer of the controller adopts the redistribution pseudo inverse (RPI) algorithm, which takes the tire utilization rate as the optimization target and the maximum driving torque of the motor as the constraint target, and effectively distributes the required yaw moment to each wheel. The proposed control system is simulated and verified under J-turn and single shift line condition, and the control effect is reflected by comparison control in the uncontrolled, fuzzy PI control and variable universe fuzzy control. The simulation results show that it can make the vehicle track the reference better and enhance vehicle's handing and stability, and that the control algorithm is effective and feasible.

Keywords: Distributed drive electric vehicle · Direct yaw moment control · Variable universe fuzzy control

1 Introduction

Due to the growing global energy crisis and environmental pollution, the electric vehicle has been widely studied in recent years [1]. As a result, the distributed drive electric vehicle is developed rapidly, which replaces the traditional internal combustion engine and the complicated transmission mechanism with the full-hub motor drive with fast response and high-precision torque control [2, 3]. And also the yaw moment is derived by actively adjusting the torque of each wheel, which provides a new idea for

The Project was Supported by the Key Laboratory of Expressway Construction Machinery of Shaanxi Province, 300102259513.

the electric vehicle to achieve the line-controlled yaw stability control, and improves the stability, safety and comfort of the whole vehicle.

The key of DYC is to calculate a required yaw moment to allow the vehicle to track the expected path by determining the operating state of the vehicle. The main idea of fuzzy control in DYC is to use the deviation between actual value and reference of vehicles as the input of fuzzy controller, and then based on expert knowledge and control experience, fuzzy rules are formulated to finally obtain the required yaw moment. Zhou [4] designed a fuzzy PID controller, which uses fuzzy rules to adjust the PID adjustable parameters online to realize the yaw stability control of the vehicle under complex conditions. However, the domain of the conventional fuzzy controller are solidified after the design is completed. The over and under selection of the domain will affect the control effect, which makes vehicle control more difficult in the case of changing vehicle parameters. Li [5] proposes the idea of variable universe fuzzy control (VUFC), and selects the appropriate scaling factor to make the domain size change in real time without changing the controller fuzzy rules, which achieves excellent control effects. In this paper, the scaling factor is determined by fuzzy rules to simplify the design of the variable universe fuzzy controller.

After obtaining the required yaw moment, torque distribution is required. He [6] takes the minimum of the weighted sum of the output torques as the optimization target, and adopts the generalized inverse method to complete the torque distribution, but this method does not consider any constraints, so that the solution obtained by the controller cannot be applied to some actual working conditions. Abe [7] proposed that the minimum sum of tire adhesion utilization with weight coefficient is the optimization goal, which can improve the stability of the vehicle under extreme conditions.

In this paper, a two-stage variable universe fuzzy controller is designed to improve the response speed and accuracy of the controller, and adopts RPI algorithm to complete the torque distribution effectively. And the performance of control system is evaluated in J-turn and single shift line condition.

2 Direct Yaw Moment Control System

2.1 DYC System Structure

The distributed drive electric vehicle DYC system is shown in Fig. 1. The upper layer is the motion tracking layer, the deviation between actual value and reference of yaw rate and side slip angle is used to calculate the required yaw moment. The lower layer is the torque distribution layer that adopts the RPI algorithm, which takes the tire utilization rate as the optimization target and the maximum driving torque of the motor as the constraint target, and effectively distributes the required yaw moment to each wheel.

The control variable expectations can be calculated by the 2 degree of freedom (DOF) reference model [8], the equations are as follows:

$$\gamma_d = min\left\{\left|\frac{u}{L(1+Ku^2)}\delta\right|, \left|\frac{0.85\mu g}{u}\right|\right\}sign(\delta) \tag{1}$$

$$\beta_d = 0 \tag{2}$$

Where δ is front wheel steering angle, L is wheel base, u is longitudinal speed, K is stability factor, μ is road adhesion coefficient.

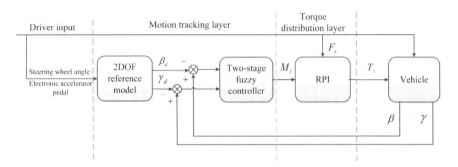

Fig. 1. Distributed drive electric vehicle DYC system

2.2 Establishment of Vehicle Model

The seven DOF vehicle model is shown in Fig. 2 [9]. The kinetic equations are follows:

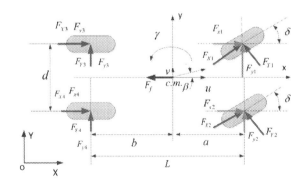

Fig. 2. 7DOF vehicle model

Longitudinal moment:

$$m(\dot{u} - v\gamma) = \sum_{i=1}^{4} F_{x_i} - F_W - F_f \tag{3}$$

Lateral moment:

$$m(\dot{v} + u\gamma) = \sum_{i=1}^{4} F_{y_i} \tag{4}$$

Yaw moment:

$$I_z\dot{\gamma} = \sum M_{z_i} \tag{5}$$

$$\sum M_{Z_i} = \frac{d}{2}(-F_{x_1}\cos\delta + F_{y_2}\sin\delta - F_{x_3} + F_{x_4} + F_{x_2}\cos\delta - F_{y_2}\sin\delta) \\ -(F_{y_3} + F_{y_3})b + ((F_{x_1} + F_{x_2})\sin\delta + (F_{y_1} + F_{y_2})\cos\delta)a \tag{6}$$

Tire rolling:

$$J_i\frac{d\omega_i}{dt} = T_{di} - T_{bi} - F_{xi}R_{wi} \tag{7}$$

Where v is lateral speed, F_W is wind resistance, F_f is rolling resistance, F_{xi} is tire longitudinal driving force, F_{yi} is tire lateral driving force, ω_i is wheel speed, T_{di} is driving torque, T_{bi} is braking torque, $R_{\omega i}$ is tire radius, J_i is wheel moment of inertia.

The wheel's longitudinal and lateral forces are derived from the tire model, and in this paper, Dugoff tire model is chosen [10].

$$S = \frac{\mu F_{zi}(1 - \varepsilon_r v_x\sqrt{\lambda_i^2 + \tan^2\alpha_i})}{2\sqrt{C_x^2\lambda_i^2 + C_y^2\tan^2\alpha_i}}(1 - \lambda_i) \tag{8}$$

$$f(S) = \begin{cases} 1 & S > 1 \\ S(2 - S) & S < 1 \end{cases} \tag{9}$$

$$F_{xi} = \frac{C_x\lambda_i}{1 - \lambda_i}f(S) \tag{10}$$

$$F_{yi} = \frac{C_y\tan\alpha_i}{1 - \lambda_i}f(S) \tag{11}$$

Where F_{zi} is tire vertical force, ε_r is adhesion performance factor, λ_i is wheel slip rate, α_i is tire side angle, C_x is tire longitudinal deflection coefficient, C_y is tire lateral deviation coefficient.

Vehicle model in Simulink is shown in Fig. 3.

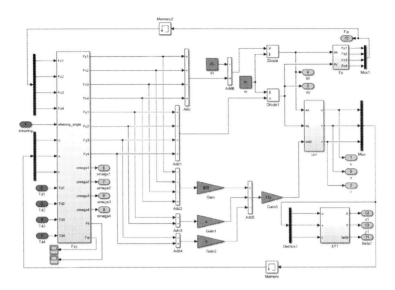

Fig. 3. Simulink model of vehicle

3   The Analysis and Design of DYC Algorithm

The block diagram of DYC algorithm is shown in Fig. 4. The algorithm is divided into two layers: In the motion tracking layer, the appropriate variables are chosen, and a two-stage variable universe fuzzy controller is applied to calculate the required yaw moment. In the lower layer, the required yaw moment is distributed efficiently and harmoniously to the four drive motors through the RPI algorithm.

3.1   Scale Factor Fuzzy Controller

The Scaling factor of the basic function has large uncertainty, and the simple function expression can't meet the accuracy requirements of the controller. Therefore, the fuzzy rule is used to describe the scaling factor in this paper. It only needs to know the law of the expansion and contraction of the universe, and no precise function model is needed, which simplifies the design of variable universe fuzzy controller.

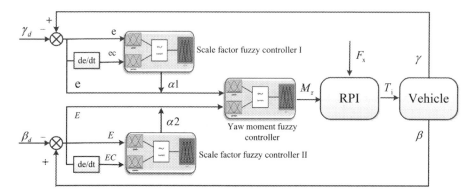

Fig. 4. Block diagram of DYC algorithm

Firstly, the yaw rate error e and its rate of change ec are calculated to determine the scaling factor α1. The fuzzy sets of input are {NB, NM, NS, ZE, PS, PM, PB}, and the basic domain of e and ec are [−0.12, +0.12] and [−1, +1]. The fuzzy sets of output are {ZE, VS, S, SB, M, B, VB}, and the basic domain of α1 is [0, 1]. The fuzzy inference rules are divided into three parts: (1) when e and ec are large and in the same direction, it indicates that vehicle body is rapidly moving away from the desired operating state, and oversteer or understeer occurs. To increase the control of the control variables, a large scaling factor is required at this time; (2) when e and ec are large and opposite, it indicates that the vehicle state is rapidly following the expected value, and a small scaling factor is required at this time; (3) when e is close to 0 and |ec| is large, it indicates that vehicle has a tendency to deviate sharply from the expected operating state, a large scaling factor is required at this time.

Secondly, the side slip angle error E and its rate of change EC are calculated to determine the scaling factor α2. The fuzzy sets of input are {NB, NM, NS, ZE, PS, PM, PB}, and the basic domain of E and EC are [−8°, +8°] and [−1, +1]. The fuzzy sets of output are {ZE, VS, S, SB, M, B, VB}, and the basic domain of α2 is [0, 1]. The fuzzy inference rules of α2 is the same as α1. The fuzzy rule is "if···then···" conditional statement. Table 1 shows fuzzy rule table of the scale factor fuzzy controller.

Table 1. Fuzzy rule of scale factor fuzzy controller

ec (EC)	e (E)						
	NB	NM	NS	ZE	PS	PM	PB
NB	VB	VB	B	B	M	S	VS
NM	VB	M	B	M	M	S	VS
NS	VB	SB	M	M	M	SB	S
ZE	M	SB	VS	ZE	B	M	VB
PS	SB	S	M	M	B	VB	VB
PM	VS	S	SB	M	B	VB	VB
PB	ZE	S	B	B	VB	VB	VB

3.2   Yaw Moment Fuzzy Controller

The inputs of yaw moment fuzzy controller are the error e of yaw rate and the error E of side slip angle. The fuzzy sets of input are {NB, NM, NS, ZE, PS, PM, PB}, and the basic domain of e and E are $[-0.12, +0.12]$ and $[-8°, +8°]$. The fuzzy sets of output are {NVB, NB, NM, NS, ZE, PS, PM, PB, PVB}, and the basic domain of M_z is $[-1000, 1000]$. According to the principle of vehicle dynamics and mature expert experience, the corresponding fuzzy rules are formulated. For example, when the vehicle is over-steered, it is necessary to apply a reverse yaw moment to the vehicle; when the vehicle is understeer, it is necessary to apply a positive yaw moment to the vehicle. Table 2 shows fuzzy rule table of the yaw moment fuzzy controller.

Table 2. Fuzzy rule of yaw moment fuzzy controller

E	e						
	NB	NM	NS	ZE	PS	PM	PB
NB	PVB	PB	PB	NB	NB	NB	NVB
NM	PVB	PM	PM	NM	NM	NM	NB
NS	PVB	PM	PM	NS	NM	NM	NB
ZE	PB	PM	PS	ZE	NS	NM	NB
PS	PVB	PM	PS	PS	NS	NM	NB
PM	PVB	PM	PM	PM	NM	NM	NB
PB	PVB	PB	PB	PB	NB	NB	NVB

3.3   The Yaw Moment Distribution Layer Design

In this paper, the redistribution pseudo inverse (RPI) algorithm is chosen, which takes the tire utilization rate as the optimization target and the maximum driving torque of the motor as the constraint target. Tire utilization is defined as the ratio of road adhesion on a single tire to the maximum adhesion that can be achieved,

$$\eta_i = \frac{\sqrt{F_{xi}^2 + F_{yi}^2}}{\mu \cdot F_{zi}}, \qquad i = 1, 2, 3, 4 \tag{12}$$

The higher the tire utilization, the smaller the vehicle stability margin. Since the lateral force of the wheel is limited to the uncontrollable actual conditions and is coupled with the longitudinal force of the tire, this paper only studies the longitudinal force distribution of the tire, and the optimization objective function is rewritten as:

$$\min_{u} J = \sum_{i=1}^{4} \frac{F_{xi}^2}{(\mu \cdot F_{zi})^2} \tag{13}$$

Rewritten into a matrix form:

$$\min_{u} J = \frac{1}{2} u^T W u \tag{14}$$

$$u = [F_{x1}, F_{x2}, F_{x3}, F_{x4}]^T \tag{15}$$

$$W = \text{diag}\left(\frac{1}{(\mu F_{z1})^2} \quad \frac{1}{(\mu F_{z2})^2} \quad \frac{1}{(\mu F_{z3})^2} \quad \frac{1}{(\mu F_{z4})^2} \right)^T \tag{16}$$

Drive moment and yaw moment can be expressed as:

$$v = \begin{bmatrix} T \\ M_z \end{bmatrix} = G[F_{x1} \quad F_{x2} \quad F_{x3} \quad F_{x4}]^T \tag{17}$$

$$G = \begin{bmatrix} R_e & R_e & R_e & R_e \\ -d & d & -d & d \end{bmatrix} \tag{18}$$

The moment distribution control problem can be described as:

$$v = G \cdot u \tag{19}$$

The G matrix is usually not a square matrix, and there is no inverse matrix, so the equation cannot be solved. From the perspective of matrix inversion, we rewrite Eq. (19) into the form of Eq. (14). When the G matrix is full rank, we obtain the generalized inverse matrix of the G matrix by mathematical solution:

$$G^+ = W^{-1} G^T (G W^{-1} G^T)^{-1} \tag{20}$$

$$u = G^+ v \tag{21}$$

The RPI algorithm adds a physical condition that the assigned torque can't exceed the maximum torque of the motor. If the allocated amount is out of range, the allocation result is corrected, and the iterative calculation is repeated and then judged again until the physical constraint is met. The RPI algorithm introduces an offset vector c for the correction. The expression is:

$$\min_{u} J = \frac{1}{2} (u + c)^T W (u + c) \tag{22}$$

Perform an iteration first and calculate the control vector:

$$u_k = -c_k + G_k^+ (v + G_0 \cdot c_k) \tag{23}$$

Where G_0 is initial G matrix, k is number of iterations, u_k and c_k are correction vector after kth iteration.

After the calculation, it is necessary to judge whether u_k exceeds the constraint range, and if it does not exceed the range, the calculation ends; if it exceeds the range, it needs to be corrected. Suppose that the ith element in the vector exceeds the constraint at the kth iteration, and the boundary value of the constraint is given:

$$u_i = \begin{cases} u_{maxi}, & u_i > u_{maxi} \\ u_{mini}, & u_i < u_{mini} \end{cases} \tag{24}$$

At the same time, the first column of the G_k matrix is zero, and the first element in c_k is the negative boundary of the constraint, and then the iterative operation is continued until u_k is within the constraint range.

4 Simulation

In order to verify the reliability of the variable universe fuzzy control system, the control performance is evaluated by J-turn condition and single shift line condition. And the control effect is reflected by comparison control in the uncontrolled, fuzzy PI control and variable universe fuzzy control.

4.1 Simulation Structure

The vehicle simulation model in Simulink is shown in Fig. 5. Vehicle parameters as follows: Vehicle mass $m = 900$ kg; Moment of inertia $I_z = 1098$ kg $*$ m^2; Height from ground to centroid $h = 450$ mm; Wheel tread $d = 1300$ mm; Wheel radius $R = 290$ mm; Distance between front axle and centroid $a = 1233$ mm; Distance between rear axle and centroid $b = 1327$ mm; $L = 2560$ mm; Front axle lateral stiffness $k1 = 10000$ N/rad; Rear axle lateral stiffness $k2 = 16000$ N/rad; Single motor maximum torque is 120 N $*$ m; Maximum speed is 750 r/min.

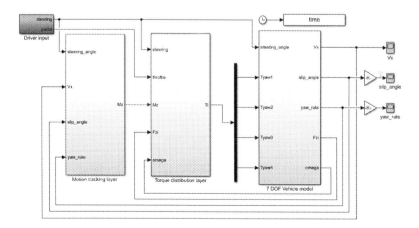

Fig. 5. The vehicle simulation model in Simulink

4.2   Simulation Result

J-Turn Condition

J-turn condition can be tested for stability in emergency avoidance situations. The initial speed of the vehicle is 90 km/h and the friction coefficient is 0.35.

As shown in Figs. 6 and 7, the vehicle's yaw rate and side slip angle can better track the reference value under VUFC, and vehicle is easier to control. And the behavior of VUFC is more stable with less phase diagram area as shown in Fig. 8. The tire utilization rate is only 0.372, and the stability margin of the vehicle is large as shown in Fig. 9.

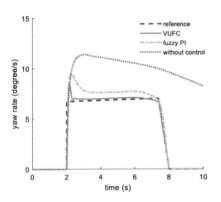

Fig. 6. Yaw rate in J-turn

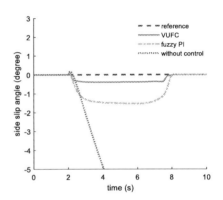

Fig. 7. Side slip angle in J-turn

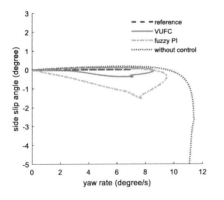

Fig. 8. Phase diagram in J-turn

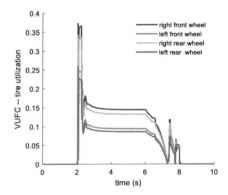

Fig. 9. Tire utilization in J-turn

Single Shift Line Condition

Single shift line condition can be tested for stability in the case of vehicle lane change. The start time for sine steering is 0.5 s, and the stop time is 2.5 s when the trajectory returns to a straight line. The initial speed of the vehicle is 100 km/h and the friction coefficient is 0.3.

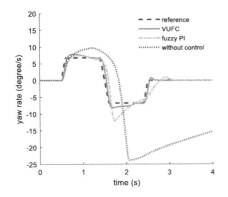

Fig. 10. Yaw rate in single shift line

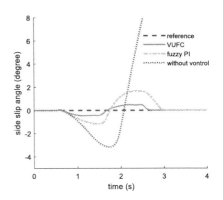

Fig. 11. Side slip angle in single shift line

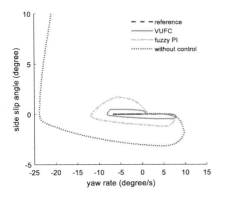

Fig. 12. Phase diagram in single shift line

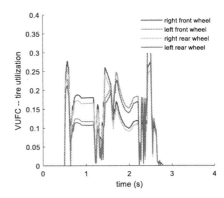

Fig. 13. Tire utilization in single shift line

Compared with fuzzy PI control, the vehicle's yaw rate and side slip angle can better track the reference value and have faster response speed and less overshoot under VUFC, and both the yaw rate and side slip angle have a large overshoot under fuzzy PI control as shown in Figs. 10 and 11. And the behavior of VUFC is more stable with less phase diagram area as shown in Fig. 12. The tire utilization rate is only 0.3, and the stability margin of the vehicle is large as shown in Fig. 13.

5 Summary

In this paper, a 7 DOF model of distributed drive electric vehicle with Dugoff tire model is established for validating the efficiency of vehicle stability control using variable universe fuzzy control system. The upper layer of controller is a two-stage variable universe fuzzy controller, and the deviation between actual value and reference of yaw rate and side slip angle is used to calculate the required yaw moment. The lower layer of the controller adopts the redistribution pseudo inverse (RPI) algorithm, which takes the tire utilization rate as the optimization target and the maximum driving torque of the motor as the constraint target, and effectively distributes the required yaw moment to each wheel. The simulation results show that vehicle driver can better track the ideal trajectory under the control in J-turn and single shift line condition. The yaw rate and side slip angle are suppressed effectively, which means VUFC system is feasible, and it strengthens the driving stability of the vehicle.

References

1. Habib, S., Khan, M.M., Abbas, F., et al.: A comprehensive study of implemented international standards, technical challenges, impacts and prospects for electric vehicles. IEEE Access **6**, 13866–13890 (2018)
2. Zhai, L., Sun, T., Wang, J.: Electronic stability control based on motor driving and braking torque distribution for a four in-wheel motor drive electric vehicle. IEEE Trans. Veh. Technol. **65**, 4726–4739 (2016)
3. Zhang, G., Zhang, H., Huang, X., et al.: Active fault-tolerant control for electric vehicles with independently driven rear in-wheel motors against certain actuator faults. IEEE Trans. Control Syst. Technol. 1–16 (2015)
4. Zhou, H., Chen, H., Ren, B., et al.: Yaw stability control for in-wheel-motored electric vehicle with a fuzzy PID method. In: 2015 27th Chinese Control and Decision Conference (CCDC). IEEE (2015)
5. Li, H., Zhihong, M., Jiayin, W.: Variable universe stable adaptive fuzzy control of nonlinear system. Sci. Chin. Ser. E Technol. Sci. **45**(3), 225–240 (2002)
6. He, P., Hori, Y.: Optimum traction force distribution for stability improvement of 4WD EV in critical driving condition. In: 2006 9th IEEE International Workshop on Advanced Motion Control. IEEE (2006)
7. Abe, M., Mokhiamar, O.: An integration of vehicle motion controls for full drive-by-wire vehicle. Proc. Inst. Mech. Eng. Part K: J. Multi-Body Dyn
8. Guvenc, B.A., Bunte, T., Odenthal, D., et al.: Robust two degree-of-freedom vehicle steering controller design. IEEE Trans. Control Syst. Technol. **12**(4), 627–636 (2004)
9. Sadri, S., Wu, C.Q.: Lateral stability analysis of on-road vehicles using the concept of Lyapunov exponents. In: IEEE Intelligent Vehicles Symposium (2012)
10. Zhang, B., Du, H., Lam, J., et al.: A novel observer design for simultaneous estimation of vehicle steering angle and sideslip angle. IEEE Trans. Ind. Electron. **63**(7), 1 (2016)

Observer and Controller Design for State-Delay Takagi-Sugeno Fuzzy Systems Subjected to Unknown Time-Varying Output Delays

Weikang Hu, Yanwei Huang$^{(\boxtimes)}$, Wenchao Huang, and Shaobin Chen

Fuzhou University, Fuzhou 350108, People's Republic of China
vvkc@foxmail.com, {sjtu_huanghao,ehwenc,shaobin308}@fzu.edu.cn

Abstract. This paper investigates the stabilization problem for Takagi-Sugeno fuzzy systems subjected to both fixed state delays and unknown time-varying output delays. First, a novel fuzzy observer is proposed to synchronously estimate the system state and the disturbance term caused by the unknown output delays. Then, along with the fuzzy observer, a fuzzy controller is designed to ensure the stability of the overall system by Lyapunov-based analysis. Finally, the effectiveness and correctness of the obtained results are verified by simulation example.

Keywords: Fuzzy systems · State delays · Unknown output delays

1 Introduction

Takagi-Sugeno (T-S) fuzzy systems have attracted continuous attention during the last few decades since many nonlinear systems in engineering fields can be characterized, at any precision, as the fuzzy form. Fruitful results have been reported for a variety of research issues on fuzzy systems, see [1,2] and reference therein. Meanwhile, inherent time-delay always exists in practical processes owing to the distributed nature of a system and communication lags, which is widely regarded as the major source of performance degradation and even instability [3,4]. In [5], a sum of squares approach to stability analysis was discussed for polynomial fuzzy systems with time-delay. In [6], a fuzzy polynomial observer was designed for time-delay fuzzy systems. The problem of robust H_∞ control was investigated for a class of nonlinear systems with state and input time-varying delays in [7].

It is noted that all the results in [5–7] were focused on systems with state delays. As a matter of fact, time delays affecting output measurements arise in a variety of applications. In [8], a distributed predictor-based controller

---

This work was supported by Guidance Projects of Industrial Science and Technology of Fujian Provence under Grant 2019H0007.

H. Yu et al. (Eds.): ICIRA 2019, LNAI 11743, pp. 169–180, 2019.
https://doi.org/10.1007/978-3-030-27538-9_15

was proposed to solve consensus problem of discrete-time heterogeneous linear multi-agent systems with constant output delays. By using the PDE-based backstepping-like design method, a high-gain observer was presented in [9] for nonlinear systems with arbitrarily large but known transport delays.

To the best of authors' knowledge, the stabilization problem for continuous-time T-S fuzzy systems subjected to both state delays and unknown time-varying output delays has not been investigated. Motivated by the above conditions, we makes the first attempt in the present paper. Two more advantages of this paper can be summarized as follows: (i) Compared with [8,9], the information of the output delays are not necessary known as a prior in our observer design procedure. (ii) The existing results in literature [10,11] can be seen as a special case of our results without state delays.

The rest of this paper is organized as below. In Sect. 2, some preliminaries are given, including some basic concepts of fuzzy system and the problem statement. Section 3 focuses the main results on fuzzy observer and controller designs. Simulation is provided in Sect. 4 and some concluding remarks are drawn in Sect. 5.

2   Preliminaries

Notations: For a symmetric matrix M, $M > 0 \, (\geq 0)$ represents that M is positive definite (or positive semi-definite). M^{-1} and M^T are the inverse and transpose of matrix A, respectively. I and 0 in block matrix are identity matrix and zero matrix have appropriate dimension, respectively. $diag\{...\}$ denotes a block-diagonal matrix. $Sym\{M\}$ denotes $M + M^T$. $\lambda_{max}(M)$ represents the maximal eigenvalue of M and $||M|| = \sqrt{\lambda_{max}(M^T M)}$.

2.1   Fuzzy Modeling of State-Delay Nonlinear System

In this paper, the original nonlinear system with time delay is delineated by the introduced T-S fuzzy modeling approach. In the T-S fuzzy modeling, several operating points are chosen for the considered nonlinear system. It should be noted that the corresponding local subsystems then can be obtained for each operating point by the virtue of system identification or linearization technique.

Consider the following nonlinear system with time delay:

$$\dot{x}(t) = f(x(t), x(t-\tau), u(t)), \tag{1}$$

where f is a nonlinear function, $x(t)$ is the state vector, $u(t)$ is the control input vector and τ denotes the constant time delay. We can represent (1) with the following T-S fuzzy model:

$\mathscr{R}^i$: **IF** $z_1(t)$ is $\mathscr{T}_1^i$ and ... and $z_p(t)$ is $\mathscr{T}_p^i$ **THEN**

$$\dot{x}(t) = A_i x(t) + A_{di} x(t-\tau) + B_i u(t), \ i \in \mathscr{L} \tag{2}$$

where $\mathscr{L} := \{1, 2, \ldots, r\}$, $\mathscr{R}^i$ is the i-th fuzzy inference rule, $\mathscr{T}_j^i (j = 1, 2, ...p)$ are fuzzy sets, $z_j(t) = [z_1(t), z_2(t), ..., z_p(t)]$ represents the premise variables, r is the number of inference rules, and $\{A_i, A_{di}, B_i\}$ is the i-th local linear subsystem.

Denote $\mathscr{T}^i = \prod_{j=1}^p \mathscr{T}_j^i$ as the inferred fuzzy set, and $h_i[z(t)]$ as the normalized membership function, it has

$$h_i[z(t)] = \frac{\prod_{j=1}^p h_{ij}[z_j(t)]}{\sum_{k=1}^r \prod_{j=1}^p h_{kj}[z_j(t)]}, \quad \sum_{i=1}^r h_i[z(t)] = 1, \tag{3}$$

where $h_{ij}[z_j(t)]$ represents the grade of membership of $z_j(t)$ in $\mathscr{T}_j^i$.

Now, we denote $z = z(t)$ for brevity. The T-S fuzzy dynamic model could be obtained via the fuzzy blending,

$$\dot{x}(t) = \sum_{i=1}^r h_i(z)\{A_i x(t) + A_{di} x(t-\tau) + B_i u(t)\}. \tag{4}$$

2.2   Problem Statement

Generally, time delays often exist in the field of feedback control systems. Here, the information of output delay is considered as unknown, and the measurement output is given by

$$y(t) = C x\left(t - d(t)\right), \tag{5}$$

where $d(t)$ denotes the unknown time-varying delays.

Now, we define the unknown delay perturbation as

$$\omega(t) = C\left[x\left(t - d(t)\right) - x\left(t\right)\right]. \tag{6}$$

The system output (5) thus becomes

$$y(t) = C x\left(t\right) + \omega(t). \tag{7}$$

Combine (4) and (7), we have the following fuzzy system:

$$\begin{cases} \dot{x}(t) = \sum_{i=1}^r h_i(z)\{A_i x(t) + A_{di} x(t-\tau) + B_i u(t)\}, \\ y(t) = C x(t) + w(t). \end{cases} \tag{8}$$

This paper aims at addressing the issue of fuzzy observer and controller design for state-delay T-S fuzzy systems with unknown output delays in continuous-time domain (8). First of all, a novel augmented observer is constructed to estimate both system state and delay perturbation caused by the unknown output delays, such that the estimation error is asymptotically stable. Then, along with the estimated system state, the stability of the overall system is ensured by employing a fuzzy controller.

In order to obtain the main results in this paper, the following lemma is proposed.

Lemma 1. *With X, Y of appropriate dimension and $\rho > 0$, the following inequality holds [12]:*

$$\rho X X^T + \frac{1}{\rho} Y^T Y \geq XY + (XY)^T. \tag{9}$$

3   Main Results

3.1   Fuzzy Observer Design

In this subsection we will construct an augmented fuzzy observer to estimate both system state and delay perturbation synchronously.

First, we define

$$x_a(t) = \begin{bmatrix} x(t) \\ w(t) \end{bmatrix}, \; E = \begin{bmatrix} I & 0 \\ 0 & 0 \end{bmatrix},$$

$$\bar{A}_i = \begin{bmatrix} A_i & 0 \\ 0 & \beta_i I \end{bmatrix}, \; \bar{A}_{di} = \begin{bmatrix} A_{di} & 0 \\ 0 & \beta_i I \end{bmatrix},$$

$$\bar{B}_i = \begin{bmatrix} B_i \\ 0 \end{bmatrix}, \; W_i = \begin{bmatrix} 0 \\ \beta_i I \end{bmatrix}, \; \bar{C} = [C \;\; I], \tag{10}$$

where β_i is positive scalar.

In term of (8) and (10), an augmented fuzzy system can be established as below:

$$\begin{cases} E\dot{x}_a(t) = \sum_{i=1}^{r} h_i(z)\{\bar{A}_i x_a(t) + \bar{A}_{di} x_a(t-\tau) \\ \qquad\qquad + \bar{B}_i u(t) - W_i(w(t) + w(t-\tau))\}, \\ y(t) = \bar{C} x_a(t). \end{cases} \tag{11}$$

Consider E is singular, the dynamic equation of the plant in (11) can be rewritten as

$$\begin{aligned} S_i \dot{x}_a(t) = \sum_{i=1}^{r} h_i(z)\{ & (\bar{A}_i - K_i \bar{C}) x_a(t) \\ & + (\bar{A}_{di} - K_{di}\bar{C}) x_a(t-\tau) + \bar{B}_i u(t) \\ & + K_i y(t) + K_{di} y(t-\tau) + L_i \dot{y}(t) \\ & - W_i(w(t) + w(t-\tau))\}, \end{aligned} \tag{12}$$

where $S_i = E + L_i \bar{C}$, $L_i = \begin{bmatrix} 0 & \tilde{L}_i^T \end{bmatrix}^T$, L_i is chosen such that S_i is nonsingular, and $\{K_i, K_{di}\}$ are the observer gains to be designed.

We design a fuzzy observer to estimate the states of (12) with the form of

$$\begin{aligned} S_i \dot{\hat{x}}_a(t) = \sum_{i=1}^{r} h_i(z)\{ & (\bar{A}_i - K_i \bar{C}) \hat{x}_a(t) \\ & + (\bar{A}_{di} - K_{di}\bar{C}) \hat{x}_a(t-\tau) + \bar{B}_i u(t) \\ & + K_i y(t) + K_{di} y(t-\tau) + L_i \dot{y}(t)\}. \end{aligned} \tag{13}$$

In practice, the fuzzy observer above can be rewritten as

$$\begin{cases} S_i \dot{\mathcal{X}}(t) = \sum_{i=1}^{r} h_i(z)\{(\bar{A}_i - K_i \bar{C})\mathcal{X}(t) \\ \qquad\qquad + (\bar{A}_{di} - K_{di}\bar{C})\mathcal{X}(t-\tau) + \bar{B} u_i(t) \\ \qquad\qquad - W_i(y(t) + y(t-\tau))\}, \\ \hat{x}_a(t) = \sum_{i=1}^{r} h_i(z)\{\mathcal{X}(t) + S_i^{-1} L_i y(t)\}, \end{cases} \tag{14}$$

where $\mathcal{X}(t)$ is an auxiliary state vector.

Define $e(t) = x_a(t) - \hat{x}_a(t)$. Subtracting (13) from (12), it has the estimation error system as follows

$$S_i \dot{e}(t) = \sum_{i=1}^{r} h_i(z)\{(\bar{A}_i - K_i\bar{C})e(t)$$
$$+ (\bar{A}_{di} - K_{di}\bar{C})e(t - \tau)$$
$$- W_i(w(t) + w(t - \tau))\}. \tag{15}$$

Define $\bar{S}_i = S_i^{-1}$ and $W_{mi} = S_i^{-1}W_i$. Pre-multiplying both sides of (15) by S_i^{-1}, we can obtain

$$\dot{e}(t) = \sum_{i=1}^{r} h_i(z)\{\bar{S}_i(\bar{A}_i - K_i\bar{C})e(t)$$
$$+ \bar{S}_i(\bar{A}_{di} - K_{di}\bar{C})e(t - \tau)$$
$$- W_{mi}(w(t) + w(t - \tau))\}. \tag{16}$$

Combine (10), $S_i = E + L_i\bar{C}$, and $L_i = \begin{bmatrix} 0 & \tilde{L}_i^T \end{bmatrix}^T$, it has $W_{mi} = \begin{bmatrix} 0 \\ \beta_i \tilde{L}_i^{-1} \end{bmatrix}$.

We can see that terms $W_{mi}(w(t) + w(t - \tau))$ can be ignored if a large matrix $\tilde{L}_i$ and a small β_i are chosen. Thus, the estimation error dynamic Eq. (16) can be simplified as

$$\dot{e}(t) = \sum_{i=1}^{r} h_i(z)\{\bar{S}_i(\bar{A}_i - K_i\bar{C})e(t) + \bar{S}_i(\bar{A}_{di} - K_{di}\bar{C})e(t - \tau)\}. \tag{17}$$

Define

$$\tilde{A}_i = \bar{S}_i(\bar{A}_i - K_i\bar{C}), \quad \tilde{A}_{di} = \bar{S}_i(\bar{A}_{di} - K_{di}\bar{C}). \tag{18}$$

Then (17) can be rewritten as

$$\dot{e}(t) = \sum_{i=1}^{r} h_i(z)\{\tilde{A}_i e(t) + \tilde{A}_{di}e(t - \tau)\}. \tag{19}$$

Theorem 1. *If there exist the positive-definite symmetric matrices $\{P_1, Q_1\}$, the positive scalar θ, and the matrices $\{M_i, M_{di}\}$, such that the following linear matrix inequalities (LMIs) are satisfied, the estimation error system (19) is asymptotically stable:*

$$\begin{bmatrix} \Theta_{11} & \Theta_{12} \\ \star & \Theta_{22} \end{bmatrix} < 0, \ \forall i \in \mathcal{L}, \tag{20}$$

where

$$\Theta_{11} = Sym\{P_1\bar{S}_i\bar{A}_i - M_i\bar{C}\} + Q_1 + \theta I,$$
$$\Theta_{12} = P_1\bar{S}_i\bar{A}_{di} - M_{di}\bar{C},$$
$$\Theta_{22} = -Q_1 + \theta I. \tag{21}$$

The corresponding fuzzy observer gains are given by

$$K_i = S_i P_1^{-1} M_i, \ K_{di} = S_i P_1^{-1} M_{di}. \tag{22}$$

Proof. Consider the following Lyapunov-Krasovskii function:

$$V_o(t) = V_{o1}(t) + V_{o2}(t), \tag{23}$$

with

$$V_{o1}(t) = e^T(t) P_1 e(t), \ V_{o2}(t) = \int_{t-\tau}^{t} e^T(\gamma) Q_1 e(\gamma) d\gamma, \tag{24}$$

where $\{P_1, Q_1\}$, are the positive-definite symmetric matrices.

Then, define $\xi^T(t) = \left[e^T(t) \ e^T(t - \tau) \right]$, along the error system (19), it has the derivative:

$$
\begin{aligned}
\dot{V}_{o1}(t) &= \dot{e}^T(t) P_1 e(t) + e^T(t) P_1 \dot{e}(t) \\
&= \sum_{i=1}^{r} h_i(z) \left\{ \xi^T(t) \begin{bmatrix} \tilde{A}_i^T P_1 + P_1 \tilde{A}_i & P_1 \tilde{A}_{di} \\ \star & 0 \end{bmatrix} \xi(t) \right\},
\end{aligned} \tag{25}
$$

$$
\begin{aligned}
\dot{V}_{o2}(t) &= e^T(t) Q_1 e(t) - e^T(t - \tau) Q_1 e(t - \tau) \\
&= \sum_{i=1}^{r} h_i(z) \left\{ \xi^T(t) \begin{bmatrix} Q_1 & 0 \\ \star & -Q_1 \end{bmatrix} \xi(t) \right\}.
\end{aligned} \tag{26}
$$

Combine (23) – (26), it has

$$\dot{V}_o(t) \leq \sum_{i=1}^{r} h_i(z) \left\{ \xi^T(t) \Lambda \xi(t) - \theta \xi^T(t) \xi(t) \right\}, \tag{27}$$

where θ is a positive scalar and

$$\Lambda = \begin{bmatrix} \bar{\Theta}_{11} & P_1 \tilde{A}_{di} \\ \star & -Q_1 + \theta I \end{bmatrix}, \tag{28}$$

with $\bar{\Theta}_{11} = \tilde{A}_i^T P_1 + P_1 \tilde{A}_i + Q_1 + \theta I$.

Recall (18), and define $M_i = P_1 \bar{S}_i K_i$ and $M_{di} = P_1 \bar{S}_i K_{di}$, it is clear that the condition (20) indicates that $\Lambda < 0$. Thus, from (27), it has

$$\dot{V}_o(t) \leq -\theta \xi^T(t) \xi(t), \tag{29}$$

which means $\dot{V}_o(t) < 0$.   □

Notes and Comments. The obtained observer design results in this section do not need any information of the time-varying output delays, which is much more practical for application. Similar technique can be found in [4, 10, 11].

3.2 Fuzzy Controller Design

This subsection is to design a fuzzy controller such that the closed-loop system is asymptotically stable.

Based on the designed observer (14), we construct the following fuzzy controller

$$u(t) = \sum_{i=1}^{r} h_i(z)\{-F_i\hat{x}(t) - F_{di}\hat{x}(t - \tau)\}$$

$$= \sum_{i=1}^{r} h_i(z)\{-[F_i\ 0]\hat{x}_a(t) - [F_{di}\ 0]\hat{x}_a(t - \tau)\}$$

$$= \sum_{i=1}^{r} h_i(z)\{-F_i x(t) - F_{di}x(t - \tau) + \bar{F}_i e(t) + \bar{F}_{di}e(t - \tau)\}, \quad (30)$$

where $\bar{F}_i = [F_i\ 0]$ and $\bar{F}_{di} = [F_{di}\ 0]$.

Thus, the closed-loop system is given by

$$\dot{x}(t) = \sum_{i=1}^{r}\sum_{j=1}^{r} h_i(z)h_j(z)\{(A_i - B_iF_j)x(t)$$
$$+ (A_{di} - B_iF_{dj})x(t - \tau)$$
$$+ B_i\bar{F}_j e(t) + B_i\bar{F}_{dj}e(t - \tau)\}. \quad (31)$$

Theorem 2. *If there exist the positive-definite symmetric matrices $\{X, U\}$, the matrices $\{N_i, N_{di}\}$ and the positive scalar ρ such that the following LMIs are satisfied, the closed-loop system (31) is asymptotically stable:*

$$\tilde{\Phi}_{ii} < 0, \ \forall i \in \mathscr{L}, \quad (32)$$

$$\tilde{\Phi}_{ij} + \tilde{\Phi}_{ji} < 0, \ i < j \leq r, \quad (33)$$

where

$$\tilde{\Phi}_{ij} = \begin{bmatrix} \tilde{\Phi}_{11} & \tilde{\Phi}_{12} & X \\ \star & -U & 0 \\ \star & \star & -\frac{1}{\rho}I \end{bmatrix}, \quad (34)$$

with

$$\tilde{\Phi}_{11} = Sym\{A_iX - B_iN_j\} + U,$$
$$\tilde{\Phi}_{12} = A_{di}X - B_iN_{dj}. \quad (35)$$

The corresponding fuzzy controller gains are given by

$$F_i = N_iX^{-1}, \ F_{di} = N_{di}X^{-1}. \quad (36)$$

Proof. Consider the following Lyapunov-Krasovskii function:

$$V_c(t) = x^T(t)P_2 x(t) + \int_{t-\tau}^{t} x^T(\gamma)Q_2 x(\gamma)d\gamma, \tag{37}$$

where $\{P_2, Q_2\}$ are positive-definite symmetric matrices.

Then, define $\vartheta^T(t) = [x^T(t)\ x^T(t-\tau)]$, along the closed-loop system (31), similar to the proof in Theorem 1, it has the derivative:

$$\begin{aligned}
\dot{V}_c(t) &= \sum_{i=1}^{r}\sum_{j=1}^{r} h_i(z)h_j(z)\Big\{\vartheta^T(t)\Phi_{ij}\vartheta(t) \\
&\quad + Sym\{x(t)P_2 B_i \bar{F}_j e(t) \\
&\quad + x(t)P_2 B_i \bar{F}_{dj} e(t-\tau)\}\Big\} \\
&= \sum_{i=1}^{r} h_i^2(z)\{\vartheta^T(t)\Phi_{ii}\vartheta(t)\} \\
&\quad + \sum_{i=1}^{r}\sum_{i<j}^{r} h_i(z)h_j(z)\vartheta^T(t)\{\Phi_{ij} + \Phi_{ji}\}\vartheta(t) \\
&\quad + \sum_{i=1}^{r}\sum_{j=1}^{r} h_i(z)h_j(z)\Big\{Sym\{x^T(t)P_2 B_i \bar{F}_j e(t) \\
&\quad + x^T(t)P_2 B_i \bar{F}_{dj} e(t-\tau)\}\Big\}
\end{aligned} \tag{38}$$

where

$$\begin{aligned}
\Phi_{ij} &= \begin{bmatrix} \Phi_{11} & \Phi_{12} \\ \star & -Q_2 \end{bmatrix}, \\
\Phi_{11} &= Sym\{P_2(A_i - B_i F_j)\} + Q_2, \\
\Phi_{12} &= P_2(A_{di} - B_i F_{dj}).
\end{aligned} \tag{39}$$

By Lemma 1, it has

$$\begin{aligned}
& Sym\{x^T(t)P_2 B_i \bar{F}_j e(t) + x^T(t)P_2 B_i \bar{F}_{dj} e(t-\tau)\} \\
& \leq \rho x^T(t)x(t) + \frac{2}{\rho}e^T(t)\Xi_1 e(t) + \frac{2}{\rho}e^T(t-\tau)\Xi_2 e(t-\tau)
\end{aligned} \tag{40}$$

where ρ is a positive scalar and

$$\begin{aligned}
\Xi_1 &= (P_2 B_i \bar{F}_j)^T (P_2 B_i \bar{F}_j), \\
\Xi_2 &= (P_2 B_i \bar{F}_{dj})^T (P_2 B_i \bar{F}_{dj}).
\end{aligned} \tag{41}$$

Thus,

$$\dot{V}_c(t) \leq \sum_{i=1}^{r} h_i^2(z)\{\vartheta^T(t)\hat{\Phi}_{ii}\vartheta(t)\}$$

$$+ \sum_{i=1}^{r}\sum_{i<j}^{r} h_i(z)h_j(z)\vartheta^T(t)\{\hat{\Phi}_{ij} + \hat{\Phi}_{ji}\}\vartheta(t)$$

$$+ \sum_{i=1}^{r}\sum_{j=1}^{r} h_i(z)h_j(z)\left\{\frac{2}{\rho}e^T(t)\Xi_1 e(t) + \frac{2}{\rho}e^T(t-\tau)\Xi_2 e(t-\tau)\right\}, \quad (42)$$

where

$$\hat{\Phi}_{ij} = \begin{bmatrix} \hat{\Phi}_{11} & \Phi_{12} \\ \star & -Q_2 \end{bmatrix},$$

$$\hat{\Phi}_{11} = Sym\{P_2(A_i - B_i F_j)\} + Q_2 + \rho I. \quad (43)$$

Define $X = P_2^{-1}$, $U = XQ_2 X$, $N_i = F_i X$ and $N_{di} = F_{di}X$. Multiplying both sides of $\hat{\Phi}_{ij} < 0$ by $diag\{X, X\}$, we can obtain

$$\begin{bmatrix} \bar{\Phi}_{11} & \tilde{\Phi}_{12} \\ \star & -U \end{bmatrix} < 0, \quad (44)$$

where

$$\bar{\Phi}_{11} = Sym\{A_i X - B_i N_j\} + U + \rho XX,$$

$$\tilde{\Phi}_{12} = A_{di}X - B_i N_{dj}. \quad (45)$$

Employing Schur complement to (44), it's clear that if the LMI conditions (32) and (33) hold, then it has

$$\hat{\Phi}_{ii} < 0, \ \forall i \in \mathcal{L} \quad (46)$$

$$\hat{\Phi}_{ij} + \hat{\Phi}_{ji} < 0, \ i < j \leq r. \quad (47)$$

Thus,

$$\dot{V}_c(t) \leq \sum_{i=1}^{r}\sum_{j=1}^{r} h_i(z)h_j(z)\left\{\frac{2}{\rho}e^T(t)\Xi_1 e(t) + \frac{2}{\rho}e^T(t-\tau)\Xi_2 e(t-\tau)\right\}. \quad (48)$$

Let

$$V_{co}(t) = V_c(t) + gV_o(t), \quad (49)$$

where g is a positive scalar.

From (29), (48) and (49), we can obtain

$$
\dot{V}_{co}(t) \leq \sum_{i=1}^{r} \sum_{j=1}^{r} h_i(z) h_j(z) \Big\{ \frac{2}{\rho} e^T(t) \Xi_1 e(t)
$$
$$
+ \frac{2}{\rho} e^T(t-\tau) \Xi_2 e(t-\tau) - g\theta \xi^T(t) \xi(t) \Big\},
$$
$$
= \sum_{i=1}^{r} \sum_{j=1}^{r} h_i(z) h_j(z) \Big\{ e^T(t) (\frac{2}{\rho} \Xi_1 - g\theta I) e(t)
$$
$$
+ e^T(t-\tau) (\frac{2}{\rho} \Xi_2 - g\theta I) e(t-\tau) \Big\}, \tag{50}
$$

Selecting

$$
g > \frac{2}{\rho\theta} \| P_2 B_i \bar{F}_j \|^2,
$$
$$
g > \frac{2}{\rho\theta} \| P_2 B_i \bar{F}_{dj} \|^2, \quad i \leq r, j \leq r, \tag{51}
$$

which indicates $\dot{V}_{co}(t) < 0$. The asymptotical stability of the system (31) is achieved. □

4   Demonstrative Example

To illustrate the viability of the above design approach, this section provides a design example.

Consider system (8) with the following parameters:

$$
A_1 = \begin{bmatrix} 0 & 10 \\ -40 & -10 \end{bmatrix}, \; A_2 = \begin{bmatrix} 0 & 10 \\ -50 & -10 \end{bmatrix},
$$
$$
A_{d1} = \begin{bmatrix} 1 & 0.5 \\ -0.4 & -0.1 \end{bmatrix}, \; A_{d2} = \begin{bmatrix} 1 & 0.5 \\ -0.5 & -0.1 \end{bmatrix},
$$
$$
B_1 = B_2 = \begin{bmatrix} 1 \\ 0 \end{bmatrix}, \; C = \begin{bmatrix} 1 & 0 \\ 0 & 1 \end{bmatrix}. \tag{52}
$$

First, choose $\beta_1 = \beta_2 = 0.001$ and $\tilde{L}_1 = \tilde{L}_2 = diag\{1, 1\}$, and solve LMIs in Theorem 1 to obtain observer gains:

$$
K_1 = \begin{bmatrix} 0.028978 & 1.1314 \\ -0.20513 & -4.1431 \\ 8.1646 & -3.3788 \\ 0.19475 & 17.78 \end{bmatrix}, K_2 = \begin{bmatrix} 0.23187 & 4.7975 \\ -1.4229 & -23.479 \\ 7.3867 & -5.3107 \\ 1.8363 & 76.079 \end{bmatrix},
$$
$$
K_{d1} = \begin{bmatrix} 0.075156 & 0.0071349 \\ 0.19141 & 0.029539 \\ -1.2999 & -0.40778 \\ -0.10994 & -0.015748 \end{bmatrix}, K_{d2} = \begin{bmatrix} 0.078177 & -3.3884 \\ -0.37428 & 10.943 \\ -0.64991 & 1.5693 \\ 0.067757 & -62.882 \end{bmatrix}. \tag{53}
$$

Then, solve LMIs in Theorem 2 to obtain controller gains:

$$F_1 = [-2.5416 \quad -38.122], \ F_2 = [-3.9678 \quad -50.614],$$
$$F_{d1} = [1 \quad 0.5], \ F_{d2} = [1 \quad 0.5]. \tag{54}$$

The closed-loop system states (original x, estimated $\hat{x}$ and output y) are shown in Fig. 1, which demonstrates the efficacy of proposed method.

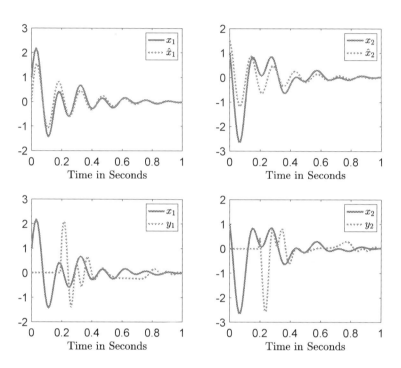

Fig. 1. Comparison of system states

5 Conclusion

The focus of this paper is to develop a fuzzy observer and controller to stabilize the fuzzy systems with fixed state delays and unknown time-varying output delays. The stability analysis for the augmented systems employ Lyapunov-based approach. All the results can be numerically solved via the well-developed LMI technique. In our future work, it would be of interest to extend the proposed techniques to a fuzzy system with unknown delays acting on the system states.

References

1. Qiu, J., Gao, H., Ding, S.X.: Recent advances on fuzzy-model-based nonlinear networked control systems: a survey. IEEE Trans. Ind. Electron. **63**(2), 1207–1217 (2016)
2. Lam, H.: A review on stability analysis of continuous-time fuzzy-model-based control systems: from membership-function-independent to membership-function-dependent analysis. Eng. Appl. Artif. Intell. **67**, 390–408 (2018)
3. Wu, A.G., Lin, Q., Fu, Y.M., Duan, G.R.: A less conservative stability condition of time-delay systems with polytopic uncertainty. Asian J. Control **15**(5), 1543–1547 (2013)
4. Zhong, Z., Zhu, Y., Ahn, C.K.: Reachable set estimation for takagi-sugeno fuzzy systems against unknown output delays with application to tracking control of AUVs. ISA Trans. **78**, 31–38 (2018)
5. Siala, F., Gassara, H., Chaabane, M., El Hajjaji, A.: Stability analysis of polynomial fuzzy systems with time-delay via sum of squares (SOS) approach. In: 14th International Conference on Sciences and Techniques of Automatic Control & Computer Engineering-STA 2013, pp. 197–200. IEEE (2013)
6. Yu, J., Qinsheng, L., Jian, W., Chunsong, H.: Polynomial observer design for time-delay polynomial fuzzy system by sum of squares approach. In: 2017 36th Chinese Control Conference (CCC), pp. 6397–6402. IEEE (2017)
7. Lian, Z., He, Y., Zhang, C.K., Shi, P., Wu, M.: Robust H_∞ control for T-S fuzzy systems with state and input time-varying delays via delay-product-type functional method. IEEE Trans. Fuzzy Syst. (2019)
8. Xu, X., Liu, L., Feng, G.: Consensus of discrete-time linear multiagent systems with communication, input and output delays. IEEE Trans. Autom. Control **63**(2), 492–497 (2018)
9. Ahmed-Ali, T., Giri, F., Krstic, M., Kahelras, M.: Pde based observer design for nonlinear systems with large output delay. Syst. Control Lett. **113**, 1–8 (2018)
10. Gao, Z.: Estimation and compensation for Lipschitz nonlinear discrete-time systems subjected to unknown measurement delays. IEEE Trans. Ind. Electron. **62**(9), 5950–5961 (2015)
11. Zhong, Z., Zhu, Y., Lin, C.M., Huang, T.: A fuzzy control framework for interconnected nonlinear power networks under TDS attack: estimation and compensation. J. Franklin Inst. (2019)
12. Liu, C., Lam, H.K.: Design of a polynomial fuzzy observer controller with sampled-output measurements for nonlinear systems considering unmeasurable premise variables. IEEE Trans. Fuzzy Syst. **23**(6), 2067–2079 (2015)

Force Control Polishing Device Based on Fuzzy Adaptive Impedance Control

Pengfei Chen, Huan Zhao$^{(\boxtimes)}$, Xin Yan, and Han Ding

School of Mechanical Science and Engineering,
Huazhong University of Science and Technology, Wuhan 430074, China
huanzhao@hust.edu.cn

Abstract. The final finishing technology of wind turbine blade is usually manual polishing and robotic polishing is a very meaningful but still hard task. This paper presents a novel strategy by combining a force control polishing device and contact force control algorithm. Specifically, the polishing device is electrically driven, which has advantage of high accuracy compared to the active control flange driven by cylinder. On the basis of this device, A fuzzy adaptive controller with a gravity compensation is proposed to adjust the damping parameter of the impedance controller to reduce the force error. The polishing device is placed on the end of Comau robot to be carried out the wind turbine blade polishing experiments. The results show that, the dynamic contact force error is 2 N and the roughness of wind turbine blade surface is 0.4 μm, which can obtain satisfactory performance of polishing.

Keywords: Wind turbine blade polishing · Force control polishing device · Fuzzy adaptive impedance control

1 Introduction

Wind turbine blades are key components of wind turbines. It is a typical large complex curved components, and it's surface roughness directly affects wind power efficiency and longevity. So it's important to polish the surface at once to keep the surface high accuracy and quality.

At present, the final finishing technology of the blades includes manual polishing and multi-axis CNC machine polishing [1]. The manual polishing process is completed by many workers who holds the polishing tool to polish the wind turbine blade. In most case, this method is stilled used today. This traditional manual polishing method has several problems: (1) poor dimensional controllability; (2) low consistency of surface accuracy and quality; (3) labor intensive; (4) harmful to worker's health due to dust pollution; (5) low efficiency. The numerical control polishing method uses multi-axes CNC machine tools to polish the wind turbine blades. It can reduce process time and the labor to improve the quality, but it has poor processing flexibility and costs a lot [2]. At the same time, it's hard to process the end part of the wind turbine that is weak rigidity. Now, industrial robot is used for the blade polishing work, it is a mobile manipulator with a fixed polishing tool. Comparing to the multi-axes CNC machine tools, not only it can combine the capabilities, large of dexterity and mobility, but also

© Springer Nature Switzerland AG 2019
H. Yu et al. (Eds.): ICIRA 2019, LNAI 11743, pp. 181–194, 2019.
https://doi.org/10.1007/978-3-030-27538-9_16

it costs less labor and money. So robot polishing has broad application prospects in the processing and manufacturing in wind turbine blades [3–5].

The robot must contact with the blade compliantly in the polishing task. In these contact tasks, not only the end-effector's position, but also the contact force should be controlled. Now the main methods of achieving contact force control are active force control and passive force control. The robot uses the controller to achieve active force control by force-position control. But general purpose force controlled robots require new control systems, new software and powerful programming environments. And it's hard to realize the force and position control at the same time because the coupled force and position [6]. On the contrast, it's more easy to achieve passive force control by using the compliant device. We just need to keep the other directions in position controlled. A compliant compliance which is attached to the robot end-effector will absorbed the kinetic energy. It could avoid the possible big forces or moments, and decouple the force/position of the polishing process of industrial robots. At the same time, it can increase flexibility and reduce the requirement to robot position accuracy. Finally the lack of continuity is accommodated and performance of the complete system is smoothed [7]. Also, when the robot is equipped with compliant device, the permitted force control gain is higher than that without it, which is desirable for improving performance and sensitiveness of force control [8].

There are two kind of compliant devices, the first one contains no source of energy such as springs and other elastic elements. The most famous compliance mechanism that is designed for assembly is the remote centre compliance (RCC) device introduced by Whitney and Newins. But it's hard to adjust the passive center and has poor universality [9]. The second one is the active actuator. Ting Huang designed force control polishing flange based on fuzzy PID to polish turbine blade. It's used for improving systems' performance, such as overshoot, rise time and integral of the absolute error [10]. But the drive mode of the end of device are cylinder driven, which has lower force error.

In many cases, impedance control outperformed the others method in terms of controlling the dynamic contact between the manipulator and environment, as well as presented more robustness in an unknown environment [11]. At the same time, fuzzy control is a rule-based control. It directly adopts language-based control rules. Depending on the user's control experience or the knowledge of relevant experts, it is not necessary to establish an accurate mathematical model of the controlled object in the design. The knowledge of input and output needs not to be obtained from a large amount of teaching data. The fuzzy control supplied a favorable option for industrial applications with many worthwhile features, as it has the ability to on-line adapt to time varying nonlinear environment [12–14].

This paper presents a force control polishing device driven by electrically with fuzzy adaptive impedance control algorithm. Comparing with the cylinder driven, the device has higher precision of contact force control. It is placed on the end of Comau robot to carry out the wind turbine blade polishing experiments. It can be shown in Fig. 1. It can adjust the distance of the robot and wind turbine blade through the step motor according to the contact force. It can keep the contact force constant when the position of the end of robot on normal direction of the blade surface changes. The controller can improve precision and robustness of force error.

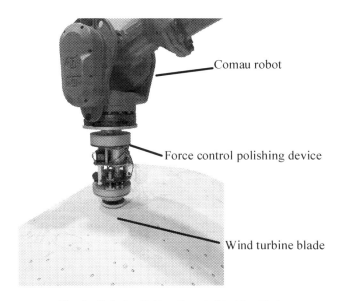

Fig. 1. Robot polishing the wind turbine blade

2 The Force Control Polishing Device

The model structure and real object of the device are shown in Figs. 2 and 3.

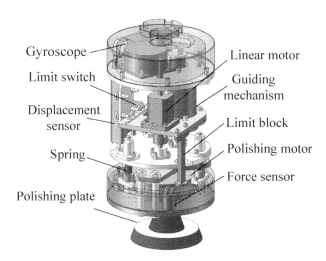

Fig. 2. Three-dimensional model of the polishing device

Fig. 3. Physical display of the polishing device

The device include linear motor, force sensor, displacement sensor, guiding mechanism, springs, polishing motor and gyroscope. Linear motor turns rotational motion of step motor into linear motion of screw. Guiding mechanism allows the polishing plate move linearly. Spring is the passive compliant part of the device.

The work principle is like that: when the device contacts with wind turbine blade, the polishing motor begins to work. The contact force can be obtained through force sensor, then using the fuzzy impedance controller to obtain the velocity of the linear motor. Finally the linear motor moves forward to change the distance between the end of device and the surface of turbine blade. At the same time, the robot holds the device to polish the blade surface and keeps the feed direction of device to be perpendicular to the blade surface at the contact point.

3   Fuzzy Adaptive Impedance Controller

It is difficult to predict and tune the control parameters of the impedance control to cope with the variations in the polishing environment. In this study, fuzzy combiner is used on-line to obtain the parameter of impedance control. The fuzzy adaptive controller is shown in Fig. 4. A control strategy composes of impedance control and fuzzy combiner for robot polishing with constant force has been established, which is called fuzzy adaptive impedance control. The control theory is shown in Fig. 5. The differences between the actual contact force f obtained by a force sensor and the desired contact force f_d, and their differentials d_{ef} are calculated. All the parameters are entered into the force control loop. At the same time, as the output of the fuzzy combiner, the impedance control parameter, damping D_m is tuned. Through position control of step motor, the motion of the device is controlled precisely and the contact force is adjusted indirectly.

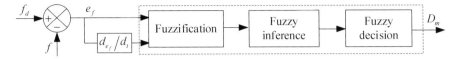

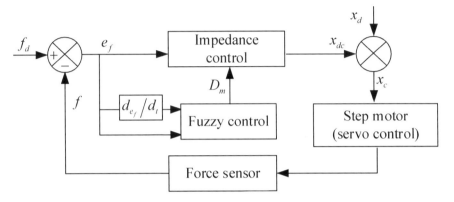

Fig. 4. The fuzzy adaptive controller

Fig. 5. Fuzzy adaptive impedance controller

3.1 Gravity Compensation Algorithm

Force sensor can obtain the measuring contact force F_0 between the polishing flange and turbine blade. Gyroscope can obtain the real angle α, β, γ between the orientation of the flange and the word coordinate system. The orientation change of the flange can cause the force sensor's measurement coordinate system to rotate relatively to the world coordinate system. As it's shown in Fig. 6. Therefore, the gravity component of the device in the normal direction of the blade surface is changed in real time, and this part of the gravitational component G must be compensated in order to obtain the actual contact force F.

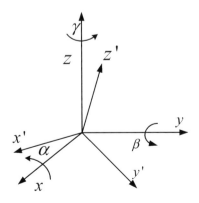

Fig. 6. The transformation of the world coordinate system and the end effector coordinate system

According to the transformation sequence of Y-X-Z from the world coordinate system to the end effector coordinate system, the transformation matrix

$$
\begin{aligned}
T &= R_Z(\alpha)R_X(\gamma)R_Y(\beta) \\
&= \begin{bmatrix}
\cos\alpha\cos\beta - \sin\alpha\sin\gamma\sin\beta & -\sin\alpha\cos\gamma & \cos\alpha\sin\beta + \sin\alpha\sin\gamma\cos\beta \\
\sin\alpha\cos\beta + \cos\alpha\sin\gamma\sin\beta & \cos\alpha\cos\gamma & \sin\alpha\sin\beta - \cos\alpha\sin\gamma\cos\beta \\
-\cos\gamma\sin\beta & \sin\gamma & \cos\gamma\cos\beta
\end{bmatrix}
\end{aligned}
\tag{1}
$$

The vector of gravity in the world coordinate system is $\overrightarrow{G_s} = [0, 0, G]$. The component G_z of the workpiece gravity on the Z axis is

$$
G_z = G\cos\gamma\cos\beta
\tag{2}
$$

The actual contact force

$$
F = F_0 - G\cos\gamma\cos\beta
\tag{3}
$$

3.2   Impedance Control

When force control polishing device contacts with turbine blade, the relation between the force error and position error can be obtained from the impedance controller. Hogan [15] first proposed the concept of impedance control, where manipulator control was invoked for tracking a motion trajectory by means of adjusting the target impedance. It can be described as

$$
M\Delta\ddot{x}_{dc} + D\Delta\dot{x}_{dc} + K\Delta x_{dc} = e_f
\tag{4}
$$

where M, D, K are gain of inertia, damping, stiffness of the polishing device. Δf is force error of desired force and actual force. Δx_{dc} is position error of desired position and actual position. By increasing the damping gain, the overshoot of the contact force reduces. If the damping gain is too large, the contact force reaches stable for a long time.

3.3   Estimation of On-Line Control Parameters

In the fuzzy combiner, the output variables are the control parameters, damping D_m. The force error e_f and rate of change of force error d_{ef} of force signal were used as inputs variables. The time-varying variables e_f and d_{ef} are updated periodically by using Eqs. (5) and (6). F_d is the desired contact force and f is the real-time force feedback signal.

$$e_f = F_d - f \tag{5}$$

$$d_{ef} = e_f(i) - e_f(i - 1) \tag{6}$$

Fuzzification is the first step of fuzzy combiner, which changes the input and output variables into the fuzzy quantity. In the discrete domain, the input and output variables are denoted as respectively. Their corresponding fuzzy quantities are defined for the rule base as {NB (negative big), NM (negative middle), NS (negative small), Z (zero), PS (positive small), PM (positive middle), PB (positive big)}. Their real variables are shown in Fig. 7 and Table 1. Fuzzification uses the scaling factors to establish the relationship between the variables in the different domains [16], and the scaling factor can be defined using Eqs. (7) and (8)

$$k_i = \frac{D_h - D_1}{R_h - D_1} \tag{7}$$

$$k_o = \frac{R_h - R_1}{D_h - D_1} \tag{8}$$

Where k_i and k_o denote the scaling factors of input and output, $[D_h, D_l]$ denotes the range of variables in the discrete domain, $[R_h, R_l]$ denotes the range of real variables.

After fuzzification, fuzzy inference is a process to establish the fuzzy rule. The membership functions of all of the variables first need to be determined. The membership function is a curve that defines how each point is mapped to a membership value between 0 and 1. In this study, the triangular membership function was used for all variables. The fuzzy rule is constructed using if-then statements, and 49 rules are defined to form the fuzzy rule base for the fuzzy combiner.

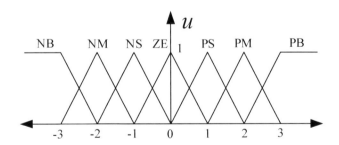

Fig. 7. Membership function of the variables

Finally, the fuzzy decision is used to obtain the fuzzy quantity of the outputs. In the actual application, according to the fuzzy value of the input, the control system uses the look-up table to obtain the fuzzy quantity of the outputs and then multiplies the corresponding scaling factor to obtain the actual control quantity [17].

Table 1. The fuzzy rules

Dm				d_{ef}			
e_f	NB	NM	NS	ZE	PS	PM	PB
NB	PB	PM	PS	ZE	ZE	ZE	ZE
NM	PB	PM	PS	ZE	ZE	ZE	NS
NS	PB	PS	PS	ZE	ZE	NS	NM
ZE	PB	PB	PS	ZE	NS	NB	NB
PS	PM	PS	ZE	ZE	NS	NM	NB
PM	PS	ZE	ZE	ZE	NS	NM	NB
PB	ZE	ZE	ZE	ZE	NS	NM	NB

4   Experiment Design and Analysis

4.1   Experimental Program Design

Figure 8 is a block diagram of the experimental program. The entire experimental procedure can be divided into two section. They are strategy of the force control and protection program section.

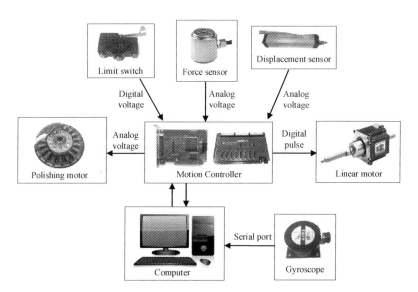

Fig. 8. Block diagram of the experimental program

We use fuzzy adaptive impedance controller to control the device to contact with wind turbine blade with constant force. At first, the voltage signals generated in the force sensors are sent to Google motion controller. The frequency of the controller is 8 kHz. We use filter to remove some noise of the force signal, then convert the voltage into force according to the sensitivity between them. Since the force sensor itself has a certain offset, the offset must be subtracted to get the contact force. The angle of device relative the word coordinate system obtained by gyroscopes is sent to computer through serial port. Then by using the gravity compensation algorithm, the actual contact force is obtained after the weight of the polishing device compensated. The control system use the pulse signal calculated by force control algorithm to control linear motor. Then the distance between the end of flange and turbine blade change. Finally, the contact force during the polishing process is approximate to the expected contact force.

The protection program section protects the experimental device from being damaged. On the one hand, it limits the actual contact force to be less than 80 N. On the other hand, it limits the position within 20 mm. Google motion controller can obtain the voltage of displacement sensor, then convert to the position of the linear motor, finally limit the position of linear motor by programming. Limit switch has the same effect by sending the digital signal to Google controller when the linear motor reached limit position. When the contact force and the position linear motor are out of range, then the motor locks immediately. The range of the force sensor is 50 N, and the precision is 0.1 N. The limit block can limit the position of polishing plate forcibly to protect the force sensor when the end of flange is overloaded. When the force control process begins, the linear motor moves forward with constant velocity before the device contacts with turbine blade. Then the polishing motor begins to work and the position of linear motor changes according the force after the flange contacts with turbine blade.

4.2   Experiment of Result

The load of Comau robot is 200 kg, and the weight of polishing device is 4.5 kg. It can be placed on the end of Comau robot to polish the turbine blade. The large wind turbine blade model is made of glass fiber, and its length and width are 1.5 m and 1.2 m. The polishing path is generated by human demonstration. The direction of contact force control of polishing device is the normal direction of the blade. Before carrying out the polishing experiments on the turbine blade, we first tested it on a plate made of glass fiber and analyzed the result. Under the force control strategy, the damping parameters of impedance control was adjusted only by fuzzy control. To verify the performance of the force control strategy, comparative milling experiments were carried out using different polishing parameters. The polishing parameters includes the contact force, the speed of the polishing motor, and the mesh number of the sandpaper. We analyzed the contact force error and the roughness of surface with different polishing situation. The roughness of the surface is measured by the hand-held roughness measuring instrument. It is shown in Fig. 9.

Fig. 9. The hand-held roughness measuring instrument

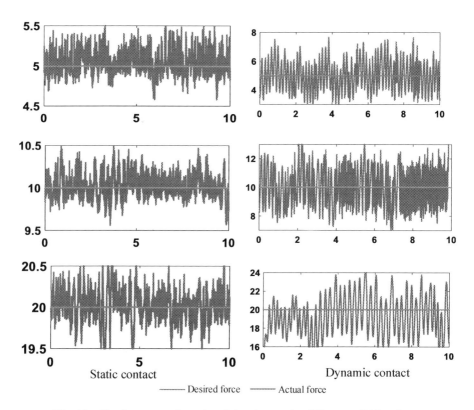

Fig. 10. The force control results of the plate under different polishing force

The experimental results show that there is no significant difference in the steady state of the contact force error. It can be controlled within 0.5 N when the polishing motor does not rotate, and 2 N when the polishing motor rotates (Fig. 10). The dynamic force error is bigger than static force error because the frictional force of the polishing plate.

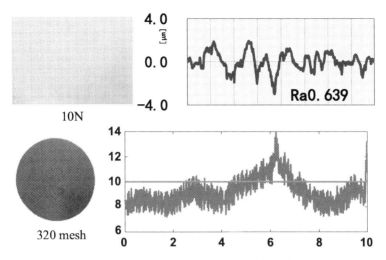

Fig. 11. The polishing results of the plate without force control

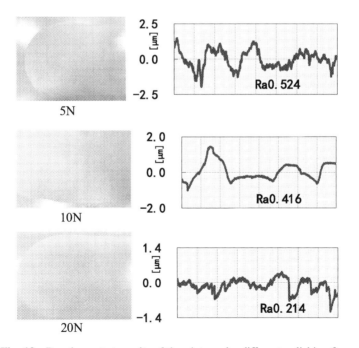

Fig. 12. Roughness test results of the plate under different polishing force

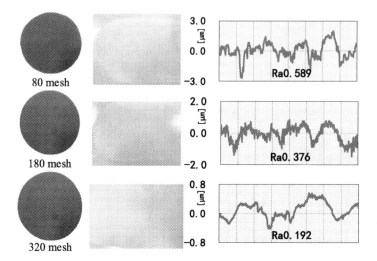

Fig. 13. Roughness testing results of the plate with sandpaper of different mesh number

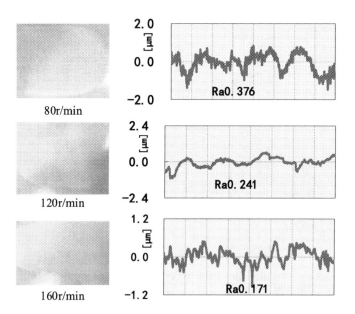

Fig. 14. Roughness testing results of the plate with sandpaper of different polishing speed

First, we polish the plate without force control. The result can be obtained in Fig. 11. The dynamic force error and the roughness of surface are greater than polishing the plater with force control. Then we use different contact force to polish the plate, and the speed of polishing motor and the mesh number of sandpaper are 80r/min and 320. The different results of experiment can be obtained in Fig. 12. The bigger contact force is, the better the plate roughness is. However, if the contact force is too large, it may lead to over-polishing. Therefore, the contact force should be controlled within a suitable range. We use sandpaper with different roughness to polish the plate, the mesh number of the sandpaper are 600, 300, 80. At the same time, the desired contact force and the speed of polishing motor are 10 N and 80 r/min. The different result of experiment can be obtained in Fig. 13. The experimental results shown the mesh number of the sandpaper is more smaller, the surface is more rough. Finally we used three different polishing velocity that are 80 r/min, 120 r/min and 160 r/min to polish the plate. The desired contact force and the mesh number of sandpaper are 10 N and 320. The result can be obtained in Fig. 14. It shown that the polishing velocity is bigger, the surface is more rough.

Based on the information obtained from the plate polishing experiment, this paper further conducted the polishing experiment on the turbine blade. The polishing parameters are that the polishing velocity is 120 r/min, the polishing force is 5 N, and the mesh number of the sandpaper is 320. As shown in Fig. 15, the steady state error of the controlled force is about 2 N. The surface quality of the turbine blade after polishing with force control has been greatly improved, and can be controlled below 0.4 μm. The surface is very smooth, and can be fully applied to the working requirements of the wind turbine blade.

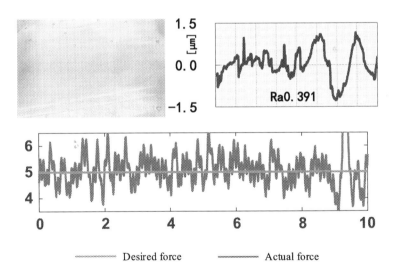

Fig. 15. The results of polishing the wind turbine blade

5 Conclusion

This paper presents a novel strategy by combining a force control polishing device and contact force control algorithm to polish the turbine blade. The device is placed on the end of the Comau robot to control the contact force between the polishing plate and the turbine blade. Then turbine blade polishing experiments are carried out to further test the performance of the proposed method. The active controlled contact force is within 2 N, and the surface roughness is about 0.4 μm. The results prove that the surface roughness and machining consistency are significantly improved with the proposed method.

Acknowledgements. This work was supported by the National Key Research and Development Program of China under Grant No. 2017YFB1301501, the National Natural Science Foundation of China under Grant Nos. 91748114 and 51535004.

References

1. Jost, P.: Grinding device for machine based grinding of rotor blades for wind energy systems. US Patent 13,580,362, 20 Dec 2012
2. Jost, P.: Grinding device for machine based grinding of rotor blades for wind energy systems. US Patent 8,900,037, 2 Dec 2014
3. Wormley, D., Agranat, E.A.: Computer controlled grinding machine for producing objects with complex shapes. US Patent 5,193,314, 16 Mar 1993
4. Kennerknecht, S., Fortin, S.: Automated method and appartus for aircraft surface finishing. US Patent 9,731,979, 13 June 2002
5. Keld Eriksen, L.: Abrading arrangement to abrade a surface of an item and method of use thereof. US Patent 13,809,277, 11 July 2013
6. Norberto Pires, J., Godinho, T., Araújo, R.: Force control for industrial applications using a fuzzy PI controller. Sens. Rev. **24**(1), 60–67 (2004)
7. Attiya, A.J., Wenyu, Y., Shneen, S.W.: Fuzzy-PID controller of robotic grinding force servo system. Int. J. Electr. Comput. Eng. (IJECE) **15**(1) (2015)
8. Xu, Y.: Control software of robot compliant wrist system. Technical reports (CIS), Report number: 564 (1990)
9. Watson, P.C.: Remote center compliance system. US Patent 4,098,001, 4 July 1978
10. Huang, T., et al.: Design of a flexible polishing force control flange. In: 2016 IEEE Workshop on Advanced Robotics and its Social Impacts (ARSO). IEEE (2016)
11. Sheng, X., Zhang, X.: Fuzzy adaptive hybrid impedance control for mirror milling system. Mechatronics **53**, 20–27 (2018)
12. Gharghory, S., Kamal, H.: Modified PSO for optimal tuning of fuzzy PID controller. IJCSI Int. J. Comput. Sci. Issues **10**, 462 (2013)
13. Wang, Y.: Direct drive electro-hydraulic servo control system design with self-tuning fuzzy PID controller. TELKOMNIKA Indonesian J. Electr. Eng. **11**, 3374–3382 (2013)
14. Ma, Q., Shi, J.: Fuzzy PID speed control of two phases ultrasonic motor. TELKOMNIKA Indonesian J. Electr. Eng. **12**, 6560–6565 (2014)
15. Hogan, N.: Impedance control: an approach to manipulation: part II—implementation. J. Dyn. Syst. Measur. Control **107**(1), 8–16 (1985)
16. King, P.J., Mamdani, E.H.: The application of fuzzy control systems to industrial processes. Automatica **13**(3), 235–242 (1977)
17. Deng, Z., et al.: Fuzzy force control and state detection in vertebral lamina milling. Mechatronics **35**, 1–10 (2016)

A Study of TSK Inference Approaches for Control Problems

Jie Li[1], Fei Chao[2], and Longzhi Yang[3]([✉])

[1] School of Computing and Digital Technologies, Teesside University,
Middlesbrough, UK
jie.li@tees.ac.uk

[2] Department of Cognitive Science, Xiamen University, Xiamen, China
fchao@xmu.edu.cn

[3] Department of Computer and Information Sciences, Northumbria University,
Newcastle upon Tyne, UK
longzhi.yang@northumbria.ac.uk

Abstract. Fuzzy inference systems provide a simple yet powerful solution to complex non-linear problems, which have been widely and successfully applied in the control field. The TSK-based fuzzy inference approaches, such as the convention TSK, interval type 2 (IT2) TSK and their extensions TSK+ and IT2 TSK+ approaches, are more convenient to be employed in the control field, as they directly produce crisp outputs. This paper systematically reviews those four TSK-based inference approaches, and evaluates them empirically by applying them to a well-known cart centering control problem. The experimental results confirm the power of TSK+ and IT2 TSK+ approaches in enhancing the inference using either dense or sparse rule bases.

Keywords: TSK · TSK+ · Fuzzy control · Fuzzy inference · Sparse rule base

1 Introduction

Fuzzy inference is a mechanism that uses fuzzy logic and fuzzy set theory to map input domains to output domains. A typical fuzzy inference system consists of two main parts, a rule base and an inference engine. Several inference engines have been developed, with the Mamdani inference [1] and the TSK inference [2] being most widely applied. Compared with the Mamdani inference approach, which takes human linguistic variables as inputs to produce fuzzy outputs and thus requires a defuzzification process to convert the fuzzy outputs to crisp values, the TSK inference approach uses polynomials as the rule consequences to directly generate crisp outputs. For better uncertainty management and performance, these fuzzy inference approaches have been extended to support interval type-2 (IT2) fuzzy sets. Generally speaking, an IT2 fuzzy set represents the membership of a given member as a crisp interval in the range of $[0, 1]$ [3].

© Springer Nature Switzerland AG 2019
H. Yu et al. (Eds.): ICIRA 2019, LNAI 11743, pp. 195–207, 2019.
https://doi.org/10.1007/978-3-030-27538-9_17

Nevertheless, a complete knowledge base (also termed as a dense rule base), which covers the entire input domains, is always required by both conventional type-1 and IT2 fuzzy inference approaches; otherwise, no rule can be fired and no results can be consequently produced if a given input does not overlap with any rule antecedent in the rule base.

Fuzzy interpolation, firstly proposed in [4], relaxes the requirement of dense rule bases, thus to alleviates the problem of lack of knowledge in the rule base. Fundamentally, fuzzy interpolation considers the neighbouring rules in the rule base by means of fuzzified polynomial (usually linear) interpolation to produce the inference results. Therefore, when given inputs do not overlap with any rule antecedent, a certain conclusion can still be obtained. Various fuzzy interpolation methods and extensions have been developed in the literature, including the works reported in [4–11] using Mamdani style inference, and [3,12] using TSK style inference. Due to the simplicity and effectiveness in representing and reasoning on human natural language, fuzzy inference and fuzzy interpolation technologies have been successfully applied to not only the control problems, such as the train operation system in Japan [13], intelligent home heating controller [14], and manufacturing scheduling and planning [15,16], but also other decision-making problems, such as cybersecurity [17–19], business [20], computer network [21], and healthcare [22].

This paper systematically reviews different types of TSK fuzzy inference approaches and their corresponding extensions, including the TSK, IT2 TSK approach, TSK+ inference approach, IT2 TSK+ inference approach. Briefly, the convention TSK and IT2 TSK approaches are only applicable to problems with dense rule bases, but TSK+ and IT2 TSK+ can work with either dense or sparse rule bases. These approaches are then applied to a well-known control problem, the cart centering problem with various sizes of rule bases for empirical evaluation. The experimental results show that the TSK+ and IT2 TSK+ inference approaches enhance the convention TSK and IT2 TSK approaches by means of broader applicability.

The rest of this paper is structured as follows: Sect. 2 introduces the relevant background theory. Section 3 reviews the four different types of TSK inference approaches. Section 4 reports the experimentation of the TSK approaches on a cart centering problem; and Sect. 5 concludes the paper and suggests probable future work.

2   Background

The relevant background theories, including fuzzy sets and interval type-2 fuzzy sets, are introduced in this section.

2.1   Type-1 Fuzzy Sets

Fuzzy logic defines the concept of the fuzzy sets that use membership functions to represent the relationships between elements and their degrees of membership, expressed in the range of $[0, 1]$ [23]. Given a type-1 fuzzy set, denoted as A, it can be expressed as:

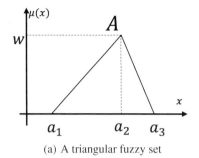
(a) A triangular fuzzy set

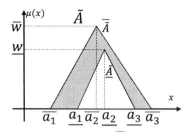
(b) LMF $\underline{\tilde{A}}$ and UMF $\overline{\tilde{A}}$ of a triangle IT2 fuzzy set $\tilde{A}$

Fig. 1. Triangle fuzzy sets

$$A = \{(x, \mu_A(x)) | \forall x \in X, \forall \mu_A(x) \in [0,1]\}, \tag{1}$$

where X is the domain of universe, $\mu_A(x)$ represents the membership for a given x. Assume that the conventional triangle membership is used to represent fuzzy set A as: $A = (a_1, a_2, a_3, w)$, as illustrated in Fig. 1(a), where $w, w \in (0,1]$, is the degree of confidence for fuzzy set A. Apprently $w = 1$, if A is a normal fuzzy set.

2.2 Interval Type-2 Fuzzy Sets

A type-2 fuzzy set, denoted as $\tilde{A}$, can be represented as:

$$\tilde{A} = \{((x, u), \mu_{\tilde{A}}(x, u)) | \forall x \in X, \forall u \in J_x \subseteq [0,1], \quad \mu_{\tilde{A}}(x, u) \in [0,1]\}, \tag{2}$$

where X is the primary domain, J_x is the primary membership for a given element x, and $\mu_{\tilde{A}}(x, u)$ denotes the secondary membership. Taken the triangle IT2 fuzzy set $\tilde{A}$ as an example, as illustrated in Fig. 1(b), It can be represented by a lower membership function (LMF), $\underline{\tilde{A}} = (\underline{a_1}, a_2, \underline{a_3}, \underline{w})$, and a upper membership function (UMF), $\overline{\tilde{A}} = (\overline{a_1}, \overline{a_2}, \overline{a_3}, \overline{w})$. In this case, $\tilde{A} = < \underline{\tilde{A}}, \overline{\tilde{A}} >$, where $(\underline{a_1}, a_2, \underline{a_3})$ and $(\overline{a_1}, \overline{a_2}, \overline{a_3})$ are respectively the three odd points of the LMF and UMF, and $\underline{w}$ and $\overline{w}$ denote respectively the degrees of confidence for $\underline{\tilde{A}}$ and $\overline{\tilde{A}}$, with $0 < \underline{w} \leq \overline{w} = 1$. The area between LMF and UMF, illustrated in grey in Fig. 1(b), thus denotes the footprint of uncertainty (FOU), which represents the uncertainty of the fuzzy set $\tilde{A}$. Obviously, a larger FOU area implies a higher level of uncertainty; and the IT2 fuzzy set degenerates to a type-1 fuzzy set when $\underline{\tilde{A}}$ coincides with $\overline{\tilde{A}}$ (i.e., the area of $FOU(\tilde{A})$ is 0).

3 TSK Fuzzy Control

Four different TSK-style fuzzy models are expressed in this section.

3.1 Conventional Type-1 TSK Fuzzy Model

Suppose that a TSK-style fuzzy rule base comprises of n rules each with m antecedents:

R_1 : **IF** x_1 is A_1^1 and $\cdots$ and x_m is A_m^1
$\quad$ **THEN** $y = f_1(x_1^1, \cdots, x_m^1) = p_0^1 + p_1^1 x_1^1 + \cdots + p_m^1 x_m^1,$

$\cdots\cdots$

R_n : **IF** x_1 is A_1^n and $\cdots$ and x_m is A_m^n
$\quad$ **THEN** $y = f_n(x_1^n, \cdots, x_m^n) = p_0^n + p_1^n x_1^n + \cdots + p_m^n x_m^n,$ $\quad$ (3)

where p_0^k and p_s^k, ($k \in \{1, 2, \cdots, n\}$ and $s \in \{1, 2, \cdots, m\}$) are constant parameters of the linear functions of rule consequences. The consequence polynomials deteriorate to constant numbers p_0^k when the outputs are discrete crisp numbers (usually to represent symbolic values). Given an input vector $(A_1^*, \cdots, A_m^*)$, the TSK engine performs inference in the following steps:

Step 1: Calculate the firing strength of each rule R_k ($k \in \{1, 2, \cdots, n\}$) by integrating the matching degrees between its antecedents and the given inputs:

$$\alpha_k = \mu(A_1^*, A_1^k) \wedge \cdots \wedge \mu(A_m^*, A_m^k),$$ $\quad$ (4)

where $\wedge$ is a t-norm usually implemented as a minimum operator, and $\mu(A_s^*, A_s^k)$ ($s \in \{1, 2, \cdots, m\}$) is the matching degree between fuzzy sets A_s^* and A_s^k:

$$\mu(A_s^*, A_s^k) = \max\{\min\{\mu_{A_s^*}(x), \mu_{A_s^k}(x)\}\},$$ $\quad$ (5)

where $\mu_{A_s^*}(x)$ and $\mu_{A_s^k}(x)$ are the degrees of membership for a given value x within the domain. Note that $\alpha_k = 0$ if there is no overlap between the given inputs and any rule antecedent; in this case, rule $R - K$ will not be fired.

Step 2: Obtain the sub-output led by each rule R_k based on the given observation $(A_1^*, \cdots, A_m^*)$:

$$f_k(x_1^*, \cdots, x_m^*) = p_0^k + p_1^k Rep(A_1^*) + \cdots + p_m^r Rep(A_m^*),$$ $\quad$ (6)

where $Rep(A_s^*)$ is the representative value or defuzzified value of fuzzy set fuzzy set A_s^*, which is often calculated as the centre of gravity of the membership function.

Step 3: Determine the final output by integrating all the sub-outputs from all the rules:

$$y = \frac{\sum_{k=1}^{n} \alpha_k f_k(x_1^*, \cdots, x_m^*)}{\sum_{k=1}^{n} \alpha_k}.$$ $\quad$ (7)

It is clear from Eq. 5 that the firing strength will be 0 if a given input vector does not overlap with any rule antecedent. In this case, no rule will be fired and the conventional TSK approach will fail.

3.2 Type-1 TSK+ Fuzzy Model

TSK+ fuzzy inference approach [3,12] is an extension of the conventional TSK fuzzy inference, which allows the TSK fuzzy inference to still be performed over a sparse rule base. Note that in a sparse rule base, the given observation may not overlap with any rule antecedent. In order to enable this extension, Eq. 5, which is used to obtain the firing strength for overlapped rules, is replaced by

$$\mu(A, A^*) = \left(1 - \frac{\sum_{i=1}^{3} |a_i - a_i^*|}{3}\right) \cdot d \cdot \frac{\min(w, w^*)}{\max(w, w^*)}, \tag{8}$$

where w and w^* denote the degrees of confidence for fuzzy sets A and A^*, respectively, and d, termed as *distance factor*, is a function of the distance between the two concerned fuzzy sets:

$$d = \begin{cases} 1 & ; \begin{array}{l} a_1 = a_2 = a_3 \\ \& \ a_1^* = a_2^* = a_3^* \end{array} \\ 1 - \frac{1}{1+e^{(-s \cdot \|A,A^*\|+5)}} & ; \quad \text{otherwise,} \end{cases} \tag{9}$$

where $\|A, A^*\|$ represents the distance between the two fuzzy sets usually defined as the Euclidean distance of their representative values, and s $(s > 0)$ is an adjustable sensitivity factor. Smaller value of s leads to a similarity degree which is more sensitive to the distance of the two fuzzy sets. Given a rule base as specified in Eq. 3 and an input vector $(A_1^*, \cdots, A_m^*)$, the TSK+ performs inferences using the same steps as those detailed in Sect. 3.1 except that Eq. 5 is replaced by Eq. 8.

In the TSK+ inference model, every rule in the rule base contributes to the final inference result to a certain degree. Therefore, even if the given observation does not overlap with any rule antecedent in the rule base, certain inference result can still be generated, which significantly improves the applicability of the conventional TSK inference system.

3.3 Conventional Interval Type-2 TSK Fuzzy Model

Generally speaking, in an IT2 TSK fuzzy model, the inputs and all the fuzzy sets in the rule antecedents are but not necessarily be IT2 fuzzy sets; and the consequence of IT2 TSK rules are zero or first order of polynomial functions, where the parameters can be either crisp values or a crisp interval. Assume that an IT2 TSK rule base is comprised of n rules as:

$$\begin{aligned} R_1 : \ & \textbf{IF } x_1 \text{ is } \tilde{A}_1^1 \text{ and } \ldots \text{ and } x_m \text{ is } \tilde{A}_m^1 \\ & \textbf{THEN } y = f_1(x_1^1, \cdots, x_m^1) = \tilde{p}_0^1 + \tilde{p}_1^1 x_1^1 + \cdots + \tilde{p}_m^1 x_m^1, \end{aligned}$$

$$\cdots$$

$$\begin{aligned} R_n : \ & \textbf{IF } x_1 \text{ is } \tilde{A}_1^n \text{ and } \ldots \text{ and } x_m \text{ is } \tilde{A}_m^n \\ & \textbf{THEN } y = f_n(x_1^n, \cdots, x_m^n) = \tilde{p}_0^n + \tilde{p}_1^n x_1^n + \cdots + \tilde{p}_m^n x_m^n, \end{aligned} \tag{10}$$

where $\tilde{A}_j^k, (j \in \{1,\ldots,m\}, k \in \{1,\ldots,n\})$ is an IT2 fuzzy set regarding input variable x_j in the kth rule, ad discussed in Sect. 2.2. The consequence is a crisp polynomial function $y = f_k(x_1, \ldots, x_m) = \tilde{p}_0^k + \tilde{p}_1^k x_1^k + \cdots + \tilde{p}_m^k x_m^k$, where $\tilde{p}_j^k$ are parameters usually being crisp intervals, represented as $[\underline{\tilde{p}_j^k}, \overline{\tilde{p}_j^k}]$. For a given input $O(\tilde{A}_1^*, \cdots, \tilde{A}_m^*)$, the steps for calculating the final inference output can be summarised as follows:

Step 1: Compute the firing strength α_k of the kth rule by

$$
\begin{aligned}
\tilde{\alpha}_k =& [\underline{\tilde{\alpha}_k}, \overline{\tilde{\alpha}_k}] = \sqcap_{j=1}^m \tilde{\mu}(\tilde{A}_j^k, \tilde{A}_j^*) \\
=& [\min(\min(\tilde{\mu}_{\tilde{A}_1^k}(x), \tilde{\mu}_{\tilde{A}_1^*}(x)), ..., \min(\tilde{\mu}_{\tilde{A}_m^k}(x), \tilde{\mu}_{\tilde{A}_m^*}(x))), \\
& \min(\max(\tilde{\mu}_{\tilde{A}_1^k}(x), \tilde{\mu}_{\tilde{A}_1^*}(x)), ..., \max(\tilde{\mu}_{\tilde{A}_m^k}(x), \tilde{\mu}_{\tilde{A}_m^*}(x)))],
\end{aligned}
\tag{11}
$$

where $\sqcap$ is the meet operation. It is clear for the Eq. 11, $\tilde{\alpha} = [0,0]$ if the given input does not overlap with any rule antecedent.

Step 2: Determine the intermediate results from individual rule based on the given input O by:

$$
\begin{aligned}
\tilde{c}^k =& \tilde{p}_0^k + \tilde{p}_1^k x_1^k + \cdots + \tilde{p}_m^k x_m^k \\
=& [\underline{\tilde{p}_0^k} + \underline{\tilde{p}_1^k} x_1 + \cdots + \underline{\tilde{p}_m^k} x_m, \overline{\tilde{p}_0^k} + \overline{\tilde{p}_1^k} x_1 + \cdots + \overline{\tilde{p}_m^k} x_m],
\end{aligned}
\tag{12}
$$

where $\tilde{c}^k$ is a crisp interval that indicates the intermediate result led by rule R_k. $\underline{\tilde{p}_j^i}$ and $\overline{\tilde{p}_j^i}, (j \in \{0, 1, \cdots, k\})$, denote the minimum and maximum values of crisp interval $\tilde{p}_j^i$, respectively.

Step 3: Generate the final output $\tilde{c}$ by:

$$
\begin{aligned}
\tilde{c} =& [\underline{\tilde{c}}, \overline{\tilde{c}}] \\
=& \int_{\tilde{c}^1 \in [\underline{\tilde{c}^1}, \overline{\tilde{c}^1}]} \cdots \int_{\tilde{c}^n \in [\underline{\tilde{c}^n}, \overline{\tilde{c}^n}]} \int_{\tilde{\alpha}^1 \in [\underline{\tilde{\alpha}^1}, \overline{\tilde{\alpha}^1}]} \cdots \int_{\tilde{\alpha}^n \in [\underline{\tilde{\alpha}^n}, \overline{\tilde{\alpha}^n}]} 1 \Big/ \frac{\sum_{i=1}^n \tilde{\alpha}^i \cdot \tilde{c}^i}{\sum_{i=1}^n \tilde{\alpha}^i}.
\end{aligned}
\tag{13}
$$

This equation can be practically implemented by computing the two extreme values of the crisp interval, minimum $\underline{\tilde{c}}$ and maximum $\overline{\tilde{c}}$, separately:

$$
\left[\underline{\tilde{c}} = \frac{\sum_{i=1}^L \overline{\tilde{\alpha}^i} \underline{\tilde{c}^i} + \sum_{j=L+1}^n \underline{\tilde{\alpha}^i} \tilde{c}^i}{\sum_{i=1}^L \overline{\alpha}_i + \sum_{j=L+1}^n \underline{\alpha}_j}, \; \overline{\tilde{c}} = \frac{\sum_{i=1}^R \overline{\tilde{\alpha}^i} \tilde{c}^i + \sum_{j=R+1}^n \underline{\tilde{\alpha}^i} \overline{\tilde{c}^i}}{\sum_{i=1}^R \overline{\alpha}_i + \sum_{j=R+1}^n \underline{\alpha}_j} \right],
\tag{14}
$$

where L and R are the *switch points* that used to make sure $\underline{\tilde{c}}$ is minimized and $\overline{\tilde{c}}$ is maximized, which can be obtained by an iterative procedure. A number of implementations on such problem have been proposed in the literature and widely used in the real world, such as the Karnik-Mendel (KM) algorithms, enhanced Karnik-Mendel algorithms (EKMA), an iterative algorithm with stop condition (ISAC), and enhanced ISAC [24]. In particular, the Karnik-Mendel (KM) algorithm is adapted in this work due to its efficiency, and the details of this approach is omitted here as this is beyond the focus of this paper.

Once the output interval or special IT2 fuzzy set is generated, type reduction or defuzzification needs to be applied. This can be readily implemented by applying a simple average operation:

$$c = \frac{\tilde{c} + \bar{\tilde{c}}}{2}. \tag{15}$$

The same as the convention type-1 TSK fuzzy inference model, the convention IT2 TSK fuzzy inference approach is only able to work with dense rule bases; otherwise, no rule can be fired and consequently, no result can be generated.

3.4 Interval Type-2 TSK+ Fuzzy Model

In order to address the requirement of a dense rule base, the conventional IT2 TSK fuzzy inference approach has also been extended to IT2 TSK+ approach to work with the sparse rule base [25]. The working procedure of this extension follows the processes introduced in Sect. 3.2, which uses Eq. 8 to obtain the firing strength of each rule instead of the overlapped matching degree. As a result, Eq. 11 can be rewrite as:

$$\begin{aligned}
\tilde{\alpha}_k &= [\underline{\tilde{\alpha}_k}, \overline{\tilde{\alpha}_k}] = \sqcap_{j=1}^{m} \tilde{\mu}(\tilde{A}_j^k, \tilde{A}_j^*) \\
&= [\mu(\underline{\tilde{A}_1^k}, \underline{\tilde{A}_1^*}) \wedge \cdots \wedge \mu(\underline{\tilde{A}_m^k}, \underline{\tilde{A}_m^*}), \mu(\overline{\tilde{A}_1^k}, \overline{\tilde{A}_1^*}) \wedge \cdots \wedge \mu(\overline{\tilde{A}_m^k}, \overline{\tilde{A}_m^*})].
\end{aligned} \tag{16}$$

From here, the final crisp output for the given input can be calculated using the same steps as detailed in Sect. 3.3.

4 Experimentation

A well-known cart centering problem, which has been considered by a conventional IT2 TSK fuzzy model with a dense rule base in [26], is re-considered in this section for evaluation and comparison purpose.

4.1 Cart Centering Control Problem

A cart can only move along a line on a plane, which assumes the plane is frictionless, and the goal of this control problem is to drive and keep the cart to the central position of this line from a given initial position, as illustrated in Fig. 2. The inputs of the controller for this problem are the current position coordinates of cart x and the current velocity of cart v, and the output of this fuzzy model is force F that should be applied on the cart. In [26], the domain of the cart position x was restricted from -0.75 m to 0.75 m; the range of cart velocity v was restricted from -0.75 m/s to 0.75 m/s; the output force F was defined between -0.18 m/s and 0.18 m/s; and the sampling time used was t $=0.1$ s. This set of parameters and constraints were also utilised in this experiment, reported herein.

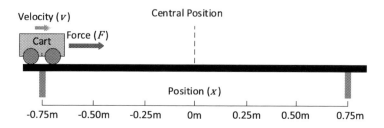

Fig. 2. The cart centering problem

4.2 Type-1 TSK Fuzzy Control

The work in [25] designed and demonstrated a 0-order IT2 TSK fuzzy model to solve this control problem, which used five linguistic values, denoted as IT2 fuzzy sets, to cover every domain of input variables x and v. In order to enable a direct comparison, the design reported in the work of [25] was adopted in this experimentation. Therefore, five type-1 fuzzy sets were created to cover the entire input domain x and v, which are negative large (NL), negative small (NS), zero (0), positive small (PS), and positive large (PL), as illustrated in Fig. 3. And five crisp values were used as the output, which are also represented as NL, NS, 0, PS and PL, which are shown in Table 1. Consequently, a dense rule base, which contains in total 25 0-order TSK fuzzy rules were generated, as listed in Table 2.

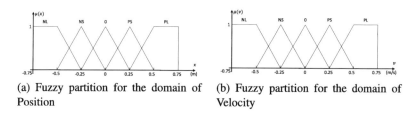

(a) Fuzzy partition for the domain of Position

(b) Fuzzy partition for the domain of Velocity

Fig. 3. Fuzzy partition on input domain

Table 1. Output values

Output Label	NL	NS	0	PS	PL
Value	−0.16	−0.08	0	0.08	0.16

Table 2. Generated dense rule base for Type-1 TSK fuzzy model with 25 rules

Velocity (v)	Position (x)				
	NL	NS	0	PS	PL
NL	PL	PL	PL	PS	0
NS	PL	PL	PS	0	NS
0	PL	PS	0	NS	NL
PS	PS	0	NS	NL	NL
PL	0	NS	NL	NL	NL

Table 3. Sparse rule base for Type-1 TSK fuzzy model with 4 rules

Velocity (v)	Position (x)	
	NL	PL
NL	PL	0
PL	0	NL

In order to evaluate the TSK+ fuzzy inference approach working with a sparse rule base, three fuzzy sets from each domain were artificiality removed from the above example to demonstrate an extremely sparse rule base, as shown in Fig. 4. As a results, only two boundary fuzzy sets of each input domain were kept, which is composed to four rules, as listed in Table 3.

Given an initial state of the cart, $x = 0.5$ m and $v = 0.5$ m/s, the conventional TSK and TSK+ fuzzy inference approaches were both employed on the dense and sparse rule base, if applicable, for system performance comparison. The results are shown in the first and second column of Fig. 6.

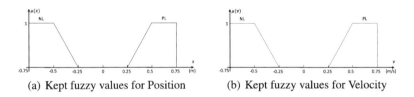

(a) Kept fuzzy values for Position   (b) Kept fuzzy values for Velocity

Fig. 4. Fuzzy partition on input domain

In particular, Fig. 5(a) and (b) demonstrated the results that produced by conventional TSK with dense rule base; the results generated by TSK+ with dense rule base are shown in Fig. 5(e) and (f); and Fig. 5(i) and (j) illustrated the results that obtained by TSK+ with only 4 boundary rules.

4.3   Type-2 Fuzzy Control

In this experiment, the IT2 TSK fuzzy model was implemented. The fuzzy rule bases detailed in Sect. 4.2 were used in this section, but all fuzzy sets were changed to IT2 fuzzy sets instead of the type-1 fuzzy sets, which are expressed in Fig. 5. In addition, instead of using crisp values, five crisp interval values were employed as the output as listed in Table 4. From here, this cart centring problem can be solved by an IT2 0-order TSK fuzzy model with a dense rule base that composed of 25 rules, as shown in Table 2. Again, three fuzzy variables from each input domain were manually removed to simulate the situation of lack of information for comparison purpose. In the same the situation as described in Sect. 4.2, only two boundary fuzzy sets, NL and PL, were kept on each input domain to construct an extremely sparse IT2 0-order rule base, which only contains 4 rules, as shown in Table 3.

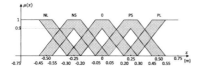
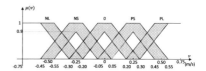

(a) IT2 membership for the domain of Position   (b) IT2 membership function for the domain of Velocity

Fig. 5. Input membership functions

Table 4. Fuzzy partition of output domain

Output label	Value	Linguistic value
NL	$[-0.18\ -0.14]$	NL
NS	$[-0.10\ -0.06]$	NS
0	$[-0.02\ 0.02]$	0
PS	$[0.06\ 0.10]$	PS
PL	$[0.14\ 0.18]$	PL

The simulated results of employing the conventional IT2 TSK and IT2 TSK+ approaches over the dense and sparse rule base, if applicable, for a given initial state of the cart, $x = 0.5$ m and $v = 0.5$ m/s, are illustrated in the third and fourth column of Fig. 6.

The experimental results show that all four approaches (conventional TSK, TSK+, conventional IT2 TSK and IT2 TSK+) performed well in controlling the cart to the target position from the given initial state. From Fig. 5(g), it is clear that the IT2 TSK+ with the dense rule base took less time (around 2.5 s) to drive the cart to the target state from the initial state with relatively smooth control, compared with the performances produced by other three approaches (around 3 s), based on the dense rule base. In term of controlling over the sparse rule base, although the TSK+ and IT2 TSK+ approaches took much longer to drive the cart to the goal position, around 35 s and 17 s, respectively; however, considering only 4 boundary rules were applied instead of a dense rule base with 25 rules, such performance indicates the power of both TSK+ and IT2 TSK+ approaches in reasoning from incomplete knowledge and system complexity reduction.

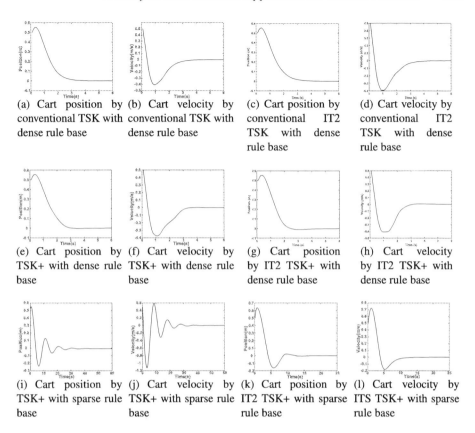

(a) Cart position by conventional TSK with dense rule base

(b) Cart velocity by conventional TSK with dense rule base

(c) Cart position by conventional IT2 TSK with dense rule base

(d) Cart velocity by conventional IT2 TSK with dense rule base

(e) Cart position by TSK+ with dense rule base

(f) Cart velocity by TSK+ with dense rule base

(g) Cart position by IT2 TSK+ with dense rule base

(h) Cart velocity by IT2 TSK+ with dense rule base

(i) Cart position by TSK+ with sparse rule base

(j) Cart velocity by TSK+ with sparse rule base

(k) Cart position by IT2 TSK+ with sparse rule base

(l) Cart velocity by ITS TSK+ with sparse rule base

Fig. 6. Performance comparison

5   Conclusion

This paper systematically reviews four different types of TSK-based fuzzy inference approaches, including the convention TSK, TSK+, IT2 TSK and IT2 TSK+, in terms of their effectiveness for control problems. Compared with the conventional TSK and IT2 TSK approaches, which are only workable with dense rule bases, the TSK+ and IT2 TSK+ are applicable to both dense and sparse rule bases significantly increasing the applicability of the TSK-based fuzzy inference systems. The experimental results demonstrate the power of the TSK+ and IT2 TSK+ in mobile cart control.

For future works, more real-world applications, such as truck backer-upper control [5], navigation of autonomous mobile robot control [27], powered exoskeleton control [28], and robotic control [29], will be considered for more thorough evaluation of the approach. And then, it is worthwhile to compare the performance between the conventional Mamdani inference approach and the Mamdani-based fuzzy interpolation approaches. In addition, it is interesting to investigate how the sparse rule base generation approaches, such as [30,31], can be applied to help generate sparse rule bases, and thus more compact TSK fuzzy models.

References

1. Mamdani, E.H.: Application of fuzzy logic to approximate reasoning using linguistic synthesis. IEEE Trans. Comput. **C–26**(12), 1182–1191 (1977)
2. Takagi, T., Sugeno, M.: Fuzzy identification of systems and its applications to modeling and control. IEEE Trans. Syst. Man Cybern. SMC **15**(1), 116–132 (1985)
3. Li, J., Yang, L., Qu, Y., Sexton, G.: An extended Takagi-Sugeno-Kang inference system (TSK+) with fuzzy interpolation and its rule base generation. Soft Comput. **22**(10), 3155–3170 (2018)
4. Kóczy, L.T., Hirota, K.: Approximate reasoning by linear rule interpolation and general approximation. Int. J. Approximate Reasoning **9**(3), 197–225 (1993)
5. Huang, Z., Shen, Q.: Fuzzy interpolation and extrapolation: a practical approach. IEEE Trans. Fuzzy Syst. **16**(1), 13–28 (2008)
6. Yang, L., Chao, F., Shen, Q.: Generalized adaptive fuzzy rule interpolation. IEEE Trans. Fuzzy Syst. **25**(4), 839–853 (2017)
7. Yang, L., Shen, Q.: Adaptive fuzzy interpolation. IEEE Trans. Fuzzy Syst. **19**(6), 1107–1126 (2011)
8. Yang, L., Shen, Q.: Closed form fuzzy interpolation. Fuzzy Sets Syst. **225**, 1–22 (2013). Theme: Fuzzy Systems
9. Naik, N., Diao, R., Shen, Q.: Dynamic fuzzy rule interpolation and its application to intrusion detection. IEEE Trans. Fuzzy Syst. **PP**(99), 1 (2017)
10. Chen, S.M., Zou, X.Y., Barman, D.: Adaptive weighted fuzzy rule interpolation based on ranking values and similarity measures of rough-fuzzy sets. Inf. Sci. **488**, 93–110 (2019)
11. Chen, S.M., Adam, S.I.: Adaptive fuzzy interpolation based on ranking values of interval type-2 polygonal fuzzy sets. Inf. Sci. **435**, 320–333 (2018)
12. Li, J., Qu, Y., Shum, H.P.H., Yang, L.: TSK inference with sparse rule bases. In: Angelov, P., Gegov, A., Jayne, C., Shen, Q. (eds.) Advances in Computational Intelligence Systems. AISC, vol. 513, pp. 107–123. Springer, Cham (2017). https://doi.org/10.1007/978-3-319-46562-3_8
13. Yasunobu, S., Miyamoto, S., Ihara, H.: Fuzzy control for automatic train operation system. IFAC Proc. Volumes **16**(4), 33–39 (1983). 4th IFAC/IFIP/IFORS Conference on Control in Transportation Systems, Baden-Baden, FRG, 20–22 April 1983
14. Li, J., Yang, L., Shum, H.P.H., Sexton, G., Tan, Y.: Intelligent home heating controller using fuzzy rule interpolation. In: 15th UK Workshop on Computational Intelligence, UKCI (2015)
15. Yang, L., Li, J., Hackney, P., Chao, F., Flanagan, M.: Manual task completion time estimation for job shop scheduling using a fuzzy inference system. In: 10th IEEE International Conference on Cyber, Physical and Social Computing (2017)
16. Yang, L., Li, J., Chao, F., Hackney, P., Flanagan, M.: Job shop planning and scheduling for manufacturers with manual operations. Expert Syst. (2018)
17. Elisa, N., Li, J., Zuo, Z., Yang, L.: Dendritic cell algorithm with fuzzy inference system for input signal generation. In: Lotfi, A., Bouchachia, H., Gegov, A., Langensiepen, C., McGinnity, M. (eds.) UKCI 2018. AISC, vol. 840, pp. 203–214. Springer, Cham (2019). https://doi.org/10.1007/978-3-319-97982-3_17

18. Zuo, Z., Li, J., Anderson, P., Yang, L., Naik, N.: Grooming detection using fuzzy-rough feature selection and text classification. In: 2018 IEEE International Conference on Fuzzy Systems (FUZZ-IEEE), pp. 1–8. IEEE (2018)
19. Zuo, Z., Li, J., Wei, B., Yang, L., Chao, F., Naik, N.: Adaptive activation function generation for artificial neural networks through fuzzy inference with application in grooming text categorisation. In: 2019 IEEE International Conference on Fuzzy Systems (FUZZ-IEEE) (2019)
20. Fu, X., Zeng, X.J., Wang, D., Xu, D., Yang, L.: Fuzzy system approaches to negotiation pricing decision support. J. Intell. Fuzzy Syst. **29**(2), 685–699 (2015)
21. Li, J., Yang, L., Fu, X., Chao, F., Qu, Y.: Dynamic QoS solution for enterprise networks using TSK fuzzy interpolation. In: 2017 IEEE International Conference on Fuzzy Systems (FUZZ-IEEE), pp. 1–6. IEEE (2017)
22. Gürsel, G.: Healthcare, uncertainty, and fuzzy logic. Digital Med. **2**(3), 101 (2016)
23. Zadeh, L.A.: Fuzzy sets. Inf. Control **8**(3), 338–353 (1965)
24. Wu, D., Nie, M.: Comparison and practical implementation of type-reduction algorithms for type-2 fuzzy sets and systems. In: 2011 IEEE International Conference on Fuzzy Systems (FUZZ-IEEE 2011), pp. 2131–2138, June 2011
25. Li, J., Yang, L., Fu, X., Chao, F., Qu, Y.: Interval type-2 TSK+ fuzzy inference system. In: 2018 IEEE International Conference on Fuzzy Systems (FUZZ-IEEE), pp. 1–8. IEEE (2018)
26. Enyinna, N., Karimoddini, A., Opoku, D., Homaifar, A., Arnold, S.: Developing an interval type-2 TSK fuzzy logic controller. In: 2015 Annual Conference of the North American Fuzzy Information Processing Society and the 5th World Conference on Soft Computing (2015)
27. Baklouti, N., John, R., Alimi, A.M.: Interval type-2 fuzzy logic control of mobile robots. J. Intell. Learn. Syst. Appl. **4**(04), 291 (2012)
28. Yin, K., Xiang, K., Pang, M., Chen, J., Anderson, P., Yang, L.: Personalised control of robotic ankle exoskeleton through experience-based adaptive fuzzy inference. IEEE Access (2019). https://doi.org/10.1109/ACCESS.2019.2920134
29. Chao, F., Zhou, D., Lin, C.M., Yang, L., Zhou, C., Shang, C.: Type-2 fuzzy hybrid controller network for robotic systems. IEEE Trans. Cybern. (2019). https://doi.org/10.1109/TCYB.2019.2919128
30. Li, J., Shum, H.P.H., Fu, X., Sexton, G., Yang, L.: Experience-based rule base generation and adaptation for fuzzy interpolation. In: 2016 IEEE International Conference on Fuzzy Systems (FUZZ-IEEE), pp. 102–109. IEEE (2016)
31. Tan, Y., Li, J., Wonders, M., Chao, F., Shum, H.P.H., Yang, L.: Towards sparse rule base generation for fuzzy rule interpolation. In: 2016 IEEE International Conference on Fuzzy Systems (FUZZ-IEEE), pp. 110–117. IEEE (2016)

Development of Ultra-Thin-Film, Flexible Sensors, and Tactile Sensation

FES Proportional Tuning Based on sEMG

Yu Zhou[1(✉)], Jia Zeng[1], Kairu Li[2], and Honghai Liu[1,2]

[1] State Key Laboratory of Mechanical System and Vibration,
Shanghai Jiao Tong University, Shanghai, China
{hnllyu,jia.zeng,honghai.liu}@sjtu.edu.cn
[2] Group of Intelligent System and Biomedical Robotics, School of Computing,
University of Portsmouth, Portsmouth, UK
{kairu.li,honghai.liu}@port.ac.uk
http://bbl.sjtu.edu.cn/

Abstract. It is evident that inappropriate functional electrical stimulation (FES) intensity is easy to trigger muscle fatigue and discomfortableness. This study proposes a FES tuning solution based on surface electromyography (sEMG), which is to form the relationship from sEMG to FES pulse width through the force. Six healthy subjects were invited to verify the proposed method based on the grip experiment. The feasibility of the estimated FES pulse width was evaluated respect to the correlation index (R) between the voluntary grip force and the FES-induced grip force. The experimental results indicated that the estimated pulse width could well induce the grip force that is similar to the voluntary force ($R > 0.9$), demonstrating the effectiveness of the proposed method and confirming the potential for improving the experience of FES in clinical settings.

Keywords: Functional electrical stimulation (FES) ·
Surface electromyography (sEMG) · Signal processing

1 Introduction

FES has been an effective neuroprosthetic technique to restore lost motor function for spinal cord injury or stroke patients through delivering electrical stimulation current to their paralyzed muscles, since first used for foot drop rehabilitation by Liberson in 1960 [1,2]. However, there still lack of clear relationship between the paralyzed muscle physiological status and FES intensity, thus FES in clinical settings is usually passive and empirically tuned by the therapist. During FES-induced muscle contraction, the motor units are recruited in a synchronous and constant order manner, which consume more energy compared with voluntary muscle contraction [3]. So the empirically predefined stimulation patterns are easier to cause excessive stimulation that will speed up muscle fatigue, especially for the SCI patients whose fatigue resistance decreases in the weak muscle [4]. Besides, the passive FES excludes the active participation of the subjects and decreases the neuromuscular activity as well as energy consumption [5,6].

© Springer Nature Switzerland AG 2019
H. Yu et al. (Eds.): ICIRA 2019, LNAI 11743, pp. 211–220, 2019.
https://doi.org/10.1007/978-3-030-27538-9_18

Thus, the relationship between the muscle status and FES intensity should be investigated to drive the closed-loop FES research forward and further improve the rehabilitation efficiency.

The muscle status can be reflected by muscle force, no matter for FES-induced muscle contraction or voluntary muscle contraction, thus we can use force as the bridge to combine muscle status and FES parameters. That is, if the relationship between muscle status and muscle force, muscle force and FES intensity are detected, then the relationship between muscle status and FES intensity can be obtained. The sEMG signal, demonstrating the physiological process of muscle contraction, is one of the dominant biological signals widely applied in human-machine interface [7]. Many studies focused on estimating muscle force information based on sEMG processing. For example, the nonnegative matrix factorization method was developed to estimate neural control information from sEMG to predict wrist force [8], the finger force with isometric contraction (all the fingers were held straight and in line with the metacarpals) was estimated based on the sEMG signals captured from forearm [9], and the FES-induced joint torque was estimated based on the evoked sEMG [10]. Thus, sEMG was applied in this study to recognise muscle status.

This study proposes an attempt of modeling the relationship between muscle status and FES parameters based on the grip movement. The Gaussian mixture regression (GMR) combined with polynomial fitting was applied as the solution of sEMG-to-FES modeling. The GMR is developed to map the sEMG-to-force relationship while the polynomial fitting represents the force-to-FES model. The findings in this study would pave the way for potential active closed-loop neuroprosthesis applications.

2 Platform Construction

The proposed method is a kind of muscle to muscle interface, as shown in Fig. 1. There are two main parts included in the frame, namely the sEMG/FES integration hardware and the FES parameter estimation algorithm. The customized integration hardware was designed in our previous study [11], which is used to acquire sEMG signals from the reference muscle and output the stimulation current to the target muscle. The raw sEMG signals are sampled at 1kHz and band-passe filtered (20–500 Hz) to remove the movement artifacts. After that, the digitized sEMG signals are transmitted to the host computer through bluetooth by the integration hardware for FES parameter estimation. The GMR is combined with polynomial fitting to form the FES parameters estimation algorithm. GMR is a probabilistic regression method which can be applied based on the parameters of a Gaussian mixture model (GMM) [12]. The pre-trained GMR model estimate muscle force F_p based on the sEMG, then the estimated force is used as the input of the pre-trained polynomial fitting model to predict the FES parameters as defined by Eqs. 1 and 2. Finally, the estimated FES current is applied to the target muscle through the integration hardware to reproduce the similar muscle force as the reference muscle.

$$f(x) = p_1 x^n + p_2 x^{n-1} + \ldots + p_n x + p_{n+1} \qquad (1)$$

$$\widehat{P} = f(F_p), \widehat{P} \in [H_l, H_u] \qquad (2)$$

where f is the mathematical model for n degrees polynomial fitting of FES-induced muscle force and FES parameters, and $\widehat{P}$ is the estimated FES parameters. The lower threshold H_l was defined as the stimulation intensity that induced the muscle contraction slightly, while the upper threshold H_u was the stimulation intensity that made the subjects feel uncomfortable.

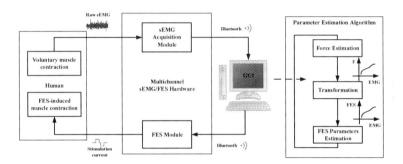

Fig. 1. The framework of the proposed sEMG to FES interface. The solid arrows represent the data/signal flow.

3 Experimental Protocols

3.1 Subjects

Six healthy subjects (aged 23 to 28; referenced as S1–S6) were invited to participate in the experiment. None of them had any history of neuromuscular disorder and each gave written informed consent prior to the experiment. All the experiment procedures in this study were approved by the SJTU School Ethics Committee.

3.2 Preliminary Experiment

The grip force and the FES pulse width were selected in this study to verify the proposed method. The grip dynamometer (Biometrics Ltd, UK) was used to measure the grip force. And the Flexor Digitorum Superficialis muscle (FDS) was selected as the target muscle for sEMG acquisition and FES stimulation. The preliminary experiment setup is shown in Fig. 2(a). The purpose of the preliminary experiment was to find the upper and lower stimulation threshold in Eq. 2 for each subject in terms of the pulse width. The results are shown in Table 1. The pulse width of the stimulation current was gradually increased from the lower threshold to the upper threshold with a constant increment and

Table 1. The FES intensity range for different subjects.

Subject	Upper threshold Pulse width (μs)	Lower threshold Pulse width (μs)
S1	390	10
S2	250	100
S3	250	50
S4	240	20
S5	290	10
S6	250	10

applied to the FDS muscle of each subject with the grip force measured. During the preliminary experiment, the stimulation frequency was fixed as 50 Hz and the current amplitude was fixed as the medium value of the lower and upper amplitude threshold of the subject when the pulse width was $100\,\mu s$.

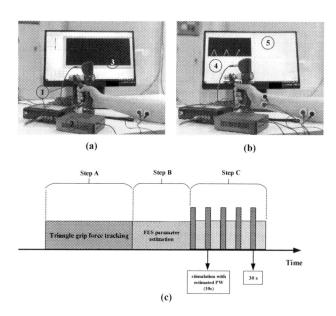

Fig. 2. (a) The preliminary experiment; (b) The formal experiment; (c) The experimental procedures; 1. The grip dynamometer; 2. The multichannel sEMG/FES hardware; 3. The grip force induced by FES; 4. The triangular grip force; 5. The recorded sEMG signals.

3.3   Formal Experiment

The formal experiment setup is shown in Fig. 2(b) and the experimental flow is shown in Fig. 2(c). The two differential sEMG electrodes were placed on the FDS muscle belly in the right hand, parallel to the direction of muscle fiber, with the reference electrodes placed on the end of the ulna. For the step A, the subjects sat comfortably in front of a computer screen and lay his right elbow on the desk. The subjects performed right hand grip and control the grip force to track the triangular wave force line displayed in the computer screen for 60 s, with sEMG from FDS and grip force recorded simultaneously. The recorded 60 s sEMG data and force data were used to estimate the FES pulse width by the proposed method during step B. After the pulse width estimation, the current with the estimated pulse width was applied to FDS muscle belly through the pair of sEMG electrodes (the frequency and the amplitude of the current were fixed as the values in the preliminary experiment) in step C. The stimulation was repeated for five times and each stimulation lasted for 10 s with a 30 s rest followed to avoid muscle fatigue. The FES-induced grip force of the right hand was recorded during the stimulation period of each subject.

4   Data Processing and Evaluation Metrics

The sEMG signals were segmented by the sliding data window with a length of 300 data points and the step size was set as 50 data points. The time domain (TD) features [13], root-mean-square values (RMS) [14] and sixth order autoregressive coefficient (AR6) [15] were calculated from each sliding data window to make up the feature vector. The feature vector was combined with the corresponding grip force to form the data sets for GMR model training and grip force estimation. The offline force estimation accuracy was determined using a five-fold estimation cross-validation.

(1) *Optimal polynomial fitting*: The optimal polynomial fitting model f in Eq. 1 that representing the relationship between the FES-induced grip force and FES current pulse width was investigated. The polynomial fitting was compared from one degree to three degrees respect to the coefficient of determination (R^2). The one-way ANOVA was applied to investigate the fitting performance between different degrees. The level of statistical significance was set at $p < 0.05$ for all statistics.

(2) *Grip force estimation accuracy*: Since the grip force is used as a bridge to link sEMG and FES parameter, the force estimation accuracy is related to FES current pulse width estimation. The coefficient of determination (R^2) and the normalized root-mean-square error (NRMSE) between the estimated values and the real values are used to quantize the estimation accuracy. And a one-way ANOVA was applied to compare the effects of different feature sets on the estimation accuracy.

(3) *Correlation between voluntary and FES − induced force*: This index is used to verify the effectiveness of the estimated FES current in retrieving

force with FES-induced muscle contraction. The FES pulse width is estimated based on the sEMG signals that respect to voluntary force in step A
in formal experiment. The normalized FES-induced force is compared with
the normalized original voluntary force in terms of the Pearsons correlation
coefficient (R).

5   Results

5.1   Optimal Polynomial Fitting

The recorded force induced by the stimulation current with different pulse width
was calculated as the average values of force during stimulation as shown in
Fig. 3(a), then the different pulse width was polynomial fitted with the corresponding FES induced force as shown in Fig. 3(b). The average goodness of fit
across all the subjects are shown in Fig. 3(c) based on the data captured in the
preliminary experiment, and the three degrees polynomial fitting shows the best
performance $(R^2 = 0.91 \pm 0.05)$. No significant differences appealed between the
effects of different fitting degrees $(p > 0.05)$. The two degrees polynomial fitting was selected to set up the mathematical model f for the rest of this study,
considering the trade-off between computing complexity and goodness of fit.

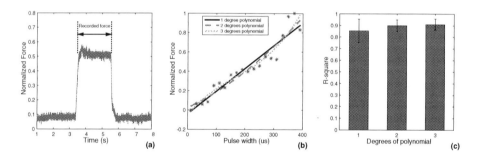

Fig. 3. (a) Demonstration for grip force calculation during FES. (b) Demonstration for
polynomial fitting process. (c) The average results for different degrees of polynomial
fitting performance across all the subjects.

5.2   Grip Force Estimation Accuracy

The grip force estimation results are shown in Fig. 4. The average results across
all the subjects revealed that GMR showed excellent performance for decoding
grip force based on the RMS feature sets $(R = 0.950 \pm 0.023, NRMSE = 6.15\% \pm 1.31\%)$ and TD feature sets $(R = 0.954 \pm 0.018, NRMSE = 5.96\% \pm 1.09\%)$. The ANOVA analysis indicated that no significant differences were found
between the performance of RMS and TD feature sets $(p = 0.954$ for R^2 and
$p = 0.919$ for $NRMSE)$. Significant differences appeared between the RMS
and AR6 feature sets $(p = 0.004$ for R^2 and $p < 0.001$ for $NRMSE)$ as well

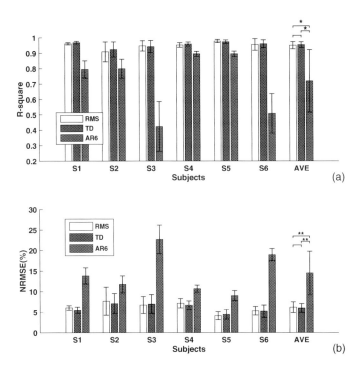

Fig. 4. The comparison of force estimation accuracy across the six subjects based on different sEMG features: (a) R^2; (b) NRMSE. Error bars represent the standard deviation. One asterisk "$*$" denotes $p < 0.05$ and two asterisks "$**$" denote $p < 0.001$.

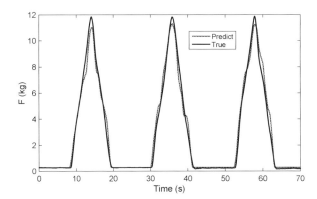

Fig. 5. Typical demonstrations of comparisons between true and predicted grip force for subject S1.

as between the TD feature sets and AR6 feature sets ($p = 0.004$ for R^2 and $p < 0.001$ for $NRMSE$). Thus, the results through the rest of this study were based on the RMS feature sets considering the computing consumption. Figure 5 shows an example of the estimation quality vividly based on the data sets of S1.

5.3   Correlation Between Voluntary and FES-induced Force

Table 2 shows the results of the similarity between the voluntary force and corresponding FES-induced force across all the subjects. The FES-induced force is highly correlated with the voluntary force ($R > 0.9$) except for S2 and the mean value across all subjects is $R = 0.93 \pm 0.08$, demonstrating that the FES estimated based on voluntary sEMG is effective to reproduce the grip force as similar as the voluntary force. Figure 6 shows an example of the differences between the estimated-FES-induced grip force and voluntary grip force.

Table 2. The Results for correlation between voluntary and FES-induced force.

Subject	S1	S2	S3	S4	S5	S6	**MEAN $\pm$ Sd**
R	0.96	0.79	0.98	0.97	0.97	0.90	**0.93 $\pm$ 0.08**

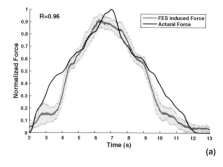 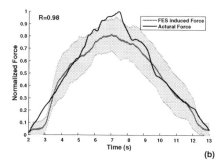

Fig. 6. Demonstrations of comparisons between voluntary force and FES-induced force based on the experimental data of S1 and S3: (a) S1, (b) S3. The light red region represents the standard deviation of the five repetitions of FES-induced grip force. The red solid line represents the average values of the five repetitions of FES-induced grip force. (Color figure online)

6   Discussion and Conclusion

This study investigated the sEMG-to-FES sequential mapping relationship based on the proposed method, which combined GMR with polynomial fitting. GMR is used to model the sEMG-to-force relationship while polynomial fitting is applied to model the force-to-FES relationship. The experimental results verified the feasibility of the proposed muscle-to-muscle interface, which is potential for the force training applications based on the closed-loop FES.

The relationship between FES current pulse width and the correlated FES-induced grip force was investigated through polynomial fitting. As shown in Fig. 3(c), the three degrees polynomial fitting shows the best performance compared with the other two kinds of fitting, indicating the non-linear relationship between the FES pulse width and FES-induced grip force. The grip force is applied as the bridge for modeling the sEMG-to-FES relationship. Thus the force estimation accuracy is vital for the sEMG-to-FES estimation. The GMR model was developed to predict grip force based on the voluntary sEMG signals captured form FDS muscle. As shown in Figs. 4 and 5, the performance of GMR was regard as excellent on proportional force prediction, based on RMS feature and TD feature. Thus, the sEMG-to-force relationship and the force-to-FES relationship were setup to ensure the accuracy of sEMG-to-FES estimation.

The FES pulse width was estimated by the proposed method based on the voluntary sEMG, then the voluntary grip force corresponding to the aforementioned voluntary sEMG was compared with the grip force induced by the FES current with estimated pulse width. The results in Table 2 and Fig. 6 indicated the high similarity of the force pattern between the voluntary muscle contraction and estimated-FES-induced muscle contraction. Thus, it revealed that the proposed method could well stimulate the target muscle to generate the desired grip force according to the voluntary grip movement intention.

As a muscle-to-muscle interface, the proposed method could be used for the closed-loop FES applications. The FES parameters can be estimated based on the target muscle contraction and be applied to the same muscle to help strengthen the muscle force. Besides, the FES intensity is adapt to muscle status, which could avoid excessive stimulation and slow down the muscle fatigue compared with the open loop FES. To drive the method to be practical for clinical applications, the random grip force will be involved in the near future. Besides, more efforts will be devoted to drive the proposed method to stroke rehabilitation, that is, the FES parameters will be estimated based on the sEMG and force captured from the reference unaffected hand muscle isometric contraction and be evaluated on the contralateral muscle in the affected hand to see wether the estimated-FES-induced contralateral muscle force is similar to the reference muscle.

Acknowledgments. This work is supported by the National Natural Science Foundation of China (No. 51575338, 51575407, 51475427,61733011) and the Fundamental Research Funds for the Central Universities (17JCYB03).

References

1. Lynch, C.L., Popovic, M.R.: Functional electrical stimulation. IEEE Control Syst. **28**(2), 40–50 (2008)
2. Liberson, W.: Functional electrotherapy: stimulation of the peroneal nerve synchronized with the swing phase of the gait of hemiplegic patients. Arch. Phys. Med. Rehabil. **42**, 101 (1961)
3. Binder-Macleod, S.A., Snyder-Mackler, L.: Muscle fatigue: clinical implications for fatigue assessment and neuromuscular electrical stimulation. Phys. Ther. **73**(12), 902–910 (1993)
4. Pelletier, C., Hicks, A.: Muscle fatigue characteristics in paralyzed muscle after spinal cord injury. Spinal Cord **49**(1), 125 (2011)

5. Edgerton, V.R., Roy, R.R.: Robotic training and spinal cord plasticity. Brain Res. Bull. **78**(1), 4–12 (2009)
6. Lotze, M., Braun, C., Birbaumer, N., Anders, S., Cohen, L.G.: Motor learning elicited by voluntary drive. Brain **126**(4), 866–872 (2003)
7. Zhou, Y., Liu, J., Zeng, J., Li, K., Liu, H.: Bio-signal based elbow angle and torque simultaneous prediction during isokinetic contraction. Sci. China Technol. Sci. **62**(1), 21–30 (2019)
8. Jiang, N., Englehart, K.B., Parker, P.A.: Extracting simultaneous and proportional neural control information for multiple-DOF prostheses from the surface electromyographic signal. IEEE Trans. Biomed. Eng. **56**(4), 1070–1080 (2009)
9. Castellini, C., Koiva, R.: Using surface electromyography to predict single finger forces. In: 2012 4th IEEE RAS & EMBS International Conference on Biomedical Robotics and Biomechatronics (BioRob), pp. 1266–1272. IEEE (2012)
10. Li, Z., Guiraud, D., Andreu, D., Benoussaad, M., Fattal, C., Hayashibe, M.: Real-time estimation of FES-induced joint torque with evoked EMG. J. Neuroeng. Rehabil. **13**(1), 60 (2016)
11. Zhou, Y., Fang, Y., Gui, K., Li, K., Zhang, D., Liu, H.: semg bias-driven functional electrical stimulation system for upper-limb stroke rehabilitation. IEEE Sens. J. **18**(16), 6812–6821 (2018)
12. Calinon, S., Guenter, F., Billard, A.: On learning, representing, and generalizing a task in a humanoid robot. IEEE Trans. Syst. Man Cybern. Part B (Cybern.) **37**(2), 286–298 (2007)
13. Hudgins, B., Parker, P., Scott, R.N.: A new strategy for multifunction myoelectric control. IEEE Trans. Biomed. Eng. **40**(1), 82–94 (1993)
14. Huang, Y., Englehart, K.B., Hudgins, B., Chan, A.D.: A Gaussian mixture model based classification scheme for myoelectric control of powered upper limb prostheses. IEEE Trans. Biomed. Eng. **52**(11), 1801–1811 (2005)
15. Khezri, M., Jahed, M.: A neuro-fuzzy inference system for semg-based identification of hand motion commands. IEEE Trans. Ind. Electron. **58**(5), 1952–1960 (2011)

Application of Haptic Virtual Fixtures on Hot-Line Work Robot-Assisted Manipulation

Yutao Chen[1], Jing Zhu[1], Min Xu[1], Hao Zhang[2], Xuming Tang[2], and Erbao Dong[1(✉)]

[1] CAS Key Laboratory of Mechanical Behavior and Design of Materials, Department of Precision Machinery and Precision Instrumentation, University of Science and Technology of China, 96 Jinzhai Road, Hefei 230026, Anhui, China
ebdong@ustc.edu.cn
[2] Huainan Power Supply Company, Anhui Electric Power Co., Ltd., 139 Huaishun South Road, Huainan 232007, Anhui, China

Abstract. This paper presents a teleoperation system combines with force feedback. The teleoperation system is mainly composed of the 6-DOF Geomagic Touch haptic device, the simulation environment and the 6-DOF UR5 manipulator. We analyzed the forward kinematics of master and slave manipulators, then we calculated the workspace of the UR5 arms. The slave manipulator is controlled by using incremental displacement and incremental rotation strategies in a space Cartesian coordinate system. Creating virtual fixtures is a way to reduce operator error and guide operator to complete tasks efficiently in teleoperation. So we built the virtual environment in simulation software based on the real environment, used a certain length of angle steel as a dangerous area in live working of distribution network, and a forbidden-region virtual fixture was established to avoid the collision of the manipulator with the steel. We tested the delay and accuracy of the system through experiments. In addition, we verified the feasibility of the designed virtual fixture.

Keywords: Hot line work robot · Teleoperation · Master-slave control · Virtual fixture

1 Introduction

Because of the characteristics of clean, easy to convert, and convenient transportation, electric energy has been widely used in various fields, whether in industrial production or in daily life. With the widespread use of electricity, people have built a huge network of electric power infrastructure to deliver electricity. However, the power infrastructure is aging, how to safely and effectively detect, repair, and replace old components without affecting people using electricity is an important issue.

Live-line maintenance is an effective solution and has become an industry norm. However, the staff is working at a high level when overhauling the distribution network. And long-term work under strong magnetic and strong electric fields will cause

© Springer Nature Switzerland AG 2019
H. Yu et al. (Eds.): ICIRA 2019, LNAI 11743, pp. 221–232, 2019.
https://doi.org/10.1007/978-3-030-27538-9_19

harm to the body. Therefore, as early as the 1980s and 1990s, countries began to study the technology of distribution network live-line working robots. Representatives include Phase1, Phase2, Phase3 developed by the Kyushu Electric Power Co. in Japan [1], and ROBTET developed by the Polytechnic University of Madrid, Spain [2]. Climbing robot for the construction overhead distribution lines at Hydro-Québec [3], DWR-I developed by Shanghai Jiaotong University, China [4]. The distribution network working robot has also evolved from the original master-slave control system to the current control system integrating visual and force feedback. The entire system is also moving from manual operation to semi-automation, even full automation [5].

However, due to the unstructured operation of the distribution network and the complexity of the operation steps, it is difficult to realize the implementation of fully automated operations at this stage. Only a small part of the simple work can be done by the robot itself. The current mainstream operation mode is still the master-slave operating system.

In teleoperation control, the initial type is the master-slave isomorphic robot, usually using the joint space mapping method. This approach is used in the teleoperation of hydraulic and pneumatic hybrid dual-arm robots [6]. It is easy to control the movement of the entire robot. But if the size of the master arm is very different from slave arm, the difference in speed between their end actuators will vary greatly. Not all master-slave teleoperation systems are isomorphic, many scholars have also studied master-slave nonisomorphic robot workspace mapping. The University of Plymouth research team used the Monte Carlo random sampling method to obtain the working space of the master-slave device [7]. They enlarged the workspace of the master device and matched with the slave, in order to maximize the overlap between the two workspaces, implement point-to-point mapping. However, since the working space of the main control hand is enlarged several times, the steering precision is reduced a lot, so it is not suitable for precise operation.

The virtual fixture was proposed by Louis B. Rosenberg of Stanford University in 1993 [8]. The manipulator needs a virtual fixture to guide the operation during master-slave teleoperation, just as a manual drawing of a straight line requires a ruler as a tool. On the one hand, the guiding tool can reduce the psychological burden of the operator, and more importantly, it can draw high-quality straight lines, and the virtual fixture has the same effect. Virtual fixtures can be divided into guidance virtual fixtures and forbidden-region virtual fixtures. A forbidden-region virtual fixture is a method for prohibiting a robot end effector from entering a certain region [9]. Atsushi Nakazawa et al. proposed the generation method for a truncated cone-shape virtual fixture, which is applicable to neurosurgical procedures in deep and narrow spaces within the brain [10].

The key research of this paper is to propose a master-slave control mapping strategy. And the forbidden-region virtual fixture concept is used to assist operator to control the master manipulator and complete the live-line maintenance work.

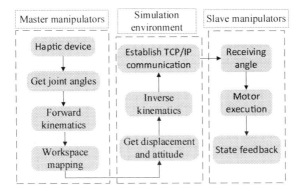

Fig. 1. Connection of the system and flow of information

2 Teleoperation System of Manipulator

The remote master-slave teleoperation system is mainly composed of three parts, namely, the master manipulator, the virtual simulation environment, and the slave manipulator. The master is the Geomagic Touch haptic device, which is used to manipulate the slave arm and apply force feedback to the hands of user, allowing them to feel the touch of the virtual object to produce a realistic tactile sensation, guiding the operator to operate. The slave devices are the UR5 arms. The system connection and information flow are shown in Fig. 1. State feedback is to keep the virtual and physical arm states consistent during initialization.

We need to build a model in a virtual environment according to the real robotic arm, including building CAD models and constraining between links and joints. The forward kinematic of the master manipulator and the inverse kinematic of the slave manipulator need to be calculated in real time. Information from each joint of the robot arm will be fed back.

2.1 Master Manipulator

The master device that we used in the paper is a 6-degree-of-freedom series joystick which equip with force feedback. As shown in Fig. 2. Three DC motors and photoelectric encoders are mounted on the wrist, shoulder and elbow joints. The motor is used to generate forces against the operator, simulating the forces and tactile sensations generated when interacting with the environment, and the encoder records the real-time rotation angle of the joint. It can simulate resistance, damping, magnetic and so on [11]. The D-H parameters of the Geomagic Touch haptic device can be calculated as shown in Table 1.

In medical applications, Geomagic Touch haptic device has long been used to simulate training surgery, such as simulators for hip replacement and resurfacing [12]. To quickly improve the proficiency of beginners in surgery and the success rate of surgery. On the MATLAB/Simulink interface, the Omni Bundle package can be used to connect and use the device. In our work, we use the C++ Software Development Kit of the haptic device for connection.

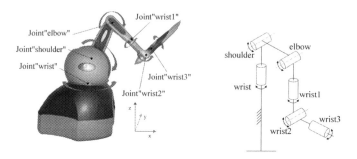

Fig. 2. Geomagic Touch haptic device

Table 1. DH parameters of Geomagic Touch haptic device

Link i	$\alpha_{i-1}(\deg)$	$a_{i-1}(mm)$	$d_i(mm)$	$\theta_i(\text{anglelimit}(\deg))$
1	0	0	125	$\theta_1 \in [-55°, 55°]$
2	$-90°$	0	0	$\theta_2 \in [-102°, 0°]$
3	0	134	0	$\theta_3 \in [-70°, 48°]$
4	$-90°$	0	132.5	$\theta_4 \in [-145°, 145°]$
5	90	0	0	$\theta_5 \in [-151°, -7°]$
6	$-90°$	0	23	$\theta_6 \in [-150°, 150°]$

2.2 Slave Manipulator

The slave arm is UR5 arm with 6-DOF, each joint has a range of motion of $\pm 360°$ with a payload of 5 kg, as shown in Fig. 3. We obtain UR5 robotic arm information via TCP/IP communication, including joint angle, position and speed information of the end effector, etc. At the same time, the socket communication port is used to send motion commands, the communication frequency is 125 Hz. The D-H parameters of the UR5 manipulator can be calculated as shown in Table 2 [13]. We use UR5 robot as the teleoperation test object of hot-line working robot.

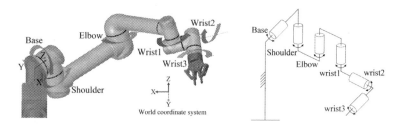

Fig. 3. Outline and structure of the UR5 arm

Table 2. DH parameters Of UR5 slave manipulator

Link i	α_{i-1}(deg)	a_{i-1}(mm)	d_i(mm)	θ_i(anglelimit(deg))
1	$0°$	0	89.2	$\theta_1 \in [-360°, 360°]$
2	$90°$	0	0	$\theta_2 \in [-360°, 360°]$
3	$0°$	-425	0	$\theta_3 \in [-360°, 360°]$
4	$0°$	-392.5	109.3	$\theta_4 \in [-360°, 360°]$
5	$90°$	0	94.75	$\theta_5 \in [-360°, 360°]$
6	$-90°$	0	82.5	$\theta_6 \in [-360°, 360°]$

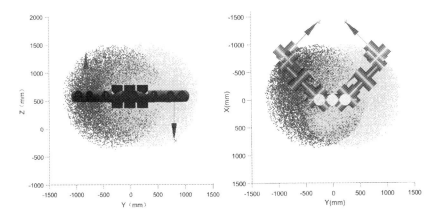

Fig. 4. The work space of slave manipulators (Color figure online)

After obtaining the D-H parameters of the UR5 single arm, we created a corresponding model in MATLAB to solve the workspace according to the shape and size of the pedestal. We use four fixed-angle links to simulate pedestals in different orientations. The manipulator of our experimental platform are mounted obliquely forward 45°, and each joint of the robot arm can rotate ±360°. Therefore, the resulting single-arm working space is approximately one sphere, and the coordinated working area is a blue-green overlapping area, as showed in Fig. 4.

2.3 Master-Slave Arm Mapping Strategy

There are many ways to map the workspace of the master-slave robotic arm, such as point-point mapping, velocity-velocity mapping, or hybrid switching mapping [14]. In our study we choose mapping the position and attitude of the master-slave arm in Cartesian coordinates. Incremental control is used for both position and attitude control of the system. For position control, we map the displacement of the force feedback device to a displacement from the end of the arm by a certain scale. The simulation of the scene and the inverse kinematics solution are all done in Simulation software. We establish control balls which are controlled by the haptic devices in the virtual scene. The position and attitude of the control balls change as that of the haptic devices

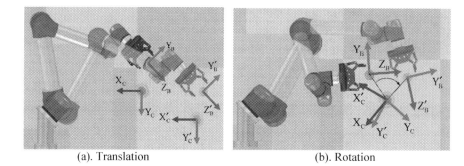

(a). Translation   (b). Rotation

Fig. 5. The teleoperation control strategy of manipulator

change. The coordinate system direction of the haptic devices and the control balls are consistent with the world coordinate. So there is no need to consider the problem of converting the robotic base coordinate system to world coordinates. Below we specifically introduce this control method, as shown in Fig. 5.

We assume that the world coordinate system is {W}, the target coordinate system before rotation is {B}, after rotation is {B'}. The coordinate system of the control sphere before rotation is {C}, after rotation is {C'}. Other coordinates are known except for the {B'} coordinate system.

Before rotation:

$$ {}^W_B T = {}^W_C T {}^C_B T \ \Rightarrow\ {}^C_B T = {}^W_C T^{-1} {}^W_B T \tag{1} $$

where T is a 4 × 4 homogeneous transformation matrix. ${}^W_B T$ represent the rotation and translation matrix of {B} coordinates system relative to {W} coordinates system.

$$ {}^W_B T = \begin{bmatrix} {}^W_B R_{Z'Y'X'} & {}^W_B X \\ 0 & 1 \end{bmatrix} \tag{2} $$

Where ${}^W_B R_{Z'Y'X'}$ represents Z-Y-X Euler angle rotation matrix, ${}^W_B X$ represents translation vector.

$$ {}^W_B R_{Z'Y'X'}(\alpha,\beta,\gamma) = \begin{pmatrix} c\alpha c\beta & c\alpha s\beta s\gamma - s\alpha c\gamma & c\alpha s\beta c\gamma + s\alpha s\gamma \\ s\alpha c\beta & s\alpha s\beta s\gamma + c\alpha c\gamma & s\alpha s\beta c\gamma - c\alpha s\gamma \\ -s\beta & c\beta s\gamma & c\beta c\gamma \end{pmatrix} \tag{3} $$

Since {B} is rotating around the origin of {C} coordinate system during the rotation

$$ {}^{C'}_{B'} T = {}^C_B T \tag{4} $$

$$ {}^W_{B'} T = {}^W_{C'} T {}^{C'}_{B'} T \tag{5} $$

In summary

$$\substack{W \\ B'}T = \substack{W \\ C'}T\substack{W \\ C}T^{-1}\substack{W \\ B}T \qquad (6)$$

We finally got the relationship between the control ball and the robot arm before and after the rotation. With this control strategy, we can control the translation and rotation of the end effector simultaneously or separately by the master arm. By reducing the gain factor of the mapping between master and slave devices, we are able to control the motion of the arm more precisely. This control strategy combines the advantage of the joint angle mapping method in terms of rotation and the advantage of point-point mapping method in terms of mobility. It is more in line with human operating habits.

3   Forbidden-Region Virtual Fixture

In the live working of the distribution network, if the mechanical arm accidentally touches the wire, it will cause serious safety accidents. Therefore, we must establish a forbidden-region virtual fixture to restrain a certain working space and prevent the operator from accidentally touching the high voltage wire during the operation error. At the same time, the operator needs to use the guidance virtual fixture to complete the task. The method of implementing a forbidden-region virtual fixture can be roughly divided into two types. One way is to create geometry through software and generate constraining force on the surface of the geometry [15]. Another way is to build force feedback through functions. We use the second way to generate constraining force here. The Mario Selvaggio research team proposed a way to create a virtual fixture geometry path in real time, based on the shape of the guided virtual fixture required in the task (e.g. in surgical anatomy) by manipulating the slave arm to capture points of interaction with the environment [16]. Xu et al. used Kinect Sensor to collect the point cloud reconstruction environment and generate potential field forces around the forbidden area to avoid the mechanical arm touching the dangerous area [17].

In this paper, we have built a virtual fixture based on the minimum distance between the end of the arm and the obstacle. With the minimum distance calculation module in simulation software, we can get the minimum distance size and direction. Then we are able to customize the threshold that needs to calculate the minimum distance to increase the calculation speed. The closer the manipulator is to the prohibited area, the greater the force in the direction of the minimum distance vector. Equation (8) reflect the relationship between the two.

$$F_h = \begin{cases} (\dfrac{K}{d_{\min}^m} - 1)T, & d_{\min} \leq \sqrt[m]{K} \\ 0, & d_{\min} > \sqrt[m]{K} \end{cases} \qquad (7)$$

$$\vec{F}_h = \begin{bmatrix} F_X \\ F_Y \\ F_Z \end{bmatrix} = \frac{F_h}{d_{\min}} \begin{bmatrix} d_X \\ d_Y \\ d_Z \end{bmatrix} = \frac{F_h}{d_{\min}} \vec{d}_{\min} \qquad (8)$$

where T is the torque we set, d_{min} is the minimum distance between the end of the arm and the forbidden area, F_h is the value of the resultant force input to the haptic device. m is a gain factor that representing how strongly the force varies with distance. K and m together determine the minimum distance at which the feedback force is generated. $\vec{d}_{min}$ and $\vec{F}_h$ are both 3×1 vectors representing the components of the minimum distance and the feedback force in the three directions of X, Y, and Z. This ensures that the direction of the force is the same as the direction of the minimum distance, guiding the operator to move away from the danger region.

4   Experiments and Results

We tested the positional accuracy and delay of the entire master-slave teleoperation system, as well as the impact under virtual fixture constraints.

4.1   Free Movement Experiment

In the test, we used the Qualisys 3D motion acquisition and analysis system to capture the displacement of the master-slave end at a frequency of 100 Hz, as shown in Fig. 6.

According to the recording frequency of the displacement point, we can get the displacement-time diagram. The gain coefficient between the master and slave arm is 2.5. First, we put fluorescent balls on the end of the master and the slave manipulators so that their trajectory can be captured by the camera. Then the operator moves the main manipulator arm in a slow motion, draws a circle with a radius of 51 cm on the horizontal plane, and tests the displacement error of the master and slave ends. The result is shown in the Fig. 7.

Fig. 6. The hardware structure of the teleoperation

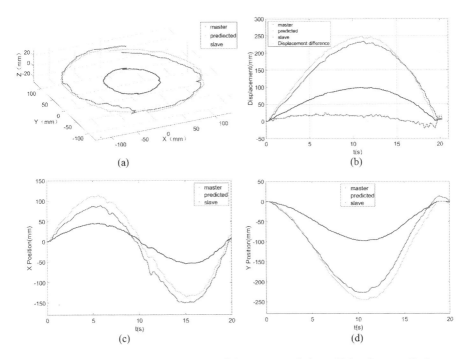

Fig. 7. Trajectory and displacement of the master and slave (Color figure online)

Figure 7(a) shows the trajectory of the master-slave arm in three-dimensional space. Where blue curve is the actual trajectory of master manipulator, the green curve is the expected slave trajectory, the red curve is the actual trajectory of the slave manipulator. Figure 7(b) shows the displacement of the master and slave end with time. Where pink curve is the difference between the expected displacement and the actual displacement of slave arm. Figure 7(c) and (d) are displacement-time diagrams in the X and Y directions, respectively.

According to Fig. 7, we get the maximum displacement difference between the master arm and the slave arm is 2.5 cm. And we can roughly find that the delay of the master and slave is 0.25 s. In this paper, we use the DLS inverse kinematics solution. The Dumping coefficient is 0.1 and the max iterations is 30.

4.2 Forbidden-Region Virtual Fixture Experiment

The biggest function of the haptic device is to feedback the interaction information between the slave arm and the environment. In our experiment, we convert the minimum distance between the robot arm and the forbidden area into the feedback force of the haptic device. We tested the case where the relationship between the minimum distance and the feedback force is an inverse proportional function, i.e. $k = 1/5$, $m = 1$, $T = 5$ N/m. The gain coefficient of the master-slave displacement is 1. We get the relationship between feedback force and minimum distance as shown in (9).

$$F_h = \begin{cases} \frac{1}{d_{\min}} - 5, & d_{\min} \leq 0.2 \\ 0, & d_{\min} > 0.2 \end{cases} \tag{9}$$

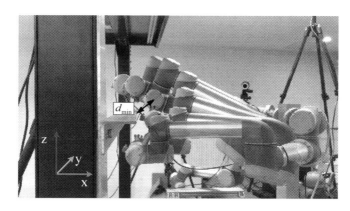

Fig. 8. Manipulator trajectory under force feedback

When $d_{\min}$ is less than 0.2 m, feedback force will be generated. The closer the distance, the greater the feedback. We perform the teleoperation experiment under this setting, and the movement of the robot arm is as shown in Fig. 8. $d_{\min}$ is the distance from the center of the end effector of the arm to the obstacle.

Because of the feedback force, the force will guide the operator to avoid obstacles. We used the Qualisys 3D motion acquisition and analysis system to extract the trajectory of the robot arm while recording the feedback force. The time of both data is synchronized by recording the time at which the haptic device reaches a particular location. The relationship between the movement trajectory and the feedback force is shown in Fig. 9. In our experiment, the forbidden area is long strip angle, so the minimum distance is always in the X-Z plane, so we show the displacement and force in the X-Z direction. We assume that during the movement of the arm, there is no change in the minimum distance point on the obstacle, and the expected motion trajectory is obtained according to the feedback force. The actual motion trajectory is basically in line with expectations, but since the point on the obstacle must change during the actual distance detection, the actual trajectory is slightly larger than the expected trajectory.

The direction of the feedback force is the minimum distance vector direction of the prohibited area and the arm, the feedback force increases as the distance decreases. The feedback force changes with time as shown in Fig. 10.

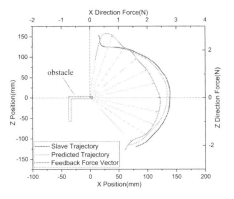

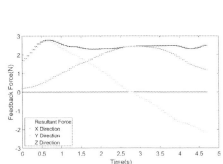

Fig. 9. Robot arm trajectory and feedback force

Fig. 10. Change of feedback force (Color figure online)

Where dark blue curve represents the resultant force, the green, magenta, and light blue curves represent the forces in the X, Y, and Z directions, respectively. Because the minimum distance vector is always in the X-Z plane, the magnitude of the force in the Y direction is 0 N. The data shows that when the feedback force is about 2.3 N, the minimum distance tends to be stable. At this time, d_{min} is about 0.13 m. Since the speed of data storage is much faster than the speed of Simulation software data update, the data in Fig. 10 is stepped.

5 Conclusion

We built a master-slave teleoperation system using Geomagic Touch haptic devices, UR5 manipulators and simulation environment. For the master-slave heterogeneous teleoperation system, we propose a position and attitude control method based on the control ball. In addition, we established a forbidden virtual fixture based on the minimum distance between the robot arm and the prohibited area. The feedback force of the haptic device can guide the operator to avoid driving slave manipulator touching the dangerous area. We tested the accuracy and latency of the teleoperation system. Virtual fixture experiment shows the feasibility of our proposed method.

As a future work, we will consider using a 3D lidar scanning environment to generate scenes automatically. And design a virtual fixture that can perform attitude constraint on the end of the arm according to the needs of the task.

Acknowledgment. The authors would like to thank Qiqiang Hu for his assistance in performing the experiments reported in this paper. The authors also thank Yin Zhu for his suggestion on the paper. The work is supported by the National Key R&D Program of China (2018YFB1307400).

References

1. Takaoka, K., Yokoyama, K., Wakisako, H., Yano, K., Higashijima, K., Murakami, S.: Development of the fully-automatic live-line maintenance robot-Phase III. In: Proceedings of the 2001 IEEE International Symposium on Assembly and Task Planning. Assembly and Disassembly in the Twenty-first Century (Cat. No. 01TH8560), pp. 423–428. IEEE (2001)
2. Aracil, R., Ferre, M.: Telerobotics for aerial live power line maintenance. In: Ferre, M., Buss, M., Aracil, R., Melchiorri, C., Balaguer, C. (eds.) Advances in Telerobotics. Springer Tracts in Advanced Robotics, vol. 31, pp. 459–469. Springer, Heidelberg (2007). https://doi.org/10.1007/978-3-540-71364-7_28
3. Allan, J.-F.: Robotics for distribution power lines: overview of the last decade. In: 2012 2nd International Conference on Applied Robotics for the Power Industry (CARPI), pp. 96–101. IEEE (2012)
4. Shouyin, L., Yanping, L., Wei, Q.: Robotic live-working for electric power lines maintenances. In: 2009 4th IEEE Conference on Industrial Electronics and Applications, pp. 1716–1719. IEEE (2009)
5. Menendez, O., Cheein, F.A.A., Perez, M., Kouro, S.: Robotics in power systems: enabling a more reliable and safe grid. IEEE Ind. Electron. Mag. **11**, 22–34 (2017)
6. Whitney, J.P., Chen, T., Mars, J., Hodgins, J.K.: A hybrid hydrostatic transmission and human-safe haptic telepresence robot. In: 2016 IEEE International Conference on Robotics and Automation (ICRA), pp. 690–695. IEEE (2016)
7. Ju, Z., Yang, C., Li, Z., Cheng, L., Ma, H.: Teleoperation of humanoid baxter robot using haptic feedback. In: 2014 International Conference on Multisensor Fusion and Information Integration for Intelligent Systems (MFI), pp. 1–6. IEEE (2014)
8. Rosenberg, L.B.: Virtual fixtures: perceptual tools for telerobotic manipulation. In: Proceedings of IEEE Virtual Reality Annual International Symposium, pp. 76–82. IEEE (1993)
9. Rydén, F., Chizeck, H.J.: Forbidden-region virtual fixtures from streaming point clouds: remotely touching and protecting a beating heart. In: 2012 IEEE/RSJ International Conference on Intelligent Robots and Systems, pp. 3308–3313. IEEE (2012)
10. Nakazawa, A., et al.: Feedback methods for collision avoidance using virtual fixtures for robotic neurosurgery in deep and narrow spaces. In: 2016 6th IEEE International Conference on Biomedical Robotics and Biomechatronics (BioRob), pp. 247–252. IEEE (2016)
11. Inoue, S., Makino, Y., Shinoda, H.: Active touch perception produced by airborne ultrasonic haptic hologram. In: 2015 IEEE World Haptics Conference (WHC), pp. 362–367. IEEE (2015)
12. Vaughan, N., Dubey, V.N., Wainwright, T.W., Middleton, R.G.: A review of virtual reality based training simulators for orthopaedic surgery. Med. Eng. Phys. **38**, 59–71 (2016)
13. Kebria, P.M., Al-Wais, S., Abdi, H., Nahavandi, S.: Kinematic and dynamic modelling of UR5 manipulator. In: 2016 IEEE International Conference on Systems, Man, and Cybernetics (SMC), pp. 004229–004234. IEEE (2016)
14. Dubey, R.V., Everett, S., Pernalete, N., Manocha, K.A.: Teleoperation assistance through variable velocity mapping. IEEE Trans. Robot. Autom. **17**, 761–766 (2001)
15. Bowyer, S.A., Davies, B.L., y Baena, F.R.: Active constraints/virtual fixtures: a survey. IEEE Trans. Robot. **30**, 138–157 (2014
16. Selvaggio, M., Fontanelli, G.A., Ficuciello, F., Villani, L., Siciliano, B.: Passive virtual fixtures adaptation in minimally invasive robotic surgery. IEEE Robot. Autom. Lett. **3**, 3129–3136 (2018)
17. Xu, X., Song, A., Ni, D., Li, H., Xiong, P., Zhu, C.: Visual-haptic aid teleoperation based on 3-D environment modeling and updating. IEEE Trans. Ind. Electron. **63**, 6419–6428 (2016)

Haptic Feedback with a Reservoir Computing-Based Recurrent Neural Network for Multiple Terrain Classification of a Walking Robot

Pongsiri Borijindakul[1], Noparit Jinuntuya[2], and Poramate Manoonpong[1,3(⊠)]

[1] Institute of Bio-inspired Structure and Surface Engineering,
College of Mechanical and Electrical Engineering,
Nanjing University of Aeronautics and Astronautics, Nanjing, China
{kobekang,poma}@nuaa.edu.cn
[2] Department of Physics, Faculty of Science, Kasetsart University,
Bangkok, Thailand
[3] CBR Embodied AI and Neurorobotics Lab,
The MærskMc-Kinney Møller Institute,
University of Southern Denmark, Odense M, Denmark
http://neutron.manoonpong.com/

Abstract. Terrain classification is an important feature for walking robots because it allows the robots to stably move and operate on the terrain. Different terrain classification techniques have been developed. The techniques include the use of different exteroceptive and proprioceptive sensors with different classification methods. Whereas these techniques have been widely used to classify flat, hard, and rough terrains, their application to soft terrains has not been fully addressed. Achieving soft-terrain classification will expand the operational range of walking robots. Thus, in this study, we propose a new technique to classify various terrains including soft ones. The technique exploits haptic feedback (expressed only through ground contact force measurement of a legged robot) and neurodynamics with the temporal memory of a reservoir computing-based recurrent neural network. We used six different terrains to evaluate the performance of the proposed technique. The terrains include sand (loose ground), foams with different softness levels (soft ground), and floor (hard ground). The experimental results show that we can successfully classify all terrains with an accuracy of above 70%. Furthermore, owing to the temporal memory of the network, if the haptic feedback is transiently missing, the network will be still be able to classify the terrain considerably well.

Keywords: Terrain classification · Soft terrains · Haptic feedback · Neural networks · Walking machines

© Springer Nature Switzerland AG 2019
H. Yu et al. (Eds.): ICIRA 2019, LNAI 11743, pp. 233–244, 2019.
https://doi.org/10.1007/978-3-030-27538-9_20

1   Introduction

Walking animals can stably move around and adapt their locomotion to the terrain. Walking robots, to achieve the same behavior, have to be able to differentiate terrain properties. Thus, terrain classification is an important feature for robots. Different terrain classification techniques have been developed [1–10]. The techniques include the use of exteroceptive sensors (e.g., a camera [5], a 2D laser range finder [7]) and/or proprioceptive sensors (e.g., joint angles [11], tactile or ground contact force sensing [8–10], and a combination of joint motor current and ground contact force [12]) with different classification methods. The typical methods include the root-mean-square value [7], discriminant function [9], support vector machines [5,10], neural networks [13], and adaptive boosting machine learning [12]. These techniques, while impressive in their own right, have been used to mainly classify flat, hard, and rough terrains. Their application to soft terrain classification has not been fully addressed. Thus, in this study, we propose a new technique to classify various terrains including soft ones. Inspired by the work of [12,13], our technique exploits two main ingredients: (i) haptic feedback (expressed only through ground contact force sensing [12]) and (ii) neurodynamics with the temporal memory of a reservoir computing-based recurrent neural network [13]. Compared with the above-mentioned techniques, which typically require multiple proprioceptive sensors [12,13] or additional exteroceptive sensors [2–5], our approach here uses only a ground contact force sensor installed in a front leg of our hexapod walking robot. This sensor, or haptic feedback, provides a direct interaction between the leg and the terrain, thereby allowing the robot to sense different terrain softnesses which might be difficult to obtain by using an exteroceptive sensor. The feedback is directly processed through a recurrent neural network. Owing to the temporal memory of the network, if the feedback is transiently missing, the network will still be able to classify the terrain considerably well. We emphasize that the embedded temporal memory of the network leads to more robust classification compared to other techniques. Thus, our proposed technique can be a basis for expanding the operational range of walking robots to cover not only flat, hard, and rough terrains but also soft terrains.

2   Bio-inspired Hexapod Walking Robot System

In this study, we used our bio-inspired hexapod walking robot system to develop our terrain classification technique. The system consists of two main parts: (1) a bio-inspired robot hardware platform (AMOSII) and (2) neural locomotion control.

2.1   Bio-inspired Robot Hardware Platform

AMOS II (Fig. 1(a)) is a bio-inspired hexapod walking robot [10]. The morphology of cockroaches inspired the robot body. The robot has six identical legs that are connected to the truck. The truck consists of two thoracic jointed segments. AMOS II has in total 19 active joints (three at each leg and one backbone joint). Its active backbone joint is inspired by a cockroach. The backbone joint provides the flexibility to the body. In addition, the body joint torque is tripled by the use of gear to achieve a more powerful body joint motion. The thoracal-coxal (TC) joint controls the forward/backward motion of the leg, the coxal-trochanteral (CTr) joint plays the role of extension and flexion of the second part of the leg, and the femoral-tibial (FTi) joint drives up/down motion of the third part of the leg. AMOSII also has six ground contact force sensors installed in its legs. In this study, we use only one ground contact force sensor at a front leg to receive haptic feedback for terrain classification.

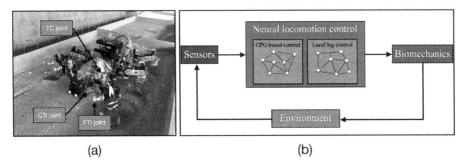

(a)   (b)

Fig. 1. (a) The bio-inspired robot hardware platform AMOSII. (b) Neural locomotion control of AMOSII.

2.2 Neural Locomotion Control

The locomotion control has been developed based on a modular structure. It consists of two main components: CPG-based control and local leg control [14] (Fig. 1(b)). The CPG-based control coordinates all leg joints of AMOS II, thereby generating insect-like leg movements and a multitude of different behavioral patterns. The patterns include forward/backward walking, turning left and right, and insect-like gaits. The local leg control using proprioceptive sensory feedback (such as ground contact force sensors) adapts the movement of an individual leg of AMOS II to deal with a change of terrain, loss of ground contact during the stance phase, or stepping on or hitting an obstacle during the swing phase. Each leg has two components facilitating local leg control: (1) an adaptive neural forward model, transforming the motor signal (efference copy) generated by the CPG into an expected sensory signal for estimating the walking state, and (2) elevation and searching control for adapting the leg motion (e.g., extension/flexion and elevation/depression). For more details of neural locomotion control, see [15].

3   Reservoir Computing-Based Recurrent Neural Network for Multiple Terrain Classification

Here we use the computational model using a recurrent neural network (RNN) of the reservoir computing (RC) type [16,17] (Fig. 2) for multiple terrain classification. Owing to the dynamic reservoir, the network with recurrent connections exhibits a wide repertoire of nonlinear activity and temporal memory. Typically, the reservoir computing-based recurrent neural network has three layers: input, hidden, and output layers. The hidden layer is constructed as a random network with N hidden recurrent neurons and fixed randomly initialized synaptic connectivity.

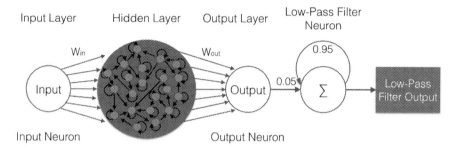

Fig. 2. Reservoir computing-based recurrent neural network for terrain classification.

The recurrent neural activity within the dynamic reservoir varies as a function of its previous activity and the current driving input signal. The discrete time state dynamics of reservoir neurons is given by:

$$\mathbf{x}(t+1) = (1-\lambda)\mathbf{x}(t) + \lambda f_{sys}(\mathbf{W}_{in}\mathbf{u}(t+1) + \mathbf{W}_{sys}\mathbf{x}(t) + b_0), \tag{1}$$

$$y(t) = \mathbf{W}_{out}\mathbf{x}(t), \tag{2}$$

where $\mathbf{x}(t)$ is the N-dimensional vector of neural state activations; $\mathbf{u}(t)$ is the input to the reservoir, which, in this case, is a single CTr-motor signal (see Fig. 1(a)); $y(t)$ is the vector of output neurons. In this study, we use one output neuron to classify different terrains. The reservoir time scale is controlled by the parameter λ, where $0 < \lambda \le 1$. Here the parameter is set to 0.9. A constant bias $b_0 = 0.001$ is applied to the reservoir neurons. $\mathbf{W}_{in}$ and $\mathbf{W}_{sys}$ are the input to reservoir weights and the internal reservoir recurrent connection weights, respectively. The output weights $\mathbf{W}_{out}$ are calculated using the recursive least squares (RLS) algorithm [18] at each time step, while the training input $\mathbf{u}(t)$ is being fed into the network. $\mathbf{W}_{out}$ are calculated such that the overall error is minimized. We implement the RLS algorithm using a fixed forgetting factor $(\lambda_{RLS} < 1)$ as follows:

$$e(t) = d(t) - y(t), \tag{3}$$

$$\mathbf{K}(t) = \frac{p(t-1)\mathbf{x}(t)}{\lambda_{RLS} + \mathbf{x}^T p(t-1)\mathbf{x}(t)}, \tag{4}$$

$$\mathbf{p}(t) = \frac{1}{\lambda_{RLS}}[\mathbf{p}(t-1) - K(t)\mathbf{X}^T(t)\mathbf{p}(t-1)], \tag{5}$$

$$\mathbf{W}_{out}(t) = \mathbf{W}_{out}(t-1) + K(t)e(t). \tag{6}$$

Here for each input set $\mathbf{u}(t)$, the reservoir state $\mathbf{x}(t)$ and network output $y(t)$ are calculated using Eqs. 1 and 2; $e(t)$ is the error calculated from the difference between the desired output $d(t)$ (here, foot contact signal) and the network output $y(t)$. $K(t)$ is the RLS gain vector and $\mathbf{p}(t)$ is the auto-correlation matrix updated at each time step. The reservoir to output weights $\mathbf{W}_{out}$ are initially set to zero. The forgetting factor λ_{RLS} is set to a value less than 1 (here, we use 0.99). The auto-correlation matrix $\mathbf{p}$ is initialized as $\mathbf{p}(0) = \mathbf{I}/\beta$, where $\mathbf{I}$ is unit matrix and β is a small constant (i.e., 10^{-4}). Details of all the fixed parameters and initial settings for the reservoir model are summarized in (Table 1). The network output $y(t)$ is finally sent to a low-pass filer neuron (i.e., a single recurrent neuron with a linear transfer function, see Fig. 2) in order to smooth the output signal. Here we set the connection weight from the output neuron to the low-pass filter neuron to 0.05 while the recurrent weight of the low-pass filter neuron is set to 0.95.

Table 1. List of network parameter settings.

Parameter	Value
Number of input neurons	1
Number of output neurons	1
Number of hidden neurons	50
Learning mode	RLS
Internal transfer funtcion (f_{sys})	Tanh
Output transfer function	Linear
Input sparsity	20
Internal sparsity	50
Forgetting factor (λ_{RLS})	0.99

RSL = the recursive least squares algorithm

Figure 3 shows the input, low-pass filter output, desired output, and error of the network. Figure 4 shows that the network can still predict the terrain although the network input which a foot contact sensor feedback is missing. Due to the temporal memory of the network, it allows the network to deal with the missing input information.

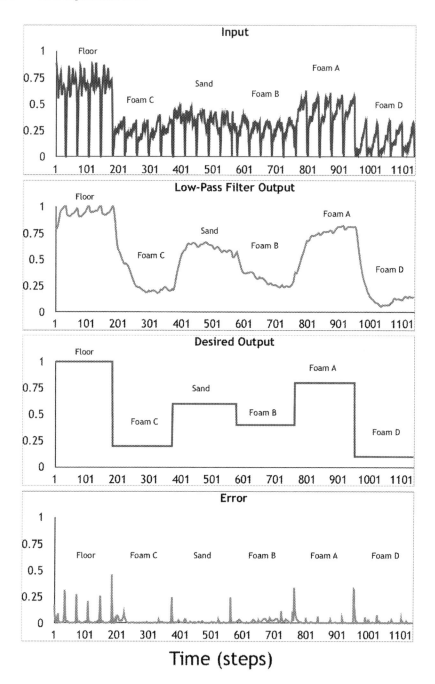

Fig. 3. Signals while the robot walked on different terrains. The first row shows the haptic feedback. The second row shows the output of the network. The third row shows the desired output and the last row shows the error between the desired output and the low-pass filter output.

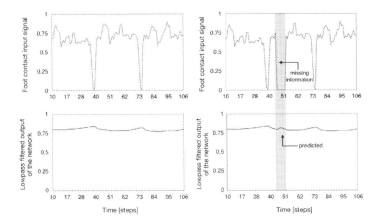

Fig. 4. An example of the prediction of lost information while the robot walked on the floor.

4 Multiple Terrain Classification

In our experiment, we chose six different terrains with different stiffnesses namely, floor, sand, foam of density $80 \, \text{kg/m}^3$ (foam A), foam of density $32 \, \text{kg/m}^3$ (foam B), foam of density $89 \, \text{kg/m}^3$ (foam C), and foam of density $37 \, \text{kg/m}^3$ (foam D) (see Fig. 5). First, we let the robot walk on the six terrains with a tetrapod gait and used the feedback from the foot contact sensor in the right front leg to indicate the terrain property. Figure 6 shows an example of the foot contact sensor feedback from the six terrains.

Fig. 5. Six different terrains for testing. The terrains include sand (loose ground), four foams with four different softness levels (soft ground), and floor (hard ground).

We applied force feedback from the robot leg to classify terrains by using our proposed reservoir computing-based recurrent neural network technique and compared with two different techniques, which are standard mean value and

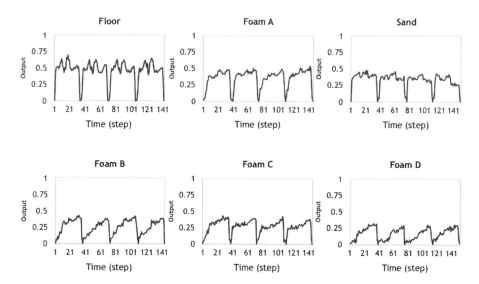

Fig. 6. Haptic feedback from the ground contact force sensor of the right front leg of AMOSII. The feedback was recorded while the robot walked on each terrain.

metrology techniques. The standard mean value technique is the wieldy used technique for analyzing data by using standard deviation. The standard deviation is a measure of how spread out numbers are and is calculated as the square root of the variance. Variance is the average of the squared difference from the mean. If y is the average value of force feedback on each terrain and Y is the outcome, then the results of force feedback are analyzed by using the standard deviation of testing values (see Eqs. 7 and 8):

$$Y = y \pm SD \tag{7}$$

$$SD = \sqrt{\frac{(x - \overline{x})^2}{n - 1}} \tag{8}$$

The metrology technique provides a high level of accuracy of data analyzed by using the expanded uncertainty. We evaluated the value of the repeatability of the measurement process to calculate the expanded uncertainty. Expanded uncertainty is the product of combined standard measurement uncertainty and a factor larger than 1. The expanded uncertainty (U) is calculated as $U =$ coverage factor k times combined uncertainty $U_c(y)$ (see Eq. 10), where k is from effective degrees of freedom. The effective degrees of freedom V_{eff} can be calculated from Eq. 11, where c_i is the sensitivity coefficients, $u(x_i)$ is the type A standard uncertainty, V_i is the degrees of freedom of $u(x_i)$, and N is the series of observations (here, N = 1). For combined uncertainty in this work, we calculated only type A uncertainty (calculated from independent repeated observations(n))

(see Eq. 13) and set type B uncertainty (evaluated using available information) to zero because the sensor has good repeatability. We demonstrated the correction of classification through the confusion matrix (Table 2).

$$Y = y \pm U \tag{9}$$

$$U = kU_c(y) \tag{10}$$

$$k = V_{eff} = \frac{U_c^4(y)}{\sum_{i=1}^{N} \frac{c_i^4 u^4(x_i)}{V_i}} \tag{11}$$

$$U_c = \sqrt{U_A^2 + U_B^2} \tag{12}$$

$$U_A = \frac{SD}{\sqrt{n}} \tag{13}$$

5   Experimental Results

Our experimental results show that the reservoir computing technique can be used to classify all types of terrains. The standard mean value technique can be used to classify only three terrains, which are foam A, foam D, and sand. This is because the average values of foam B and foam C are quite similar. The metrology technique can be used to classify only four terrains, which are foam A, foam B, foam D, and sand, whereas foam C cannot be unclassified. The standard mean value and metrology techniques both have a high percentage of unknown values because of the overlap of the average values as shown in (Table 2). The accuracy of classification of floor for the standard mean value and metrology techniques is higher than that of the reservoir computing because the terrain is even and the hardness of the floor is obviously higher than others. Moreover, the standard mean value and the metrology techniques classify terrains by using the average of input data, but the reservoir computing use both average input data and the differences in the characteristic of amplitude, therefore, if the signal looks similar, sometimes it would affect to the classification. In contrast, on the rest terrains, the reservoir computing method has higher accuracy than standard mean value and metrology technique (Fig. 7).

Table 2. Confusion matrix of three different techniques for multiple terrain classification. The vertical axis represents the actuals and the horizontal axis represents the output of the classification in percentage.

Confusion Matrix of RC Technique

Tetrapod	Floor	Foam C	Sand	Foam B	Foam A	Foam D	unknown
Floor	92	0	0	0	8	0	0
Foam C	0	72	0	20	0	8	0
Sand	0	0	84	0	16	0	0
Foam B	0	20	8	72	0	0	0
Foam A	0	0	20	0	80	0	0
Foam D	0	21	0	0	0	79	0

Confusion Matrix of SD Technique

Tetrapod	Floor	Foam C	Sand	Foam B	Foam A	Foam D	unknown
Floor	100	0	0	0	0	0	0
Foam C	0	0	0	0	0	8	92
Sand	0	0	48	24	0	0	28
Foam B	0	8	0	4	0	0	88
Foam A	0	0	12	0	60	0	28
Foam D	0	0	12	0	0	40	28

Confusion Matrix of Metrology Technique

Tetrapod	Floor	Foam C	Sand	Foam B	Foam A	Foam D	unknown
Floor	100	0	0	0	0	0	0
Foam C	0	0	0	4	0	20	76
Sand	0	0	48	24	0	0	28
Foam B	0	8	0	40	0	0	52
Foam A	0	0	12	0	60	0	28
Foam D	0	0	12	20	0	60	8

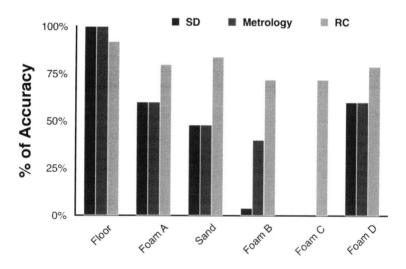

Fig. 7. The comparative accuracy chart of the three different methods on the six different terrains.

6   Conclusion

In this work, we demonstrated the performance of our reservoir computing-based recurrent neural network for multiple terrain classification by using haptic feedback. The reservoir computing technique can successfully classify all terrains with an accuracy of above 70% compared with the standard mean value and the metrology techniques, which cannot classify all terrains. Moreover, the proposed technique is also able to predict the missing or incomplete information while the robot walked and still can classify the terrain considerably well. In future work, we will implement ground contact force feedback from all legs to get more precise input data and complete terrain information to improve the terrain classification. We will also use the output of the classification method to allow the robot adapt its locomotion to the terrain.

Acknowledgments. This work was supported by the Capacity Building on Academic Competency of KU Students from Kasetsart University, Thailand, the Thousand Talents program of China, and the National Natural Science Foundation of China (Grant No. 51861135306).

References

1. Williamson, D., Kottege, N., Moghadam, P.: Terrain characterisation and gait adaptation by a hexapod robot. In: Australasian Conference on Robotics and Automation (ARAA), Brisbane, QLD, Australia (2016)
2. Stejskal, M., Mrva, J., Faigl, J.: Road following with blind crawling robot. In: International Conference on Robotics and Automation (ICRA), pp. 3612–3617. IEEE, Stockholm (2016). https://doi.org/10.1109/ICRA.2016.7487544
3. Krebs, A., Pradalier, C., Siegwart, R.: Comparison of boosting based terrain classification using proprioceptive and exteroceptive data. In: Khatib, O., Kumar, V., Pappas, G.J. (eds.) Experimental Robotics. Springer Tracts in Advanced Robotics, vol. 54, pp. 93–102. Springer, Heidelberg (2008). https://doi.org/10.1007/9783642001963_11
4. Homberger, T., Bjelonic, M., Kottege, N., Borges, P.V.K.: Terrain-dependant control of hexapod robots using vision. In: Kulić, D., Nakamura, Y., Khatib, O., Venture, G. (eds.) International Symposium on Experimental Robotics (ISER). Springer Proceedings in Advanced Robotics, vol. 1, pp. 92–102. Springer, Cham (2017). https://doi.org/10.1007/978-3-319-50115-4_9
5. Zenker, S., Aksoy, E.E., Goldschmidt, D., Wörgötter, F., Manoonpong, P.: Visual terrain classification for selecting energy efficient gaits of a hexapod robot. In: International Conference on Advanced Intelligent Mechatronics, pp. 577–584. IEEE/ASME, Wollongong (2013). https://doi.org/10.1109/AIM.2013.6584154
6. Hoepflinger, M.A., Remy, C.D., Hutter, M., Spinello, L., Siegwart, R.: Haptic terrain classification for legged robots. In: International Conference on Robotics and Automation, pp. 577–584. IEEE, Anchorage (2010). https://doi.org/10.1109/ROBOT.2010.5509309

7. Kesper, P., Grinke, E., Hesse, F., Wörgötter, F., Manoonpong, P.: Obstacle/gap detection and terrain classification of walking robots based on a 2D laser range finder. In: 16th International Conference on Climbing and Walking Robots and the Support Technologies for Mobile Machines (CLAWAR), Australia, pp. 419–426 (2013). https://doi.org/10.1142/9789814525534_0053

8. Mrva, J., Faigl, J.: Tactile sensing with servo drives feedback only for blind hexapod walking robot. In: 10th International Workshop on Robot Motion and Control (RoMoCo). IEEE, Poznan (2015). https://doi.org/10.1109/RoMoCo.2015.7219742

9. Walas, K.: Tactile sensing for ground classification. J. Autom. Mobile Robot. Intell. Syst **7**(2), 18–23 (2013)

10. Wu, X.A., Huh, T.M., Mukherjee, R., Cutkosky, M.: Integrated ground reaction force sensing and terrain classification for small legged robots. IEEE Robot. Autom. Lett **1**(2), 1125–1132 (2016)

11. Best, G., Moghadam, P., Kottege, N., Kleeman, L.: Terrain classification using a hexapod robot. In: Guivant, J., Eaton, R. (eds.) Proceedings of the Australasian Conference on Robotics and Automation (ACRA), Sydney, Australia, pp. 1–8 (2013)

12. Hoepflinger, M.A., Remy, C.D., Hutter, M., Spinello, L., Siegwart, R.: Haptic terrain classification for legged robots. In: 2010 IEEE International Conference on Robotics and Automation, pp. 2828–2833. IEEE, Anchorage (2010). https://doi.org/10.1109/ROBOT.2010.5509309

13. Jonas, D., Cauwenbergh, R.V., Wyffels, F., Waegeman, T., Schrauwen, B.: Terrain classification for a quadruped robot. In: 2013 12th International Conference on Machine Learning and Applications, vol. 1, pp. 185–190. IEEE, Miami (2013). https://doi.org/10.1109/ICMLA.2013.39

14. Manoonpong, P., Parlitz, U., Wörgötter, F.: Neural control and adaptive neural forward models for insect-like, energy-efficient, and adaptable locomotion of walking machines. Front. Neural Circ. **7**(12), 1–28 (2013)

15. Steingrube, S., Timme, M., Wörgötter, F., Manoonpong, P.: Self-organized adaptation of simple neural circuits enables complex robot behavior. Nat. Phys. **6**, 224–230 (2010)

16. Jaeger, H., Hass, H.: Harnessing nonlinearity: predicting chaotic systems and saving energy in wireless communication. Science **304**(5667), 78–80 (2004)

17. Dasgupta, S., Wörgötter, F., Manoonpong, P.: Information dynamics based self-adaptive reservoir for delay temporal memory tasks. Evolving Syst. **4**(4), 235–249 (2013)

18. Jaeger, H.: Adaptive nonlinear system identification with echo state networks. In: Advances in Neural Information Processing Systems, pp. 593–600 (2003)

Robotic Technology for Deep Space Exploration

Kinematic Characteristics Analysis of a Double-Ring Truss Deployable Antenna Mechanism

Bo Han[1], Yundou Xu[1,2], Jiantao Yao[1,2], Dong Zheng[1],
and Yongsheng Zhao[1,2(✉)]

[1] Parallel Robot and Mechatronic System Laboratory of Hebei Province,
Yanshan University, Qinhuangdao 066004, Hebei, China
`yszhao@ysu.edu.cn, 1440731168@qq.com`
[2] Key Laboratory of Advanced Forging & Stamping Technology
and Science of Ministry of National Education, Yanshan University,
Qinhuangdao 066004, Hebei, China

Abstract. Deployable antenna is the key equipment of satellites and other spacecraft, it can realize the information transmission between the spacecraft and earth. In order to enrich the mechanism configurations of space deployable antenna, a double-ring truss deployable antenna mechanism is proposed in this paper, and it is decomposed into a plurality of mechanism units. Based on screw theory, degree of freedom (DOF) of the mechanism is analyzed, the result showed that it has only one DOF. Then, velocities of each component in the double-ring truss deployable mechanism unit are analyzed, their angular velocities and linear velocities were obtained. Finally, a three-dimensional model of this mechanism is established in Solidworks software, based on the three-dimensional model, numerical calculation and simulation verification are carried out, and simulation results verified the correctness of the theoretical analysis. The double-ring truss deployable mechanism proposed in this paper has a good application prospect in the field of aerospace, and the analysis method based on screw theory provides a good reference for other spatial deployable mechanisms.

Keywords: Double-ring truss · Deployable antenna · Screw theory · DOF · Kinematics

1 Introduction

Due to the limited space of launchers, most of the mechanisms in aerospace engineering are deployable mechanisms, they have widely applied in the satellite platforms, space stations and other spacecraft. One of the important applications of deployable mechanisms in the field of aerospace is used as deployment and supporting mechanism for large-diameter space antennas [1]. The space deployable antenna adopts a combination of a mesh-shaped reflecting surface and a truss supporting framework [2], at present, in orbit operation antennas mainly have the truss deployable antenna, ring truss deployable antenna and the radial rib deployable antenna. [3, 4].

© Springer Nature Switzerland AG 2019
H. Yu et al. (Eds.): ICIRA 2019, LNAI 11743, pp. 247–259, 2019.
https://doi.org/10.1007/978-3-030-27538-9_21

Ring truss deployable antenna has high folding rate and light weight, and its weight does not increase in proportion with the increase of diameter, this characteristics make it to be the ideal form of large diameter space antenna [5]. The AstroMesh antenna developed by NGST in the United States in 2000 is a successful in-orbit application of the ring truss deployable antenna [6]. Escrig F proposed the Pactruss double-ring truss deployable antenna mechanism in 1985 [7], Datashvili et al. developed a double-ring deployable truss which has a 6 m diameter [8], You et al. developed a prototype of a double-ring deployable truss based on the scissors mechanisms [9]. Guan et al. developed several prototypes of ring truss deployable antenna mechanisms [10, 11]. Shi et al. studied the double-ring truss deployable mechanisms based on graph theory [12], and reference [13] also proposed a large deployable antenna mechanism. Although the relevant researchers have done some research works, but there are still few types of the ring truss deployable antennas in orbit.

In terms of the kinematic characteristics analysis of the deployable mechanisms, Xu et al. proposed a method of DOF analysis for the tetrahedral truss deployable antenna mechanism [14]. Wei et al. studied the mobility of the Hoberman switch-pitch ball [15], Cai et al. studied the kinematics of the Hoberman's linkage consisting of a series of scissor like elements [16]. Chen et al. studied the kinematic characteristics of the Bricard and Bennett linkages when constructing the space deployable mechanisms [17, 18], the references [19] and [20] separately analyzed the DOF, kinematics and dynamics of the scissors mechanism combination units. This references analyzed different mechanisms, but a unified and concise analysis method has not been formed.

This paper proposed a double-ring truss deployable antenna mechanism, its DOF and velocity characteristics are analyzed based on screw theory, and the simulation verification are carried out. The research in this paper aims to lay the foundation for the subsequent research and application of this deployable mechanism and to provide references for the kinematics analysis of other spatial deployable mechanisms.

2   Double-Ring Truss Deployable Antenna Mechanism

Double-ring truss deployable mechanism is shown in Fig. 1, it mainly includes the inner ring truss, the outer ring truss and a plurality of scissors mechanism units.

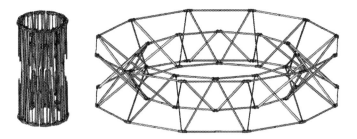

Fig. 1. Double-ring truss deployable antenna mechanism.

The two figures shown in Fig. 1 are the fully folded state and the fully deployed state of the double-ring truss deployable antenna mechanism. Its general configuration is the half-deployed state, the inner and outer ring truss mechanisms have the same structure, they are all composed of 3R (R represents the revolute joint) mechanisms which are connected through the node disks, and the inner and outer ring truss mechanisms are connected by the scissors mechanism units. The double-ring truss deployable mechanism can be decomposed to a closed loop deployable mechanism unit, a plurality of non-closed loop deployable mechanism units and two planar 3R mechanisms, the half-deployed state of the double-ring truss deployable mechanism and its structural decomposition are shown in the Fig. 2.

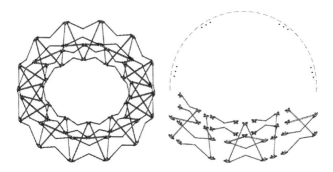

Fig. 2. Half-deployed state and its structural decomposition.

3 DOF Analysis of Double-Ring Truss Deployable Mechanism

3.1 DOF Analysis of the Closed Loop Deployable Mechanism

As shown in Fig. 3, coordinate system O-XYZ is established for the closed loop deployable mechanism, and each node disk is numbered with an uppercase letter. Origin O is located at the center of the bottom node disk, X axis is pointed by the node disk where the origin O located to the other node disk, Z axis straight up and the Y axis is determined by the right hand rule.

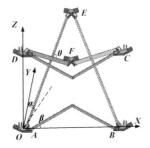

Fig. 3. Closed loop deployable mechanism unit and the coordinate system.

Set the length on the scissors rod connected to the inner node disk is l, the length connected to the outer node disk is L, and the length of the two links between the outer node disks is q, the distance between the axes of the R joints on the inner node disks and the center is m, and the distance between the axes of the R joints on the outer node disks and the center is n. As shown in Fig. 3, the angle between the projection of the scissors rod on the XOY plane and the Y axis is α, the angle between the two connected scissors rods is θ, and the angle between the links connecting the outer node disks and the X axis is β. Then, in the Fig. 3, the parameters have the following relationship:

$$(L+l)\cos\frac{\theta}{2}\sin\alpha = q\cos\beta \tag{1}$$

In the closed loop deployable mechanism unit shown in Fig. 3, the number of the rods are indicated by the number of the connected node disks, such as that the number of the scissors rod between the node disks A and E is AE, the two links connecting the node disks C and D are CD_1 and CD_2. Based on graph theory and screw theory, the components are represented by circles, the joints are represented by lines, and the motions at different joints are represented by the numerical unit twists, such as that the motion of the joint between the scissors rods AE and DF is $\$_1$, in this way, the screw constraint topology can be obtained, as shown in the Fig. 4.

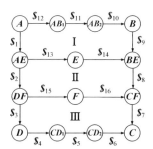

Fig. 4. Screw constraint topology of the closed loop deployable mechanism unit.

Position coordinate of the joint 11 which is connected link AB_1 and AB_2 is:

$$r_{11} = (n+q\cos\theta \quad 0 \quad q\sin\theta) \tag{2}$$

The axis direction of the joint 11 is:

$$S_{11} = (0 \quad 1 \quad 0) \tag{3}$$

According to screw theory, the unit twist of the joint 11 can be obtained:

$$\$_{11} = [0 \quad 1 \quad 0 \quad -q\sin\theta \quad 0 \quad n+q\cos\theta]^{\mathrm{T}} \tag{4}$$

Similarly, the expressions of the other unit twists shown in Fig. 4 can be obtained. Use the ω to indicate the angular velocity value of the joints, for the three closed loops of I-III shown in Fig. 4, the corresponding screw constraint equations can be established as follows:

$$\begin{cases} \omega_1\$_1 - \omega_9\$_9 - \omega_{10}\$_{10} - \omega_{11}\$_{11} - \omega_{12}\$_{12} + \omega_{13}\$_{13} + \omega_{14}\$_{14} = 0 \\ \omega_2\$_2 - \omega_8\$_8 - \omega_{13}\$_{13} - \omega_{14}\$_{14} + \omega_{15}\$_{15} + \omega_{16}\$_{16} = 0 \\ \omega_3\$_3 + \omega_4\$_4 + \omega_5\$_5 + \omega_6\$_6 - \omega_7\$_7 - \omega_{15}\$_{15} - \omega_{16}\$_{16} = 0 \end{cases} \tag{5}$$

where the ω_i represents the angular velocity of the joint i, 0 is a 6×1 null matrix.
Equation (5) can be written in a matrix form as follows:

$$MN = 0 \tag{6}$$

where

$$N = \begin{bmatrix} \omega_1 & \omega_2 & \omega_3 & \cdots & \omega_{14} & \omega_{15} & \omega_{16} \end{bmatrix} \tag{7}$$

$$M = \begin{bmatrix} M_2 & M_1 & M_3 & M_4 \\ M_5 & M_6 & M_1 & M_7 \\ M_8 & M_9 & M_1 & M_{10} \end{bmatrix}, \quad \begin{cases} M_1 = (0 \quad 0 \quad 0 \quad 0) \\ M_2 = (\$_1 \quad 0 \quad 0 \quad 0) \\ M_3 = (-\$_9 \quad -\$_{10} \quad -\$_{11} \quad -\$_{12}) \\ M_4 = (\$_{13} \quad \$_{14} \quad 0 \quad 0) \\ M_5 = (0 \quad \$_2 \quad 0 \quad 0) \\ M_6 = (0 \quad 0 \quad 0 \quad \$_8) \\ M_7 = (-\$_{13} \quad -\$_{14} \quad \$_{15} \quad \$_{16}) \\ M_8 = (0 \quad 0 \quad \$_3 \quad \$_4) \\ M_9 = (\$_5 \quad \$_6 \quad -\$_7 \quad 0) \\ M_{10} = (0 \quad 0 \quad -\$_{15} \quad -\$_{16}) \end{cases} \tag{8}$$

where the 0 is a 6×1 null matrix.

The screw constraint matrix M is an 18×16 matrix, DOF of the closed loop deployable mechanism unit corresponds to the dimension of the null space of the screw constraint matrix, it can be calculated by the Matlab software:

$$rank(M) = 15 \tag{9}$$

The number of columns in matrix M is 16, so that we can obtain that the DOF of the closed loop deployable mechanism unit is 1.

3.2 DOF Analysis of the Combination Mechanism and the Whole Double-Ring Truss Deployable Mechanism

There are two types of non-closed loop deployable mechanisms in the whole mechanism, they have the same configuration, only the size of the components are different, since the component size cannot affect the DOF of the mechanism, the two types of non-closed loop deployable mechanism units can be uniformly processed when analyzing the DOF of the overall mechanism. The combination of a closed loop mechanism unit and a non-closed loop mechanism unit is shown in the Fig. 5.

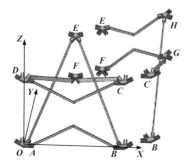

Fig. 5. Combination mechanism.

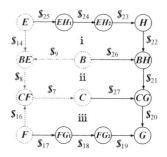

Fig. 6. Screw constraint topology of the non-closed loop deployable mechanism unit.

In Fig. 5, the closed loop deployable mechanism unit on the left side is the mechanism unit in Fig. 3. Similarly, the screw constraint topology of the non-closed loop deployable mechanism in Fig. 5 can be obtained, as shown in Fig. 6.

The screw constraint equations corresponding to Fig. 6 can be obtained:

$$\begin{cases} -\omega_9\$_9 + \omega_{14}\$_{14} - \omega_{22}\$_{22} - \omega_{23}\$_{23} - \omega_{24}\$_{24} - \omega_{25}\$_{25} + \omega_{26}\$_{26} = \mathbf{0} \\ \omega_7\$_7 + \omega_8\$_8 + \omega_9\$_9 - \omega_{21}\$_{21} - \omega_{26}\$_{26} + \omega_{27}\$_{27} = \mathbf{0} \\ -\omega_7\$_7 - \omega_{16}\$_{16} + \omega_{17}\$_{17} + \omega_{18}\$_{18} + \omega_{19}\$_{19} - \omega_{20}\$_{20} - \omega_{27}\$_{27} = \mathbf{0} \end{cases} \quad (10)$$

where the $\mathbf{0}$ is a 6×1 null matrix.

Through combining Eqs. (5) and (10), the set of screw constraint equations of the combination mechanism can be obtained:

$$\begin{cases} \omega_1\$_1 - \omega_9\$_9 - \omega_{10}\$_{10} - \omega_{11}\$_{11} - \omega_{12}\$_{12} + \omega_{13}\$_{13} + \omega_{14}\$_{14} = \mathbf{0} \\ \omega_2\$_2 - \omega_8\$_8 - \omega_{13}\$_{13} - \omega_{14}\$_{14} + \omega_{15}\$_{15} + \omega_{16}\$_{16} = \mathbf{0} \\ \omega_3\$_3 + \omega_4\$_4 + \omega_5\$_5 + \omega_6\$_6 - \omega_7\$_7 - \omega_{15}\$_{15} - \omega_{16}\$_{16} = \mathbf{0} \\ -\omega_9\$_9 + \omega_{14}\$_{14} - \omega_{22}\$_{22} - \omega_{23}\$_{23} - \omega_{24}\$_{24} - \omega_{25}\$_{25} + \omega_{26}\$_{26} = \mathbf{0} \\ \omega_7\$_7 + \omega_8\$_8 + \omega_9\$_9 - \omega_{21}\$_{21} - \omega_{26}\$_{26} + \omega_{27}\$_{27} = \mathbf{0} \\ -\omega_7\$_7 - \omega_{16}\$_{16} + \omega_{17}\$_{17} + \omega_{18}\$_{18} + \omega_{19}\$_{19} - \omega_{20}\$_{20} - \omega_{27}\$_{27} = \mathbf{0} \end{cases} \quad (11)$$

where the $\mathbf{0}$ is a 6×1 null matrix.

Equation (11) can be written in a matrix form:

$$PQ = \mathbf{0} \quad (12)$$

where

$$Q = [\omega_1 \quad \omega_2 \quad \omega_2 \quad \dots \quad \omega_{25} \quad \omega_{26} \quad \omega_{27}]^T \tag{13}$$

In Fig. 5, the scissors mechanism connected by the node disks B, C, E and F and the joints on them are shared by the two mechanism units, when calculating the DOF of the combination mechanism, the repeated twists should be removed, that is, one of the $\$_7$, $\$_8$, $\$_9$, $\$_{14}$ and $\$_{16}$ are removed, corresponding to the red dotted line in Fig. 6. The coefficient matrix P in Eq. (12) can be written as follows:

$$P = \begin{bmatrix} M & 0_{18 \times 11} \\ 0_{18 \times 16} & M' \end{bmatrix} \tag{14}$$

where M is the matrix M in the Eq. (6), the matrix M' is as follows:

$$M' = \begin{bmatrix} M'_1 & M'_2 & M'_3 \\ M'_1 & M'_4 & M'_5 \\ M'_6 & M'_7 & M'_8 \end{bmatrix}, \quad \begin{cases} M'_1 = (0 \quad 0 \quad 0) \\ M'_2 = (0 \quad -\$_{22} \quad -\$_{23} \quad 0) \\ M'_3 = (-\$_{24} \quad -\$_{25} \quad \$_{26} \quad 0) \\ M'_4 = (-\$_{21} \quad 0 \quad 0 \quad 0) \\ M'_5 = (0 \quad 0 \quad -\$_{26} \quad \$_{27}) \\ M'_6 = (\$_{17} \quad \$_{18} \quad \$_{19}) \\ M'_7 = (-\$_{20} \quad 0 \quad 0 \quad 0) \\ M'_8 = (0 \quad 0 \quad 0 \quad -\$_{27}) \end{cases} \tag{15}$$

From Eq. (14), the following equation can be obtained:

$$rank(P) = rank(M) + rank(M') \tag{16}$$

Substituting the mechanism parameters, the rank of the matrixes can be obtained:

$$rank(M) = 15, rank(M') = 11 \tag{17}$$

DOF of the combination mechanism can be obtained:

$$t = u - rank(P) = 27 - 26 = 1 \tag{18}$$

where the t represents the DOF, the u is the columns of the matrix P.

Since the matrix M' is a full rank matrix, the Eq. (18) can also be written as:

$$\begin{aligned} t &= u_M + u_{M'} - rank(M) - rank(M') \\ &= [u_M - rank(M)] + [u_{M'} - rank(M')] \\ &= u_M - rank(M) \end{aligned} \tag{19}$$

It can be seen from Eq. (19) that the DOF of the combination mechanism still depends on the matrix M, the number of DOF is the same as that of the closed loop deployable mechanism.

When the non-closed loop deployable mechanism unit is continuously added on the combination mechanism, it can be known from the above analysis that the DOF of the overall mechanism is still the same as that of the single closed loop deployable mechanism. Similarly, it can be analyzed that the whole double-ring truss deployable mechanism is the same as that of the single closed loop deployable mechanism, the DOF number of the whole double-ring truss deployable mechanism is 1.

4   Velocity Analysis of the Double-Ring Truss Deployable Mechanism

In order to analysis the velocity of the mechanism, based on the mechanism division in Fig. 5, dividing the whole mechanism into a plurality of the same unit combination mechanisms, as shown in the Fig. 7.

Fig. 7. A plurality of unit combination mechanisms.

4.1   Velocity Analysis of the Unit Combination Mechanism

It can be seen from the above analysis that the unit combination mechanism has only one DOF, so that if one of the inputs is given, such as the ω_1, the angular velocities in Eq. (11) can be solved. The screw velocities of each component in the closed-loop I shown in Fig. 4 can be obtained by the vector operation:

$$
\begin{cases}
V_A = \mathbf{0} \\
V_{AE} = \omega_1 \$_1 \\
V_{AB_1} = \omega_{12} \$_{12} \\
V_E = \omega_1 \$_1 + \omega_{13} \$_{13} \\
V_{AB_2} = \omega_{12} \$_{12} + \omega_{11} \$_{11} \\
V_B = \omega_{12} \$_{12} + \omega_{11} \$_{11} + \omega_{10} \$_{10} \\
V_{BE} = \omega_1 \$_1 + \omega_{13} \$_{13} + \omega_{14} \$_{14}
\end{cases}
\tag{20}
$$

where the V_i represents the screw velocity of the component i.

The screw velocities of the components in the closed-loop II can be obtained based on the screw velocities in the closed-loop I:

$$\begin{cases} V_{DF} = V_{AE} + \omega_2 \$_2 \\ V_F = V_{AE} + \omega_2 \$_2 + \omega_{15} \$_{15} \\ V_{CF} = V_{AE} + \omega_2 \$_2 + \omega_{15} \$_{15} + \omega_{16} \$_{16} \end{cases} \tag{21}$$

Similarly, the screw velocities of the components in the closed-loop III and the closed-loops in the Fig. 6 can be obtained. According to the character of the screw velocity, the angular velocity vector of each component can be expressed as:

$$\boldsymbol{\omega}_i = \omega(\boldsymbol{V}_i) \tag{22}$$

where the $\omega(\cdot)$ is a vector represents the first three of the screw velocity.

The centroid linear velocity of the component i can be obtained as:

$$\boldsymbol{v}_i = v(\boldsymbol{V}_i) + \omega(\boldsymbol{V}_i) \times \boldsymbol{r}_i \tag{23}$$

where the $v(\cdot)$ is a vector represents the last three of the screw velocity, $\boldsymbol{r}_i$ is a distance vector from the coordinate origin to the centroid of the component.

4.2   Velocity Analysis of the Whole Double-Ring Truss Deployable Mechanism

Since the double-ring truss deployable mechanism is a completely central symmetrical mechanism, the sizes of the unit combination mechanisms are identical, and they are symmetric about the ring center, so that if the coordinate system is established at each unit combination mechanism, the velocities of the components which have the same position in their self-coordinate system are identical.

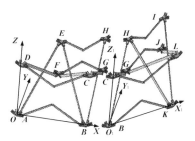

Fig. 8. Two unit combination mechanisms and the coordinate systems.

Take the node disk B and K in Fig. 8 as an example, they have the follow relationship:

$$^O v_B = {}^{O_1} v_K, \quad {}^O \omega_B = {}^{O_1} \omega_K \tag{24}$$

The whole mechanism can be divided into N unit combination mechanisms, and the coordinate systems $O\text{-}XYZ \sim O_{N-1}\text{-}X_{N-1}Y_{N-1}Z_{N-1}$ can be established, as shown in Fig. 9.

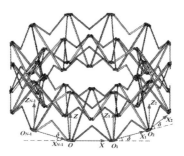

Fig. 9. Double-ring truss deployable mechanism and the coordinate systems.

Select the $O\text{-}XYZ$ to be the fixed coordinate system, the velocities of the components in the fixed coordinate system can be expressed as follows:

$$\begin{cases} {}^O v_i = {}^O_{O_j} R \, {}^{O_j} v_i + \sum_{k=1}^{j} {}^O_{O_{k-1}} R \, {}^{O_{k-1}} v_{O_k} \\ {}^O \omega_i = {}^O_{O_j} R \, {}^{O_j} \omega_i + \sum_{k=1}^{j} {}^O_{O_{k-1}} R \, {}^{O_{k-1}} \omega_{O_k} \end{cases} \tag{25}$$

where i is the component number, and j is the coordinate number.

The expression of the rotational transformation is:

$$^O_{O_j} R = \begin{bmatrix} \cos j\delta & -\sin j\delta & 0 \\ \sin j\delta & \cos j\delta & 0 \\ 0 & 0 & 1 \end{bmatrix} \tag{26}$$

Through the above analysis and calculation, the angular velocities and linear velocities of the components in the whole mechanism can be solved.

5   Simulation Verification

Structural and physical parameters are shown in Table 1.

Table 1. Structural and physical parameters.

Parameter	Value
Length of the inner rod	236 mm
Length of the outer rod	150 mm
Length of the scissors rod	516.5 mm
Distance between the R joints and center on the inner node disk	30 mm
Distance between the R joints and center on the outer node disk	18.5 mm
Angle input function	$2.5t^2$
Simulation time	5.8 s

The subdivision number of the double-ring truss deployable mechanism model is 12, use Adams software and Matlab software to simulate and verify the correctness of the above analysis. The results of the angular velocities and linear velocities of the components are shown in Figs. 10 and 11.

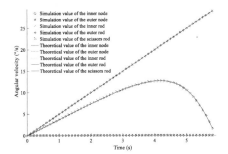

Fig. 10. Angular velocities.   Fig. 11. Linear velocities.

It can be seen from Figs. 10 and 11 that the simulation results and the theoretical values of the components are consistent, which effectively shows the correctness of the theoretical analysis.

6   Conclusion

Ring truss deployable antenna is an important type in the space antennas, in this paper, a double-ring truss deployable antenna mechanism is proposed, and its DOF was analyzed, the result showed that it has only one DOF, the velocities of the components in the mechanism were deduced based on the screw theory, and simulation results verified the correctness of the analysis.

The double-ring truss deployable mechanism proposed in this paper has only one DOF, it can be better applied in the field of aerospace, and the theoretical analysis method used in this paper can also be well used in other deployable mechanisms.

Acknowledgements. This research was co-supported by the National Natural Science Foundation of China (No. 51675458), the Key Project of Natural Science Foundation of Hebei Province of China (No. E2017203335) and the Youth Top Talent Project of Hebei Province Higher Education of China (No. BJ2017060).

References

1. Hu, F., Song, Y.P., Zheng, S.K., et al.: Advances and trends in space truss deployable antenna. J. Astronaut. **39**, 111–120 (2018)
2. Santiago-Prowald, J., Baier, H.: Advances in deployable structures and surfaces for large apertures in space. Ceas Space J. **5**, 89–115 (2013)
3. Li, T.: Deployment analysis and control of deployable space antenna. Aerosp. Sci. Technol. **18**(1), 42–47 (2012)
4. Deng, Z.Q., Huang, H.L., Li, B., et al.: Synthesis of deployable/foldable single loop mechanisms with revolute joints. J. Mech. Robot. **3**(3), 031006 (2011)
5. Xu, Y., Guan, F.L., Chen, J.J., et al.: Structural design and static analysis of a double-ring deployable truss for mesh antennas. Acta Astronaut. **81**(2), 545–554 (2012)
6. Meguro, A., Tsujihata, A., Hamamoto, N., et al.: Technology status of the 13 m aperture deployment antenna reflectors for engineering test satellite VIII. Acta Astronaut. **47**(2–9), 147–152 (2000)
7. Escrig, F.: Expandable space structures. Int. J. Space Struct. **1**(2), 79–91 (1985)
8. Datashvili, L., Endler, S., Wei, B., et al.: Study of mechanical architectures of large deployable space antenna apertures: from design to tests. Ceas Space J. **5**(3–4), 169–184 (2013)
9. You, Z., Pellegrino, S.: Cable-stiffened pantographic deployable structures part 2: mesh reflector. AIAA J. **35**(8), 1348–1355 (1997)
10. Dai, L., Guan, F.L., Guest, J.K.: Structural optimization and model fabrication of a double-ring deployable antenna truss. Acta Astronaut. **94**(2), 843–851 (2014)
11. Xu, Y., Guan, F.L.: Structure-electronic synthesis design of deployable truss antenna. Aerosp. Sci. Technol. **26**(1), 259–267 (2013)
12. Shi, C., Guo, H.W., Liu, R.Q., et al.: Configuration optimization and structure design of the double-layer hoop deployable antenna mechanism. J. Astronaut. **37**(7), 869–878 (2016)
13. Han, B., Xu, Y.D., Yao, J.T., et al.: Design and analysis of scissors linkage double ring truss deployable antenna mechanism. Manned Spacefl. **23**(3), 306–310 (2017)
14. Xu, Y.D., Liu, W.L., Chen, L.L., et al.: Mobility analysis of a deployable truss-antenna mechanism-method based on link-demolishing and equivalent idea. Acta Aeronaut. Astronaut. Sin. **38**(9), 316–327 (2017)
15. Wei, G.W., Ding, X.L., Dai, J.S.: Mobility and geometric analysis of the Hoberman switch-pitch ball and its variant. J. Mech. Robot. **2**(3), 031010 (2010)
16. Cai, J.G., Xu, Y.X., Feng, J.: Kinematics analysis of Hoberman's Linkages with the screw theory. Mech. Mach. Theory **63**(63), 28–34 (2013)

17. Chen, Y., You, Z.: On mobile assemblies of Bennett linkages. Proc. Math. Phys. Eng. Sci. **464**(2093), 1275–1293 (2008)
18. Chen, Y., You, Z., Tarnai, T.: Threefold-symmetric Bricard linkages for deployable structures. Int. J. Solids Struct. **42**(8), 2287–2301 (2005)
19. Sun, Y.T., Wang, S.M., Li, J.F., et al.: Mobility analysis of the deployable structure of SLE based on screw theory. Chin. J. Mech. Eng. **26**(4), 793–800 (2013)
20. Sun, Y.T., Wang, S.M., Mills, J.K., et al.: Kinematics and dynamics of deployable structures with scissor-like-elements based on screw theory. Chin. J. Mech. Eng. **27**(4), 655–662 (2014)

Conceptual Design of Ejection, Aerostat and Rolling Group Detectors

Qunzhi Li[1], Chao Ma[2(✉)], Wangjun Zhang[1], Han Wang[1], and Zhihui Zhao[1]

[1] Beijing Institute of Spacecraft System Engineering, Beijing, China
[2] Beijing Key Laboratory of Intelligent Space Robotic Systems Technology and Applications, Beijing Institute of Spacecraft System Engineering, Beijing, China
machaodn@163.com

Abstract. Floating exploration in near Mars is a new mode between orbiting detection and landing detection, synthesized with the advantages of orbiter's global coverage and rover's high image definition. Rolling exploration on Martian surface has the better characteristic of anti-tilting than mature wheeled roaming detection on Martian surface presently. It can adapt to complex environment of Martian surface. Combined with the two new modes, floating exploration technology in near Mars and rolling exploration technology on Martian surface is presented. By Joint exploration of ejection, aerostat and rolling group detectors, the larger ranges and higher accuracy of extraterrestrial three-dimensional stereo-exploration is achieved. It has the characteristics of various exploration mode, multi-dimension, low cost and high reliability.

Keywords: Mars Exploration · Ejection · Aerostat detection · Rolling detection · Group detectors

1 Introduction

Human exploration of extraterrestrial objects has a history of several decades. However, there are great limitations on the detection methods, scope and capability. In particular, the flying around survey can only use remote sensors to detect. The range, efficiency and ability of rover detection are limited, which cannot deal with the complex planetary surface environment. In order to obtain more detailed detection data of extraterrestrial objects, breaking through the limitations of existing detection methods, ranges and capabilities has become one of the urgent problems to be solved in the field of deep space exploration.

Mars near-Surface floating exploration is a new type of exploration between surround exploration and landing exploration, which combines the advantages of the global coverage of the orbiter and high resolution of the rover. The detection method has undergone a lot of ground tests and already has a success on-orbit practice. The rolling detection of Martian surface has better anti-overturning ability than the current wheel-type rover. It can fit for the complex environment of Martian surface. The rolling

H. Yu et al. (Eds.): ICIRA 2019, LNAI 11743, pp. 260–272, 2019.
https://doi.org/10.1007/978-3-030-27538-9_22

detection is still in the stage of principle verification, and there are no on-orbit examples.

The conceptual design of the ejection floating and rolling group detector is proposed in this paper. Through the combined exploration of floating/rolling (space-ground), the three-dimensional exploration of extraterrestrial objects with wider scope and higher accuracy can be realized. It has the characteristics of diversified detection forms, high dimensionality, low cost and high reliability.

2   Domestic and International Research

The two detection methods of near-Surface floating and surface rolling will play an important role in planetary exploration. Near-Surface floating exploration is a new form of exploration between surround detection and landing detection, which combines the global coverage advantages of orbiters and the high definition of rovers. Compared with the current wheeled planetary surface rover, the planetary surface rolling detector has better anti-overturning ability. It can overcome the poor anti-overturning characteristics of wheeled, legged, wheeled-legged. So, it can be better adapted to the complex environment of planetary surface.

2.1   Planet Near-Surface Floating Detector

Due to the limitation of mass, volume and power consumption, the near-surface floating detector has a short flight life. It cannot carry a large number of payloads for long-term scientific observation and data collection as the orbiter or lander. By balancing the observation accuracy and range, it can be seen that the float balloon detector is suitable for short-term observation of a specific scientific target.

At present, only the former Soviet Union successfully launched the Vega-Venus-Halley Comet Detector in 1985 with two balloon detectors (Vega-1/Vega-2) [1], which successfully realized the floating detection of Venus' atmospheric environment. Russia-Vega-D [1], Russia/France-Mars96, US-Planetary Balloon Program [1], US-MABVAP Mars Exploration Balloon [2–4], France-MIR, China-Mars Balloon Exploration and so on have carried out and are carrying out balloon near-surface floating exploration at different stages. Balloon near-surface floating exploration will expand into a new form of deep space exploration [5, 6].

2.2   Rolling Detector on the Planetary Surface

The planetary surface rolling detector is not only flexible in motion, but also has good sealing ability, which makes it well adapted to the changes of planetary environment and suitable for the surface topographic detection. Because of its small size, the planetary surface rolling detector can be released to the planetary surface as a load of the planetary near-surface floating detector or surface rover for rolling detection.

The method of planetary surface rolling detection is still in the stage of principle verification, and there are no in-orbit examples [7, 8]. Relevant countries include Finland/Italy-wheel-driven spherical detector [9], Britain/United States-independent hemisphere-driven spherical detector [10], Sweden/Canada-counterweight-driven spherical detector, Iran/United States/India-omnidirectional four-drive spherical detector, United States-wind-driven spherical detector [11], United States-reconnaissance force counterweight-driven detector [12], and China Beijing University of Posts and Telecommunications [13], Shanghai Jiaotong University, Beijing University of Aeronautics and Astronautics [14, 15] and so on.

3 Analysis of Links and Parameters

Analysis of Martian Atmospheric Parameters. The preliminary analysis shows that under the same local conditions, the changes of atmospheric parameters with longitude can be neglected, so only the changes with latitude and height are considered. The lower the optical depth near the Martian surface, which the clearer the Martian weather will be (the optical depth is 0.3, 1, 3, corresponding to sunny, small dust storms and big dust storms respectively), the higher the atmospheric density will be. Comparing the results of 10 o'clock and 16 o'clock local time, the atmospheric density does not change much with the local time within 100 km, which changes within 20% range. But the wind speed at 10 o'clock and 16 o'clock varies greatly, and the maximum difference can reach 2 times.

Inter-detector Link Analysis Conclusion. The links between Mars float, rolling detectors and Mars landing probe conform to CCSDS proximity link protocol, and can realize one-way communication with a maximum of 1 km. The corresponding code rate is 2048 kbps, and the link margin is more than 4 dB, which can meet the mission requirements.

Analysis Conclusion of Thermal Control Demand. Before landing, the floating and rolling group detectors are in the entering cabin. The floating detectors are mainly facing the equipment in the cabin, which in a vacuum environment. The radiation temperature boundary is the main part, and they are in the vacuum environment. The temperature in the entering cabin is between −50 °C–70 °C, so the floating detectors can be safely stored in this environment. After the Mars floating and rolling group detectors land on the Martian surface, they will stay for about 5 to 10 days, that unlock, inflate and deploy during the day, and then carry out the floating exploration mission. In the Martian landing patrol area, the lowest ambient temperature at night is about −110 °C (storage temperature), and the highest ambient temperature during the day is about 70 °C (working temperature). In order to ensure the low temperature storage index of the detector cabin, the thermal insulation design of the whole cabin is the main part of the detector. When the temperature of the Martian surface is low, the temperature control heating circuit should be designed to keep the cabin warm. When the detector is released, the heat consumption of the equipment is large, and there is no need for temperature control heating in the cabin.

Analysis Conclusion of Different Gas Source Devices. The method of self-contained gas cylinder is feasible, and the mass and volume of liquid hydrogen are acceptable.

Considering the safety of gas, helium is finally chosen. The method of preparing hydrogen from dry powder has higher requirement in temperature or pressure, and it is not feasible. The method of preparing hydrogen from electrolytic water consumes more energy and needs too much water, it is also not feasible.

Analytical Conclusions of Floating Detection. Aiming at the mass of the whole system not exceeding 10 kg, the altitude of the floatation is -1 km, and the maximum carrying capacity of the balloon is 2.3 kg (the attached weight of the balloon is 0.3 kg). The balloon system with 12 g/m^2 material weighs about 3.63 kg (8L cylinder) which corresponds to 12 g/m^2 skin material. The diameter of balloon is about 8.9 m.

Analysis Conclusion of Rolling Detection. The rolling sphere is designed with a mass of 2 kg. The gas in the sphere is made of conventional helium. The use of the cylinder is consistent with that of the floating detector. The rolling binocular camera is installed at the bearing end of the rolling detector. During the process of being far from the lander, it will have the stereo images of the local Martian surface, to provide the most reliable basic data for the safe movement and scientific exploration of the Mars probe.

4   Conceptual Design of Floating-Rolling Detectors

The conceptual design of ejection space-ground group detectors is described below. After the probe (lander) lands on the Martian surface, many small space probes will be ejected one by one. During ejection, it inflates, cuts off and seals. After that, each small space-ground detector is an independent individual, which can float, roll on the Martian surface. They carry different loads to carry out scientific exploration, and transmit the detection data back to exploration. Detection data are sent back to Surface by the lander.

The object of exploration is planets with atmosphere such as Mars. The targets are described below. (1) Martian atmospheric gradient environment, including atmospheric composition, atmospheric density, pressure, temperature field, vertical wind, wind speed and so on; (2) high-resolution imaging of Martian surface topography and geomorphology; (3) the fine detection of magnetic anomalies in the Martian crust; (4) electromagnetic flux in the UV band of Martian surface; (5) the ionizing radiation intensity of Martian surface; (6) the precise Martian gravity field; (7) the Natural Source Sound Detection near Martian surface, etc.

Ejection space group detectors are placed in the inner box of Mars probe. After landing, the box doors are opened successively under the control of the motor. An internal spring device ejects these ejection space group detectors into the Martian sky or surface on Mars, as shown in Fig. 1.

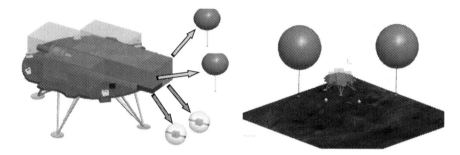

Fig. 1. Diagram of ejection state of space-ground group detectors.

4.1 Preliminary Configuration Design

General Configuration. The Ejection Space Ground Group Detectors are placed in the inner box of the Mars Probe. It is divided into two layers, 20 boxes. The upper layer carries 10 floating detectors, and the lower layer carries 10 rolling detectors. The whole box is driven by a motor, and the side of the main box carries cylinders, etc. as shown in Fig. 2. Each time the distance of a unit box size can be moved (Fig. 1), 20 floating and rolling detectors need to be moved five times to release. The Martian rover can be placed on the top of the entire box.

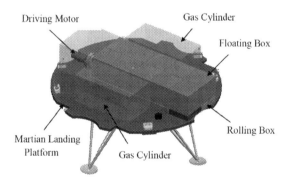

Fig. 2. Diagram of the detectors on the Martian landing platform.

Configuration of Floating Detector. The configuration of the whole floating detector is shown in Fig. 3. The batteries are distributed on the top and bottom of the cabin, the mid-board is the satellite module, the UHF transmitting module and the UHF transmitting antenna are arranged on the side board, and the cameras and plug-ins are arranged on the bottom board. As shown in Fig. 3, the outer envelope size of the closing state of the antenna of the floating detector is 130 mm × 130 mm × 133 mm. The outer envelope size of the deployment state of the antenna is 310 mm × 130 mm × 133 mm.

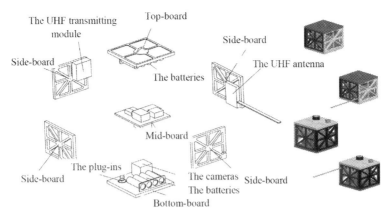

Fig. 3. The configuration and deployment/closing state of antenna of the floating detector.

Configuration of Rolling Detector. The configuration of the whole rolling detector, as shown in Fig. 4, is composed of sphere module (including shell, axle assembly, swing hammer, etc.), satellite, power supply, inter-device communication module, load (camera) interface and so on. The central axle assembly is internally equipped with satellite affair, power supply, inter-device communication module, etc.

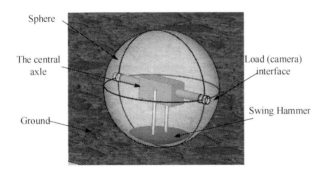

Fig. 4. The configuration of the rolling detector.

4.2 Overall Composition

Ejection floating and rolling group detectors consist of four parts: the floating detector, the rolling detector, the supporting inflatable system and the ejection device, which are placed on the Mars landing platform. Among them, the floating detector is divided into seven parts: balloon module, satellite module management, power module, inter-device communication module, micro camera, structure thermal control module and load module. The rolling detector is divided into six parts: sphere module, satellite module management, power module, inter-device communication module, camera module and load module. The inflatable system and ejection device are non-floating and rolling.

4.3   Flight Programming

The ejection floating and rolling group detectors are mounted on the Mars landing platform. During the long-term flight of Mars transfer, the landing platform provides mechanical fixing, power supply, heat preservation, etc. to complete the necessary state inspection and supplementary charging. The flight program is designed as follows.

Time to Release. After landing the Martian surface, the Mars probe completes the necessary on-orbit test and establishes its working state. And then, the ground staff choose to send the power-up instructions of ejection floating and rolling group detectors. During this period, the communication module is controlled by the satellite module management and operates regularly. During the initial life period of the Martian surface, it works for about 10 min every day. During the 5–10 Martian days before the release of the ejection floating and the rolling detector, the landing platform provides the early survival power demand. When ejection floating and rolling group detectors are released, power supply for pyrotechnics, electric blasting valve, disconnection and release channel are provided by landing platform.

Release trigger conditions: (1) The wind speed on the Martian surface is no more than 1 m/s, and the angle between the wind direction on the Martian surface and the departure direction of the Martian rover is more than 45°. (2) Mars time is around 10 a.m. The Martian surface is clear and dust-free, and the optical depth $\tau < 0.5$.

Release Process. After receiving the release instructions, the ejection device completes a unit movement driven by the motor. Thereafter, the explosive cutting device unlocks the balloon bag. After about 2 s, the electric blasting valve detonates and the gas path opens. The high-pressure cylinder fills the balloon (about 350 s). When the balloon is filled with, the pipeline of the working balloon is separated. After about 2 s, the explosive unlocking device unlocks, the balloon floater springs up, and the balloon floater detaches from the landing platform. The balloon carries the floating detector to begin aerial exploration. It ascends and finally levitates over the landing platform in the area of 1 km. At the same time, the sphere of rolling detector is inflated and ejected, which is inflated, cut off and sealed in the ejection process. After that, each small space-to-ground detector is a separate individual that can float and roll on the Martian surface.

Inter-device Communication. Ejection floating and rolling group detectors do not communicate directly to the Earth. Their engineering telemetry and load data are transmitted to the Martian lander. After ejection, floating and rolling group detectors move up to 1 km away from the Martian lander, the detector and the Martian lander constitute a one-way inter-device communication link.

Detection. After the exploration of ejection floating and rolling group detectors started, the floating detector was carried by balloon and floated to the upper part of the Mars landing platform. In this process, the floating detector completed the video shooting of the detector area aiming at the Mars landing platform, and the detection of the atmospheric composition. The rolling detector completed the Martian surface topography exploration under the driving module of the sphere.

5 Simulation Verification

5.1 The Whole Process of Near-Ground Floating and Rolling Detection

The Ejection Space Ground Group Detectors are placed inside the built-in box of the Mars probe. The probe carries the Mars Rover to the Martian surface and the Martian

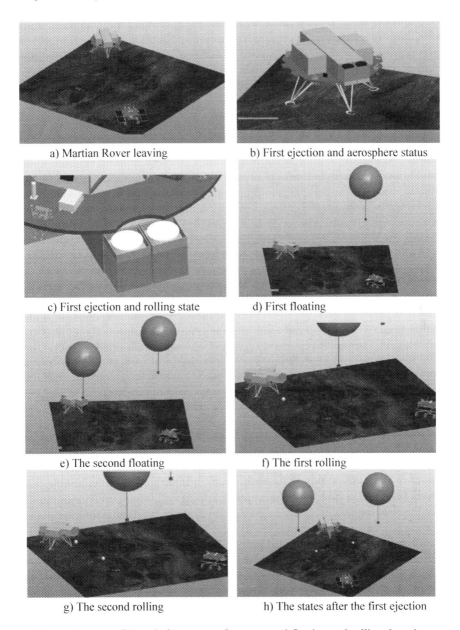

a) Martian Rover leaving

b) First ejection and aerosphere status

c) First ejection and rolling state

d) First floating

e) The second floating

f) The first rolling

g) The second rolling

h) The states after the first ejection

Fig. 5. Diagram of the whole process of near-ground floating and rolling detection.

Rover leaves (Fig. 5a). Then, under the control of the motor, the door of the box opens sequentially, and the floating and rolling detectors are released (Fig. 5b, c). An internal spring device ejects these Ejection Space-ground detectors into the Martian sky (Fig. 5d, e) or surface (Fig. 5f, g), inflatable, cut off and sealed during ejection. When ejection is completed for the first time, the floating and rolling states are shown in Fig. 5h. They are carrying different loads to carry out scientific exploration, transmitting the detection data back to the lander, which then returning to the Earth in a unified way.

5.2   Simulation and Verification of Near-Surface Floating Detection

The preliminary flight parameters of the balloon are estimated as shown in Fig. 6. The flight time is about 400 s from the nominal altitude of −1 km. The buoyancy of the balloon is about 6.88 kg before the balloon carries the floating detector out of the Mars landing platform. That is to say, the maximum force exerted on the Mars landing platform during the balloon lift-off is about 6.88 kg.

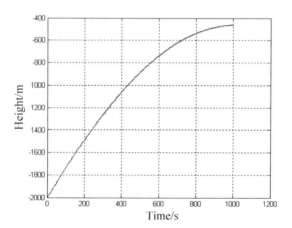

Fig. 6. Preliminary flight parameters of balloon liftoff.

5.3   Simulation and Verification of Surface Rolling Detection

The prototype model of rolling detector is imported into ADAMS software. Contact constraints are added between the spherical shell and the ground. Rotation constraints 1 and rotation drive 1 are added to the rotating joint between the spherical shell and the central axis assembly, and rotation constraints 2 and rotation drive 2 are added to the rotating joint between the central axis assembly and the swing hammer. The simulation results are examples of straight line and climbing simulation. The rotary drive 1 and the rotary drive 2 are controlled to make the rolling detector move uniformly along a straight line and climb a slope of 10°. Figure 7 shows the position change curve of the center of the rolling detector type.

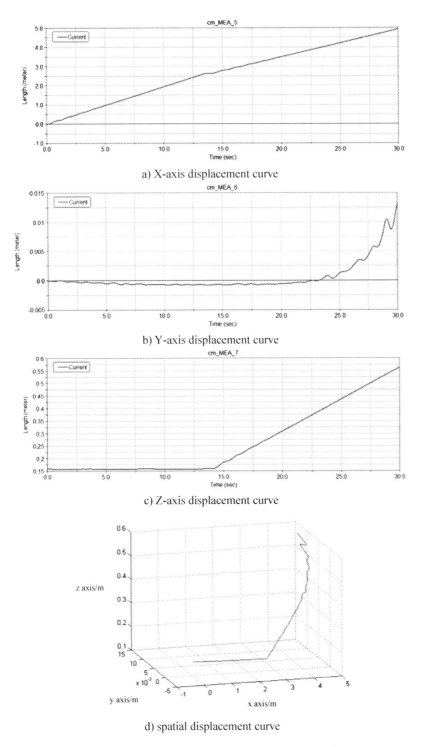

a) X-axis displacement curve

b) Y-axis displacement curve

c) Z-axis displacement curve

d) spatial displacement curve

Fig. 7. Rolling detector center position curve.

From the X-axis displacement curve, we can see that the motion of other positions is smooth except for the track fluctuation at the interface of plane and slope. From the displacement curve of Y axis, we can see that the position deviation of rolling detector is slight. At the end of climbing motion, the position deviation of Y axis of rolling detector is about 10 mm. From the Z-axis displacement curve, it can be seen that the position of the Z-axis center fluctuates slightly up and down due to the interaction between the spherical crust and the ground, and it is slightly obvious at the interface of the plane and the slope, which is caused by the deformation and the interaction between the surface's crust and the ground. Rolling detector rotation drive 1 moment curve is shown in Fig. 8.

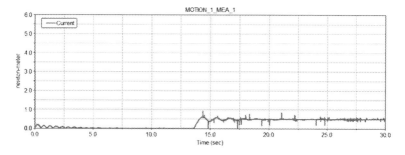

Fig. 8. Rotary drive 1 torque curve.

It can be seen from the moment curve of rotating drive that the impact of the initial rolling detector's motion acceleration is 5.5 Nm. When the rolling detector moves smoothly in the plane, the moment keeps a very small positive value. In order to reduce the initial moment impact of the rolling detector motion, the initial acceleration should not be too large when the rolling detector motion is controlled.

6   Conclusion

Mankind has made a great success in exploring extraterrestrial objects by using space probes. However, there are great limitations in detection mode, scope and capability. In order to obtain further detailed information of extraterrestrial objects, it is necessary to carry out research and practice on new exploration methods. Floating and rolling exploration is a new way of detecting extraterrestrial objects.

New Detection Methods: Floating and rolling detection is a new type of detection between surround detection and landing rover detection. It combines the global coverage of orbiter and the high definition advantages of lander and rover. It breaks through the limitations of existing detection methods, ranges and capabilities. And it is simple compared with surround detection, and is low development cost and low energy consumption.

Unique Exploration Perspective: Mars floating and rolling exploration has always been one of the hotspots of extraterrestrial space exploration, which can provide a unique perspective for scientific observation. Floating detection can fly close to the Martian surface, nearly 100 times the observation distance of orbiter, and 1000 times larger than the range of Martian Rover activity in the same time.

Mature Exploration Platform: Although Mars has atmosphere, it is only equivalent to the atmospheric density at the altitude of 35 km on Earth, which poses a great challenge to Martian floating detection. Plans for the float exploration of extraterrestrial objects such as Mars and Titan have been implemented for many years, forming a relatively systematic theoretical and research system. The research of rolling detectors has also formed a relatively systematic theoretical and research system.

Acknowledgment. This research was supported, in part, by the National Natural Science Foundation of China (No. 51875393) and by the China Advance Research for Manned Space Project (No. 030601).

References

1. Tian, L.L., Fang, X.D.: NASA aerospace research and progress, space return and remote sensing, vol. 33, no. 1, p. 81, February 2012
2. Heun, M.K., Cathey, H.M., Haberle Jr., R.: Mars balloon trajectory model for mars geoscience aerobot development, p. 1500, AIAA (1997)
3. Jeffery, L.H., Michael, T.P., Viktor, V.K.: Mars balloon flight test results. In: AIAA Balloon Systems Conference, Seattle, Washington, pp. 1–12 (2009)
4. Fairbrother, D.A.: Development of planetary balloons. In: NASA Goddard Space Flight Center's Wallops Flight Facility, Balloon Program Office, Code 820, Wallops Island, VA, USA (2007)
5. Lei, Y.P., Yang, C.X.: Research on temperature distribution of mars overpressure balloon. J. Aeronaut. Sch. Aeronaut. Sci. Eng. **33**(2), 234–241 (2012). Beijing University of Aeronautics and Astronautics
6. Zhou, C.Q., Min, C.H., Wu, X.Y., et al.: The influence of ground wind on the selection of sounding balloon sites. Guizhou Meteorol. **30**(6), 30–32 (2006)
7. Bicchi, A., Balluchi, A., Prattichizzo, D., et al.: Introducing the sphericle: an experimental testbed for research and teaching in nonholonomy. In: Proceedings of the IEEE International Conference on Robotics and Automation, pp. 2620–2625 (1997)
8. Bhattacharya, S., Agrawal, S.K.: Spherical rolling robot: a design and motion planning studies. IEEE Trans. Robot. Autom. **16**(6), 835–839 (2000)
9. Bruhn, E.C., Pauly, K., Kaznov, V.: Extremely low mass spherical rovers for extreme environments and planetary exploration enabled with mems. In: Proceedings of the 8th International Symposium on Artifical Intelligence Robotics and Automation in Space-iSAIRAS, Munich, Germany (2005)
10. Otani, T., Urakubo, T., Maekawa, S., et al.: Position and attitude control of a spherical rolling robot equipped with a gyro. In: IEEE AMC 2006, Istanbul, Turkey, pp. 416–421 (2006)
11. Hajos, G.A.: An overview of wind-driven rovers for planetary exploration, NASA, Langley Research Center, Hampton, VA (2005)

12. Munk, J.R.: StratSat-the wireless solution. In: The 3rd Stratospheric Platform Systems Workshop, Tokyo, pp. 45–51(2001)
13. Liu, D.L.: Research on motion analysis and control technology of a spherical mobile robot. Ph.D. Dissertation, Beijing University of Posts and Telecommunications (2009)
14. Onda, M., Morikawa, Y.: High-altitude lighter-than-air powered platform. Soc. Automot. Eng. Trans. **16**(1), 2216–2223 (1991)
15. Onda, M.: A ground-to airship microwave power transmission experiment for stationary aerial platform. In: AIAA LTA Systems Conference, Florida, p. 19 (2006)

Experimental Research on Dynamic Characteristics of Truss Structure for Modular Space Deployable Truss Antenna

Dake Tian[1(✉)], Rongqiang Liu[2], Lu Jin[1], Hongwei Guo[2], and Zongquan Deng[2]

[1] School of Mechanical Engineering, Shenyang Jianzhu University, Shenyang 110168, China
tiandake@sjzu.edu.cn
[2] School of Mechanical and Electrical Engineering, Harbin Institute of Technology, Harbin 150001, China

Abstract. In order to accurately research the dynamic characteristics of truss structure for modular space deployable truss antenna, dynamic experiments are carried out. Based on the basic theory of dynamics and the characteristics of antenna structure, a set of dynamic experimental system is designed, and the modal experiments under free boundary conditions are carried out by means of single-point input and multi-point output. The experimental results show that the autocorrelation coefficients of all the modes of the antenna structure are 100%, and the correlation functions between the modes are small, the maximum value is only 15.45%, which shows that the experimental results are correct. The maximum relative error of natural frequency is only 10.59%. In addition, the experimental mode shapes with the frequency of 32.781 Hz and 58.003 Hz are all in good agreement with the first and the third mode shapes of finite element analysis. The experimental method proposed in this paper can provide reference for modal analysis of other large space deployable truss structures.

Keywords: Deployable antenna · Modular structure · Dynamics experiment

1 Introduction

Space deployable antenna is a new space structure with the rapid development of space science and technology, which plays an important role in high-resolution earth observation, satellite communication and deep space exploration [1–4]. Space deployable antenna has become the frontier and hotspot of the research of space powers and scholars at home and abroad. Due to the limitation of the rocket payload module, the deployable antenna is in a closed state when the rocket is launched. After the satellite enters orbit, it gradually expands until it is locked. The deployable antenna changes from a mechanism state to a stable structure. However, due to the large aperture and low stiffness of the antenna, many dynamic problems may arise in the stage of attitude adjustment and on-orbit operation, such as structural coupling interference between the antenna and the satellite body, strong vibration caused by the impact of space debris and meteorites, etc. Therefore, it is very important for the design

© Springer Nature Switzerland AG 2019
H. Yu et al. (Eds.): ICIRA 2019, LNAI 11743, pp. 273–282, 2019.
https://doi.org/10.1007/978-3-030-27538-9_23

of satellite system to analyze and study the dynamics of deployable antenna structure and understand its dynamic behavior and characteristics [5, 6].

In this paper, the dynamic characteristic experiment of truss structure for a modular space deployable truss antenna composed of seven modules is carried out. Based on the basic theory of dynamics and the characteristics of antenna structure, a dynamic experimental system is designed. The modal experiments of the truss structure under free boundary conditions are carried out. The experimental results are analyzed. The dynamic experiments and analysis can be taken as a reference of modal analysis for other large space deployable truss structures.

2 Basic Theory of Dynamics

The basic dynamic equations of general multi-degree-of-freedom systems can be expressed as:

$$[M]\{\ddot{u}\} + [C]\{\dot{u}\} + [K]\{u\} = \{P(t)\} \tag{1}$$

where [M]——mass matrix;
     [C]——damping matrix;
     [K]——stiffness matrix;
     $\{\ddot{u}\}$——node acceleration vector;
     $\{\dot{u}\}$——node velocity vector;
     $\{u\}$——node displacement vector;
     $\{P(t)\}$——external Force Function vector。

The main work of structural dynamics analysis is to calculate the natural frequencies and main modes of structures. This work is also the basis of structural dynamic response analysis. The analysis of natural frequencies and main modes of structures can be summarized as eigenvalue and eigenvector problems [7].

For the case of undamped free vibration, that is, both [C] and $\{P(t)\}$ are zero in Eq. (1), then the free vibration equation can be obtained:

$$[M]\{\ddot{u}\} + [K]\{u\} = 0 \tag{2}$$

For linear systems, [M] and [K] are n-order square matrices, and the characteristic equation can be obtained:

$$\left| [K] - \omega^2 [M] \right| = 0 \tag{3}$$

The eigenvalue $\lambda_i(\lambda_i = \omega_i^2)$ and the corresponding eigenvector $\{\phi_i\}$ can be obtained from Eq. (3). ω_i is the angular frequency(rad/s) of the i th mode of the structure and $\{\phi_i\}$ is the corresponding mode shape.

The relationship between modal stiffness K_{ii}, modal mass M_{ii} and λ_i is as follows:

$$\lambda_i = K_{ii}/M_{ii} = \omega_i^2 \tag{4}$$

The displacement vector $\{u_i\}$ in physics is replaced by modal coordinate ξ_i, i.e. $\{u\} = [\phi]\{\xi\}$, substitution formula (1), and left multiplied by $[\phi]^T$, a new formula can be got:

$$[\phi]^T[M][\phi]\{\ddot{\xi}\} + [\phi]^T[C][\phi]\{\dot{\xi}\} + [\phi]^T[K][\phi]\{\xi\} = R(t) + [\phi]^T\{N\} \tag{5}$$

Assuming that the modal damping $[\phi]^T[C][\phi]$ is a diagonal matrix, the non-coupled equations of motion can be obtained by removing the non-linear external force term according to the orthogonality of the modal.

$$M_{ii}\ddot{\xi} + C_{ii}\dot{\xi} + K_{ii}\xi = R_i(t), \quad (i = 1, 2, 3, \cdots) \tag{6}$$

In this way, the order of the structural equation is converted from the degree of freedom of the original system to the mode of $[\phi]$ matrix. After the response of each mode is obtained, the response of the system can be obtained by superposing them according to $\{u\} = [\phi]\{\xi\}$[8].

3   Experimental Research

3.1   Experimental Conditions

(1) Structural Composition and Parameters

The modular space deployable truss antenna consists of seven modules, each module is mainly composed of rigid support truss and flexible cables. Each module is composed of mesh surface and truss structure [9, 10]. The structure of the module is shown in Fig. 1. Mesh surface is formed in parabolic shape, which is the working part of the deployable truss antenna. Each truss structure of module consists of six basic frames located in a radial direction from a center vertical beam. Basic frame can be deployed and stowed. The basic module is composed of hinges, spring, wires, motor and members etc. (see Fig. 2). The deployment force is generated by the spring which is installed in the center beam. The module can be deployed and stowed by the slider, which is attached to the diagonal beam and spring, and slides along the center beam. During the process of deployment, the motor installed in the bottom of the module controls the speed of the deployment through drive cable and pulls the slider to the bottom of center beam gradually, until the module realizes deployment state completely. After deployment truss structure is locked by the locking mechanism and it has high stiffness. Crossing cable can also improve the stiffness and strength of structure.

The beam length of the module is 600 mm, the height of the module is 150 mm, and the size of the envelope rectangle of the expanded antenna is 3000 mm × 3118 mm. The structural parameters of the truss structure are as follows: the material is aluminium alloy 2A12, elastic modulus is E = 70GPa, density is 2840 kg/m^3, Poisson's ratio is 0.31; the outer diameter × wall thickness of the central beam is 12 mm × 1 mm, the upper beam, the lower beam, the side beam and the diagonal beam are 10 mm × 1 mm; the diameter of the crossing cable is 1 mm, elastic modulus is E = 150GPa, and the pre-tightening force is 200 N.

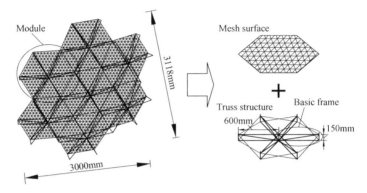

Fig. 1. Structure of deployable truss antenna and module.

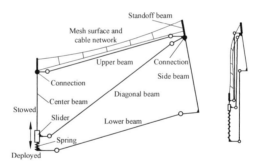

Fig. 2. Structure of basic frame.

(2) Establishment of Experimental System

In order to understand the inherent characteristics of structure for deployable truss antenna, modal experiments of the structure in unconstrained free state are carried out. Because of the large size of antenna, the suspension method is used to test. The object is suspended by flexible elastic rope on the microgravity experimental device. The center of each module is selected as the suspension point, i.e. seven-point suspension. The counterweight block with the same mass of the module is suspended at the other end of the elastic rope to eliminate the influence of gravity field as far as possible. The advantage of using elastic rope suspension is that the stiffness of the elastic rope is very low and almost zero compared with the structure under test. When using the elastic rope to carry out the experiment, the rigid body modes of the structure can also be generated, but the vibration modes of the structure will not be affected. Therefore, this method can simulate the free boundary conditions more accurately.

In this paper, a set of dynamic experimental testing system is designed. The scheme is shown in Fig. 3. The test system is mainly composed of microgravity experimental device, exciter, power amplifier, acceleration sensor, signal acquisition and processing system, rubber rope and so on.

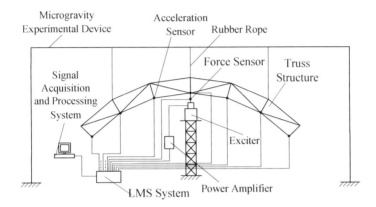

Fig. 3. Dynamic test system of truss structure of deployable truss antenna.

Microgravity experimental device is the framework of dynamic experimental system, which is used to suspend deployable antenna [11, 12]; rubber rope is used to separate the measured object from the frame, eliminating the external influence on the measured object; exciter is a device that generates excitation force, which can make the stimulated object obtain a certain form and size of vibration; acceleration sensor is a sensor that can measure the acceleration of the object. Power amplifier and signal acquisition and processing system are used to amplify, collect and analyze the measured signals.

Both the exciter and the power amplifier are produced by Jiangsu Energy Electronics Technology Co., Ltd. The models are JZK-2 exciter and YE587 series amplifier respectively. The acceleration values in x, y and z direction can be measured simultaneously by using three-way KISTLER acceleration sensor. The signal acquisition and processing system adopts LMS SCADAS III signal conditioning and data acquisition system produced by Belgium LMS Company. The system can provide users with complete, high-quality, low-cost solutions, and has been widely used in high-speed data acquisition and signal conditioning.

3.2   Dynamics Experiment

In the experiment, the single-point input and multi-point output mode experiment is used. The exciter is placed in different positions for testing. The center of the truss structure is determined as the excitation point, and the direction is vertical to the ground. The signal is a random signal of white noise. The sensors and key points are numbered. Choosing the center and boundary points of each module as test points, there are seven key points for each module. When the junction between the module and the module is counted as a point and the coincidence point is removed, so the deployable antenna has 31 key points.

Six key points are tested at a time until 31 key points are tested. The distribution of measurement points is shown in Fig. 4, and the field photos are shown in Fig. 5.

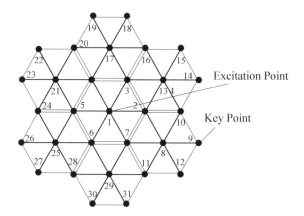

Fig. 4. Distribution of key points.

(a)   (b)

Fig. 5. Dynamic test field of truss structure. (a) Testing instrument. (b) Signal acquisition and processing system.

4   Results Analysis

4.1   Verification of Correctness

Through the analysis and processing of the data collected by LMS system, the natural frequencies of the supporting truss are obtained. However, because the deployable antenna structure is a rigid-flexible coupling system and the designed dynamic experimental system is also complex, it is difficult to directly judge whether the experimental results are correct or not. Therefore, the correctness of the experimental results should be analyzed and verified first.

According to the theory of modal analysis, all modes of the system should be orthogonal to each other, that is, the correlation coefficient of any two groups of modes is 0. However, because the experimental process can not be carried out under the theoretical assumptions, the collected signals will inevitably deviate from the real signals, which will directly lead to the deviation between the experimental results and the theory. After analysis and calculation, the histogram of autocorrelation function is shown in Fig. 6.

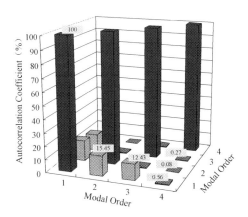

Fig. 6. Columnar section of autocorrelation function of modal.

The diagonal values in the figure are the autocorrelation coefficients of the modes of each order, which are all 100% because of their own comparison; the non-diagonal elements are the values of the correlation functions of the modes of each order. It can be seen from the figure that the correlation functions between the modes are small, and the maximum correlation coefficient is only 15.45%. This shows that the experiment has stimulated the low-order modes of the supporting truss very well, and the modal confidence is very high.

4.2 Analysis of Test Results

From the data acquisition system, the first four natural frequencies of the supporting truss are 32.781 Hz, 58.003 Hz, 66.396 Hz and 74.170 Hz, respectively. The experimental data are processed by the analysis software provided by LMS, and the two modes of the truss structure are obtained as shown in Fig. 7.

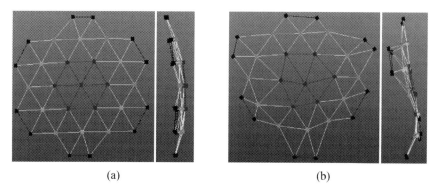

(a)   (b)

Fig. 7. Vibration mode obtained from experiment. (a) Vibration mode (32.781 Hz). (b) Vibration mode (58.003 Hz).

Comparing the experimental results with the theoretical analysis [13], it is found that the measured fourth-order natural frequencies correspond to the first, third, fourth and fifth-order natural frequencies of the finite element analysis, respectively, as shown in Table 1.

Table 1. Comparison between finite element analysis and experiment.

Modal order	Finite element result (Hz)	Experiment result (Hz)	Relative error (%)
1	29.643	32.781	10.59
2	29.644	——	——
3	58.027	58.003	0.41
4	68.461	66.396	3.02
5	72.133	74.170	2.82

It can be seen from the table that the maximum relative error between the theoretical and experimental results is only 10.59%, and the experimental results are in good agreement with the simulation results. In addition, the experimental mode shapes with the frequency of 32.781 Hz are in good agreement with the first mode shapes of finite element analysis, and the experimental mode shapes with the frequency of 58.003 Hz are in good agreement with the third mode shapes of finite element analysis. Therefore, the comparison of natural frequencies and modes has been further validated by theoretical analysis and experimental research.

In theoretical analysis, the first two natural frequencies of the structure are very close, while only 32.781 Hz natural frequencies are measured near the frequency band in the experiment. It is preliminarily determined that the analysis software can hardly distinguish the second natural frequencies so close due to the influence of the experimental environment, experimental instruments and other objective conditions. Therefore, only the first natural frequencies are obtained here. In addition, in the finite element analysis, from the fourth natural frequency, local modes of the support truss appear, and large bending deformation occurs in the internal members of the module. However, in the experiment, it is difficult to fix the sensor on the cross section of the member because of the cylindrical shape. Therefore, only the vibration modes corresponding to the second frequency are obtained in the experiment. The higher-order modal experiment of the truss structure will be a future research content of this topic.

5   Conclusions

(1) The autocorrelation coefficients of all modes of the antenna structure are 100%. The correlation functions between the modes are small, and the maximum value is only 15.45%. This shows that the experimental results are correct. At the same time, it also shows that the designed dynamic experimental system can meet the requirements of the modal experiment of the deployable antenna structure.

(2) Compared with the experimental results, the maximum relative error of the natural frequency is only 10.59%. The theoretical analysis is correct because it agrees well with the experimental results.

(3) The second-order and higher-order modes were not measured in the experiment. In the follow-up experiments, more in-depth research will be carried out on the testing instruments and structural improvement in order to obtain more comprehensive and accurate dynamic characteristics of the structure.

Acknowledgment. This project is supported by Key Program of National Natural Science Foundation of China (No. 51835002) and Liaoning Natural Fund Guidance Plan (2019).

References

1. Tibert, A.G.: Optimal design of tension truss antennas. In: 44thAIAA/ASME/ASCE/AHS Structures, Structural Dynamics, and Materials Conference, pp. 2051–2060, AIAA, Norfolk, Virginia (2003)
2. Liu, H.P., Luo, A.N., Zhang, T.M., et al.: Vibration analysis of circle truss of the astromesh deployable antenna. In: 3rd International Conference on Measuring Technology and Mechatronics Automation, pp. 1116–1119, Shanghai, China (2011)
3. Yang, G.G., Yang, D.W., Du, J.L., et al.: Method for deployable mesh antenna cable network structures' form-finding design based on force density. J. Mech. Eng. **52**(11), 34–41 (2016)
4. Meguro, A., Harada, S., Watanabe, M.: Key technologies for high-accuracy large mesh antenna reflectors. Acta Astronaut. **53**(11), 899–908 (2003)
5. Ando, K., Mitsugi, J., Senbokuya, Y.: Analyses of cable-membrane structure combined with deployable truss. Comput. Struct. **74**(1), 21–39 (2000)
6. Meguro, A., Tsujihata, A., Hamamoto, N., et al.: Technology status of the 13 m aperture deployment antenna reflectors for engineering test satellite VIII. Acta Astronaut. **47**(2–9), 147–152 (2000)
7. Shang, Y.J.: Finite Element Principle and ANSYS Application Guide, 1st edn. Tsinghua University Press, Beijing (2006)

8. Li, S.J.: Design parameters optimization and deployment experiment study of the rocker-bogie suspension for lunar exploration rover. Harbin Institute of Technology, Harbin (2009). (in Chinese)

9. Tian, D.K., Liu, R.Q., Deng, Z.Q., Guo, H.W.: Geometry modeling of truss structure for space deployable truss antenna with multi-modul. J. xi'an Jiaotong Univ. **45**(1), 111–116 (2011). (in Chinese)

10. Tian, D.K., Guo, H.W., Deng, Z.Q., Liu, R.Q.: Optimization of structural parameters for space deployable truss antenna with multi-module. J. Huazhong Univ. Sci. Technol. (Nat. Sci. Ed.), **40**(3), 49–53 (2012). (in Chinese)

11. Tsunoda, H., Hariu, K., Kawakami, Y., et al.: Deployment test methods for a large deployable mesh reflector. J. Spacecraft Rockets **34**(6), 811–816 (1997)

12. Tsunoda, H., Hariu, K., Kawakami, Y., et al.: Structural design and deployment test methods for a large deployable mesh reflector. In: AIAA/ASME/ASCE/AHS/ASC Structures, Structural Dynamics and Materials Conference, pp. 2963–2971. AIAA, Kissimmee (1997)

13. Tian, D.K.: Design and experimental research on truss structure for modular space deployable antenna, Harbin Institute of Technology, Harbin (2011). (in Chinese)

The Study of Wheel Driving Torque Optimization of Mars Rover with Active Suspension in Obstacle Crossing

Tang Ling[1], Liu Tao[1], Wei Shimin[1(✉)], and Liu Yafang[2,3]

[1] Beijing University of Posts and Telecommunications, Beijing 100876, China
wsmly@bupt.edu.cn
[2] Beijing Institute of Spacecraft System Engineering, Beijing 100094, China
[3] Beijing Key Laboratory of Intelligent Space Robotic Systems Technology and Applications, Beijing 100094, China

Abstract. Aiming at the problem of excessive driving torque of Mars rover in the process of obstacle crossing, a wheel driving torque optimization algorithm of rover wheels obstacle crossing ability of Mars rover is proposed. By using the redundant degrees of freedom of Mars rover to obtain the optimal configuration in the process of obstacle crossing, and the torque can be optimized. Based on the hybrid coordinate system method, the kinematics model of the Mars rover is established. Quasi-static method is used to calculate and analyze the torques of the front wheels, the middle wheels and the rear wheels of the Mars rover respectively in the process of obstacle crossing. And on this basis, the constraints of obstacles crossing are obtained. The result shows that the driving torques are reduced by 10.26%, 43.43% and 9.77% respectively for the front wheels, middle wheels and rear wheels, by using the wheel torque optimization algorithm.

Keywords: Obstacle crossing · Optimal configuration ·
Wheel torque optimization

1 Introduction

There are some complex landforms on the Mars [1], such as cross-wind ridges caused by weathering [2], chaotic topography caused by sublimation of ice-rich materials [3], craters [4], highlands [5], canyons and hills between canyons and craters. These harsh environments bring challenge to the mobility of Mars rovers.

The mobility of Mars rover on Mars surface has always been the research focus. The Mars rover with active suspension can change the configuration of the rover in order to enhance its traffic capacity [6]. Sutoh [7] studied the influence of wheel-spines on the Mars rover travel smoothness, and concluded that increasing the number of wheel-spines can improve the mobility. In addition, Sutoh [8] also proposes a new method for estimating the traveling performance of a wheeled rover over a slope, and proves that the effectiveness of the method. However, the above papers mainly focus on the analysis of the performance of the rover climbing performance. The performance of obstacle crossing is also an important part of rover mobility. Yongming [9] and others used quasi-statics to analyze the climbing ability of the Mars rover passing the same obstacle,

H. Yu et al. (Eds.): ICIRA 2019, LNAI 11743, pp. 283–293, 2019.
https://doi.org/10.1007/978-3-030-27538-9_24

and shows that the rear wheel has the best obstacle-climbing capability, the middle wheel is the worst, and the front wheel is moderate. Du [10] had proposed that the obstacle can be surmounted by lifting the wheels. However, the efficiency of lifting the wheels to surmount the obstacle is low, and in the process of lifting the wheels, the passive wheels support is higher. Gao [11] built a Mars rover model to analyze the mobility of the rover, such as obstacle crossing and slope climbing. Yubo [12] analyzed the force of Mars rover in the process of crossing the obstacle which height is less than the radius of the wheel, but that paper did not use the redundant degree of freedom of the Mars rover to optimize the torque of the Mars rover. Chen Shirong [13, 14] made a dynamic analysis of obstacle crossing and analyzed the stability of obstacle crossing for Mars rover. However, that paper focused on the structure design of Mars rover and there is no analysis of the optimal configuration in the process of obstacle crossing, ignoring the influence of configuration on torque, only considering the obstacle crossing condition of Mars rover, and did not optimize the torque.

In this paper, the redundant degree of freedom of the Mars rover is used to optimize the torque in the process of obstacle crossing by changing the configuration of the Mars rover. Ensure that the torque of the Mars rover wheel is within the passing range of the Mars soil. The chapters of this paper are distributed as follows. Firstly, the kinematics of Mars rover is analyzed and the kinematics model is established. Secondly, the quasi-static analysis of obstacle crossing of the Mars rover is carried out, and the constraints of each wheels are determined. Furthermore, Adams is used to simulate and analyze the wheel torque optimization algorithm of Mars rover. Finally, the conclusion.

2   Kinematics Analysis of Mars Rover

The structure diagram of Mars rover is shown in Fig. 1. The rover consists of the carriage, the differential, the angle adjustment mechanism, the main rocker, the vice rocker arm, the clutch, the steering joint of wheel and the wheel. The configuration of the Mars rover can be changed by adjusting the swing angle of main rocker arm and changing the state of clutch which can be set to brake and free.

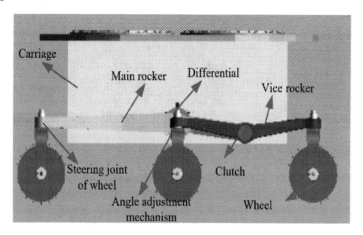

Fig. 1. A structure diagram of the mars rover with active suspension.

The description of the rover coordinate system is shown in Fig. 2. The origins of all the coordinate frames are located at the geometry center of the rover components, and the z-axis are the rotation axis of the joints. The directions of the three axes are shown in the figure, and they satisfy the right-hand rule. The joint i usually contains the coordinate frame $O_{\bar{i}}$ and O_i, and they belong to two interconnected parts. At the initial time, the position and posture of frame $O_{\bar{i}}$ and O_i are the same, so some descriptions of frame $O_{\bar{i}}$ are omitted in the figure. O_{cm} is the center of mass coordinate frame of carriage. O_{di}, $i = 1, 2$ is the coordinate frame of differential and d_i is the angle of the differential. The gear transmission relation of angle adjusting mechanism is simplified to two rotational joints, which are the joints of the differential shaft i between the front main rocker and the rear main rocker, respectively represented as a coordinate system O_{hfi} and O_{hri}, $i = 1, 2$. The motion constraint relation of two joints of the angle adjustment mechanism i is $h_{fi} = -\frac{h_{ri}}{2}$, $i = 1, 2$, in which h_{fi} and h_{hi} are the rotation angles of the joints.O_{bi}, $i = 1, 2$ is the coordinate frame of clutch i. b_i, $i = 1, 2$ is the rotation angle of the clutch i.O_{ti}, $i = 1, \cdots, 6$ is the steering joint coordinate frame of the wheel$i$. t_i, $i = 1, \cdots, 6$ is rotation angle of the steering joint of wheel i.O_{wi}, $i = 1, \ldots, 6$ is the drive joint coordinate frame of wheel i. w_i, $i = 1, \cdots, 6$ is rotation angle of the drive joint of the wheel i.

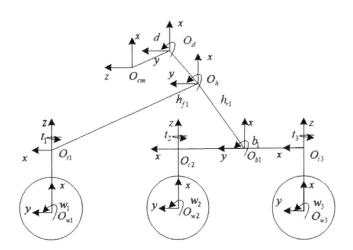

Fig. 2. -y side coordinate frames of the mars rover.

$P_{i-1}^{\bar{i}}$ and $C_{i-1}^{\bar{i}}$ are the position and attitude transformation matrixes of coordinate frame $O_{\bar{i}}$ relative to coordinate frame O_{i-1}. $P_{\bar{i}}^{i}$ and $C_{\bar{i}}^{i}$ are the position and attitude transformation matrixes of coordinate frame O_i relative to coordinate frame $O_{\bar{i}}$. Since coordinate frame $O_{\bar{i}}$ and coordinate frame O_i overlap, so $P_{\bar{i}}^{i} =$ zeros $(3, 1)$. θ_i is the rotation angle of joint i, and $C_{\bar{i}}^{i}$ is given by

$$C_i^i = \begin{bmatrix} \cos\theta_i & -\sin\theta_i & 0 \\ \sin\theta_i & \cos\theta_i & 0 \\ 0 & 0 & 1 \end{bmatrix} \tag{1}$$

The position and attitude transformation matrix of coordinate frame O_i relative to coordinate frame O_{i-1} can be expressed as

$$C_{i-1}^i = C_{i-1}^{\tilde{i}} C_i^i \tag{2}$$

$$P_{i-1}^i = P_{i-1}^{\tilde{i}} + P_i^i \tag{3}$$

The transformation matrix of coordinate frame O_{i-1} and coordinate frame O_i can be expressed as

$$T_{i-1}^i = \begin{bmatrix} C_{i-1}^i & P_{i-1}^i \\ 0 & 1 \end{bmatrix} \tag{4}$$

Therefore, the relationship between the coordinate frames of the rover can be obtained by transformation matrix.

T_b^{cm} is the coordinate transformation matrix from O_b to O_{cm}, which is given by $T_b^{cm} = T_d^{cm} T_h^d T_b^h$, and take $H_b^{cm} = T_b^{cm}(1,4) \cdot T_{wi}^{cm}, i = 1,4$ is the coordinate transformation matrix from O_{wi} to O_{cm}, which is given by $T_{wi}^{cm} = T_d^{cm} T_h^d T_{ti}^h T_{wi}^{ti}$, take $H_i^{cm} = T_{wi}^{cm}(1,4); L_i^{cm} = T_{wi}^{cm}(3,4)$. $T_{wi}^{cm}, i = 2,3,5,6$ is the coordinate transformation matrix from O_{wi} to O_{cm}, which is given by $T_{wi}^{cm} = T_d^{cm} T_h^d T_{bi}^h T_{ti}^{bi} T_{wi}^{ti}$ take $H_i^{cm} = T_{wi}^{cm}(1,4); L_i^{cm} = T_{wi}^{cm}(3,4)$. Moreover, the angle of clutch is related with the terrain and the swing angle of main rocker arm. The clutch angle which caused by the swing of main rocker arm can be calculated by the following:

The vector of the coordinate system O_{c20} in the x direction of O_{c10} coordinate system is parallel to the vector of the coordinate system O_{c2} in the x direction of O_{c10} coordinate system. These relationships can be expressed as $X_{c10}^{c20} // X_{c10}^{c2}$, where $X_{c10}^{c20} = T_{c10}^{c20}[1 \ 0 \ 0 \ 0]^T$, $X_{c10}^{c2} = T_{c10}^{c2}[1 \ 0 \ 0 \ 0]^T$. The equation can be written as

$$X_{c10}^{c20}(1) X_{c10}^{c2}(2) - X_{c10}^{c20}(2) X_{c10}^{c2}(1) = 0 \tag{5}$$

3   Static Analysis of Mars Rover Obstacles Crossing

There are some unstructured terrains on the surface of Mars, such as hillsides and obstacles. These unstructured terrains pose a challenge to the safe travel of Mars rovers. It is necessary to analyze the driving performance of Mars rovers. Obstacle crossing ability is an important part of Mars rover mobility. The obstacle crossing process of Mars rover can be divided into: two front wheels crossing the obstacle at the same time, two middle wheels crossing the obstacle at the same time, and two rear wheels crossing the obstacle at the same time. The following is a static analysis of the obstacle crossing process of the Mars rover.

3.1 Analysis of Front Wheels Obstacle Crossing of Mars Rover

Figure 3 is a force analysis diagram of two front wheels of Mars Rover crossing obstacles on the rigid terrain at the same time. As shown in this picture, $N_i, i = 1 - 3$ is the wheel support, $F_i, i = 1 - 3$ is the wheel friction, G is the carriage gravity, F_b is the gravity of clutch, the gravity of the others can be neglected.

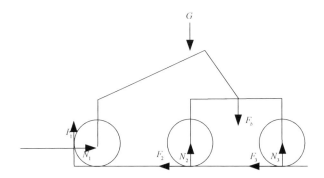

Fig. 3. Analysis of front wheel obstacle crossing

$$F_1 + N_2 + N_3 = G + F_b \tag{6}$$

$$F_2 + F_3 = N_1 \tag{7}$$

$$F_1\left(L_1^{cm} + R\right) + F_2\left(H_2^{cm} + R\right) + F_3\left(H_3^{cm} + R\right) + F_b L_b^{cm} = N_1 H_1^{cm} + N_3 L_3^{cm} \tag{8}$$

$$F_i = \mu N_i, \ i = 1 - 3 \tag{9}$$

The Eqs. (6)–(9) can be solved jointly:

$$N_1 = \frac{\mu(G + F_b)}{\mu^2 + 1} \tag{10}$$

$$N_2 = \frac{(G + F_b)}{\mu^2 + 1} - \frac{\left(\mu L_1^{cm} + \mu R + R\right)\frac{\mu(G + F_b)}{\mu^2 + 1} - F_b L_b^{cm}}{L_3^{cm}} \tag{11}$$

$$N_3 = \frac{\left(\mu L_1^{cm} + \mu R + R\right)\frac{\mu(G + F_b)}{\mu^2 + 1} - F_b L_b^{cm}}{L_3^{cm}} \tag{12}$$

According to the analysis of obstacle crossing of front wheel, the front main rocker arm needs to move clockwise around the clutch in the process of obstacle crossing, and the rotational dynamic torque needs to be greater than the rotational resistance moment so that the front wheels can cross the obstacle. The force inequality is shown in inequality (13):

$$F_1\left(R+L_1^b\right) > N_1 H_1^b + GL_b^{cm} \tag{13}$$

Equations (10)–(12) is brought into inequality (13). By changing the swing angle of the main rocker arm, the configuration of the Mars rover and L_b^{cm} can be changed. According to inequality (13), the rotational resistance moment decreases and the front wheel torque is optimized.

3.2   Analysis of Middle Wheels Obstacle Crossing of Mars Rover

Figure 4 shows the force diagram of the two middle wheels when the front wheels cross the obstacle smoothly and the middle wheels contact the obstacle. At this moment, the static equilibrium equations are as follows:

$$N_1 + F_2 + N_3 = G + F_b \tag{14}$$

$$F_1 + F_3 = N_2 \tag{15}$$

$$F_1\left(H_1^{cm} + R\right) + N_1 L_1^{cm} + F_2 R + F_3\left(H_3^{cm} + R\right) + F_b L_b^{cm} = N_2 H_2^{cm} + N_3 L_3^{cm} + GL_b^{cm} \tag{16}$$

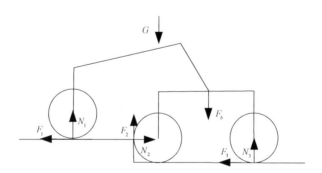

Fig. 4. Analysis of middle wheel obstacle crossing

The Eqs. (14)–(16) can be solved jointly and the results are shown as following:

$$N_1 = G + F_b - \frac{\mu^2(G+F_b)}{\mu^2+1} - \frac{(G-F_b)L_b^{cm} - \frac{\mu(G+F_b)}{\mu^2+1}\left(\mu R + \frac{1}{\mu}L_1^{cm}\right)}{\mu R - L_1^{cm} - L_3^{cm}} \tag{17}$$

$$N_2 = \frac{\mu(G + F_b)}{\mu^2 + 1} \tag{18}$$

$$N_3 = \frac{(G - F_b)L_b^{cm} - \frac{\mu(G+F_b)}{\mu^2+1}\left(\mu R + \frac{1}{\mu}L_1^{cm}\right)}{\mu R - L_1^{cm} - L_3^{cm}} \tag{19}$$

Analysis for the torque of the clutch assembly when the middle wheels cross the obstacle, the force inequality is shown in inequality (20).

$$F_2\left(R + L_2^b\right) + F_3\left(R + H_3^b\right) > N_2 H_2^b + N_3 L_3^b \tag{20}$$

Equations (17)–(19) is brought into inequality (20). The optimal configuration can be obtained by changing the swing angle of the main rocker arm. Therefore, the torque is optimized.

3.3 Analysis of Rear Wheels Obstacle Crossing of Mars Rover

According to Fig. 5, a quasi-static analysis is carried out:

$$N_1 + N_2 + F_3 = G + F_b \tag{21}$$

$$F_1 + F_2 = N_3 \tag{22}$$

$$F_1\left(R + H_1^{cm}\right) + N_1 L_1^{cm} + F_2\left(R + H_2^{cm}\right) + F_b L_b^{cm} = F_3\left(L_3^{cm} - R\right) + N_3 H_3^{cm} \tag{23}$$

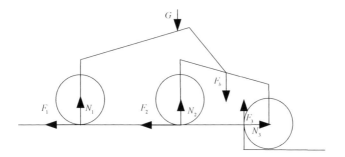

Fig. 5. Analysis of rear wheel obstacle crossing

Equation (21)–(23) can be solved jointly and the following can be obtained:

$$N_1 = \frac{\mu^2(G + F_b)\left(L_3^{cm} - R\right) - (\mu^2 + 1)F_b L_3^{cm}}{(\mu^2 + 1)L_1^{cm}} \tag{24}$$

$$N_2 = G + F_b - \frac{\mu^2(G + F_b)(L_3^{cm} - R) - (\mu^2 + 1)F_b L_3^{cm}}{(\mu^2 + 1)L_1^{cm}} - \frac{\mu^2(G + F_b)}{\mu^2 + 1} \quad (25)$$

$$N_3 = \frac{\mu(G + F_b)}{\mu^2 + 1} \quad (26)$$

According to the force diagram in Fig. 5, the following conditions are needed for the rear wheels to cross the obstacle:

$$F_3(L_3^b - R) + N_3 L_3^b > F_2(H_2^b + R) + N_2 L_2^b \quad (26)$$

Equations (24)–(25) is brought into inequality (26). The torque can be optimized by changing the configuration and adjusting L_1^{cm}, L_3^{cm} and L_b^{cm}. Therefore, the torque is optimized.

4 Simulation and Analysis

The Mars rover mobility is very important for the Mars Rover to travel on the surface of Mars. In order to verify the correctness of the wheel driving torque optimization algorithm, the high-fidelity dynamic models are established based on Adams software. As is shown in the Fig. 6, the simulation models include the dynamic model of the Mars rover and the unstructured terrain model. The simulation parameters are set according to Mars rover prototype and Mars environment and the simulation parameters are set as shown in Table 1. In this paper, simulation analysis is carried out for each optimal configuration.

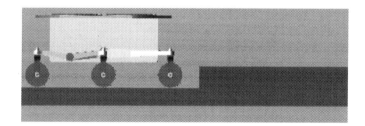

Fig. 6. The unstructured terrain

Table 1. Simulation parameters

Parameter	Value
Gravitational acceleration	3.72 m/s^2
Quality of Mars rover	247.14 kg
Wheel diameter	0.3 m
Obstacle height	0.15 m
Friction coefficient of rigid terrain	0.8
Wheel speed	10.5°/s
μ	0.7

The wheel torque is obtained by simulating and analyzing different optimal configurations for different terrain. For the curves, the Butterworth low pass filter with a cut-off frequency of 20 Hz is used.

4.1 Driving Torque Analysis of Front Wheels Obstacle Crossing

Figure 7 is the driving torque curve of the front wheel in the process of obstacle crossing. Figure 7a is the curve of obstacle-crossing torque of the Mars rover front wheel. The front wheels contact the obstacle on 12 s. The maximum torque of the front wheel during the obstacle-crossing process is 24345 Nmm. Figure 7b is the curve of wheel obstacle-crossing torque of the Mars rover front wheel after adjusting configuration. The front wheels contact the obstacle on 11.19 s. The maximum torque of front wheel in the process of obstacle crossing is 21847 Nmm. Compared with non-optimization, the torque decreases by 10.26%.

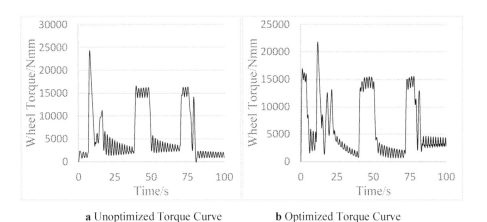

a Unoptimized Torque Curve   b Optimized Torque Curve

Fig. 7. Front Wheel obstacle crossing torque curve

4.2 Middle Wheels Obstacle Crossing

Figure 8 is the driving torque curve of the middle wheel in the process of obstacle crossing. Figure 8a is the curve of obstacle crossing torque of the Mars rover middle wheel. The middle wheels contact the obstacle on 52.63 s. The maximum torque of the middle wheel during the obstacle-crossing process is 17328 Nmm. Figure 8b is the curve of wheel obstacle crossing torque of the Mars rover middle wheel after adjusting configuration. The middle wheels contact the obstacle on 47.71 s. The maximum torque of middle wheel in the process of obstacle crossing is 9803 Nmm. Compared with non-optimization, the torque decreases by 43.4268%.

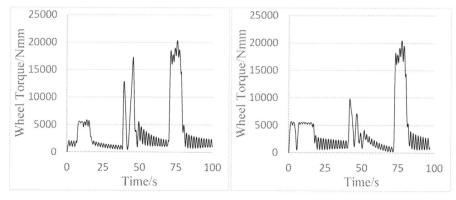

a Unoptimized Torque Curve   **b** Optimized Torque Curve

Fig. 8. Middle wheel obstacle crossing torque curve

4.3   Rear Wheels Obstacle Crossing

Figure 9 is the driving torque curve of the rear wheel in the process of obstacle crossing. Figure 9a is the curve of obstacle crossing torque of the Mars rover rear wheel. The rear wheels contact the obstacle on 84.24 s. The maximum torque of the rear wheel during the obstacle crossing process is 18561 Nmm. Figure 9b is the curve of wheel obstacle-crossing torque of the Mars rover rear wheel after adjusting configuration. The rear wheels contact the obstacle on 82.4 s. The maximum torque of rear wheel in the process of obstacle crossing is 16747 Nmm. Compared with non-optimization, the torque decreases by 9.77%.

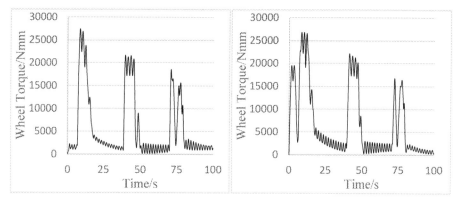

a Unoptimized Torque Curve   **b** Optimized Torque Curve

Fig. 9. Optimized rear wheel obstacle crossing torque curve

5   Conclusion

In this paper, the wheel driving torque optimization algorithm of the Mars rover with active suspension is proposed. By using the Adams simulation, the results show that the torque of the front wheels, middle wheels and rear wheels can be reduced by 10.26%, 43.4268%, 9.27% respectively through the proposed wheel torque optimization algorithm.

Aiming at the obstacle crossing situation of rear wheels, the optimization effect of rear wheels is not obvious because the front wheels and the middle wheels have exceeded the obstacle and the rear wheels are running on the flat ground. There are speed matching problems among the three wheels. The speed matching problem will be studied in the future.

References

1. Kipp, D.: Terrain safety assessment in support of the Mars Science Laboratory mission. In: IEEE Aerospace Conference Proceedings, pp. 1–8. IEEE, Montana (2012)
2. Berman, D.C., et al.: High-resolution investigations of transverse aeolian ridges on Mars. Icarus **312**(15), 247–266 (2018)
3. Gallagher, C., et al.: Formation and degradation of chaotic terrain in the Galaxias regions of Mars implications for near-surface storage of ice. Icarus **309**(15), 69–83 (2018)
4. Ziyuan, O.: The Mars and its environment. Spacecraft Environ. Eng. **29**(6), 591–601 (2012)
5. Wang, J., et al.: Lunar terrain auto identification based on DEM topographic factor and texture feature analysis. In: International Conference on Intelligent Computation Technology & Automation, pp. 534–537. IEEE, Nanchang (2016)
6. Zheng, J., Liu, Z., Gao, H., et al.: A novel active deform and wheel-legged suspension of Mars rover. In: IEEE International Conference on Robotics & Biomimetics, pp. 7–12. IEEE, Qingdao (2017)
7. Sutoh, M., Ito, T., Nagatani, K., et al.: Influence evaluation of wheel surface profile on traversability of Mars rovers. In: IEEE/SICE International Symposium on System Integration, pp. 67–72. IEEE, Sendai (2010)
8. Sutoh, M., et al.: Traveling performance estimation for planetary rovers over slope. In: IEEE/SICE International Symposium on System Integration, pp. 884–889. IEEE, Kyoto (2011)
9. Yongming, W., Xiaoliu, Y., Wencheng, T.: Analysis of obstacle-climbing capability of planetary exploration rover with rocker-bogie structure. In: International Conference on Information Technology & Computer Science, pp. 329–332. IEEE, Kiev (2009)
10. Du, J., Ren, M., Zhu, J., Liu, D.: Study on the dynamics and motion capability of the planetary rover with asymmetric mobility system. In: The 2010 IEEE International Conference on Information and Automation, pp. 682–687. IEEE, Harbin (2010)
11. Gao, H., Fan, X., Deng, Z., et al.: Simulation and experiments analysis of mobility performance in deployable manned lunar vehicle. Manned Spaceflight **22**(3), 323–327 (2016)
12. You, B., Tian, B., Ding, L., et al.: Planet rover operation mode selection strategy. J. Harbin Univ. Sci. Technol. **23**(02), 40–45 (2018)
13. Shirong, C., et al.: Control and simulation on getting over flight of step for wheeled robot. J. Mach. Des. **24**(01), 13–15 (2007)
14. Chen, S., et al.: Research on lunar terrain trafficability of lunar rover of rocker and bogie. University of Science and Technology of China (2009)

Designing, Modeling and Testing of the Flexible Space Probe-Cone Docking and Refueling Mechanism

Longfei Huang[1]([⊠]) [iD], Zhi Li[1], Jianbin Huang[1], Wenlong Wang[2], Wen Li[3], Bo Meng[1], Yujia Pang[1], Xu Han[1], and Zhimin Zhang[1]

[1] Qian Xuesen Laboratory of Space Technology,
Beijing 100094, People's Republic of China
huanglongfei@qxslab.cn
[2] Beijing Institute of Spacecraft System Engineering,
Beijing 100094, People's Republic of China
[3] Beijing Institute of Control Engineering,
Beijing 100090, People's Republic of China

Abstract. According to the requirements of docking and refueling satellites for deep space exploration, the paper presents a docking and refueling mechanism under a weak impact rendezvous and docking conditions. The flexible rod is adopted in the design of the mechanism to achieve the soft connection, while the rigid peripheral rod implements the correction and the rigid locking. The damping device of the mechanism absorbs the colliding energy. Moreover, it adopts the floating gas-liquid coupling interface and the electrical interface to further realize the high-precision gas/liquid/circuit connection. The multi-body dynamics model of satellites is established by using Lagrange analytical mechanics, and the deformation of flexible components during the collision process is described by using modal superposition method, then flexible docking and refueling dynamics model of satellites is established. The multi-condition dynamic simulation test shows that the mechanism can achieve reliable docking and refueling within the range of weak impact speed of 0.25 m/s, lateral docking tolerance of 20 mm and angle tolerance of $\pm 5°$. The prototype of docking and refueling mechanism was developed and experiment was performed, and the docking performance and circuit connection test was performed in the linear motion platform, also the interface sealing and propellant transmission test was performed in dedicated refueling system. The test results show that the mechanism can achieve the desired function and performance.

Keywords: Docking and refueling mechanism · Flexible space probe-cone · Dynamical model · Weak impact docking

1 Introduction

With the continuous improvement of the space electronic technology and the maturity of the satellite platform, the shortage of fuel carried by satellites has gradually become the main factor that restricts the satellite's life. Especially for satellites in the field of

© Springer Nature Switzerland AG 2019
H. Yu et al. (Eds.): ICIRA 2019, LNAI 11743, pp. 294–306, 2019.
https://doi.org/10.1007/978-3-030-27538-9_25

deep space exploration, sufficient fuel is the basic condition for long-distance exploration over a long period of time. It is a basic requirement for the space systems, which improve the response capability to major emergency events through the orbit maneuver. Future spacecraft will not be possible or necessary to bring full propellant from the ground all at once [1]. Therefore, the spacecraft system which can accept on-orbit refueling is one of the important development trends of space system. This shows that safe and reliable docking and refueling technology has become a prerequisite for on-orbit servicing [2].

However, in the complex space environment, to realize successfully rendezvous and docking of two spacecraft under high-speed orbit, a series of key problems need to be solved, including the light and small design of the docking mechanism, the dynamics analysis of the docking collision process, and the control of collision suppression etc.

There have been many years of exploration and research about on-orbit docking facilities, such as the Russian space station rendezvous and docking facility, the U.S. rapid transit plan, the XSS series, the DART project, the RSGS project, the AAReST project, the ESA ROGER project in DLR, ROTEX project in DLR, TECSAS project in Japan, ETS-VII project in Japan. According to the different ways of docking capture mechanism, there are several types of conical rod, claw, electromagnetic for different tracks, different target objects. However, the spacecraft inevitably has residual relative velocities when it is docked, and these docking mechanisms all attempt to weaken the impact of the docking process through structural design or precise control, such as using the spring-damping device, electromagnetic non-contact device or other ways to reduce the impact of the collision [3].

It should be noticed that the conical rod type docking mechanism is simple in structure and light in weight, and can make full use of the weak impact velocity of the two spacecraft to achieve effective alignment of the contact capture. By utilizing the conical surface of the passive device for isotropic guidance and racemization, the control accuracy of the Relative attitude between spacecraft can be reduced [4]. In view of the docking and refueling of satellite, it is feasible to use the flexible rod as the buffer device to realize the collision cushion directly at the butted rod end.

The dynamics of flexible impact belongs to the flexible multibody system dynamics theory system. Dupac studied the nonlinear dynamics of the impact of the flexible mechanism. In their study, the flexible rod was modeled as a concentrated mass and assumed that the model was subjected to an external collision of periodic elastic spheres [5]. Kovecses carried out the research on the collision model of flexible arm and ball, solved the model numerically and carried out the related experiments, and compared the results with the experimental data [6]. Vgasarayani studied the collision model between continuous system and rigid body obstacle using the method of recovery coefficient, and proposed a continuous system collision dynamics model based on element impulse feedback. The limitations of applying the existing recovery factor method to the simulation of continuous system crash are discussed [7]. Kim carried out a study of the contact dynamics control of flexible multi-body systems [8]. The German Aerospace Research Center conducted a research on the impact vibration of the flexible rod and controlled the post-collision vibration of the flexible rod by direct velocity feedback; Escalona et al. proposed a new numerical method for solving the problem of flexible bar subjected to axial collision [9].

Aiming at the on-orbit refueling satellites, this paper designs a universal docking interface with soft docking, rigid locking, gas/liquid coupling and electrical floating connection, establishes the flexible docking dynamic model and carries out the simulation analysis, and verified by ground test.

2   Flexible Docking and Refueling Mechanism Design

2.1   Mechanism Design

Docking and refueling mechanism consists of the active part and the passive part, which were installed in the active (service) spacecraft and passive (be serviced) spacecraft respectively. The docking mechanism adopts the layout of the center of the circumference and the periphery. And the center pole is flexible. After the soft docking is realized, 3 sets of peripheral rigid rods are connected rigidly. The flexible centering rod can correct the deviation of the two spacecraft's pitch/yaw direction and the deviation of the horizontal (radial) position when the initial docking is completed. The deviation of the two spacecraft's roll is corrected when the three side rods complete the initial docking and provide rigidity after the spacecraft is connected. The center rod is driven by a motor and has limit control during the extension and retraction movements. The Hall proximity switch provides the feedback signal after the extension is in place. The center pole and the surrounding rods unlock by the use of electromagnet. In order to avoid mechanical interference, additional mechanisms and electrical connectors are used floating connection, while designing high-precision guide and pre-tightening device, to provide additional gas and liquid anti-interference circuit connection capability. The overall configuration of the docking and refueling mechanism shows in Fig. 1.

2.2   Docking Principle

After entering the capture envelope, the two spacecraft will still have some pose deviation after the end of the rendezvous, and the docking and refueling mechanism will overcome the position and attitude deviation and establish the connection between the two spacecraft in three steps. Process diagram as shown below:

Achieve Passive Spacecraft Capture Through the Center Pole and Establish a Soft Connection. In the initial state, the center rod is folded into the active end support structure. Before the start of capture, the center rod extends out into the tapered hole of the passive part under the driving of the motor, and the passive end locking/unlocking component hugs the head of the center rod to realize the flexible capture. The process of extending and locking the center rod is as follows: the motor drives the lead screw to rotate through the reducer, the lead screw rotates to move the support along the guide rod within the main structure, and the center rod gradually extends under the movement of the support. After the center rod head contacts the receiving cone of the passive part, the center rod slides into the center hole of the locking/unlocking assembly under the guiding action of the cone surface, and the head of the center rod is clamped by the locking claw, what achieves the flexible capture. The Hall contact switch of rod head feeds back lock signal (Fig. 2).

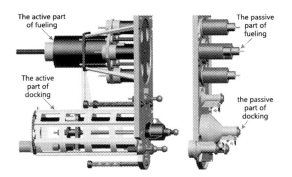

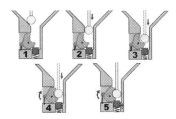

Fig. 1. The configuration of the mechanism.

Fig. 2. Lock/unlock components working process

Establish a Rigid Connection. After the initial calibration of attitude deviation is completed, the two spacecraft will be tensioned with each other through the center rod, and the posture deviation will be corrected during the process to finally form the connection pre-tightening force.

When the interface receives the lock signal, the motor reverses. The lead screw drives the movable bracket to slide in the main structure, and the central rod contracts. The center pole pulls in the active part and the passive part closer together. The relative position and orientation of the active part and the passive part are adjusted through the three conical guides of the passive end. The heads of the three peripheral levers enter the taper hole of the passive end and are locked by the three locking/unlocking components.

After the capture is completed, the center pole retracts the last paragraph. Accurate position alignment is achieved with a pre-designed guide cone on the active part. In the case of continuous tension to determine the preload to meet the requirements, the motor stops working, and the brake starts, then the rigid connection is completed.

2.3   Establish Gas, Liquid, Circuit and Other Functions Connection

While the rigid connections established, the gas connector, hydraulic connector and electrical connector, which distributed in the active part and the passive part, complete the docking action. The electrical connector insertion force is provided by the drive assembly and the pull-out force is provided by the guide separation assembly. Air connector, hydraulic connector insertion force provided by the connector itself (Fig. 3).

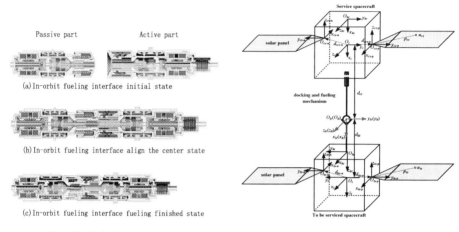

Fig. 3. Refueling interface.

(a) In-orbit fueling interface initial state

(b) In-orbit fueling interface align the center state

(c) In-orbit fueling interface fueling finished state

Passive part   Active part

Fig. 4. The structural form of the soft connection assembly

3   Flexible Docking Dynamics Modeling and Controlling

3.1   System Description

Considering the structural form of the soft connection assembly, the whole system can be regarded as a multi-body open-loop tree system with a center rigid body and a number of rigid and flexible attachments, as shown in Fig. 4, which is divided into the following components.

- Service spacecraft's center body and its internal moving parts (such as reactive momentum wheel, etc.), can be regarded as a central rigid body.
- The flexible rod of the docking mechanism is a first-order flexible attachment, with only flexible vibration. Modal superposition method is used to describe the dynamic characteristics and the modal order is n.
- Service spacecraft's solar panel is a second-order flexible attachment with only flexible vibrations, and the modal order is m.
- To be serviced spacecraft's center body and its internal moving parts (such as reactive momentum wheel, etc.) are the first-order rigid attachment, only the relative three-axis rotation from the center of the front-end is considered. That is the attitude rotation between the coordinate system $(O_t\ x_t\ y_t\ z_t)$ and the coordinate system $(O_{lc}\ x_{lc}\ y_{lc}\ z_{lc})$.
- To be serviced spacecraft's solar panel is a third-order flexible attachment with only flexible vibrations, and the modal order is m.

Based on the Lagrangian analytical mechanics theory, the following flexible docking dynamics model can be obtained.

$$M\ddot{q} + \dot{\theta}_1 D_1 + \dot{\theta}_1^2 D_2 + D_3 = NF_N + \tau F_\tau \tag{1}$$

Where M is a generalized mass matrix with a dimension of $(n + m + 6) \times (n + m + 6)$; θ_1 is the offset angle between the service spacecraft and target spacecraft; F_N, F_τ represent vertical impact force and tangential impact force; q, D_1, D_2, D_3, N, τ all are $(n + m + 6) \times 1$-dimensional vectors; q is Generalized variable; and N, τ are coefficient matrix of impact force.

It is assumed that the contact between the flexible rod and the passive part at the time of collision is the ideal point-to-surface contact. The normal distance from the end of the flexible rod to the surface of the passive part is δ, which can be used as the judgment criterion for collision.

$$\begin{cases} \delta > 0 & Not\ separated \\ \delta = 0 & Contact\ or\ separated \\ \delta < 0 & Depth\ embedded \end{cases} \tag{2}$$

According to the relative position of spacecraft and flexible rod in the service spacecraft installation position, the mathematical relationship of δ can be given.

When $\delta \leq 0$, vertical impact force F_N can be given.

$$F_N = F_k + F_d \tag{3}$$

Where F_K is spring restoring force, and F_d is damping force during contact. Spring restoring force F_K is determined by Hertz contact theory.

$$F_k = k\delta^{3/2} \tag{4}$$

Where k is the contact stiffness and related to the contact body's geometry and material. Nonlinear damping model is used to determine the damping force during contact.

$$F_d = C_1 \delta \dot{\delta} \tag{5}$$

Where, C_1 is the damping coefficient, which is related to the recovery factor e and contact stiffness k. During the contact sliding process, the flexible rod will slide along the passive part docking cone surface, so the tangential contact force is actually the tangential sliding friction force.

$$F_\tau = \mu F_N \tag{6}$$

Where, μ is the sliding friction coefficient. Solar panels can be simplified to the homogeneous isosceles cantilever model. Only the horizontal deformation of the solar panels is considered, while ignoring the surface deformation and so on. The deformation u_s at any point i on the solar panel is represented in its own coordinate system.

$$\mu_s = \varphi_s \eta_s = \begin{bmatrix} 0 & \cdots & 0 & \cdots & 0 \\ 0 & \cdots & 0 & \cdots & 0 \\ \varphi_{S1} & \cdots & \varphi_{Si} & \cdots & \varphi_{Sm} \end{bmatrix} \eta_S \tag{7}$$

Where φ_s is $3 \times m$-dimensional mode shape matrix, η_s is $m \times 1$-dimensional regularized modal coordinate array, m is the number of modalities to retain for model reduction.

By using the method of separating variables, we can get a homogeneous cantilever beam of equal cross-section frequency equation.

$$\cos \beta L \cosh \beta L = -1 \tag{8}$$

Where, L is the length of cantilever beam. The natural frequency of each order is

$$\Lambda_{si} = \beta_i^2 \sqrt{\frac{EI}{\rho_l}} = \frac{\lambda_i^2}{L^2} \sqrt{\frac{EI}{\rho_l}} \tag{9}$$

Where EI is the bending stiffness and ρ_L is the linear density. The mode shape function corresponding to each natural frequency is shown as below.

$$\varphi_{si} = \cosh \beta_i y - \cos \beta_i y + \zeta_i (\sinh \beta_i y - \sin \beta_i y) \tag{10}$$

Where, the coefficients can be listed as below.

$$\beta_i = \frac{\lambda_i}{L}, \lambda_i = \begin{cases} 1.875 & i = 1 \\ 4.694 & i = 2 \\ (i - 0.5)\pi & i \geq 3 \end{cases} \tag{11}$$

$$\zeta_i = -\frac{\sinh \beta_i L - \sin \beta_i L}{\cosh \beta_i L + \cos \beta_i L} = -\frac{\cosh \beta_i L + \cos \beta_i L}{\sinh \beta_i L + \sin \beta_i L} \tag{12}$$

Due to the light weight of the flexible rod, the short collision contact time during docking, and little influence on the lateral attitude of the whole star by its axial motion. Therefore, when analyzing the transverse vibration mode of the flexible rod, it can be approximated as the cantilever modal treatment. The expression of the vibration mode function of the flexible rod corresponding to each natural frequency is listed as below.

$$\Phi_i(x) = \cosh k_i x - \cos k_i x + \zeta_i (\sinh k_i x - \sin k_i x) \tag{13}$$

Where, l_l is the length of the flexible rod. According to the above equation, any order mode function of solar panels and flexible rod can be solved.

3.2 Controller Design

The controller is mainly composed of control circuit, bus interface circuit, telemetry acquisition circuit, controller power supply control circuit, power conversion circuit, motor power control circuit, motor pulse control circuit and motor drive circuit. By controlling the motor of positive rotation and reverse rotation, the center rod extends forward or backward. The capture hand is opened by responding to the in-position signal at the top of the center pole assembly near the switch. By detect the force sensor, whether the passive part of the pre-load has meted the requirements can be determined. Trigger the brake when it meets the requirements.

The ground controller mainly realizes the function, such as the drive of the brushless DC motor, the signal acquisition in place, the control of the electromagnet, the communication and recording of data through the host computer and hardware devices. The relationship between the controller and the external devices is shown as Fig. 5.

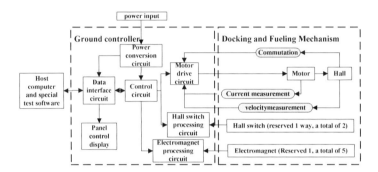

Fig. 5. The relationship between ground controller and devices

4 Simulation and Analysis

4.1 Dynamic Process

The docking process is divided into two steps.

- The motor rotates, and then drives the center rod to the passive end and into the hole. Because of the relative docking velocity of spacecraft after weak impacting or the forward movement of the mechanism, the center rod pushes the locking cam, and locking block enters into locking position by the action of the spring. The cam locks the center rod.
- Motor rotates reversal. As the center rod into the passive side is locked, so it will pull the active end closer to the passive end. The three spring rods contact the passive end docking plate and create compression. The three auxiliary probes enter the passive acceptance cone. Consistent with the principle of central lever locking, the three auxiliary probes are cam-locked and the relative positions of the active end and the passive end are tightened to be consistent. So far the docking is completed.

A total of 17 components in the model, that shows in Table 1. The model has a total of 25° of freedom: 12° of freedom including the main body of the active end and the passive end, a translational degree of freedom of the center rod. Each of the center lock block and the auxiliary lock blocks 1–3 has one degree of translational freedom. Each of the center cams 1–3 and the auxiliary cams 1–3 has one rotational degree of freedom, and each of the auxiliary bars 1–3 has a translational freedom degree.

There are 13 springs in the model. Each of the auxiliary springs 1–3 includes one compression spring. Each of the passive end center lock block and the auxiliary lock blocks 1–3 has one compression spring, and each of the center cams A–C and the auxiliary cams 1–3 has one extension spring.

Table 1. Components in the model

Part	Components	Identification	Part	Components	Identification
The active end	The main body	ActivePart	The passive end	The main body	PassivePart
	The center rod	CentralRod		The center lock block	Block
	Drive shaft	DriveShaft		The center cams A–C	CamA–C
	Auxiliary rod 1–3	Rod1–3		The auxiliary bars 1–3	Block1–3
				The auxiliary cams 1–3	Cam1–3

4.2   Working Conditions

There are eight kinds of conditions for simulation analysis.

- Condition1: 0 m/s initial velocity, o° attitude angular and 100 mm axial distance;
- Condition2: 0.25 m/s axial initial velocity docking;
- Condition3: Increase initial lateral velocity in (2);
- Condition4–6: Increase 5° relative attitude angles in directions of X, Y, Z in (3);
- Condition7: 0.25 m/s axial velocity and 0.5°/s relative attitude angular velocity;
- Condition8: 20 mm lateral tolerance, 0.25 m/s axial relative velocity and 0.5°/s relative attitude angular velocity.

4.3   Result and Analysis

Simulation results show that the mechanism can successfully complete the docking in 8 conditions. The results are shown in Figs. 6, 7 and 8 and Table 2.

Table 2. The results of the analysis.

Condition	Docking time(s)	The maximum attitude change angle(°)			Whether succeed
1	174	0.50	−0.04	−1.86	Yes
2	157	0.24	−0.06	−1.85	Yes
3	157	−13.64	−6.36	5.82	Yes
4	161	−4.37	−3.71	11.28	Yes
5	157	5.0	−8.20	4.20	Yes
6	161	−7.23	−14.10	5.81	Yes
7	157	−12.88	−6.53	5.6	Yes
8	157	1.80	−6.24	3.34	Yes

It can achieve the capture with tolerance of ±20 mm lateral distance and ±5° relative angular deviation under the condition of relative axial velocity of 0.25 m/s and relative angular velocity of 0.5°/s. While the docking mechanism of ETS-VII can achieve the capture with tolerance of ± 50 mm lateral distance and ±1.5° relative angular deviation under the condition of relative axial velocity of 0.015 ± 0.008 m/s and relative angular velocity of 0.15°/s. It can be seen from the displacement and force curve of the docking that the flexible rod can slide well along the docking tapered surface with a collision force of ≤ 40 N. The ultimate locking contact force between the mechanisms is no greater than 70 N because of the damping.

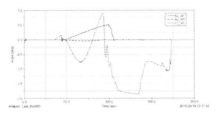

Fig. 6. Time-domain curves of relative attitude angles in three directions of active end and passive end under typical operating conditions.

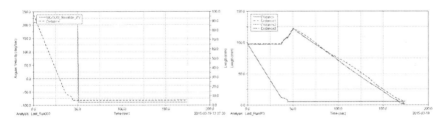

Fig. 7. The distance between the center rod and the locking cam (left). Distance between the corresponding locking cam and the center rod or auxiliary probe (right).

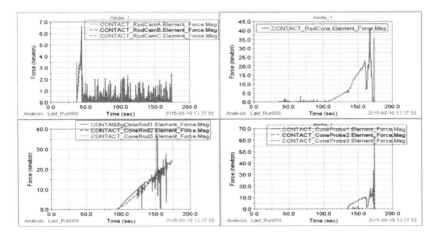

Fig. 8. Curve of collision force

5   Testing

The docking performance and circuit connection test was performed in the linear motion platform. The interface sealing and propellant transmission test was performed in dedicated refueling system.

5.1   The Docking Performance and Circuit Connection Test

The principle prototype of docking Mechanism was developed. And the linear motion platform was built, what supports to complete the docking performance and circuit connection multiple tests. A. The process of the test shows in Fig. 9.

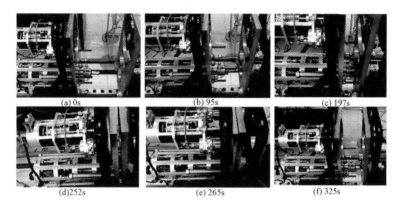

(a) 0s   (b) 95s   (c) 197s

(d)252s   (e) 265s   (f) 325s

Fig. 9. The process of the docking performance and circuit connection

The mechanism successfully realized docking performance and built circuit connection within 256 s. Then, the mechanism successfully unlocked the connection after gas, liquid, circuit and other function connection has been established (There is no gas and liquid in this test). The test results show that the mechanism can achieve the desired function and performance.

5.2   The Interface Sealing and Propellant Transmission Test

Although the fact that gas and liquid were not really added to the test, the interface sealing and propellant transmission test was performed in dedicated refueling system. The process of the test shows in Fig. 10.

Fig. 10. The interface sealing and propellant transmission

In the test, the transmission medium was deionized water and the pressurized gas was nitrogen. Propellant from the active end of the tank to the passive end of the tank is the forward transmission. The propellant is transferred backwards from the passive end tank to the active end tank. Repeat the cycle to complete the simulated liquid propellant filling volume 40 kg. Body structure can withstand 3 MPa pressure. The gas and liquid leak rate is less than 1×10^{-8} Pam^3/s. Through the test of propellant transmission, it's proved that the interface of the mechanism has good sealing performance. The test results show that mechanism performs normal during text.

6   Conclusion

This paper presents a docking and refueling mechanism under weak impact rendezvous and docking conditions, which fulfil the requirements of docking and refueling satellites. The flexible rod is adopted in the design of the mechanism to realize the soft connection, while the rigid peripheral rod realizes the correction and the rigid locking. The damping device of the mechanism absorbs the colliding energy. Moreover, it adopts the floating gas-liquid coupling interface and the electrical interface to further realize the high-precision gas/liquid/circuit connection. The satellites multi-body dynamics model is established by using the Lagrange analytical mechanics, and the deformation of flexible components during the collision process is described by using modal superposition method, and then the flexible docking and refueling dynamics model of satellites is established. The multi-condition dynamic simulation tests show that the mechanism can achieve reliable docking and refueling within the range of weak impact speed of 0.25 m/s, lateral docking tolerance of 20 mm and angle tolerance of $\pm 5°$. The prototype of docking and refueling mechanism was developed and test was performed, which shows that the mechanism can achieve the desired function and performance.

References

1. Sullivan, B.R., Akin, D.L., Roesler, G.: Parametric investigation of satellite servicing requirements, revenues and options in geostationary orbit. In: AIAA SPACE 2015 Conference and Exposition 2015, p. 4477 (2015)
2. Meng, B., Hang, J., Li, Z., Huang, L., et al.: The orbit deployment strategy of OOC system for refueling near-earth orbit satellites. Atca Astronaut. **159**, 486–498 (2019)
3. Dawei, Z., Hao, T., Yang, Z.: Dynamics analysis and parametric design of rod-like cone-type docking mechanism. J. Aeronaut. **29**(6), p1717–p1718 (2008)
4. Rivera, D.E., Motaghedi, P.: Modeling and simulation of the Michigan aerospace autonomous satellite docking system II. In: Proceedings of SPIE, vol. 5799 (2005)
5. Dupac, M., Marghitu, D.B.: Nonlinear dynamics of a flexible mechanism with impact. J. Sound Vib. **289**, 952–966 (2006)
6. Kovecses, J., Cleghorn, W.L.: Impulsive dynamics of a flexible arm: analytical and numerical solutions. J. Sound Vib. **269**, 183–195 (2002)

7. Vgasarayani, C.P., McPhee, J., Birkett, S.: Modeling impacts between a continuous system and a rigid obstacle using coefficient of restitution. J. Appl. Mech. **77**, 021008 (2010)
8. Kim, S.-W.: Contact Dynamics and Force Control of Flexible Multi-Body Systems. McGill University, Montreal (1999)
9. Escalona, J.L., Mayo, J., Dominguez, J.: A new numerical method for the dynamic analysis of impact loads in flexible beams. Mech. Mach. Theory **34**, 765–780 (1999)

Dynamics Modeling Method of Module Manipulator Using Spatial Operator Algebra

Tao Xiao$^{(\boxtimes)}$, Xiaodong Zhang, and Minghua Xiong

Beijing Key Laboratory of Intelligent Space Robotic Systems Technology
and Applications, Beijing Institute of Spacecraft System Engineering,
Beijing, People's Republic of China
txiao163@126.com

Abstract. Spatial Operator Algebra (SOA) was an operator theory based on Lie Group and Screw, and it implemented a recursion algorithm of O(n) with clear physical meanings. In order to increase the efficiency of dynamics modeling of modular manipulator, a kind of efficient modeling method using SOA is proposed in this paper. The conceptual design of basic modules is presented and the mathematical relationship between each module is described by the transformation matrix. Thereafter, a dynamics modeling method of modular manipulator is proposed based on Spatial Operator Algebra which has the characters of concise format and efficient calculation. Finally, a simulation for the 6-DOF modular manipulator is carried out and compared with ADAMS model, to verify the effectiveness and validity of this method.

Keywords: Modular manipulator · Dynamics modeling ·
Spatial Operator Algebra

1 Introduction

For the requirement of manipulator functions, the manipulators are usually designed as modular manipulator system, which can be build different configurations to adapt to the different working environments or tasks by changing the way of combination of connecting rods and joints [1]. Carnegie Mellon University, Toshiba Company, German SCHUNK company carried out several researches on the modular manipulator, and achieved certain results.

In order to control the motion of modular manipulator and complete different tasks, the dynamics model of the modular manipulator needs to be established repeatedly since the configuration is continuously reconstructed. Therefore, it is of great theoretical significance and application value to conduct efficient modeling research of modular manipulator. Most scholars adopt the Newton-Euler method [2] and the Lagrange method [3] to establish the dynamics model of modular manipulator. Newton-Euler method is an earlier developed and mature dynamics modeling method,

Supported by Key R&D Projects of the Ministry of Science and Technology (2017YFB1300204).
Supported by the National Natural Science Foundation of China (61733001).

H. Yu et al. (Eds.): ICIRA 2019, LNAI 11743, pp. 307–319, 2019.
https://doi.org/10.1007/978-3-030-27538-9_26

which is effective in simple systems. But it is not suitable for complex system with more degrees of freedom (DOF) due to its computational complexity $O(n^3)$, where n is the number of degrees of freedom. The Lagrange method is to analyze the manipulator system from the point of view of energy, whose computational complexity is $O(n^2)$. WANG W [4] proposed the kinematics method of modular manipulator by the expression of the motion helix and the force spiral. Since the method is based on the Lagrange method, its computational complexity is also $O(n^2)$. Due to the reconfigurable characteristics of modular manipulator, uncertainties of degrees of freedom and other factors need to be considered during its dynamic modeling procedure. Thus, the modeling methods mentioned above is not effective for the system with more degrees of freedom, and cannot be adapted well to satisfy the needs of the rapid modeling of space remote manipulator during the reconstruction process.

SOA is different from the Newton-Euler method in establishing coordinate systems. It is spatially recursive and has a clearer mathematical expression, whose computational complexity grows more slowly as the number of degrees of freedom increases [5]. Therefore, this paper studies a kind of faster and more effective method to establish the dynamics model for modular manipulator based on the SOA algorithm.

In the following, Sect. 2 gives the mathematical description of modular manipulator. Section 3 establishes the dynamics model of modular manipulator and Sect. 4 is the simulation. The summary of the paper is given in Sect. 5.

2   Mathematical Description of Modular Manipulator

Compared to a conventional manipulator, the modular manipulator is easily to construct a variety of different configurations and adapt to a lot of complex tasks. This is because many of the joints or connecting rods of the modular manipulator are the same or similar, which makes it convenient to combine into different configurations and replace it in the case of failure. Thus, we will present the conceptual design of the modular manipulator first.

2.1   Conceptual Design of the Modular Manipulator

The design of joint and connecting rods modules are the foundation of a modular manipulator. This paper only considers these basic modules, and then combines them into different configurations. Designed modules can be built in a simulation environment to meet the different requirements. The kinematics and dynamics modeling can be used to realize the motion control and inspection of the modular manipulator.

Joint modules are usually divided into two categories, revolute joint module and prismatic joint module. If the revolute joints are used rationally, the modular manipulator can reach any pose in the workspace. And considering that the revolute joint module is more suitable to the integrated management of the module, so only the revolute joint module is designed in this paper. The basic configuration of the revolute joint module is cylindrical, with mounting holes for connection with other modules. At the same time, for a modular manipulator, the base module and the end-effector module are designed. The base module plays the role of a solid support of the modular manipulator, and the end-effector module is mainly used for special tasks such as grasping or capturing. After the design of the basic module is finished, joints and links can be connected in different ways to construct different configurations to meet the different configuration requirements.

2.2 Mathematical Relationship

After presenting the conceptual design of joint and link modules and designing a modular manipulator with end-effector, the mathematical relationship between various modules should be obtained. Since it is important to establish kinematics and dynamics models of the modular manipulator and accurately describe its changing configurations.

For same type of modules, mass, center of mass and other parameters are exactly same, so the corresponding parameters can be reused in the modeling of the modular manipulator. Thus, the mathematical description matrices of modules obtained in this way have strong reusability.

Another feature of modular manipulator is the variability of its configuration, and it often needs to reconstruct to choose the appropriate working configuration. After reconstructed, the modeling and solution of the modular manipulator have to be repeated. In the repeated combination process, the information of mathematical relationship of modules is stored in a specific form of combination, and cumbersome recursive superposition operation for each joint and connecting rod is no longer needed.

The parameters of the mathematical description are combined into a 3-order matrix.

$$
\mathbf{M}_{abk} = \begin{bmatrix} a_x & b_x & k_x \\ a_y & b_y & k_y \\ a_z & b_z & k_z \end{bmatrix} \tag{1}
$$

Where $[a_x, a_y, a_z]^T$ denotes the direction vector at the interface of one end of the joint or link to the center of mass, $[b_x, b_y, b_z]^T$ denotes the direction vector at the center of mass of the joint or link to the interface at the other end, $[k_x, k_y, k_z]^T$ denotes the direction vector at the interface of one end of the joint or link to the interface of the other end.

Through mathematical relationship between modules of modular manipulator, the modeling process can be greatly simplified and the calculation efficiency of modeling the corresponding modular manipulator can be improved in the process of repeated modeling and solving.

3 Dynamics Model of Modular Manipulator

Assume that the manipulator is composed of n links and n joints. Each link is numbered 1 to n in sequence from the end-effector to the base, where the base is numbered $n + 1$. The joints from the end of the modular manipulator to the base are numbered joint 1 to joint n in sequence. As illustrated in Fig. 1, coordinate systems based on the SOA method are established, which help to analyze the kinematic relationship of the modular manipulator.

3.1   Symbol Description

As shown in Fig. 1, some symbols in this paper are expressed as follows:

J_k: The kth joint.
m_k: The mass of the kth link.
Σ_I: Inertial coordinate system, which is the foundation of all the recursive computations.
Σ_k: Coordinate system of the kth link, which is located at position of J_k.
C_k: The centroid of the kth link.
a_k: The vector from J_k to C_k.
b_k: The vector from C_k to J_{k+1}.
$P_c(k)$: The vector from J_k to $C_k.a_k$
p_k: The joint vector k expressed in inertial coordinate system.

During dynamics modeling of the modular manipulator, the mathematical description of the designed modules is used to establish coordinate systems. The first and the second column of $\mathbf{M}_{abk}$ is and b_k here, respectively. In the continuous recursion of joints and links, it's not necessary to repeat the calculation for each joint and link. In fact, only the first column and the second column of $\mathbf{M}_{abk}$ need calculation.

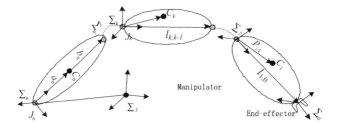

Fig. 1. Coordinate systems based on SOA method

3.2   Dynamic Recursive Calculation

Based on the SOA method, to obtain the transformation relationship between adjacent links, we firstly define the velocity of the kth joint as follows:

$$V(k) = \begin{pmatrix} \omega_k \\ v_k \end{pmatrix} \tag{2}$$

Where v_k and ω_k denote the velocity and angular velocity of the kth joint. Thus, the acceleration of the kth joint is calculated:

$$\alpha(k) = \begin{pmatrix} \dot{\omega}_k \\ \dot{v}_k \end{pmatrix} \tag{3}$$

Then the force and torque of the kth joint is defined as follows:

$$f(k) = \begin{pmatrix} N_k \\ F_k \end{pmatrix} \tag{4}$$

And the inertial matrix of kth link is:

$$M(k) = \begin{pmatrix} I_k & m_k \tilde{p}_c(k) \\ -m_k \tilde{p}_c(k) & m_k E \end{pmatrix} \tag{5}$$

Where I_k denotes the inertial tensor matrix of link k with respect to Σ_k, $\tilde{p}_c(k)$ denotes an antisymmetric matrix of $P_c(k)$, and E is a three-dimensional unit matrix. Define the state transition matrix of Joint k as $H(k) = \begin{bmatrix} h^T(k) & 0 & 0 & 0 \end{bmatrix}$, where $h(k)$ denotes the rotational axis vector of the joint, which is a three-dimensional column vector. If the base is fixed, $H(n+1) = diag\begin{bmatrix} 1 & 1 & 1 & 1 & 1 & 1 \end{bmatrix}$.

The space transfer operator will be defined to realize the outward recursive calculation (from n to 0) of the velocity and acceleration, and the inward recursive calculation (from 0 to n) of the force and torque of the modular manipulator. The recursive operator of force and torque is defined as:

$$\phi(k+1, k) = \begin{pmatrix} E & \tilde{l}(k+1, k) \\ 0 & E \end{pmatrix} \tag{6}$$

Its transpose matrix can realize the velocity recursion and acceleration recursion, which is written as:

$$\phi^T(k+1, k) = \begin{pmatrix} E & 0 \\ -\tilde{l}(k+1, k) & E \end{pmatrix} \tag{7}$$

Where $\tilde{l}(k+1, k)$ is the vector of joint $k+1$ to joint k.

Define $\tilde{y} \cdot x = x \times y$, then the recursive relationship between adjacent links can be expressed as follows:

The recursion of velocity and acceleration for joints:

$$\begin{aligned} V(k) &= \phi^T(k+1, k)V(k+1) + H^T(k)\dot{\theta}(k) \\ \alpha(k) &= \phi^T(k+1, k)\alpha(k+1) + H^T(k)\ddot{\theta}(k) + a(k) \end{aligned} \tag{8}$$

Where $k = n, n-1, \cdots, 1$.

The recursion of force and torque for joints:

$$\begin{aligned} f(k) &= \phi(k, k-1)f(k-1) + M(k)\alpha(k) + b(k) \\ T(k) &= H(k)f(k) \end{aligned} \tag{9}$$

Where $k = 1, 2, \cdots n$. And in (8) and (9), $a(k)$ and $b(k)$ denote the Carioles force and the centrifugal force of the modular manipulator respectively. If the joint is a revolute joint:

$$a(k) = \begin{pmatrix} \omega(k+1) \times h(k)\dot{\theta}(k) \\ \omega(k+1) \times [\omega(k+1) \times l(k+1,k)] \end{pmatrix}$$
$$b(k) = \begin{pmatrix} \omega(k) \times [I(k)\omega(k)] \\ m(k)\omega(k) \times [\omega(k) \times P_c(k)] \end{pmatrix} \quad . \tag{10}$$

The velocity operator of the modular manipulator is defined as $V = [V(1), \cdots, V(n-1), V(n)]^T$. And the acceleration operator, the force operator, and the torque operator are given as α, f, T. Thus (8) and (9) can be expressed as:

$$\begin{aligned} V &= H^T \phi^T \dot{\theta} \\ \alpha &= \phi^T H^T \ddot{\theta} + \phi^T a \\ f &= \phi(M\alpha + b) \\ T &= Hf \end{aligned} \tag{11}$$

Where the mass matrix, the state transition matrix and the space transfer operator of modular manipulator are expressed as:

$$\begin{aligned} M &= diag[M(1), \cdots, M(n-1), M(n)] \\ H &= diag[H(1), \cdots, H(n-1), H(n)] \end{aligned} \tag{12}$$

$$\phi = \begin{pmatrix} I & 0 & 0 & \cdots & 0 \\ \phi(2,1) & I & 0 & \cdots & 0 \\ \vdots & \vdots & \ddots & \cdots & \vdots \\ \phi(n-1,1) & \cdots & \cdots & I & 0 \\ \phi(n,1) & \phi(n,2) & \cdots & \phi(n,n-1) & I \end{pmatrix} \tag{13}$$

Joint torque of modular manipulator can be derived from (11) as:

$$\begin{aligned} T &= M_G \ddot{\theta} + C \\ M_G &= H\phi M \phi^T H^T \\ C &= H\phi(M\phi^T a + b) \end{aligned} \tag{14}$$

Where M_G denotes the generalized mass matrix of the modular manipulator, C denotes the nonlinear term, which contains the Coriolis force and the centrifugal force of the system. It can be seen from (14) that the dynamics model of modular manipulator through SOA method has a more intuitionistic expression than the dynamical equation through the Newton-Euler method. The flow chart of the modeling algorithm is shown in Fig. 2.

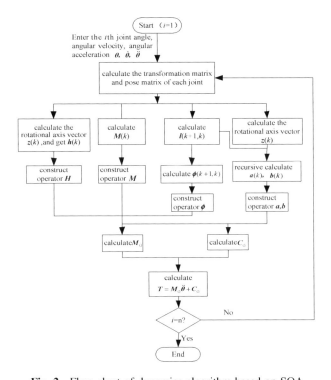

Fig. 2. Flow chart of dynamics algorithm based on SOA

3.3 Forward Dynamics Algorithm by Mass Matrix

The operator in the bias-free robot dynamics equations is symmetric positive definite. This follows from (14). If such an operator can be modeled as the covariance of an output from a known, causal, and finite-dimensional linear system driven by white noise, the operator can be factored and inverted efficiently by the use of standard techniques from filtering, detection, and estimation theory [6, 7].

$\mathbf{M_G} = H\phi M\phi^T H^T$ is positive definite, define $\mathbf{M_G}$ as:

$$\mathbf{M_G} = (I + H\phi K)D(I + H\phi K)^{\mathrm{T}} \tag{15}$$

Where D is symmetric matrix, and $(I + H\phi K)^{-1} = I - H\psi K$, and the operator can be factored as:

$$\mathbf{M_G^{-1}} = (\mathbf{I} - \mathbf{H\psi K})^{\mathrm{T}}\mathbf{D}^{-1}(\mathbf{I} - \mathbf{H\psi K}) \tag{16}$$

The operator $\mathbf{P}, \mathbf{D}, \mathbf{G}, \boldsymbol{\psi}, \mathbf{K}$ can be calculated by Eq. (17) recursively [11]:

$$
\begin{aligned}
&\mathbf{P}(0) = 0 \\
&for \quad k \quad = \quad 1 \cdots n \\
&\mathbf{P}(k) = \boldsymbol{\psi}(k, k-1)\mathbf{P}(k-1)\boldsymbol{\psi}^*(k, k-1) + \mathbf{M}(k) \\
&\mathbf{D}(k) = \mathbf{H}(k)\mathbf{P}(k)\mathbf{H}^*(k) \\
&\mathbf{G}(k) = \mathbf{P}(k)\mathbf{H}^*(k)\mathbf{D}^{-1}(k) \\
&\bar{\tau}(k) = \mathbf{I} - \mathbf{G}(k)\mathbf{H}(k)
\end{aligned}
\tag{17}
$$

$$
\begin{aligned}
\boldsymbol{\psi}(k+1, k) &= \boldsymbol{\phi}(k+1, k)\bar{\tau}(k) \\
\mathbf{K}(k+1, k) &= \boldsymbol{\phi}(k+1, k)\mathbf{G}(k) \\
end \quad loop
\end{aligned}
$$

Form Eqs. (12), (16):

$$
T' = \mathbf{T} - \mathbf{H}\boldsymbol{\phi}\left[\mathbf{M}\boldsymbol{\phi}^T \mathbf{a} + \mathbf{b} + \mathbf{B}\mathbf{f}(0)\right]
\tag{18}
$$

$$
\boldsymbol{\vartheta} = (\mathbf{I} - \mathbf{H}\boldsymbol{\psi}\mathbf{K})^T \mathbf{D}^{-1}(\mathbf{I} - \mathbf{H}\boldsymbol{\psi}\mathbf{K})T'
\tag{19}
$$

From the Eqs. (16), (18), (19), get the $O(n)$ recursive algorithm:

$$
\begin{cases}
\hat{\mathbf{z}}(0) = 0 \quad \mathbf{T}'(0) = 0 \\
\quad for \ k = 1 \cdots n \\
\hat{\mathbf{z}}(k) = \boldsymbol{\psi}(k, k-1)\hat{\mathbf{z}}(k-1) + \mathbf{K}(k, k-1)\mathbf{T}'(k-1) \\
\quad \boldsymbol{\varepsilon}(k) = \mathbf{T}'(k) - \mathbf{H}(k)\hat{\mathbf{z}}(k) \\
\quad \mathbf{v}(k) = \mathbf{D}^{-1}(k)\boldsymbol{\varepsilon}(k) \\
\quad end \quad loop
\end{cases}
\tag{20}
$$

$$
\begin{cases}
\quad \boldsymbol{\lambda}(n+1) = 0 \\
\quad for \ k = n \cdots 1 \\
\boldsymbol{\lambda}(k) = \boldsymbol{\psi}^T(k+1, k)\boldsymbol{\lambda}(k+1) + \mathbf{H}^T(k)\mathbf{v}(k) \\
\hat{\boldsymbol{\theta}}(k) = \mathbf{v}(k) - \mathbf{K}^T(k+1)\boldsymbol{\lambda}(k+1, k) \\
\quad end \quad loop
\end{cases}
\tag{21}
$$

3.4 Algorithm Complexity Analysis

Compared with Newton Euler method or Lagrange method, the algorithm based on SOA has lower computational complexity. The multiplication operation is expressed by the letter C, and the addition operation is expressed by the letter J. The calculation of each step is $k = 1, \cdots, n$, and the calculation results are all relative to the inertial coordinate system Σ_I.

The algorithm complexity of each step in the dynamic modeling method based on SOA is analyzed, and the computation of its multiplication and addition is counted. Because the dynamic model based on space operator algebra is solved by matrix recurrence, many "0" elements are included in the matrix, and the computation of multiplication and addition with the "0" element is very small, so we can define the multiplication and addition of the "0" element as zero plus multiplication, and indicate the total amount of computation by letter L.

(1) When calculating the rotation matrix R_k, the D-H parameter and the current step angle of modular manipulator should be used in the calculation process. The result will be used for the conversion calculation of $h(k)$, $\tilde{l}(k+1,k)$, and I_k from the local coordinate system to the inertial coordinate system, and the computation amount is $[27nC + 27nJ]$.

(2) When calculating the space transfer operator $\phi(k+1,k)$, it can be seen from the formula (6) that it is composed of a matrix, which can be combined by the known adjacent joint vectors of modular manipulator and the rotation matrix in step 1, and the computation amount is $[9nC + 6nJ]$.

(3) When the angular velocity $\omega(k)$ of the connecting rod is calculated, the formula (8) is used to be recursively solved and the amount of calculation is $[3nC + 3nJ]$.

(4) When the Coriolis acceleration $a(k)$ is calculated, the formula (10) is used to be recursively solved and the amount of calculation is $[30nC + 18nJ]$. Among them, the amount of zero plus multiplication is $L = [9nC + 9nJ]$.

(5) When calculating the moment of inertia $I(k)$ of each rod, the relative coordinate system is transformed from the known moment of inertia of each rod relative to its own coordinate system, its transformation is $R_k I(k) R_k^T$, and the computation amount is $[27nC + 18nJ]$.

(6) When calculating the centroid vector $P_c(k)$, the calculated rotation matrix is calculated from the known centroid vectors of each bar relative to its own coordinate system, combined with step 1, the computation amount is $[9nC + 6nJ]$.

(7) When the centrifugal acceleration $b(k)$ is calculated, the formula (10) is used to be recursively solved and the calculation amount is $[39nC + 24nJ]$. Among them, the amount of zero plus multiplication is $L = [9nC + 9nJ]$.

(8) When the joint acceleration $\alpha(k)$ is calculated, the formula (8) is recursively solved and the calculation amount is $[42nC + 42nJ]$. Among them, the calculation amount of zero plus multiplication is $L = [21nC + 21nJ]$.

(9) When the inertia mass matrix $M(k)$ of the rod is calculated, the formula (5) can be used and the calculation amount is $[21nC]$. Among them, the calculation amount of zero plus multiplication is $L = [6nC]$.

(10) When calculating the force $f(k)$ at each joint, the formula (12) is recursively solved and the calculation amount is $[72nC + 72nJ]$. Among them, the calculation amount of zero plus multiplication is $L = [18nC + 18nJ]$.

(11) When the torque $T(k)$ of each joint is calculated, the formula (12) is recursively solved and the calculation amount is $[6nC + 5nJ]$. Among them, the computation amount of zero plus multiplication is $L = [3nC + 3nJ]$.

Based on the sum of multiplication and addition of the above calculation steps, we can get the total computation amount of joint torque based on spatial operator algebra. $(285nC + 221nJ)$, if we remove the zero plus multiplier, the total amount of computation is $(228nC + 170nJ)$. The computational complexity of the dynamic equations based on the Newton Euler and Lagrange method is $O(n^3)$ and $O(n^2)$ respectively for the modular manipulator's degree of freedom, compared with which, the computational complexity of SOA is reduced to $O(n)$. For the multi-DOF modular manipulator, the computational efficiency has been greatly improved.

4 Simulation Results

This section will present the simulation and verify the effectiveness of the proposed dynamics modeling method for the modular manipulator. The simulation object is a 6-dof modular manipulator, and its dynamic calculation is programmed by MATLAB.

The dynamics calculation requires path planning in advance as the input of the program. The trajectory of modular manipulator is designed and the whole run time is 200 s. As shown as Fig. 3, the trajectory of end-effector is designed as follow:

Step1: move 300 mm along Z direction in the base coordinate system in 20 s;
Step2: move 1/4 circle curve in 160 s;
Step3: move 300 mm along − X direction in base coordinate system in 20 s.

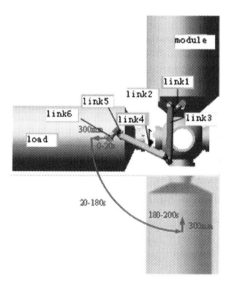

Fig. 3. The trajectory of a 6-dof modular manipulator

Based on the SOA method, the joint torque curve of the manipulator is obtained by the dynamic recursive equation. In order to verify the validity and effectiveness of calculation, the comparison is made with ADAMS model and the results of simulations are shown as Fig. 4, 5, 6, 7, 8 and 9.

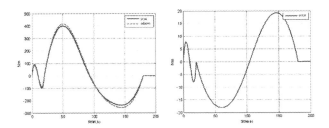

Fig. 4. Joint 1 torque curves and the torque error

The maximal error of joint1 torque is 19 Nm.

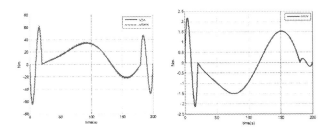

Fig. 5. Joint 2 torque curves and the torque error

The maximal error of joint1 torque is 2.2 Nm.

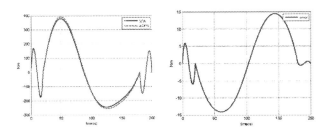

Fig. 6. Joint 3 torque curves and the torque error

The maximal error of joint3 torque is 14 Nm.

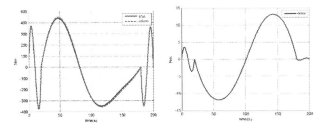

Fig. 7. Joint 4 torque curves and the torque error

The maximal error of joint4 torque is 13 Nm.

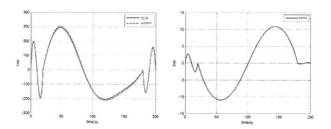

Fig. 8. Joint 5 torque curves and the torque error

The maximal error of joint5 torque is 11.5 Nm.

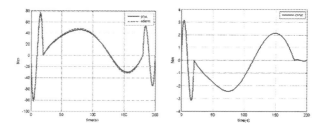

Fig. 9. Joint 6 torque curves and the torque error

The maximal error of joint6 torque is 3.2 Nm.

As shown in Fig. 4, 5, 6, 7, 8 and 9 compared with the ADAMS model, the maximal error of joint torque is 19Nm, which is the 4.75% of maximal output torque. The simulation results indicate the correctness and validity of the dynamics modeling method proposed in this paper. Moreover, for computer processor Intel(R) Core(TM) i3-2120 CPU @3.30Ghz, the calculation of dynamics equation costs 0.4 s by SOA, while it costs 1.5 s by Newton-Euler method, which proves the high efficiency of the modeling method based on SOA for modular manipulator.

5   Conclusion

In this paper, a modular manipulator of 6-DOF is taken as the research object. The basic structure of a complete module system is analyzed, and the advantages of modular design are expounded. Then, the dynamics modeling method for modular manipulator by SOA is introduced, whose complexity is analyzed and the simulation is carried out to verify the correctness and high efficiency. The simulation results shows that the efficiency of dynamics modeling calculation is increased by 375% and the accuracy of maximal error of joint output torque is less than 4.75%. Therefore, the simulation shows the dynamics modeling method for modular manipulator proposed in this paper is of great significance in engineering applications.

References

1. Li, Y., Liu, Y.: Hybrid kinematics and dynamics analysis for a mobile modular manipulator. In: 2003 Canadian Conference on Electrical and Computer Engineering, IEEE CCECE 2003, vol. 3, pp. 1767–1770. IEEE (2003)
2. Yim, M., Duff, D.G., Roufas, K.D.: PolyBot: a modular reconfigurable robot. In: 2000 Proceedings of IEEE International Conference on Robotics and Automation, ICRA, San Francisco, vol. 1, pp. 514–520. IEEE (2000)
3. Shen, J.: Research on dynamics and control of reconfigurable modular manipulator. Harbin Institute of Technology (2006)
4. Wang, W.: Dynamics analysis of reconfigurable robots based on screw theory. J. Mech. Eng. **44**(11), 99–104 (2008)
5. Rodriguez, G.: Spatial operator algebra for multibody systems dynamics. J. Astronaut. Sci **40** (1), 27–50 (1992)
6. Meldrum, D.R.: Indirect adaptive control of multi-link serial manipulators using Kalman filtering and Bryson-Frazier smoothing in Electrical Engineering, Stratford University (1993)
7. Wei, C., Zhao, Y.: Recursive computation of space multibody dynamics using spatial operator algebra. J. Astronaut. **30**(6), 2105–2220 (2009)

Object Dimension Measurement Based on Mask R-CNN

Zuo Wei[1], Bin Zhang[1(✉)], and Pei Liu[2,3]

[1] School of Software Engineering, Xi'an Jiaotong University,
Xi'an 710049, Shaanxi, China
`weizuo@stu.xjtu.edu.cn`, `bzhang82@mail.xjtu.edu.cn`
[2] School of Electronic and Information Engineering, Xi'an Jiaotong University,
Xi'an 710049, Shaanxi, China
`57269529@qq.com`
[3] China Academy of Aerospace Standardization and Product Assurance,
Beijing 100071, China

Abstract. An object dimension measurement system based on Mask R-CNN and monocular vision is introduced to perform non-contact measurement of the two-dimensional size of objects in irregular shape. Firstly, Mask R-CNN is used for detecting all objects to be measured and segmenting each object from the image captured by the camera. Secondly, edge contour extraction is conducted for all object regions and then the minimum bounding rectangle of each object contour can be obtained. Thirdly, according to the result of system calibration, the actual size of each pixel in the image can be acquired. Finally, the actual size of minimum bounding rectangle of objects contour can be calculated. The size of minimum bounding rectangle represents the two-dimensional size of an object. The experimental results show that the object dimension measurement system can accurately and rapidly measure the two-dimensional size of several irregular objects at a time, and the measurement system is robust to the change of ambient light.

Keywords: Dimension measurement · Mask R-CNN · Contour feature

1 Introduction

In the industrial environment, the size of product is one of the most important control elements, so it is particularly significant to measure the size of product accurately. Size information can be used for classifying products into different levels and checking whether the product is qualified. In traditional industrial process, the typical method of dimension measurement is that measuring workers perform manual measurement on products to be measured using measuring tools such as vernier caliper, micrometer or tape measure. Although the traditional measurement method is simple, it requires a large number of labor resources and the measurement efficiency is low. It can only measure a single object at a time, and the measurement result cannot be processed in time to meet the needs

© Springer Nature Switzerland AG 2019
H. Yu et al. (Eds.): ICIRA 2019, LNAI 11743, pp. 320–330, 2019.
https://doi.org/10.1007/978-3-030-27538-9_27

of large-scale automated production. In addition, the accuracy of measurement results is greatly affected by human factors.

With the rapid development of image processing technology, many dimension measurement methods based on digital image processing have emerged. An object dimension feature measurement method based on image segmentation [1] segments image by OTSU, extracts minimum bounding rectangle for region of object, and then utilizes the geometry math for object size. Non-contact dimension measurement of mechanical parts based on image processing [2] uses Hough transform algorithm to detect the circle and line on mechanical parts, and then measures the size of mechanical parts of specific specifications. Bend tube spatial parameter measurement method based on multi-vision [3] adopts the matching method based on central axis to acquire the 3-D coordinates of the bend tube spatial central axis from different points of view, and then calculates the bend tube external diameter from the edge lines. A method to improve the accuracy of crack length using machine vision [4] proposed by Khalili et al. measures the crack length of mechanical tool by utilizing machine vision, image capturing and image processing techniques.

However, the result of dimension measurement based on traditional digital image processing is easily influenced by environmental factors and has poor stability. When application scenarios or ambient illumination have changed, it is usually difficult to accurately detect the object from the image. The dimension measurement method based on traditional digital image processing has low practical accuracy, thus it is usually used in specific application scenarios for specific object dimension measurement.

In order to solve the problems mentioned above, an object dimension measurement system is designed in this paper, which combines deep learning with digital image processing technology. Firstly, we use Mask R-CNN [5] to detect all objects to be measured and segment each object from the image which is captured by the camera. Then, edge contour extraction is conducted for all object regions and the minimum bounding rectangle of each object contour can be obtained. According to the result of system calibration, the actual size of each pixel in the image can be known. Finally, the actual size of minimum bounding rectangle of object contour can be calculated. The size of minimum bounding rectangle represents the two-dimensional size of an object. The object dimension measurement system proposed in this paper can accurately and rapidly measure the two-dimensional size of several objects at a time, and the measurement system is robust to the change of ambient light.

2   Background

Mask R-CNN is an instance segmentation model proposed by He et al. which extends Faster R-CNN [6] by adding a branch for predicting segmentation masks on each Region of Interest (RoI), in parallel with the existing branch for classification and bounding box regression. The mask branch is a small full convolutional network (FCN) [7] applied to each RoI, predicting a segmentation mask in a pixel-to-pixel manner.

Mask R-CNN consists of four parts, namely Feature Pyramid Network (FPN) [8], Region Proposal Network (RPN), ROIAlign and functional network [9], and functional network includes three branches for classification, bounding box regression and segmentation masks. The structure of Mask R-CNN is shown in Fig. 1.

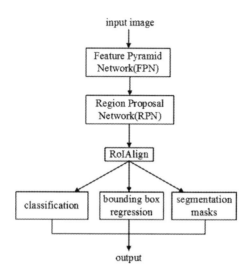

Fig. 1. The structure of Mask R-CNN.

A feature pyramid is a basic component in recognition system for detecting objects at different scales. A deep convolutional neural network computes a feature hierarchy layer by layer, and the feature hierarchy has an inherent multiscale, pyramidal shape. FPN relies on an architecture that combines the bottom-up downsampling pathway of deep convolutional neural network with the top-down upsampling pathway by means of lateral connection to merge the low-resolution, semantically strong features with high-resolution, semantically weak features. Each lateral connection merges feature maps of the same spatial size from the bottom-up pathway and the top-down pathway. The feature pyramid based on the above architecture has rich semantics at all levels and is built quickly from a single input image scale.

RPN takes an image of any size as input and outputs a set of rectangular object proposals, each with an objectness score. Anchor mechanism is used to generate region proposals in RPN, and an anchor is a box with preset coordinates and size in the input image. Each point in the five feature maps output by FPN corresponds to three anchors with different scales and aspect ratios in the input image, and RPN can perform classification and bounding box regression for each anchor. The classification in RPN can classify an anchor as object or background without determining the specific category of object. The bounding box regression in RPN can revise the width, height and coordinates of each anchor. After classification and bounding box regression, some proposals highly overlap with each other. To reduce redundancy, non-maximum suppression (NMS) is adopted to filter out more accurate object proposals based on classification scores.

In RoIAlign layer, bilinear interpolation and pooling are adopted to transform the features of all object proposals into uniform size to use for classification, bounding box regression and segmentation tasks in functional networks. RoIAlign layer transforms the feature size of all object proposals to 7×7 for classification and bounding box regression tasks, and transforms the feature size of all object proposals to 14×14 for segmentation tasks.

In Functional Network, taking features output by RoIAlign layer as input, the branch for classification classifies each proposal into a specific category, the branch for bounding box regression fine-tunes the width, height and coordinates of each region proposal, and the branch for segmentation uses FCN to semantically segment each object.

3 Algorithm

3.1 Calibration of the Measurement System

The principle of digital camera is shown in Fig. 2. Rectangular ABCD refers to the digital sensor of the camera, and point O stands for the center point of the digital sensor. Rectangular $A_1 B_1 C_1 D_1$ refers to the scene captured when the camera is focused, and point O_1 refers to the center point of the scene captured as the camera focused, point G represents the center point of the camera lens. Line segment OG means the focal length of the camera lens, and line segment $O_1 G$ signifies the object distance from the photographed object to the camera lens. When the camera captures an image, objects at points A_1, B_1, C_1 and D_1 are mapped to points A, B, C, and D of the digital sensor of the camera respectively through the center point G of the camera lens.

Obviously the polyhedron GABCD and the polyhedron $GA_1 B_1 C_1 D_1$ are geometrically similar, then:

$$\frac{OG}{O_1 G} = \frac{AB}{A_1 B_1} = \frac{AD}{A_1 D_1} \tag{1}$$

Assume that the size of the digital sensor of the camera is $a \times b$, that is, the length of AB is a and the length of AD is b, the focal length of the camera lens OG is f, the distance between the camera lens and the object to be measured is fixed to u, that is, the length of $O_1 G$ is u. Put the above system parameters into Eq. (1), and calculate the length of $A_1 B_1$ and $A_1 D_1$ as follows:

$$A_1 B_1 = a \times \frac{u}{f} \tag{2}$$

$$A_1 D_1 = b \times \frac{u}{f} \tag{3}$$

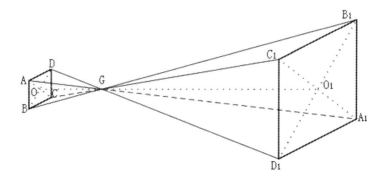

Fig. 2. The principle of digital camera.

If the resolution of the camera is $m \times n$, m corresponds to AB and n corresponds to AD, the actual size of each pixel in the image can be calculated as follows:

$$pixelSize = \frac{A_1 B_1}{m} = \frac{a \times u}{f \times m} \tag{4}$$

or

$$pixelSize = \frac{A_1 D_1}{n} = \frac{b \times u}{f \times n} \tag{5}$$

3.2   Object Dimension Measurement

When the object dimension measurement system works, camera is used for capturing an image of objects to be measured, Mask R-CNN is used for detecting all objects in image and segmenting each object from background, edge contour extraction is used for extracting all object contours and then the minimum bounding rectangle of each object contour can be obtained. The size of minimum bounding rectangle represents the two-dimensional size of an object.

The algorithm of the object dimension measurement is as follows:

Step 1. Capture an image of objects to be measured with the camera;

Step 2. Detect all objects to be measured and segment each object from background in Mask R-CNN;

Step 3. Extract the contour features of all object regions;

Step 4. Obtain the minimum bounding rectangle of each object contour;

Step 5. According to the result of system calibration, the actual size of each pixel in the image can be known. Calculate the actual size of minimum bounding rectangle of object contour, and the size of minimum bounding rectangle represents the two-dimensional size of an object.

4   Experiments and Results

The object dimension measurement system proposed in this paper consists of two parts: the hardware system and the software system (see Fig. 3).

The hardware system consists of a front-end processing unit and a back-end server. The front-end processing unit includes a camera, a monitor, a microcontroller and a measurement platform. The camera is used for capturing an image of objects to be measured; the monitor is used for displaying the result of the dimension measurement; the microcontroller is used for controlling the camera to capture images, controlling the monitor to display the results of the dimension measurement and being responsible for the network communication between the front-end processing unit and the back-end server; the measurement platform is used for placing objects to be measured, fixing the camera and keeping the distance between the camera and objects to be measured constant. The back-end server which includes GPU and CPU is used for receiving images from the front-end processing unit, detecting objects in the image, calculating objects dimension, and transmitting the result of the object dimension measurement to the front-end processing unit through the network.

The software system is composed of image acquisition module, result display module, network communication module, Mask R-CNN module, contour feature extraction module, MBR (Minimum Bounding Rectangle) calculation module and size calculation module.

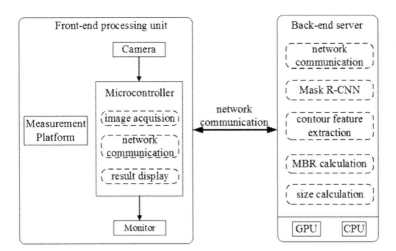

Fig. 3. Composition of the object dimension measurement system.

In this paper, we take the dimension measurement of tools as an example to verify the availability and stability of our system. There are five types of tools, namely forcep, screwdriver, knife, meter and hammer. The number of sample used for training and testing Mask R-CNN is 2000, and each sample typically contains one to five tools. 1500 samples in dataset are used for training Mask R-CNN, and the rest are used for testing Mask R-CNN. When training Mask R-CNN, We fine-tune the model, which is pre-trained on ImageNet, on our labeled dataset. The training and testing process are completed on the back-end server (NVIDIA Tesla K40c).

The camera DFK22AUC03 used in this experiment is produced by The Imaging Source company, which has a resolution of 744×480, and has a digital sensor size of $4.464\,mm \times 2.880\,mm$. The focal length of the camera lens used in this experiment is $5\,mm$. The distance between the camera lens and the tools to be measured on the measurement platform is fixed at $70\,cm$. When the system is calibrated, the actual size of each pixel in the image is calculated to be $0.84\,mm$ through these system parameters.

After the training of the Mask R-CNN and the system calibration are completed, the object dimension measurement can be performed. The result of object dimension measurement is shown in Fig. 4.

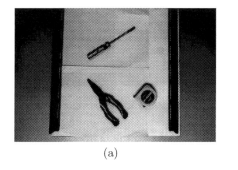
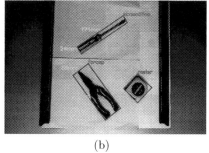

(a)   (b)

Fig. 4. (a) The original image of objects to be measured; (b) The result image of object dimension measurement.

The intermediate results of the dimension measurement are shown in Fig. 5.

In order to evaluate the accuracy of the object dimension measurement of our system, we manually measure the size of a group of tools and compare it with the measurement results of our system, as is shown in Table 1.

Compared with the results of manual measurement, the average error of the system is 2.1 mm. The average time it takes to perform dimension measurement on NVIDIA Tesla K40c is 0.6 s. The measurement system performs better for objects with lower height.

In order to evaluate the robustness of our measurement system to the change of ambient light, we conduct a check experiment by changing the ambient light. With the ambient light changed, the results of the object dimension measurement are shown in Fig. 6. It is found that illumination intensity, facula and halo have little influence on the result of object dimension measurement, thus our measurement system is robust to the change of ambient light.

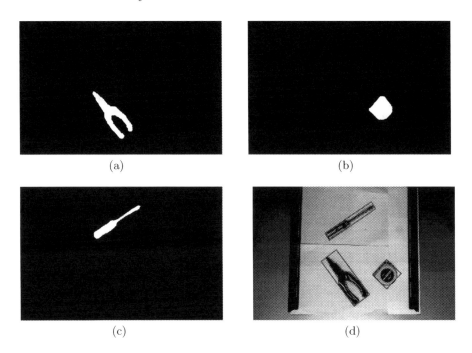

Fig. 5. The intermediate results of the object dimension measurement; (a) The segmentation result of the forcep in Mask R-CNN; (b) The segmentation result of the meter in Mask R-CNN; (c) The segmentation result of the screwdriver in Mask R-CNN; (d) The result of contour extraction and minimum bounding rectangle calculation for all objects region.

Table 1. The results of dimension measurement system and manual measurement.

No.	Sample type	Results of our measurement system (mm)	Results of manual measurement (mm)	Average error (mm)
1	forcep	167×58	167×57	0.5
2	forcep	150×50	152×52	2.0
3	forcep	169×58	168×56	1.5
4	screwdriver	171×24	175×22	3.0
5	screwdriver	170×25	173×22	3.0
6	screwdriver	160×22	157×25	3.0
7	meter	63×60	63×60	0.0
8	meter	55×59	57×57	2.0
9	knife	153×37	150×40	3.0
10	hammer	138×67	135×70	3.0

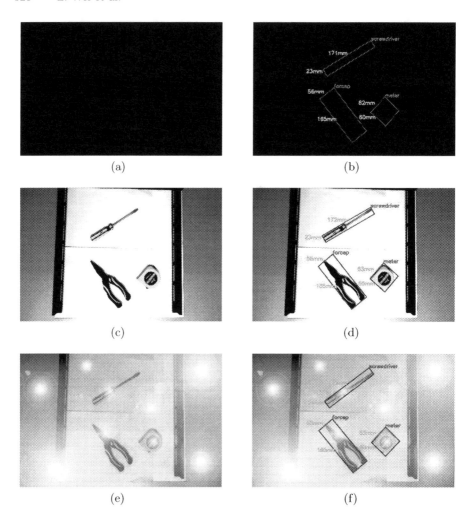

Fig. 6. (a) The original image of objects to be measured under the condition of weak ambient light; (b) The result of the object dimension measurement under the condition of weak ambient light; (c) The original image of objects to be measured under the condition of strong ambient light; (d) The result of the object dimension measurement under the condition of strong ambient light; (e) The image of objects to be measured under the condition of facula and halo; (f) The result of the object dimension measurement under the condition of facula and halo.

As is shown in Fig. 7, we also conduct an experiment to measure dimension of some different tools. we can draw a conclusion from the result of experiment that the measurement result would not be affected by the orientation of objects and the system has an ability of generalization.

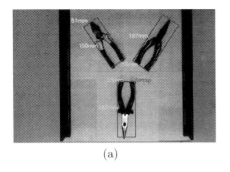 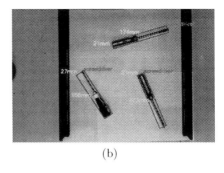

(a)   (b)

Fig. 7. The result images of object dimension measurement.

5 Conclusion

The object dimension measurement system proposed in this paper combines deep learning with digital image processing technology. Firstly, we use Mask R-CNN to detect all objects to be measured and segment each object from the image which is captured by the camera. Then, edge contour extraction is conducted for all object regions and the minimum bounding rectangle of each object contour can be obtained. According to the result of system calibration, the actual size of each pixel in the image can be known. Finally, the actual size of minimum bounding rectangle of objects contour can be calculated. The size of minimum bounding rectangle represents the two-dimensional size of an object. The object dimension measurement system proposed in this paper can accurately and rapidly measure the two-dimensional size of several irregular objects at a time, and the measurement system is robust to the change of ambient light.

Acknowledgements. This work is supported by National Natural Science Foundation of China (61603291), Natural Science Basic Research Plan in Shaanxi Province of China (2018JM6057), and Fundamental Research Funds for the Central Universities.

References

1. Wang, Y., Wang, P.F., Yang, Y.W.: Object dimension feature measurement based on image segmentation. Comput. Technol. Dev. **28**(2), 191–195 (2018)
2. Li, Y.F., Han, X.X., Li, S.Y.: Non-contact dimension measurement of mechanical parts based on image processing. In: International Congress on Image and Signal Processing, pp. 974–978. IEEE, Shenyang (2015)
3. Zhang, T., Tang, C., Liu, J.: Bend tube spatial parameter measurement method based on multi-vision. Chin. J. Sci. Instrum. **34**(2), 260–267 (2013)
4. Khalili, K., Vahidnia, M.: Improving the accuracy of crack length measurement using machine vision. Procedia Technol. **19**, 48–55 (2015)
5. He, K., Gkioxari, G., Dollár, P., Girshick, R.: Mask R-CNN. In: International Conference on Computer Vision (ICCV), pp. 693–696. IEEE, Venice (2017)

6. Ren, S., He, K., Girshick, R., Sun, J.: Faster R-CNN: towards real-time object detection with region proposal networks. IEEE Trans. Pattern Anal. Mach. Intell. **39**(6), 1137–1149 (2017)
7. Long, J., Shelhamer, E., Darrell, T.: Fully convolutional networks for semantic segmentation. IEEE Trans. Pattern Anal. Mach. Intell. **39**(4), 640–651 (2014)
8. Lin, T.Y., Dollar, P., Girshick, R., He, K., Hariharan, B., Belongie., S.: Feature pyramid networks for object detection. In: Conference on Computer Vision and Pattern Recognition (CVPR), pp. 936–944. IEEE, Honolulu (2017)
9. Peng, Q., Song, Y.: Object recognition and localization based on mask R-CNN. J. Tsinghua Univ. (Sci. Technol.) **59**(2), 135–141 (2019)

Research on Spatial Target Classification and Recognition Technology Based on Deep Learning

Yujia Pang[1][⊠][iD], Zhi Li[1], Bo Meng[1], Zhimin Zhang[1],
Longfei Huang[1], Jianbin Huang[1], Xu Han[1], Yin Wang[1],
and Xiaohui Zhu[2]

[1] Qian Xuesen Laboratory of Space Technology,
Beijing 100094, People's Republic of China
pangyujia@qxslab.cn
[2] China Academy of Space Technology,
Beijing 100094, People's Republic of China

Abstract. With the progress of human space technology, mankind stepped into more distant space. Due to the long distance from the earth in deep space exploration, higher requirements were put forward for intelligent cognition of targets and environment. In this paper, the space target classification and recognition technology based on deep learning was studied by taking the classification of three types of satellites as an example. A satellite simulation sample set for deep learning was established, and a ResNet multi-layer convolutional neural network model suitable for spatial target characteristics was constructed. The training and test of satellite intelligent classification were completed, and the feature extraction results of the neural network were visualized. The accuracy rate of satellite classification identification for the remote sensing satellites, communication satellites and navigation satellites reached 90%, which provided a reference for the development of intelligent classification and identification technology of space targets in the field of deep space exploration.

Keywords: Deep space exploration · Intelligent cognition · Deep learning

1 Introduction

Deep space exploration vehicles are human messengers to outer space. With the progress of ground artificial intelligence technology, it has become possible for space intelligent robots to independently carry out target recognition, environment recognition, navigation and positioning, decision control, health management and energy supply [1]. In the process of deep space flight, there will be many unexpected events and accidents, which put forward higher requirements for autonomous mission decision-making and control ability of on-orbit space intelligent robots [2]. Before autonomous decision-making and control, space intelligent robots need to recognize the environment and target accurately [3]. The recognition of space targets mainly

H. Yu et al. (Eds.): ICIRA 2019, LNAI 11743, pp. 331–340, 2019.
https://doi.org/10.1007/978-3-030-27538-9_28

includes the types, surface features and motion states of space targets, including asteroids, comets, artificial space debris, abandoned spacecrafts and so on.

Taking the classification and recognition of three kinds of satellites as an example, this paper discussed the application of deep learning in intelligent classification of space targets. The three types of satellites were remote sensing satellites, communication satellites and navigation satellites.

In order to classify three kinds of satellites intelligently, the ResNet neural network model was adopted, and a simulation sample set was established for deep learning. The training and test of the neural network for satellite classification has been completed. The classification accuracy of the three satellites reached 90%. Research on spatial target classification and recognition technology based on deep learning described in this paper could provide references and basis for subsequent intelligent cognitive technology of deep space exploration.

2   Establishment of Neural Network Training Sample Set

Target recognition based on deep learning usually requires thousands of training samples [4]. In order to improve the recognition accuracy of the deep neural network model, it is necessary to establish satellite sample set under the condition of space optical imaging. The construction method of the sample set was to build 3D models of different types of satellites and to simulate the space environment for 3D models imaging.

2.1   Construction Requirements

The satellite 3D model design adopted the modeling tools and considered the model proportion, imaging effect, texture pattern, etc. The cognitive scope mainly includes three types of targets: remote sensing satellite, communication satellite and navigation satellite. The satellite image samples can reflect the key payload and surface features of the satellite, including solar panel, polyimide film, secondary surface mirror, payload, star sensor, thruster, docking ring, antenna, etc. The surface texture information of the satellite model was set according to the true reflectivity of the materials used on each part.

2.2   Construction Method

In the process of building the satellite 3D models and simulating the space imaging environment, the space black background, vacuum, and direct sunlight were taken into account. As most of the satellite payloads point to the earth, in order to reflect the surface features of satellites as far as possible, in the process of simulation imaging of key payloads and characteristics, it is necessary to avoid to image the very top of satellites. Thus, cone of 60° angle from top of the satellite was excluded from imaging view, shown as follows:

In order to increase the diversity and richness of satellite samples, random imaging was adopted. As the spatial illumination direction may come from any direction, and different illumination directions have great influence on visible light imaging effect, the direction of sunlight incident in the imaging process was randomly generated in the satellite 4π space. Again because of the space vacuum environment without air scattering factor influence, image contrast is very big. If the angle of light and camera is too large, imaging effect will be influenced greatly. So the angle between light beam and camera imaging axis was set to be less than 45°, shown in Fig. 1.

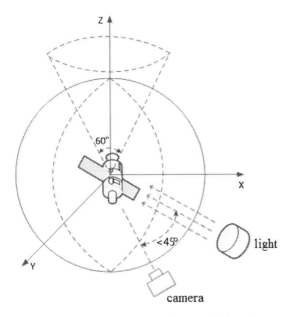

Fig. 1. Schematic diagram of 3D model imaging

The samples of imaged satellite are shown as follows (Figs. 2, 3 and 4):

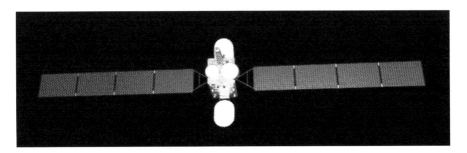

Fig. 2. Imaging example of communication satellite model

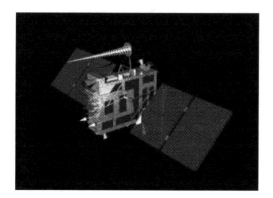

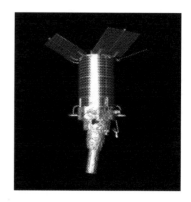

Fig. 3. Example of navigation satellite

Fig. 4. Example of remote sensing satellite

3   Establishment of Neural Network Model

3.1   ResNet Network

The ResNet residual network model was used for satellite classification, and was implemented by Tensorflow. The ResNet network model allows a certain proportion of original input to be retained in the residual network calculation of each layer, which reduces the sensitivity and training complexity of neural network structure to depth. ResNet residual network improves the performance that the accuracy decreases due to the continuous increase of network depth in deep learning [5].

3.2   Construction of Neural Network Model

The neural network was constructed as follows:

- All kinds of satellite images were processed to 640×360 resolution images.
- The neural network model was composed of 1 convolutional layer, 3 residual learning modules and 1 full connection layer.
- Each residual learning module included 2 residual learning units, and each residual learning unit adopted a 2-layer structure. Thus, each residual learning module included 4 convolution operations, so the network had a total of 14 layers.
- The Relu activation function was adopted. The network model optimization algorithm adopted Momentum algorithm, and the initial learning rate is 0.1.

In conclusion, the ResNet neural network model structure used for satellite classification was shown in the following Table 1:

Table 1. Structure table of neural network model used for satellite classification

Layer	Output	Structure
Conv0	640×360	3×3, 16, stride 1
ConV1_x	640×360	$\begin{bmatrix} 3 \times 3, & 16 \\ 3 \times 3, & 16 \end{bmatrix} \times 2$
ConV2_x	320×180	$\begin{bmatrix} 3 \times 3, & 16 \\ 3 \times 3, & 32 \end{bmatrix} \times 2$
ConV3_x	160×90	$\begin{bmatrix} 3 \times 3, & 64 \\ 3 \times 3, & 64 \end{bmatrix} \times 2$
Full connection	1×3	Average pool, fc, softmax

Among them, Conv0 is the initial convolutional layer, ConV1_x is the first residual learning module, ConV2_x is the second residual learning module, ConV3_x is the third residual learning module, and Full connection is the full connection layer.

Input images entered the initial convolution layer and the 1st–3rd residual learning module successively. After average pooling operation in the full connection layer, full connection operation was carried out. Finally, classification probability statistics was calculated through the classifier, so as to determine the application type corresponding to the target satellite.

4 Training and Test of Neural Network for Satellite Classification

4.1 Image Resolution

In order to keep the detailed features and improve classification accuracy, image resolution used for training and test of multilayer convolution neural network should not be too low. At the same time, in order to save computing resources and improve the working efficiency of the processor, the sample image resolution can not be too high. The sample image resolution of the satellite classification neural network introduced in the paper can not be less than 256×256. Therefore, before the image sample was sent to the neural network, the image resolution was reduced to 640×360 in proportion, and the aspect ratio remains unchanged.

4.2 Image Preprocessing

Before feeding training samples into the deep learning neural network, image processing methods such as rotation, translation and flip were used to increase the number of samples. The rotation angle was $0°–360°$ random. The translation distance was not more than 1/32 of the image length or width, which avoided the satellite body moving out of the image.

4.3 Training Set and Test Set

All satellite samples were randomly divided into training set and test set. The number ratio of training sample to test sample was about 3:1. There was no cross sample between training set and test set. The training set and test set samples can cover three types of satellites evenly. The training set and test set were labeled data. The training set was used for neural network training, and the test set was used for neural network test during and after training.

4.4 Training and Test Results

During the training process, 10 images in the training sample set were randomly selected and sent to the neural network for processing and learning until the whole training sample set was finished. This was called a training cycle. Generally, in order to achieve higher classification accuracy, hundreds of cycles of autonomous recognition training were needed.

The training and test results of the neural network model for satellite classification were shown as follows (Figs. 5 and 6):

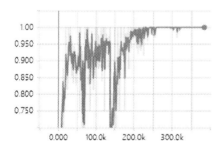

Fig. 5. Training accuracy

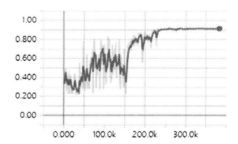

Fig. 6. Test accuracy

4.5 Satellite Prediction

Satellite sample images were randomly selected from the test sample set and sent to the trained neural network model for type prediction. The results were shown as follows (Figs. 7, 8 and 9):

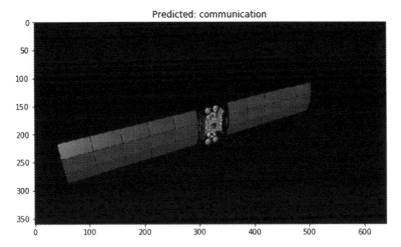

Fig. 7. The predicted result of a communication satellite

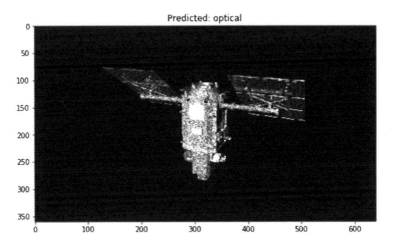

Fig. 8. The predicted result of one remote sensing satellite

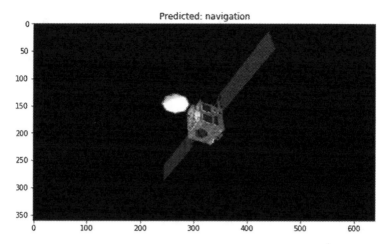

Fig. 9. The predicted result of a navigation satellite

The predicted results of the above satellites were consistent with the actual situation.

5   Visualization of Neural Networks

In order to better understand the features learned by the artificial neural network in the process of target classification, feature maps were visualized in the three dimensions of width, height and depth (number of channels) [6]. Following picture is a satellite and was sent to the trained neural network for prediction (Fig. 10).

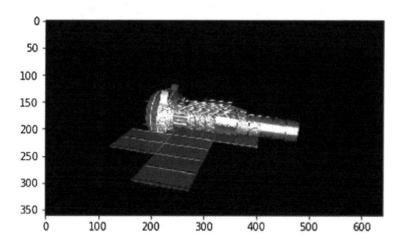

Fig. 10.   One satellite sample sent to neural network after training for predicted

Feature maps of an activation layer output are shown as follows (Fig. 11):

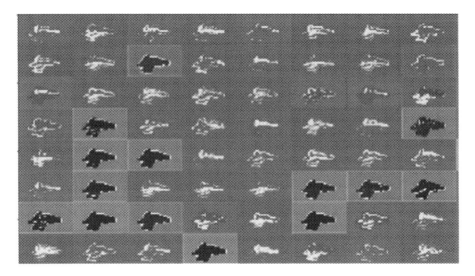

Fig. 11. Feature maps extracted by the neural network

The figure above showed features that were obtained through the neural network by different filters (convolution kernels). At last, the neural network would synthesize the feature extraction results of each channel through the full connection layer, and drew a conclusion to determine which type the satellite belonged to.

6   Conclusion

The satellite classification based on deep learning introduced in this paper can establish a deep neural network model suitable for on-orbit autonomous recognition of space targets through off-line training. By collecting visible images of the target satellite in orbit and using the deep convolutional neural network model trained successfully for real-time recognition, the autonomous on-orbit recognition of satellite classification can be realized. This technology can provide effective reference for deep space exploration application of deep learning technology.

Future research direction of our work team is feature detection and feature location of spatial targets using deep learning, so that artificial intelligence could be applied on space technology.

References

1. Lin, Y., Li, D., Wang, Y.: Current status and analysis of space robot. Spacecr. Eng. **24**(5) (2015)
2. Liu, S., Chen, Y., Xing, L.: Method of agile imaging satellites autonomous task planning. Comput. Integr. Manuf. Syst. **22**(4), 928–934 (2016)
3. Robotics, Tele-Robotics and Autonomous Systems Roadmap. National Aeronautics and Space Administration (2012)
4. Sun, Y., Wang, X., Tang, X.: Deep learning face representation from predicting 10,000 classes. In: IEEE Conference on Computer Vision and Pattern Recognition (2014)
5. He, K., Zhang, X., Ren, S.: Deep residual learning for image recognition. In: 2016 IEEE Conference on Computer Vision and Pattern Recognition (CVPR) (2016)
6. Chollet, F.: Deep Learning with Python. Posts & Telecom Press, Beijing (2018)

Planetary Rover Path Planning Based on Improved A* Algorithm

Weihuai Wu, Xiaomei Xie[⊠], Mingzhu Wei, Nian Liu, Xin Chen,
Peng Yan, Mechali Omar, and Limei Xu

School of Aeronautics and Astronautics,
University of Electronic Science and Technology of China,
Chengdu 611731, China
mayxiezhou@uestc.edu.cn

Abstract. Developing a space rover with ability to explore robustly and autonomously the unknown outer space landscape like Moon and Mars has always been a major challenge, since the first roving remote-controlled robot, Lunokhod 1, landed on the moon. Path planning is one of important task when the rover travels a certain distance without the human control. To traverse safely on the harsh and complex planetary surface, the terrain environmental information and the ability of the roving vehicle to overcome obstacles should be taken into account. In this paper, an improved A* algorithm is proposed via introducing both the environmental characteristics (such as surface slope and surface toughness) and the rover's traversability as the constraint conditions. Comparison of the performance of the proposed A* algorithm relative to the original A* algorithm is conducted based on MATLAB platform. Numerical simulations indicate that the improved A* algorithm has shorter path and higher planning success rate.

Keywords: Path planning · Environmental characteristics · Traversability · A* algorithm

1 Introduction

The application of the first rover landed on the out space can be dated back to November 17, 1970 the Soviet Luna 17 spacecraft landed the first roving remote-controlled robot, Lunokhod 1, on the Moon. After that, several planetary rovers, such as Apollo lunar roving vehicle, China's Yutu lunar rover and Mars rovers (Sojourner, Spirit and Opportunity, and the Curiosity), have been used to explore the Moon and Mars. It is noted that all these rovers are driven by the human tele-operators. So the autonomous navigation ability of the rover is needed in the near future, while path planning is one important problem [1]. Path planning is that the rover searches for an optimal or suboptimal path from the starting position to the target position in the motion space according to some optimization criteria (such as minimum energy consumption, shortest walking route, shortest walking time, etc.), so that the lunar rover can safely and bypass all obstacles in the motion process. In the past few decades, people have applied different path planning algorithms to the launched rovers [2].

© Springer Nature Switzerland AG 2019
H. Yu et al. (Eds.): ICIRA 2019, LNAI 11743, pp. 341–353, 2019.
https://doi.org/10.1007/978-3-030-27538-9_29

Sojourner rover is the first rover deployed by the United States on Mars. National Aeronautics and Space Administration (NASA) applied a Go To Waypoint reactive algorithm [3] similar to Tangent Bug algorithm [4]. Since only the sensor information from the rover is used, the algorithm is simple and the computation is small. Although such algorithm works well in most environments, it lacks completeness. In other words, there is no guarantee that the algorithm will halt, or that the robot will be able to find the goal even if a path exists. The algorithm also tends to produce lengthy paths in natural terrain (relative to the optimal path). It mainly used to verify the application of new technologies needed to travel longer distances (50 km) on the surface of Mars.

Rocky7 applies a sensor-based Wedge bug response algorithm that is also based on the Tangent Bug algorithm [5]. The algorithm considers the height and slope of obstacles in obstacle avoidance and uses A* algorithm to search for the local optimal path. The disadvantages of the algorithm are the limitation of the rover as a point and the difficulty of the obstacle boundary detection, which bring some difficulties to the application of the algorithm.

Maimone et al. [6] uses a rasterized network to mark the terrain on NASA's Mars Rovers Spirit and opportunity, and built a digital elevation map (DEM) based on the grid position and corresponding terrain height in order to use the D* algorithm [7, 8] in DEM map for global path planning. The algorithm not only has the ability of secondary planning, but also considers the terrain traversability factor and improves the obstacle climbing capability of the rover. But the disadvantage is that the amount of terrain data is huge, and the processor performance must be very high. Since the errors of the gyroscope and the accelerometer will increase when rover crosses complex terrain, new positioning mechanism such as visual odometer must be introduced [9].

In 2013, China successfully deployed a lunar rover called Yutu. The improved heuristic A* search algorithm has been employed to find the optimal driving path in the three-dimensional digital elevation map of the moon while considering the limitation of the automatic environment recognition ability and the limitation of the algorithm itself. For the result of path planning, a manual correction strategy is introduced to ensure the correctness and optimality of path searching [10].

The lunar surface is a highly complex and unstructured environment. The autonomous safe driving of lunar rovers on surface is not only related to the topographic information, but also related to the obstacle-crossing ability of the lunar moving vehicle itself. At the same time, the computing power of the lunar rover and path length should be taken into account to realize the autonomous navigation. Therefore, finding a path planning method with low computational complexity, traversability of simple terrain and shortest path is the first issue we should consider. In order to solve this problem, based on the A* algorithm, this paper not only introduces the environmental characteristics, but also considers the constraints of the rover when formulating the path cost function of the algorithm, and presents a path planning algorithm based on the environmental characteristics.

This paper is organized as follows. Section 2 introduces the environmental characteristics of the lunar terrain. Section 3 demonstrates the principle of the classic A* algorithm and the improved algorithm. Section 4 shows the performance of our algorithm by simulations. The conclusion is presented in the Sect. 5.

2   Environmental Characteristics of Lunar Terrain

The environmental characteristics of lunar surface is critical to plan the path of the rover during exploration. In this paper, two main features including slope and roughness of lunar surface are used to describe environmental features [11].

2.1   Lunar Slope

The slope of any point on surface of a natural terrain is defined as the angle between the fitting plane of the point and the horizontal plane [12]. It indicates the degree of inclination of the ground surface at the point, which is numerically equal to the angle θ between the unit normal vector $\vec{n}$ of the fitting plane and the unit vector $\vec{m}$ parallel to z-axis, as shown in Fig. 1. The z-axis is the height coordinate axis of the three-dimensional map. Here, the slope of the center grid point I_{ij} denoted by θ is calculated as follows.

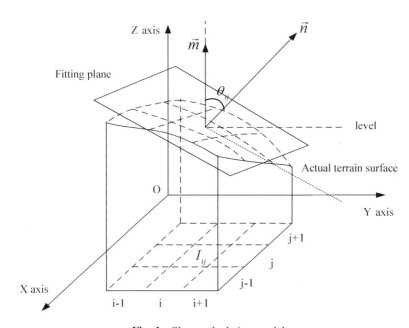

Fig. 1. Slope calculation model

In terms of Fig. 1, the analysis area is an arbitrary sub-area on the map containing 9 grids (elevation points) (x_i, y_i, z_i), $i = 1, 2. \ldots .9$, where (x_i, y_i) is the coordinate position of the point on the grid map, and z_i is the elevation value corresponding to the point. We assume the mathematical expression of the fitting plane is

$$Ax + By + Cz + D = 0 \tag{1}$$

or

$$z = -\frac{A}{C}x - \frac{B}{C}y - \frac{D}{C} \tag{2}$$

Let $a_0 = -\frac{A}{C}, a_1 = -\frac{B}{C}, a_2 = -\frac{D}{C}$, Eq. (2) is further transformed into Eq. (3)

$$z = a_0 x + a_1 y + a_2 \tag{3}$$

For nine grid points in the sub-region, the above plane Eq. (3) is calculated by the nine points fitting. Hence, to determine the terms a_0, a_1 and a_2, Eq. (4) should be minimum.

$$S = \sum_{i=1}^{9} (a_0 x_i + a_1 y_i + a_2 - z_i)^2 \tag{4}$$

In this context, Eq. (5) is established by considering $\frac{\partial S}{\partial a_k} = 0, k = 0, 1, 2$. Namely,

$$\begin{cases} a_0 \sum x_i^2 + a_1 \sum x_i y_i + a_2 \sum x_i = \sum x_i z_i \\ a_0 \sum x_i y_i + a_1 \sum y_i^2 + a_2 \sum y_i = \sum y_i z_i \\ a_0 \sum x_i + a_1 \sum y_i + a_2 n = \sum z_i \end{cases} \tag{5}$$

Solving Eq. (5) can get the values of a_0, a_1 and a_2. The normal vector $\vec{n}$ of the plane Eq. (3) is $\vec{n} = (a_0, a_1, -1)$.

Since the normal vector of the horizontal plane $Z = 0$ is $\vec{m} = (0, 0, 1)$, the angle between the normal vector $\vec{n}$ of the fitting plane and the plane $Z = 0$ is ϕ, as shown in Fig. 1. Thus, we have

$$\cos \theta = |\cos \langle \vec{m}, \vec{n} \rangle| = \frac{1}{\sqrt{a_0^2 + a_1^2 + 1^2}} \tag{6}$$

According to (6), the slop angle θ of the grid point I_{ij} can be obtained.

$$\theta_{ij} = \arccos \frac{1}{\sqrt{a_0^2 + a_1^2 + 1}} \tag{7}$$

2.2   Moon Surface Roughness

In actual environment, besides the steep slope, there is also uneven surface which threatens the safety of rovers. Here, roughness is used to measure the safety of the lunar rover passing through uneven surface. Generally speaking, the roughness of a terrain is defined as the ratio of surface area S_{surface} of a surface unit to its projected area S_{flat} on a horizontal plane [13].

$$R = S_{\text{surface}}/S_{\text{flat}} \tag{8}$$

In practice, the roughness of the terrain can be expressed by fitted the mean deviation. However, because a grid has a small size and its fitting plane does not reflect the actual topographical features, a window area (3×3 grids) is used to calculate the fitted mean deviation. It is easy to know that the distance from each elevation point in the window area (nine grids) to this fitting plane is

$$d_i = \frac{|a_0 x_i + a_1 y_i + a_2 - z_i|}{\sqrt{a_0^2 + a_1^2 + (-1)^2}}, \ i = 1, \cdots, 9 \tag{9}$$

Based on (9), the average of distances from 9 grid points to the fitting plane is:

$$\overline{D} = \frac{1}{9} \sum_{i=1}^{9} |d_i| = \frac{1}{9} \sum_{i=1}^{9} \frac{|a_0 x_i + a_1 y_i + a_2 - z_i|}{\sqrt{a_0^2 + a_1^2 + (-1)^2}} \tag{10}$$

The fitted mean deviation $\overline{D}_{ij}$ of each grid in the window area is equal to the average distance of 9 grids to the fit plane.

$$\overline{D}_{ij} = \overline{D} = \frac{1}{9} \sum_{i=1}^{9} |d_i| = \frac{1}{9} \sum_{i=1}^{9} \frac{|a_0 x_i + a_1 y_i + a_2 - z_i|}{\sqrt{a_0^2 + a_1^2 + (-1)^2}} \tag{11}$$

3   Proposed Improved A* Algorithm

The A* algorithm was originally proposed by Hart et al. based on the Dijkstras algorithm in 1968 [14]. It combines the advantages of Dijkstras algorithm and Best-First Search (BFS) and is the most popular one of the graph search algorithms.

3.1   Principle of Classic A* Algorithm

The principle of the classic A* algorithm is to design a cost estimation function (12).

$$f(n) = g(n) + h(n) \tag{12}$$

The evaluation function $f(n)$ is the estimated value of the minimum cost path from the starting grid to grid n and then to the target grid. The function $g(n)$ is the actual cost of elapsed path from the starting grid to the grid n. The heuristic function $h(n)$ is the estimated cost of the possible optimal path from the grid n to the target grid.

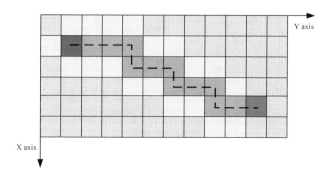

Fig. 2. A path for manhattan distance (Color figure online)

It is noted that a good heuristic function $h(n)$ is important when determining the minimum cost estimate from any grid n to the target grid. The standard heuristic function is based on the Manhattan distance. Referring to Fig. 2, red grid is the grid n which two-dimensional coordinates are (x_n, y_n), green grid is the target grid and its corresponding two-dimensional coordinates are (x_t, y_t). The coordinate value of each grid is an integer. Assuming the pure distance movement cost between two adjacent grids is L m (not considering terrain and diagonal movement, shown in Fig. 2, then the estimated cost $h(n)$ from grid n to target grid can be expressed as Eq. (13).

$$h(n) = L * (abs(x_t - x_n) + abs(y_t - y_n)) \tag{13}$$

3.2   Improved A* Algorithm

The classic A* algorithm uses Manhattan distance to calculate the movement between adjacent grids. However, the planetary rover can move in the diagonal direction on the map. Thus, we use a different heuristic function. Referring to Fig. 3, red grid is the grid n defined by the two-dimensional coordinates (x_n, y_n), green grid is the target grid and its two-dimensional coordinates are (x_t, y_t). The coordinate value of each grid is an integer. We assume that the movement cost between two adjacent diagonal grids can be simply $\sqrt{2}L$ m, then the estimated cost $h(n)$ from grid n to target grid can be expressed as Eq. (16).

According to mathematical knowledge, the following (14), (15), (16) can be obtained.

$$h\_diagonal(n) = min(abs(x_t - x_n), \ abs(y_t - y_n)) \tag{14}$$

$$h\_straight(n) = (abs(x_t - x_n) + abs(y_t - y_n)) \tag{15}$$

$$h(n) = \sqrt{2}L * h\_diagonal(n) + L * (h\_straight(n) - 2 * h\_diagonal(n)) \tag{16}$$

Where, $h\_diagonal(n)$: the number of steps that can be moved along a diagonal line; $h\_straight(n)$: the number of steps in Manhattan distance. All slash steps are multiplied

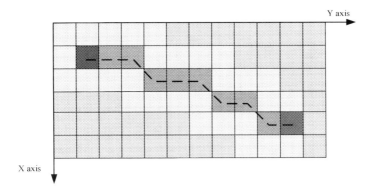

Fig. 3. A path for diagonal distance (Color figure online)

by $\sqrt{2}L$, and all line steps (Manhattan distance steps minus 2 times slash steps) are multiplied by L.

Moreover, for classic A* algorithm, we simply divide the grids in the map into obstacles (not passable) and barrier-free (passable), without considering that the lunar rover has certain obstacle-crossing ability and can climb over some relatively simple obstacles. Taking the Yutu as an example, it can generally climb a slope below 20° or a step below 20 cm safely. The trafficability of the robot at the grid point I_{ij} can be obtained by judging whether the grid point meets the safety requirements. That is, whether the gradient θ_{ij} of the grid is less than the maximum safety gradient θ_{max}, and whether the roughness $\overline{D}_{ij}$ of the grid is less than the maximum safety roughness $\overline{D}_{max}$. If they are less than or equal to safety value, the grid satisfies the condition of passibility; otherwise, the grid is directly determined to be unsafe [15].

In the actual test, we get many paths satisfying the conditions of accessibility. How to choose an optimal path among these paths is a problem worth studying. Here we may take the shortest path length as the optimization criterion. Assume that the path from grid n to the target grid is divided into e straight steps and f oblique steps. For terrain slope, the additional length of traveling through the grid are W. Similarly, for terrain roughness, the additional length of traveling through the grid are E, then the estimated cost $h\,(n)$ from grid n to target grid can be expressed as Eq. (17).

$$h(n) = \sqrt{2}L * h\_diagonal(n) + L * (h\_straight(n) - 2 * h\_diagonal(n)) + W + E \tag{17}$$

Where, $W = \sum\limits_{i=1}^{f} L * \left(\frac{1.4}{\cos\theta_i} - 1.4\right) + \sum\limits_{k-1}^{e} L * \left(\frac{1}{\cos\theta_k} - 1\right)$, and $E = \sum\limits_{i=1}^{f} \sqrt{2} * \overline{D}_i + \sum\limits_{k=1}^{e} \overline{D}_k$.

The pseudocode of the improved A* algorithm is provided in Table 1.

Table 1. The pseudocode of the improved A* algorithm

Algorithms 1 Improved A* algorithm
___

Require: θ_{max} : Maximum safety gradient

Require: $\bar{D}_{max}$: Maximum safety roughness

Require: (x_0, y_0, z_0) :The coordinates of the starting grid n_{start}

Require: (x_t, y_t, z_t) :The coordinates of the target grid n_{target}

1:/* **Search for a path from start grid** n_{start} **to target grid** n_{target} **and return the result */**

2:**function Evaluation**(n)

3       $h\_diagonal(n)=min\big(abs(x_t - x_n),\ abs(y_t - y_n)\big)$

4:      $h\_straight(n)=\big(abs(x_t - x_n) + abs(y_t - y_n)\big)$

5:      $f = h\_diagonal(n)=min\big(abs(x_t - x_n),\ abs(y_t - y_n)\big)$

6:      $e = abs(x_t - x_n) + abs(y_t - y_n)-2*min\big(abs(x_t - x_n),\ abs(y_t - y_n)\big)$

7:      $W = \sum\limits_{i=1}^{f} L * \left(\dfrac{1.4}{\cos\theta_i}-1.4\right)+\sum\limits_{k=1}^{e} L * \left(\dfrac{1}{\cos\theta_k}-1\right)$

8:      $E = \sum\limits_{i=1}^{f} \sqrt{2} * \bar{D}_i + \sum\limits_{k=1}^{e} \bar{D}_k$

9:      $h(n) = \sqrt{2}\,L*h\_diagonal(n)+L*\big(h\_straight(n)-2*h\_diagonal(n)\big)$
        $+W + E$

10:     $f(n) = g(n) + h(n)$

11:     **return** $f(n)$

12:**end function**

13:**function Traversability**(n)

14:      if $\theta_n > \theta_{max}$ OR $\bar{D}_n > \bar{D}_{max}$ then

15:          $Traversability(n) < 0$

16:          **ignore this grid n, grid n is not safe**

17:      else

18:          $Traversability(n) > 0$

19:      **end if**

20:      **return** $Traversability(n)$

21:**end function**

22:**function UpdateState(** n, n' **)**

23:
$$c(n,n') = \sqrt{2}\,L*h\_diagonal\left(n,n'\right)$$
$$+L*\left(h\_straight\left(n,n'\right) - 2*h\_diagonal\left(n,n'\right)\right)$$
$$+W(n,n') + E(n,n')$$

24:    **if** Traversability$\left(n'\right) < 0$ **OR** $n' \in$ CLOSED **then**

25:        **Ignore this** n'

26:    **else**

27:        **if** $n' \in$ OPEN **then**

28:            **if** $g(n') > g(n) + c(n,n')$ **then**

29:                $parent(n') = n$

30:                $g(n') = g(n) + c(n,n')$

31:                Evaluation(n')

32:            **else**

33:                **ignore this** n'

34:            **end if**

35:        **else**

36:            OPEN.Insert(n' ,Evaluation(n'))

37:            parent(n')=n

38:            $g(n') = g(n) + c(n,n')$

39:        **end if**

40:    **end if**

41:**end function**

42:**function Main()**

43:    $g(n_{start}) = 0$

44:    OPEN=$\varnothing$

45:    CLOSED=$\varnothing$

46:    OPEN.Insert(n_{start}, Evaluation(n_{start}))

47:    **while** OPEN $\neq \varnothing$ **do**

48:        n=OPEN.minEvaluation(n)

49:        CLOSED = CLOSED $\bigcup n$

50:        **if** $n = n_{target}$ **then**

51:            **return** "Find the optimal path"

52:        **else**

53:            n' are adjacent 8 grids of n

54:            **for all** n' **do**

55:            updateState $\left(n,n'\right)$

56:        **end if**

57:    **end while**

58:    **return** "Path planning failed"

59:**end function**

4   Simulation Experiments

Because there is no detailed digital elevation map (DEM) of local lunar surface, the interpolation method is used in MATLAB R2018A to build the grid map similar to the planetary surface environment. The map consists of three hillsides, four deep pits and rough ground. The classic A* algorithm and the improved A* algorithm are used to plan the path on the map. The experimental results are shown in Fig. 4. The size of the map is 100 m × 100 m, the size of unit grid is 1 m × 1 m. The blue points in the map are the unsafe grids (the slope is greater than 20° or the roughness is greater than 0.2 m) that the lunar rover cannot pass through. The starting point and target point on the map are produced randomly. For example, the starting point coordinate and the target point coordinate illustrated in Fig. 4 are (5 m, 5 m) and (59 m, 82 m) respectively.

As shown in Fig. 4, the red solid path planned by the improved A* algorithm is not only shorter, but also traverses some safe terrain obstacles. However, the black-dotted path planned by the classic A* algorithm passes through dangerous terrain that the lunar rover cannot cross. It means such path planning has actually failed and further proves that the improved A* algorithm is more suitable for the complex unstructured environment of the lunar surface.

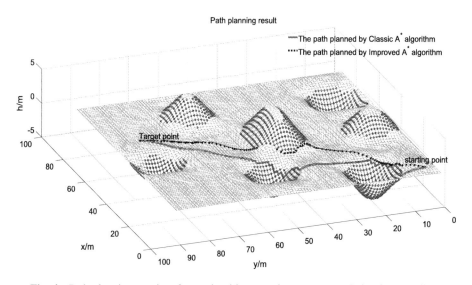

Fig. 4. Path planning results of two algorithms on the same map (Color figure online)

Changing the starting point and target point on the map and running both the classic and improved A* to get a new couple of paths, 50 different experiments are repeatedly done. The numerical simulation results are summarized in Figs. 5 and 6 respectively. Figure 5 presents the length of each path planned by each algorithm. Figure 6 illustrates that whether the planning path is successful for each experiment for each algorithm.

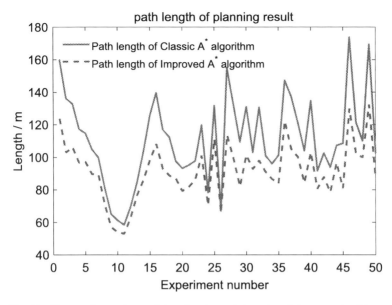

Fig. 5. 50 sets of experimental data for the path lengths of the two algorithms.

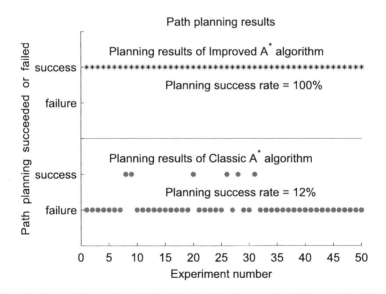

Fig. 6. 50 sets of experimental data for the planning results of the two algorithms.

The numerical results shown in Fig. 5 indicate that the path length of the improved A* algorithm for most of the 50 experiments is shorter than the path length of the classic A* algorithm. It can be seen from Fig. 6, the improved A* algorithm is definitely able to successfully plan a safe path, while the classic A* algorithm tends to pass some dangerous terrain and results in a low planning success rate.

5   Conclusion

A* algorithm is often used to solve the shortest path problem because of its simple principle and low computation. It uses the heuristic function to reduce the search space and improve the search efficiency, so the heuristic function plays a key role in the A* algorithm. To traverse safely on the harsh and complex planetary surface, the terrain environmental information and the ability of the roving vehicle to overcome obstacles should be taken into account. In this paper, we introduce the obstacle-crossing ability of lunar rover, lunar slope and moon surface roughness into the heuristic function of the algorithm, and allow the lunar rover to move obliquely which is more like to the actual movement of the lunar rover on the lunar surface. The simulation results show that the improved A* algorithm has higher planning success rate and shorter path than the classic A* algorithm for unstructured and complex lunar environment.

Acknowledgment. The author would like to acknowledge the support from the Advanced Research Project of Manned Space under Grant No. 0603(17700630), the National Natural Science Foundation of China under Grant No. 61803075, the Fundamental Research Funds for the Central Universities under Grant No. ZYGX2018KYQD211.

References

1. Wong, C., Yang, E., Yan, X., Gu, D.: Adaptive and intelligent navigation of autonomous planetary rovers—a survey. In: 2017 NASA/ESA Conference on Adaptive Hardware and Systems (AHS), Pasadena, CA, pp. 237–244 (2017)
2. Grotzinger, J.P., et al.: Mars science laboratory mission and science investigation. Space Sci. Rev. **170**(1–4), 5–56 (2012)
3. Wilcox, B., Nguyen, T.: Sojourner on Mars and lessons learned for future planetary rovers. SAE Technical Paper 10.4271/981695 (1998)
4. Laubach, S.L., Burdick, J., Matthies, L.: An autonomous path planner implemented on the Rocky 7 prototype microrover. In: Proceedings of 1998 IEEE International Conference on Robotics and Automation (Cat. No. 98CH36146), Leuven, Belgium (1998)
5. Laubach, S.L., Burdick, J.W.: An autonomous sensor-based path-planner for planetary microrovers. In: Proceedings of 1999 IEEE International Conference on Robotics and Automation (Cat. No. 99CH36288C), Detroit, MI, USA (1999)
6. Maimone, M., Biesiadecki, J.J., Tunstel, E., Cheng, Y., Leger, C.: Chapter 3: Surface navigation and mobility intelligence on the Mars exploration rovers (2006)
7. Maimone, M.W., Leger, P.C., Biesiadecki, J.J.: Overview of the mars exploration rovers' autonomous mobility and vision capabilities. In: Proceedings of 2007 IEEE International Conference on Robotics and Automation (2007)
8. Stentz, A.: The D* algorithm for real-time planning of optimal traverses. CMU Technical report CMU-RI-TR-94–37 (1994)
9. Carsten, J., Rankin, A., Ferguson, D., Stentz, A.: Global path planning on board the Mars exploration rovers. In: 2007 IEEE Aerospace Conference, Big Sky, MT (2007)
10. Wu, W., Zhou, J., Wang, B., Liu, C.: Key techniques in the teleoperation of the Yutu no. 3 "Yutu" lunar rover. Sci. China Inf. Sci. (2014)
11. Chavez-Garcia, R.O., Guzzi, J., Gambardella, L.M., Giusti, A.: Learning ground traversability from simulations. IEEE Robot. Autom. Lett. **3**(3), 1695–1702 (2018)

12. Brooks, R.: A robust layered control system for a mobile robot. IEEE J. Robot. Autom. **2**(1), 14–23 (1986)
13. Moore, I.D., Grayson, R.B., Ladson, A.R.: Digital terrain modeling: a review of hydrological, geomorphological, and biological applications. Hydrol. Process **5**, 3–30 (1991)
14. Hart, P.E., Nilsson, N.J., Raphael, B.: A formal basis for the heuristic determination of minimum cost paths. IEEE Trans. Syst. Sci. Cybern. SSC4 **4**(4), 100–107 (1968)
15. Hadsell, R., Scoffier, M., Muller, U., LeCun, Y., Sermanet, P.: Mapping and planning under uncertainty in mobile robots with long-range perception. In: Proceedings of IEEE/RSJ International Conference on Intelligent Robots and Systems, pp. 1–6. IEEE (2008)

A Self-calibration Method
of Lander Manipulator for Deep Space
Exploration Mission

Qingxuan Jia, Wen Shao, Gang Chen$^{(\boxtimes)}$, Yifan Wang, and Lanpu Li

Beijing University of Posts and Telecommunications, Beijing 100876, China
buptcg@163.com

Abstract. In view of the characteristics of the lander in deep space exploration mission, a self-calibration method of kinematics parameters is proposed; it uses the hand-eye camera at the end of the manipulator as the measuring equipment to calibrate the kinematics parameters of the manipulator carried on the lander. By establishing the kinematic model contains the relative pose of manipulator's base coordinate and target coordinate, and then establishing the kinematic error model of the lander manipulator system to realize the kinematics parameters calibration. The method realizes the kinematics parameters calibration under the condition of unknown of the relative pose of base coordinate system and target coordinate system, and calibrates the manipulator base coordinates in inertial system and the hand-eye relation at the same time. Through simulation experiments, it is verified that the self-calibration method proposed in this paper can obtain accurate kinematics parameters and effectively improve the accuracy of the lander manipulator terminal pose.

Keywords: Self-calibration · Deep space exploration · Lander manipulator

1 Introduction

For the deep space exploration mission, it has the long mission cycle and the complex deep space environment, the lander equipped with manipulator is a trend. Therefore, the lander can use the manipulator to realize a series of operating tasks such as autonomous sampling, autonomous carrying and autonomous assembly. In order to realize the unmanned sampling return, the lander needs to use its equipped manipulator to complete the task of autonomous sampling, which is required to accurately reach the designated sampling area and bring back samples with more research value [1]. In addition, the construction of the outland base (such as lunar base) needs more manipulators to complete various tasks such as load carrying and assembly operation [2]. These complex missions put forward higher requirements for the operation accuracy of the manipulators.

Supported by the National Natural Science Foundation of China (No. 61573066), and "the Fundamental Research Funds for the Central Universities" (No. 24820182018RC29).

H. Yu et al. (Eds.): ICIRA 2019, LNAI 11743, pp. 354–366, 2019.
https://doi.org/10.1007/978-3-030-27538-9_30

After the completion of machining and assembly of the manipulator, the absolute position and attitude accuracy of the manipulator are mainly ensured by the control system. As the main parameter of the manipulator control, the kinematics parameter of the manipulator has a great influence on the absolute position and attitude accuracy of the manipulator [3]. Under the influence of strong vibration and impact in the launching process and the gravity different, the kinematic parameters of lander manipulator will change [4]. Therefore, before the implementation of the deep space exploration operation mission of the manipulator, its kinematic parameters must be calibrated.

The calibration of kinematic parameters of a manipulator generally includes four steps: error modeling, pose measurement, parameter identification and precision compensation [5]. The traditional method of the calibration of kinematic parameters based on the model often relies on external measurement equipment to provide data. Limited by the conditions of deep space exploration, only the lander itself can reach the detection area, and there is no external measurement equipment support, so the self-calibration method of the manipulator needs to be considered. Due to the development of visual measurement technology and the importance of vision sensing, the deep space exploration lander must be equipped with a high-performance visual system, so visual self-calibration method can be adopted. Zhou [6] takes a 7-DOF space manipulator as the research object, established the absolute pose error model of the manipulator with D-H method, and calibrated the kinematics parameters of the manipulator. Richter [7] used the global camera to identify the marker points set on the manipulator, and the camera obtained the displacement of the marker points to achieve robot calibration. Because the global camera has a larger field of view, its measurement accuracy is relatively low, so the hand-eye camera is adopted for calibration with higher precision. Li [8] measured the terminal pose with the hand-eye camera, and identified the kinematic parameter error according to the pose error model. Wang [9] proposed a kinematics in-orbit self-calibration method for space manipulator based on POE formula, and used the binocular camera at the end of the space manipulator and the chess board for calibration. All the above methods are implemented on the premise that the base and target pose are known. However, considering the operational characteristics of the deep space exploration lander, the working space of the manipulator often far away from the main part, which can be regarded as the manipulator's base, and the pose of the base and the target are not known.

Therefore, this paper will focus on the situation of the lander manipulator base and target pose are unknown, on this basis of establish kinematics error model contains hand-eye camera coordinate system and target coordinate system, propose a self-calibration method of the lander manipulator. The method realizes the kinematics parameters calibration under the condition of unknown of the relative pose of base coordinate system and target coordinate system, and calibrates the manipulator base coordinates in inertial system and the hand-eye relation at the same time. Final, the method is verified by designing simulation experiment.

2 Kinematic Modeling

2.1 Research Object

In this paper, the manipulator equips on the lander for deep space exploration is taken as the research object, and its structure is shown in Fig. 1. The main part of the lander can be regarded as the manipulator base. The manipulator is composed of rotating joints and links with n degree of freedom. The hand-eye camera is mounted on the end of the manipulator.

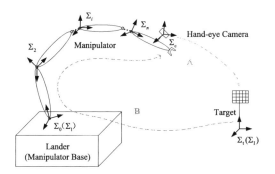

Fig. 1. Structural representation of manipulator

The inertial system is set to coincide with the target coordinate system in this paper, and the transformation relationship between the base coordinate system of the manipulator and the target coordinate system is integrated into the kinematic model of the lander, which is equivalent to a zero-DOF link. The hand-eye camera can be used as a measuring device in the calibration process. The pose transformation relationship between the target coordinate system and the hand-eye camera coordinate system can be obtained, as shown by arrow A in the Fig. 1. Therefore, in order to make closed chain for the self-calibration of the kinematic parameters of the manipulator, it is necessary to establish the pose relationship shown by arrow B in the Fig. 1.

2.2 Description of Kinematic Relationship

The kinematic model needed for the calibration of kinematic parameters of manipulator needs to meet the principles of integrality, continuity and minimum parameters [10]. Zhuang [11] put forward the CPC (Complete and Parametrically Continuous) model, it makes up for the D-H model of integrality and continuity. In order to eliminate the problem of the parameter redundancy, the MCPC (Modified Complete and Parametrically Continuous) [12] model was put forward. In this paper, the method of MCPC model is adopted.

Intermediate Link Coordinate Systems. The MCPC model uses 4 parameters (α, β, x, y) to describe the transformation relationship between the intermediate link coordinate systems. Where, α and β are used to describe the angle between adjacent joint axes, x and y are used to describe the offset between adjacent joint axes. The MCPC coordinate system of the ith link can be established as shown in Fig. 2. According to the established MCPC coordinate system, the specific values of each parameter can be obtained through the manipulator structure.

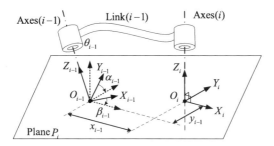

Fig. 2. Establishment of intermediate link coordinate system

Through the MCPC method, $^{i-1}_i T$ the transformation matrix from link i coordinate system to link $i-1$ coordinate system can be described as

$$^{i-1}_i T = \mathrm{Rot}\left(X, \alpha_{i-1}\right) \mathrm{Rot}\left(Y, \beta_{i-1}\right) \mathrm{Trans}\left(X, x_{i-1}\right) \mathrm{Trans}\left(Y, y_{i-1}\right) \tag{1}$$

Base Coordinate System. For the base coordinate system $\sum_0$ of the manipulator, it fixed to the base of the manipulator as a reference coordinate system. In order to simplify the calculation, the coordinate axis Z_0 of the base coordinate system is often parallel to the axis of the first joint, and when the manipulator is in the initial configuration, the coordinate system $\sum_0$ and the coordinate system $\sum_1$ coincide.

Hand-eye Camera Coordinate System. MCPC model for the establishment of the tool coordinate system is different from the intermediate link coordinate system. In order to complete description of the tool coordinate system, on the base of the intermediate link coordinate system build rules, adding two parameters γ_n and z_n to describe the relation of the last link coordinate system and tool coordinate system.

For the manipulator of the deep space exploration lander, the hand-eye camera and the tool are also installed on the last link of the manipulator, so the hand-eye camera coordinate system can be described in the same way as the tool coordinate system. Thus, the specific expression of the transformation matrix from the hand-eye camera coordinate system to the last link coordinate system $^n_c T$ described by the MCPC model can be obtained as follows

$$^n_c T = \mathrm{Rot}(X, \alpha_n) \mathrm{Rot}(Y, \beta_n) \mathrm{Rot}(Z, \gamma_n) \mathrm{Trans}(X, x_n) \mathrm{Trans}(Y, y_n) \mathrm{Trans}(Z, z_n) \tag{2}$$

Target Coordinate System. The description of the transformation relationship between the target coordinate system and the base coordinate system $^t_0 T$ is similar to the hand-eye camera coordinate system in MCPC model, 6 parameters (α_t, β_t, γ_t, x_t, y_t, z_t) are used to describe it.

2.3   Kinematic Modeling

The relation between the lander manipulator system coordinate systems and the kinematics parameters of the lander manipulator can be obtained. By multiplying the transformation matrix between coordinate systems, the kinematic model of the lander manipulator system can be obtained as

$$\begin{matrix}^1_c T = {}^1_t T \, {}^t_0 T \, {}^0_1 T \, {}^1_2 T \cdots {}^{n-1}_n T \, {}^n_c T\end{matrix} \tag{3}$$

Where, $^1_c T$ indicates the transformation matrix of the hand-eye camera coordinate system $\sum_c$ with respect to the inertial system $\sum_1$; $^1_t T$ indicates the transformation matrix of the target coordinate system $\sum_t$ with respect to the inertial system $\sum_1$; $^1_t T = I_4$.

3   Kinematic Error Modeling

3.1   Intermediate Link Error Model

For the intermediate link coordinate system, let $^i_{i+1}T^N$ and $^i_{i+1}T^A$ be the nominal transformation matrix and the actual transformation matrix which means that $\sum_{i+1}$ is relative to $\sum_i$. Make the first-order approximation of transformation matrix differentiation and get

$$\mathrm{d}T_i = {}^i_{i+1}T^A - {}^i_{i+1}T^N = {}^i_{i+1}T^N \cdot \varDelta_i \tag{4}$$

Where, $\varDelta_i \in \Re^{4 \times 4}$ is the pose error matrix which means that the link $i+1$ coordinate system relative to the link i coordinate system.

The pose error matrix $\varDelta_i$ in the formula (4) can be expressed as

$$\varDelta_i = \begin{bmatrix} 0 & -\delta_{iz} & \delta_{iy} & d_{ix} \\ \delta_{iz} & 0 & -\delta_{ix} & d_{iy} \\ -\delta_{iy} & \delta_{ix} & 0 & d_{iz} \\ 0 & 0 & 0 & 0 \end{bmatrix} \tag{5}$$

Where, $\boldsymbol{\delta}_i = [\delta_{ix}, \delta_{iy}, \delta_{iz}]^T$ and $\boldsymbol{d}_i = [d_{ix}, d_{iy}, d_{iz}]^T$ respectively indicates the attitude error and position error.

The $\mathrm{d}T_i$ can be written as the following linear form

$$\mathrm{d}T_i = \frac{\partial T_i}{\partial \alpha_i} \Delta\alpha_i + \frac{\partial T_i}{\partial \beta_i} \Delta\beta_i + \frac{\partial T_i}{\partial x_i} \Delta x_i + \frac{\partial T_i}{\partial y_i} \Delta y_i \tag{6}$$

In order to get the correspondence between parameter errors and pose errors, the partial derivative in formula (6) is transformed as follows

$$\frac{\partial T_i}{\partial \alpha_i} = T_i^N \cdot Q_\alpha, \quad \frac{\partial T_i}{\partial \beta_i} = T_i^N \cdot Q_\beta, \quad \frac{\partial T_i}{\partial x_i} = T_i^N \cdot Q_x, \quad \frac{\partial T_i}{\partial y_i} = T_i^N \cdot Q_y \qquad (7)$$

Combined with Eq. (4), we can get

$$\Delta_i = Q_\alpha \Delta \alpha_i + Q_\beta \Delta \beta_i + Q_x \Delta x_i + Q_y \Delta y_i \qquad (8)$$

According to Eqs. (5) and (8), the pose error can be expressed as

$$D_i = \begin{bmatrix} d_{ix} & d_{iy} & d_{iz} & \delta_{ix} & \delta_{iy} & \delta_{iz} \end{bmatrix}^T = \begin{bmatrix} k_i^1 & k_i^2 & k_i^3 & k_i^4 \\ k_i^5 & k_i^6 & 0 & 0 \end{bmatrix} \begin{bmatrix} \Delta \alpha_i \\ \Delta \beta_i \\ \Delta x_i \\ \Delta y_i \end{bmatrix} \qquad (9)$$

Where, the specific value of the coefficient matrix is as follows

$$k_i^1 = \begin{bmatrix} -y_i s\beta_i \\ x_i s\beta_i \\ y_i c\beta_i \end{bmatrix}, \ k_i^2 = \begin{bmatrix} 0 \\ 0 \\ -x_i \end{bmatrix}, \ k_i^3 = \begin{bmatrix} 1 \\ 0 \\ 0 \end{bmatrix}, \ k_i^4 = \begin{bmatrix} 0 \\ 1 \\ 0 \end{bmatrix}, \ k_i^5 = \begin{bmatrix} c\beta_i \\ 0 \\ s\beta_i \end{bmatrix}, \ k_i^6 = \begin{bmatrix} 0 \\ 1 \\ 0 \end{bmatrix}$$
$$(10)$$

Where, $s\varphi$ is the abbreviation of $\sin \varphi$, and $c\varphi$ is the abbreviation of $\cos \varphi$.

3.2 Hand-eye Camera Coordinate System Error Model

Use dT_n to represent the differential of the hand-eye camera coordinate system relative to the transformation matrix of the last link coordinate system. Similarly, it can be expressed as follows

$$dT_n = \frac{\partial T_n}{\partial \alpha_n} \Delta \alpha_n + \frac{\partial T_n}{\partial \beta_n} \Delta \beta_n + \frac{\partial T_n}{\partial \gamma_n} \Delta \gamma_n + \frac{\partial T_n}{\partial x_n} \Delta x_n + \frac{\partial T_n}{\partial y_n} \Delta y_n + \frac{\partial T_n}{\partial z_n} \Delta z_n \qquad (11)$$

Let the nominal transformation matrix of the hand-eye camera coordinate system relative to the last link coordinate system is T_n^N, we can get

$$\frac{\partial T_n}{\partial \gamma_n} = T_n^N \cdot Q_\gamma, \quad \frac{\partial T_n}{\partial z_n} = T_n^N \cdot Q_z \qquad (12)$$

Similar to the derivation of the intermediate link error model, the resulting expression is as follows

$$\Delta_n = Q_\alpha \Delta\alpha_n + Q_\beta \Delta\beta_n + Q_\gamma \Delta\gamma_n + Q_x \Delta x_n + Q_y \Delta y_n + Q_z \Delta z_n \qquad (13)$$

Furthermore, the last link parameter error model $D_n = [d_{nx}, d_{ny}, d_{nz}, \delta_{nx}, \delta_{ny}, \delta_{nz}]^T$ can be obtained as follows

$$D_n = \begin{bmatrix} k_n^1 & k_n^2 & k_n^3 & k_n^4 & k_n^7 & k_n^8 \\ k_n^5 & k_n^6 & 0 & 0 & k_n^9 & 0 \end{bmatrix} [\Delta\alpha_n \quad \Delta\beta_n \quad \Delta x_n \quad \Delta y_n \quad \Delta\gamma_n \quad \Delta z_n]^T \qquad (14)$$

Where, the specific value of the coefficient matrix is as follows

$$\begin{cases} k_n^1 = \begin{bmatrix} -y_n s\beta_n - z_n c\beta_n s\gamma_n \\ -z_n c\beta_n c\gamma_n + x_n s\beta_n \\ c\beta_n(y_n c\gamma_n + x_n s\gamma_n) \end{bmatrix}, & k_n^2 = \begin{bmatrix} z_n c\gamma_n \\ -z_n s\gamma_n \\ -x_n c\gamma_n + y_n s\gamma_n \end{bmatrix}, & k_n^3 = \begin{bmatrix} 1 \\ 0 \\ 0 \end{bmatrix}, & k_n^4 = \begin{bmatrix} 0 \\ 1 \\ 0 \end{bmatrix} \\ k_n^5 = \begin{bmatrix} c\beta_n c\gamma_n \\ -c\beta_n s\gamma_n \\ s\beta_n \end{bmatrix}, & k_n^6 = \begin{bmatrix} s\gamma_n \\ c\gamma_n \\ 0 \end{bmatrix}, & k_n^7 = \begin{bmatrix} -y_n \\ x_n \\ 0 \end{bmatrix}, & k_n^8 = \begin{bmatrix} 0 \\ 0 \\ 1 \end{bmatrix}, & k_n^9 = \begin{bmatrix} 0 \\ 0 \\ 1 \end{bmatrix} \end{cases} \qquad (15)$$

The target parameter error model D_t has the same form with the last link parameter error model D_n.

3.3   Lander Manipulator System Error Model

Let ${}^1_c T^N$ and ${}^1_c T^A$ be the nominal transformation matrix and the actual transformation matrix of the hand-eye camera coordinate system relative to the inertial system.

$$ {}^1_c T^A = {}^1_c T^N + dT \qquad (16) $$

Substitute formula (3) into formula (16) further deduces and ignores high-order small quantities, and we can get

$$ {}^1_c T^A \approx {}^1_c T^N + dT_t \cdot {}^0_c T^N + \sum_{i=1}^{n} \left({}^1_{i-1} T^N \cdot dT_{i-1} \cdot {}^i_c T^N \right) + {}^1_n T^N \cdot dT_n \qquad (17) $$

Substitute formula (4) into formula (17) and we can get

$$ dT = {}^t_c T \cdot \left({}^0_c T^{-1} \cdot \Delta_t \cdot {}^0_c T + \sum_{i=1}^{n} \left({}^i_c T^{-1} \cdot \Delta_{i-1} \cdot {}^i_c T \right) + \Delta_n \right) \qquad (18) $$

Where, the transformation matrices on the right side of the equation without the right superscript are nominal values, the same below.

The pose error matrix Δ which means that the hand-eye coordinate system $\sum_c$ is relative to base coordinate system $\sum_0$ is

$$\Delta = {}^0_c T^{-1} \cdot \Delta_t \cdot {}^0_c T + \sum_{i=1}^{n} \left({}^i_c T^{-1} \cdot \Delta_{i-1} \cdot {}^i_c T \right) + \Delta_n \tag{19}$$

Let $U_i = {}^i_c T = {}^i_{i+1} T\, {}^{i+1}_{i+2} T \cdots {}^{n-1}_n T\, {}^n_c T,\ i = 0,\ 1,\ \ldots,\ n,\ n+1,\ U_{n+1} = I_4,\ U_i$ is homogeneous transformation matrix. Substitute it into (19) and we can get

$$\Delta = (U_0)^{-1} \cdot \Delta_t \cdot U_0 + \sum_{i=1}^{n+1} (U_i)^{-1} \cdot \Delta_{i-1} \cdot U_i \tag{20}$$

The general formula of U_i can be written as $U_i = \begin{bmatrix} n_i & o_i & a_i & p_i \\ 0 & 0 & 0 & 1 \end{bmatrix} \in \Re^{4\times4}$ By rewriting the pose error matrix Δ shown in formula (20) into the pose error vector, we can deduce that the pose error of the hand-eye camera coordinate system $\sum_c$ relative to the inertial system $\sum_1$ is

$$D = \sum_{i=0}^{n+1} \left(\begin{bmatrix} (n_i)^T & (p_i \times n_i)^T \\ (o_i)^T & (p_i \times o_i)^T \\ (a_i)^T & (p_i \times a_i)^T \\ 0_{1\times3} & (n_i)^T \\ 0_{1\times3} & (o_i)^T \\ 0_{1\times3} & (a_i)^T \end{bmatrix} \begin{bmatrix} d_{ix} \\ d_{iy} \\ d_{iz} \\ \delta_{ix} \\ \delta_{iy} \\ \delta_{iz} \end{bmatrix} \right) = J'_e \cdot \Omega \tag{21}$$

Where, $\Omega = [\Delta\alpha^T, \Delta\beta^T, \Delta\gamma^T, \Delta x^T, \Delta y^T, \Delta z^T]^T$ is kinematic parameter error vector, $\Delta\alpha = [\Delta\alpha_t, \Delta\alpha_0, \ldots, \Delta\alpha_n]^T,\quad \Delta\beta = [\Delta\beta_t, \Delta\beta_0, \ldots, \Delta\beta_n]^T,\quad \Delta x = [\Delta x_t, \Delta x_0, \ldots, \Delta x_n]^T,$ $\Delta y = [\Delta y_t, \Delta y_0, \ldots, \Delta y_n]^T,\ \Delta\gamma = [\Delta\gamma_b, \Delta\gamma_n]^T,\ \Delta z = [\Delta z_t, \Delta z_n]^T;\ J'_e$ is error Jacobian matrix, which indicates the mapping relationship between the end pose error of the manipulator and the kinematic parameter error.

D in Eq. (21) is the representation of the end pose error in the hand-eye camera coordinate system. In practical applications, the mapping relationship between the pose error of the hand-eye camera and the kinematic parameter error in the inertial coordinate system is needed. We can get

$$D_1 = J_e \cdot \Omega = T_s \cdot J'_e \cdot \Omega \tag{22}$$

Where, T_s indicates the pose of hand-eye camera under the inertial system.

4 Parameter Identification and Accuracy Compensation

4.1 Initial Kinematics Parameters of the Base Coordinate System

Because the target located far away from the main structure of the lander, the kinematics parameters of base coordinate system relative to the target coordinate system transformation matrix ${}_{0}^{t}T$ are difficult to obtain. Before identifying the kinematics parameters of the manipulator, the initial kinematics parameters of the base coordinate system relative to the target coordinate system need to be solved.

Since the lander manipulator forms a closed-loop kinematics relationship by the hand-eye camera identifying target, the initial kinematics parameters of the manipulator system can be solved through the kinematics equation.

Through the transformation of formula (3) can obtain

$$
{}_{0}^{t}T = {}_{c}^{t}T^{A} \cdot {}_{c}^{n}T^{-1} \cdot {}_{n}^{0}T^{-1}
\tag{23}
$$

According to the above formula, a set of the transformation relation between the base coordinate system of manipulator and the target coordinate system can be obtained through the single measurement of the hand-eye camera; the measurement can be expressed as

$$
{}_{0}^{t}T = \begin{bmatrix}
n_x & o_x & a_x & p_x \\
n_y & o_y & a_y & p_y \\
n_z & o_z & a_z & p_z \\
0 & 0 & 0 & 1
\end{bmatrix}
\tag{24}
$$

The initial kinematics parameter of ${}_{0}^{t}T$ can be obtained, and its specific expression is

$$
\begin{cases}
\alpha_t = \arctan\left(-\frac{a_y}{a_z}\right), \ \beta_t = \arctan\left(-\frac{a_x}{\sqrt{n_x^2 + o_x^2}}\right), \ \gamma_t = \arctan\left(-\frac{o_x}{n_x}\right) \\
x_t = p_x c\beta_t c\gamma_t + c\alpha_t\left(p_y s\gamma_t - p_z c\gamma_t s\beta_t\right) + s\alpha_t\left(p_y c\gamma_t s\beta_t + p_z s\gamma_t\right) \\
y_t = p_z c\gamma_t s\alpha_t - s\gamma_t\left(p_x c\beta_t + p_y s\alpha_t s\beta_t\right) + c\alpha_t\left(p_y c\gamma_t + p_z s\beta_t s\gamma_t\right) \\
z_t = p_x s\beta_t + p_z c\alpha_t c\beta_t - p_y c\beta_t s\alpha_t
\end{cases}
\tag{25}
$$

The initial kinematics parameters of ${}_{0}^{t}T$ can be obtained through the above formula, which can be substituted into the error model of the pose of the hand-eye camera, and can be corrected as a group of kinematics parameters in the process of parameter identification and precision compensation.

4.2   Kinematic Error Model Solution and Accuracy Compensation

Kinematic Error Model Solution. The pose error of frame $\sum_c$ relative to frame $\sum_I$ can be obtained through the measurement of the hand-eye camera as

$$D_1 = {}_c^1 T^A - {}_c^1 T^N \tag{26}$$

Through the formula (22), the kinematics parameters error can be obtained as

$$\Omega = J_e^\dagger D_1 \tag{27}$$

Where, $J_e^\dagger$ indicates the pseudo-inverse of the error Jacobian matrix J_e.

In the MCPC model, the manipulator system has $4n + 12$ kinematics parameters. However, the pose error obtained by one measurement can only list 6 equations. When the number of unknowns is greater than the number of equations, the unique solution cannot be obtained. Therefore, the overdetermined equations should be constructed through multiple measurements to complete the solution.

Accuracy Compensation. In order to ensure the accuracy of the kinematics parameters, the algorithm is usually iterated many times until the error is satisfied. After the kinematics parameter error is obtained, the kinematics parameter after the calibration of the manipulator is

$$E = E^N + \Omega \tag{28}$$

Where, E is the calibration value of kinematic parameters, namely the kinematic parameters after calibration; E^N is the nominal value of kinematic parameters, namely the kinematic parameters of the manipulator structure design. The transformation matrix between the coordinate systems of each link can be calculated by using the formula (1).

According to the kinematics parameters after calibration, the relation between the base coordinate system and the inertia system and the hand-eye relation can be obtained respectively.

5   Simulation Results

MATLAB software is used to verify the calibration method proposed in this paper. The 8-DOF modular manipulator is taken as the research object. Its physical diagram and MCPC model are shown in Fig. 3, and its MCPC parameters are shown in Table 1. Using 50 randomly generated configuration groups, the position error and attitude error of the manipulator system before and after calibration were compared respectively, and the scatter diagram of the position and attitude error before and after calibration was shown (see Figs. 4 and 5).

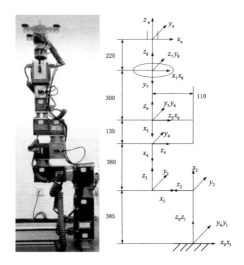

Fig. 3. 8-DOF robot (left) and kinematics model (right)

In order to carry out simulation verification for calibration, parameter errors are set of $\pm 0.005°$ or ± 0.005 m for each kinematics parameter in the manipulator system. By taking the sum of nominal kinematics parameter values and parameter error values as the actual kinematics parameter values, the actual transformation relation ${}_{c}^{I}T^{A}$ between hand-eye camera coordinate system $\sum_{c}$ and the inertial system $\sum_{I}$ was obtained.

Table 1. Nominal values of kinematics parameters of the 8-DOF manipulator

Link i	α_i (°)	β_i (°)	γ_i (°)	x_i (mm)	y_i (mm)	z_i (mm)
0	0	0	/	0	0	/
1	0	−90	/	385	0	/
2	0	90	/	−110	0	/
3	0	90	/	−380	0	/
4	0	0	/	−135	0	/
5	0	−90	/	0	0	/
6	−90	0	/	0	−300	/
7	90	0	/	0	0	/
8	0	0	0	0	0	220

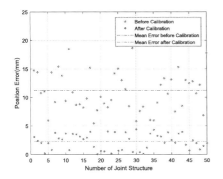

Fig. 4. Position error

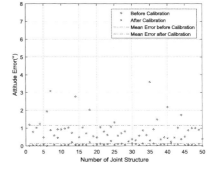

Fig. 5. Attitude error

Table 2. Comparison of the pose error before and after calibration

Pose error	Before		After	
	Max	Mean	Max	Mean
Position error (mm)	22.9	11.2	4.4	2.2
Attitude error (°)	7.42	1.15	0.89	0.13

From Table 2, the mean value and the maximum value of position error after calibration is 80.4% and 92.1% lower than that before calibration respectively; The mean value and the maximum value of attitude error before calibration is 88.7% and 88.0% lower than that before calibration respectively. It can be seen that the position accuracy and attitude accuracy of the manipulator after calibration have been significantly improved.

6   Conclusion

In this paper, a self-calibration method for the kinematics parameters of the lander manipulator is proposed. According to the mission characteristics of the lander in deep space exploration, the error model including the relationship between the manipulator base coordinate system and the target coordinate system and the relationship between the hand and eye are established. On this basis, the initial kinematics parameters between the base coordinate system and the target are solved, and a self-calibration method for the kinematics parameters of the lander manipulator is designed. The kinematics parameters of the manipulator were calibrated when the pose of the manipulator base and target were unknown. Take the 8-DOF modular manipulator as research object designing simulation experiment, and the experimental results prove that the calibration method can reduce the position error and attitude error effectively by obtaining accurate kinematics parameters, and then improve the operating accuracy of the lander manipulator.

References

1. Weixin, Jiao: Semi-global leaderless consensus of circular motion with input saturation. Spacecraft Environ. Eng. **35**(02), 103–110 (2018)
2. Yuan, Y., Zhao, C., Hu, Z.: Prospect of lunar base construction scheme. J. Deep Space Explor. **6**(4), 374–381 (2018)
3. Chen, G., Li, T., Chu, M., et al.: Review on kinematics calibration technology of serial robots. Int. J. Precis. Eng. Manuf. **15**(8), 1759–1774 (2014)
4. Liu, D., Li, H., Li, Z.: Calibration strategy of space manipulator system on-orbit servicing fine operation. J. Astronaut. **38**(06), 630–637 (2017)
5. Marwan, A., Simic, M., Imad, F.: Calibration method for articulated industrial robots. Procedia Comput. Sci. **112**, 1601–1610 (2017)
6. Zhou, W., Wei, B., Li, H., et al.: Accurate calibration of kinematic parameters in long-reach space manipulator. Manned Spaceflight **22**(4), 466–470 (2016)
7. Richter, L.: Robust real-time robot/camera calibration. Robot. Transcranial Mag. Stimulation 63–84 (2013)
8. Li, H., Jiang, Z., He, Y., et al.: Vision-based space manipulator online self-calibration. In: 2009 IEEE International Conference on Robotics & Biomimetics, pp. 1768–1772. IEEE Computer Society, Washington (2009)
9. Wang, Y., Wei, Q., Hu, C., et al.: A self-calibration method for space manipulators based on POE formula. J. Beijing Univ. Aeronaut. Astronaut. **44**(11), 2336–2342 (2018)
10. Schroer, K., Albright, S.L., Grethlein, M.: Complete, minimal and model-continuous kinematic models for robot calibration. Robot. Comput. Integr. Manuf. **13**(1), 73–85 (1997)
11. Zhuang, H., Roth, Z.S., Hamano, F.: A complete and parametrically continuous kinematic model for robot manipulators. IEEE Trans. Robot. Autom. **8**(4), 451–463 (1992)
12. Zhuang, H., Wang, L.K., Roth, Z.S.: Error-model-based robot calibration using a modified CPC model[J]. Robot. Comput. Integr. Manuf. **10**(4), 287–299 (1993)

A Hybrid Deep Reinforcement Learning Algorithm for Intelligent Manipulation

Chao Ma, Jianfei Li, Jie Bai, Yaobing Wang$^{(\boxtimes)}$, Bin Liu,
and Jing Sun

Beijing Key Laboratory of Intelligent Space Robotic Systems Technology
and Applications, Beijing Institute of Spacecraft System Engineering,
Beijing, China
`machaodn@163.com, yaobing_cast@163.com`

Abstract. Conventional collaborative robots can solve complex problems through programming approaches. But the current tasks are different and non-repetitive, many problems cannot be solved by conventional programming methods. Deep reinforcement learning provides a framework for solving robotic control tasks using machine learning techniques. However, the existing model-free deep reinforcement learning algorithms lack unified framework for comparing sample efficiency with final performance. In this paper, a hybrid deep reinforcement learning framework and its application in robot control are proposed based on the existing model-free deep reinforcement learning algorithms. In the acting process, the distributed actors acting with the environment are used to acquire the data, while prior actors are used to solve the cold boot problem of the algorithm. In the learning process, prioritized experience replay and multi-step learning are designed for the improvement on the final performance. Simulations are represented to show the practicality and potential of the proposed algorithm. Results show that the hybrid deep reinforcement learning algorithm in this paper has a significant improvement on the final performance and sample efficiency while it can ensure the stability and convergence.

Keywords: Deep reinforcement learning · Robot control · Data flow · Hybrid deep reinforcement learning

1 Introduction

Conventional collaborative robots can solve complex problems through programming approaches [1]. But the current tasks are different and nonrepetitive, many problems cannot be solved by conventional programming methods. Deep reinforcement learning provides a framework for solving robotic control tasks using machine learning techniques. However, the existing model-free algorithms lack unified framework for comparing sample efficiency with final performance. In this paper, we investigate the application of framework integrated with off-the-shelf deep reinforcement learning algorithms, and a hybrid deep reinforcement learning algorithm is proposed. Simulations show this combination of deep reinforcement learning algorithm can obtain better final performance and sampling efficiency.

© Springer Nature Switzerland AG 2019
H. Yu et al. (Eds.): ICIRA 2019, LNAI 11743, pp. 367–377, 2019.
https://doi.org/10.1007/978-3-030-27538-9_31

The remaining parts of the paper are organized as follows. The background and research methodologies are described in Sect. 1. As the foundation of deep reinforcement learning, the establishments of the basis representation of deep reinforcement learning are reviewed in Sect. 2. Then the improvements of data flow algorithm and a hybrid deep reinforcement learning algorithm are proposed in Sect. 3. The simulation tasks are proposed in Sect. 4. In Sect. 5, typical simulations are represented to show the practicality and potential of the proposed algorithm. The conclusions are summarized in Sect. 6.

2   Background

In this section, we formulate robot control tasks as standard reinforcement learning problems, and introduce the necessary algorithmic foundations on which we demonstrate the methods for this work.

2.1   Reinforcement Learning

We consider a reinforcement learning process where an agent interacts with an environment modeled as a Markov Decision Process (MDP) [2]. An MDP is defined by a tuple (S, A, P, R, γ), where S is the state space, A is the action space, R is the reward function set, γ is the discount factor and P is the transition dynamics. When time t, the agent states at the state s_t, selects an action a_t according to the policy, according to the dynamics $P(s_{t+1}|s_t, a_t)$, and receives a reward $R_{t+1}(s_t, a_t)$ (or R_{t+1}). Here, if we define the discounted reward as:

$$G_t = R_{t+1} + \gamma R_{t+2} + \gamma^2 R_{t+3} + \ldots + \gamma^{T-t} R_{T+1} = \sum_{k=t}^{T} \gamma^{k-t} R_{k+1} \tag{1}$$

The goal of reinforcement learning is to learn a policy maximizing the expected discounted reward over the agent's trajectory $\tau = (s_0, a_0, R_1, s_1, a_1, R_2 \ldots, s_T)$, which is $J = \mathbb{E}_{s \sim \rho, a \sim \pi}[G_0]$.

Policies. $\pi(a|s)$: stochastic policy, where actions are drawn from a probability distribution defined by $a \sim \pi(a|s)$. $\mu(s)$: deterministic policy, where actions are deterministically selected by a mapping $a = \mu(s)$.

Value Function. $V^\pi(s)$: state-value function, defined as the expected return when starting from state s and following policy π thereafter:

$$V^\pi(s) = \mathbb{E}_\pi\left[\sum_{k=t}^{T} \gamma^{k-t} R_{k+1}|s_t = s\right] \tag{2}$$

$Q^{\pi}(s, a)$: action-value function, defined as the expected return by taking the action a from state s, then following π thereafter:

$$Q^{\pi}(s, a) = \mathbb{E}_{\pi}\left[\sum_{k=t}^{T} \gamma^{k-t} R_{k+1} | s_t = s, a_t = a\right] \tag{3}$$

2.2 Actor-Critic Framework

The approach to reinforcement learning problems can be available to two alternative methods. The first one is value function approaches (Critic-only). These methods are based on estimating the value-action function Q^{π} of being in a given state, then the policy is implicitly derived from Q^{π} as $\pi(s) = \mathrm{argmax}_{a \in A} Q^{\pi}(s, a)$. The other available method is *policy search* (Actor-only). In the policy search methods, policies are represented by a variety of approaches and can be directly optimized to maximize the cumulative reward, given:

$$\mathcal{J}(\pi_{\theta}) = \mathbb{E}_{\pi_{\theta}}[f_{\pi_{\theta}}(\cdot)] \tag{4}$$

where $f_{\pi_{\theta}}(\cdot)$ represents the total reward of the trajectory.

Actor-Critic framework is composed of value function approaches and policy search methods, where the Critic estimates the value function according to the temporal difference (TD) learning, while the Actor updates the policy parameters according to the learned value function [3].

2.3 Deep Reinforcement Learning

Aforementioned reinforcement learning algorithms have been extended to the high-dimensional continuous control domain, by deploying deep neural networks as powerful non-linear function approximators for value-action functions and policies, which are called as deep reinforcement learning (DRL). They usually take the observations as input (e.g., raw pixel images from Atari emulators or joint angles of robot arms), and output either the Q-values, from which greedy actions are selected, or policies that can be directly used to execute agents.

Many useful mechanisms have also been proposed that can be added on top of the existing DRL algorithms. These mechanisms generally work orthogonally with the algorithms, and some can accelerate the DRL training by a large margin. Here, we just cover the most influential model-free DRL algorithms and DRL mechanisms.

The first family of DRL algorithms are Deep Q-networks (DQN) [4] and Deep Deterministic Policy Gradient (DDPG) [5]. DQN algorithm combines convolutional neural networks in deep learning and Q-learning in reinforcement learning to realize end-to-end direct control from pixel input to output. However, as a value-based method, DQN cannot be used to solve high-dimensional continuous tasks. DDPG expands DQN based on Actor-Critic framework to handle continuous tasks. As we all know, reinforcement learning is a sequential decision-making problem and the data generated are time-dependent, which leads that supervised learning algorithms are not available to DQN. Hence some tricks are applied to eliminate/reduce data correlation.

Two DRL mechanisms are employed in DQN/DDPG: target network and experience replay. See [5] for more details.

The second family of DRL algorithms are Asynchronous Advantage Actor-Critic (A3C) [6] and A2C [7]. A3C deploy multiple actor-learners to collect experiences and accumulate gradients calculated to update network parameters. Profit from mechanism, different actors collect samples at the same time so that data correlation is much smaller. Recent works find that the asynchrony in A3C does not necessarily lead to improved performance compared to the synchronous version: A2C, which serves as a standard algorithm in OpenAI baselines.

The third family of DRL algorithms are Trust Region Policy Optimization (TRPO) [8] and Proximal Policy Optimization (PPO) [9]. TRPO aims to find a formalization to weigh the advantages of policies for optimizing large nonlinear policies, with guaranteed monotonic improvement. However, TRPO adopts the 2nd-order conjugate gradient solution, which shows a low update efficiency and a difficult implementation. PPO, as an improved algorithm, adopts 1st-order stochastic gradient descent solution, which shows a high update efficiency and an easy implementation. Kullback-Leibler divergence and importance sampling are employed in improving the learning efficiency of the algorithm. PPO serves as a standard algorithm.

3   Algorithm

3.1   Data Flow

We first conduct an instance: Generative Adversarial Network (GAN) [10], which can be divided into the generator and the discriminator. The generator generates a false picture according to a given distribution, where the goal is to generate as realistic an image as possible so that the discriminator judges it is real. The discriminator judges the authenticity of an input image, where the goal is to separate the images generated by the generator from the images of the real world. In other words, the generator is a process of generating data, and the discriminator is a process of consuming data.

Moreover, we summarize the principle: data flow, which can be depicted into a process from data generating to data consuming in the data-driven learning. Similarly, we can define data flow in reinforcement learning. We can define the part for data generation as the actor and for the data consumption as the learner. The actor generates data and supplies sample experiences to the learner, which is referred as the acting, while the learner consumes data and provides the actor with update parameters, which is considered as the learning. In this way, we can transfer reinforcement learning as a standard data flow process, which can be shown in Fig. 1.

Fig. 1. The actor generates data and supplies sample experiences to the learner, while the learner consumes data and provides the actor with update parameters.

3.2   Improvement of Algorithms

DRL algorithms can be improved including but not limited to new frameworks and unified mechanisms. Deep learning frameworks such as DistBelief [11] can make large-scale neural networks efficient to implement for an expanded DRL framework, where some progress has been made on effective use of computational resources such as Gorila [12] and Ape-X [13]. In addition, some mechanisms can be unified to nature DRL algorithms for the state-of-the-art performance. Rainbow [14] expands nature DQN with Double Q-Learning, Prioritized Replay Buffer, Dueling Networks, Multi-step Learning, Distributional Network, Noisy Network, et al.

3.3   Hybrid Deep Reinforcement Learning

We decompose the deep reinforcement learning algorithms according to data flow, where we decouple acting from learning and adopt the asynchronous methods. The first component acting, interacts with the environment, generates its own trajectories of experience and stores the data in a memory buffer. The second component learning, samples a minibatch of experience from the memory and update the network parameters. Based on the distributed architecture, both the actors and the learners can be possessed of multiple distributed workers. We adopt the GA3C [15] to our architecture, where multiple actors run on multi-core CPUs to generate the experience, while a single learner runs on a GPU to sample from the memory buffer and update network parameters. The new DRL framework is called Hybrid Deep Reinforcement Learning (HDRL).

Rainbow combining improvements in DQN-based can only solve the discrete environments, while HDRL can handle both continuous control tasks and discrete environments combining improvements in DDPG-based. The fusion of DRL mechanisms in HDRL are listed in Fig. 2.

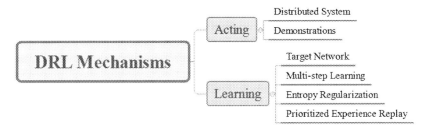

Fig. 2. HDRL can be divided into two parts: acting and learning, both of which contains some DRL mechanisms.

4   Simulations

In order to verify the performance of HDRL on high-dimensional continuous control environments especially for robot control tasks, we have trained on a set of MuJoCo problems (Benchmarks) and contact manipulating tasks.

4.1   Benchmarks

Benchmarking tasks have been performed in two continuous control domains (Reacher-v2(a) and Hopper-v2(b)), which were implemented in the MuJoCo physics simulator. Hopper-v2 is a hopper walker with action, state dimensionalities $|\mathcal{S}| = 13$ and $|\mathcal{A}| = 3$ respectively. Reacher-v2 is a manipulator with $|\mathcal{S}| = 13$ and $|\mathcal{A}| = 2$, which receives reward for catching a randomly-initialized moving ball. Reward function of Hopper-v2 and Reacher-v2 can be seen in Ref [16] (Fig. 3).

Fig. 3. Continuous control environments in MuJoCo simulator: (a) Reacher-v2, (b) Hopper-v2.

4.2   Contact Manipulating Tasks

A co-simulation platform of Python and V-REP is built for the simulation to complete position control and force control task in orthogonal spaces by two DOF arm. Consider the planar manipulator with two revolute joints shown in Fig. 4. The end-effector of the robot moves along the constraint plane. The task requires that the end-effector are under force control in z-direction to track the constant force, while position control in the x-direction to track the constant velocity. Here is task modeling for reinforcement learning as follows.

Fig. 4. Two link planar manipulator on a plane in V-REP simulator.

Action Space Design. Setting action space into torque-value of two motors, that is $a = [\tau_1, \tau_2]^T$, and action space dimension $|\mathcal{A}| = 2$.

State Space Design. Considering all of associated states with the task, containing the joint's position $q = [q_1, q_2]^T$ and velocity $\dot{q} = [\dot{q}_1, \dot{q}_2]^T$, the end-effector's position $X = [X, Z]^T$ and velocity $\dot{X} = [\dot{X}, \dot{Z}]^T$, contact force in z-direction F_z. As a rule of thumb, we can choose state space dimension $|\mathcal{S}| = 8 \sim 20$. Therefore, we can preserve all of states without filtering. Finally, the states can be chosen as $s = [q_1, q_2, \dot{q}_1, \dot{q}_2, X, Z, \dot{X}, \dot{Z}, F_z]^T$, and state space dimension $|\mathcal{S}| = 9$.

Reward Design. Considering desire velocity is $\dot{X}_d = [0.02, 0]^T$ and desired contact force is $F_d = [0, -10]^T$. Setting initialized states in x-direction $X_0 = x_0 + \epsilon$, where ϵ is an initialized noise. Define the one type of termination states (reach) is $X_{ter1} = x_0 + 0.06$, while the other type of termination states (out of contact) equivalent to X_{ter2}, so termination states are $X_{ter} = X_{ter1} \, or \, X_{ter2}$. Finally, reward function is defined by

$$R_{t+1} = \begin{cases} -(\lambda_1 \|\dot{X}^{targ} - \dot{X}_t\| + \lambda_2 \|F_z^{targ} - F_{zt}\|), & \text{if } X \neq X_{ter} \\ 0, & \text{if } X = X_{ter1} \\ -100, & \text{if } X = X_{ter2} \end{cases} \quad (5)$$

where λ_1 and λ_2 are the reward coefficients, to adjust the target weight. We set $\lambda_1 = 10$ and $\lambda_2 = 0.07$ in this simulation.

5 Results

In this section, we mainly discuss final performance and sampling efficiency of DRL algorithms and control performance of DRL algorithms vs. traditional force control algorithm proposed in Ref. [17].

5.1 DRL Performance

On the MuJoCo environments, we consider DDPG, A2C, PPO and HDRL with 1 M frames trained, respectively. See Fig. 5. for average return curves of Hopper-v2 and Fig. 6. for average return curves of Reacher-v2.

Compared to Baselines (DDPG, A2C and PPO), the average return curve of HDRL shows a faster rising speed in the early stage of training. Meanwhile, it exerts a higher result when the algorithm converges. In other word, HDRL demonstrates a scale up improvement in sampling efficiency and final performance in terms of Baselines.

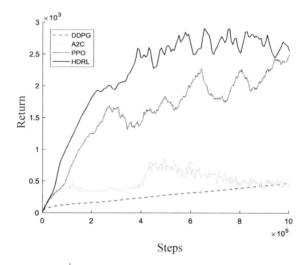

Fig. 5. Average return curves of Hopper-v2 via different DRL algorithms.

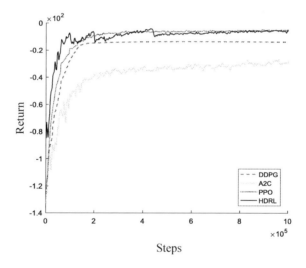

Fig. 6. Average return curves of Reacher-v2 via different DRL algorithms.

Similarly, we consider HDRL and DDPG with 1 M frames trained on contact manipulating tasks, respectively. See Fig. 7. For average return curve. Results shows that HDRL also demonstrates a scale up improvement in sampling efficiency and final performance compared to DDPG.

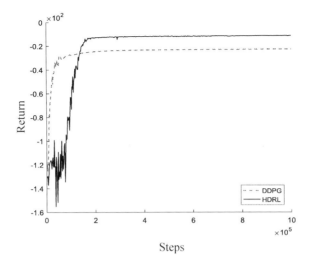

Fig. 7. Average return curves of contact manipulating task via different DRL algorithms.

5.2 Control Performance

Traditional control (TC) algorithm and DRL (HDRL) algorithm are used to demonstrate control performance of the contact manipulating task, respectively. See Fig. 8. for tracking the contact force in z-direction and Fig. 9. for tracking the velocity in x-direction.

Results shows that DRL algorithm can not only complete the contact manipulating task, but also show the same level of control precision (position control precision) as traditional control algorithm, or exceed the control precision (force control precision) of traditional control algorithm. More contact manipulating task simulation can be tested for the application of DRL algorithms.

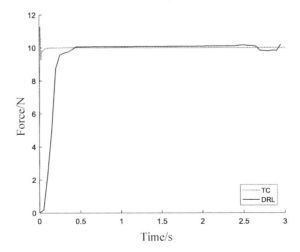

Fig. 8. Tracking the contact force in z-direction of TC and DRL algorithm.

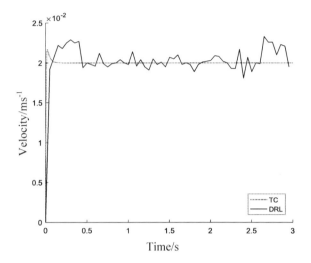

Fig. 9. Tracking the velocity in *x*-direction of TC and DRL algorithm.

6   Conclusions

In this paper, a hybrid deep reinforcement learning framework and its application in robot control are proposed based on the existing model-free deep reinforcement learning algorithms. In the acting process, the distributed actors acting with the environment are used to acquire the data, while prior actors are used to solve the cold boot problem of the algorithm. In the learning process, prioritized experience replay and multi-step learning are designed for the improvement on the final performance. The performance of this algorithm is verified and compared with that of the existing baselines through benchmark tasks in order to shed light on the potential application of the proposed framework. Simulations result show that the hybrid deep reinforcement learning algorithm in this paper has a significant improvement on the final performance and sample efficiency compared with the baselines, while it can ensure the stability and convergence.

Acknowledgment. This research was supported, in part, by the National Natural Science Foundation of China (No. 51875393) and by the China Advance Research for Manned Space Project (No. 030601).

References

1. Vecerik, M., Hester, T., Scholz, J., et al.: Leveraging demonstrations for deep reinforcement learning on robotics problems with sparse rewards. arXiv preprint arXiv:1707.08817 (2017)
2. Tai, L., Zhang, J., Liu, M., et al.: A survey of deep network solutions for learning control in robotics: from reinforcement to imitation. arXiv preprint arXiv:1612.07139 (2016)
3. Barto, G., Sutton, S., Anderson, W.: Neuronlike adaptive elements that can solve difficult learning control problems. IEEE Trans. Syst. Man Cybern. **5**, 834–846 (1984)

4. Mnih, V., Kavukcuoglu, K., Silver, D., et al.: Playing Atari with deep reinforcement learning. In: Neural Information Processing Systems (2013)
5. Lillicrap, P., Hunt, J., Pritzel, A., et al.: Continuous control with deep reinforcement learning. arXiv preprint arXiv:1509.02971 (2015)
6. Mnih, V., Badia, P., Mirza, M., et al.: Asynchronous methods for deep reinforcement learning. arXiv preprint arXiv:1602.01783 (2016)
7. Wu, Y., Mansimov, E., Grosse, B., et al.: Scalable trust-region method for deep reinforcement learning using kronecker-factored approximation. In: Neural Information Processing Systems, pp. 5279–5288 (2017)
8. Schulman, J., Levine, S., Abbeel, P., et al.: Trust region policy optimization. In: 32nd International Conference on Machine Learning (ICML 2015), pp. 1889–1897 (2015)
9. Schulman, J., Wolski, F., Dhariwal, P., et al.: Proximal policy optimization algorithms. arXiv preprint arXiv:1707.06347 (2017)
10. Goodfellow, I., Pouget, J., Mirza, M., et al.: Generative adversarial nets. In: Neural Information Processing Systems, pp. 2672–2680 (2014)
11. Dean, J., Corrado, G., Monga, R., et al.: Large scale distributed deep networks. In: 25th International Conference on Neural Information Processing Systems (2012)
12. Nair, A., Srinivasan, P., Blackwell, S., et al.: Massively parallel methods for deep reinforcement learning. arXiv preprint arXiv:1507.04296 (2015)
13. Horgan, D., Quan, J., Budden, D., et al.: Distributed prioritized experience replay. arXiv preprint arXiv:1803.00933 (2018)
14. Hessel, M., Modayil, J., Hasselt, H., et al.: Rainbow: combining improvements in deep reinforcement learning. arXiv preprint arXiv:1710.02298 (2017)
15. Babaeizadeh, M., Frosio, I., Tyree, S., et al.: Reinforcement learning through asynchronous advantage actor-critic on a gpu. arXiv preprint arXiv:1611.06256 (2016)
16. Google. https://github.com/openai/gym/tree/master/gym/envs/mujoco. Accessed 06 May 2019
17. Li, J., Liu, L., Wang, Y., et al.: Adaptive hybrid impedance control of robot manipulators with robustness against environment's uncertainties. In: 2015 IEEE International Conference on Mechatronics and Automation, pp. 1846–1851. IEEE (2015)

Virtual-Sensor-Based Planetary Soil Classification with Legged Robots

Shuang Wu[(✉)], Lei Chen, Bin Liu, Chu Wang, Qingqing Wei,
and Yaobing Wang

Beijing Key Laboratory of Intelligent Space Robotic System Technology
and Applications, Beijing Institute of Spacecraft System Engineering,
Beijing 100094, China
shuangwu_ll@163.com

Abstract. The estimation of soil properties is crucial for legged robots during planetary exploration missions. A virtual-sensor-based soil classification approach for legged robots is proposed in this paper. Instead of installing extra force sensors on the foot of the robot, joint motion information from joint position sensors and current signals from joint motors on the leg are recorded and used as the dataset in classification. The collected data is decomposed using the Discrete Wavelet Transform and assigned a soil type by a Support Vector Machine (SVM). This approach is validated on a dataset acquired from a high-fidelity simulation model of a hexapod robot, and the classification accuracy of more than 90% was achieved. Different SVM models are used in classification for comparative analysis, and the contributions of the different signals to the classification performance are evaluated. Experimental results demonstrate that the proposed approach can estimate the soil properties with a good performance and rapid forecasting speed.

Keywords: Soil classification · Virtual sensor · Legged robots

1 Introduction

Planetary exploration is a challenging task for mobile robots because of the difficulty of anticipating the soil mechanical properties for motion control. To safely traverse fine-grained, granular and other inaccessible terrain, estimating of soil mechanical properties is critical, since soil conditions can strongly influence robots' stability.

Terramechanics is one way to simulate the mechanical properties of soil [1–3]. Brunskill et al. [4] designed several tests to measure some fundamental macroscopic properties to characterize Martian soil. Ding et al. [5] analyzed the foot-soil interaction mechanics for legged robots based on the knowledge of terramechanics. However, this kind of method has its limitation to describe the uncertainty exists in terrain modeling.

Terrain classification for legged robots has been investigated using machine learning techniques [6–8]. Brooks and Iagnemma [9] proposed a self-supervised terrain classification approach for wheeled robots, which can enable the wheeled robots to learn to predict mechanical properties of distant terrain. Walas et al. [10] described a

© Springer Nature Switzerland AG 2019
H. Yu et al. (Eds.): ICIRA 2019, LNAI 11743, pp. 378–385, 2019.
https://doi.org/10.1007/978-3-030-27538-9_32

walking robot controller for negotiation of terrains with different traction characteristics. Three perception systems were used to gather information for characterizing the terrain class, and a Support Vector Machine (SVM) were used as a classifier for terrain classification. Kolvenbach [11] proposed a haptic inspection method using legged robots for various Martian soils. In that method, the impact data recorded from sensors placed in the foot was used as sample sets in soil classification. However, the sensors on feet are easily damaged due to its frequently impacting with various terrains and barriers, which reduce the robustness of the control system.

Virtual sensor is a good way to solve this problem, which is an indirect measurement method that analyze and study the data from the alternative sensors instead of the data form the required sensors. Ablameyko et al. [12] developed a virtual sensor based on empirical data using an artificial neural network. Gonzalez-de-Santos et al. [13] have verified that the virtual sensor is a feasible way to apply to the robotic sensor system, and the joint position, position error and velocity can be used to estimate the force exerted on the bottom of the foot.

In this paper, we propose a classification approach based on virtual instrument technique for soils with different hardness by using a legged robot. Instead of using impact forces recorded from sensors placed on the foot of the robot, joint motion information from joint position sensors and current signals from joint motors on the leg are used as the dataset in classification. Then the dataset is decomposed by the Discrete Wavelet Transform (DWT), and classified into different categories based on the different soil types using the SVM. Due to the classifier is trained offline, it only takes a very little time to predict the soil type during the robot's walking. Moreover, without installing any other sensors on the foot, our approach can largely reduce the complexity of the mechanical system while improve its robustness.

The rest of this study is organized as follows. The scheme of the proposed virtual-sensor-based classification is given in Sect. 2. The classification method is designed in Sect. 3. The classification results are reported in Sect. 4. Finally, the conclusions are drawn in Sect. 5.

2 Virtual-Sensor-Based Classification Scheme

In order to anticipate soil mechanical properties for legged robots, the interaction between robots and different kinds of terrains can be recorded and used as datasets to implement soil classification. The impact forces exerted on feet has been used in soil classification and got a good result. However, it requires extra force sensor and IMU installed on feet which would increase the complexity of the hardware system while also lower the system robustness. According to the virtual sensor technique, the statistical dependence between measurements from different sensors can be estimated by data-driven methods, and then a virtual sensor can be built from other physical measurements and used in place of its own physical measurement [14]. Based on this conception, the dependence between the joint state from the joint sensor and the impact forces from the force sensor on feet can be obtained by data training. Here we extended this idea and built the dependence between the joint state and the soil properties by data training in order to implement soil classification.

The classification approach developed in this study consists of three parts: data collection, feature extraction and classification. In the first part, the joint positions, joint velocities and joint motor current are collected from one leg of a robot, which are as the dataset. Then the features were extracted from the dataset using DWT in the second part. In the last part, soil classification is implemented with the extracted features using SVM method. The schematic overview of our approach is shown in Fig. 1, where the leg with two joints is taken as the example, while this approach is suitable for any multi-joint legged robots.

The implementation of this approach can be divided into two phases: offline training and online prediction. In the offline training phase, we designed several trajectories for the robot walking on various soils, and the dataset is collected during the robot walking. These dataset is used for training after the collection. The trained SVM classifier can be obtained in this phase. In the online prediction phase, the current data during the robot walking in exploration tasks are also recorded. These data are used for prediction with the trained SVM classifier, and the soil type can be estimated at that moment.

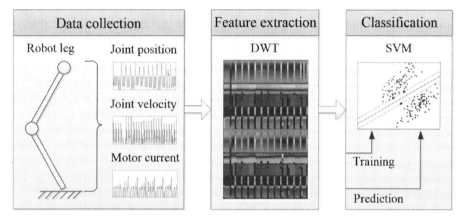

Fig. 1. The schematic overview of the virtual-sensor-based classification approach

3 Method

3.1 Data Collection

The dataset was acquired based on a high-fidelity hexapod robot simulation model which was constructed in ADAMS. We set different contact parameters between feet and soil to simulate the robot walking on different types of soil. Instead of a physical robot, the simulation model was used here to validate our approach. This approach will be implemented on a physical robot in our future work.

We designed several trajectories for the robot walking based on Bezier curve. The robot is walking followed these trajectories with different velocities between 50 mm/s to 100 mm/s. Thus the foot of the robot can contact with the ground at different angles and velocities. A set of 13 data samples was collected from a foot on one soil (one contact was seen as one sample). Because 4 types of soil (ST-1, ST-2, ST-3, ST-4) were designed in this test, this result in a total amount of 52 data samples recorded with the robot. The sampling frequency of 100 Hz and sampling time of 10 s were adopted during the sampling process. For the simulation model used here, the joint torque is used to take the place of the motor current, and each sample includes joint state (joint position and joint velocity), joint torque, and the corresponding soil type.

3.2   Feature Extraction

Before classification, the DWT is used to extract the features from the data collected during the robot walking.

The Wavelet Transform was developed as an alternative to the short time Fourier Transform to overcome problems related to its frequency and time resolution properties. The DWT is a special case of the Wavelet Transform that provides a compact representation of a signal in time and frequency that can be computed efficiently [15]. For the above advantages, DWT has been used to extract features from motion or force information on robots [11, 16, 17].

Here we get the features using the Daubechies wavelet with four vanishing moments to ensure exchange-ability of wavelet coefficients within each scale of decomposition.

3.3   Classification

Support Vector Machine (SVM) [18] classifier is used in this study as it can get a better result with small-size training sample set and has excellent generalization ability which are very important for its application in planetary exploration with legged robots. Since the collection of sample data on planets is an expensive and challenging task, in many cases the number of training samples is insufficient for a proper learning of classification systems. As a direct implementation of the structure risk minimization inductive principle, SVM provides good performances such as global optimization and good generalization abilities, and especially for classifying high-dimensional data when a limited number of training sample are available [19–21].

In this research, the classification is performed using the Classification Learner App, which is contained in the Statistics and Machine Learning toolbox of Matlab. Among the datasets acquired in the simulation, 80% of the them are used for training, and 20% for validation. Five-fold cross-validation technique is employed to improve the prediction accuracy. The one-vs-one SVM with different kernel functions are used as classifiers in the training. The kernel functions used in this study are as follows:

Linear function

$$K(x_i, x_j) = x_i^T x_j \tag{1}$$

Polynomial function (Quadratic: d = 2 and Cubic: d = 3)

$$K(x_i, x_j) = (\gamma x_i^T x_j + r)^d, \gamma > 0 \tag{2}$$

Radial Basis function (Gaussian function)

$$K(x_i, x_j) = \exp\left(-\gamma \|x_i - x_j\|^2\right), \quad \gamma > 0 \tag{3}$$

Here, γ, r, and d are kernel parameters.

4   Results and Discussion

In this work, 4 different types of SVM: Linear SVM, Quadratic SVM, Cubic SVM, and Medium Gaussian SVM are used to execute classification for comparative analysis. The classification confusion matrices for these SVM models on the validation dataset are shown in Fig. 2. Results of classification accuracy of these SVM models are shown in Table 1. As can be seen from the results, the Cubic SVM has the highest classification accuracy of 92.3%. Although its training time is a bit longer, it will not add extra computational burden on the online prediction because of the offline training scheme. The classification accuracy for the Cubic SVM classification related to the selected signals are shown in Table 2, where also shows the corresponding number of total features. The Torque signals demonstrate a higher individual accuracy compared to the joint state signals. These results above show the validity of the proposed virtual-sensor-based soil classification approach.

The proposed soil classification approach has three main advantages. First, instead of installing extra sensors, this approach only uses the exist sensors for data collection, which can lower the hardware complexity of the robot and improve the system robustness. Second, the offline training and online prediction scheme makes it only takes a litter time to estimate the soil type during exploration tasks. Third, this approach is concise with clear concept, and can be easily applied to the legged robots.

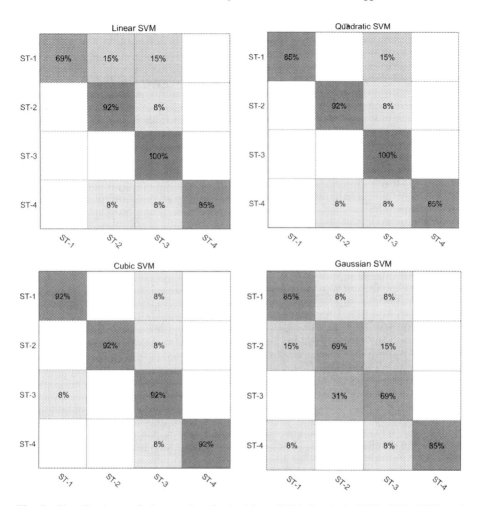

Fig. 2. Classification confusion matrices for the Linear SVM, Quadratic SVM, Cubic SVM, and Medium Gaussian SVM on the validation dataset.

Table 1. Comparison of different SVM models.

SVM model	Accuracy	Train time (sec)	Prediction speed (obs/sec)
Linear	86.5%	20.82	~22
Quadratic	90.4%	21.07	~21
Cubic	92.3%	27.05	~22
Medium Gaussian	76.9%	35.66	~24

Table 2. Accuracy of the Cubic SVM classification related to selected signals.

	No. total features	Classification accuracy				
		ST-1	ST-2	ST-3	ST-4	Overall
Joint state	2012	92%	31%	31%	92%	61.5%
Torque	1006	85%	92%	100%	85%	90.4%
Joint state + Torque	3018	92%	92%	92%	92%	92.3%

5   Conclusions

In order to improve the locomotor efficiency of legged robots during planetary exploration, we propose a virtual-sensor-based soil classification approach for legged robots. The soil classification approach is based on the virtual sensor technique, which can estimate the interaction effects between soils and feet by analysis of the information from joints on legs. The joint motion and motor current signals are acquired from joint position sensor and joint motor on the leg. The features are extracted from the acquired signals using the DWT, and then classified by a SVM. This approach is validated on a dataset collected from a high-fidelity simulation model of a hexapod robot, and the classification accuracy of more than 90% was achieved. Without installing any extra sensors on feet, the proposed approach can achieve a high classification accuracy with low hardware complexity and high robustness. For the future, the approach will be implemented and executed on a physical hexapod robot to further verify its validity and robustness.

Acknowledgement. This research was supported in part by the National Natural Science Foundation of China (No. 51875393) and by the China Advance Research for Manned Space Project (No. 030601).

References

1. Janosi, Z., Hanamoto, B.: Analytical determination of drawbar pull as a function of slip for tracked vehicles in deformable soils: mechanics of soil-vehicle systems: Edizoni Minerva Technica. Editione Minerva Tecnica, Torino (1962)
2. Wong, J.Y., Reece, A.R.: Prediction of rigid wheel performance based on the analysis of soil-wheel stresses part I. Performance of driven rigid wheels. J. Terramech. **4**(1), 81–98 (1967)
3. Komizunai, S., Konno, S., Abiko, A., et al.: Slip characteristics identification for biped walking of a humanoid robot on sand. In: Proceedings of Eighth International Conference on Flow Dynamics, pp. 9–11 (2011)
4. Brunskill, C., Patel, N., Gouache, T.P., et al.: Characterisation of martian soil simulants for the ExoMars rover testbed. J. Terrramech. **48**(6), 419–438 (2011)
5. Ding, L., Gao, H., Deng, Z., et al.: Foot–terrain interaction mechanics for legged robots: modeling and experimental validation. Int. J. Robot. Res. **32**(13), 1585–1606 (2013)
6. Mrva, J., Faigl, J.: Feature extraction for terrain classification with crawling robots. Inf. Technol. Appl. Theory **1422**, 179–185 (2015)

7. Degrave, J., Van Cauwenbergh, R., Wyffels, F., et al.: Terrain classification for a quadruped robot. In: 12th International Conference on Machine Learning and Applications, vol. 1, pp. 185–190. IEEE (2013)
8. Kertész, C.: Rigidity-based surface recognition for a domestic legged robot. IEEE Robot. Autom. Lett. **1**(1), 309–315 (2016)
9. Brooks, C.A., Iagnemma, K.: Self-supervised terrain classification for planetary surface exploration rovers. J. Field Robot. **29**(3), 445–468 (2012)
10. Walas, K.: Terrain classification and negotiation with a walking robot. J. Intell. Rob. Syst. **78**(3–4), 401–423 (2015)
11. Kolvenbach, H., Bärtschi, C., Wellhausen, L., et al.: Haptic inspection of planetary soils with legged robots. IEEE Robot. Autom. Lett. **4**(2), 1626–1632 (2019)
12. Ablameyko, S., Goras, L., Gori, M., Piuri, V.: Neural Networks for Instrumentation Measurement and Related Industrial Applications, vol. 185. IOS Press, Amsterdam (2003)
13. Gonzalez de Santos, P., Garcia, E., Estremera, J.: Virtual sensors for walking robots. In: Gonzalez de Santos, P., Garcia, E., Estremera, J. (eds.) Quadrupedal Locomotion: An Introduction to the Control of Four-legged Robots, pp. 191–211. Springer, London (2006). https://doi.org/10.1007/1-84628-307-8_8
14. Masson, M.H., Canu, S., Grandvalet, Y., et al.: Software sensor design based on empirical data. Ecol. Model. **120**(2–3), 131–139 (1999)
15. Tzanetakis, G., Essl, G., Cook, P.: Audio analysis using the discrete wavelet transform. In: Proceedings of Conference in Acoustics and Music Theory Applications, vol. 66 (2001)
16. Jaber, A.A., Bicker, R.: Industrial robot backlash fault diagnosis based on discrete wavelet transform and artificial neural network. Am. J. Mech. Eng. **4**(1), 21–31 (2016)
17. Jakovljevic, Z., Petrovic, P.B., Mikovic, V.D., et al.: Fuzzy inference mechanism for recognition of contact states in intelligent robotic assembly. J. Intell. Manuf. **25**(3), 571–587 (2014)
18. Vapnik, V.N.: Statistical Learning Theory. Wiley, New York (1998)
19. Chi, M., Feng, R., Bruzzone, L.: Classification of hyperspectral remote-sensing data with primal SVM for small-sized training dataset problem. Adv. Space Res. **41**(11), 1793–1799 (2008)
20. Su, J., Yi, D., Liu, C., et al.: Dimension reduction aided hyperspectral image classification with a small-sized training dataset: experimental comparisons. Sensors **17**(12), 2726 (2017)
21. Li, C., Wang, J., Wang, L., et al.: Comparison of classification algorithms and training sample sizes in urban land classification with Landsat thematic mapper imagery. Remote Sens. **6**(2), 964–983 (2014)

Virtual Force Senor Based on PSO-BP Neural Network for Legged Robots in Planetary Exploration

Chu Wang[✉], Shuang Wu, Lei Chen, Bin Liu, Qingqing Wei,
and Yaobing Wang

Beijing Key Laboratory of Intelligent Space Robotic System Technology
and Applications, Beijing Institute of Spacecraft System Engineering,
Beijing 100094, China
wangchu711@126.com

Abstract. The foot force of the legged robot plays a decisive role in the balance of the fuselage. Especially when walking on the irregular road surface and the less rigid road surface, the change of the foot end support force will change the attitude of the robot body, which will affect the stability. In addition, the change of foot force is also closely related to the flexibility of the movement of the leg of the robot. When the movement of the foot end has a transition from free space to constrained space, only the position control will not meet the requirements of the leg for the flexibility of the movement. This paper addresses the design of virtual sensors for terrain adaptation developed with the aims of simplifying the hardware of the legged robot or increasing the reliability of the sensorial information available. The virtual force sensor (VFS) is developed based on particle swarm optimization (PSO) BP neural network and can estimate the forces exerted by the feet from data extracted from joint-position, joint-velocity, and joint-torque, which are mandatory in all robotic systems. The force estimates are used to detect foot/ground contact. Several simulations carried out with the hexapod robot are reported to prove the efficacy of this method. This method simplifies the hardware of the robot, reduces design, construction and maintenance costs while enhancing the robustness of the robot and the reliability of its behavior.

Keywords: Virtual force sensor · Particle swarm optimization algorithm · BP neural network · Legged robot

1 Introduction

With the development of science and technology, the scope of human exploration of nature is gradually expanding. For areas where human beings cannot enter or are not suitable for entry (such as the moon, Mars, and disaster scenes), robot devices are the best choice to utilized for on-the-spot exploration. At present, there are two main types of robots used for exploration in complex unknown environments. One is the wheeled robot that moves on wheels, and the other is the legged robot based on bionic walking. The advantage of the wheeled robot is that the control strategy is relatively simple, and

© Springer Nature Switzerland AG 2019
H. Yu et al. (Eds.): ICIRA 2019, LNAI 11743, pp. 386–397, 2019.
https://doi.org/10.1007/978-3-030-27538-9_33

the walking efficiency is high in a flat area, but the disadvantage is that it lacks adaptability to an unknown complex terrain. Legged robots can span larger obstacles (such as ditch, ridge, etc.), and the robot's legs have a large degree of freedom to make their movements more flexible, and thus more adaptable to complex terrain. Therefore, one of the main advantages of legged robots is their great adaptability to irregular, unstructured terrain [1–3]. However, the major complexity of the control algorithms, the mechanical devices and electronic hardware that go into these robots is a negative aspect of this essential characteristic. This complexity is one of the main drawbacks that have kept legged robot from expanding to real applications [4–6].

The aim of legged robot control strategy is to tracking the desired contact force between the foot and the environment. Consequently, the force sensor is required to sense the foot force in real time, and also needs to adjust the control parameters in real time to adapt to the variation of the environment [7, 8]. In space exploration, the difficulty of acquiring contact forces and adjusting control parameters in real time is greatly increased due to the unknown of environmental parameters and unstructured planet surface statement in space exploration, and the reliability of force sensors in harsh environments, as well as limited by the timeliness of telemetry data transmission [9, 10].

Virtual sensor is a soft sensing strategy that can process complex data of multiple sets of physical signals through certain algorithms and provide indirect measurement data to the control system. It has the corresponding functions of actual physical sensors and is a virtual reality and virtual instrument. A fusion technology developed by interdisciplinary research such as sensors. The virtual sensor is mainly for measuring the cost that is difficult to directly measure or directly measure, and the related quantity is measured by modeling, and then the measured signal is processed, and the target quantity information can be indirectly obtained [11]. In a sense, it is a mathematical model that can be used to achieve the output of the measured data by creating an extended system model based on the raw data. Therefore, starting from the idea of virtual sensor technology application, the key technology and implementation process of virtual sensor are fully considered, and the virtual sensor model which can accurately sense the foot end force and foot-environment action parameters of foot robot is applied to the planet [12–14]. The compliant control of the detected foot robot provides accurate parameters.

This paper addresses the design, development, and testing of virtual force sensors, which can be defined as systems that infer sensorial magnitudes by monitoring of other available magnitudes. The objective of this work is either to substitute or to complement the information on terrain given normally by physical sensors on legged robot for planetary exploration. These objectives have been motivated by the necessity of simplifying the hardware of legged robots and reducing their design, construction, and maintenance costs while enhancing the robustness of the machine and the reliability of its behavior. This virtual force sensor is based on a neural network. The position, velocity and torque information at the joint of the motor are used as input to estimate the supporting force and friction between the foot and the ground. Virtual sensors are intended to generate different estimates of the forces exerted by the feet. These estimates can emulate the information given by force sensor installed on the foot. The force estimates are to be employed to detect the contact between the foot and the ground at the end of leg transference.

2   PSO-BP Neural Network

2.1   Back-Propagation Learning Algorithm

Back-Propagation (BP) neural network was blossomed by Rumelhart and McCelland in 1986, which is a multi-layer feedforward network model trained according to the error reverse propagation algorithm. The back-propagation (BP) algorithm is mainly composed of two parts, namely, the positive propagation of the signal and the reverse propagation of the error. Forward communication is the key attribute value input from the input layer to the hidden layer for processing, and then to the output layer. If the output and the desired output are biased, the deviation is propagated back along the neural network, and the threshold and weight are continually modified to achieve the prediction target.

As a feed-forward network composed of nonlinear change units, BP model is widely used due to its strong nonlinear interpolation ability and the ability to obtain mathematical mapping reflecting the internal laws of experimental data. Under the condition of reasonable structure and appropriate weight, the neural network can approximate any nonlinear continuous function and apply the error gradient descent algorithm to minimize the mean square error between the network output value and the actual one

2.2   PSO-Based Training Algorithm

Particle swarm optimization algorithm (PSO) is a randomly optimal algorithm based on swarm intelligence. The algorithm can be used to solve optimization problem and it is brought forward through the inspiration of the biology model of bird seeking foods. In the algorithm, the solution for each optimization problem can be considered as seeking a flying bird in the sky, and each bird is a "particle". Each particle has an adaptive value determined by the optimized function; the velocity of each particle will determine its direction and distance. Then, the particles will follow the optimal particle searching in the solution space.

Suppose the search space is a D-dimensional space and the number of particle swarm is n, then the particle i of swarm can be represented by a D-dimensional vector: $x_i = (x_{i1}, x_{i2}, ..., x_{iD})$, $i = 1, 2, ..., n$. the speed of particle is $V_i = (V_{i1}, V_{i2}, ..., V_{iD})$, $i = 1, 2, ..., n$. PSO algorithm can be described as follow:

- Step 1. Randomly initialize a group of m particles with positions and velocities.
- Step 2. Calculate the fitness value of each particle.
- Step 3. Calculate the position of the best fitness value of each particle from its historical movement, which called p_{best}.
- Step 4. Calculate the position of best fitness value of all particles from global historical movement, which called g_{best}.
- Step 5. Speed and position of particles are updated using the following formulas.

$$V_i^{t+1} = \omega^t V_i^t + c_1 \tau_1 \left(p_{best}^t - x_i^t\right) + c_2 \tau_2 \left(g_{best}^t - x_i^t\right) \tag{1}$$

$$X_i^{t+1} = X_i^t + V_i^{t+1} \tag{2}$$

where V_i^t is the velocity of particle i at iteration t. As V_i^t is uncontrollable, a particle will cycle beating in the problem space, in order to inhibit the erratic beating, the speed is often limited to a value within $[-v_{max}, v_{max}]$; X_i^t represents the position of particle i at iteration t; τ_1 and τ_2 are two uniform random number from $[0, 1]$; c_1 and c_2 are learning factor which also called acceleration constants as they control how far a particle can move in a single iteration. Generally, $c_1 = c_2 = 1.8$ were used. As previously introduced, p_{best}^t and g_{best}^t are the individual best position and the global best position of all particles at iteration t, respectively. The variable ω^t is inertia weight at iteration t which is defined by Eq. (3) below. A larger inertia weight led to the global exploration and a smaller inertia weight tends to facilitate the local exploration to fine-tune the current search area.

$$\omega^t = \omega_{max} - (\omega_{max} - \omega_{min}) \times \frac{iter}{it_{max}} \tag{3}$$

where ω_{max} and ω_{min} are the maximum value and the minimum value of inertia weight, which are suggested to be 0.9 and 0.4, respectively; $iter$ is the iteration t; it_{max} is the maximum value of iteration number.

- Step 6. If the end condition is not satisfied, loop back to step 2 again. The end condition usually is a predetermined it max value or adapts fitness value.

2.3   The Hybrid PSO-BP Algorithm

The utilization of BP model weights and thresholds has great influence on the prediction accuracy, so the optimization of neural network weights can effectively improve the prediction performance. The BP neural network optimized by Particle Swarm Optimization algorithm is also called PSO-BP algorithm, it takes the weights and biases of neurons trained as one particle for PSO algorithm. The fundamental idea of PSO-BP algorithm can be described as follows:

- Step 1. Normalize the training dataset and the testing dataset into $[-1, 1]$.
- Step 2. Randomly initialize a group of m particles with the number is m, including positions and speed velocities.
- Step 3. Compute every particle's fitness value: Referring to complexity of training dataset, LM algorithm or the Conjugate gradient algorithm is used to train the BP neural network. When the dataset is simple, the LM algorithm is used, otherwise Conjugate algorithm is chosen. Update the weights and biases of each neuron using current g_{best} value. The performance function selects the MSE function: where MSE denotes the mean sum of squares of the network errors.
- Step 4. Update particles' speed and position using the Eqs. (1) and (2).

- Step 5. If the end condition is not satisfied, go to step 2 again, or else, go to step 6. The end station usually is set to a previously determined it_{max} or adapts fitness value.
- Step 6. Update the weights and biases of BP neural network by PSO algorithm and the network can be used for forecasting.
- Step 7. Renormalize the forecasting results from $[-1, 1]$.

3   Construction of VFS for Legged Robot

3.1   Dynamic Simulation Model

The planetary detection hexapod robot consists of six legs, as shown in Fig. 1. Each leg adopts a plane parallel two-degree-of-freedom design scheme to ensure that the robot can realize the full-configuration motion in the main motion direction of the forward and backward translation. The configuration of each leg of the hexapod robot is shown in the Fig. 2. The single leg is a five-bar linkage mechanism with three passive joints, which constitutes a parallelogram structure ABCD. The mechanism is driven by a motor-connected reducer to drive two rods AB and AD respectively.

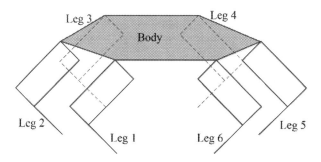

Fig. 1. Dynamic simulation model of hexapod robot.

3.2   Virtual Force Sensor Design

The contact force of the legged robot plays a decisive role in the balance of the fuselage. Especially when walking on irregular and small rigid terrain, Variations in the force of the foot will cause the posture of the robot body to change, which may affect the stability of the legged robot. Artificial intelligence technology can be applied to establish foot force recognition model. Utilizing the real-time joint motor parameters as input, after training and learning, it is possible to predict the foot force online and build a virtual sensor to replace the conventional physical sensor.

Certain dynamic parameters of legged robot are already measured by existing measurement sensors. Other parameters, such as the state of contact and the contact force, necessary or desirable for legged robot monitoring or control are not currently measured, either because those measurements would be too costly or too slow to be of use in real time. The approach is to use the suite of available sensor measurements along with neural networks with online learning capabilities to develop "virtual sensors" for the parameters that are needed but cannot be easily or rapidly measured. The data from these virtual sensors can then be used for performance monitoring and to make legged robot control decisions.

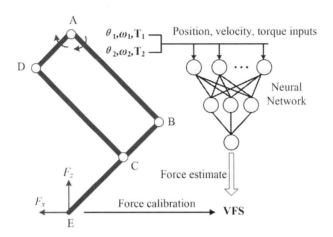

Fig. 2. Configuration of each leg of hexapod robot.

3.3   VFS Based on PSO-BP Algorithm

Here we propose the use of neural networks to correlate the foot forces with the available sensorial magnitudes, and so implementing a virtual sensor. Joint position and speed are the main motion variables that determine the system's working conditions during leg motion.

To solve the ground-detection problem, a nonlinear feed-forward neural network (multilayer perceptron) with one hidden layer and sigmoidal activation functions was selected. This network is widely extended in the modeling of nonlinear static systems and in the implementation of virtual sensors.

Previous research dedicated that dynamic effects due to joint inertia or friction hysteresis were not relevant in the hexapod robot's normal operation. Accordingly, the use of some well-known dynamic network architectures or the inclusion of past inputs in a static network did not prove to enhance the system's performance. Therefore, the static approach of the feed-forward network was found to be sufficient to model the system for this particular platform.

The torque, the position and the speed of each leg joint have been selected as input magnitudes for the network. Since the leg consists of two joints, the network has a total of six input neurons. The number of hidden neurons has been fixed at five empirically, a selection based on the quality of the results and the training cost. The number of output neurons is one in the case of the virtual switch and the virtual one axis force sensor.

The specific process of VFS for legged robot based on PSO-BP algorithm is shown in Fig. 3.

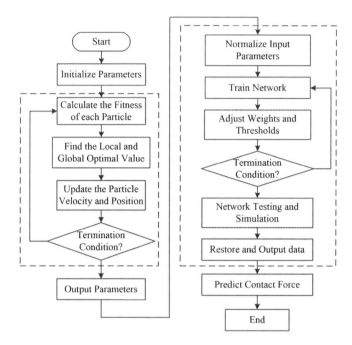

Fig. 3. The specific process of VFS based on PSO-BP algorithm.

4   Simulation and Analysis

4.1   Parameters Initialization of PSO-BP Model

In this study, the training and validation sample data are obtained by dynamic simulation result. The input layer parameters of the PSO-BP model for VFS are the angle, angular velocity and torque parameters of the two joint motors. Considering the availability of parameters during the actual test, the joint motor current will be used instead of the torque parameter as the input parameter of the virtual sensor in further test.

The *Premnmx* function is applied to normalize the input and output parameters to the interval $[-1, 1]$. Under the condition of the initialization of weights and thresholds, the transfer functions between input layer, hidden layer and output layer are set to *Tansig* and *Purelin* respectively, and the training function is *Trainlm*. The number of network training is set at 10,000, the number of hidden nodes is 8, the target error is 0.001, and the learning rate is 0.01.

The particle number of particle swarm is 100 and the maximum number of allowable iterations is 10,000. Acceleration constants $c_1 = c_2 = 1.8$, and maximum limiting velocity $v_{max} = 1$. The inertia weight of PSO algorithm can neither be too large nor too small, because it determines the balance between global search ability and local search ability of velocity update.

The network output is the estimate of the module of the foot force in Z-axis and X-axis directions.

4.2   Training Sample Set

The examples used to train the network must accurately represent all the possibilities that can be found, but kept as low as possible to accelerate the calibration process. In order to delimit the problem, the possible foot trajectories have been limited to the trajectories in the continuous gaits the robot currently uses. Therefore, the trajectory used in the training examples are Bezier curve. The training examples are then selected attempting to represent all the possible foot speeds. The Bezier curve foot trajectories and speed values were selected with the aim of uniformly covering the whole leg work space and the whole speed range (25 to 50 mm/s), respectively. The total number of examples used to train the network (the result of the combination of those foot speeds and trajectories) was 44, summing up to 44000 samples. The training procedure was accomplished with the help of MATLAB software in an external computer.

4.3   Test Sample Set

Several simulations were performed in order to obtain the test sample set, which is designed to validate the virtual force sensor in different situations that could be encountered in practice. Thus, the examples represent Bezier curve trajectories executed within the leg work space and the speed range employed in normal locomotion. Other working conditions were discarded as they are not expected to appear during the ground detection process. This example set was divided into two subsets, each intended to evaluate a specific aspect of the virtual sensors' performance:

Sample set I: This set was used to test the repeatability of the system at a single operating point. All the examples corresponded to a single randomly chosen operating point.

Sample set II: This set was intended to test the accuracy of the estimates in working conditions not represented in the training process. It included examples for the foot speeds and trajectories most dissimilar to those found in the training set, while remaining within the considered speed range and leg work space.

5   Result and Discussion

Figure 4 illustrates the accuracy of the estimate obtained with the virtual force sensor in sample set I along Z-axis and X-axis. The relative error of the estimate has been used to characterize the accuracy of the estimate for sample set I in Fig. 5. The relative error e_r can be calculated by Eq. (4).

$$e_r = (F_{VFS} - F_{SIM})/F_{SIM} \times 100\% \tag{4}$$

where F_{VFS} is the estimated force of virtual force sensor and F_{SIM} is the force of simulation result.

In Fig. 5, it can be observed that the relative error of the sample set I prediction result in the Z-axis direction is not below 2.5%, and for the X-axis result, the maximum relative error is less than 3.5%. The virtual force sensor's prediction for sample set II also yields good results, but its prediction accuracy is slightly lower than Set I. The maximum relative error of the set II prediction result in the Z-axis direction is about 4.5%, and the relative error in the X-axis direction is less than 4%.

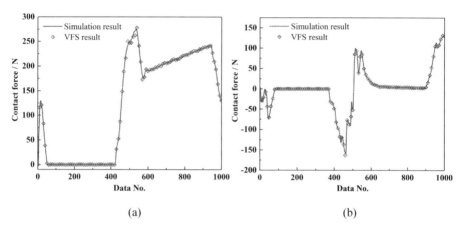

Fig. 4. Example of force estimation in sample set I along: (a) Z-axis and (b) X-axis.

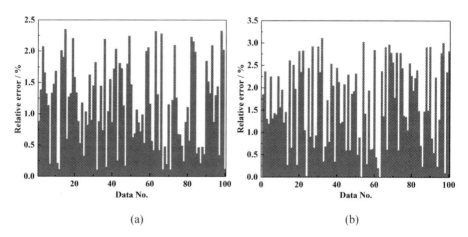

Fig. 5. Relative error of the virtual force sensor in the examples in sample set I along: (a) Z-axis and (b) X-axis.

Figure 8 demonstrates the estimated force along Z-axis with different speeds and contact stiffness. It can be found that the mean value of estimation error in alternative speed condition and contact stiffness condition ranged from 2.3% to 4.4% for the sample set II. The virtual force sensor showed very good precision in the experiments mimicking the operating conditions considered in the training set. In addition, this force estimation system showed excellent generalization features, obtaining a similar degree of precision for any trajectory and foot speed throughout the entire normal working range. It is evident that the estimate's accuracy depends on the foot speed (the higher the speed, the lower the correlation), the dependence on foot trajectory has not been found to be systematic. The enhanced performance of this virtual force sensor is the consequence of the improved richness of the analog information used to establish the relationship between magnitudes (Figs. 6 and 7).

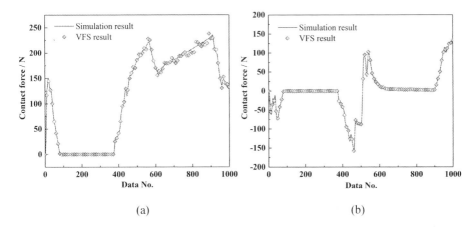

Fig. 6. Example of force estimation in sample set II along: (a) Z-axis and (b) X-axis.

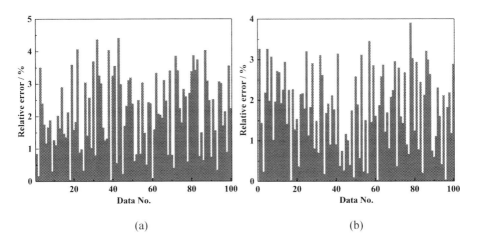

Fig. 7. Relative error of the virtual force sensor in the examples in sample set II along: (a) Z-axis and (b) X-axis.

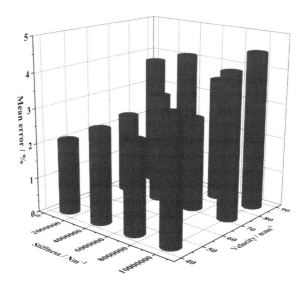

Fig. 8. Mean error of estimated force along Z-axis in different speeds and contact stiffness condition.

6   Conclusion

The development and testing of a contact force detection system for legged robot has been described. Joint position, joint velocity, and joint torque signals have been chosen as a feasible set of inputs for a virtual sensor to estimate the forces exerted by the robot's foot. These inputs can be drawn from the joint-position sensors available in most robotic systems, so the implementation of this virtual sensor does not result in an extra hardware burden. Data driven virtual sensors have been found to be a suitable choice for developing a common sensorial system for several robotic platforms. The use of PSO-BP neural networks to process the input information and generate a convenient output has been proved experimentally to be an adequate solution in a real walking robot.

High quality outputs were obtained for all parameters for normal operating conditions. Estimation errors ranged from 2.5% to 4.5%. This level of accuracy demonstrates feasibility of the virtual sensor concept for this application. Because this method is easy to adapt to other machines, it is a good choice for simplifying the hardware of a servo-controlled system, or for providing it with low-cost sensor redundancy. As these results have been found promising, future work will focus on the creation of similar virtual sensors for other purposes in legged robot locomotion. The most immediate objectives in such applications are the detection of obstacles during the leg-transfer phase and the estimation and control of forces during the leg-support phase.

Acknowledgement. This research was supported, in part, by the National Natural Science Foundation of China (No. 51875393) and by the China Advance Research for Manned Space Project (No. 030601).

References

1. Ding, L.: Foot-terrain interaction mechanics for legged robots: modeling and experimental validation. Int. J. Robot. Res. **32**(13), 1585–1606 (2013)
2. Zhang, J.P.: An ATPSO-BP neural network modeling and its application in mechanical property prediction. Comput. Mater. Sci. **163**, 262–266 (2019)
3. Wilcox, B.H.: ATHLETE: a cargo handling and manipulation robot for the moon. J. Field Robot. **24**(5), 421–434 (2007)
4. Estremera, J.: Neural virtual sensors for terrain adaptation of walking machines. J. Robot. Syst. **22**(6), 299–311 (2005)
5. Sharf, I.: Identification of contact dynamics parameters for stiff robotic payloads. IEEE Trans. Rob. **25**(2), 240–252 (2009)
6. Zhang, L.: Study of a new improved PSO-BP neural network algorithm. J. Harbin Inst. Technol. (New Ser.) **20**(5), 206–212 (2013)
7. Krzysztof, W.: Terrain classification and negotiation with a walking robot. J. Intell. Robot Syst. **78**, 401–423 (2015)
8. Lankarani, H.M.: A contact force model with hysteresis damping for impact analysis of multibody systems. J. Mech. Des. **112**(3), 369–376 (1990)
9. You, L.J.: Reconstruction and prediction of capillary pressure curve based on particle swarm optimization-back propagation neural network method. Petroleum **4**, 268–280 (2018)
10. Che, Z.H.: PSO-based back-propagation artificial neural network for product and mold cost estimation of plastic injection molding. Comput. Ind. Eng. **58**, 625–637 (2010)
11. Ren, C.: Optimal parameters selection for BP neural network based on particle swarm optimization: a case study of wind speed forecasting. Knowl.-Based Syst. **56**, 226–239 (2014)
12. Wang, H.S.: Cost estimation of plastic injection molding parts through integration of PSO and BP neural network. Expert Syst. Appl. **40**, 418–428 (2013)
13. Irawan, A.: Optimal impedance control based on body inertia for a hydraulically driven hexapod robot walking on uneven and extremely soft terrain. J. Field Robot. **28**(5), 690–713 (2011)
14. Silva, M.F.: Modelling and simulation of artificial locomotion systems. Robotica **23**(5), 595–606 (2005)

A Smooth Gait Planning Framework for Quadruped Robot Based on Virtual Model Control

Jian Tian[1], Chao Ma[2(✉)], Cheng Wei[1,2], and Yang Zhao[1,2]

[1] Department of Aerospace Engineering, Harbin Institute of Technology,
Harbin 150000, China
tj15704618301@163.com
[2] Beijing Key Laboratory of Intelligent Space Robotic Systems Technology
and Applications, Beijing Institute of Spacecraft System Engineering,
Beijing 100094, China
machaodn@163.com

Abstract. The smooth gait of robot plays an essential role in the locomotion, which influences by constraint from ground. Most of the planning algorithms centered on the characteristics of periodicity and amplitude of joint angles, and lost sight of the continuity of displacement and velocity of food trajectories. In this paper, the rhythmicity of robot body was studied in linear motion, according of which the smooth gait constrained by boundary conditions was planned by Hermite interpolation. In order to ensure the stability of robot posture during the movement, the strategy of virtual model control (VMC) was introduced and PD control method was used to track joint angles. The results and feasibility were verified by dynamics simulations finally.

Keywords: Quadruped robot · Smooth gait · Planning framework ·
Virtual model control

1 Introduction

In the movement of quadruped robot, joint angles calculated from gait trajectory are tracked to realize various forms of locomotion. An excellent gait planning can not only guarantee the smoothness of joint angles to minimize the driven torque, but also reduce attitude deviation of the robot body. Nevertheless, as a result of the contact with ground during the movement, the smoothness of gait trajectory a goal that is not easy to achieve.

To achieve stable walking of the quadruped robot, various gait generators and control strategy of stability have been investigated. The paper [8] focused on aperiodic motion gait to adapt unknown terrain and ensure motion stability, and the simulation results verified the proposed method. Neural oscillators were applied to match spring-mass system to keep jumping in a pronk gait in [9], which prepared primary techniques for center pattern generator. In order to

© Springer Nature Switzerland AG 2019
H. Yu et al. (Eds.): ICIRA 2019, LNAI 11743, pp. 398–410, 2019.
https://doi.org/10.1007/978-3-030-27538-9_34

achieve powered autonomous running robots, paper [4] presents the mechanical systems, models and control strategies employed to generate and control leg thrust in the KOLT quadruped running robot. The contribution [3] presented experiments of an adaptive locomotion controller on a compliant quadruped robot. The paper [18] proposed a reliable gait planning and control algorithm for the pet robot by Dasarobot, Korea, and integrated several online gaits to realize a compact and efficient gait form. The roll and pitch dynamics of a biologically inspired quadruped water runner robot are analyzed in [15], and a stable robot design is proposed and tested. In the paper [19], a software architecture was presented to accomplish locomotion task based on learning algorithms and rapid recovery and replanning techniques. The paper [13] develop an inverse-dynamics controller for floating-base robots under contact constraints that can minimize any combination of linear and quadratic costs in the contact constraints and the commands.

Cheetah-cub was used to study a series of locomotion experiments with fast trotting gaits in [16], and the major advantages was analysis, such as motion velocity, self-stability and so on. The paper [7] provides an overview about StarlETH: a compliant quadruped robot that is designed to study fast, efficient, versatile, and robust locomotion. Using model-based control strategies, the medium dog-sized machine is capable of various gaits ranging from static walking to dynamic running over challenging terrain. Based on relevant theoretical and practical aspects in impedance control, the paper [2] investigate the model-based controller design to the overall stability and performance assessment. A modular controller for quadruped robot was designed to adapt rough terrain in [1], in which center pattern generator and virtual model control was applied to improve performance during locomotion. Gait transition is an important method to enhance the efficiency of locomotion and adapt complex terrain environment. The paper [10] presented a gait transition control method for a quadruped walking robot based on the observation on the locomotion behaviors of quadruped animals. Kinematic Motion Primitives (kMPs) was presented in [12] to describe the transfer of walking, trotting and galloping of quadruped robot. A real-time system was presented in [11] to enable a highly capable dynamic quadruped robot to maintain an accurate six-degree of-freedom pose estimate. A planning/control framework for quasi-static walking of quadruped robots was proposed in paper [5], implemented for a demanding application in which regulation of ground reaction forces is crucial. In paper [6], a planning algorithm of foot trajectory with low force and low energy consumption was proposed, which was analysed in MATLAB environment. The paper [14] reviewed various of hydraulic quadruped robot, and concluded that the effective and reasonable control strategy is the combination of three methods based on model, CPG and intelligent method.

The paper [17] introduced RoboCat-1 and HyQ to establish a control framework based on CoM trajectory generator and virtual admittance control, which inspired us to accomplish this paper with the modular planning and control method. To achieve a locomotion with minor ground impact, the relative velocity between foot and ground was set to zero at the moment of lifting and landing. With this in mind, the motion acceleration of body trajectory was identified

using a periodical function with adjustable amplitude, and Hermite interpolation
was applied to generate gait constrained by boundary conditions. The body attitude control strategy was virtual model control simplified by decoupled partial
admittance. Finally, the simulation results presented the effectiveness of control
strategy and effect influenced by motion velocity and stride in trotting.

2   The Model and Reference of Mechanical Structure

The 3-D model of quadruped robot was built according to a relatively popular
style with 12 actuated joint motor and 18 freedoms in the whole multi-body
system, including 6 body freedoms and 12 joint freedoms. As shown in Fig. 1,
the laser radar and vision camera installed on the top and front of the body
respectively are applied to build a perception system for navigation of robot.
The joints from top to bottom of each leg are named as abduction joint, hip
joint and knee joint.

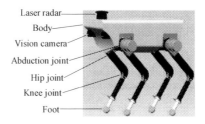

Fig. 1. 3-D model of quadruped robot

The coordinate system and kinematics vectors are defined in Fig. 2. The coordinates fixed on ground, body and abduction joint represent the initial reference,
body and abduction coordinate system. r_b, r_h and r_f defined in the initial reference are the displacements of center of mass, abduction reference and foot. The
vectors r_{bh} and r_{hf} are used to relative displacement among the coordinates
mentioned above. The variables θ_A, θ_H and θ_K demonstrate the three joints in
each leg.

3   Gait Trajectory Generation

3.1   Motion Analysis

The displacement of quadruped robot is implemented by the supporting force
from ground through legs. According to the research of gait forms with regard
to quadruped animals, there are various common gaits used in locomotion for
different requirements, such as walk, trot, bound, etc. Trot is determined to be
the research objective due to its extensive applicability.

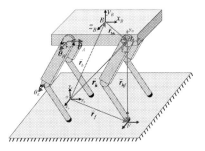

Fig. 2. Coordinate and vector representation

In the gait form of trot, as shown in Figs. 3 and 4, there are two legs contacting ground at every moment. In order to realize uniform motion of quadruped robot, the acceleration during one period should satisfy that the integral condition is zero. That is:

$$\int_0^{T_s} a_m d\tau = 0 \tag{1}$$

where a_m is the acceleration of robot body, and T_s is the period with double supporting legs. According to the Eq. (1), a_m can be set to:

$$a_m = A \cdot \sin(\omega \cdot t + \varphi) \tag{2}$$

where A is the amplitude of acceleration, $\omega = \frac{2 \cdot \pi}{T_s}$ is the motion frequency, and is initial phase at every cycle.

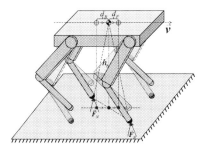

Fig. 3. Gait analysis of trot

The variable v in Fig. 3 is the velocity of robot, and the desired velocity can be defined as:

$$v_d = -\frac{A}{\omega} \cos(\omega \cdot t + \varphi) + v_{mean} \tag{3}$$

where v_{mean} is the average velocity through the whole period. The displacement of robot body can be integrated from Eq. (3):

$$s_d = -\frac{A}{\omega^2} \sin\left(\omega \cdot t + \varphi\right) + v_{mean} \cdot t + s_0 \tag{4}$$

where s_0 is the initial displacement in inertial reference. After one period locomotion, the incremental displacement of s_d is:

$$\Delta s_d = Str = v_{mean} \cdot T_s \tag{5}$$

where the variable Str is the stride of robot.

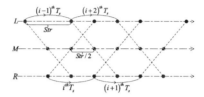

Fig. 4. Foothold of trot

3.2   Gait Generator

According to the trajectory of robot body, the gait modality is devised with swing phase and support phase as shown in Fig. 5. In order to reduce impact between the foots and ground, the position and relative velocity are assumed to be consistent during phase switching as shown in Fig. 6.

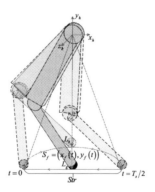

Fig. 5. Trot gait analysis

In one period, the constraints and boundary conditions are presented in following equation:

$$x_f = \begin{cases} -Str & t = 0 \ or \ T_s \\ 0 & t = T_s/4 \\ Str & t = T_s/2 \\ 0 & t = 3*T_s/4 \end{cases} \tag{6}$$

$$y_f = \begin{cases} -L_g & t = 0 \quad or \quad \frac{T_s}{2} \leq t \leq T_s \\ -L_h & t = \frac{T_s}{4} \end{cases} \tag{7}$$

Based on above conditions, segmented Hermite interpolation is used to construct gait trajectory, as shown in Fig. 6.

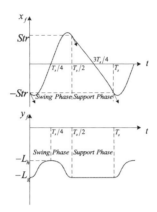

Fig. 6. Position coordinate planning

4 Control Strategy of Body Attitude

During motion processes, the attitude of robot body is adjusted through the force passed from legs and ground more deeply. As shown in Fig. 7, attitude error can be decomposed into rolling, yawing and pitching, indicated by angle errors θ, φ and ψ between desired axes of coordinate and actual ones. To eliminate and decouple above errors, partial control admittances are applied in the method of virtual model control. The height differences of hip joints and yaw angle are selected as control admittances that are identified as δ and η in Figs. 7 and 8. So the desired joint torques aimed at height differences can be designed as follows:

$$\begin{aligned} \tau^{hd} &= -J_y^T \cdot F^{att} \\ &= -J^T \cdot k_{att} \cdot \delta \cdot \zeta \end{aligned} \tag{8}$$

where J_y is the component in y direction of real-time Jacobian matrix of legs. k_{att} and ζ indicate the control coefficient of height differences and detection symbol of ground contact, that is:

$$\zeta = \begin{cases} 0 & F_N = 0 \\ 1 & F_N \neq 0 \end{cases} \tag{9}$$

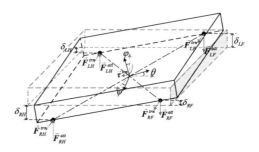

Fig. 7. The schematic figure depicting VMC

The second control admittance is the yaw angle mainly influenced by lateral force where other forces are ignored to ensure the velocity of forward direction. So the turning torque acting on joints can be designed as:

$$
\begin{aligned}
\tau^{yaw} &= -J_z^T \cdot F^{trn} \\
&= -J_z^T \cdot k_{trn} \cdot \eta \cdot \zeta
\end{aligned}
\tag{10}
$$

where J_z is the component in z direction of real-time Jacobian matrix of legs and k_{trn} is the control coefficient of yaw angle.

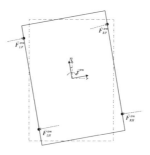

Fig. 8. Control strategy of yaw angle

5   Analysis of Robot Locomotion

According to gait planning strategy before-mentioned, a dynamics model is built based on Sect. 2 to realize various conditions on flat surface.

5.1   Parameters of Simulation

Take the quadruped robot in Fig. 1 as an example, the main kinematic and dynamics parameters are illustrated in Table 1. The dynamics model was established based on Lagrange's dynamical equations, and the simulation model is shown in Fig. 9.

Table 1. Kinematic and dynamics parameters

Structural parts	L (m)	m (kg)
Body	0.55 * 0.1 * 0.35	30
Hip-knee	0.3	0.5
Knee-foot	0.35	0.3
Degrees of freedom	3 (each leg) * 4(Number of legs) +6(body)	

Fig. 9. Simulation model of quadruped robot

The quadruped robot is mainly composed of three kind of body structure and twelve degrees of freedom, where should be noted that abduction joints and hip joints are intersected at one point in each leg. In the simulation model, the motion direction is opposite to the coordinate reference in Fig. 2, so the desired displacement of robot body is represented in Fig. 10 under conditions that $v_{mean} = 0.2\,\text{m/s}$ and $Str = 0.08\,\text{m}$. The coefficient of virtual model control are set as $k_{att} = 50$ and $k_{trn} = 1000$.

For the condition of linear locomotion, abduction joint angles are set to zero, and the others are desired to be periodic change. Hip and knee angle curves of LF leg and RF leg are shown in Figs. 11 and 12 respectively.

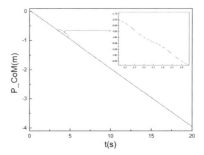

Fig. 10. Desired displacement of robot body under one condition

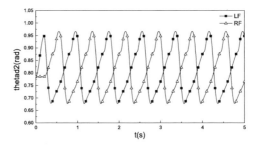

Fig. 11. Desired angles of hip joints

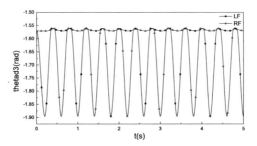

Fig. 12. Desired angles of knee joints

By adopting the planning algorithm in this paper, the desired angles of both hip and knee joints can be set smoothly throughout swing and support phase, to reduce the peak value of control torque. And in the gait of trot, there are 90° out of phase between joint angles of LF and RF legs.

5.2   Traveling Velocity

With the proposed trajectory generator and gait planning algorithms, the desired motion velocity and stride will both influence the desired angles of leg joints.

Firstly, the velocity was changed with 0.1, 0.2, and 0.3 m/s and the stride was set as constant in the simulation. The quaternion of robot body is output in Fig. 13.

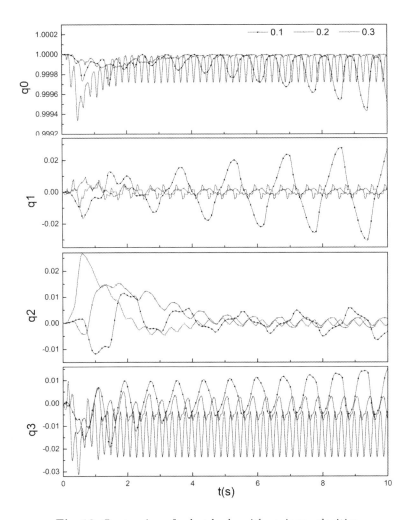

Fig. 13. Quaternion of robot body with various velocities

From above curves, preliminary conclusion can be obtained by analyzing the quaternion of robot body. Since the fact of $v_{mean} \cdot T_s = Str$ from Eq. (5), the support period with double legs and the velocity of body exist anti-proportional relationship with a constant of stride. As motion velocity decreasing, the support period increases leading to the divergence of q1, which implies that the roll angle of body presents unstable trend.

5.3   Analysis of Attitude Control

For the condition of moving on flat terrain, yaw angle is the mainly control admittance that influences motion direction. In this paper, the coefficient k_{trn} was adjusted to study the control effect, and the quaternion of robot body was output in Fig. 14.

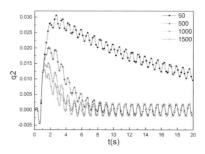

Fig. 14. Quaternion 2 of robot body with different k_{trn}

For the locomotion on flat terrain, the control coefficient of direction is much more important than others. As curves shown above, the increase of k_{trn} significantly shortens the time until the yaw angle is stable especially compared with the condition of smaller value.

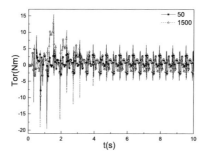

Fig. 15. Abduction joint torque of LF leg

Nevertheless, the control torque of abduction joint did not present much more difference except the beginning as shown in Fig. 15. Once into the stable movement stage, control torque almost has the similar tendency within $7N \cdot m$.

6   Concluding Remarks

In this paper, a planning and control framework was established for quadruped robot to realize smooth trajectory of joint angles and stable locomotion. According to the requirement of uniform motion, the period acceleration of body displacement was generated to decrease impact from ground. Based on the planned trajectory, trot gait was divided into swing phase and support phase. Hermite interpolation was applied to satisfy constraints and boundary conditions at the phase exchange moment. In order to achieve stable movement, virtual model control was simplified in the attitude control strategy.

Finally, dynamics simulations targeted at the proposed framework were accomplished and results verified the feasibility of algorithm. The smooth curves of joint angles were generated and in trot gait, travelling velocity would influence the roll angle of body under the condition of constant stride. For motion on flat terrain, the coefficient of direction control was an essential value to shorten convergence time of robot body.

Acknowledgments. This research was supported, in part, by the National Natural Science Foundation of China (No. 51875393) and by the China Advance Research for Manned Space Project (No. 030601).

References

1. Ajallooeian, M., Pouya, S., Sprowitz, A., Ijspeert, A.: Central pattern generators augmented with virtual model control for quadruped rough terrain locomotion. In: Proceedings - IEEE International Conference on Robotics and Automation, May 2013
2. Boaventura, T., Buchli, J., Semini, C., Caldwell, D.G.: Model-based hydraulic impedance control for dynamic robots. IEEE Trans. Robot. **31**(6), 1324–1336 (2015)
3. Buchli, J., Ijspeert, A.J.: Self-organized adaptive legged locomotion in a compliant quadruped robot. Auton. Rob. **25**(4), 331 (2008). https://doi.org/10.1007/s10514-008-9099-2
4. Estremera, J., Waldron, K.J.: Thrust control, stabilization and energetics of a quadruped running robot. Int. J. Robot. Res. **27**, 1135–1151 (2008)
5. Focchi, M., del Prete, A., Havoutis, I., Featherstone, R., Caldwell, D.G., Semini, C.: High-slope terrain locomotion for torque-controlled quadruped robots. Auton. Robots **41**(1), 259–272 (2017). https://doi.org/10.1007/s10514-016-9573-1
6. Hui-shu, M., Jian-Jun, F.: Foot trajectory planning and optimization simulation of low foot-terrain impact by quadruped robot based on the Trot Gait. J. Electr. Electron. Eng. **6**(1), 26 (2018). http://sciencepg.com/journal/paperinfo?journalid=239&paperId=10029462
7. Hutter, M., Gehring, C., Höpflinger, M.A., Blösch, M., Siegwart, R.: Toward combining speed, efficiency, versatility, and robustness in an autonomous quadruped. IEEE Trans. Robot. **30**(6), 1427–1440 (2014)
8. Jeong, K.M., Oh, J.H.: An aperiodic straight motion planning method for a quadruped walking robot. Auton. Robots **2**(1), 29–41 (1995). https://doi.org/10.1007/BF00735437
9. Kimura, H., Akiyama, S., Sakurama, K.: Realization of dynamic walking and running of the quadruped using neural oscillator. Auton. Robots **7**(3), 247–258 (1999). https://doi.org/10.1023/A:1008924521542

10. Koo, I.M., et al.: Biologically inspired gait transition control for a quadruped walking robot. Auton. Robots **39**(2), 169–182 (2015). https://doi.org/10.1007/s10514-015-9433-4
11. Ma, J., Bajracharya, M., Susca, S., Matthies, L., Malchano, M.: Real-time pose estimation of a dynamic quadruped in GPS-denied environments for 24-hour operation. Int. J. Robot. Res. **35**, 631–653 (2015)
12. Moro, F.L., et al.: Horse-like walking, trotting, and galloping derived from kinematic Motion Primitives (kMPs) and their application to walk/trot transitions in a compliant quadruped robot. Biol. Cybern. **107**(3), 309–320 (2013). https://doi.org/10.1007/s00422-013-0551-9
13. Righetti, L., Buchli, J., Mistry, M., Kalakrishnan, M., Schaal, S.: Optimal distribution of contact forces with inverse dynamics control. Int. J. Robot. Res. **32**, 280–298 (2013)
14. Shao, J., Ren, D., Gao, B.: Recent advances on gait control strategies for hydraulic quadruped robot. Recent Patents Mech. Eng. **11**, 15–23 (2018)
15. Soo Park, H., Floyd, S., Sitti, M.: Roll and pitch motion analysis of a biologically inspired quadruped water runner robot. Int. J. Robot. Res. **29**, 1281–1297 (2010)
16. Sprowitz, A., Tuleu, A., Vespignani, M., Ajallooeian, M.: Towards dynamic trot gait locomotion design, control, and experiments with cheetah-cub, a compliant quadruped robot. Int. J. Robot. Res. **35**, 649–655 (2013)
17. Ugurlu, B., Havoutis, I., Semini, C., Kayamori, K., Caldwell, D.G., Narikiyo, T.: Pattern generation and compliant feedback control for quadrupedal dynamic trot-walking locomotion: experiments on RoboCat-1 and HyQ. Auton. Robots **38**(4), 415–437 (2015). https://doi.org/10.1007/s10514-015-9422-7
18. Yi, S.: Reliable gait planning and control for miniaturized quadruped robot pet. Mechatronics **20**(4), 485–495 (2010). http://www.sciencedirect.com/science/article/pii/S0957415810000747
19. Zico Kolter, J., Ng, A.Y.: The Stanford LittleDog: a learning and rapid replanning approach to quadruped locomotion. Int. J. Robot. Res. **30**(2), 150–174 (2011). https://doi.org/10.1177/0278364910390537

An Adaptive Parameter Identification Algorithm for Post-capture of a Tumbling Target

Jia Xu, Yang Yang, Yan Peng, Xiaomao Li, Shuanghua Zheng, and Jianxiang Cui[✉]

Shanghai University, Shanghai 200444, China
cuijianxiang@shu.edu.cn

Abstract. In this paper, a new parameter identification scheme is proposed for an unknown tumbling target captured by the space manipulator. Due to the unknown and various dynamic parameters of the target and the strong nonlinear characteristics of the manipulator, it is difficult to achieve the capture operation with high tracking accuracy and low energy consumption. Aiming at the challenge, the parameter identification model of free-floating space manipulator is established based on the momentum conservation principle. Then, the VDW-RLS (variable data-window-size recursive least square) algorithm is applied to identify the inertia parameters. VDW-RLS algorithm can adjust the size of data window online according to the change of system parameters. SimMechanics simulation platform is employed to implement the three-dimensional model of 7-DOFs manipulator system. Simulation results show that the proposed algorithm has a fast tracking performance and low misalignment in the inertial parameter identification of the multi-DOFs space manipulator, and the control effect can be further improved by using the identified dynamic parameters.

Keywords: Space manipulator · Parameter identification ·
Momentum conservation · VDW-RLS algorithm

1 Introduction

In recent years, many advanced space robots have been developed for on-orbit servicing operations, such as capturing space debris, recovering failed satellites, and assembling large space modules. One of the most challenging for orbital operations of the malfunctioning satellite is that the system is difficult to stabilize when a tumbling satellite is grasped by the manipulator [1, 2]. During the tumbling target capturing task, the system uncertainties caused by large payload with unknown inertial parameters will degrade the system performances severely [3]. Therefore, it is of great importance to stabilize the compound system, after a tumbling target docked to a servicing spacecraft, before a service job can be performed.

Several articles have been published to address accurate estimation of the inertial parameters of the target online during the operation of spacecraft for autonomous on-orbit service missions. The most methods are based on vision [4, 5], force [6] and momentum [7, 8]. In which, the vision-based and force-based approach requires the

© Springer Nature Switzerland AG 2019
H. Yu et al. (Eds.): ICIRA 2019, LNAI 11743, pp. 411–422, 2019.
https://doi.org/10.1007/978-3-030-27538-9_35

space manipulator to be equipped with specific sensors, and the corresponding identification algorithm is more susceptible to signal noise. On the contrast, the method based on momentum conservation principle is more suitable, since the parameter identification requires only velocity measurement.

The recursive least-squares (RLS) algorithm is widely used for linear online identification algorithm [9]. However, owing to using all datasets from the beginning of the iterative calculation, RLS is close to saturation with the increase of the number of iterations, and the tracking performance gradually deteriorates [10]. Thus it is difficult to be applied for strongly nonlinear space manipulator. In addition, the finite-data-window RLS (FDW-RLS) algorithm only processes the latest fixed amount of data in the datasets [11], which can improve the speed of tracking time-varying parameters. However, the reduction of the number of datasets also increases the misalignment error of time-varying parameters.

Aiming to the problems, an improved RLS algorithm, variable data-window-size RLS (VDW-RLS) [12], is proposed to improve the tracking accuracy and speed of variable load at the tip of manipulator in this study. The performance of VDW-RLS in terms of convergence rate, tracking accuracy, misadjustment error, and stability depends on the window size. This algorithm can adaptively decrease the window size for rapid tracking when the system parameters vary. On the contrary, it increases the window size when the system parameters remain constant.

The contents of this paper are organized as follows. In Sect. 2, the basic coupling momentum equations of space manipulator are briefly reviewed. An adaptive identification algorithm VDW-RLS for estimating the inertial parameters after capturing an unknown tumbling target is presented in Sect. 3. The simulation is performed to verify the feasibility of the proposed scheme in Sect. 4, and the conclusion and future work are given in Sect. 5.

2   Preliminaries

After the end-effector captured the target to form a new system, the inertial parameters of the last link change. For the multi-DOFs strongly nonlinear space manipulator, the on-orbit stability control of the post-captured problem requires the precise inertial parameters of the system. In this section, the parameter recognition algorithm based on momentum conservation for unknown tumbling target captured by a space manipulator is presented. It is assumed that the attitude control actuators are off and the whole system is not disturbed by external force/torque within the parameter identification process. It means the whole post-captured system satisfies the conservation of momentum.

Figure 1 shows a simplified model of a multi-links space manipulator mounted on the base of the service spacecraft, with the target captured by the manipulator. The target is considered to be part of the last link. P and L represent the linear and angular momentum of the compound system, which can be calculated from (1) and (2), respectively [13].

$$P = \sum_{i=0}^{n} m_i \dot{r}_i \tag{1}$$

$$L = \sum_{i=0}^{n} (I_i \omega_i + r_i \times m_i \dot{r}_i) + \sum_{i=1}^{n} (J_{im} \omega_{im}) \tag{2}$$

where $r_i \in R^3$ is the position vector of the center of mass of the link i; $I_i \in R^{3 \times 3}$ is the inertia tensor of the center of mass of link i; $\omega_i \in R^3$ is the angular velocity of link i.

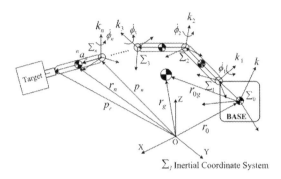

Fig. 1. Schematic diagram of space robot and target satellite.

The velocity change is measurable and the kinematics and dynamics parameters of the space robot are known, except for the inertia parameters change of the last link. Therefore, Eqs. (1) and (2) can be decomposed into known and measured terms, in which the square brackets are used to distinguish the unknown items.

$$P = \sum_{i=0}^{n-1} m_i \dot{r}_i + [m_n \dot{r}_n] \tag{3}$$

$$L = \sum_{i=0}^{n-1} (I_i \omega_i + r_i \times m_i \dot{r}_i) + [I_n \omega_n + r_n \times m_n \dot{r}_n] \tag{4}$$

3   Online Parameter Identification Algorithm

3.1   Dynamic Parameter Identification Model

The Eq. (3) can be rewritten to Eq. (5), in which the unknown quantities in square brackets to be identified are put on the right side of the equation [14].

$$-\left(v_0 + \omega_0 \times (p_n - r_0) + \sum_{j=1}^{n} (k_j \times (p_n - p_j))\dot{q}_j\right)$$

$$= u\left[\frac{1}{m_n}\right] + \left(\tilde{\omega}_0^I R_n + \sum_{j=1}^{n} \dot{q}_j \tilde{k}_j^I R_n\right)[{}^n a_n] \tag{5}$$

where $(\tilde{\cdot})$ represents the skew symmetric matrix of $(\cdot)$.

Then, the angular momentum equation can be obtained from (4):

$$L - k = \tilde{u}^I R_n{}^n a_n + {}^I R_n I_n{}^n \omega_n \tag{6}$$

where $k = \sum_{i=0}^{n-1} (I_i \omega_i + r_i \times m_i \dot{r}_i) + \sum_{i=1}^{n} (J_{im}\omega_{im}) + u \times p_n$.

The angular momentum of the tumbling target after capture is unknown. However, because of the momentum conservation of the combined system after capture, the angular momentum increment in the moment is zero, and the increment in the moment of formula (7) can be given.

$$-\Delta k = \Delta(\tilde{u}^I R_n)^n a_n + \Delta\Omega_n i_n \tag{7}$$

where the matrix $\Delta\Omega_n$ and the vector i_n are defined as follows:

$$\Delta\Omega_n = \Delta\left[{}^I R_n \begin{bmatrix} {}^n\omega_{nx} & {}^n\omega_{ny} & {}^n\omega_{nz} & 0 & 0 & 0 \\ 0 & {}^n\omega_{nx} & 0 & {}^n\omega_{ny} & {}^n\omega_{nz} & 0 \\ 0 & 0 & {}^n\omega_{nx} & 0 & {}^n\omega_{ny} & {}^n\omega_{nz} \end{bmatrix}\right],$$

$$i_n = [I_{11}, I_{12}, I_{13}, I_{21}, I_{22}, I_{33}]^T.$$

Combining (5) and (7) into a matrix form, and factor out the mass of the last link m_n, the position of the center of mass relative to the coordinate system of the last link ${}^n a_n$, and the inertial tensor ${}^n I_n$. Hence the standard linear equation for estimating can be obtained as follows.

$$-\begin{bmatrix} v_0 + \omega_0 \times (p_n - r_0) + \sum_{j=1}^{n} (k_j \times (p_n - p_j))\dot{q}_j \\ \Delta k \end{bmatrix}$$

$$= \begin{bmatrix} u & \tilde{\omega}_0^I R_n + \sum_{j=1}^{n} \dot{q}_j \tilde{k}_j^I R_n & 0 \\ 0 & \Delta(\tilde{u}^I R_n) & \Delta\Omega_n \end{bmatrix}\begin{bmatrix} \frac{1}{m_n} \\ {}^n a_n \\ i_n \end{bmatrix} \tag{8}$$

It is noticed that the multiple sets of measurement data are required to determine the parameters in Eq. (8). As a result, it can be written as a simplified linear regression equation with noise terms added to form a control of auto-regressive (CAR) model with control variables.

$$y(t) = \varphi(t)w + \xi(t) \tag{9}$$

where $w = \begin{bmatrix} \frac{1}{m_n} & {}^n a_n & i_n \end{bmatrix}^T$ is the parameter to be identified; $\xi(t)$ denoted the gaussian white noise; the input $\varphi(t)$ and output $y(t)$ of the identification model are defined as follows.

$$\varphi(t) = \begin{bmatrix} u & \tilde{\omega}_0^l R_n + \sum_{j=1}^{n} \dot{q}_j \tilde{k}_j^l R_n & 0 \\ 0 & \Delta(\tilde{u}^l R_n) & \Delta\Omega_n \end{bmatrix} \tag{10}$$

$$y(t) = - \begin{bmatrix} v_0 + \omega_0 \times (p_n - r_0) + \sum_{j=1}^{n} (k_j \times (p_n - p_j))\dot{q}_j \\ \Delta q \end{bmatrix} \tag{11}$$

3.2   Online Parameter Estimation Algorithm

The VDW-RLS algorithm is used to identify the CAR model. Figure 2 shows a model for online estimating of inertial parameters of the combined system, where ZOH is used to discrete continuous signals.

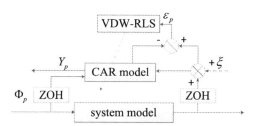

Fig. 2. Structure for estimation of CAR model parameters for MSDM.

At time t, the least square estimation of the cost function is:

$$\hat{w}_p(t) = \left[\Phi_p(t)^T \Phi_p(t)\right]^{-1} \Phi_p(t)_T Y_p(t) \tag{12}$$

where $\hat{w}_p(t)$ is the system parameter to be identified based on the latest p window datasets, and input and output data matrix are defined as follows.

$$\Phi_p = \begin{pmatrix} \varphi^T(t-p+1) \\ \vdots \\ \varphi^T(t-1) \\ \varphi^T(t) \end{pmatrix} \in R^{np \times m}, \quad Y_p = \begin{pmatrix} y^T(t-p+1) \\ \vdots \\ y^T(t-1) \\ y^T(t) \end{pmatrix} \in R^{np \times 1} \tag{13}$$

Therefore, the recursive equation of identifying unknown parameters by VDW-RLS algorithm is obtained.

$$K(t-1) = P(t-1)\varphi(t-p) + \frac{P(t-1)\varphi(t-p)\varphi^T(t-p)P(t-1)}{I - \varphi^T(t-p)P(t-1)\varphi(t-p)}\varphi(t-p) \quad (14)$$

$$\widehat{w}_{p-1}(t-1) = \widehat{w}_p(t-1) - K(t-1) \times \left[y(t-p) + \varphi^T(t-p)\widehat{w}_p(t-1)\right] \quad (15)$$

$$P(t) = K(t-1)\varphi(t) - \frac{K(t-1)\varphi(t)\varphi^T(t)K(t-1)}{I + \varphi^T(t)K(t-1)\varphi(t)}\varphi(t) \quad (16)$$

$$\widehat{w}_p(t) = \widehat{w}_{p-1}(t-1) + P(t) \times \left[y(t) - \varphi^T(t)\widehat{w}_{p-1}(t-1)\right] \quad (17)$$

To update the parameter from $\widehat{w}_{p-1}(t-1)$ to $\widehat{w}_p(t)$, the identification process needs to be divided into two steps. In the first step, the last group of data in the window size $[t-p, t-1]$ is deleted. Here, removing the oldest data by Eqs. (14) and (15) can be called a 'downdate' operation. At this time, $\widehat{w}_{p-1}(t-1)$ is then obtained, and the total number of window size is temporarily reduced by one, as shown in Fig. 3(a). In a second step, the update group of data with the dataset $\varphi(t)$ and $y(t)$ are added. Here, estimating the latest data by Eqs. (16) and (17) can be called an 'update' operation. Next, $\widehat{w}_p(t)$ is obtained by the intermediate term $\widehat{w}_{p-1}(t-1)$, and the total number of window size becomes p, as shown in Fig. 3(b).

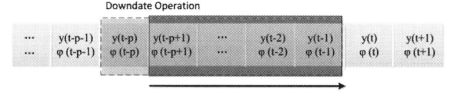

(a)   VDW-RLS with removing the oldest dataset

(b)   VDW-RLS with adding the newest dataset

Fig. 3. VDW-RLS identification process diagram.

It is noticed that the window size p is not a constant value, which can be adjusted in real time according to the posteriori error. According to the p-th observation results and the corresponding posterior error, the cost function can be defined as (18).

$$J = \varepsilon_p^T(t)\varepsilon_p(t) = \sum_{k=1}^{p}\left[Y_p(t) - \Phi_p(t)\hat{w}_p(t)\right] \tag{18}$$

When the system is in a steady state, the expectation of its cost function is given by (19).

$$E(J) = \sigma_v^2(p - m) \tag{19}$$

where σ_v^2 with covariance of zero represents gaussian white noise; p is defined as the window size, m is the size of parameters to be identified in Eq. (9).

While the system is in a transient state, the expectation of its cost function is given by (20).

$$E(J) = E\left[\sum_{i=t-p+1}^{t}\varepsilon^2(i)\right] = C_p(t) \tag{20}$$

Finally, according to the system state, the size of the specific data window is determined by the following criterion.

$$p(t+1) = \begin{cases} p_{\min}, \text{ if } C_p(t) > \sigma_v^2(p(t) - m) \\ p(t) + 1, \text{ if } C_p(t) \leq \sigma_v^2(p(t) - m) \ \& \ p(t) < p_{\max} \\ p_{\max}, \text{ if } C_p(t) \leq \sigma_v^2(p(t) - m) \ \& \ p(t) = p_{\max} \end{cases} \tag{21}$$

4 Simulation and Discussion

4.1 Simulation Setup

A 7-DOFs space manipulator mounted on a free-floating satellite base was used as the platform to verify the validity of the proposed method. It is assumed that the target rotates around the central axis of the system at constant speed. The end-effector immediately locked up after capturing the target. The inertial parameters of the target are determined to achieve better stability control effect in post-capture. To simulate the free tumbling motion of the target before capturing, the initial angular pulse $L_x = L_y = L_z = 2.5\,\text{kgm}^2/\text{s}$ is applied on the inertia axis of the end-effector.

After the impulse was applied at the end effector, the algorithm based on the conservation of angular momentum was implemented to identify the mass m_n, the center of mass position ${}^n a_n$ and the inertial tensor of the last link i_n.

SimMechanics multi-body dynamics simulation software was selected as the modeling tool of system dynamics. The specific parameters of the free-floating base and 7-DOFs space manipulator are listed in Table 1. The input data size M is 10; p_{min} and p_{max} are respectively set as 11 and 60 (Fig. 4 and Table 3).

4.2   Experimental Results and Discussion

Figure 5 shows the variation of the identification window size, during the identification process from target 1 to target 2. It can be found that the target changes between iterations interval [150, 200]. To track the inertia parameters more quickly, the number of window size adaptively decreased to 11, that is the minimum number of window p_{min}. As the number of iterations increased, the identification algorithm tends to be stable, and the number of the window size gradually returned to the maximum number of window p_{max}.

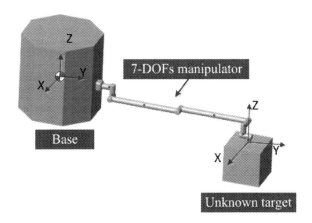

Fig. 4. The combined system model after capturing a tumbling target.

Table 1. D-H parameters of the 7-DOFs space manipulator.

Link i	$\theta_i(°)$	d_i(mm)	a_{i-1}(mm)	$\alpha_{i-1}(°)$
1	θ_1	700	0	0
2	θ_2	500	0	−90
3	θ_3	300	3700	−90
4	θ_4	300	3700	0
5	θ_5	700	0	0
6	θ_6	500	0	90
7	θ_7	300	0	90

Table 2. Simulation parameters of the 7-DOFs space manipulator.

Link i	Mass (kg)	$I_{xx}(\text{kg} \cdot \text{m}^2)$	$I_{yy}(\text{kg} \cdot \text{m}^2)$	$I_{zz}(\text{kg} \cdot \text{m}^2)$
0	3000	8011.60	6343.10	8011.60
1	40	1.80	0.53	1.87
2	35	0.86	0.49	0.94
3	160	224.12	1.93	224.23
4	160	224.12	1.93	224.23
5	40	1.80	0.53	1.87
6	35	0.86	0.49	0.94
Target 1	68	31.41	−50.40	13.05
Target 2	90	132.10	−126.10	−84.92

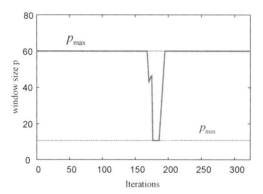

Fig. 5. Variation of the identification window size.

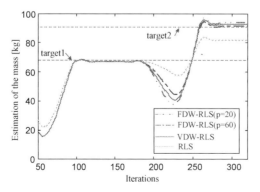

Fig. 6. Estimation result of mass.

Table 3. Identification effects of four identification algorithms.

Error/Iteration numbers	FDW-RLS ($p = 20$)	FDW-RLS ($p = 60$)	VDW-RLS	RLS
Target 1	0.84/125	0.86/125	0.79/124	0.70/120
Target 2	3.15/292	1.59/297	2.87/292	9.17/296

(a)   **(b)**

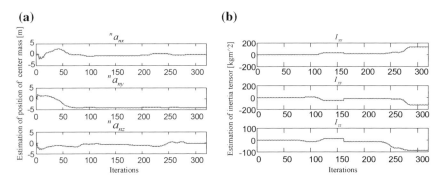

Fig. 7. Estimation result of (a) the center of mass position and (b) the inertia tensor.

Table 4. Misalignment errors of the center of mass position and the inertia tensor.

Error	$^{n}a_{nx}$, m	$^{n}a_{ny}$, m	$^{n}a_{nz}$, m	I_{xx}, kgm^2	I_{yy}, kgm^2	I_{zz}, kgm^2
Target 1	0.02	0.12	0.08	3.02	8.90	4.92
Target 2	0.19	0.32	0.25	8.74	6.39	9.05

(a)   **(b)**

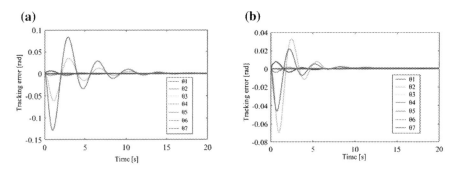

Fig. 8. PD control results. (a) Controller based on estimated inertial parameters (b) controller based on identification results.

The identification effect of different identification algorithms under the same working condition is shown in Fig. 6. The form of $1/m_n$ in Eq. (8) is adopted to identify the last link's mass. $1/m_n$ is extremely large at the beginning of identification and it has no reference significance. Therefore, we observe the identification results after 50 iterations. When target 1 is identified, all the RLS algorithms can converge rapidly and reach the steady state value.

Identification parameters changed after 170th iteration indicating that target 1 was released and target 2 was captured. In the target 2 identification process, FDW-RLS algorithm with $p = 20$ rapidly converged at the 292th iteration and reached a steady state first. Because it only used the latest updated 20 datasets, it has the highest misalignment error. Compared with the other two algorithms, the FDW-RLS algorithm with $p = 60$ and the algorithm proposed in this paper share lower misalignment error. This is due to the fact that when the steady state occured, the two algorithms adopted the same datasets. From Table 2, it can be seen that the conventional RLS algorithm comparatively has the largest steady-state error. Because of using all datasets from the beginning of identification, the RLS algorithm gradually tended to be saturated. Hence we can conclude that RLS cannot provide better tracking performance in the continuous identification process. On the contrast, the proposed algorithm can achieve better tradeoff effect in tracking speed and tracking performance.

Figure 7 is the results of estimation of the position of the center of mass and inertial tensor identified by VDW-RLS algorithm. From the Table 4, it can be seen that the misalignment errors are within the acceptable range.

Given a desired point in the Cartesian coordinate system and the desired angle of each joint, the error between the desired position and the actual position measured by the sensor was taken as the input of PD linear controller of the space manipulator. The output of the controller was the driving torque of each joint. Figure 8(a) shows the joint stabilization accuracy of the controller designed with estimated inertial parameters instead of using identification results. Figure 8(b) is a PD controller designed with the inertial parameters obtained by the algorithm proposed in this paper. Although both of them can meet the accuracy requirement of $\pm 1e-04$ rad, the PD control designed with identification results can depress the overshoot (12.03%), shorten the stable time (6.25 s), and improve the control accuracy (0.003 rad) to acquire a better control process.

The simulation results presented in this section demonstrate the importance of the VDW-RLS algorithm in post-capturing a tumbling target control.

5 Conclusion

In this paper, a new identification algorithm is proposed for the unknown tumbling target captured by a multi-DOFs space manipulator. The parameter identification model of free-floating space manipulator is established based on the principle of momentum conservation. The proposed algorithm is improved based on the RLS identification algorithm, and it can adaptively adjust the size of identification window in the identification process. It has a fast tracking performance in the transient state and low misalignment error in the steady-state. Matlab/Simlink and SolidWorks were used to build the simulation platform. The simulation results show that the proposed algorithm can provide better identification effect in the continuous identification of target. In the future, after capturing the unknown tumbling target, the coupling effect between the satellite and the space manipulator will be considered to design a coordination control scheme to achieve the rapid stability of the whole system.

Acknowledgement. This study was supported by National Natural Science Foundation of China (Grant No. 61773254), Shanghai Sailing Program (Grant No. 17YF1406200), Shanghai Young Eastern Scholar Program (Grant No. QD2016029), and Shanghai civil-military integration program (Grant No. JMRH-2018-1043).

References

1. Wang, M., Luo, J., Yuan, J.: Detumbling strategy and coordination control of kinematically redundant space robot after capturing a tumbling target. Nonlinear Dyn. **92**(3), 1023–1043 (2018)
2. Aghili, F.: Coordination control of a free-flying manipulator and its base attitude to capture and detumble a noncooperative satellite. In: IEEE/RSJ International Conference on Intelligent Robots & Systems. IEEE Press (2009)
3. Stolfi, A., Gasbarri, P., Sabatini, M.: A combined impedance-PD approach for controlling a dual-arm space manipulator in the capture of a non-cooperative target. Acta Astronautica **139**, 243–253 (2017)
4. Aghili, F., Parsa, K.: Motion and parameter estimation of space objects using laser-vision data. J. Guid. Control Dyn. **32**(2), 538–550 (2009)
5. Hillenbrand, U., Lampariello, R.: Motion and parameter estimation of a free-floating space object from range data for motion prediction. In: 8th International Symposium on Artificial Intelligence, Robotics and Automation in Space, DLR (2005)
6. Murotsu, Y., Senda, K., Ozaki, M.: Parameter identification of unknown object handled by free-flying space robot. J. Guid. Control Dyn. **17**(3), 488–494 (1994)
7. Yoshida, K., Abiko, S.: Inertia parameter identification of a free-flying space robot. Trans. Jpn. Soc. Mech. Eng. AIAA **68**(672), 2002–4568 (2002)
8. Ou, M., Dang, H., Pham, K.: On-orbit identification of inertia properties of spacecraft using a robotic arm. J. Guid. Control Dyn. **31**(6), 1761–1771 (2012)
9. Wilson, E., Lages, C., Mah, R.: On-line gyro-based, mass-property identification for thruster-controlled spacecraft using recursive least squares. In: Symposium on Circuits & Systems. IEEE (2002)
10. Goodwin, G.C., Teoh, E.K., Elliott, H.: Deterministic convergence of a self-tuning regulator with covariance resetting. IEE Proc. D Control Theory Appl. **130**(1), 6–8 (1983)
11. Ding, F., Xiao, Y.: A finite-data-window least squares algorithm with a forgetting factor for dynamical modeling. Appl. Math. Comput. **186**(1), 184–192 (2007)
12. Yu, S.C., Cho, H.: Variable data-window-size recursive least-squares algorithm for dynamic system identification. Electron. Lett. **51**(4), 341–343 (2015)
13. Chu, Z., Ma, Y., Cui, J.: Adaptive reactionless control strategy via the PSO-ELM algorithm for free-floating space robots during manipulation of unknown objects. Nonlinear Dyn. (2017)
14. Nguyen-Huynh, T.C., Sharf, I.: Adaptive reactionless motion and parameter identification in postcapture of space debris. J. Guid. Control Dyn. **36**(2), 404–414 (2013)

Review of Research on the Chinese Space Station Robots

Youyu Wang[1(✉)], Daming Li[1], Chengwei Hu[1], Yaobing Wang[1],
Zixin Tang[1], and Nian Wang[2]

[1] Beijing Key Laboratory of Intelligent Space Robotic System Technology
and Applications, Beijing Institute of Spacecraft System Engineering,
Beijing 100094, China
tjuyu@139.com
[2] Beijing Spacecrafts, Beijing 100094, China

Abstract. For life extension and construction of large space facilities, we hope to break through the weight and outline restriction of the rocket by using the on-orbit assembly technology with space mobile robots. The Chinese Space Station robots are designed for the missions of relocking spacecraft sections, docking assistance, installing equipment, maintaining the space station and extra vehicular activity (EVA) of astronaut. Therefore, it will lay a foundation for the construction of the Chinese Space Station (CSS). The Chinese Space Station robots will be highly integrated robotic system, combining technologies of mechanics, electronics, thermotics, vision and computer control. The key technologies of the robots are described, such as high-precision servo control and human-computer interaction. The Chinese Space Station robots provide the Chinese researchers and engineer a great opportunity for developing and advancing their space robotics technologies and experience.

Keywords: Spacecraft · Chinese Space Station · Manipulator · Robot

1 Introduction

With the development of space exploration, new application requirements are put forward for large spacecraft or other large space facilities such as international space station (ISS). Large spacecraft is difficult to constructed by one shoot, limited by the bearing ability of rocket, so we hope to break through the weight and outline restriction of the rocket by using the on-orbit assembly technology with space mobile manipulators, in order to satisfy the need of large space facilities in the future space mission; on the other hand the space robot on-orbit service system should be built to recycle the bad spacecraft and this orbital succor and life extension of old spacecraft. Both side need to research the on-orbit construction and maintenance technologies, especially the technologies with space robot.

The succeed on-orbit large space facilities are the ISS and the MIR space station. Compared to the MIR space station, the ISS has many manipulator systems and a humanoid robot, which is the direction indicator for the space station. The Chinese Space Station Manipulator system (CSSM), consisting of two robotic arms, as a

© Springer Nature Switzerland AG 2019
H. Yu et al. (Eds.): ICIRA 2019, LNAI 11743, pp. 423–430, 2019.
https://doi.org/10.1007/978-3-030-27538-9_36

primary tool for the construction and services of the Chinese Space Station, will perform the missions of relocking spacecraft sections, docking assistance, installing equipment, maintaining the Space Station and extra vehicular activity (EVA) of astronaut [1, 2]. Therefore, it will lay a foundation for the construction of the Chinese Space Station (CSS). Since it is a highly integrated robotic system, combining technologies of engineering mechanics, electronics, thermotics, vision and computer control, the development of the Space Station faces many technical challenges and therefore, makes a huge challenge for the design and implementation of the robotic system. Compared with Russia and USA as well as some other developed countries, China has a big technology gap in materials, electronics, manufacturing, testing, etc. The Chinese Space Station provides the Chinese researchers and engineers a great opportunity for developing and advancing their space robotics technologies and experience.

Since 2007, the Institute of Spacecraft System Engineering of CAST has started the research of the CSSM system [3–5]. A principle prototype and an engineering prototype have been designed and constructed for the verification of the design concepts and associated new technologies. Since 2013, the space humanoid robot is developed and the principle prototype has been constructed. The key technologies, such as the system design and analysis, kernel mechanism assembly design, modeling and simulation, control design, functional tests, and environmental tests have been accomplished. The next paper will present an introduction of the major robotic arm of the CSSM system (CSSCM) and the space humanoid robot for the Chinese Space Station.

2   Comparison of Different Space Robots

The most representative extravehicular space station manipulator is the Canada's Mobile Servicing System (MSS) [6], which is developed for the construction and maintenance of the International Space Station (ISS). The MSS includes a large-scale Space Station Remote Manipulator System (SSRMS) (17.6 m long, 7 degrees of freedom) and a Special Purpose Dexterous Manipulator (SPDM) (3.5 m long, 15 degrees of freedom). The system is initially installed on the US module of the ISS [7] and has played a key role for servicing the ISS. In addition, the ISS is also equipped with another large space robotic system: The European Robotic Arm (ERA) (11.3 m, long, 7 degrees of freedom) [8] and the Japanese Experiment Module Remote Manipulator System (JEMRMS) (length 9.9 m, 6 degrees of freedom, with a 2 m-long 6-DOF small manipulator installed at the end) [9].

The first space humanoid robot named Robonaut 2 has been sent to the International Space Station as a good assistant for the EVA of astronaut. With 42 independent degrees-of-freedom (DOF's) and over 350 sensors, Robonaut 2, shown in Fig. 1, is an impressive example of mechatronic integration. Encompassing two 7-DOF arms, two 12-DOF hands, a 3-DOF neck and a single DOF waist, the system includes 50 actuators with collocated, low-level joint controllers embedded throughout. The system also integrates built-in computing and power conversion inside its backpack and torso.

The CSSCM is a 10.5-m long, 7-DOF robotic manipulator, and its other performances to be achieved are listed in Table 1 with comparison to the existing space robotic manipulators [10, 11]. It is shown that the performances of the CSSCM are similar to the existing space manipulators, especially the payload capacity, precision and speed being on the high end. A space humanoid robot is developed by the Beijing Institute of Spacecraft System Engineering of CAST, whose main performances are compared to the Robonaut 2 in Table 2 [12]. It is shown that the performances of the space humanoid robot of CAST are similar to the Robonaut 2 in payload capacity and pose accuracy.

Table 1. Performances of the manipulators

	SSRMS	JEMRMS	ERA	CSSCM
Length (m)	17.6	9.9	11.3	10.5
Mass (kg)	1,800	757	619	738
Max payload (kg)	116,000	7,000	8,000	25,000
Joints	7	6	7	7
Stopping distance (m)	0.6	0.3	0.4	0.4
c (mm)	45	50	40	45
Pose accuracy (deg)	0.71	1.8	1	1
Translation (m/s)	0.012–0.36	0.02–0.06	0.01–0.2	0.05–0.6
Rotation (deg/s)	0.04–4	0.5–2.5	0.15–3.0	0.04–4

Table 2. Performances of the humanoid robot

	Robonaut 2	Humanoid robot of CAST
Mass (kg)	149.5	99
Arm DOF's	7	7
Waist DOF's	1	2
Neck DOF's	3	2
Fingers	5	5
Hands DOF's	12	13
Arm payload (N)	90	100
Finger payload (N)	22.5	25

3   Main Technical Highlights

The main body of the CSSCM consists of seven rotational joints, two end-effectors, an arm computer, two booms and a vision system, as shown in Fig. 1. The arm mechanism features 3 shoulder joints, 1 elbow joint and 3 wrist joints. The symmetry architecture of the arm allows for relocation of the arm like a walking warm. Joints are the kernel elements of the manipulator, which is used for the motion function. An end-effector is a target-capture tool of the manipulator, which is used for capturing, locking and releasing a target or for attaching to the Station. The vision system has three cameras distributed on the shoulder, the elbow and the wrist locations. The shoulder and the wrist cameras have the function of target recognition and measurement, while the elbow camera has the function of video surveillance. The function of the two boom assemblies is to provide the required long and stiff structural connections between the shoulder, elbow, and wrist. The control function consists of thermal controls and temperature sensors distributed among the robotics controls. The robotic control system consists of arm, joint, and end-effector controls. Arm control is performed by the arm computer units which are the control center. Joint control function is performed by seven joint electronics units, while end-effector control is performed by two end-effector electronics units. The arm control software can be downloaded to the arm computer units from the appropriate data management system. The arm computer units receive commands from the data communications function and sensory data from the joint electronics units as well as the end-effector electronics units.

Recently, a space humanoid robot with changeable end-effector is developed by the Beijing Institute of Spacecraft System Engineering of CAST. The space humanoid robot has 31-DOF (which can be expanded to 44-DOF), hundred sensors and four operation modes. The changeable end-effector is useful in different mission, including multi-fingered dexterous hand and multifunctional tools. With the special interface of CSSCM, the space humanoid robot can easily realize large scope movement and smart operation. Experiments to confirm the reliability of the space humanoid robot have been successfully conducted, demonstrating the tracking of flexible structures. The design of the space humanoid robot with changeable end-effector has been qualified to be manufactured and tested, as shown in Fig. 2, which lays the foundation to support the construction of the space station and the development of the on-orbit assembly technology of China. The CSSCM and the humanoid robot can be assembled together with a power and data grapple fixture (PDGF) to be a whole space robot system, as shown in Fig. 3, which can deal with more difficult on-orbit tasks.

Fig. 1. The principle prototype of CSSCM

Fig. 2. The prototype of space humanoid robot

Fig. 3. The whole robot system in the CSS

4   Key Technologies Analysis

The key technologies of the Chinese Space Station robots are described in this section, especially for the on-orbit assembly technology.

4.1   System Design and Optimization Technique

Considering the characteristics of diversification, real time information interaction for the on-orbit assembly and maintenance mission, the robot requires more degrees of freedom and interfaces, which increase the difficulty of system design and decrease the reliability of work process. Therefore, the top-level plan and strategy design should be researched considering the special mission application in the system design of robot and the mechanical system should be developed for multi-function requirements including capture, connection replacement, reconfiguration, movement, refueling and so on. Otherwise, the long life and high reliability request of the system should be considered at the same time by using collaborative and redundancy design.

4.2   High-Precision Servo Control

The precision of space robot is influenced by various system errors and random errors, such as assembly backlashes, control errors and sensors errors which are very difficult to avoid. However, the system errors including the mechanical production errors, mechanical assemble errors, base body positioning errors, and the errors conducted by payload can be deal with by proper calibration or control compensation to get higher control precision of robot endpoint. High precision servo control system has two control architectures, a centralized control and a distractive control [2]. For the characters of dispersed position of the manipulator joints and functional complexity of single joint, if the centralized control architecture is used, the problems such as the signal interference and the disaccording of time-sharing control system is difficult to resolve. Thus, the manipulator control system adopts a distributed control architecture.

So the high-precision servo control architecture should be adopted to improve the performance of robot and dynamics and friction compensations should be added. To adjust the position of the robot due to structure vibration and the misalignment of target, the tip needs to be precisely tracked and controlled using on-orbit sensors such as vision and accelerometers.

4.3 High Reliability Trajectory Planning

For the high reliability trajectory planning, the conventional inverse kinematics solution should be extended to satisfy various constraints such as disturbance minimization, complex exterior layout, collision avoidance, minimal cost, trajectory optimization and so on. Collisions and obstacles have great significant influence on system performance. Careful trajectory planning and control with fault tolerance are highly recommended to avoid collisions and obstacles in the environment. Different trajectory planning methods such as the least torque trajectory for capture operations, the least disturbance to the base, and the minimal time trajectory can also be implemented for special mission needs.

4.4 Flexible Multi-body System Dynamics Modeling and Simulation

When the robot moves in orbit, the flexibilities of its booms and joints give significant impact to the dynamic performance of the manipulator, and even affect the safety of the system, hence the flexible multi-body dynamics modeling and simulation are a critical tool for the design, analysis and verification of the manipulator system.

Focusing on the expected tasks of space robot, joint dynamics model is established in accordance with the principle of joint motors, planetary gears and other joint components, nonlinear friction, backlash, stiffness, load change impacts are considered. On the other hand, the dynamics model of the whole space robot is also established. Finite element method is used to model the flexible booms. Flexible end-effector should be considered, which is employed for simulation of a capture process of target.

4.5 Object Recognition and Measurement

Object recognition and measurement for space robot is usually implemented by a vision system with cooperative target [13], which is mature and used abroad in the space, but sub millimeter level or further distance measurement still have difficulty in improving accuracy. Recently, capturing technology of non-cooperative target, aiming at on-orbit servicing of spacecraft, has been focused on research in the field of space robot technology. In order to measure the relative pose between the two non-cooperative spacecrafts in the capture task, the method based on object recognition and measurement for the non-cooperative spacecraft should be studied in three parts: Camera calibration, object recognition and pose estimation.

4.6   Human-Computer Interaction

The complicated mission of space usually needs the space robot to have more degrees of freedom, the tradition method with front-panel instruction way of the direct control can't adapt for complicated actions, while the use of human actions and gestures to control the robot can replace complex program operations, and humans can manipulate and interact with the robots easily and conveniently. Human motion and gesture recognition based on video is an indispensable key technology in the new generation of human-computer interaction technique, which will become increasingly common.

4.7   Longevity Lubrication for the Joint

In order to maintain the stability of joint lubrication requirements for the space robot to work normally in the space station, the lubrication methods and materials needs to be properly selected or developed.

(1) Grease lubricating materials are used for transmission mechanisms having light loads and high speeds.
(2) Solid lubricating materials are used for mechanisms having heavy-duty and low speed applications.
(3) The test of space environment adaptability is conducted for various lubricating materials.

4.8   Long-Duration Power Supply and Energy-Efficient Operation Technique

The independent power supply module should be mounted on the space robot system for long-duration power supply to maintain independence from the system resources. Both the long-duration power supply and the energy-efficient operation are required for life extension of on-orbit robot system. The easy charged battery will be used for long-duration power supply.

4.9   Ground Test and Verification

For a large space robot, it is difficult to physically test at the system level to verify the actual performance on-orbit in ground gravity. Like everyone else in the space robotics industry, we are using a combination of digital simulation, semi-physical test, and planar physical test to fully cover orbit missions of the robotic system on the ground. Flotation platform and suspension system is used in the physical test, to obtain data performances and make mutual authentication with digital results.

5   Conclusions

The Chinese Space Station robots are highly integrated robotic system, combing technologies of engineering mechanics, electronics, thermotics, vision and computer control. The development of the Chinese Space Station robots contains many unsolved technical problems, at least to the Chinese development team, and therefore faces huge challenges for the design and implementation of the robotic system. The Chinese Space Station robots take on the missions of relocking spacecraft sections, assisting docking station cabins, installing equipment, and maintaining the Space Station.

This paper presents some technical solutions for the Chinese Space Station robots, it also describes the research results of nine key technologies such as the high-precision joint servo control, multi-constrained trajectory planning, and the verification and validation of the space robotic system. Research results obtained so far has indicated that our design of the Chinese Space Station robots have been qualified to be manufactured and tested, which lays the foundation to support the construction of the Chinese Space Station.

Acknowledgement. This research was supported in part by the National Natural Science Foundation of China (No. 51875393 and No. 5192780006) and by the China Advance Research for Manned Space Project (No. 030601).

References

1. Zhou, J.P.: Chinese space station project overall vision. Manned Spacefl. **19**(2), 1–10 (2013)
2. Yu, D.Y., Sun, J., Ma, X.R.: Suggestion on development of Chinese space manipulator technology. Spacecr. Eng. **16**(4), 1–8 (2007)
3. Zhang, K.F., Zhou, H., Wen, Q.P., et al.: Review of the development of robotic manipulator for international space station. Chin. J. Space Sci. **30**(6), 612–619 (2010)
4. Yu, D.Y., Pan, B., Sun, J.: A literature review on dynamic modeling and analysis of the joints in space manipulator. Spacecr. Eng. **19**(2), 1–10 (2010)
5. Zhang, X., Shao, Z.: Adaptive high precision position control of servo actuator with friction compensation using LuGre model. J. Beijing Inst. Technol. **20**(1), 105–110 (2011)
6. Stieber, M.E., Trudel, C.P., Hunter, D.G.: Robotic system for the international space station. In: Proceedings of the 1997 IEEE International Conference on Robotics and Automation Albuquerque, New Mexico, pp. 3068–3073 (1997)
7. Gibbs, G., Sachdev, S.: Canada and the international space station program: overview and status. Acta Astronautica **51**(1), 591–600 (2002)
8. Mozzon, J.M., Crausaz, A., Favre, E., Baker, F.: Torque control design of the European robotic arm. In: Proceedings of the 50th European Space Conference, Tarragona, Spain, pp. 335–342 (1998)
9. Shiraki, K., Ozawa, K., Matsueda, T., et al: JEMRMS development status. In: Proceedings of the 44th Congress of the International Astronautical Federation, Graz, Austria, pp. 1–5 (1993)
10. Patten, L., Evans, L., Oshinowo, L., et al: International space station robotics: a comparative study of ERA, JEMRMS and MSS. In: Proceedings of the 7th ESA Workshop on Advanced Space Technologies for Robotics and Automation 'ASTRA 2002' ESTEC, Noordwijk, The Netherlands, pp. 1–8 (2002)
11. Qin, W.B., Chen, M., Zhang, C.F., et al.: Surveys on large-scale mechanism of space station. Aerosp. Shanghai **27**(4), 32–42 (2010)
12. Diftler, M.A., et al.: Robonaut 2 – initial activities on-board the ISS. In: Proceedings of the IEEE Aerospace Conference, Big Sky, Montana, pp. 1–12 (2012)
13. Chen, L., Jia, Y.D., Li, M.X.: An FPGA-based RGBD imager. Mach. Vis. Appl. **23**(3), 513–525 (2012)

Wearable Sensing Based Limb Motor Function Rehabilitation

Design of a Sensor Insole for Gait Analysis

Kamen Ivanov[1,2], Zhanyong Mei[3], Ludwig Lubich[4], Nan Guo[5],
Deng Xile[6], Zhichun Zhao[7], Olatunji Mumini Omisore[1], Derek Ho[5],
and Lei Wang[1(✉)]

[1] Shenzhen Institutes of Advanced Technology, Chinese Academy of Sciences,
Shenzhen 518055, China
{kamen, omisore, wang.lei}@siat.ac.cn
[2] Shenzhen College of Advanced Technology,
University of Chinese Academy of Sciences, Shenzhen 518055, China
[3] College of Cyber Security, Chengdu University of Technology,
Chengdu 610059, China
zhanyongm99@163.com
[4] Faculty of Telecommunications, Technical University of Sofia,
Sofia 1000, Bulgaria
lvl@tu-sofia.bg
[5] Department of Materials Science and Engineering,
City University of Hong Kong, Kowloon, Hong Kong
nanguo-c@my.cityu.edu.hk, derekho@cityu.edu.hk
[6] Xi'an Polytechnic University, Shaanxi 710048, China
[7] College of Information Science and Technology,
Chengdu University of Technology, Chengdu 610059, China

Abstract. There is an increasing interest in the application of instrumented insoles in sport and medicine to obtain gait information during activities of daily living. Despite the high number of research works dedicated to smart insole design, there is a lack of discussions on strategies to optimize the design of the force sensing electronic acquisition module. Such strategies are needed to achieve a small form factor while maintaining reliable kinetic data acquisition. In the present work, we describe our implementation of a smart insole and demonstrate channel multiplexing to optimize electronic component count. We discuss the details of the analog part, including the analog-to-digital conversion, optimal sampling frequency selection, and methods to reduce errors and influences of component imperfections. We demonstrated a complete framework for insole signal processing developed in Python. We used the insole prototype to collect data from twenty volunteers and implemented a basic algorithm for person recognition. As a result, we achieved a reasonable classification accuracy of 98.75%.

Keywords: Smart insole · Channel multiplexing · GaitPy ·
Person recognition · Gait analysis

© Springer Nature Switzerland AG 2019
H. Yu et al. (Eds.): ICIRA 2019, LNAI 11743, pp. 433–444, 2019.
https://doi.org/10.1007/978-3-030-27538-9_37

1 Introduction

Recent technological advancements determine the rapid development of biomedical wearables, including those intended for gait analysis. Apart from intuitive applications of patient rehabilitation, diabetes ulcers monitoring, and sports performance evaluation, gait analysis is considered a candidate in less typical applications, such as evaluation of worker footwear [1] or biometric recognition [2]. In more simplistic gait analysis applications, motion sensors integrated into mobile phones already have an established role. In short-time laboratory experiments, to reflect limb motion finely, special, high-performance motion sensors are used [3]. On the other side, the evaluation of plantar pressure distribution is essential for understanding lower limb functioning [4]. Wearables for measuring plantar pressure arise, and are still in the research phase, with few commercial examples. For obtaining complete information of human gait in environments of daily living, efforts are to develop the so-called *sensor shoes, insoles* or *socks*. As these devices possess computing capabilities, they are also known as *smart wearables*. They contain miniature inertial and force sensors to collect both kinematic and kinetic data. Such combination allows for synchronized multimodal data capture and application of sensor data fusion algorithms to reflect gait phenomena completely. Inertial sensing units possess nine or six degrees of freedom; that is, they provide three-axis acceleration, angular speed, and in some cases also magnetic field sensing. Main challenges in using inertial sensing units are to deal with the drifts, and these are addressed sufficiently by strategies such as *Zero Velocity Update* and the application of *Kalman filtering*. As to force sensors, currently, several technologies can serve gait analysis. Force sensitive resistors (FSR) include resistive and piezoresistive sensors. Piezoelectric, capacitive and even optical sensing are also explored [5, 6].

Advantages of FSR are the low cost, simple fabrication process, their optimal thickness, mechanical strength and the fact that they can accept custom shapes [7]. Related challenges include low accuracy and repeatability, the effects of drifts, hysteresis, temperature sensitivity, fabrication tolerances, and non-linear current-voltage characteristic [8]. Also, in FSR, conductance is the parameter that changes relatively linearly with the applied force [9, 10]. Hence, one choice is to connect the sensor in a simple voltage divider, capture directly the non-linearly changing voltage over the sensor and deal with the non-linearity using software methods. Another commonly-applied approach is to use a transimpedance amplifier. Its output voltage changes linearly with the current through the sensor, and, respectively, with the applied force. For a single sensor, the added power consumption and required area on the board of such a hardware stage, are neglectable, and it is worth using it. However, to obtain a fuller picture of plantar pressure distribution, at least several force sensors are required. That comes in contradiction with efforts for a small electronic module with low power consumption, that, eventually, to be integrated within the body of the smart insole/shoe. Thus, it is needed to apply channel multiplexing, i.e., to use only a single analog channel to serve multiple FSRs. Such an approach requires to consider the selection of a multiplexing scheme, specifics of the analog-to-digital conversion, the selection of optimal sampling frequency, and avoiding the influence of electronic component imperfections. In the vast amount of research works dedicated to instrumented insole design, there is little attention on analyzing the FSR signal acquisition module. In many cases, ready electronic kits are used, and even if channel multiplexing is utilized, signal acquisition is not discussed in detail [11, 12].

In the present work, we describe our design of a smart insole prototype and provide a discussion on the aspects mentioned above.

2   System Design

2.1   Hardware Scenario

The proposed hardware configuration is illustrated in Fig. 1a. An essential design decision to make is to determine the number of force sensors and sampling frequency as a trade-off between several contradicting factors. The amount of captured data has to be moderate to fit the bandwidth-limited communication channel and preserve the battery charge.

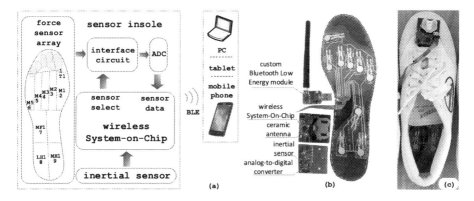

Fig. 1. Proposed sensor insole (a) block diagram (b) prototype (c) insole assembled in a shoe.

On the other side, to obtain enough information about the pressure under the main foot areas, a high number of sensors are required. If the foot is scanned to create its model before use, the number of sensors could be significantly reduced [13]. However, such an approach may not be user-friendly and may be challenging to apply to users with foot anatomical deviations. In wearables with a high number of sensors, the sampling frequency goes as low as 25–50 Hz [14]. In case of fast motions, such rates are suboptimal, while in many cases a sampling frequency of 100 Hz is still an acceptable choice.

In our proposed design we used nine force sensors, located under the toe (T1), metatarsal (M1 – M5), midfoot (MF7), and heel (LH1, MH1) areas, respectively. Circular sensors of type FlexiForce are often used in insole prototypes because of their superior characteristics compared to other existing FSRs [9]. We selected sensors of type A301, with a diameter of the active sensing area of 9.53 mm. Based on previous research on the maximum plantar pressure range, we selected the sensor version with a range of 445 N [6, 10]. A drawback to choosing a sensor with a large range is that its sensitivity and accuracy in a narrower range would be low. As explained below, the overall sensitivity of the system also depends on the design choices of the interface circuit. Sensors were affixed on a flexible printed circuit board inserted between two flexible polyvinyl chloride sheets – a hard, 0.5 mm thick lower one that does not allow sensor sinking and a soft upper one with a thickness of 0.8 mm. The entire design is based on a wireless system-on-chip nRF52832 by Nordic. A channel multiplexing scheme is used for the sensor signal acquisition. The obtained signal is digitized through an external, single-channel 12-bit analog-to-digital converter (ADC) of type ADS7042. At a supply voltage of 2.5 V and a sampling frequency of 1 MHz, the power consumption of the ADC is less than 180 μA. The control board is attached at the frontal part of the shoe as shown in Fig. 1c, thus reflecting well the trajectory of the foot. It contains an incorporated inertial sensor of type BMI160. Without the application of power-preserving strategies, at the lowest level of transmission power, during active data transfer, the consumption of the device does not exceed 2.4 mA. Data are transferred to the host device using Bluetooth Low Energy (BLE) technology. For the reception at a personal computer (PC), we have developed a custom data receiving module that pairs with left and right insole and transfers all the received data through a virtual serial port.

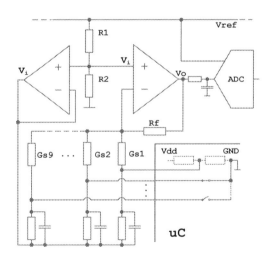

Fig. 2. Proposed force sensor interface circuit (sensor 2 active).

2.2   Interface Circuit

The proposed interface circuit is shown in Fig. 2. The key design decision is how to complement the transimpedance amplifier with channel multiplexing capability and an appropriate ADC. In many modern ADCs, there is a feature to select the supply voltage as the reference one. We make use of it, to obtain the conductance directly, as follows:

$$V_i = V_{ref} \frac{R2}{R1 + R2} = \sigma V_{ref}; \quad Gs = \frac{\left(\frac{ADC\ reading}{ADC\ levels} - \sigma\right)}{\sigma Rf} \tag{1}$$

In this way, the measurement does not depend on the value of the analog supply voltage. However, as the sensor current-voltage characteristic at fixed forces is non-linear [8], to avoid the effects of that nonlinearity, the analog supply was taken from a precise 2.5 V regulator. Lower values of Vi and Rf determine lower sensitivity and large force range of the sensor [9].

At a time, only one sensor is active. Selection is made through general purpose I/O pins of the microcontroller, acting as digital switches. The active sensor is connected to the ground, while the rest of the sensors are inactive and their corresponding pins of the microcontroller are set in a high-impedance state by configuring them as inputs. As denoted in Fig. 2, these switches are not ideal, and in a high-impedance state, they still have some conductivity, which allows inactive sensors to influence the reading of the active one. Also, concerning noise immunity, it is not recommended to have sensor pins floating. To address these problems, we connected inactive sensors trough high-impedance resistors to Vi. These resistors have a much lower value than the parasitic resistance in a high-impedance state of the pin. Thus, the both ends of the inactive sensors have the potential of Vi, and any influence over the active sensor is prevented. While a sensor is active, the series resistor gets connected between Vi and the ground, which does not impact the measurement, and leads to negligible current. For providing a low-impedance path for external disturbances, capacitors are connected in parallel to series resistors. To avoid the influence of the series resistor of the active sensor on Vi, Vi for the series resistors is taken through a buffer.

Before passing a signal for analog-to-digital conversion, it has to go through an anti-aliasing filter. In the suggested approach, however, sensor switching is equivalent to sampling. Thus, it is not possible to apply an anti-aliasing filter directly before the multiplexing stage, and this problem remains open. It is well known that systems, where multiplexing is used to read sensors, require a proper anti-aliasing solution [15]. However, in many smart insole designs channel multiplexing was applied but the anti-aliasing issue was not discussed [16]. Apart from the thermal noise, there is a variety of undesired interference signals well beyond the Nyquist band that can enter the signal processing tract. A possible solution would be to apply a nonuniform sampling scheme that does not require band limiting. In our implementation, we rely on the fact that the components of the eventual interference signals will be very low in amplitude compared to the strong signals from the sensors. As the presence of an anti-aliasing filter before the ADC is imperative, we still used a first-order RC filter with a cut-off frequency much higher than that required for a single channel. In choosing it, it is critical to ensure that its time constant is low enough in respect to the selected sampling frequency to avoid the "memory effect" – having the reading from the previous sensor influencing the reading from the active one.

In some designs, the sensors are connected in voltage dividers with corresponding series resistors to the input of the ADC. However, the current-voltage characteristic of the force sensors is non-linear [8]. In this case, the voltage at the ends of the sensor depends non-linearly on the applied force, as well as on the analog supply voltage. Thus, it would be challenging to derive a model that takes into account all relationships. In contrast, the transimpedance amplifier maintains a constant voltage over the sensor.

For the ADC, an intriguing approach would be to use the microcontroller built-in one to optimize component count. However, in the case of nRF52832 and *Vdd* selected as a reference voltage, the gain for the input stage has to be chosen between 0.6 or 1. In the former case the conversion error turns out to be unacceptably large, while in the second, the input range is limited.

2.3   Firmware Implementation

Sensor insole firmware involves inertial sensor data reading, force sensor control and reading, as well as Bluetooth Low Energy-based data transmission. All sensors were sampled at 100 Hz. All operations were interrupt-driven, and data reading used buffering. For the inertial sensor, its internal buffer was utilized, while for the force sensors two alternatively switched buffers were organized in the memory of the microcontroller and used as described in [3].

Force sensor data reading and sensor switching were controlled by a timer, and the conductance was calculated on-board. Timer interrupts were generated at a frequency ten times higher than the one of a single channel. In each interrupt event, the subsequent sensor was read, and the next one was activated. Thus, there was enough time for the voltage "tail" of the previous sensor to fade out and the output voltage corresponding to the newly activated sensor to settle. As to wireless transmission, data were structured into four types of packets – for the left and right inertial sensor and left and right force sensors, respectively. Packets were distinguished by the header and contained fields for packet counter and a checksum. Force sensor data packets also contained information about insole size. Information about battery level was also transferred. At the receiver side, packets were passed to a virtual serial port without alteration. The receiver board was configured to connect insoles automatically.

2.4   Gait Analysis Python Framework

To receive, visualize and store sensor insole signals on a personal computer, we developed the whole required framework, entirely in Python. We called it **GaitPy**. It is illustrated in Fig. 3 and its components are explained in the next sections.

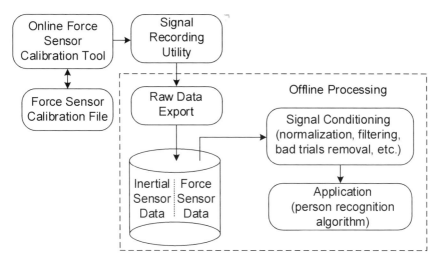

Fig. 3. Structure of the gait analysis framework **GaitPy** developed by us in Python.

3 Evaluation

To cover most common foot sizes, we manufactured six pairs of insoles of different sizes; according to the Continental European system, these are standard sizes of 37, 38, 39 (female sizes), and 41, 42, 43 (male sizes). Each insole was inserted into an ordinary sports shoe (Fig. 1c).

3.1 Sensor Calibration

Before use, both the inertial and force sensors need calibration. In practice, calibration procedures could be complex. Since the presented project is in the initial stage of development, we limited the calibration steps to the basic ones. For the inertial sensor, we asked the subjects to stand still for more than ten seconds and used the obtained signals to judge for the levels of the offsets, which were then used during the offline signal processing. As to force sensors, we performed static calibration as instructed in [17]. Though dynamic calibration is desirable, static calibration is still acceptable in cases of normal, relatively low-speed walking. The calibration setup is illustrated in Fig. 4a. For the calibration of force sensors, we developed a utility in Python, that accepts real-time data for each tested force point, records the conductance for it, and builds the line of the best fit. The user interface of the application is shown in Fig. 4b.

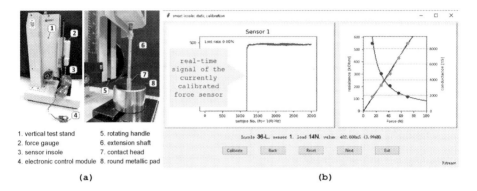

1. vertical test stand   5. rotating handle
2. force gauge   6. extension shaft
3. sensor insole   7. contact head
4. electronic control module 8. round metallic pad

(a)   (b)

Fig. 4. Sensor calibration: (a) calibration setup (b) user interface of the force sensor static calibration utility developed by us.

To avoid the influence of signal variations, when obtaining a calibration point, the last 100 samples were averaged. Before calibration, we explored data of several subjects to find the maximum conductance/force, which we used to set the upper limit of the signal range. Based on that, for each sensor the conductance at five equidistant force points was captured, namely 14 N, 28 N, 42 N, 56 N and 70 N. For each point, the force was increased from zero to the desired value. We performed calibration for six pairs of insoles of different sizes, thus, having calibrated 108 force sensors in total. Sensors were calibrated after being incorporated into the insole, at the same temperature as the one of conducting the subsequent data collection [7, 17]. For the calibration, a force gauge was used in combination with a custom metallic head that matched in diameter the active area of the sensor. Calibration data of the sensors were stored in a JSON file and used to obtain the force values. It was interesting to compare the calibration results between sensors. Results are shown in Fig. 5 and reveal that characteristics of sensors from the same batch could differ significantly, hence the need to develop advanced methods of calibration and utilization, that can address these differences.

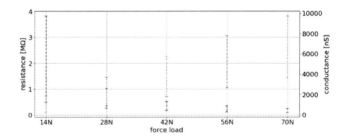

Fig. 5. Comparison of the force-conductance ranges during calibration of 108 force sensors.

3.2 Classification of Insole-Collected Data for Person Recognition

In terms of individual sensor accuracy, limits are guaranteed by the manufacturer, and by proper calibration procedure before use. However, force signal validation of the complete device during regular use is challenging as it would involve a simultaneous measurement from both the tested prototype and a pressure sensitive gold standard device. As we elaborated, thin-film sensor signals are to be considered qualitative rather than quantitative [18]. Also, recently, there is an increased interest in methods for person recognition based on human gait, especially continuous authentication, where gait patterns serve as a weak biometric [19]. For this reason, we considered it reasonable to demonstrate the operating capability of the sensor insole by proving that data collected from our prototype contain discriminative information allowing to identify a user. Thus, to prove the capability of the designed prototype, we performed an experiment for person recognition.

Host Data Acquisition Utility. For visualization of insole signals during signal acquisition and storing them on the hard disk of the personal computer, we developed a utility in Python. Its user interface is shown in Fig. 6.

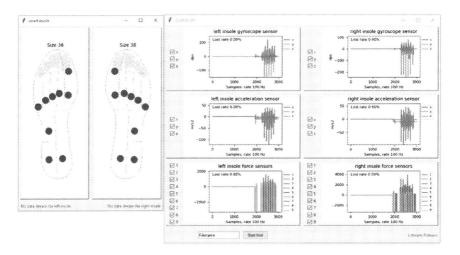

Fig. 6. The user interface of the utility for insole signal capturing.

As an interpretive language, Python is known for the lower execution speed compared to other types of programming languages; on the other side, it allows fast and convenient software prototyping. To ensure successful data recording, the utility stores the raw data in a binary file directly, together with the data transfer protocol overhead. For the visualization, the number of displayed signal samples were reduced, which does not impact human perception while lowers the requirement towards processing. During the recording, the utility also indicates lost and corrupt packets to allow for timely undertaking of corrective actions.

Subjects and Experimental Protocol. We recruited twenty healthy volunteers who were selected to cover the available six sizes of the prototype. Before the experiment, each participant was informed about the experimental procedure and signed an informed consent form. The experiment was approved by the ethics committee of the University of Technology of Chengdu and conformed to the Declaration of Helsinki. Each participant was asked to wear a pair of shoes with an incorporated insole, and walk straight at a self-selected speed over a walkway with a length of seven meters at least twenty times.

Data Processing and Classification Algorithm. In total, 472 trials without lost packets were collected and processed. Both force and inertial data from the left and right foot were used. A set of features were extracted, that included maximum, minimum, mean, range, zero-crossing rate, root-mean-square values, variance, standard variance, skewness, and kurtosis. For the recognition, we applied a random forest classifier with default parameter settings, as this classifier was found to have superior performance when applied on features of gait [20]. The data were divided into an 80%-training set and 20%-testing set, and 5-fold cross-validation was performed. Obtained accuracy was as high as 98.75%. Figure 7 shows the resultant confusion matrix and representative signals from the insole.

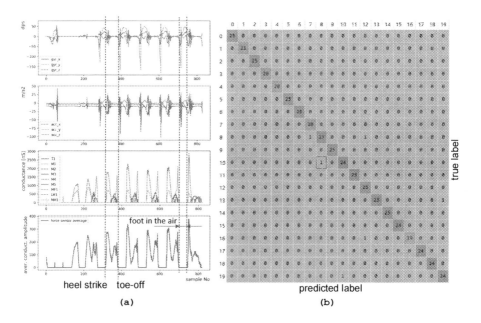

Fig. 7. (a) A representative example of signals captured by the sensor insole (b) Resultant confusion matrix of classification for person recognition.

4 Conclusion

In the present work, we described our implementation of a smart insole device; we make the following contributions:

(1) Suggested and demonstrated a force sensor channel multiplexing circuit for sensorized insole design to optimize the component count.

(2) Pointed out an important issue that might be present in some of the existing smart insole research prototypes where channel multiplexing was used; namely, many of them may not have an appropriate anti-aliasing filtering. This matter deserves more attention in new sensor insole designs.

(3) Developed and demonstrated a gait analysis framework called *GaitPy* that contains convenient tools for calibration and signal recording and was developed entirely in Python language.

(4) Demonstrated that data collected from sensor insole contain discriminative information allowing to identify a user by his gait pattern, thus proving the operational capability of the device.

In our further work on smart insoles, we will focus on solutions to address the anti-aliasing filtering issue in designs with channel multiplexing, advanced sensor calibration schemes, internal sensor synchronization, optimizing the volume of transferred data and algorithmic solutions for intelligent data processing. In terms of application, we plan to explore the use of smart insole for driver foot movements tracking [21, 22].

Acknowledgments. This project was supported in parts by the Key Project 2017GZ0304 of the Science and Technology Department of Sichuan province, Key Program of Joint Funds of the National Natural Science Foundation of China, grant U1505251, The Enhancement Project for Shenzhen Biomedical Electronics Technology Public Service Platform, and the Outstanding Youth Innovation Research Fund of SIAT-CAS, grant Y8G0381001.

References

1. Ochsmann, E., Noll, U., Ellegast, R., Hermanns, I., Kraus, T.: Influence of different safety shoes on gait and plantar pressure: a standardized examination of workers in the automotive industry. J. Occup. Health **58**, 404–412 (2016)

2. Connor, P., Ross, A.: Biometric recognition by gait: a survey of modalities and features. Comput. Vis. Image Underst. **167**, 1–27 (2018)

3. Ivanov, K., Mei, Z., Li, H., Du, W., Wang, L.: A custom base station for collecting and processing data of research-grade motion sensor units. In: Perego, P., Andreoni, G., Rizzo, G. (eds.) MobiHealth 2016. LNICST, vol. 192, pp. 11–18. Springer, Cham (2017). https://doi.org/10.1007/978-3-319-58877-3_2

4. Mei, Z., Ivanov, K., Zhao, G., Li, H., Wang, L.: An explorative investigation of functional differences in plantar center of pressure of four foot types using sample entropy method. Med. Biol. Eng. Comput. **55**, 537–548 (2017)

5. Crea, S., Donati, M., De Rossi, S.M.M., Oddo, C.M., Vitiello, N.: A wireless flexible sensorized insole for gait analysis. Sensors **14**, 1073–1093 (2014)

6. Razak, A.H.A., Zayegh, A., Begg, R.K., Wahab, Y.: Foot plantar pressure measurement system: a review. Sensors **12**, 9884–9912 (2012)
7. Schofield, J.S., Evans, K.R., Hebert, J.S., Marasco, P.D., Carey, J.P.: The effect of biomechanical variables on force sensitive resistor error: implications for calibration and improved accuracy. J. Biomech. **49**, 786–792 (2016)
8. Paredes-Madrid, L., Palacio, C.A., Matute, A., Parra Vargas, C.A.: Underlying physics of conductive polymer composites and force sensing resistors (FSRs) under static loading conditions. Sensors **17**, 2108 (2017)
9. TekScan: FlexiForce Sensors User Manual
10. Tekscan: FlexiForce Standard Model A301, datasheet
11. Gonzalez, I., Fontecha, J., Hervas, R., Bravo, J.: An ambulatory system for gait monitoring based on wireless sensorized insoles. Sensors **15**, 16589–16613 (2015)
12. Lee, W., Hong, S.-H., Oh, H.-W.: Characterization of elastic polymer-based smart insole and a simple foot plantar pressure visualization method using 16 electrodes. Sensors **19**, 44 (2018)
13. Ghaida, H.A., Mottet, S., Goujon, J.-M.: Foot modeling and smart plantar pressure reconstruction from three sensors. Open Biomed. Eng. J. **8**, 84–92 (2014)
14. Hegde, N., Bries, M., Sazonov, E.: A comparative review of footwear-based wearable systems. Electronics **5**, 48 (2016)
15. Tsai, D., Yuste, R., Shepard, K.L.: Statistically reconstructed multiplexing for very dense, high-channel-count acquisition systems. IEEE Trans. Biomed. Circuits Syst. **12**, 13–23 (2018)
16. Majewski, C., Perkins, A., Faltz, D., Zhang, F., Zhao, H., Xiao, W.: Design of a 3D printed insole with embedded plantar pressure sensor arrays. Presented at the Proceedings of the 2017 ACM International Joint Conference on Pervasive and Ubiquitous Computing and Proceedings of the 2017 ACM International Symposium on Wearable Computers, Maui, Hawaii (2017)
17. Tekscan Inc.: Calibration Quick Start Guide for FlexiForce Sensors. Rev A, 06 October 2008
18. Interlink Electronics, Inc.: FSR Force Sensing Resistors, Integration Guide, Document part number EIG-10000 Rev. C
19. Yeh, K., Su, C., Chiu, W., Zhou, L.: I walk, therefore i am: continuous user authentication with plantar biometrics. IEEE Commun. Mag. **56**, 150–157 (2018)
20. Schneider, O.S., MacLean, K.E., Altun, K., Karuei, I., Wu, M.M.A.: Real-time gait classification for persuasive smartphone apps: structuring the literature and pushing the limits. Presented at the Proceedings of the 2013 International Conference on Intelligent User Interfaces, Santa Monica, California, USA (2013)
21. Wu, Y., Boyle, L.N., McGehee, D.V.: Evaluating variability in foot to pedal movements using functional principal components analysis. Accid. Anal. Prev. **118**, 146–153 (2018)
22. © Neurico company. https://neurico.com. Accessed 27 Apr 2019

Multiple Features Fusion System
for Motion Recognition

Jiang Hua[1,2], Zhaojie Ju[3], Disi Chen[3], Dalin Zhou[3], Haoyi Zhao[4],
Du Jiang[5,6], and Gongfa Li[1,2(✉)]

[1] Key Laboratory of Metallurgical Equipment and Control Technology
of Ministry of Education, Wuhan University of Science and Technology,
Wuhan 430081, China
ligongfa@wust.edu.cn
[2] Precision Manufacturing Research Institute,
Wuhan University of Science and Technology, Wuhan 430081, China
[3] School of Computing, University of Portsmouth, Portsmouth PO1 3HE, UK
[4] Research Center of Biologic Manipulator and Intelligent Measurement
and Control, Wuhan University of Science and Technology,
Wuhan 430081, China
[5] Hubei Key Laboratory of Mechanical Transmission and Manufacturing
Engineering, Wuhan University of Science and Technology,
Wuhan 430081, China
[6] 3D Printing and Intelligent Manufacturing Engineering Institute,
Wuhan University of Science and Technology, Wuhan, China

Abstract. Surface EMG signal is a signal source that can reflect the movement state of human muscles accurately. However, there are still problems such as low recognition rate in practical applications. It is necessary to study how they can be exploited effectively for a more accurate extraction. The paper combines two time domain features and nonlinear feature to get the feature vector for subsequent pattern recognition. The paper chooses the generalized regression neural network (GRNN) as the classifier for hand motion pattern recognition. The proposed method in this paper not only realizes the feature extraction of signals, but also ensures the high classification accuracy. The feature, RMS-SampEn-WL, obtains the highest recognition rate above 97% compared with the two time features. The new sEMG feature is effective and suitable for hand motion pattern recognition. Finally, we hope to establish a robust recognition system based on sEMG.

Keywords: Surface EMG signal · GRNN classifier · RMS-SampEn-WL

1   Introduction

The pattern recognition technology used in surface electromyography (sEMG) signals for identifying human motions is widely involved in human-computer interaction, biomimetic prosthetics, diagnosis in clinical applications and the development of rehabilitation equipment [1].

© Springer Nature Switzerland AG 2019
H. Yu et al. (Eds.): ICIRA 2019, LNAI 11743, pp. 445–455, 2019.
https://doi.org/10.1007/978-3-030-27538-9_38

The research is more challenging compared to other widely used bioelectrical signals because of its randomness [2]. sEMG is a biological signal that is collected on the surface of the skin [3]. The muscle control information can be collected to control electrical powered prostheses [4]. So this method based on sEMG Signal is widely used in a series of clinical applications [5].

Therefore, many researchers have begun to study the features of the sEMG signals. They have re-evaluated the performance of the commonly used Hudgins' time domain features [6]. Autoregressive (AR) model analysis is also a common method to get signal feature [7]. Willison amplitude(WAMP) and sample entropy (SampEn) using six different sEMG data sets containing over 60 subject sessions and 2500 separate contractions [8]. In addition, multiple features are studied or evaluated to improve the hand motion classification accuracy [9]. A set of time domain features is proposed that can estimate the EMG signal power spectrum characteristics using five different EMG data sets [10].

The current research on the physiological mechanism of human motion is still in the exploratory stage [11]. Therefore, in the process of pattern recognition, it is still lack of a standard in these aspects: selection of the sampled muscle groups, the extraction of sEMG features, and the modeling of continuous motions [12]. Universally, researchers determine the program mainly based on previous experience, these subjective factors may bring more uncertainty into the experimental conclusions [6].

Obtaining the active segment data of continuous sEMG signals accurately is the primary procedure to complete the classification of action patterns [13]. Especially in the mode of supervised machine learning, a sufficient data samples of different action types is the premise and guarantee of the classifier with excellent performance.

The purpose of the pattern classification is to determine which model the features fit. A good pattern classifier should have a smaller amount of computation, a higher recognition rate, and a stronger generalization ability. Support vector machine (SVM), linear discriminant analysis (LDA), k-nearest neighbor (KNN), multi-layer perceptron neuron network (MLP) and random forest (RF) classification algorithm are put forward [14].

In view of the above situations, this paper focuses on proposing an exploratory research to fuse multiple features for improving sEMG classification. We prove that the pre-processed sEMG frequency domain signals have a large loss through experimental analysis, so the time domain features are extracted for classifying. The nonlinear dynamic feature can construct a multidimensional dynamic model based on a one-dimensional time series to extract more hidden information. So large amounts of experiments have been conducted to explore how features fuse can achieve a better performance. The time domain features this paper choose are root mean square (RSM) and Waveform length (WL), the nonlinear dynamic feature is sample entropy (SampEn). The experimental result shows that this new feature can improve the accuracy of different hand motions classification based on sEMG after comparing the new feature with traditional time domain features. The feature contributes to the accurate human-machine interaction between intelligent prosthetic hand and users.

The remainder of this paper is organized as follows. Section 2 describes the methods to capture and process sEMG signals. Section 3 indicates the experimental results about the feature extraction and performance evaluation. Section 4 draws the conclusion and gives the discussion of future work.

2 Related Work

2.1 Collection of Signals

We collect the sEMG signals of nine hand motions from 10 subjects. All of them were healthy able-bodied subjects, without any prior neuromuscular disorders.

sEMG is usually collected by one or more electrodes were placed on the skin surface. Electrode shift and electrode distribution will obviously affect the recognition accuracy of the hand motion. Experiments use a 16-channel electrode sleeve to collect experimental data. In this paper the electrodes are modified from traditional disposable electrodes by gel removing means. Elastic fabrics are used to fix electrodes in advance. This method can reduce the time and position error of arranging electrodes. To obtain better skin impedance, the subjects must use alcohol to wash the forearm skin before the experiment. The scene of wearing the sleeve is shown in Fig. 1.

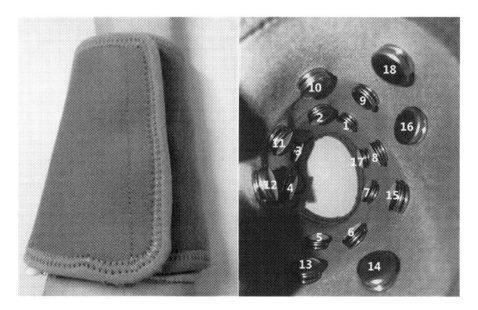

Fig. 1. It shows the scene of wearing the sleeve.

The 9 motions include hand closure (HC), hand open (HO), wrist flexion (WF), wrist extension (WE), thumb force on index finger (TI), middle finger (TM), ring finger (TR) and the little finger (TL), in addition to these hand motions also include a rest action (RE). The experimental hand motions are showed in Fig. 2.

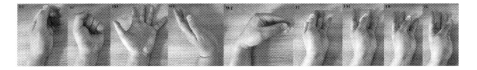

Fig. 2. The experimental hand motions

In the experiment, 10 trials were repeated for each motion. The repeated method is to rest for 5 s, keep the action for 5 s, repeat 10 times. If you have finished a motion, there will be a ten-minute break to avoid muscle fatigue. The hand motions are collected for 3 consecutive days, using the same collection method. So the temporal and spatial differences of the same individual in myoelectric signals can be obtained.

2.2 Signal Preprocessing

In order to achieve a high recognition rate of the classification results, the raw sEMG signals need to be preprocessed. The EMG signals contain a variety of noises due to its instability. The preprocessing includes two steps of noise reduction and feature selection. The digital noise filtering is combined with wavelet transform to reduce the true signal waveform as much as possible.

The captured sEMG signal consists of 4 phases: The relax state of a hand, The dynamic process for forming a hand motion, the steady state for maintaining a hand motion and the dynamic procedure for releasing a hand motion. In the experiment, sEMG signals sampling frequency is set to 1 kHz based on the Nyquist Sampling Theorem.

Power frequency interference caused by the nonlinear characteristics of hardware must be removed first. The power frequency of experimental equipment is 50 Hz. To eliminate these interferences, the experiment uses a 20-step 50 Hz comb filter to remove power frequency noise. The comb filter results are shown in Fig. 3.

The preprocessed signals still contain a large amount of data that will affect the operation speed. Therefore, the valid signals should be extracted as a feature value before the sEMG signals put into the classifier. The main function of feature extraction is to make classification easier and more intuitive by way of mapping complex signals from high-dimensional space to low-dimensional space.

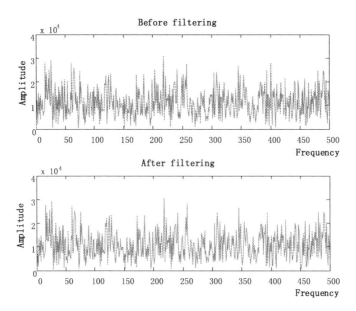

Fig. 3. Comparing the two graphs, it can be found that the filter mainly deals with the signals at an integer multiple of 50 Hz.

Many scholars have done a lot of work on feature extraction and pattern recognition. The time domain methods treat the sEMG signals as a function of time, and obtain some features by time domain analysis. The time domain methods are widely used in feature extraction of sEMG signals because of the lower computation in algorithm complexity. However, even small changes in muscle activity will cause significant influence. The frequency domain methods of sEMG signals are relatively stable because of the signals transformed into power spectrum and the waveform change little. But the sEMG signals will have a great loss in the process of extracting features.

This paper compares two time-domain features and nonlinear feature to prove the effectiveness. Two time domain features include root mean square (RMS) and waveform length (WL).

RMS is the measure of the amplitude of the EMG signal, which can be expressed as (1).

$$RMS = \sqrt{\frac{1}{N} \sum_{i=1}^{N} x_i^2} \tag{1}$$

N is the length of the window. Similar to RMS, the absolute value of the integral and the mean absolute value (MAV) have been proven to have the same performance in manual identification.

WL refers to the cumulative length of the EMG waveform. WL is related to the waveform amplitude, frequency and time. Where N represents the length of the signal and X_n represents the EMG signal in a segment. It can be formulated as (2).

$$WL = \sum_{i=1}^{N-1} |x_{i+1} - x_i| \tag{2}$$

Although the two methods have been widely used, they ignore the robustness of stochastic sEMG signals. The number of motor units and action potentials vary dramatically during the process of exercise, and the motion-neural system has many nonlinear characteristics. So the nonlinear dynamics methods can construct a multidimensional dynamic model to extract more hidden information. This paper chooses the main nonlinear method sample entropy (SampEn).

SampEn similar to the approximate entropy is used to measure the randomness of dynamic system expressed in time series. However, it has been used to reduce the error caused by the comparison of its own data. The equation of SampEn is defined as (3).

$$SampEn(m, r, N) = -In\frac{A}{B} \tag{3}$$

As is defined in (1), r is the threshold generally given, N is the number of samples and m is a given embedding dimension.

So the sample entropy, time domain features RMS and WL are used as eigenvalues to form feature vectors.

$$feature = \{RMS, WL, SampEn\} \tag{4}$$

3   Experimental Result

3.1   Feature Extraction

In this paper, the EMG signals are collected simultaneously by 16 channels, so the dimension of the three features is: 1 * 48. The mean value of the 16 channels is taken as the valid description to perform the feature vector. As shown in Table 1, the mean values of the three features under the nine motions.

Table 1. The mean values of the three features under the nine motions.

	RMS	WL	SampEn
Re	7.1262	1.8368*e3	0.9410
HC	183.1176	4.3872*e4	0.9133
HO	125.5576	2.5299*e4	1.5337
WE	42.9087	1.1577*e4	1.1249
WF	50.0360	1.3359*e4	1.3516
TI	58.4510	9.3138*e3	1.1672
TM	75.1499	1.3223*e4	1.4571
TR	102.8147	2.1140*e4	0.9705
TL	28.5878	6.6026*e3	1.0930

It can be clearly seen that the mean values of three features extracted from the signals are significantly different. In order to further show the difference of the feature vector, this paper takes ten sample points of the action to draw a scatter plot, as shown in Fig. 4.

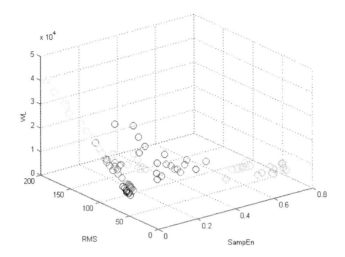

Fig. 4. A scatter plot of RMS-SampEn-WL (Color figure online).

It can be seen from Fig. 4 that the distribution of the nine hand movements is relatively discrete, although the distribution areas of the black and red portions are close. So this part of the area is enlarged, as shown in Fig. 5.

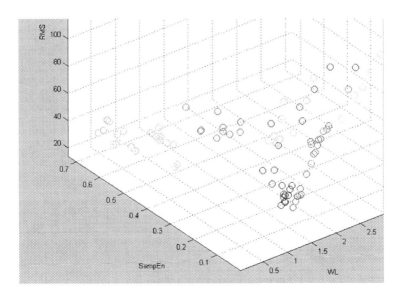

Fig. 5. The enlarged area of the black and red portions (Color figure online).

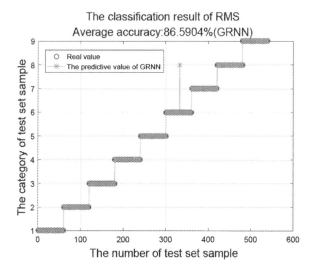

Fig. 6. The classification result of RMS.

It can be found that the distribution area has obvious interval. Therefore, it is feasible to extract the sample entropy, RMS and WL as the features of hand motions recognition for classification and recognition research.

3.2 Performance Evaluation

After completing the preparations such as noise reduction and feature extraction, the features need to be put into the appropriate classifier. The classifier is particularly important to realize the final hand motion classification and recognition. Currently, there are many types of widely used classifiers, and they have their own advantages and shortcomings. It is necessary to analyze the best hand motion classifiers through certain comparative experimental analysis. By summarizing and analyzing the existing work, this chapter chooses the generalized regression neural network (GRNN) as the classifier for hand motion pattern recognition.

Firstly, the feature vectors and corresponding action labels of the 9 groups of motions are equally divided into two groups, which are used as the training data set and the test data set respectively. At the same time, the data will be normalized. The data scaling involved in this paper mainly refers to scale the feature value WL to avoid the excessively dominant feature vector. After the parameters are optimized, the scaled training data set is imported into the GRNN classifier.

This paper compares the fusion feature with two time features to prove the effectiveness of the proposed method. The test data set is put into the classifier model to complete the test, and the GRNN classification performance is shown in Figs. 6, 7 and 8.

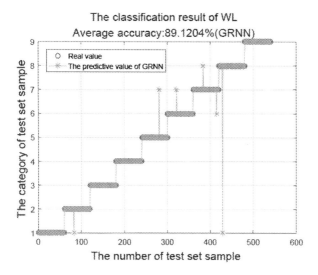

Fig. 7. The classification result of WL.

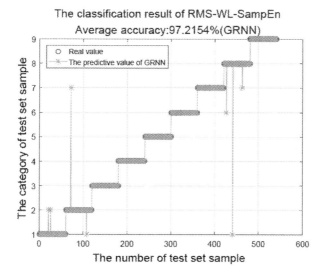

Fig. 8. The classification result of RMS-SampEn-WL.

As shown in Figs. 6 and 7, the classification rate of RMS is 86.5904%, the classification rate of WL is 89.1204%. The classification result of RMS-SampEn-WL is 97.2145%. So the fusion feature is more excellent and reliable for hand motion pattern recognition.

4 Conclusion

In the paper, a multiple features fusion system for motion recognition is proposed. The feature, RMS-WL-SampEn, obtains the highest recognition rate by the GRNN classifier compared with two time feature (average 87% and 89%). The new sEMG feature is effective and suitable for the sEMG pattern recognition. The results obtained from this experiment represent that the fusion feature can be a better way to increase the accuracy. The accuracy of the motion recognition was significantly improved to 97%, which made the system more robust.

Although the feature extraction of static gestures is studied, there are still many problems to be further discussed. The feature dimension and redundant information can be reduced that will increase the speed of operation. Future research will use more subjects and more dynamic motions for data collection. Therefore, more efforts will be used in ensuring real-time processing for hand motion recognition. The selection of features need to be further studied, and the method used to reduce the dimension needs to be further determined. Finally, we hope to establish a real-time recognition system based on sEMG by optimizing the algorithm.

Acknowledgements. This work was supported by Grants of National Natural Science Foundation of China (Grant Nos. 51575407, 51505349, 51575338, 51575412, 61733011), the Grants of National Defense Pre-Research Foundation of Wuhan University of Science and Technology (GF201705) and Open Fund of the Key Laboratory for Metallurgical Equipment and Control of Ministry of Education in Wuhan University of Science and Technology (2018B07).

References

1. Yang, W., Yang, D., Liu, Y., Liu, H.: A 3-DOF hemi-constrained wrist motion/force detection device for deploying simultaneous myoelectric control. Med. Biol. Eng. Comput. **56**(9), 1669–1681 (2018)
2. Yang, D., Zhao, J., Gu, Y., Jiang, L., Liu, H.: Estimation of hand grasp force based on forearm surface EMG. In: 2009 International Conference on Mechatronics and Automation, Changchun, China, pp. 1795–1799. IEEE (2009)
3. Fang, Y., Zhou, D., Li, K., Ju, Z., Liu, H.: A force-driven granular model for EMG based grasp recognition. In: 2017 IEEE International Conference on Systems, Man, and Cybernetics (SMC), Banff, AB, pp. 2939–2944. IEEE (2017)
4. Yang, D., Zhao, J., Gu, Y., Jiang, L., Liu, H.: EMG pattern recognition and grasping force estimation: improvement to the myocontrol of multi-DOF prosthetic hands. In: 2009 IEEE/RSJ International Conference on Intelligent Robots and Systems, St. Louis, MO, USA, pp. 516–521. IEEE (2009)
5. Li, G.F., Jiang, D., Zhou, Y.L., Jiang, G.Z., Kong, J.Y., Gunasekaran, M.: Human lesion detection method based on image information and brain signal. IEEE Access **7**, 11533–11542 (2019)
6. Sun, Y., et al.: Gesture recognition based on kinect and sEMG signal fusion. Mobile Netw. Appl. **23**(4), 797–805 (2018)
7. Jiang, X., Merhi, L.-K., Xiao, Z.G., Menon, C.: Exploration of force myography and surface electromyography in hand gesture classification. Med. Eng. Phys. **41**, 63–73 (2017)

8. Koiva, R., Hilsenbeck, B., Castellini, C.: Evaluating subsampling strategies for sEMG-based prediction of voluntary muscle contractions. In: 2013 IEEE 13th International Conference on Rehabilitation Robotics (ICORR), Seattle, WA, USA, pp. 1–7. IEEE (2013)

9. Cheng, W.T., Sun, Y., Li, G.F., Jiang, G.Z., Liu, H.H.: Jointly network: a network based on CNN and RBM for gesture recognition. Neural Comput. Appl. **31**(Suppl. 1), 309–323 (2018)

10. Liao, Y., et al.: Simultaneous calibration: a joint optimization approach for multiple kinect and external cameras. Sensors **17**(7), 1491 (2017)

11. Nielsen, J.L.G., Holmgaard, S., Jiang, N., Englehart, K.B., Farina, D., Parker, P.A.: Simultaneous and proportional force estimation for multifunction myoelectric prostheses using mirrored bilateral training. IEEE Trans. Biomed. Eng. **58**(3), 681–688 (2011)

12. Phinyomark, A., Scheme, E.: EMG pattern recognition in the era of big data and deep learning. Big Data Cogn. Comput. **2**(3), 21 (2018)

13. Triolo, R.J., Moskowitz, G.D.: The theoretical development of a multichannel time-series myoprocessor for simultaneous limb function detection and muscle force estimation. IEEE Trans. Biomed. Eng. **36**(10), 1004–1017 (1989)

14. Wu, J., Sun, L., Jafari, R.: A wearable system for recognizing american sign language in real-time using IMU and surface EMG sensors. IEEE J. Biomed. Health Inform. **20**(5), 1281–1290 (2016)

Classification Methods of sEMG Through Weighted Representation-Based K-Nearest Neighbor

Shuai Pan, Jing Jie$^{(\boxtimes)}$, Kairui Liu, Jinrong Li, and Hui Zheng

Zhejiang University of Science and Technology,
Liuhe Road 318#, Hangzhou 310023, Zhejiang, China
Jingjie@zust.edu.cn

Abstract. As a valuable bio-electrical signal, surface electromyography (sEMG) can be adopted to predict the user's motion gestures in human-machine interaction, but its validity severely depends on the accuracy of patterns recognition. In order to improve the recognition accuracy, the paper introduced a weighted representation-based k-nearest neighbor (WRKNN) to classify different hand motion patterns based on the forearm sEMG signals. All the signals were collected from 8 able-bodied volunteers through a sEMG acquisition system with 16 channels, and the root mean square (RMS) feature with the window size of 300 ms and the window shift of 100 ms were used to acquire the feature data. Based on the average classification accuracy and the standard deviation, the proposed algorithm and its improved version (weighted local mean representation-based k-nearest neighbor, WLMRKNN) were compared with k-nearest neighbor (KNN) and BP neural network. The experimental results show that WRKNN and WLMRKNN are superior to KNN and BP network with the best classification accuracy, and can be widely applied in the pattern recognition of sEMG in future.

Keywords: sEMG · Pattern recognition · Classification · K-nearest neighbor

1 Introduction

Recently, many researchers have investigated sEMG in various fields as sEMG has several advantages. Firstly, sEMG signals are collected non-invasively by simply placing electrodes on the skin surface of the subjects' forearm. This method has low cost and no damage to human body [1]. Secondly, sEMG signals are the electrical manifestations of the human brain's intentions. Ding, et al. [2] points out that the sEMG can predict the intention of the motion because sEMG is ahead of the actual motion. sEMG also contains abundant information such as muscle force, joint torque, joint moment, etc., so it is more acceptable for users to use simple and convenient human-computer interaction mode based on brain control. Finally, sEMG signals can be used with a variety of other bio-electrical signals to make gesture classification more accurate, such as sonomyography (SMG), electroencephalography (EEG), electroneurography (ENG) and so on [1]. Wu, et al. [3] proposed a new strategy of fusing EEG and sEMG to control multi-degree of freedom prosthetic hand. The average

© Springer Nature Switzerland AG 2019
H. Yu et al. (Eds.): ICIRA 2019, LNAI 11743, pp. 456–466, 2019.
https://doi.org/10.1007/978-3-030-27538-9_39

classification accuracy of 10 subjects was over 98.33%. Although they reached a high accuracy, the control method was not based on human brain's intentions.

With the development of technology, there are some commercial prosthetic hand which can improve disabled people's quality of life, such as I-limb. In the latest product, I-limb introduced a muscle control method which used specific muscle signals as triggers. However, it is suitable only for advanced users who can operate open/closing gestures comfortably and consistently, and there are only few gestures can be discriminated. As we known, high classification accuracy, robustness and rapidity are essential for the sEMG-based pattern recognition systems in real-time control and rehabilitation applications. In order to increase the accuracy of pattern recognition, researchers have done a lot of work in three aspects. In the data acquisition aspect, Fang, et al. [4, 5] proposed a novel electrodes configuration to reduce the influence of electrodes shift and used several filters to make the sEMG signals cleaner, including low pass filter, band pass filter and notch filter. In the feature extraction aspect, features are divided into three groups, including time domain, frequency domain, and time and frequency domain features. The most common features are root mean square (RMS), median frequency (MDF) and wavelet transform coefficients (WTC), respectively. However, in addition to the three features mentioned above, there are numerous features which can improve classification accuracy such as waveform length (WL), autoregressive coefficients (AR), sample entropy (SampEN) [6], peak frequency (PKF), etc. In order to explore an appropriate feature vector or optimal feature combination. Phinyomark, et al., Reference [7] evaluated thirty-seven features in space which aims to avoid the usage of redundant features. In reference [8], the authors compared the possible combinations of 2, 3 and 4 out of 50 features in order to find the best feature combination which can obtain the highest classification accuracy with LDA classifier. In reference [9], features were investigated for different time window sizes and noise levels.

Last aspect is about the classifiers, there are various types of classifiers, such as k-nearest neighbor (KNN) [10], support vector machine (SVM), artificial neural network (ANN), Naïve Bayes (NB), linear discriminant analysis (LDA), and so on. In reference [11], the authors compared three classifiers including KNN, QDA and LDA. The results show that KNN is better than QDA and LDA. In reference [12], the authors used variable learning rate based neural network and reached the best average accuracy of 95% in real control experiment. Although there are several works compared different classifiers, there are few classifiers can be applied in clinical or industrial applications. KNN and LDA are able to calculate fast, but their classification accuracy is not well enough to reach the application level, while neural network or SVM algorithm can achieve high classification accuracy, but they require huge computational costs. In order to be applied in clinical or industrial environments, classification algorithms need to possess some necessary characteristics, such as high classification accuracy, strong robustness and rapidity. So, in this study, we introduce two new classification algorithm to deal with sEMG signals first, including a weighted representation-based k-nearest neighbor (WRKNN) and its improved version called weighted local mean representation-based k-nearest neighbor (WLMRKNN) [13]. In the two classifiers, the categorical representation-based distance is taken as the classification decision, and the test samples are classified into the class with the minimum representation-based distance. The introduced classification algorithms not only have the best average accuracy and the smallest standard deviation, but also have fast computing speeds similar to linear learning algorithm. It proves that WRKNN and WLMRKNN are valid classification methods and can be used widely in sEMG applications like real-time control, rehabilitation training and clinical medicine in the future.

The remainder of the paper is organized as follows. Section 2 describes the methodology about the subjects, sEMG data acquisition and classification algorithms in this study. Section 3 presents the experiment set, results and the discussion. Finally, Sect. 4 provides the conclusions and future works.

2   Methodology

In this section, the subjects and data acquisition, including sEMG collecting device and collecting process, are first introduced, then the WRKNN and WLMRKNN algorithms are reviewed in details.

2.1   Subjects

8 normal volunteers between the ages of 23 and 29 (7 males and 1 female) participated in this study. Each volunteer was informed well before the experiment and consented to participate in this study.

All the volunteers were asked to complete 5 gestures, including hand close (HC), hand open (HO), wrist side flexion (WSF), wrist extension (WE) and wrist flexion (WF) in a trial, as depicted in Fig. 1. Each gesture was required to maintain more than 12 s in order to obtain 10 s stable sEMG data. There is about a 10 s break between each gesture, so each trial contains 110 s sEMG data in total. In order to avoid the influence of electrode shift, all the volunteers are asked to continuously test and record sEMG data 3 times under the same sleeve wearing position. For 8 volunteers, a total of 24 data sets were collected, each data set contains 5 gestures and each gesture contains 10 s stable data which was regarded as the effective gesture signal. In other words, the effective gesture signal data used in each trial is the 50 s, and the total effective gesture signal is 1200 s.

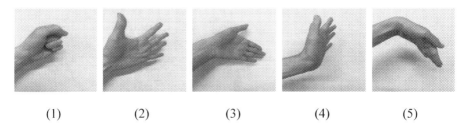

(1)   (2)   (3)   (4)   (5)

Fig. 1. Pictures of five gestures. 1 Hand close, 2 Hand open, 3 Wrist side flexion, 4 Wrist extension and 5 Wrist flexion

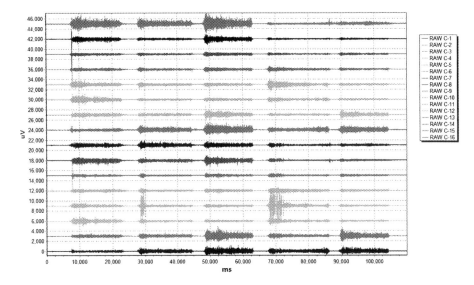

Fig. 2. 16-channel sEMG signals

2.2 Data Acquisition

In this study, the ELONXI EMG 100-Ch-Y-RA acquisition device and a EMG sleeve are used to collect sEMG signals (The EMG acquisition device and the EMG sleeve were from Hangzhou Elonxi Technology Co. Ltd). A total of 18 dry electrodes are used in the EMG sleeve, each electrode is modified from standard disposable Ag/AgCl ECG electrodes, which is widely used for EMG signal collection. 16 of the 18 dry electrodes are used to collect sEMG signals from each participant's forearm, another two dry electrodes are reference and bias electrodes, respectively. The example of 16-channel sEMG signals is shown in Fig. 2, and from left to right, the gestures represented by signal waving section are followed by hand close, hand open, wrist side flexion, wrist extension and wrist flexion. A novel sEMG electrodes array using improved bipolar montage was used in EMG sleeve, more details can be found in reference [5]. The raw sEMG signals are filtered through a low pass filter, a band pass filter of 20 Hz to 500 Hz and a notch filter of 50 Hz, because most of the effective frequencies of sEMG signals are between 20 Hz and 500 Hz, and 50 Hz power line noise is the main contamination source. According to Shannon sampling theorem, the sampling frequency is set to 1000 Hz.

2.3 Classification Algorithms

WRKNN and WLMRKNN classification algorithms are both proposed in reference [13]. Based on UCI and UCR data sets and the face databases, the authors compared them with LMKNN (local mean-based k-nearest neighbor) [14], MLMNN (multi-local means-based nearest neighbor) and so on. Results showed that WRKNN performs best in the face databases and WLMRKNN performs best in the UCI and UCR data sets, but both of them are superior to the other competing classifiers. So, we introduced WRKNN and WLMRKNN into the classification of sEMG, and try to improve the recognition accuracy. The two classification algorithms are reviewed in details below.

Weighted Representation-Based K-Nearest Neighbor (WRKNN). WRKNN is a weighted extension of the LMKNN [14]. The main idea of WRKNN is as follows. Firstly, choose k nearest neighbors of test sample y from each class j by using Euclidean distance, it is calculated by

$$d(y, x_i^j) = \sqrt{(y - x_i^j)^T (y - x_i^j)} \tag{1}$$

where x_i^j indicates the ith training sample from class j and denotes the k-nearest neighbor as $X_{kN}^j = [x_{1N}^j, x_{2N}^j, \cdots, x_{kN}^j]$. Secondly, represent the test sample y as the linear combination of categorical k nearest neighbors which can be defined as

$$y = x_{1N}^j \eta_1^j + x_{2N}^j \eta_2^j + \cdots + x_{kN}^j \eta_k^j = X_{kN}^j \eta^j \tag{2}$$

where η_i^j indicates the ith coefficient of ith nearest neighbor from class j. Thirdly, solve the optimal representation coefficient η^{j*} which can be defined as

$$\eta^{j*} = \arg \min_{s^j} \left\{ \left\| y - X_{kN}^j \eta^j \right\|_2^2 + \lambda \left\| T^j \eta^j \right\|_2^2 \right\} \tag{3}$$

$$= \left((X_{kN}^j)^T X_{kN}^j + \lambda (T^j)^T T^j \right)^{-1} (X_{kN}^j)^T y \tag{4}$$

Where λ is the regularization coefficient, T^j is the distance matrix between test sample and each nearest neighbor, W^j is defined as

$$T^j = \left\{ \begin{matrix} \left\| y - x_{1N}^j \right\|_2 & & 0 \\ & \ddots & \\ 0 & & \left\| y - x_{kN}^j \right\|_2 \end{matrix} \right\} \tag{5}$$

Then calculate the categorical representation-based distance between the test sample and k-local mean vectors in class j as

$$r_k^j(y) = \left\| y - X_{kN}^j \eta^{j*} \right\|_2^2 \tag{6}$$

Finally, classify the test sample y into the class with the minimum categorical representation-based distance among all the classes, the definition can be expressed as

$$l_y = \arg \min_{l_j} \left(r_k^j(y) \right), j = 1, 2, \ldots, C \tag{7}$$

Weighted Local Mean Representation-Based K-Nearest Neighbor (WLMRKNN).
WLMRKNN is a weighted extension of the MLMNN [15] and can be regarded as an
improved one of WRKNN. The main difference between WLMRKNN and WRKNN is
that WLMRKNN uses k local mean vectors to represent the test sample $\mathbf{y}$, while
WRKNN uses k nearest neighbors to represent the test sample $\mathbf{y}$. The main idea of
WLMRKNN is as follows. Firstly, choose k-nearest neighbors of test sample $\mathbf{y}$ from
each class j by using Euclidean distance, it is calculated by

$$d\left(\mathbf{y}, x_i^j\right) = \sqrt{\left(y - x_i^j\right)^T \left(y - x_i^j\right)} \tag{8}$$

where x_i^j indicates the ith training sample from class j and denotes the k nearest
neighbors as $X_{kN}^j = \left[x_{1N}^j, x_{2N}^j, \cdots, x_{kN}^j\right]$. Secondly, calculate categorical k local mean
vectors of k nearest neighbors from each class which can be expressed as

$$\bar{x}_{iN}^j = \frac{1}{i} \sum\nolimits_{h=1}^i x_{hN}^j (\mathrm{i} = 1, 2 \cdots, k) \tag{9}$$

where $\bar{x}_{iN}^j$ indicates the ith local mean vector from class j, and represent the test sample
$\mathbf{y}$ as the linear combination of categorical k local mean vectors which can be defined as

$$y = \bar{x}_{1N}^j s_1^j + \bar{x}_{2N}^j s_2^j + \cdots + \bar{x}_{kN}^j s_k^j = \bar{X}_{kN}^j s^j \tag{10}$$

where s_i^j indicates the ith coefficient of ith local mean vector from class j. Thirdly, solve
the optimal representation coefficient s^{j*} which can be defined as

$$s^{j*} = \arg\min_{s^j}\left\{\left\|y - \bar{X}_{kN}^j s^j\right\|_2^2 + \gamma\left\|W^j s^j\right\|_2^2\right\} \tag{11}$$

$$= \left(\left(\bar{X}_{kN}^j\right)^T \bar{X}_{kN}^j + \gamma\left(W^j\right)^T W^j\right)^{-1} \left(\bar{X}_{kN}^j\right)^T y \tag{12}$$

where γ is the regularization coefficient, W^j is the distance matrix between test sample
and each local mean vector, W^j is defined as

$$W^j = \left\{ \begin{array}{ccc} \left\|y - \bar{x}_{1N}^j\right\|_2 & & 0 \\ & \ddots & \\ 0 & & \left\|y - \bar{x}_{kN}^j\right\|_2 \end{array} \right\} \tag{13}$$

Then calculate the categorical representation-based distance between the test sample
and k-local mean vectors in class j as

$$\bar{r}_k^j(y) = \left\|y - \bar{X}_{kN}^j s^{j*}\right\|_2^2 \tag{14}$$

Finally, classify the test sample y into the class with the minimum categorical representation-based distance among all the classes, the definition can be expressed as

$$l_y = \arg\min_{l_j} \left(\bar{r}_k^j(y) \right), j = 1, 2, \ldots, C \tag{15}$$

3   Experiments and Discussions

3.1   Experiment Set

In the paper, WRKNN and WLMRKNN are applied to solve the pattern recognition of sEMG. Their performance are compared with KNN and two kinds of BP neural networks from the reference [16] (Here, noted as BP neural network1 and BP neural network2). Among those algorithms, KNN, WRKNN and WLMRKNN, were analyzed under the MATLAB-2017b platform, while the other two neural networks, BP neural network1 and BP neural network2 were analyzed under the ANACONDA-PYTHON-3.5 platform.

In terms of feature extraction, since RMS is the most representative time-domain feature with many advantages such as large information and quick calculation efficiency, this paper takes RMS feature as the evaluation criteria for the above classification algorithms. The window size and the window shift of RMS feature are 300 ms and 100 ms, respectively. In terms of parameter selection, k value used by KNN and WRKNN is 5 and k value used by WLMRKNN is 4. The super-parameters used in BP neural network1 are 0.5 for learning rate, 1 for mini-batch size, 30 for the number of iterations and 30 for the number of hidden layer neurons. The super-parameters used in BP neural network2 are 0.3 for learning rate, 0.001 for regularization coefficient, 10 for mini-batch size, 40 for the number of iterations and 100 for the number of hidden layer neurons. All parameters are obtained after several times of debugging and comparison, with high overall performance and high repeatable rate of target accuracy.

3.2   Results and Discussions

The classification accuracy of five classification algorithm for the same individual with different data sets is shown in Table 1. The first column of Table 1 indicates that the first data set of each individual is regarded as the training set, the other two data sets are regarded as the test set, and the first data set is classified with the other two data sets respectively. The generalization performance of each classification algorithm can be reflected by using different data sets better than by using k-fold cross-validation method because each individual's state is different when collecting each data set, including muscle force, forearm fatigue, the slight deviation of electrode position after doing different gestures, and the psychological state.

For each training set and test set, the best classification accuracy among the five classification algorithms is emphasized in Table 1 using bold and italic forms.

Table 1. Classification accuracy of five classification algorithms for the same individual with different data sets

Training data \test data	Classification algorithms				
	KNN	BP neural network1	BP neural network2	WLMRKNN	WRKNN
CYB1\CYB2	81.58%	95.04%	96.24%	*100.00%*	*100.00%*
CYB1\CYB3	60.59%	87.52%	89.50%	*100.00%*	*100.00%*
CYX1\CYX2	43.96%	95.04%	96.03%	*99.01%*	98.42%
CYX1\CYX3	79.21%	*98.81%*	97.42%	77.03%	77.82%
SK1\SK2	80.00%	79.40%	80.00%	93.66%	*98.45%*
SK1\SK3	98.42%	93.66%	89.90%	*99.60%*	*99.60%*
TP1\TP2	69.50%	60.39%	64.55%	77.62%	*78.61%*
TP1\TP3	78.42%	72.27%	72.27%	79.60%	*79.80%*
YJX1\YJX2	99.60%	*100.00%*	*100.00%*	*100.00%*	*100.00%*
YJX1\YJX3	*100.00%*	*100.00%*	*100.00%*	96.24%	97.23%
YKJ1\YKJ2	79.60%	96.23%	92.67%	*97.43%*	95.64%
YKJ1\YKJ3	82.18%	*100.00%*	98.21%	98.22%	97.43%
ZJN1\ZJN2	89.11%	85.14%	88.11%	98.02%	98.61%
ZJN1\ZJN3	81.98%	*99.40%*	94.45%	84.55%	85.94%
CHF1\CHF2	87.13%	98.81%	98.81%	*100.00%*	*100.00%*
CHF1\CHF3	96.04%	99.00%	*99.40%*	98.42%	98.61%

From Table 1, it can be clearly found that WRKNN classification algorithm obtains the best classification performance, showing the best classification accuracy in 9 training sets and test sets, accounting for 56.25% of the total 16 training sets and test sets. The times with the best classification accuracy for the other four classification algorithms, KNN, WLMRKNN, BP neural network1, BP neural network2 are 1, 7, 5, 3, accounting for 6.25%, 43.75%, 31.25% and 18.75% of the total, respectively. it can be found that the percentage of times that WRKNN obtains the best classification accuracy is 12.5% higher than the second one. it is worth noting that the sum of the percentage of times that the 5 classification algorithms show the best classification accuracy is not 100%. Because when the accuracy reaches 100%, the accuracy cannot be further improved. Therefore, when two or more classification algorithms show the classification accuracy of 100%, it is considered that these algorithms all show the best classification accuracy. In addition, to reflect the excellent classification performance of WRKNN more intuitively, the classification accuracy of five classification algorithms for the same individual with different data sets is shown in Fig. 3 with a line chart.

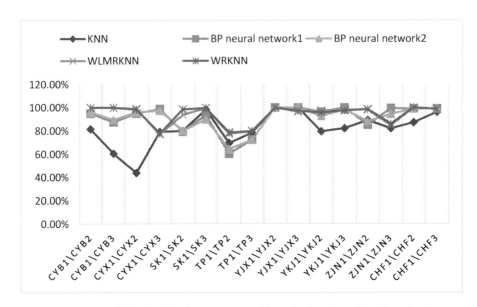

Fig. 3. Line chart of the classification accuracy of five classification algorithms for the same individual with different data sets

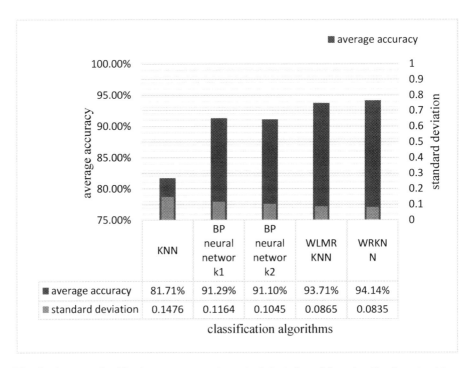

Fig. 4. Average classification accuracy and standard deviation of five classification algorithms

Figure 4 shows the average classification accuracy and standard deviation of five classification algorithms for a total of 16 training sets and test sets from 8 volunteers. In Fig. 4, it can be clearly found that WRKNN obtains the highest average classification accuracy of 94.14%, which is 0.43% higher than WLMRKNN with the second classification accuracy of 93.71%, and 12.43% higher than KNN with 81.71% average classification accuracy. WRKNN classification algorithm not only obtains the best average classification accuracy of 94.14%, but also obtains the best deviation of 0.0835, which shows that WRKNN classification algorithm has the best classification robustness.

4 Conclusions

This paper introduced new classification algorithms called WRKNN and WLMRKNN to classify the motion patterns of sEMG, and compared them with other classification algorithms such as KNN and BP neural network. The results show that WRKNN is the best classification algorithm with the best classification performance and robustness because it obtains the highest average classification accuracy of 94.14% and the lowest classification deviation of 0.0835. It is confirmed that WRKNN can be widely used in real-time control, rehabilitation training, clinical medicine applications. In the future research, we will do in-depth research on the practical application of electrode shift and environmental noise in order to obtain better classification algorithms and feature combinations.

References

1. Fang, Y., Hettiarachchi, N., Zhou, D., et al.: Multi-modal sensing techniques for interfacing hand prostheses: a review. IEEE Sens. J. **15**(11), 6065–6076 (2016)
2. Ding, Q.-C., Xiong, A.-B., Zhao, X.-G., Han, J.-D.: A review on researches and applications of sEMG-based motion intent recognition methods. Acta Automatica Sinica **42**(1), 13–25 (2016). (in Chinese)
3. Wu, C.-C., Xiong, P.-W., Zeng, H., Xu, B.-G., Song, A.-G.: A control strategy for prosthetic hand based on EEG and sEMG. Acta Automatica Sinica **44**(4), 676–684 (2018). (in Chinese)
4. Fang, Y., Liu, H.: Robust sEMG electrodes configuration for pattern recognition based prosthesis control. In: 2014 IEEE International Conference on Systems, Man, and Cybernetics (SMC), San Diego, CA, USA, pp. 2210–2215. IEEE (2014)
5. Fang, Y., Zhu, X., Liu, H.: Development of a surface EMG acquisition system with novel electrodes configuration and signal representation. In: Lee, J., Lee, M.C., Liu, H., Ryu, J.-H. (eds.) ICIRA 2013. LNCS (LNAI), vol. 8102, pp. 405–414. Springer, Heidelberg (2013). https://doi.org/10.1007/978-3-642-40852-6_41
6. Richman, J.S., Randall, M.J.: Physiological time-series analysis, using approximate entropy and sample entropy. Am. J. Physiol. Heart Circulatory Physiol. **278**(6), H2039–H2049 (2000)
7. Phinyomark, A., Phukpattaranont, P., Limsakul, C.: Feature reduction and selection for EMG signal classification. Expert Syst. Appl. **39**(8), 7420–7431 (2012)

8. Phinyomark, A., Quaine, F., Charbonnier, S., Serviere, C., Tarpin-Bernard, F., Laurillau, Y.: EMG feature evaluation for improving myoelectric pattern recognition robustness. Expert Syst. Appl. **40**(12), 4832–4840 (2013)

9. Zardoshtikermani, M., Wheeler, B.C., Badie, K., et al.: EMG feature evaluation for movement control of upper extremity prostheses. IEEE Trans. Rehabil. Eng. **3**(4), 324–333 (1995)

10. Cover, T.M., Hart, P.E.: Nearest neighbor pattern classification. IEEE Trans. Inf. Theory **13**(1), 21–27 (1967)

11. Kim, K.S., Choi, H.H., Moon, C.S., et al.: Comparison of k-nearest neighbor, quadratic discriminant and linear discriminant analysis in classification of electromyogram signals based on the wrist-motion directions. Curr. Appl. Phys. **11**(3), 740–745 (2011)

12. Zhao, J., Xie, Z., Jiang, L., et al.: EMG control for a five-fingered underactuated prosthetic hand based on wavelet transform and sample entropy. In: 2006 IEEE/RSJ International Conference on Intelligent Robots and Systems, Beijing, China, pp. 3215–3220. IEEE (2006)

13. Gou, J., et al.: Locality constrained representation-based K-nearest neighbor classification. Knowl.-Based Syst. **167**, 38–52 (2019)

14. Mitani, Y., Hamamoto, Y.: A local mean-based nonparametric classifier. Pattern Recogn. Lett. **27**(10), 1151–1159 (2006)

15. Gou, J., et al.: A multi-local means based nearest neighbor classifier. In: IEEE International Conference on Tools with Artificial Intelligence, Boston, MA, USA, pp. 448–452. IEEE Computer Society (2017)

16. Goodfellow, I., Bengio, Y., Courville, A.: Deep Learning. MIT Press, Cambridge (2016)

A Soft Capacitive Wearable Sensing System for Lower-Limb Motion Monitoring

Xingxing Ma[1], Jiajie Guo[1(✉)], Kok-Meng Lee[1,2], Luye Yang[1], and Minghui Chen[1]

[1] The State Key Laboratory of Digital Manufacturing Equipment and Technology, School of Mechanical Science and Engineering, Huazhong University of Science and Technology, Wuhan 430074, China
jiajie.guo@hust.edu.cn
[2] George W. Woodruff School of Mechanical Engineering, Georgia Institute of Technology, Atlanta, GA 30332, USA

Abstract. Human limb motion monitoring has been a challenging task for robotic applications in unstructured environments, because traditional sensing methods are limited in conforming to compliant human bodies and adapting to unpredictable external disturbances. Motivated by the need to capture rotation angles of lower-limb joints in real time, this paper proposes a soft wearable sensing system based on a network of soft capacitive sensors that can be stretched with joint bending. The capacitance of the sensing module changes with the sensor deformations thus its deviated value from the initial installation state is closely related to the joint rotation angle. The sensor fabrication is developed with shape deposition molding, and the sensing electronics are designed to improve signal transmission and sensing robustness. The sensing system is calibrated with machine vision and its performance is evaluated in walking tests with different speeds. An illustrative example is presented to verify the proposed method capable to monitor human lower-limb motions in practice.

Keywords: Lower-limb motion measurement · Soft Strain Sensor · Wearable robotics · Sensor network · Capacitive sensing

1 Introduction

Robotic assistive devices (like prostheses and exoskeletons) play an increasingly important role in improving human life quality as well as our understanding of human natural motions. It is convenient to capture human motions by the optical tracking of passive retroreflective or active markers on targeted anatomical landmarks [1]. Though visual methods, like Vicon, can ensure high precisions and reliability of measurements, it is time-consuming, expense-costly and often limited to static and controlled environments. At the same time, optical motion capture systems usually require tedious post-processing and kinematic model development in addition to marker occlusion issues. Kinect systems, utilizing depth images, are user friendly with reduced deploying cost as compared to their earlier approaches [2, 3], but are also impractical for applications involving exoskeletons or prostheses. On the other hand, these optical

© Springer Nature Switzerland AG 2019
H. Yu et al. (Eds.): ICIRA 2019, LNAI 11743, pp. 467–479, 2019.
https://doi.org/10.1007/978-3-030-27538-9_40

instruments exhibit limited performances in outdoor environments. Recently, Ultra-sound imaging systems have also been successfully used to estimate human lower-limb movements; however, because of the slow processing rate of 3 to 6 frames per second (FPS), they generally have difficulties in meeting real-time requirements [4]. Inertial sensing provides a cost-effective alternative to optical technologies in practice [5], where inertial measurement units (IMUs) attached to a human body collect acceleration and orientation data during motions. For example, measurements from a single leg-worn IMU were incorporated to monitor human locomotion activities [6]. However, inertial sensing suffers from sensor noises and data drifts that usually require for signal filtering [7] and sensor fusion [8].

Soft sensors, seamlessly conforming to musculoskeletal structures and soft tissues via large deformations, are competent for human motion sensing with merits of wearable, adaptable and robust properties [9]. They provide wearable devices with intimate and comfortable human-machine interfaces without seriously interfering human natural movements [10, 11]. There have been many emerging prototypes for various applications, including the soft sensing glove for virtual reality [12], the stretchable sensor for measuring elbow flexion rotation [11], the soft exosuits for assisting motions of upper-limbs [13] and lower-limbs [10, 14]. While soft resistive sensors response to applied strain with the changing resistance [10, 14], they suffer from several disadvantages such as electrical resistivity changes due to particle network disruption at large strains [15, 16], fluid content variation with evaporation or hygro-scopic effects when used in resistive-based sensing motifs [16–18]. To overcome these limitations, capacitive sensors provide an alternative approach where a dielectric layer sandwiched between two conductive electrodes changes its thickness in response to an applied deformation [19, 20].

Motivated by the need to capture rotation angles of lower-limb joints in real time, this paper proposes a soft wearable sensing system based on a network of soft capacitive sensors that can be stretched with joint bending. The wearable system is featured with simple fabrication of soft capacitive sensors, adaptability to natural motions with acceptable sensing accuracy, and expandability via the CAN-bus communication protocol. The rest of the paper is organized with the system design of soft sensing module and electronic components, experimental results of sensor calibration and system verification, and evaluation analysis of sensing performance.

2   System Description

Figure 1 shows the capacitive wearable sensing system comprised of two components, namely the capacitive sensing module with stretchable capability to adapt to lower-limb motions and the electronic component to process and transmit measured data. Six soft capacitive sensors are attached on the surface of tights with nylon hook-and-loop fasteners at each lower-limb joint as described in the following:

- two sensors for hip joint angles dorsally placed on each gluteus;
- two sensors for knee joint angles frontally placed on each thigh with inextensible webbing routed across the knees to the shins;
- two sensors for ankle joint angles attached to the heels.

The hook-and-loop fasteners were cut into a rectangular shape and sewn to the desired positions on the running tights. Since nylon distinguishes itself with a much higher elastic modulus (about 4GPa) than that of the sensor material (80 kPa for Ecoflex 00-30), it is guaranteed that strains of joint bending are transformed and captured by elongation of the stretchable capacitive sensors.

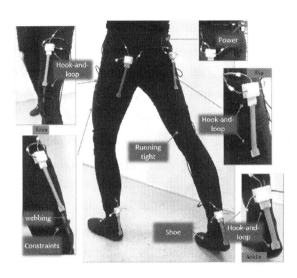

Fig. 1. The wearable sensing system for lower-limb motion monitoring.

2.1 Soft Sensing Module

With the design concept of a capacitance varies with an elongation strain, the sensing module is developed as a soft parallel capacitor with the stretchable capability. The change of capacitance ΔC can be determined as a function of the rotated joint angle $\Delta\theta$ as follows

$$\Delta C = \varepsilon_o \varepsilon_r \frac{w}{d} l(\Delta\theta) \tag{1}$$

where ε_0 is the dielectric constant of the air, ε_r is the relative dielectric constant of the dielectric layer, w and d are the width and distance between the parallel capacitor electrodes, respectively, and l is the electrode length dependent on the rotated joint angle $\Delta\theta$. While the above relation provides physical insights between ΔC and $\Delta\theta$, it will be calibrated in experiment.

Figure 2 illustrates the fabrication process of a sensing module using shape deposition molding (SDM) and the prototype dimensions are 12 mm wide, 90 mm long and 3 mm thick. The deformable structure of the sensing module was made by Ecoflex 00-30 and the capacitor electrode plates were made from liquid metal. In Fig. 2 (a), the Ecoflex-A and Ecoflex-B solutions were mixed in equal proportions and poured into the empty cavity formed by the base mold 1 and mold 2. Then, the base layer of the sensing module was demolded after 4 h curing. As shown in Fig. 2(b), a spraying system printed an electrode plate with EGaIn droplets on the base layer groove, and a thin copper sheet 3 was attached to the base layer to secure a rigid connection between the electrode and copper wire. Thereafter in Fig. 2(c), the base layer mold 1 and the second layer mold 4 were enclosed to create a cavity for forming the dielectric layer, after which the same procedure as Fig. 2(b) was repeated to print the second electrode plate with EGaIn (Fig. 2d). When all electrode plates were fabricated, the sealing layer was cured within the cavity formed by the mold 5 and the base mold 1 as shown in Fig. 2(e). Finally, the clamping ends, cast with PU8400 solution using the molds 6 and 7 (Fig. 2f), were fastened to the hoop-and-loop.

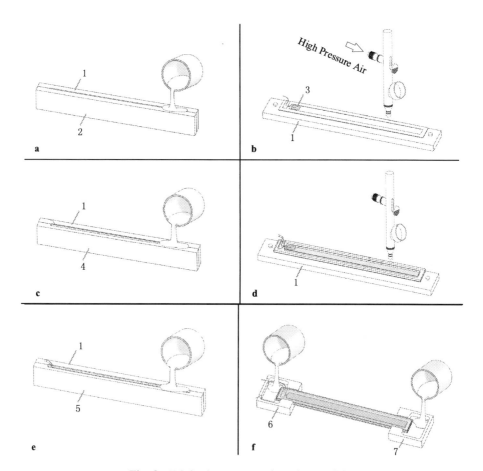

Fig. 2. Fabrication process of sensing module.

2.2 Electronic Components

It is desired that the data-acquisition system is capable of multi-channel signal-transmission for the sensor network (Fig. 1) and is fast enough to capture dynamic characteristics of human lower-limb motions. Because capacitance tends to change under environmental disturbances, robustness to external noises is also expected for the capacitive sensing system.

For the above reasons, a schematic of the data-acquisition system is proposed as shown in Fig. 3, where the controller area network (CAN) bus connects each soft capacitive sensor and the main circuit in serial, for the ease of sensor installation and device communication without a host computer. Within each soft sensor, the sensing circuit collects analog capacitance signals and convert them to digital angle data before they are sent to the main process circuit via the CAN bus cable. In this way, the measured results would not be seriously affected by the capacitance of long wires as well as external disturbances. The main circuit serves as a hub for measured data from sensors, where the UART and bluetooth modules provide wired and wireless options to transmit data to a distant server or hand-held device. This protocol is based on messages that are recognized by specific identification bits within every data package. Its transmission speed of 1 Mbit/s in theory is fast enough to support for maximum 126 sensors when data are collected at 8Kbit/s. The electronics in the soft sensor is powered either by a 3.6 V lithium battery or through a power line along with the CAN bus cable.

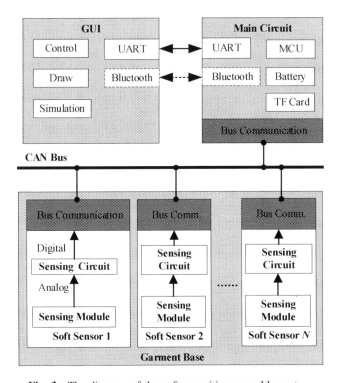

Fig. 3. The diagram of the soft capacitive wearable system.

Figure 4 illustrates connection details between the sensing module and sensing circuit within the soft sensor. Two copper wires individually connecting to the capacitor electrodes (described in Fig. 2) come out from one clamping end of the soft sensor, and they are soldered to the input pins of a 24-Bit capacitance-to-digital converter (Analog AD7746) on the STM32-based sensing circuit. The circuit is designed in a compact size (23 mm × 28 mm × 1.6 mm) to be housed in a fixation box fastened to a hook-and-loop on the running tights. Specifications of the converter AD7746 are listed in Table 1, where the sampling rate between 10 and 90 Hz is appropriate for general human-body motions, and the sensing range (−4–4 pF) can be expanded by connecting a constant capacitor in serial. The AD7746 converter transforms the analog measured signal into digital data, and the on-board STM32 handles the data transmission to the main circuit. Besides, other ports on the sensing circuit are designed for the CAN communication, powering and noise reduction. With the stray capacitance due to mutual influence among the soft sensors and electronic components nearby, the capacitive sensing could be contaminated with environmental noises. However, it is found in practice that the signal-to-noise ratio is substantially increased by connecting the ground pins of all sensing circuits with the human body. In this way, the human subject was requested to wear a metal ring as the common ground in this work. It is probably because the stray effects on the wearable capacitive sensors are attenuated by introducing the human body as the reference ground.

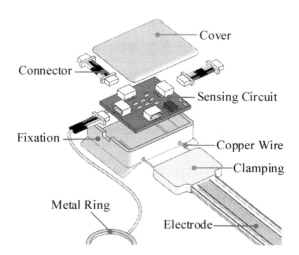

Fig. 4. Installation of sensing circuit.

Table 1. Specifications of Analog AD7746.

Resolution (aF)	4	Sampling rate (Hz)	10 to 90
Accuracy (fF)	4	Voltage (V)	2.7 to 5
Linearity (%)	0.01%	Current (mA)	0.7
Range of measured capacitance (pF)			−4–4 pF

2.3   Graphical User Interface (GUI)

To qualitatively verify the measured results and real-time monitor human lower-limb motions in practice, the simulation platform has been developed (Fig. 5) as a graphical user interface (GUI) in Windows operating system with C# programming. Eight input channels are available for signal processing and gait analysis. To simulate natural human motions with the measured data, a human musculoskeletal model is built in the three-dimensional space with Unity, where its limb motions are characterized by rotation angles of joints connecting 55 bones.

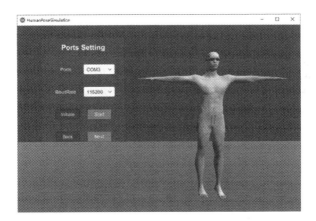

Fig. 5. Simulation platform.

3   Experimental Validation

The proposed wearable sensing system has been experimentally evaluated with machine vision in walking tests. Two experiments were conducted as follows:

(1) The theoretical sensing model (1) is calibrated with the capacitances measured from the wearable sensing system and the joint rotation angles obtained with the Vicon motion capture system.

(2) An illustrative example is presented to verify the calibrated sensing model by simulating human walking motions with the measured joint rotation angles in real time with different human subjects.

In the above experiments, the participants were required to stand upright for 20 s after putting on the sensing system to record the initial capacitances that represent the installation states of each soft sensors. In this way, the capacitance change ΔC in (1) is calculated from the measured data subtracted by the initial values averaged over the standing time. Each of the walking tests lasted for 2 min.

There were six infrared cameras utilized in the optical motion capture system, where 16 markers were attached to the subject lower limbs based on the modified Cleveland Clinic marker set. As shown in Fig. 6, the markers were placed on the anatomical landmarks, namely the bilateral anterior superior iliac spines, bilateral apex of iliac crests, dorsal aspect at the L5-sacral interface, lateral calcaneal tuberosities and the superior aspect of the first and fifth metatarsophalangeal joints. The triad marker clusters were placed on the femoral and tibiae.

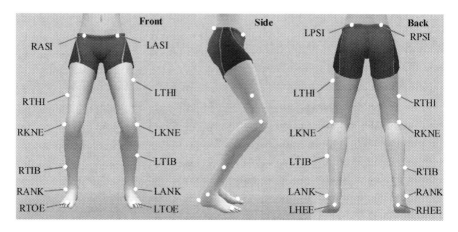

Fig. 6. Positions of Markers.

3.1 Sensor Calibration with Walking

The walking tests for the sensor calibration were performed on a treadmill at the speed of 4 km/h. Because the vision sampling rate of 100 Hz was different from that of the capacitive sensing system (90 Hz), pulse signals was intrigued to coordinate the start and end of data collection in both systems. As shown in Fig. 7 where the right hip data were employed for example, the raw signals from the soft sensor and motion capture system were collected simultaneously during the same time period and they were sampled at 100 Hz with spline interpolation for data synchronization. Polynomial fitting was performed to obtain the relationship between the changes in capacitances and joint angles measured in 60 cycles. The zoom-in plot in Fig. 7 shows the validation result for the right hip in one gait cycle. Table 2 provides a summary of parametric values in the data fitting. The angles of the right hip and ankle joints can be approximated using a linear regression with the correlation coefficient $R^2 = 0.98$ and 0.78, respectively; and the knee angle is fitted with the quadratic function of the capacitance change with $R^2 = 0.95$.

Table 2. Calibrated models.

Joints	$\Delta\theta = a\Delta C^2 + b\Delta C + c$			
	a	b	c	Correlation R^2
Hip	0	7.43	1.93	0.98
Knee	3.42	19.77	−2.80	0.95
Ankle	0	11.90	1.00	0.78

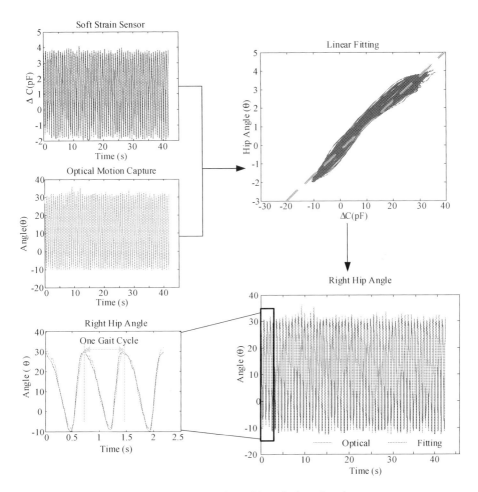

Fig. 7. Sensor calibration with optical motion data.

3.2   Real-Time Evaluation

The human walking motion can be simulated with the measured joint angles in real time using the human-body model (Fig. 5). The experiment involves two participants whose information is listed in Table 3, where the calibrated models (Table 2) obtained with the first subject were applied to simulate the motions of the second one. A video of the second subject's walking was recorded and snapshots of the lower-limb states were compared against the simulation results for one gait cycle (Fig. 8). Although it is only qualitative comparison, the simulation is capable to capture typical features of limb motions during walking as shown in the video frames. It is noted that the two subjects have different heights and weights. After the first subject finished the calibration with the walking speed of 4 km/h, the soft sensors were doffed and donned on the second one without recalibration, and the second subject walked at a random speed as he felt comfortable. The above observations indicate the potential application of the proposed method to gait pattern identification and motion intent recognition which require qualitative estimation, while the sensing precision of the soft sensors among a larger group of human subjects needs further investigation.

Table 3. Information about the participants.

Subject	Gender	Height (cm)	Weight (kg)	Age
Subject1	Male	171	61	24
Subject2	Male	164	55	22

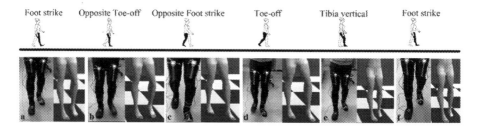

Foot strike   Opposite Toe-off   Opposite Foot strike   Toe-off   Tibia vertical   Foot strike

Fig. 8. Real-time comparison between simulated and experimental results.

4 Analysis and Discussion

To further evaluate the system sensing precision and consistency on the same person after sensor calibration, Fig. 9 compares results measured with the wearable sensing system and optical motion sensing, where three joints of the right lower-limb were analyzed at the speeds of 3 km/h and 5 km/h using the calibrated models at 4 km/h in Table 2. Employing twenty gait-cycles data for analysis, the mean values of the soft sensor results are plotted in solid lines while those from optical measurements are presented by dashed lines; the shaded green and red curves indicate one standard deviation about the means of the soft sensor and optical measured results, respectively. In this way, a thicker line represents a greater signal variation. It is observed that the soft sensor signals have a similar variation with that of optical measurements, which is probably due to the participant's natural motion patterns. The mean absolute errors (MAEs) between both sensing methods are shown for each joint, where the MAEs tend to increase with the walking speed from about 10° for 3 km/h to 15° for 5 km/h. Besides, the MAEs for the knee and ankle appear to be larger than that for the hip joint, which is because the complexity of anatomical joint structure may contribute to the sensing noises with the effects of muscle distributions, tissue deformations, and non-linear condyle shapes on the soft sensor deformations. In summary, the proposed wearable sensing system provides an alternative practical approach to lower-limb motion monitoring with an acceptable variation and mean absolute error of less than 15° when compared with optical motion sensing.

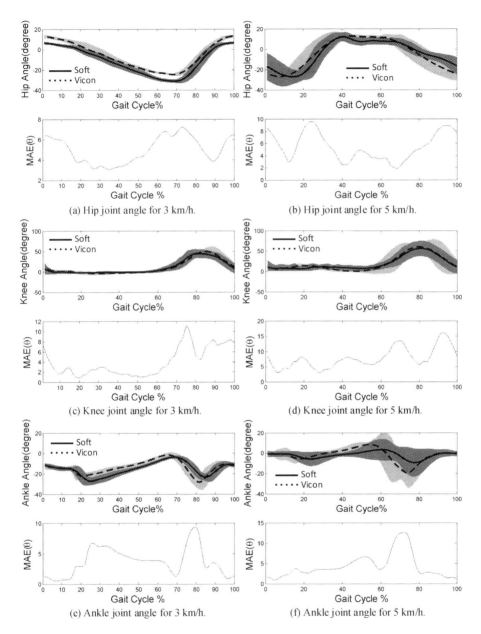

Fig. 9. Performance evaluation with walking tests at different speeds.

5 Conclusion

This paper has proposed a compliant wearable sensing system for human lower-limb motion monitoring. The wearable system is developed based on a network of soft capacitive sensors that can be stretched with joint bending, thus rotation angles of the human joints can be captured with capacitance changes. The soft sensors are sewn to running tights to conform to human limb motions. Fabrication of the sensing module has been presented with the shape deposition molding process, and the electronic sensing components have been designed to connect all sensors in serial so that measured data are transmitted through a CAN bus cable. The simulation platform has been established to qualitatively verify the measured results and real-time monitor human lower-limb motions in practice. The sensing system has been calibrated in experiment and its performance is evaluated in walking tests with different speeds. The proposed wearable sensing system provides an alternative approach to lower-limb motion monitoring with an acceptable variation and mean absolute error of less than $15°$ when compared with optical motion sensing.

Acknowledgements. This research was supported by the National Natural Science Foundation of China (Grant 51875221, 51505164, U1713204) and the International Science & Technology Cooperation Program of China (Grant 2016YFE0113600).

References

1. Zhou, H., Hu, H.: Human motion tracking for rehabilitation—a survey. Biomed. Signal Process. Control **3**(1), 1–18 (2008)
2. Asaeda, M., Kuwahara, W., Fujita, N., Yamasaki, T., Adachi, N.: Validity of motion analysis using the Kinect system to evaluate single leg stance in patients with hip disorders. Gait Posture **62**, 458–462 (2018)
3. Clark, R.A., et al.: Reliability and concurrent validity of the Microsoft Xbox One Kinect for assessment of standing balance and postural control. Gait Posture **42**(2), 210–213 (2015)
4. Jahanandish, M.H., Fey, N.P., Hoyt, K.: Lower-limb motion estimation using ultrasound imaging: a framework for assistive device control. IEEE J. Biomed. Health Inf. 1 (2019). https://doi.org/10.1109/JBHI.2019.2891997
5. Filippeschi, A., Schmitz, N., Miezal, M., Bleser, G., Ruffaldi, E., Stricker, D.: Survey of motion tracking methods based on inertial sensors: a focus on upper limb human motion. Sensors **17**(6), 1257 (2017)
6. Bartlett, H.L., Goldfarb, M.: A phase variable approach for IMU-Based locomotion activity recognition. IEEE Trans. Biomed. Eng. **65**(6), 1330–1338 (2018)
7. Yun, X., Bachmann, E.R.: Design, implementation, and experimental results of a quaternion-based Kalman filter for human body motion tracking. IEEE Trans. Robot. **22**(6), 1216–1227 (2006)
8. Tao, Y., Hu, H., Zhou, H.: Integration of vision and inertial sensors for 3D arm motion tracking in home-based rehabilitation. Int. J. Robot. Res. **26**(6), 607–624 (2007)
9. De Rossi, D., Veltink, P.H.: Wearable technology for biomechanics: e-textile or micromechanical sensors? IEEE Eng. Med. Biol. Mag. **29**(3), 37–43 (2010)
10. Mengüç, Y., et al.: Wearable soft sensing suit for human gait measurement. Int. J. Robot. Res. **33**(14), 1748–1764 (2014)

11. Votzke, C., Daalkhaijav, U., Mengüç, Y., Johnston, M.L.: Highly-stretchable biomechanical strain sensor using printed liquid metal paste. In: 2018 IEEE Biomedical Circuits and Systems Conference (BioCAS), 17–19 October 2018, pp. 1–4 (2018)
12. Kim, S., Jeong, D., Oh, J., Park, W., Bae, J.: A novel All-in-One manufacturing process for a soft sensor system and its application to a soft sensing glove. In: 2018 IEEE/RSJ International Conference on Intelligent Robots and Systems (IROS), 1–5 October 2018, pp. 7004–7009 (2018)
13. Xiloyannis, M., Cappello, L., Binh, K.D., Antuvan, C.W., Masia, L.: Preliminary design and control of a soft exosuit for assisting elbow movements and hand grasping in activities of daily living. 4 (2017). https://doi.org/10.1177/2055668316680315
14. Asbeck, A.T., Schmidt, K., Walsh, C.J.: Soft exosuit for hip assistance. Robot. Auton. Syst. 73, 102–110 (2015)
15. Muth, J.T., et al.: Embedded 3D Printing of strain sensors within highly stretchable elastomers. Adv. Mater. 26(36), 6307–6312 (2014)
16. Rosset, S., Shea, H.R.: Flexible and stretchable electrodes for dielectric elastomer actuators. Appl. Phys. A 110(2), 281–307 (2013)
17. Cheung, Y.-N., Zhu, Y., Cheng, C.-H., Chao, C., Leung, W.W.-F.: A novel fluidic strain sensor for large strain measurement. Sens. Actuators A 147(2), 401–408 (2008)
18. Chossat, J., Park, Y., Wood, R.J., Duchaine, V.: A soft strain sensor based on ionic and metal liquids. IEEE Sens. J. 13(9), 3405–3414 (2013)
19. Larson, C., et al.: Highly stretchable electroluminescent skin for optical signaling and tactile sensing. Science 351(6277), 1071–1074 (2016)
20. Sun, J.-Y., Keplinger, C., Whitesides, G.M., Suo, Z.: Ionic skin. Adv. Mater. 26(45), 7608–7614 (2014)

Pattern Recognition and Machine Learning

Fault Diagnosis and Prediction Method of SPC for Engine Block Based on LSTM Neural Network

Chunying Jiang[✉], Ping Jin, Yuxiang Kang, and Changlong Ye

Shenyang Aerospace University, 37# Daoyi South Street, Shenbei New District, Shenyang, Liaoning, China
jiangchunying@hotmail.com

Abstract. Aiming at the problem of insufficient data volume and data time series being ignored during analysis in current quality statistical process control. A statistical process control (SPC) quality analysis and prediction model based on principal component analysis (PCA) and Long Short-Term Memory (LSTM) is proposed. Firstly, based on the normalization of the data, the key process affecting the production quality is determined based on the PCA model. The size of the previous time is the input of the LSTM, the size of the next time is the output, and the LSTM model is trained. Predictions show that LSTM has a prediction accuracy of over 92%. Secondly, combined with SPC's conventional control chart, cumulative Sum (CUSUM) control chart and exponentially weighted moving average (EWMA) control chart, the LSTM prediction value is analyzed for the small deviation problem in production, and the measurement of the data of the machining center in the actual production process is used to validates the proposed method. The results show that the proposed prediction model has high precision and good stability and can be used for quality management and predictive testing in the production process.

Keywords: LSTM neural network · Principal component analysis · Statistical process control

1 Preface

Intelligent fault diagnosis technology can effectively classify and predict mechanical parts faults, which has positive significance for reducing production cost, ensuring product quality and improving production efficiency.

In recent years, domestic and foreign scholars have conducted a lot of research on intelligent fault diagnosis and prediction methods. Literature [1] proposes a framework for real-time production quality data acquisition, small sample data conversion processing and BP neural network prediction. Aiming at the problem of signal nonlinearity and data redundancy in oil temperature trend prediction, the literature [2] proposed a gearbox oil temperature trend prediction model based on principal component analysis and SPC-dynamic neural network. Literature [3] uses dynamic neural network to predict the fault of hydraulic servo system. The above methods ignore the timing problem of fault occurrence in fault diagnosis and prediction. In view of this, in order to

© Springer Nature Switzerland AG 2019
H. Yu et al. (Eds.): ICIRA 2019, LNAI 11743, pp. 483–492, 2019.
https://doi.org/10.1007/978-3-030-27538-9_41

use the fault time series as a reliability index, the literature [4] proposes a fault time series prediction method based on cyclic neural network.

Through in-depth research analysis and accumulation, fault diagnosis and prediction method of statistical process control (SPC) based on principal component analysis (PCA) and Long Short-Term Memory (LSTM) neural network is proosed. To enable effective fault prediction in the production of mechanical parts.

2   Model Based on PCA and LSTM Neural Networks

2.1   Data Standardization Processing and PCA Dimensionality Reduction

The PCA model can eliminate redundant dimensions of data and improve computational efficiency. First, a Pearson correlation coefficient (Eq. 1) is introduced to calculate the correlation between the variables to determine the number of principal components.

$$r_{mn} = \frac{\sum_{i=1}^{k}(X_i - \bar{X})(Y_i - \bar{Y})}{\sqrt{\sum_{i=1}^{k}(X_i - \bar{X})^2}\sqrt{\sum_{i=1}^{k}(Y_i - \bar{Y})^2}} \tag{1}$$

The eigenvalues λ_i ($\lambda 1 \geq \lambda 2 \geq \ldots \geq \lambda p \geq 0$) of the correlation coefficient matrix R and the corresponding eigenvectors ai, $a_i = (a_{i1}, a_{i2}, \ldots a_{ip})$ (i = 1, 2, ..., p) are obtained by the characteristic equation $|\lambda E - R| = 0$ [5].

Finally, the data is transformed into a new space constructed by k feature vectors, and the expression of the principal component is obtained, as shown in Eqs. 2–3.

$$F_i = \frac{\lambda_i}{\sum_{k=1}^{p}\lambda_k} \times 100\% \quad (i = 1, 2, \ldots, p) \tag{2}$$

$$F_s(n) = \sum_{k=1}^{n}F_k \quad (n = 1, 2, \ldots, p) \tag{3}$$

In the formula: F_i is the main component contribution rate, and F_s is the cumulative algebraic sum of the first n principal component effective contribution rates.

If the cumulative algebra of the principal component contribution rate is $\geq 85\%$, the principal component information of the original data is guaranteed to be retained.

2.2   LSTM Neural Network Algorithms and Modeling

LSTM determines whether the input information is useful by adding a cell. Among them, three thresholds of input, forgetting, and output are set in the cell to achieve the purpose of filtering information. The addition of the threshold concept effectively curbs the problem that the gradient disappears from expansion. Figure 1 below shows the cell structure of the LSTM [6]. The LSTM model is the LSTM cell as a cell of hidden layer. It has a long-term memory function and has been continuously evolved as shown in Fig. 1. Its forward calculation method can be expressed as:

$$f_t = \sigma\big(W_f[h_{t-1}, x_t] + b_f\big) \tag{4}$$

$$i_t = \sigma\big(W_i[h_{t-1}, x_t] + b_i\big) \tag{5}$$

$$\tilde{C}_t = \tanh(W_C[h_{t-1}, x_t] + b_C) \tag{6}$$

$$C_t = f_t * C_{t-1} + i_t * \tilde{C}_t \tag{7}$$

$$o_t = \sigma\big(W_o[h_{t-1}, x_t] + b_o\big) \tag{8}$$

$$h_t = o_t * \tanh(C_t) \tag{9}$$

In the formula: f_t represents the forgotten threshold; i_t represents the input threshold; o_t represents the output threshold; $\tilde{C}_t$ is the cell state at the previous moment, is the candidate vector; C_t is the current cell state (where the current loop occurs); W represents the weight coefficient matrix; b represents the offset vector; h_{t-1} is the output of the previous time unit; h_t is the output of the current unit; σ is Sigmoid Function; tanh is a hyperbolic tangent activation function; subscript t represents time.

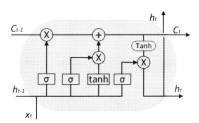

Fig. 1. LSTM hidden layer cell structure

The BPTT (Back-propagation Through Time) algorithm is used to train the LSTM. LSTM retains useful information, eliminates useless information, and works in one-to-two-out operation to improve the training accuracy and accuracy of the algorithm under repeated operations [7].

2.3 Prediction Model Accuracy Verification

Taking the acquired three-coordinate measurement data as an input variable, it is recorded as:

$$\hat{y}_{t+1} = f(X_t, y_t) \tag{10}$$

Where: y_t is the time series of mechanical parts production before time t and at time t; $X_t = [x_{i,t}]$ is the relevant variable set, which can affect the production time series of mechanical parts; $x_{i,t}$ are m time t which respectively constitute X_t as the set of historically relevant variables before the moment; $\hat{y}_{t+1}$ is the predicted value of the next moment of the system.

Standardize the data processing, use PCA analysis to perform dimensionality analysis, obtain a new set of time series variables, train the LSTM model, and establish an algorithm model based on PCA and LSTM neural network to prepare for subsequent SPC analysis. Compare the model predictions with the machining center measurements, as shown in Fig. 2. The relative error of the model test results is shown in Fig. 3. The results show that the prediction accuracy of LSTM can reach over 92%.

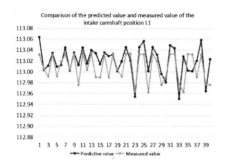

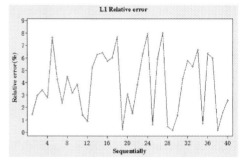

Fig. 2. L_1 predicted and measured value comparison chart

Fig. 3. L_1 relative error map

3 Multi-graph Joint Statistical Process Control Analysis

The standardized data obeys the standard normal distribution. Based on the principle of "3 Times Standard Deviation", Shewhart's conventional control chart is used to monitor the abnormal data fluctuations in production. The control limits are unified: UCL = +3, CL = 0, LCL = −3.

$\bar{x}$ Diagram Control Boundary:
$$\begin{cases} UCL = \bar{\bar{x}} + A_2\bar{R} \\ CL = \bar{\bar{x}} \\ LCL = \bar{\bar{x}} - A_2\bar{R} \end{cases} \quad \left(\bar{\bar{x}} = \frac{1}{n}\sum_{i=1}^{n}\left(\frac{1}{m}\sum_{j=1}^{m} x_{ij} \right) \right) \quad (11)$$

R Diagram Control Boundary:
$$\begin{cases} UCL = D_4\bar{R} \\ CL = \bar{R} \\ LCL = D_3\bar{R} \end{cases} \quad \left(\bar{R} = \frac{1}{n}\sum_{i=1}^{n}(x_{i\,max} - x_{i\,min}) \right) \quad (12)$$

In the formula: m is the sample capacity of the data, n is the number of sample groups of the data, and A_2, D_3, and D_4 are constants, and the measurement value control chart coefficient table can be checked.

3.1   Applying CUSUM and EWMA Small Deviation Control Chart

The idea of the Cumulative Sum (CUSUM) control chart is based on the maximum likelihood ratio, CUSUM control chart is responsible for displaying the cumulative sum of the differences between the data sample values and the target values. Equation as follows:

$$C_i = \sum_{j=1}^{i} \left(x_j - \mu_0\right) \tag{13}$$

Where: C_i is the cumulative sum of the i-th sample; x_j is the average of the j-th sample sub-group; μ is the target value of the process mean.

The Exponentially Weighted Moving Average (EWMA) control chart calculates the exponentially weighted moving flat values from the averages after calculating the average of the data in each subarray.

Since both the CUSUM control chart and the EWMA control chart have better detection power, it can better realize the fluctuation monitoring of small deviation (1–1.5 standard deviation) in the data, and make up for the shortage of the small deviation display of the Shewhart control chart. In this paper, the CUSUM control chart and the EWMA control chart and the Shewhart control chart are combined with the three-picture linkage analysis.

3.2   SPC Analysis Under Small Deviations

Based on the Shewhart control chart, CUSUM control chart, EWMA control chart, the statistical process control theory is applied to analyze the small deviations in the data to monitor the smoothness of data fluctuations. Determine whether the process capability Cpk meets the process capability evaluation criteria.

Under the premise that the process capability meets the process capability evaluation criteria, the PCA-LSTM method is combined with three control charts to perform SPC micro-deviation analysis. The steps are as follows:

(1) Find key processes that reflect quality levels based on PCA analysis.
(2) LSTM model training and prediction.
(3) Determination of control chart parameters and control boundary.
    The control boundary of the Shewhart control chart are: UCL = +3, CL = 0, LCL = −3.
    The upper and lower limit determination values of the CUSUM control map are assumed to be H. If the sampled data value exceeds the upper and lower limit determination value H, it is possible to determine that the monitored process data is abnormal and monitor the abnormality. Referring to the relevant literature, the CUSUM control chart parameters are selected as h = 5, k = 0.5, and H = 5σ.
(4) Drawing of the Shewhart control chart. The standardized processed data is monitored by the $\bar{x} - R$ control chart for production quality status.
(5) Drawing of the CUSUM control chart. The data after standardization is monitored by the cumulative sum method. The deviation between the upper and lower

expected values of the measured sample data needs to be calculated separately. The calculation formula is as follows:

$$S_H(v) = \max\{0,\ x_i - (\bar{x} + Q) + S_H(v-1)\} \tag{14}$$

$$S_L(v) = \max\{0,\ (\bar{x} + Q) - x_i + S_L(v-1)\} \tag{15}$$

$$S_H(0) = S_L(0) = 0 \tag{16}$$

In the formula: x_i is the value of the i-th sample after normalization conversion; Q is the allowable offset amount, generally taken $Q = \frac{t\sigma}{2}$, and t is the control parameter.

(6) Drawing of the EWMA control chart. The EWMA statistic formula is:

$$Z_i = \lambda X_i + (1 - \lambda)Z_{i-1} \tag{17}$$

In the formula: λ is the EWMA control chart coefficient, $0 < \lambda < 1$; Z_i is the EWMA control chart statistic; X_i is the extracted random variable sequence.

(7) Determine whether the data is in a stable controlled state according to the control chart. If it is stable, continue to monitor. If it is unstable, analyze the cause and eliminate the influencing factors.

A flowchart of an algorithm model based on PCA and LSTM, SPC is shown in Fig. 4.

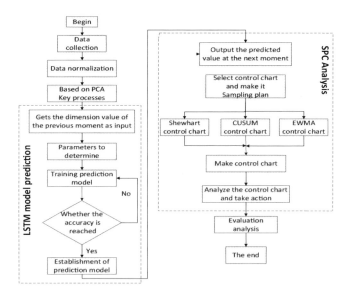

Fig. 4. Algorithm model based on PCA and LSTM, SPC

4   Application Examples and Results Analysis

In order to prove the rationality of the viewpoint and the practicability of the method, this paper takes the measured value of Hexagon multi-point coordinate measuring instrument of a factory automobile engine block machining center as the data source, and uses MATLAB programming to carry out modeling and data processing. Use Minitab for partial SPC control chart analysis. The measurement control room is shown in Fig. 5.

Fig. 5. View of measurement control room

The data is collected in real time by the coordinate measuring unit's three coordinate meter, and the air intake hole 1 camshaft hole position L_1, the air inlet hole 2 camshaft hole position L_2, the air intake hole 1 camshaft hole position degree S_1, the air intake hole 1 cylindricity S_2, the air intake hole 2 cylindricity Q_1, the vent hole 2 camshaft hole position L_3 are initially selected. Six three-coordinate measured variables are used as quality feature data, and each quality feature data can be used as one independent sampling. The six quality feature data were each selected from 540 groups of values measured in time series, with the first 500 groups being analyzed and trained, and the last 40 groups being tested for accuracy and check prediction.

4.1   Model Training and Accuracy Analysis

Combined with the above data standardization processing method, based on the standardization processing of 500 sets of instance data (the processing result is shown in Fig. 6), the PCA dimension reduction method is used to select 5 parameters as the quality characteristic data (the air intake hole 2 cylindricity Q_1 is not selected, because the data fluctuates drastically after standardization, which affects the prediction accuracy). In order to effectively utilize the timing function of the LSTM, the quality characteristic data of the first five moments is the input of the LSTM, and the data of the next moment is the output, and then the LSTM is trained. The number of training samples selected is 500, and the number of test samples is 40. Set the number of cells in the LSTM to 40, the target accuracy to 10^{-4} and the number of iterations to 2000 (Fig. 9).

The model training error results are shown in Fig. 7 below. After 2000 iterations of training, the relative error reaches 2%, meeting the training requirements. The test data is predicted by the trained model and the prediction result is shown in Fig. 8 below. The prediction result is inverse normalized and the partial prediction results are shown in Table 1 below. The error and standard deviation between the predicted target value and the actual value are as follows: Table 1 shows. Conclusion of the comparison with BP neural network is more accurate and the relative error is smaller (Literature [1]).

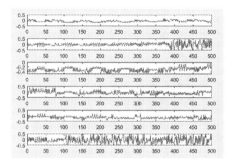

Fig. 6. Standardized processing results

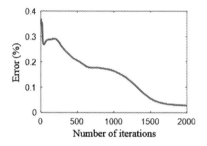

Fig. 7. LSTM training error map

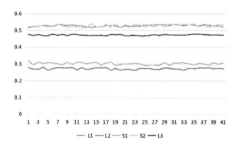

Fig. 8. Prediction results

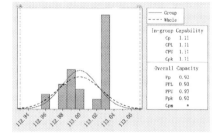

Fig. 9. Process capability analysis

Table 1. LSTM prediction results and error and C_{pk}

	L_1	L_2	S_1	S_2	L_3
1	0.5145	0.2759	0.3172	0.5215	0.474
2	0.5207	0.2676	0.2927	0.5228	0.4667
3	0.5223	0.2652	0.3089	0.5241	0.473
...	...	...	...	...	...
40	0.5314	0.2774	0.2951	0.5224	0.4745
Error (%)	0.017	0.01	0.064	0.001	−0.001
Sd (%)	0.028	0.037	0.038	0.002	0.043
C_{pk}	1.11	1.27	1.23	1.07	1.16

4.2   SPC Control Chart Analysis Based on LSTM Prediction Results

First, judge whether the process capability meets the standard, calculate the value of C_{pk} to be 1.18, which is in the range of normal process capability. Figure 8 shows the process capability analysis of the air intake hole 1 camshaft hole position L_1, and Table 1 shows the process capability index C_{pk} table. Then, the C_{pk} of the five quality feature data are in compliance with the standard, and the SPC analysis can be performed next.

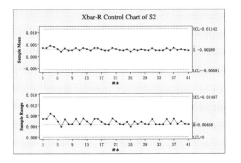

Fig. 10. Xbar-R control chart of S_2

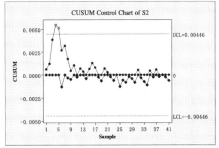

Fig. 11. CUSUM control chart of S_2

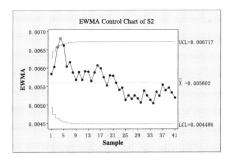

Fig. 12. WMA control chart of S_2

Next, based on the SPC method, the relevant Shehart control chart is drawn. As shown in Fig. 10.

From the Shehart control chart of X-R, the sample mean difference and the sample range are within the control limits. In order to analyze the prediction within the small deviation control limit, the CUSUM control chart is combined to further analyze the prediction data. As shown in Fig. 11.

In the CUSUM control chart, there are two initial points in the predicted value outside the control limit, indicating that the measured data is offset and a measurement fault will occur. The EWMA control chart is further combined to analyze the predicted data and the fault point.

Compared with the CUSUM control chart, EWMA control chart has better detection force in the case of small deviation. After data reference and multiple attempts, the appropriate parameter pairs are selected as $\mu = 0.10$, $L = 2.7$, $\lambda = 0.05$, $L = 3$. As shown in Fig. 12.

At this time, the measured value at the time of production is observed in advance. After the shutdown check of the machining center, it is found that the clamp is loose and the installation position is shifted. After the error is corrected, the production and measurement are continued, and the data are within the allowable range of the control limit.

5   Conclusion

Effective fault diagnosis and prediction methods are problems that need to be solved as soon as possible in the field of mechanical parts production. Fault prediction based on LSTM cyclic neural network is an effective means to solve this problem. This paper proposes a fault prediction model based on LSTM cyclic neural network, Principal Component Analysis and Statistical Process Control, including training, parameter selection, result prediction and quality analysis. The results show that the prediction accuracy of LSTM can reach over 92%, which verifies the applicability of LSTM cyclic neural network model in the field of fault prediction. Further research on quality management and quality monitoring techniques will be helpful.

References

1. Cao, J., Yin, C., Liu, F., Li, J.-C., Yin, Q.: Research and application on dynamic statistical process control of key process in multi-varieties and small-batch machining workshop. China Mech. Eng. **22**(23), 2822–2827 (2011)
2. Huang, Z., Tian, L., Xiang, D.: WEIei hybrid. J. Tsinghua Univ. (Sci. Technol.) **58**(6), 539–546 (2018)
3. Zhang, R., Qiu, L.: Fault detection of hydraulic servo-system based on dynamic neural network **38**(3), 46–49 (2002)
4. Wang, X., Wu, J., Liu, C., Yang, H., Du, Y., Niu, W.: Exploring LSTM based recurrent neural network for failure time series prediction. J. Beijing Univ. Aeronaut. A **44**(4), 772–784 (2018)
5. Sun, W., Chen, J., Li, J.: Decision tree and PCA-based fault diagnosis of rotating machinery. Mech. Syst. Signal Process. **21**(3), 1300–1317 (2006). http://kns.cnki.net/kcms/detail/detail.aspx?filename=SJES13012100145247&dbcode=SJES
6. Ma, X., Tao, Z., Wang, Y., Yu, H., Wang, Y.: Long short-term memory neural network for traffic speed prediction using remote microwave sensor data. Transp. Res. Part C **54**, 187–197 (2015). http://kns.cnki.net/kcms/detail/detail.aspx?filename=SJES3020B5D814FC272C4693E3441D2527AB&dbcode=SJES
7. das Chagas Moura, M., Zio, E., Lins, I.D., Droguett, E.: Failure and reliability prediction by support vector machines regression of time series data. Reliab. Eng. Syst. Saf. **96**(11), 1527–1534 (2011). http://kns.cnki.net/kcms/detail/detail.aspx?filename=SJES13011501716145&dbcode=SJES

Real Time Object Detection Based on Deep Neural Network

Tarek Teama[1], Hongbin Ma[1(✉)], Ali Maher[2], and Mohamed A. Kassab[3]

[1] Beijing Institute of Technology, No. 5 South Zhong Guan Cun Street,
Haidian, Beijing 100081, People's Republic of China
`eng.tarek.teama@gmail.com`, `mathmhb@qq.com`
[2] Military Technical College, Cairo, Egypt
`ali_mtc@hotmail.com`
[3] Beihang University, Beijing, China
`mohamedkassab99@gmail.com`

Abstract. In this research we focus on using deep learning for the training of real time detection of defected Nails and Nuts on a high speed production line using You Only Look Once (YOLO) algorithm for real time object detection and trying to increase the precision of detection and decrease the problems facing real time object detection models like Object occlusion, different orientation for objects, lighting conditions, undetermined moving objects and noise. A series of experiments have been done to achieve high prediction accuracy, the experimental results made on our costumed pascal visual object classes (VOC) dataset demonstrated that the mean Average Precision (mAP) could reach 85%. The proposed model showed very good prediction accuracy on the test dataset.

Keywords: Computer vision · Deep learning · Visual servoing ·
YOLOv2 · Convolutional Neural Network · Object detection

1 Introduction

Now a days visual perception is very important for robots to do some tasks like grasping [1], tracking and detection of objects, it provides rich and detailed information about the environment the agent is moving in. The main purpose of visual servoing [2] techniques is to control a dynamic system by means visual extracted features. Over the last years deep learning made great contributions in the field of computer vision like:

1. Object classification, detection and tracking
2. Direct human robot interaction
3. Object location prediction for grasping in visual servoing systems.

Most of the recent researches in visual servoing, are trying to propose different solutions based on deep learning throughout using different configurations of

© Springer Nature Switzerland AG 2019
H. Yu et al. (Eds.): ICIRA 2019, LNAI 11743, pp. 493–504, 2019.
https://doi.org/10.1007/978-3-030-27538-9_42

Convolutional Neural Networks (CNN). We briefly explain YOLO and YOLOV2. YOLO algorithm [3] is one of the frameworks that are used recently in most of applications for real time object detection and tracking. Object detection task is accomplished by detecting (localize) each target in the input image then recognize it, the localization task is carried out by the regression network while the recognition task is carried by the classification network, as a result of combining both networks in a unified system, the detection deep proposals [4,6,7], can not be utilized in real-time application system.

In the algorithms based on regression [3,5] instead of selecting interesting parts of an image (RCNN), they predict classes and bounding boxes for the whole image in one run of the algorithm. As YOLO's name exactly means that the algorithm is looking through the whole image only once and putting the bounding boxes on every object in the image where the algorithm thinks that there is a probability that this object exists in that area of the image and then remove the bounding boxes with lower existence probability percentage, the threshold may differs from application to another.

As shown in Fig. 1 firstly the image is divided into cells typically $S \times S$ grid, each cell is responsible for a constant number of bounding boxes (B) and class probability (c). Secondly YOLO puts all the bounding boxes inside the image, finally the bounding boxes with low object probability are been removed and only boxes with high object probability which contains the highest shared area still exist, this is done through a process called non-maximum suppression (NMS) and the amount of filters needed in the last layer is calculated through.

$$F = B \times (C + 5) \tag{1}$$

In Eq. (1), F represents the last layer total number of filters needed in the last layer, B is the number of bounding boxes, while C is the total number of classes, the number 5 represents the bounding box predictions related outputs.

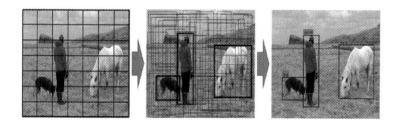

Fig. 1. YOLO object detection sequence

Redmon et al. [8] proposed a new version YOLOv2 to improve YOLO accuracy, darknet-19 network was designed by removing the full connection layers of the network, and batch normalization [9] was applied to each layer. Referring to the anchor mechanism of Faster R-CNN, k-means clustering was used to obtain the anchor boxes. In addition, the predicted bounding boxes were retrained with direct prediction. Since in this paper we are using a costumed dataset and that doesn't contain any general objects so we calculated the anchors for our dataset using K-means [10] clustering method.

2   Related Works

In this section, we will highlight some of the most recent state of arts on real time object detection, tracking and visual servoing.

2.1   Human Robot Interaction

The problem of direct human robot interaction [17] (HRI) still facing some challenges on how to make HRI much more safe for human workers. A proposed solution was introduced in [11] which focuses on the problem of the robots working with human directly and help transferring objects between human and robot with safe environment for the human worker and the other problem is detecting and tracking both the object position and the human position to grasp the object efficiently from the human worker.

2.2   Object Detection and Visual Servoing

A system was introduced [12] to locate and grasp a leaf from a plant using a single camera, the task of picking a leaf can be divided into three parts, firstly determining the position of the leaf and identifying it in the image space using CNN, secondly transforming its position into cartesian space, finally using of visual servoing to control the robot for picking the leaf using Monoscopic Depth Analysis (MDA) as a control scheme.

2.3   Defect Inspection

Defects inspection is one of the most important tasks in production lines, an efficient Automated Optical Inspection equipment (AOI) [13] was introduced which uses artificial neural network based on deep learning to detect features and classify defects on touch panel glass with area of $43 \times 229.4 \, mm^2$, the training and classification of the stored defect images are processed through the ZF-Net neural network. This system introduced excellent accuracy in detecting and classifying defects.

3   Proposed System

3.1   Problem Definition

In this research our purpose is to leverage the prediction accuracy of the 9 layers YOLOv2-tiny algorithm to be comparable with the prediction accuracy of the 24 layers YOLOv2 while maintaining the high speed detection advantage of

YOLOv2-tiny and keep tracking of the defected object on a production line until it is grasped and removed from the production line and obtaining very accurate predictions to the defected object with the exact location of that object.

During this work we faced three main challenges, the first one was the detection of very small objects on high speed production line, the second was the noise produced due to the mechanical parts movements over the production line, while the last one was the randomly placed objects with different orientations that also may results in having lots of occluded objects. Our dataset is composed of only two classes nuts and nails.

3.2 Dataset Creation

First a custom dataset of nuts and nails with different orientations, occlusions and lighting conditions have been created that contains 3000 jpg images, this dataset created by first taking real-time videos with video frame rate 60 fps and then annotating these videos using ViTBAT Video annotation tool [14], this dataset consists of six video sequences with 3000 fully annotated frames of resolution 1920×1080 pixels. Each target is annotated by a bounding box across non-successive frames; then the tool automatically interpolates the bounding box locations and sizes in skipped frames for each target as shown in Fig. 2.

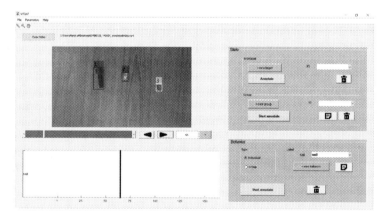

Fig. 2. The annotating process of nuts and nails by the video tracking and behavior annotation tool (ViTBAT)

Figure 3 shows a sample images from our dataset after cutting the video frames by MATLAB into sequence of images, the dataset images was divided randomly into 70% training, 15% validation and 15% testing.

3.3 Enhancing YOLOv2-Tiny Detection Accuracy

Since decreasing the number of layers will decrease the accuracy three approaches were applied to leverage YOLOv2-tiny 9 layers detection accuracy to be compa-

Fig. 3. Dataset sample

rable with the original 24 layers YOLOv2 network. The first one was to investigate the impact on the mAP and average loss throughout changing the network input image resolution from 416×416 to 608×608, which contributed to raising the mAP as shown in Table 1, however the anchor boxes that were used inside YOLOv2-tiny was not suitable for detecting very small objects.

Table 1. Input image resolution change impact on (mAP)

Model	mAP (%)	
	416×416	608×608
YOLOv2	71	72
YOLOv2-tiny	37	58

The second one was to calculate the anchor boxes and this is done through using k-mean clustering with Euclidean distance. We obtain anchors for the training dataset as follows:

As shown in Eq. (2) each bounding box (width and height) tuple is multiplied by the ratio between the network input resolution and the size of the input image contains that bounding box.

$$(w_r, h_r) = \left(\frac{W_n}{W_i} \times w_t, \frac{H_n}{H_i} \times h_t \right) \tag{2}$$

where, (w_t, h_t) and (w_r, h_r) are the ground truth bounding boxes and re-scaled bounding boxes width and height, respectively. (W_n, H_n) and (W_i, H_i) are the network input resolution and the input image width and height, respectively.

After that all of the re-scaled bounding boxes are being clustered through using k-mean clustering algorithm. The obtained k centroid tuples (w_c, h_c) were divided by the feature map stride $feat_{st}$ as shown in Eq. (3) of the network, here the network contains 5 max pooling layers with stride 2 then $feat_{st} = 32$. We know have k (w_a, h_a) tuples, each one is the resulting anchor's width and height.

We calculated anchor's from $k = 1$ until $k = 22$, then through using silhouette average coefficient we managed to obtain the optimum number of k clusters that are suitable for our training dataset, where $k = 9$ so we choose 9 anchor boxes and the last convolutional layer output feature map (filter size) was set to 63 (Fig. 4).

$$(w_a, h_a) = \left(\frac{w_c}{feat_{st}}, \frac{h_c}{feat_{st}} \right) \tag{3}$$

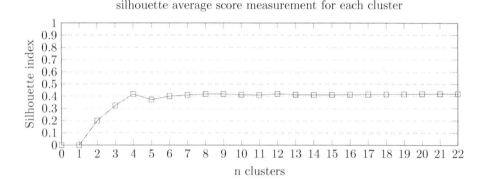

Fig. 4. Silhouette average score measurement

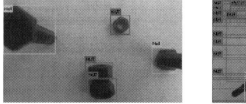 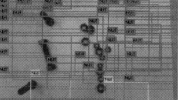

Fig. 5. Impact of our optimum number of anchors on YOLOv2-tiny detection accuracy

The impact of the silhouette measure [15] to estimate the optimum number of anchor's on the detection results is illustrated qualitatively in Fig. 5, where the right figure demonstrates the detection results with default visual object class (VOC) [16] anchors, while the left one with our evaluated anchors. The last step we needed to solve the issue of the decreased prediction accuracy due to the challenges we mentioned in Sect. 3.1.

We have done some dataset augmentations by choosing 15 images from our training dataset and using OpenCV on each image to add some transformations to those images, we included 34 image transformations which are cropping, resizing, padding each image, flipping the image, inverting image, superpixel image, adding light to the image from dark to full brightness, adding light color, saturation, hue image, multiply image for RGB colors with different ranges, gaussian blur, averaging blur, median blur, bilateral blur, opening image, closing image, morphological gradient image, top hat, black hat, sharpen image, embossing image, edge image, adaptive gaussian noise, salt noise alone, pepper noise alone and combined salt and pepper noise, contrast, applying canny edge detector, gray scale image transformation, image scaling, image translation, image rotation and image geometric transformation. Each image of the 15 images produces 139 new images which includes all of these image transformations and this led to an increase in our overall dataset images to reach 5085 images which can be found on that link https://github.com/tarek212/NUTS-and-NAILS-Dataset (Fig. 6).

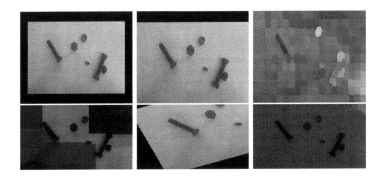

Fig. 6. Dataset augmentation samples (Color figure online)

4   Experiments

4.1   Environment

The hardware environment of the experiment is shown in Table 2, the operating system was Ubuntu 16.04, the models were implemented on the darknet platform framework.

4.2   Analysis of Training Stage

After combining all of the three approaches to train our model on YOLOv2 and YOLOv2-tiny on our training dataset. Figure 7 shows the average loss curve with the mean average precision (mAP%), where the upper one demonstrates

Table 2. The hardware environment. GPU; central processing unit (CPU).

Hardware	Environment
Computer	MSI GAMING LAPTOP
CPU	Intel(R) Core(TM) i5-7300HQ CPU @ 2.50 GHz, 4 Cores
GPU	Nvidia GTX 1060
Video Memory	6 GB
CUDA	Version 9.0
CUDNN	Version 7.0

YOLOv2 average loss and (mAP) improvement, where the bottom figure demonstrate the effectiveness of combining the three approaches on YOLOv2-tiny with average loss 0.4966 and (mAP) almost between 82% to 83% with 40000 iterations of training, with average IOU that reaches to 82% and average recall that reaches to 90%.

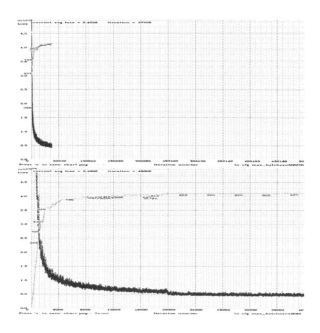

Fig. 7. YOLOv2 Vs YOLOv2-tiny training average loss and (mAP)

From the results obtained we managed to reach a comparable accuracy with YOLOv2 as shown in the comparison on Table 4, and with low computation cost and with maintaining the high speed detection advantage of YOLOv2-tiny as we needed high speed detection to work with robot arm. As shown in Table 3 the used resources during the training process is high in YOLOv2 and the weights file size is large compared to the used resources in YOLOv2-tiny which is low and the weights file size is very small.

Table 3. Environment used resources during training process and weights file size

Network	Resources used	
	GPU DRAM (GB)	Weight file sized (MB)
YOLOv2 24 layers	4.5	202.8
YOLOv2-tiny 9 layers	1.418	44.2

Table 4. Training results

Model	Input resolution	Anchors	Average loss	mAP %
YOLOv2	608 × 608	9	0.4536	83
YOLOv2-tiny	608 × 608	9	0.4966	82

4.3 Analysis of Test Stage

The performances of YOLOv2 tiny using the test dataset with a IOU threshold = 0.5 were compared using the recall, precision and average IOU as the evaluation metrics, as shown in Table 5. For object detection, a very important metric for measuring the performance of a model is mAP. As shown in Table 6. Figure 9 shows the detection results of the YOLOv2-tiny model, it shows good results with both single and multiple object detection and during the test on real time videos the model shows high detection speed with minimum 50 fps and maximum 100 fps. with prediction accuracy that ranges from 65% to 99% depending on the orientation, lighting condition and occlusion. Finally, the proposed detector delivers the detection results to a decent linear velocity kalman filter to track the defective parts as presented in [17]. The defective parts rejection process can be accomplished by means of assemble robot arm derived with the tracked defective object under ROS transportation protocol (Fig. 8).

Table 5. Testing results on real time videos

Model	Recall (%)	Precision (%)	Avg. IOU (%)	Speed (fps)	mAP (%)
YOLOv2	80	78	75	5–20	72
YOlOv2-tiny	85	84	82	50–100	82.21

Table 6. Testing results on test dataset for images and videos

Model	Nail (%)	Nut (%)
YOLOv2	77	76
YOLOv2-tiny	79.02	85.41

Fig. 8. YOLOv2 detection results

Fig. 9. YOLOv2-tiny testing results

5   Conclusion

A real-time object detection system has been presented through using YOLOv2-tiny, the presented solution has the ability to detect nails and nuts on high speed production line also we improved the overall prediction accuracy and maintained the detection speed advantage of YOLOv2-tiny by doing some dataset augmentations through using opencv library. These data augmentations were carried out to achieve efficient training that capable of increasing the detection prediction accuracy during testing on images and real time videos.

Through using cyclic learning rate during the training processes we managed to obtain the best learning rate for the model to converge faster which has been set to 0.00001, increasing the input image resolution from 416×416 to 608×608 and using K-means clustering to obtain the anchors and to obtain the optimum number of anchor boxes we used the silhouette coefficient measurement, which improved the overall feature extraction process.

In spite of the use of the 9 layers YOLOv2-tiny which should decrease the accuracy of the detection, we managed to maintain high speed real-time object detection and with comparable prediction accuracy with the 24 layers YOLO, and we managed also to maintain low computation cost as shown in Table 3, so this model is suitable to work in an embedded systems environment without using alot of its resources.

However due to our limited computing power we couldn't use YOLOv3 which is more accurate, and we still have one challenge which is the probability that an object appear on the production line during the detection that is not one of the two classes, since our dataset is relatively low so in future work we will collect more actual nuts and nails data to further study how to improve the accuracy and speed of defects detection on a high speed production line. Finally implementing a tracking system to be able to track the defected objects on the production line and apply our model on robot arm.

References

1. Sanchez-Lopez, J.R., Marin-Hernandez, A., Palacios, E.: Visual detection, tracking and pose estimation of a robotic arm end effector, April 2011. https://www.researchgate.net/publication/239918179
2. Tsarouchi, P., Michalos, G., Makris, S., Chryssolouris, G.: Vision system for robotic handling of randomly placed objects. Procedia CIRP **9**, 61–66 (2013). https://doi.org/10.1016/j.procir.2013.06.169
3. Redmon, J., Divvala, S., Girshick, R., Farhadi, A.: You only look once: unified, real-time object detection. In: Proceedings of the IEEE Conference on Computer Vision and Pattern Recognition (CVPR), Las Vegas, NV, USA, June 2016, pp. 779–788 (2016)
4. Girshick, R., Donahue, J., Darrell, T., Malik, J.: Rich feature hierarchies for accurate object detection and semantic segmentation. In: Proceedings of the IEEE Conference on Computer Vision and Pattern Recognition, pp. 580–587 (2014). https://doi.org/10.1109/CVPR.2014.81
5. Girshick, R.: Fast R-CNN. In: 2015 IEEE International Conference on Computer Vision (ICCV), pp. 1440–1448 (2015). https://doi.org/10.1109/ICCV.2015.169
6. Ren, S., He, K., Girshick, R., Sun, J.: Faster R-CNN: towards real-time object detection with region proposal networks. IEEE Trans. Pattern Anal. Mach. Intell. **39** (2015). https://doi.org/10.1109/TPAMI.2016.2577031
7. He, K., Gkioxari, G., Dollár, P., Girshick, R.: Mask R-CNN. In: IEEE International Conference on Computer Vision (ICCV), pp. 2980–2988 (2017). https://doi.org/10.1109/ICCV.2017.322
8. Redmon, J., Farhadi, A.: YOLO9000: better, faster, stronger. In: Proceedings of the IEEE Conference on Computer Vision and Pattern Recognition (CVPR), Honolulu, HI, USA, July 2017, pp. 6517–6525 (2017)
9. Ioffe, S., Szegedy, C.: Batch normalization: accelerating deep network training by reducing internal covariate shift. In: International Conference on Machine Learning, Lille, France, July 2005, pp. 448–456 (2005)
10. Sang, J., et al.: An improved YOLOv2 for vehicle detection. Sensors **18** (2018). http://www.mdpi.com/1424-8220/18/12/4272. https://doi.org/10.3390/s18124272
11. Wang, Y., Ewert, D., Vossen, R., Jeschke, S.: A visual servoing system for interactive human-robot object transfer. Autom. Control Eng. J. **3** (2015). https://doi.org/10.12720/joace.3.4.277-283
12. Ahlin, K., Joffe, B., Hu, A.-P., Mcmurray, G., Sadegh, N.: Autonomous leaf picking using deep learning and visual-servoing. IFAC-PapersOnLine **49**, 177–183 (2016). https://doi.org/10.1016/j.ifacol.2016.10.033

13. Ye, R., Pan, C.-S., Chang, M., Yu, Q.: Intelligent defect classification system based on deep learning. Adv. Mech. Eng. **10**(03) (2018). https://doi.org/10.1177/1687814018766682

14. Biresaw, T.A., Nawaz, T., Ferryman, J., Dell, A.I.: ViTBAT: video tracking and behavior annotation tool. In: 2016 13th IEEE International Conference on Advanced Video and Signal Based Surveillance (AVSS), pp. 295–301 (2016). https://doi.org/10.1109/AVSS.2016.7738055

15. Maher, A., Taha, H., Zhang, B.: Realtime multi-aircraft tracking in aerial scene with deep orientation network. J. Real-Time Image Proc. **15**(3), 495–507 (2018)

16. Everingham, M., Van Gool, L., Williams, C.K., Winn, J., Zisserman, A.: The pascal visual object classes (VOC) challenge. Int. J. Comput. Vis. **88**(2), 303–338 (2010)

17. Maher, A., Li, C., Hu, H., Zhang, B.: Realtime human-UAV interaction using deep learning. In: Zhou, J., et al. (eds.) CCBR 2017. LNCS, vol. 10568, pp. 511–519. Springer, Cham (2017). https://doi.org/10.1007/978-3-319-69923-3_55

A Fast and Robust Template Matching Method with Rotated Gradient Features and Image Pyramid

Yanjiao Si[1], Wenchao Wang[1,2], Zelong Zheng[2], and Xu Zhang[1,2(✉)]

[1] School of Mechatronic Engineering and Automation, Shanghai University,
No. 99 Shangda Road, BaoShan District, Shanghai 200444, China
xuzhang@shu.edu.cn
[2] HUST-Wuxi Reasearch Institute, No. 329 YanXin Road, Huishan District,
Wuxi 214100, China

Abstract. In the field of industrial inspection, it is an urgent need to recognize and locate objects with similar transformation in real time. Current traditional methods cannot keep high robustness in illumination change, clutter, occlusion and other environments, and cannot match objects correctly when there is a rotation angle between the scene object and the given template. In order to solve the above problems, a fast and robust rotated template matching method is proposed in this paper. First, the algorithm uses the gradient of object edge points as the basic data of similarity measure function which has high robustness; Second, image pyramid technology is selected to reduce algorithm complexity; For edges, the maximum pyramid is designed to preserve the shape information to the greatest extent, and for gradients, the mean pyramid is designed to fully consider the neighborhood information. Third, down-sampling of feature points is adopted in accelerating the algorithm and combining rotated feature with image pyramid is adopted in solving rotated matching problem. Last, the least square adjustment is applied to improve the pose accuracy.

Keywords: Similarity measure function ·
Maximum and mean image pyramid · Feature point down-sampling ·
Least squares fine adjustment

1 Introduction

Target recognition and location is an important research content of computer vision and image processing field. It refers to find target objects from specific scenes and has been widely used in military, aircraft navigation, medical diagnosis, security monitoring, industrial production line and other fields. Generally, compared with the complexity and time-consuming of 3D model, portable 2D method is more popular.

There are a lot of recognition and location algorithms. In the traditional field, Lessen first proposed the MAD [1] method. Its basic operation process is to extract a part of the region of interest from the scene image as a model image, then slide the model image in a large search image, and compare the similarity between the model image and the sub-region of the search image covered by the model image. If there is a target object in the

H. Yu et al. (Eds.): ICIRA 2019, LNAI 11743, pp. 505–516, 2019.
https://doi.org/10.1007/978-3-030-27538-9_43

search image and it can be recognized and located correctly, the coordinates of the target object in the search image and the rotation angle relative to the template image will be given out. The similarity measure function is defined to evaluate the recognition result.

Based on MAD, many variants have been developed. Similarity measure formulas are similar to each other, such as SAD, SSD and MSD [2, 3]. The difference between these methods is only to find the L1 distance or L2 distance between the model image and the search image, and whether to average the distance. So they have the same problem and are very sensitive to the change of illumination. Until the appearance of NCC [4] method which has a high robustness to the change of illumination.

Literature [5] uses the mean square distance between the edge points of the model image and the nearest edge points of search image to detect, and applies distance transformation to solve the time-consuming problem. There is a disadvantage of this method, if partial edges of model image do not appear in the search image, the distance between the partial model points and the nearest scene points may be very large, which will lead to a very large similarity measure score, that is a false match. In order to solve the problem, another distance is proposed, which is based on Haussdorff distance of two point sets. Using mean Haussdorff distance as similarity measure, the literature [6] first binarizes the image, then generates Voronoi map, then changes the rigid body, and finally calculates Haussdorff distance. In the literature [7], Haussdorff distance is modified by a single item. In the literature [8], a search path is proposed to minimize the Haussdorff distance, so that the transformation matrix between template and target location of the search image can be obtained.

To solve the problem of rotation, a recognition and location method based on directional codes is proposed in reference [9]. This method extracts the gradient direction angles of all points in the image, then counts the direction code histogram of the search image, finally compares the similarity between the model image and the search image through shift traversal analysis. It has strong robustness to light fluctuation caused by scattering interference, partial occlusion and strong illumination. But the amount of calculation is too large to be applied in practice. In reference [10–12], a method of circular projection is proposed. In this method, the target object is rotated clockwise and counter-clockwise when the angle of the object changes, and then it can be correctly identified and located by projection operation. Literature [13, 14] proposed Logarithmic Polar Fourier Transform (LPFT), which converts the rotation problem of pictures in Cartesian coordinate system into translation problem in Logarithmic Polar coordinate system, and adjusts the template according to the rotation angle obtained by Fourier Transform.

In all approaches above, the existing problems can be roughly divided into two categories: first, the robustness based on gray features is poor, and the occlusion problem cannot be handled; second, the computational complexity and storage space based on distance features are too large to be applied in practice. As an improvement in this paper, shape information is proposed as the basic data of matching, which can solve the occlusion problem while ensuring robustness. To solve the problem of rotation, a Hierarchical Generalized Hough Transform method is proposed in the literature [15]. The pyramid is used to reduce the size of the cumulative group and greatly reduce the amount of computation. Inspired by this algorithm, a combination of rotational gradient features and image pyramids is applied, which requires less computation and storage space. Shape information is also selected as matching data in literature [16]. But due to the early termination strategy used in the literature, the pipeline performance of the machine is interrupted and the real-time performance of the algorithm is affected. In view of this, feature points down-sampling as an alternative is proposed in this paper to give full play to the pipeline performance of the machine, ensure the real-time performance of the algorithm.

In the field of deep learning, convolutional neural networks are good at classifying target objects and identifying the approximate rectangular frame of the object. It is difficult to accurately locate the target. In the industrial field, the target object needs to be accurately positioned, and the result of the positioning method proposed in this paper is pixel-level and is easily extended to sub-pixel level, and the precision is much higher than the convolutional neural network. At the same time, the convolutional neural network requires a large number of sample pictures for training, and these pictures are difficult to provide in the industrial field, and may not find a sample of problems in the entire production line, so there is no convolutional neural network method to accomplish this.

2   The Fast and Robust Rotated Template Matching Algorithm

Recognition and location process is generally divided into two stages: offline stage is template creation, online stage is template search. The offline phase does not require real-time, but the online phase needs real-time. The search process is to slide every instance of the template on the search image and compare the similarity between the template and the sub-region of the search image covered by the template. The overall process is shown in Fig. 1. The similarity measure function [17] largely affects the recognition of positioning effects. A good similarity measure function needs to have high enough robustness and operational efficiency.

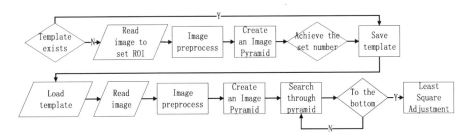

Fig. 1. Flow chart of template matching

2.1   Maximum and Mean Image Pyramid

Image pyramid [18] is a kind of image processing technology, which can be obtained by successive down-sampling of images and stacking them layer by layer from large to small. The image pyramid can reduce the complexity of the algorithm on exponential scale and greatly improve the efficiency of calculation. For every layer added to the image pyramid, the template points and scene points will be reduced by four times, that is to say, each layer of the pyramid can be speeded up by $4 \times 4 = 16$ times. Therefore, if a complete search is performed at the fourth level of the pyramid, the number of calculations is 4096 times less than that of the original image.

No matter how many layers of pyramids are created, one basic requirement is that the basic outline of the object can be preserved at the top of the image pyramid. For the traditional method, the edges fade to disappear as the number of layers increases. So in order to preserve the shape information of high-level object to the greatest extent, a maximum pyramid is designed. Its design principle is that in the 2 neighborhood of the current layer picture, as long as one pixel is 255, the corresponding position pixel of the higher layer picture is set to 255. For the gradient pyramid, the influence of gradients in the neighborhood is fully considered, the mean value of the gradient in the 2 neighborhood of the current layer image is regarded as the gradient of the corresponding position of the higher layer.

As you can see from Fig. 2, the edge of the fourth layer pyramid created by the traditional method is very light, and it is almost impossible to distinguish the edge contour. On the contrary, the edge contour created by the maximum pyramid is still clear.

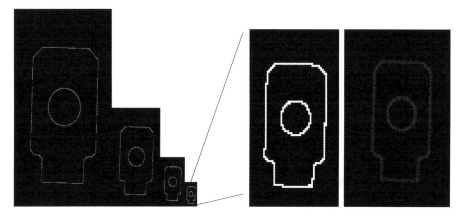

Fig. 2. Comparing the 4-level pyramid effect maps, the left is the maximum pyramid and the right is the traditional method.

2.2   Feature Extraction and Down-Sampling

The features used in the algorithm are image edge points and gradients, which can be obtained by edge processing. In this paper, canny algorithm is used. After canny processing, the edge graph and the gradient graph in X and Y directions can be obtained.

The number of feature points obtained by feature extraction may be tens of thousands. It is not necessary to calculate the similarity measure of all feature points. Usually only a part of feature points is needed to recognize objects correctly. Therefore, the most discrete sampling of feature points is carried out, and the sampling standard is the number of feature points and the most discrete degree. Assuming P is the original point set and S is the selected point set and the threshold dist is the number ratio of P to S. The sampling process is: traversing the feature point set, pressing the first feature point into the output array as the selected point, then calculating the distance between each candidate point and the selected point. If the distance meets distance threshold requirement, then the candidate point will be classified. If not, the starting position of the feature point set will be returned and the distance threshold will be relaxed for re-searching. This cycle lasts until the number of samples is reached. The effect is shown in the Fig. 3.

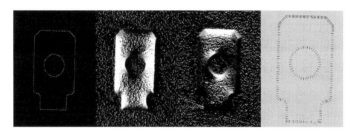

Fig. 3. Characteristic maps, from left to right are edge map, X-direction gradient map, Y-direction gradient map, and down-sampling map.

2.3 Mixing Rotated Gradient Features into Image Pyramid

In order to find the object with rotation correctly in the search image, the feature must be rotated. There are two ways to acquire rotated features: (1) Rotate the original image, and then extract the features of the rotated image. This is because some features are anisotropic and have different emphasis in different directions; (2) only extract the original image features, and then rotate the obtained features. In this way, we know in advance that the extracted features are isotropic and have the same proportion in all directions. Using the geometric center (the intersection of diagonals) of the template image as the rotation center of the original image, and expressing the coordinates of the edge points obtained above as relative to the rotation center, this will be helpful to the later search operation.

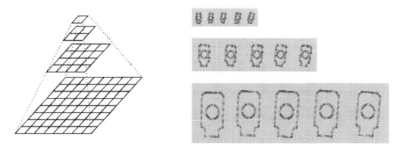

Fig. 4. Combination of rotating gradient and image pyramid

Considering that the pixel of the edge point far from the center of rotation in high-level images will change greatly during the rotation process. So we need to restrict the rotational step size. Large images use small rotational step size, small images use large rotational step size. The rotational step can be multiplied by 2 layer by layer and enlarged layer by layer. If the rotational step of the original resolution image at the bottom of the pyramid is 0.5°, the rotational step can be set 1°, 2°, 4°, 8° and so on. But the step size should not be too large. If the pyramid sampling exceeds 5 layers, the rotational step will exceed 16°, which is a very large span. So we should set an upper limit for the step size, if it exceeds 8°, it will not increase. The results are shown in Fig. 4.

The image rotational center can be divided by 2 step by step. In the process of image rotation, the span between the start angle and the end angle of rotation may not be an integer multiple of the rotational step. The following strategies can solve this problem: reduce the end angle of rotation until the angle span is an integer multiple of the rotational step.

2.4   Automatic Determination of Pyramid Layers

The size of the image is the first factor to be considered when setting the pyramid layers of the image. Because the image is sampled at intervals of 2, it will shrink to a point at the end, which is expressed by formula $K_{max} \leq \log_2 \min(M_w, M_h)$. Another factor to consider is the number of feature points at the current level. It is necessary to ensure that the image at the top of the pyramid still has enough feature points after screening. Literature [17] gives that the number of points is 4. If the number of pyramid layers is L, after sampling step by step, we find that the number of feature points is less than 4 on the top level, the number of pyramid layers will be automatically reduced within the system until the number of feature points at the top meets the minimum limit of 4. If the minimum number of feature points cannot be guaranteed until the original image that means the creation of the pyramid failed.

The method of automatic determination of image pyramid layer proposed in this paper is as follows: (1) The input image is extracted and the feature map is obtained; (2) Set the initial number of layers of the pyramid, set L = 0; (3) For feature maps, image pyramids are created layer by layer from L level; (4) Sampling feature points at current level according to sampling rate ratio; (5) If the edge point N is greater than 40 and less than 60, use the current pyramid layer number and jump out of the process; (6) If the edge point N is greater than 60, then set L += 1 and jump step (3); (7) If the edge point N is greater than 0 and less than 40, set L = 0 and divide the sampling rate by 1.5, finally jump step (3); (8) Cycle steps (3) to (7) until step (5) is satisfied.

2.5   Pose Adjustment Based on Least Squares

The search process is a step-by-step search from coarse to fine based on image pyramid. The results obtained at the top of the pyramid are mapped to the bottom. Generally speaking, a full-angle traversal is carried out at the top of the pyramid, and the results are mapped to the next level, that means multiplying the coordinates by 2. Locating the search area in the lower level in a small range around the mapping coordinates, searching in this small region of interest and taking the maximum of the range as the search result to continue mapping to the lower level. This process is repeated until no matching object is found or until the original resolution level is reached.

Moreover, due to the continuous down-sampling of images, the resolution of high-level images is reduced, the blurring degree is increased, and the contour information is less, so the detection score is generally low. Therefore, the higher the image pyramid level is, the more loosely searching threshold is needed to ensure that the correct target location can be retained; but this threshold cannot be set too low, otherwise too many potential locations will flow to the next level, which will reduce the computational efficiency.

The results obtained by the above process cannot meet the accuracy requirements, the pose needs to be further adjusted. The method used in this paper is to find the nearest scene point corresponding to the template point, then calculate the distance between the model point and the feature line, finally minimize the distance. The feature line is defined by the tangent of the nearest scene point.

There are two ways to get the nearest point. One is to draw a rectangle around the edge point of the transformed template. The rectangle is shown in the red box in Fig. 5. The distance between the scene points and the template points is calculated by traversing all the edge points of the search image within the red box. The nearest point has the smallest distance, as the feature point A. Another method is to use the inter-section of the straight line in the gradient direction of the template point and the edge of the scene as the nearest point, as the feature point B.

The second method is recommended for both methods. The first method has the problem that if the rectangular box is too large, the second closest point with the same distance may be obtained symmetrically above feature point A, which has a slight effect on stability. However, the number of points in this case is very few, so the impact is not significant. The acquisition method of nearest neighbor points and the corresponding relationship between feature features and feature lines are shown in Fig. 5.

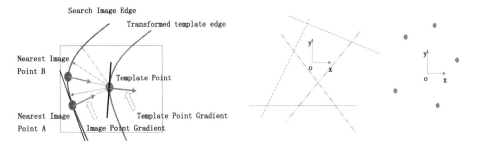

Fig. 5. Least squares adjustment, the left is the nearest point acquisition, and the right is the feature line and feature point.

3   Experimental Evaluation of the Algorithm

This part will evaluate the algorithm from experiment and application.

3.1   Experiment Setup

In this section the experimental set-up for evaluation is explained in detail. Collect a large number of pictures under different conditions and test them in groups. The size of the photographed image is 2592 × 1544, 8-bit gray scale image. The experiment was carried out in two series with 500 pieces in each: the first series used laboratory parts to test and supply the influencing factors artificially. The selected model is shown in the first one of Fig. 6, the size is 532 × 601; The second series applied the algorithm to the practical application of AOI-PCB chip defect machine to verify the performance of the algorithm from a practical point of view. The model of seven kinds of PCB chips is shown in other parts of Fig. 6. Note that the first three chips are much smaller in size than the latter four. The operating platform is: notebook, win10 system, i7 7700HQ processor, 1050ti graphics card and 8G memory.

Fig. 6. Eight types of models for testing

3.2   Robustness

Robustness evaluation is tested in four cases: (1) linear change of illumination; (2) non-linear change of illumination; (3) noise and clutter; (4) occlusion and edge loss. The test results are as Fig. 7. Among them, the first three in the first line are linear change and the last three are non-linear change. Under each condition, three pictures of normal brightness, extreme brightness and extreme darkness are taken for testing. In the second line, the first two are salt and pepper noise and gauss noise, the second two are laser beam interference under bright and dark conditions, and the last two are occlusion and partial edge loss under bright and dark conditions.

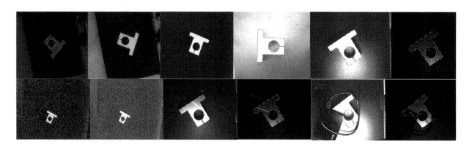

Fig. 7. Robustness test results of the algorithm

It can be seen from the results that the algorithm can be identified stably under different harsh conditions.

3.3 Accuracy

Accuracy test is carried out from three aspects: relocation accuracy, rotation accuracy and translation accuracy. At the same time, it is compared with the methods in literature [19]. The key algorithm used in this paper is the core algorithm of the mature commercial software library halcon. The recognition and positioning of halcon is regarded as the gold standard in the industry, and the detection effect is excellent. Although the paper is far away, it still has reference value. The test results are as Fig. 8. The first line represents relocation accuracy test, which are aggregation degree, angle error, X direction position error and Y direction position error respectively. The second line represents the translation and rotation accuracy tests, which are angle error, X direction error and Y direction error respectively.

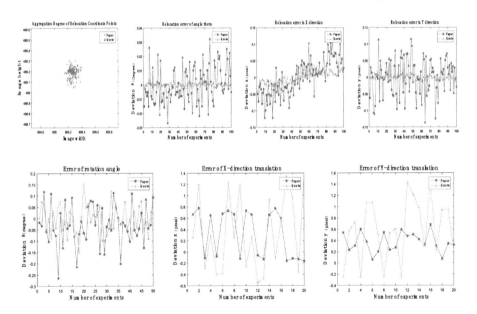

Fig. 8. The accuracy test results of the algorithm.

From the results, we can see that the repositioning accuracy in the literature is very high, and the results of multiple matching almost have no change. The repositioning accuracy of the proposed algorithm fluctuates in a very small range. Among the results, the maximum X-direction error does not exceed 0.15 pixels, the maximum Y-direction error does not exceed 0.15 pixels, and the maximum angle error does not exceed 0.03°. The rotational accuracy of proposed method is similar to that of literature. As for translation accuracy, the method in this paper has higher accuracy, the maximum deviation of X direction is no more than 0.8 pixels, and the maximum deviation of Y direction is no more than 0.7 pixels. Compared with the literature method, the deviation of X direction is 1.2 pixels and the deviation of Y direction is 1.4 pixels.

3.4   Time Consuming

Three different templates are used to evaluate the time-consuming of the algorithm. Three new models are shown in Fig. 9. From the results of the Table 1, we can see that the matching speed of the algorithm in this paper is still far from that of the literature. The problem lies in the degree of parallelization. The method used in this paper only uses openMP for parallel operation.

Table 1. Time-consuming test of algorithm

Model	[0°, 360°] [ms]		Model size	Search image size	Edge points of template in this paper
	Paper	Literature			
—	59	23.43	432 × 661	2592 × 1944	23
=	60	26.76	556 × 582	2592 × 1944	26
≡	65	27.04	296 × 262	2592 × 1944	21

Fig. 9. Three other types of models

3.5   PCB Chip

PCB chip test is the practical application of this method. All pictures are taken from real scenes. All pictures include illumination, noise, clutter, occlusion, edge distortion and other bad conditions, which can fully verify the performance of the algorithm. The results of seven of these tests are as Fig. 10. The average correct recognition rate and detection time are 98.4% and 24 ms respectively. The common features of unrecognized pictures are as follows: (1) there is solder paste on the chip surface, which makes the scene pictures different from the template pictures; (2) the proportion of pixels occupied by chip in scene image is too small, and there are more texture edges in the position of the PCB board where the chip is located, which makes the extracted chip edge features confused with texture features, and ultimately leads to the failure of recognition.

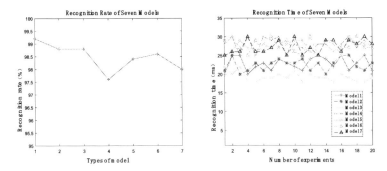

Fig. 10. Statistical results of PCB bad point chip testing

4 Conclusion

In this paper, a fast and robust rotated template matching algorithm is proposed. The main innovations are as follows: firstly, gradient is used as the basic matching data to greatly improve the stability; secondly, maximum pyramid is designed to retain the shape information of the object to the greatest extent, and mean pyramid is designed to fully consider the influence of neighborhood gradient; thirdly, feature point down-sampling is applied to accelerate the algorithm; fourthly, combining the rotated gradient feature with the image pyramid, reducing the computational complexity and storage space while guaranteeing the stability.

A performance evaluation show that the correct recognition rate is almost stable at 98%, and the average time is 50 ms. The evaluation also shows that accuracies of 0.7 pixel and 0.25° can be achieved on real images.

Acknowledgement. This research was partially supported by the key research project of Ministry of science and technology (Grant no. 2018YFB1306802 and no. 2017YFB1301503) and the National Nature Science Foundation of China (Grant no. 51575332).

References

1. Brown, L.G.: A survery of image registration techniques. ACM Comput. Surv. **24**(4), 325–376 (1992)
2. Barnea, D.I., Silverman, H.F.: A class of algorithms for fast digital image registration. IEEE Trans. Comput. **C-21**(2), 179–186 (1972)
3. Vanne, J., Aho, E., Hamalainen, T.D., et al.: A high-performance sum of absolute difference implementation for motion estimation. IEEE Trans. Circ. Syst. Video Technol. **16**(7), 876–883 (2006)
4. Stefano, L.D., Mattoccia, S., Mola, M.: An efficient algorithm for exhaustive template matching based on normalized cross correlation. IEEE Computer Society (2003)
5. Brogefors, G.: Hierarchical chamfer matching: a parametric edge matching algorithm. IEEE Trans. Pattern Anal. Mach. Intell. **10**(6), 849–865 (2002)
6. Li, S., Hu, P., Yang, C.: Algorithm and application of Voronoi graph generation for graphic components. Comput. Eng. **31**(10), 42–44 (2005)

7. Bai, C., Qi, C., Yang, Y., et al.: Hausdorff matching for fast detection of PCB benchmark markers. Optoelectron. Laser **17**(4), 498–501 (2006)
8. Klauck, C., Muller, H., Chew, L.P., et al:. Geometric pattern matching under euclidean motion. Comput. Geom. **7**(1) (1997)
9. Ullah, F., Kaneko, S.I.: Using orientation codes for rotation-invariant template matching. Pattern Recogn. **37**(2), 201–209 (2004)
10. Tsai, D.M., Chiang, C.H.: Rotation-invariant pattern matching using wavelet decomposition. Pattern Recogn. Lett. **23**(1–3), 191–201 (2002)
11. Prokop, R.J., Reeves, A.P.: A survey of moment-based techniques for unoccluded object representation and recognition. CVGIP Graph. Models Image Process. **54**(5), 438–460 (1992)
12. Choi, M.S., Kim, W.Y.: A novel two stage template matching method for rotation and illumination invariance. Pattern Recogn. **35**(1), 119–129 (2002)
13. Harris, C.G., Stephens, M.: A combined corner and edge detector. In: Alvey Vision Conference, pp. 147–151 (1988)
14. Tanaka, K., Sano, M., Ohara, S., et al.: A parametric template method and its application to robust matching. In: Computer Vision and Pattern Recognition, pp. 620–627 (2000)
15. Ulrich, M., Steger, C., Baumgartner, A., et al.: Real-time object recognition using a modified generalized Hough transform. Pattern Recogn. **36**(11), 2557–2570 (2003)
16. Steger, C.: Similarity measures for occlusion, clutter, and illumination invariant object recognition (2001)
17. Steger, C.: Occlusion, clutter, and illumination invariant object recognition. In: International Archives of Photogrammetry and Remote Sensing, vol. XXXIV, Part 3A, pp. 345–350 (2002)
18. Tanimoto, S.L.: Template matching in pyramids. Comput. Graph. Image Process. **16**(4), 356–369 (1981)
19. Ulrich, M., Steger, C.: Empirical performance evaluation of object recognition methods. In: Christensen, H.I., Phillips, P.J. (eds.) Empirical Evaluation Methods in Computer Vision, pp. 62–76. IEEE Computer Society Press, Los Alamitos (2001)

Surface Defect Inspection Under a Small Training Set Condition

Wenyong Yu[1], Yang Zhang[1], and Hui Shi[2(✉)]

[1] School of Mechanical Science and Engineering,
Huazhong University of Science and Technology,
Wuhan 430074, People's Republic of China
[2] School of Mechanical and Electronic Engineering,
Wuhan University of Technology,
Wuhan 430074, People's Republic of China
clove_shi@163.com

Abstract. The detection of surface defects in industrial production is an important technology for controlling product quality. Many researchers have applied deep learning methods to the field of surface defect detection. However, obtaining defect sample data in industrial production is difficult, and the number of samples available to train detection networks is not sufficient. Based on the you only look once (YOLO) detection system, we propose a lightweight small sample detection network (SSDN) to overcome the problem of fewer samples in surface defect detection. The SSDN is demonstrated to be a suitable network to represent defect image features as it is better at feature extraction and easier to train. We used only 10/type images to train the SSDN model without data enhancement techniques and achieved excellent results (average accuracy 99.72%) on defect detection benchmark data. Experimental results verify the robustness of the model.

Keywords: Surface detection · YOLO · Small training set · Machine vision

1 Introduction

Surface defect detection is one of the key methods for controlling product quality. Compared with other detection methods, machine vision-based methods have gradually become a trend in surface defect detection because they have many advantages, including high precision, good real-time performance and strong stability. These machine vision-based methods occur in many industrial applications, such as bottle cap inspection [1], civil infrastructure inspection [2], tire inspection [3], solar wafer inspection [4], fabric inspection [5, 6], thin-film-transistor liquid-crystal display (TFT-LCD) inspection [7], and inspection of fasteners on catenary support devices [8]. These methods can mainly be divided into three categories:

1. Traditional image analysis and processing technology;
2. Image feature extraction algorithms combined with machine learning methods;
3. Deep learning detection methods based on convolutional neural networks.

Based on image analysis and processing technology, the combination of grayscale transformation, filtering, morphological processing and segmentation [9, 10] is generally

© Springer Nature Switzerland AG 2019
H. Yu et al. (Eds.): ICIRA 2019, LNAI 11743, pp. 517–528, 2019.
https://doi.org/10.1007/978-3-030-27538-9_44

used to cause significant differences between the image target area (defect area) and background, and then the target area is detected.

To achieve better performance of the detection algorithm, the image feature extraction algorithm combined with the machine learning method [11–15] has been applied to surface defect detection.

With the development of convolutional neural networks (CNNs) in recent years, deep learning based on CNNs has become a common method for detection tasks. CNNs can not only automatically learn to represent image features but also extract more abstract image features through a deeper convolution layer. Compared with handcrafted features, image features obtained by CNNs have stronger adaptability and robustness. Wang et al. [16] used two cascading CNNs to achieve an average accuracy of 99.8%, but the accuracy of locating defects is poor.

Girshick et al. [17] and Uijlings [18] developed a region CNN (R-CNN) to obtain a more accurate location of the detected object. However, an R-CNN is not an end-to-end training algorithm, which requires a high demand on the computing power. To meet the requirement of real-time detection tasks, Redmon et al. [19] developed a fast single-shot detection (SSD) method named you only look once (YOLO). In the Pascal Visual Object Classes (VOC) dataset, YOLO can process 45 frames/s while maintaining excellent accuracy. In addition to YOLO, some algorithms achieve state-of-the-art results on object detection tasks, such as SSD [20] and feature pyramid networks (FPNs) [21].

However, in practical applications, these data-driven detection network models require a large number of image data samples for training. Obtaining defect image samples is difficult, especially for high-end processed parts produced in small quantities. Even if some data enhancement methods are used to expand the number of surface defect sample images, the detection network model is still easy to overfit with poor results. Therefore, we propose a small sample detection network (SSDN) to overcome the problem of a small sample size in product surface defect detection.

The rest of this paper is organized as follows. Section 2 reviews the region proposal method for network detection, the architecture of CNNs and the loss function. Section 3 shows the data samples used to verify the SSDN model, some experimental equipment, detection network parameter settings and experimental details of the detection algorithm. Section 4 concludes this paper.

2 Methodology

The surface defect detection task not only encounters difficulties due to insufficient samples for network learning but also requires a high-speed detection network. Compared with the SSD [20] and faster R-CNN [22] detection networks, the YOLO detection system achieves the fastest detection speed on the Microsoft Common Objects in Context (MS COCO) dataset [23] without sacrificing detection accuracy [19]. In the YOLO detection system, the improved YOLOv2 [24] and YOLOv3 [25] developed on the basis of YOLO improve the detection speed and accuracy. In addition, the YOLO detection system launched tiny-YOLOv3, and the detection speed reached 171 frames/s. Therefore, we developed a small sample defect detection model based on the YOLO detection system for surface defect detection, as shown in Fig. 1. The SSDN contains region proposal, the loss function and CNNs. Before training the network, the defect image is resized to a certain size. The detection network identifies anchor boxes on the image to predict the type and location of the defect. Position and size of the anchor box are adjusted by the loss function. And finally the exact location and type of defect are obtained.

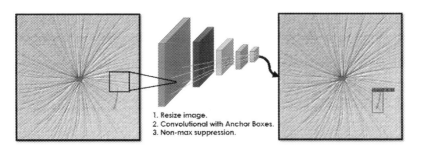

1. Resize image.
2. Convolutional with Anchor Boxes.
3. Non-max suppression.

Fig. 1. The SSDN System. Processing images with the SSDN is simple and straightforward. Our system (1) resizes the input image to 416 × 416, (2) runs a single convolutional network with anchor boxes on the image, and (3) thresholds the resulting detections by the model's confidence.

2.1   CNNs with Anchor Boxes

In the detection network, the region proposal method frames possible defect regions in the image. Therefore, the selection of region proposal methods has a considerable influence on the detection results [18, 22, 26, 27]. To quickly identify precise defect locations in defect detection tasks, we use the region proposal method of YOLOv3 [25]. For an input image, the detection network generates a feature map of size $S \times S$. The anchor box generates 2 bounding boxes at each feature map pixel, and each bounding box predicts five values, namely, t_x, t_y, t_w, t_h and t_o. (t_x, t_y) are the coordinates of the predicted bounding box. t_w and t_h are the width and height of the bounding box, respectively. t_o is the confidence score of the bounding box. The confidence scores reflect the possible size of the bounding box and the accuracy of the prediction. The definition of confidence is defined in (1).

$$Pr(\text{defection}) * IoU_{pred}^{truth} = \sigma(t_o) \tag{1}$$

If no defect exists in the bounding box, then $Pr(\text{defection})$ is equal to 0; otherwise, $Pr(\text{defection})$ is equal to the intersection over union (IoU) between the predicted bounding box and the ground truth. σ is a sigmoid function.

To constrain the center of the bounding box in the current cell and stabilize the network model training, and the sigmoid function σ is used to normalize t_x and t_y in the predicted values. The actual position and size of the predicted defect box can be obtained by (2).

$$\begin{cases} b_x = \sigma(t_x) + c_x \\ b_y = \sigma(t_y) + c_y \\ b_w = p_w e^{t_w} \\ b_h = p_h e^{t_h} \end{cases} \tag{2}$$

As Fig. 2 shows, (c_x, c_y) is the offset position of the cell relative to the upper left corner of the picture. (b_x, b_y) is the position of the predicted bounding box, and (b_w, b_h) are the width and height of the predicted bounding box, respectively. (t_w, t_h) are the width and height of the prediction, respectively. p_w, p_h is the priori setting of the bounding box.

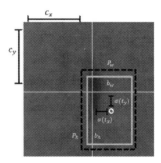

Fig. 2. A bounding box with dimensional prior and position prediction. The width and height of the box are predicted as offsets from cluster centroids. Center coordinates of the box relative to the location of the filter application are predicted using a sigmoid function.

The loss function is used to measure the difference between the predicted result and the ground truth. The YOLO network system [19] uses the loss function to correct the center and the bounding box of each prediction. The loss function indicates the performance of the detection model, with a lower loss indicating higher performance.

$$Loss = \lambda_{coord} \sum_{i=0}^{s^2} \sum_{j=0}^{B} \mathbb{1}_{ij}^{obj} [(t_{x_i} - \hat{t}_{x_i})^2 + (t_{y_i} - \hat{t}_{y_i})^2]$$

$$+ \lambda_{coord} \sum_{i=0}^{s^2} \sum_{j=0}^{B} \mathbb{1}_{ij}^{obj} [(\sqrt{t_{w_i}} - \sqrt{\hat{t}_{w_i}})^2 + (\sqrt{t_{h_i}} - \sqrt{\hat{t}_{h_i}})^2] + \sum_{i=0}^{s^2} \sum_{j=0}^{B} \mathbb{1}_{ij}^{obj} (t_{o_i} -$$

$$\hat{t}_{o_i})^2 + \lambda_{noobj} \sum_{i=0}^{s^2} \sum_{j=0}^{B} \mathbb{1}_{ij}^{noobj} (t_{o_i} - \hat{t}_{o_i})^2 + \sum_{i=0}^{s^2} \mathbb{1}_i^{obj} \sum_{c \in classes} (p_i(c) - \hat{p}_i(c))^2 \tag{3}$$

where (t_{xi}, t_{yi}) represent the standard box position coordinates, $(\hat{t}_{x_i}, \hat{t}_{y_i})$ represent the predicted box position coordinates, $(\sqrt{t_{wi}}, \sqrt{t_{hi}})$ represent the standard box width and height, respectively, and $(\sqrt{\hat{t}_{w_i}}, \sqrt{\hat{t}_{h_i}})$ indicate the predicted box width and height, respectively. The λ_{coord} and λ_{noobj} variables are used to increase the importance of the box with the object and reduce the importance of the box without the object. In the experiment, $\lambda_{coord} = 5$ and $\lambda_{noobj} = 0.5$. t_{oi} represents the *IoU* confidence of the standard box, and $\widehat{t}_{o_i}$ represents the *IoU* confidence of the predicted box. $p_i(c)$ represents the standard box category, and $\hat{p}_i(c)$ represents the predicted box category. If $\mathbb{1}_{ij}^{obj}$ is 1, then the jth bounding box predictor in the cell is responsible for this prediction; otherwise, it is 0. $\mathbb{1}_i^{obj}$ indicates whether the target appears in the cell, and if so, then the occurrence is 1; otherwise, it is 0. If $\mathbb{1}_{ij}^{noobj}$ is 0, then the jth bounding box predictor in the cell is responsible for this prediction; otherwise, it is 1.

2.2 CNN Design

The CNN has an excellent effect on image feature extraction. As the convolutional layer deepens, the ability of the network to express images becomes stronger. The deeper network layers have more abstract semantic features, but the network layer is deepened, and the parameters increase. More sample data are needed to train the network. According to the characteristics of surface defect features, fewer convolution kernels and fewer convolutional layers will be considered in training.

We balance the network layer parameters and the representation capabilities of the enhanced feature extraction network as much as possible using as many 1 × 1 convolutional layers as possible in the feature extraction network [28]. YOLOv2 considers the size diversity of the target, and the background difference may be less indistinguishable. Both the SSD [20] and the faster R-CNN [22] use different feature maps to accommodate different scales of the target. YOLOv2 uses a different method to connect shallow feature maps (14 × 14) to deep feature maps. By superimposing the adjacent features of the shallow feature map to different channels, the model is fused with fine-grained features.

Compared with YOLOv2, the feature extraction network layer of surface defect detection is smaller, and the effect of the BN layer acceleration optimization in the shallow convolution network is not significant [29]. For another reason, in the small sample case, the data used to detect model training are very limited (10–30). Batch normalization is unstable when the batch is small, and the effect is poor. Therefore, the batch normalization layer is removed from the feature extraction network.

For a more accurate position of the defect, the feature map (26 × 26) with higher resolution and the feature map (13 × 13) with lower resolution are used as the predicted feature maps in the prediction, and 26 × 26 + 13 × 13 cells are obtained. Each cell generates two different sizes of anchor boxes. Two kinds of feature maps exist in the proposed network structure shown in Fig. 3.

- Feature map 1: Add some convolution layers after the base network and output the box information.
- Feature map 2: Sample from the convolutional layer of the penultimate layer in scale 1, add it to the feature map of the last 13 × 13 layer, and output the box information again after convolution, which is twice as large as scale 1.

The input image size is 416 × 416, and the feature map size obtained after five maximum pooling iterations is 13 × 13. The structure of the network is divided into four residual network modules, five maximum pooling layers and two convolution layers. When the image features are extracted by the residual module and the convolutional layer, the size is not changed, and the maximum pooling layer is used to narrow the feature map. The layer marked by the rectangular box with dotted lines is used as the final defect detection output feature.

Type	Filters	Size/Stride	Input	Output
Conv	32	3×3/1	416×416	416×416
MaxPool		2×2/2	416×416	208×208
Conv	32	1×1/1	208×208	208×208
Conv	64	3×3/1	208×208	208×208
Residual				
MaxPool		2×2/2	208×208	104×104
Conv	64	1×1/1	104×104	104×104
Conv	128	3×3/1	104×104	104×104
Residual				
MaxPool		2×2/2	104×104	52×52
Conv	128	1×1/1	52×52	52×52
Conv	256	3×3/1	52×52	52×52
Residual				
MaxPool		2×2/2	52×52	26×26
Conv	128	1×1/1	26×26	26×26
Conv	256	3×3/1	26×26	26×26
Residual				
MaxPool		2×2/2	26×26	13×13
Conv	128	1×1/1	13×13	13×13
Avgpool			Global	
Connected				
Softmax				

Fig. 3. Feature extraction layer network structure.

3   Experiment and Results

In this section, we provide a brief description of the defect detection image dataset for evaluating the SSDN model, introduce the implementation details of the model, and provide the comparison results of the model.

3.1   Experimental Setup

Dataset Description: We use the DAGM2007 defect image dataset, a benchmark dataset in the field of defect detection, to test the model [25]. The DAGM2007 dataset was artificially generated but is very similar to the problems encountered in industrial production. The dataset has a total of ten categories, each of which contains 1,000 (2,000) defect-free images and 150 (300) defect images, as illustrated in Fig. 4, which are stored in grayscale 8-bit PNG format. Each dataset is generated by a different texture model and defect model. This dataset is highly challenging for two main reasons: the defect characteristics of the same type of defect sample vary greatly, and some defect areas are very small and similar to the background texture.

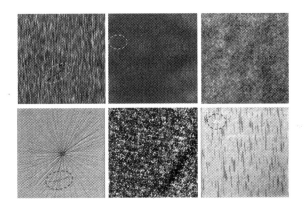

Fig. 4. Sample images with corresponding bounding boxes.

To verify the effect of the model, we chose the DAGM dataset to test the network model. The number of images used for training was 10 sheets/class, 20 sheets/class and 30 sheets/class. The verification data included 10 sheets per class. When training the detection network, we pretrained the feature extraction network but did not enhance the image dataset.

Implementation Details: The program implementation of our detection model was performed in Python 3.6 and the deep learning frameworks TensorFlow and Keras. The program was tested in CUDA 9.0 and CUDNN 5.1 on a computer with an Intel CPU Xeon X5 @** GHz CPU, with 128 GB DDR4 memory, Ubuntu 16.04, and the graphics processing unit (GPU) was a NVIDIA GTX-1080Ti with 11 GB of video memory. The optimization algorithm used by the network was Adam. The number of iteration steps of all networks was 4,000. Since our network model overcomes the defect detection problem of limited training samples, the number of samples used in training was very small. Therefore, the batch size in network training was uniformly set to 2.

IoU was defined as follows:

$$IoU(G_T, P_M) = \frac{Area(G_T \cap P_M)}{Area(G_T \cup P_M)} \tag{4}$$

where G_T the is ground truth, and P_M is the result of detection, as shown in Fig. 5.

For the IoU setting in the detection network, considering the positioning accuracy requirements of industrial detection, we set $IoU = 0.30$ during training and testing, indicating that as long as some defective areas are marked by the bounding box, the box mark indicates that the defect area is correctly detected.

Widely used indicators for defect detection include the detection rate (TPR), false alarm rate (FNR), and detection accuracy (Acc). These metrics are defined as follows:

$$TPR = \frac{TP}{N_{defect}} \times 100\% \tag{5}$$

$$FNR = \frac{TN}{N_{defect-free}} \times 100\% \tag{6}$$

$$Acc = \frac{TP + TN}{TP + FN + TN + FP} \times 100\% \tag{7}$$

where TP and FN refer to the ratios of defective samples that are detected as defective and defect-free, respectively. TN and FP refer to the ratios of defect-free samples that are correctly detected as defect-free and falsely detected as defective, respectively. Similarly, $N_{defect-free}$ and N_{defect} designate the total numbers of corresponding samples.

Fig. 5. Intersection over union (IoU).

3.2   Experimental Results and Discussion

In the field of surface defect detection, data-driven supervisory inspection models generally require a large number of defect samples to be trained to achieve a better detection effect. In this section, to accurately evaluate the effect of the SSDN model, we experimented with the small sample defect detection model under the three numbers of training samples.

Table 1. Results of six datasets with different numbers of training samples.

Sample size	Evaluation indicator	Sample category					
		1	2	3	4	5	6
10	TPR	130/130	130/130	124/130	130/130	122/130	280/280
	TNR	1000/1000	1000/1000	1000/1000	1000/1000	1000/1000	2000/2000
	Acc	100%	100%	99.20%	100%	99.29%	100%
20	TPR	120/120	120/120	119/120	120/120	117/120	270/270
	TNR	1000/1000	1000/1000	0/1000	1000/1000	1000/1000	2000/2000
	Acc	100%	100%	99.91%	100%	99.73%	100%
30	TPR	110/110	110/110	109/110	110/110	109/110	260/260
	TNR	1000/1000	1000/1000	1000/1000	1000/1000	1000/1000	2000/2000
	Acc	100%	100%	99.91%	100%	99.91%	100%

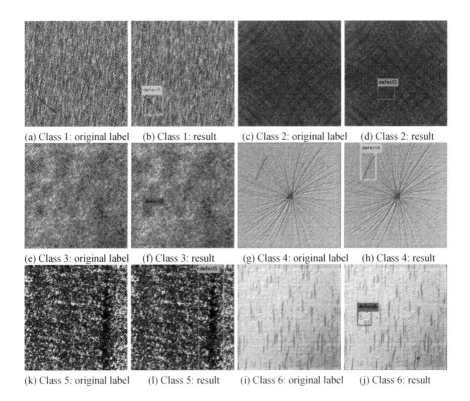

(a) Class 1: original label   (b) Class 1: result   (c) Class 2: original label   (d) Class 2: result

(e) Class 3: original label   (f) Class 3: result   (g) Class 4: original label   (h) Class 4: result

(k) Class 5: original label   (l) Class 5: result   (i) Class 6: original label   (j) Class 6: result

Fig. 6. Final defect detection results of the proposed SSDN model with 10 samples per category.

Table 1 shows the performance of six defect samples typical of DAGM under three different training datasets. For the data samples 1, 2, 4 and 6, the TPR, FNR and Acc achieve the same accuracy under three training sample numbers, but the accuracy of the defect area positioning is different. As the training samples increase, the positioning accuracy increases. Although the detection model performs slightly worse when the number of training samples is 10, and the result of sample 3 is the worst, the Acc is still higher than 99.20%, which satisfies the requirements of the industrial field for the detection algorithm. Therefore, in Fig. 6, we show the detection effect of the detection model in the training of each of the 10 samples.

3.3   Comparison of Defect Detection Performances

In this section, we present the results of some detection methods on the surface defect image data, in particular, the 12-class CNN [30], SIFT and ANN [31], Weibull [32] and the 11-layer CNN [16]. As shown in Table 2, our model can achieve a maximum average accuracy of 99.72% on the defect detection dataset. Compared to the other methods, we train the detection network model to use fewer data samples, which enables our detection model to be better able to cope with the harsh conditions in the industrial inspection field.

Table 2. Defect detection results obtained with different methods.

Class	12-class CNN [30]	SIFT & ANN [31]	Weibull [32]	11-layer CNN [16]	Our model
TPR (%)					
1	100	94.3	-	100	100
2	100	99.4	87.0	100	100
3	98.8	96.9	97.2	99.7	99.17
4	100	92.5	-	100	100
5	100	100	94.9	100	97.50
6	-	-	-	-	100
TNR (%)					
1	97.3	91.3	-	100	100
2	100	100	98.0	100	100
3	100	100	100	100	100
4	98.7	-	-	93.2	100
5	99.5	100	100	100	100
6	-	-	-	-	100
Average accuracy (%)					
	99.43	97.16	96.18	99.29	99.72

4   Conclusions

In this paper, we propose a light detection model named the SSDN to detect defects in industrial defect images using a very small sample. Based on the YOLO detection system, the anchor method generates an approximate defect proposal area and uses lightweight feature extraction modules (CNNs) to obtain a feature with a better image representation. Finally, the model classifies and locates the defect area. The SSDN is an end-to-end training network that does not use data enhancement methods to augment the defect data. It requires only a small number of surface defect sample images to train the network and achieve an excellent test result. In addition, the SSDN has good generalization performance and solves the detection problems of various surface defect samples. To improve the model's tolerance and stability to the number of training samples, more experiments will be conducted in the future.

Acknowledgments. This work is supported by a grant from the National Natural Sciences Foundation of China (51775214). All the authors are grateful for the funding. In addition, the authors especially thank the contributors to the DAGM2007 surface defect databases.

References

1. Zhou, W., et al.: A sparse representation based fast detection method for surface defect detection of bottle caps. Neurocomputing **123**, 406–414 (2014)
2. Feng, C., Liu, M.Y., Kao, C.C., Lee, T.Y.: Deep active learning for civil infrastructure defect detection and classification. Mitsubishi Electric Research Laboratories (2017). https://www.merl.com/publications/docs/TR2017-034.pdf. Accessed 6 June 2018
3. Zhang, Y., Li, T., Li, Q.: Defect detection for tire laser stereography image using curvelet transform based edge detector. Opt. Laser Technol. **47**(4), 64–71 (2013)
4. Li, W.C., Tsai, D.M.: Wavelet-based defect detection in solar wafer images with inhomogeneous texture. Pattern Recogn. **45**(2), 742–756 (2012)
5. Mei, S., Yang, H., Yin, Z.: An unsupervised-learning-based approach for automated defect inspection on textured surfaces. IEEE Trans. Instrum. Meas. **67**(6), 1266–1277 (2018)
6. Mei, S., Wang, Y., Wen, G.: Automatic fabric defect detection with a multi-scale convolutional denoising autoencoder network model. Sensors **18**(4), 1064 (2018)
7. Wang, X., Dong, R., Li, B.: TFT-LCD mura defect detection based on ICA and multi-channels fusion. In: 2016 3rd International Conference on Information Science and Control Engineering (ICISCE), pp. 687–691. IEEE, Beijing (2016)
8. Chen, J., Liu, Z., Wang, H., Núñez, A., Han, Z.: Automatic defect detection of fasteners on the catenary support device using deep convolutional neural network. IEEE Trans. Instrum. Meas. **67**(2), 257–269 (2018)
9. Lin, H.D.: Tiny surface defect inspection of electronic passive components using discrete cosine transform decomposition and cumulative sum techniques. Image Vis. Comput. **26**(5), 603–621 (2008)
10. Aiger, D., Talbot, H.: The phase only transform for unsupervised surface defect detection. In: Proceedings of the 2010 IEEE Conference on Computer Vision and Pattern Recognition (CVPR), pp. 295–302. IEEE, San Francisco (2010)
11. Huang, J.X., Li, D., Ye, F., et al.: Detection of surface defection of solder on flexible printed circuit. Opt. Precis. Eng. **18**(11), 2443–2453 (2010)
12. Dalal, N., Triggs, B.: Histograms of oriented gradients for human detection. In: International Conference on Computer Vision & Pattern Recognition (CVPR 2005), vol. 1, pp. 886–893. IEEE, San Diego (2005)
13. Ojala, T., Pietikäinen, M., Mäenpää, T.: Multiresolution gray-scale and rotation invariant texture classification with local binary patterns. IEEE Trans. Pattern Anal. Mach. Intell. **24**(7), 971–987 (2002)
14. Cortes, C., Vapnik, V.: Support-vector networks. Mach. Learn. **20**(3), 273–297 (1995)

15. Rätsch, G., Onoda, T., Müller, K.R.: Soft margins for AdaBoost. Mach. Learn. **42**(3), 287–320 (2001)
16. Wang, T., Chen, Y., Qiao, M., Snoussi, H.: A fast and robust convolutional neural network-based defect detection model in product quality control. Int. J. Adv. Manuf. Technol. **94**(9–12), 3465–3471 (2018)
17. Girshick, R., Donahue, J., Darrell, T., Malik, J.: Rich feature hierarchies for accurate object detection and semantic segmentation. In: Proceedings of the IEEE Conference on Computer Vision and Pattern Recognition, pp. 580–587. IEEE, Columbus (2014)
18. Uijlings, J.R., Van De Sande, K.E., Gevers, T., Smeulders, A.W.: Selective search for object recognition. Int. J. Comput. Vis. **104**(2), 154–171 (2013)
19. Redmon, J., Divvala, S., Girshick, R., Farhadi, A.: You only look once: unified, real-time object detection. In: Proceedings of the IEEE Conference on Computer Vision and Pattern Recognition, pp. 779–788. IEEE, Las Vegas (2016)
20. Liu, W., et al.: SSD: single shot multibox detector. In: Leibe, B., Matas, J., Sebe, N., Welling, M. (eds.) ECCV 2016. LNCS, vol. 9905, pp. 21–37. Springer, Cham (2016). https://doi.org/10.1007/978-3-319-46448-0_2
21. Lin, T.Y., Dollár, P., Girshick, R., He, K., Hariharan, B., Belongie, S.: Feature pyramid networks for object detection. In: Proceedings of the IEEE Conference on Computer Vision and Pattern Recognition, pp. 2117–2125. IEEE, Hawaii (2017)
22. Ren, S., He, K., Girshick, R., Sun, S.: Faster R-CNN: towards real-time object detection with region proposal networks. IEEE Trans. Pattern Anal. Mach. Intell. **39**(6), 1137–1149 (2016)
23. Lin, T.-Y., et al.: Microsoft COCO: common objects in context. In: Fleet, D., Pajdla, T., Schiele, B., Tuytelaars, T. (eds.) ECCV 2014. LNCS, vol. 8693, pp. 740–755. Springer, Cham (2014). https://doi.org/10.1007/978-3-319-10602-1_48
24. Redmon, J., Farhadi, A.: YOLO9000: better, faster, stronger. In: Proceedings of the IEEE Conference on Computer Vision and Pattern Recognition, pp. 7263–7271. IEEE, Hawaii (2017)
25. Redmon, J., Farhadi, A.: YOLOV3: an incremental improvement. arXiv preprint arXiv: 1804.02767 (2018)
26. Zeiler, M.D., Fergus, R.: Visualizing and understanding convolutional networks. In: Fleet, D., Pajdla, T., Schiele, B., Tuytelaars, T. (eds.) ECCV 2014. LNCS, vol. 8689, pp. 818–833. Springer, Cham (2014). https://doi.org/10.1007/978-3-319-10590-1_53
27. Simonyan, K., Zisserman, A.: Very deep convolutional networks for large-scale image recognition. In: Proceedings of the International Conference on Learning Representations (ICLR), San Diego (2015)
28. Lin, M., Chen, Q., Yan, S.: Network in network. arXiv preprint arXiv:1312.4400 (2013)
29. Pedoeem, J., Huang, R.: YOLO-LITE: a real-time object detection algorithm optimized for non-GPU computers. arXiv preprint arXiv:1811.05588 (2018)
30. Weimer, D., Scholz-Reiter, B., Shpitalni, M.: Design of deep convolutional neural network architectures for automated feature extraction in industrial inspection. CIRP Ann. **65**(1), 417–420 (2016)
31. Siebel, N.T., Sommer, G.: Learning defect classifiers for visual inspection images by neuro-evolution using weakly labelled training data. In: 2008 IEEE Congress on Evolutionary Computation (IEEE World Congress on Computational Intelligence), pp. 3925–3931. IEEE, Hong Kong (2008)
32. Timm, F., Barth, E.: Non-parametric texture defect detection using Weibull features. In: Image Processing: Machine Vision Applications IV, vol. 7877, p. 78770J. International Society for Optics and Photonics, San Francisco (2011)

A Collision-Free Path Planning Method Using Direct Behavior Cloning

Zijing Chi, Lei Zhu, Fan Zhou, and Chungang Zhuang[✉]

State Key Laboratory of Mechanical System and Vibration,
School of Mechanical Engineering, Shanghai Jiao Tong University,
Shanghai 200240, China
cgzhuang@sjtu.edu.com

Abstract. An effective path planning approach based on deep learning for robotic arms is presented in this paper. Direct behavior cloning is applied to extract the obstacle avoidance policy in collision-free paths generated by reliable motion planners, such as RRT* algorithm in our case. Behavior cloning is the simplest form of imitation learning, also known as Learning from Demonstration (LfD), where an agent tries to learn a policy to recover the expert's action with respect to the state of the environment. The designed policy in this paper gives the obstacle avoidance action in a scene knowing the pose of the obstacle, the initial and the goal configurations. The action is taken each time the state changes and thus this method is able to achieve online motion planning regardless of whether the environment is static or dynamic. We build a simulation environment with V-REP and Python client program to collect the state-action dataset and validate the trained policies. Policy models with and without visual input are constructed and tested in the same experiment setting to determine the best solution. Results show that the policy model with accurate obstacle pose input handles the path planning issue well.

Keywords: Path planning · Imitation learning · Behavior cloning ·
Obstacle avoidance · Robot manipulation

1 Introduction

Path planning/motion planning is a fundamental issue in robot manipulation aiming to find a collision-free path in the form of a sequence of continuous configuration points from the initial configuration towards the given goal configuration. In contrast, trajectory planning problem, which will not be discussed in this paper, focuses on the explicit parametrization of time taking into account the kinematics and dynamics constraints, while path planning deals only with the spatial information. There are many well-developed algorithms in the field of robotic path planning and sampling-based methods like PRM and RRT have gained popularity in robotic arm path planning for their probability completeness, high calculation efficiency, and generality.

With the rapid development of machine learning methods, reinforcement learning (RL) methods hold promise for solving high-level robotic issues. RL methods try to learn a policy which is a mapping from state to action, which is suitable to design a

© Springer Nature Switzerland AG 2019
H. Yu et al. (Eds.): ICIRA 2019, LNAI 11743, pp. 529–540, 2019.
https://doi.org/10.1007/978-3-030-27538-9_45

dynamic robot control system. The frontier of RL in robotic studies [1] is focusing on the end-to-end training with visuomotor policies of several simple tasks, mainly on the grasping task where there are few constraints in the way. There is a lack of study in terms of obstacle avoidance policy using reinforcement learning, especially when it comes to high-dimensional robotic arms.

One major issue in RL is the design of reward function, which can be hard depending on the task complexity. The sparse reward is relatively easy for design but adverse for training [2]. Another holdback is that RL can be data-inefficient in terms of training since it typically goes through thousands of unsuccessful trials to converge. Imitation learning is a feasible alternative when a reliable expert is available.

In this paper, we show that direct behavior cloning has the potential to learn an obstacle avoidance policy of high-dimensional robotic arms. We introduce a reliable method to construct the dataset containing the states and actions of each path planning episode in a simulation software. The details of different model architectures are discussed deeply and all models are verified through experiments under the same configuration. It is feasible to transfer the trained policy to the real-world scenario theoretically if given a valid perception procedure. Compared with classic path planning methods, the policy based method is suitable for online planning since it only predicts the next movement at each step and keeps observing the environment whether it is static or dynamic. The main contribution of this paper is an effective definition of state and action of the policy to overcome the complexity of the obstacle avoidance problem.

The remainder of this document is organized as follows. Section 2 gives a survey on the papers related to imitation learning and path planning of robotic arms. Section 3 describes the dataset construction details. The methodology is further discussed in Sect. 4 to determine the architecture. Section 5 demonstrates the experiment results of several policy models and Sect. 6 gives the conclusion and future plans.

2   Related Works

A large number of recent researches [3, 4] worked on the modification of RRT and its extension methods such as RRT*, RRT-connect, etc., especially on the tradeoff between calculation efficiency and stability. Many of them aimed to accelerate the planning speed by adjusting the sampling procedure taking advantage of experiences. Ichter et al. [5] used Conditional Variational Autoencoder (CVAE) to bias the sampling distribution to regions where the optimal path is most likely to lie from the experience of past planning results. The method was proved to be general and significantly faster than RRT* with uniform sampling.

While end-to-end training of visuomotor policies has become a spotlight in RL researches, it often requires an enormous dataset [6]. Imitation learning can help to achieve a good result more data-efficiently if provided expert demonstrations. Rahmatizadeh et al. [7] collected a demonstration dataset of pick and place task and pushing task in a virtual environment built in the Unity3D game engine to train a policy network that can be performed in the real world where the pose information was acquired by the Microsoft Kinect sensor and object with markers. The network employed long short memory (LSTM) and mixture density network (MDN) to improve the learning accuracy. This combination of LSTM and MDN is also seen in another work of Rahmatizadeh et al. [8], where direct behavior cloning was adopted for vision-based multi-task learning from demonstration. A special trick combining variational autoencoder (VAE) with generative adversarial network (GAN) to encode the input images to a low-dimensional feature space was found to be able to overcome the sim-to-real transfer problem, which is also a hot topic in researches. Zhang et al. [9] proposed an adversarial discriminative sim-to-real transfer approach to reduce the number of labeled real images when doing transfer learning in visuomotor tasks. The network consists of a perception module predicting the object position from raw images and a control module determining the joint angle velocities so the adversarial discriminative transfer only takes place in the perception module. Yan et al. [10] followed the DAgger framework with a simple expert having knowledge of the necessary information to conduct a certain sphere grasp task. It dealt with the sim-to-real problem by separating the whole network into a vision module and a controller module, while the vision module processed the input image into a binary mask regardless of the real image or the simulated image.

Some papers utilized the combination of imitation learning and reinforcement learning achieve better results. Zhu et al. [11] showed that reinforcement learning assisted with a small amount of demonstration data performed significantly better than training with reinforcement learning or imitation learning alone for diverse visuomotor skills. Sadeghi et al. [12] employed LSTM to train a visual servoing controller which is trained with simulated data and can transfer to a real-world robot as well following the DAgger framework to copy the optimum action simply towards the target object. Besides learning from demonstration, the network also predicts the value function as an RL object to obtain a better result.

With all the works mentioned above, few have paid attention to solve the problem when an obstacle is in the way. Thomas et al. [13] leveraged prior knowledge from CAD files to generate a geometric motion plan and learned a controller using GPS, which outperforms model-free RL methods when the transition dynamics of the system is known, for complex assembly tasks. However, the action of the policy is the torque control command and GPS is employed not to handle the path planning but to handle the dynamics. However, GPS can be regarded as a special form of supervised learning whose expert is an optimal controller in some way and is not needed when a mature expert is available in the given task, as is the case in path planning problem. Pham et al. [14] corrected the output action from the RL model by solving a constrained optimization problem to ensure that the action lay in the non-collision space. The obstacle avoidance was not implemented by the RL algorithm but the optimization part. Our work attends to achieve collision-free path planning simply by behavior cloning. It mainly refers to the methodology applied in the imitation learning works mentioned above to determine the best architecture for the obstacle avoidance task.

3 Problem Definition and Dataset Preparation

3.1 Problem Definition

Let $X \in R^d$ be defined as the state space of d dimensions. For each scene, X_{free}, $X_{obs} \in$ X denote the free space and the obstacle space respectively, x_{init}, $x_{goal} \in X_{free}$ denote the initial state and the goal state of the agent. The solution of the path planning problem is a continuous function $f(s)$, $s \in [0, 1]$ that satisfies $f(0) = x_{init}$, $f(1) = x_{goal}$, and for any $s \in [0, 1]$, $f(s) \in X_{free}$. Usually, the function is obtained by interpolating a non-empty finite-length tuple σ and the distance between any two adjacent elements should be small enough.

3.2 Dataset Construction

Building up an experiment environment to collect the data required to perform imitation learning of robotic arm path planning task with a real robot and hard coding can take tremendous effort. Data sampling is also ineffective due to the time needed for a robot to execute the planned motion and spatial information acquisition of the obstacle, not to mention the difficulty of changing the position of the obstacle manually for a mass of times. As far as the problem presented in this paper is concerned, building a dataset with a simulation system is an ideal alternative. There are several popular simulator systems integrated with a development environment suitable for robotic scenarios such as V-REP, Gazebo with ROS, and Mujoco with OpenAI Gym. We choose V-REP for its powerful module integration and variety of model library. The custom scene in V-REP is controlled by built-in Lua script and Python client program, which also processes the data sent from V-REP to form the dataset. Table 1 describes the whole dataset construction flow in detail.

The server side. A simple scene with four walls, a single UR5 robot, and a cuboid obstacle is constructed inside V-REP, as illustrated in Fig. 1. There are vision sensors in three orthogonal perspectives recording current state in the form of images at each step. In case of vision input models, a small cuboid whose position and orientation is set to that of the tip of the UR5 robot in the goal configuration provides supplementary visual guidance information. The colors of the walls and lights are reset randomly before every motion execution process and the positions of the light sources change continuously during the process, such that the RGB distribution has a large variability to avoid huge bias in terms of supervised learning. The UR5 model is attached with a

Fig. 1. The front and upper view of the scene at the initial and goal configurations. (Color figure online)

non-threaded script written in Lua containing the main functions of path planning and collision check, which can be called by the Python client program. The path planning function calculates the shortest path within several attempts given the initial configuration, the goal configuration, and the collision pairs by calling the OMPL library interface integrated by default plugin. With multiple path planning algorithms available by related OMPL API, RRT* is adopted considering it is capable of approximating the optimal path theoretically if given enough sampling number, thus decreasing the uncertainty of actions at the same state, which can lead to higher regression precision when applying supervised learning. The obstacle is a $5 \times 50 \times 20$ cm^3 cuboid and the visual guidance target is a $3 \times 3 \times 10$ cm^3 cuboid, with one surface in a different color. Figure 1 shows the images from the front and upper view of the scene at the initial and goal configurations.

Table 1. Dataset construction flow.

Dataset Construction Flow
Construct the simulation scene with embedded script in V-REP
Set the distributions in the client's side of x_{init}, $[p_{obs}, o_{obs}]$ and x_{goal}.
$N = 0$
While $N < N_{max}$
Sample from the distributions and set the values to the scene in the server's side
If $x_{init}, x_{goal} \in X_{free}$
Call the path planning function in the server's side and return the path σ if exists
$t = 0$
While $t < length(\sigma)$
Move the robot to the configuration $\sigma(t)$
Save the current images in every view
Save the action $a_t = \sigma(t+1) - \sigma(t)$ with $\sigma(t)$
$t = t + 1$
Save the pose of the obstacle $[p_{obs}, o_{obs}]$
$N = N + 1$

The client side. The client application is written in Python and its main functionality is achieved by a derived class of vrep_env[1], a project aiming to wrap V-REP remote API to create a gym environment analogous to OpenAI. The initial and goal configurations along with the position and orientation of the obstacle are randomly reset at the beginning of each session, then the robot is set to the initial and goal configurations respectively to check the collision situations. The distributions of x_{init} and x_{goal} are set to be two multivariate normal distributions with diagonal covariance matrices, and p_{obs}, o_{obs} both obey uniform distributions. The current scene will be skipped directly if a collision occurs at any configuration, else path planning is

---

[1] https://github.com/ycps/vrep-env.

executed at the server side by calling the script function. The planned path σ returned from the server side is a sequence of configuration points in-between and has been uniformly interpolated such that (1) $\sigma(0) = x_{init}$, (2) $\sigma(N) = x_{goal}$, (3) for any $i < N$, $\|\sigma(i+1) - \sigma(i)\|_2 = \|\sigma(1) - \sigma(0)\|_2$.

After the client receives a valid path σ, it sets the robot to the configurations in path sequentially and makes an observation at each step until the robot has reached the goal pose. All the observations along with the scene configuration including the initial configuration, the goal configuration, the position and the orientation of the obstacle are stored in the same directory. All the directories are later divided into the training set and the validation set. The UR5 robot is not attached with any end-effector so the 6th DoF is redundant and thus gets removed in the dataset.

4 Method

4.1 Policy Definition

The state and action definitions of the imitation learning problem are yet to be determined. In several papers, the image input is trained in the vision module to predict the target object position and gets separated from the controller module. This modularity solution decreases the training difficulty compared to end-to-end training and there are plenty of researches in pose estimation methods to be referred to. Analogously, the supervised learning model applied in our solution can be composed of a controller module and a vision module which predicts the positions and orientations of the obstacle, target object and the current joint angles of the robot. The tuple of the vision model inputs can be defined as a scene configuration $\vartheta = (\theta_t, \theta_{goal}, p_{obs}, o_{obs})$ and it is possible to obtain through a perception module by various means, even solely through a monocular camera. The use of position and orientation alone limits this model to the scenario of a certain obstacle, but the complexity would become too high to handle as for random obstacles. As a matter of fact, it is obvious that an unseen obstacle of smaller size is also applicable with this trained policy if the policy works well. In the reinforcement learning theory, the images can be regarded as the observation of the pivotal state and the vision module undertakes the mapping from observation to state. This mapping procedure can also be accomplished by traditional machine vision methods with higher stability. Therefore, this paper focuses on the controller module design.

In the other hand, the mapping from images to some certain state values is a compression process which may cause loss of some important information such as the distance between the robot and the obstacle. In view of this, end-to-end model with image input is also tested in this paper. Auxiliary inputs such as the current configuration and the goal configuration are also applied to accelerate training since they are easy to acquire and non-expensive in terms of training. Though the configurations can also be retrieved by deep learning method [15], the model architecture would become too complicated and out of our research.

The action of the imitation problem can be directly defined as the joint angle increment $a_t = x_{t+1} - x_t$. The L2 norms of actions by this definition are constrained to around 0.1 during data collection. During training, however, this action output is found to be ineffective and causes a low success rate. Instead of direct increment, another idea is to set the action as the obstacle avoidance vector by subtracting the joint angle vector towards goal configuration of the same L2 norm, that is, $a_t = (x_{t+1} - x_t) - \varphi_t$, where

$$\varphi_t = \frac{\|x_{t+1} - x_t\|_2}{\|x_{goal} - x_t\|_2} (x_{goal} - x_t), \tag{1}$$

as illustrated in Fig. 2. By this definition, a_t should be close to a zero vector when approaching the goal configuration. When applying the policy of this model, the controller simply executes

$$x_{t+1} = x_t + \frac{C}{\|x_{goal} - x_t\|_2} (x_{goal} - x_t) + a_t \tag{2}$$

to the next configuration, where a_t is the model output and C is equal to 0.1 as mentioned above. By this mean, the robot is guaranteed to approach the goal pose since a_t is relatively small supposing the supervised learning procedure succeeds. As long as obstacle avoidance action is concerned, the wrist joints do not have a great influence on the spatial occupation, so the action only takes the first three dimensions and set the rest to 0.

Though RRT* algorithm is able to approximate the optimal collision-free path, the related API in V-REP does not offer sampling counts parameter to guarantee the convergence, thus the uncertainty in path planning dataset cannot be avoided. In that case, MDN is applied, where the outputs of the model are the parameters of a mixture Gaussian distribution.

4.2   Architecture

For the deterministic controller module, it receives four inputs as the state: the current configuration, the goal configuration, the position of the obstacle and the orientation of the obstacle. Each input is processed with three fully connected layers, one of which is attached with a kernel regularizer and a batch normalization layer to avoid overfitting, then the processed vectors are concatenated to be input to the final four fully connected layers to predict the final action. Particularly, the position and orientation of the obstacle are merged first after two fully connected layers before concatenating with the other two inputs. As in the MDN controller module, the output layer is replaced by a custom MDN layer containing parameters of 10 Gaussian kernels.

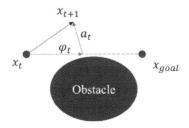

Fig. 2. The definition of obstacle avoidance action.

The model for image input should have at least two image inputs from different perspectives because the relative spatial relationship between the robot and the obstacle can hardly be predicted from a single view. Each image input is processed by a modified VGG16 network and the latent vectors are concatenated together with the processed vectors of the current configuration and goal configuration analogous to the controller module. The modified VGG net removes some convolutional layers and adds more batch normalization layers and kernel regularizers to avoid overfitting. Figure 3 (b) illustrates the detail of the image model. For the MDN model, the output layer is simply replaced with an MDN layer. The model with LSTM had been trained but turned out to work poorly in the experiment, so it is not covered in detail in this paper.

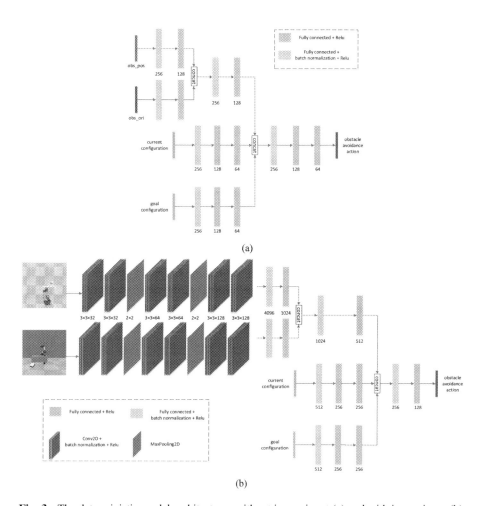

Fig. 3. The deterministic model architectures without image input (a) and with image input (b).

4.3   Training

The deterministic models were trained with loss function of direct mean squared error from the defined obstacle avoidance action

$$e_{mse} = \left\| a_{pred} - a_{true} \right\|^2 \tag{3}$$

while the loss function for the MDN model was the negative logarithm likelihood.

$$g_i(a_{true}|x) = \frac{1}{(2\pi)^{\frac{n}{2}} det(S_i(x))} \exp\left(-\frac{1}{2} \left\| S_i(x)^{-1}(a_{true} - \mu_i(x)) \right\|^2 \right), \tag{4}$$

$$e_{MDN} = -\ln\left\{ \sum_{i=0}^{m} \alpha_i(x) g_i(a_{true}|x) \right\}. \tag{5}$$

To avoid too many parameters of the MDN output, the covariance matrix of each Gaussian distribution was set to a diagonal matrix. The data in each scene consisted of the pose of obstacle and a sequence of configurations representing the path. Those data were loaded and reconfigured into a sequence of scene configuration tuple in the data generator to feed the training process. All the models were constructed and trained with Keras on TensorFlow backend, and were optimized using Adam optimizers. The learning rates of non-image deterministic model, non-image MDN model and image model were 0.01, 0.0008 and 0.001 respectively, and they shared the same learning rate decay of 0.01. The computation that non-image models required was moderate and could be run on an Intel i7 CPU, while the image model was run on an NVIDIA GeForce 1080Ti GTX graphics card. The best models (with minimum validation mean squared error) during training were saved. Figure 4 shows the training curves of different models. It is evident that the deterministic model fit better than the MDN model. The intention of using MDN was to avoid the failure of training because of the uncertainty in the output actions. Since the MDN model showed higher training error than the deterministic model, the application of MDN was no longer necessary for the image-input model and only the deterministic model was tested. The image-input

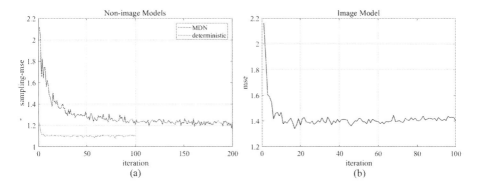

Fig. 4. Training curves of different models.

model turned out worse, possibly due to the larger bias of visual input in the unseen scenes. This result indicated that the vision module applied in this paper failed to extract more useful information in the recorded images for obstacle avoidance.

5   Experiment Validation

To evaluate the effectiveness of each policy architecture, the trained policy models were loaded in the client side of the experiment environment to execute the online path planning. Each time the robot had come to a given path point, the policy calculated a new obstacle avoidance action according to the updated scene configuration and added the normalized joint angle vector towards the goal configuration to form the final action. The obstacle avoidance action would be amplified a bit before adding to the final action to enhance the success rate. The action taken could be two times larger than the policy output to guarantee a higher success rate, at the cost of increasing the time needed to reach the goal. The max time step of each episode was set to 100. The size of the obstacle was slightly decreased (10% in our experiment) since there were regression errors and the expert might get too close to the obstacle as RRT* algorithm calculated the shortest path. If the L2 norm of the distance between the current joint angles and the goal joint angles in the configuration space was under a threshold, the path planning session was regarded as a successful attempt.

There were a proportion of scenes that the obstacle was not in the way between the initial pose and the goal pose, so it would also have succeeded to interpolate linearly in the configuration space to get the planned path. Therefore, the linearly interpolated path was also implemented each time as a contrast to manifest the validity of the obstacle avoidance policy. Table 2 shows the success rate of different models in 200 valid path planning scenes. The obstacle avoidance success rate is defined as $s_o = \frac{n_s - n_l}{200 - n_l}$, indicating the likelihood that the trained policy can execute a successful path planning while taking no obstacle avoidance action will lead to a collision. The scene configurations during validation were sampled from the same distribution of the training dataset and were identical for three policy models.

Table 2. Results comparison of different models and linear interpolation

Model type	Success count (n_s)	Success rate (s_a)	Obstacle avoidance success rate (s_o)
Non-image			
Deterministic	192	96%	94.41%
MDN	152	76%	66.43%
Image			
Deterministic	105	52.5%	33.57%
Linear interpolation success count (n_l)	57		

As the non-image deterministic model showed the best fitting result, the success rate of this policy model also proved to be the highest, and the MDN model failed more often. The image deterministic model worked much poorly than the non-image model. Besides the higher regression error of training, shrinking the obstacle caused a mismatch of the image domain, leading to the far worse execution result. Keeping the size of the obstacle the same to that of the dataset would also make the collision-free path planning harder than the non-image models.

6 Conclusion and Future Works

In this paper, we present a method of employing imitation learning to solve the problem of high-dimensional robotic arm path planning where an obstacle is in the way. A reliable procedure to construct the dataset required in simulation environment with remote client program is also introduced. Models with different architectures are discussed and tested in experiments by running different trained policy models in the same experiment setting and comparing to the linearly interpolated path. Results show that the action given by the policy is able to avoid collision with an obstacle smaller than the seen obstacle. The deterministic model functions better than the MDN model and the model with vision input works as well as the model with direct configuration input.

In the future, the vision module which acquires the pose of the obstacle from a monocular camera or a depth sensor will be supplemented in the real environment to complete the path planning network and validate in experiments. Furthermore, the dataset will be enriched and inverse reinforcement learning method will be attempted to achieve a possibly better policy.

Acknowledgment. This research work is supported in part by National Natural Science Foundation of China under grant No. 51775344.

References

1. Amarjyoti, S.: Deep reinforcement learning for robotic manipulation-the state of the art. arXiv preprint arXiv:1701.08878 (2017)
2. Riedmiller, M., et al.: Learning by playing solving sparse reward tasks from scratch. In: 35th International Conference on Machine Learning (ICML), vol. 80, pp. 4344–4353 (2018)
3. Gammell, J.D., Srinivasa, S., Barfoot, T.D.: Informed RRT*: optimal sampling-based path planning focused via direct sampling of an admissible ellipsoidal heuristic. In: 2014 IEEE International Conference on Intelligent Robots and Systems (IROS), pp. 2997–3004 (2014)
4. Tahir, Z., Qureshi, A.H., Ayaz, Y., Nawaz, R.: Potentially guided bidirectionalized RRT* for fast optimal path planning in cluttered environments. Robot. Auton. Syst. **108**, 13–27 (2018)
5. Ichter, B., Harrison, J., Pavone, M.: Learning sampling distributions for robot motion planning. In: 2018 IEEE International Conference on Robotics and Automation (ICRA), pp. 7087–7094 (2018)

6. Kalashnikov, D., et al.: Scalable deep reinforcement learning for vision-based robotic manipulation. In: Proceedings of the 2nd Conference on Robot Learning (CoRL), pp. 651–673 (2018)
7. Rahmatizadeh, R., Abolghasemi, P., Behal, A., Bölöni, L.: From virtual demonstration to real-world manipulation using LSTM and MDN. In: 32nd AAAI Conference on Artificial Intelligence, pp. 6524–6531 (2018)
8. Rahmatizadeh, R., Abolghasemi, P., Bölöni, L, Levine, S.: Vision-based multi-task manipulation for inexpensive robots using end-to-end learning from demonstration. In: 2018 IEEE International Conference on Robotics and Automation (ICRA), pp. 3758–3765 (2018)
9. Zhang, F., Leitner, J., Ge, Z., Milford, M., Peter, C.: Adversarial discriminative sim-to-real transfer of visuo-motor policies. arXiv preprint arXiv:1709.05746 (2017)
10. Yan, M., Frosio, I., Tyree, S., Kautz, J.: Sim-to-real transfer of accurate grasping with eye-in-hand observations and continuous control. In: Neural Information Processing Systems (NIPS) Workshop on Acting and Interacting in the Real World: Challenges in Robot Learning (2017)
11. Zhu, Y., et al.: reinforcement and imitation learning for diverse visuomotor skills. In: 14th Proceedings of Robotics: Science and Systems (2018)
12. Sadeghi, F., Toshev, A., Jang, E., Levine, S.: Sim2Real viewpoint invariant visual servoing by recurrent control. In: Proceedings of the 2018 IEEE Computer Society Conference on Computer Vision and Pattern Recognition (CVPR), pp. 4691–4699 (2018)
13. Thomas, G., Chien, M., Tamar, A., Ojea, J.A., Abbeel, P.: Learning robotic assembly from CAD. In: 2018 IEEE International Conference on Robotics and Automation (ICRA), pp. 1–9 (2018)
14. Pham, T., Magistris, G.D., Tachibana, R.: Optlayer-practical constrained optimization for deep reinforcement learning in the real world. In: 2018 IEEE International Conference on Robotics and Automation (ICRA), pp. 6236–6243 (2018)
15. Miseikis, J., et al.: Robot localisation and 3D position estimation using a free-moving camera and cascaded convolutional neural networks. In: 2018 IEEE/ASME International Conference on Advanced Intelligent Mechatronics (AIM), pp. 181–187 (2018)

3D Pose Estimation of Robot Arm with RGB Images Based on Deep Learning

Fan Zhou, Zijing Chi, Chungang Zhuang$^{(\boxtimes)}$, and Han Ding

State Key Laboratory of Mechanical System and Vibration,
School of Mechanical Engineering, Shanghai Jiao Tong University,
Shanghai 200240, China
cgzhuang@sjtu.edu.cn

Abstract. In the field of human-robot interaction, robot collision avoidance with the human in a shared workspace remains a challenge. Many researchers use visual methods to detect the collision between robots and obstacles on the assumption that the robot pose is known because the information about the robot is obtained from the controller and hand-eye calibration is conducted. Therefore, they focus on the motion prediction of obstacles. In this paper, a real-time method based on deep learning is proposed to directly estimate the 3D pose of the robot arm using a color image. The method aims to remove the hand-eye calibration when the system needs to be reconfigured and increase the flexibility of the system by eliminating the requirement that the camera fixed relative to the robot. Our approach has two main contributions. One is that the method estimates the 3D position of the robot base and the relative 3D positions of the predefined key points of the robot to the robot base separately different from other deep learning methods considering the limitations of the dataset. The other is that some datasets are collected through another trained network to avoid tedious calibration process, and the trained network will be reused in the pose estimation task. Finally, the experiments are conducted. The results show that a fully trained system provides an accurate 3D pose estimation for the robot arm in the camera coordinate system. The average errors of the 3D positions of the robot base and the predefined key points are 2.35 cm and 1.99 cm respectively.

Keywords: Deep learning · 3D pose estimation · Robot arm ·
Dataset generation · Collision detection

1 Introduction

In recent years, many robot manufacturers have launched collaborative robots like Baxter and Sawyer, which usually have sophisticated collision detection system [1]. The system senses the collision between the robot body and obstacles in time, and then controls the power output of the robot joint to reduce the damage. Although this solution reduces the risk of the collision to some extent, the collision should be avoided entirely in some sensitive environments. In order to detect the collision in advance, many researchers propose various methods based on one or more vision sensors to conduct collision detection and further collision avoidance trajectory planning [2]. In these safety monitoring systems, vision sensors are usually fixed relative to the robot,

© Springer Nature Switzerland AG 2019
H. Yu et al. (Eds.): ICIRA 2019, LNAI 11743, pp. 541–553, 2019.
https://doi.org/10.1007/978-3-030-27538-9_46

and hand-eye calibration is performed to make sure the collision detection in the same coordinate system, which means the relative motion between sensors and robots should be avoided. Though there are automatic calibration procedures, the calibration is still time-wasting [3]. Besides, these methods assume that the robot information is obtained from the controller. When the data associated with the robot (e.g., joint angle, robot model) are not available in some cases, it is necessary to estimate the robot pose using other methods. Lastly, for most of the work in robot arm collision avoidance, the collision between the end-effector and obstacles is the main point of focus, and other robot joints are not investigated [4].

There are many researches based on deep learning focus on the pose estimation from a single monocular image, most of which aim to estimate the human pose in the human-computer interaction field. In terms of the pose estimation in the robotics field, the 6D pose estimation of a target object in the pick-and-place task is the main research focus. The traditional approaches usually align the 3D CAD model and 3D point clouds given by the visual sensors using iterative closest point algorithms [5]. In recent researches, deep learning methods are widely applied to the pose estimation for objects [6, 7]. Different from the human pose estimation task, these methods need to use synthetic data or create own data corresponding to their task, and then train the deep neural networks on the dataset to guarantee the robustness of the model. As for the pose estimation of the robot arm, some researches work on the traditional visual methods, but few deep learning methods. One major limitation in the deep learning methods is that these methods do not take into account the fact that the dataset is not sufficient for the position estimation task of the robot base because the datasets are collected from only a few viewpoints.

In this paper, a real-time method based on deep learning is proposed to achieve the 3D pose estimation for the robot arm in the camera coordinate system using color images. The method has two main contributions. One is that two different datasets are collected to estimate the 3D position of the robot base and the relative 3D positions of the predefined key points of the robot to the robot base separately considering the limitations of the dataset. The other is that another network is trained to avoid tedious calibration process during the dataset generation, and the network will be reused in the pose estimation task. The intermediate supervision is adopted in the pose estimation task to guide the training. The proposed method can be applied to the safety monitoring system where hand-eye calibration is infeasible because of the continuously relative motion between the camera and the robot. Besides, when the system needs to be reconfigured, the method can eliminate a series of repetitive preprocess procedures including hand-eye calibration. The method also can be used to detect the collision between all joints of the robot and obstacles because the positions of all joints are obtained.

This paper is organized as follows. In Sect. 2, a survey on the methods related to the pose estimation task is given. The system setup and datasets collection for the robot is presented in Sect. 3. Then, we show the architecture of the system and elaborate on the role of each part in Sect. 4. The training of the system and experimental results are presented in Sect. 5. At last, the conclusion is presented in Sect. 6.

Fig. 1. Color images of UR5 robot in the Pose-dataset and Base-dataset at different viewpoints. These datasets include a variety of backgrounds, which provide more robustness.

2 Related Work

There are some researches worked on the pose estimation for robot arm with visual methods. Gratal et al. [8] simplified the pose estimation task by detecting the markers such as LED lights attached to the arm. The limitation of this approach is that these markers must always be in sight of the camera, which constraints the possible pose of the robot arm in space. Other methods used the RGB-D cameras to build the 3D model and detect the robot arm in the space, achieving the localization and tracking of the manipulator for grasp task without markers [9, 10]. Bohg et al. [11] presented a real-time approach to achieve the marker-less robot pose estimation. In the method, the estimation problem was transformed into a pixel-wise part classification problem, and a depth image with each pixel classified to be robot or background was used as input to train a random decision forest. Later on, they employed a random regression forest trained on synthetically generated data for the pose estimation task [12]. This method also used depth images to estimate the angular joint positions without any prior knowledge from the joint encoders, and the approach also worked on real depth images (Fig. 1).

As for deep learning method for the pose estimation of the robot arm, only a few researchers focus on the related work. Miseikis et al. [13] collected some datasets and trained the multi-objective network for robot pose estimation and localization tasks. On the other hand, there are many studies on the pose estimation of the human body in the 2D image or the 3D space. Stacked hourglass networks was a typical detection-based architecture, which was proposed by Newell et al. [14] to estimate the 2D pose of human in color image considering the relationship between multiple key points. However, it is not suitable for real-time tasks due to the large network structure. Mehta et al. [15] proposed a method to estimate both 2D and 3D pose of human. In their approach, the 3D pose was estimated by taking the value from the point in location maps corresponding to the key point in heat maps. These detection-based methods usually generate a likelihood heat map for each key point, and the point with the maximum likelihood in the heat map is taken as the key point. As a matter of fact, such "taking-maximum" operation is not differentiable [16], and it is just a post-processing method which is not included in the training process of the network. More importantly, it leads to quantization errors [16] because the resolution of the heat map is very low after multiple down-sampling and convolution operations on the input image.

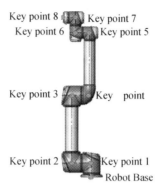

Fig. 2. The robot base and the predefined eight key points in UR5 robot body.

3   System Setup and Dataset Collection

For there is a lack of relevant datasets for pose estimation in the robotics field, researchers have to create their datasets for different tasks. In our work, we create our datasets by using a Kinect sensor and a UR5 robot in our lab. Different from the datasets collected in [13], our datasets consist of two parts, one is used to estimate the robot pose named Pose-dataset, and the other is used to estimate the 3D position of the robot base named Base-dataset, both of them are measured in the camera coordinate system. The depth information from the Kinect sensor is only used during the generation of the Base-dataset.

The specific collection of the Pose-dataset is similar to [13]. There are two main differences. In our work, eight key points are defined inside the UR5 robot body, which are at the intersection of the centerlines of the two adjacent links illustrated in Fig. 2 (Table 1).

Table 1. The description of abbreviations in the paper

Abbreviations	Description
Pose-dataset	The dataset is collected through hand-eye calibration. It is used to estimate the relative 3D positions of the predefined key points to the robot base in the camera coordinate system
Base-dataset	The dataset is collected through the Collection-Net. It is used to estimate the 3D position of the robot base in the camera coordinate system
Collection-Net	The network is trained on the pose-dataset to collect the base-dataset quickly and reused in the pose estimation task
Pose-Net	The network is trained on the pose-dataset to estimate the relative 3D positions of the predefined key points to the robot base
Base-Net	The network is trained on the base-dataset to estimate the 3D position of the robot base in the camera coordinate system

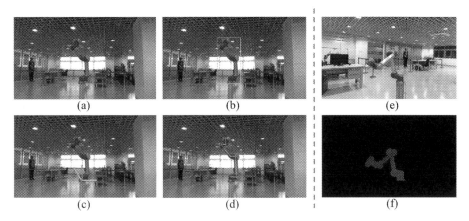

Fig. 3. The example of the color image and the ground truth data in the Pose-dataset (a–d) and Base-dataset (e–f). (a) An original color image in the Pose-dataset. (b) The ground truth bounding box. (c) The ground truth 3D position of the robot base in the camera coordinate system. (d) The ground truth 3D positions of the key points marked on the color image. (e) An original color image in the Base-dataset. (f) The depth image of the robot aligned with the color image.

The robot pose in the camera coordinate system can be obtained through these key points. Another difference is that each instance in our datasets contains a 1920 × 1080 pixels color image and the ground truth data. The ground truth data include pixel coordinates, cartesian coordinates of the key points, and a rough bounding box generated according to the key points in the color image. In the end, we created 8 Pose-dataset from 8 viewpoints, and the number of samples per dataset was kept at 1500 (Fig. 3).

In fact, the position of the robot base is fixed in the camera coordinate system at each viewpoint, so the number of viewpoints in the Pose-dataset is too small to train the network for estimating the 3D position of the robot base. Unfortunately, it is cumbersome to increase the size of the datasets for locating the robot base by only adding the number of viewpoints. Because it is necessary to perform hand-eye calibration at each viewpoint, and a single viewpoint has little contribution to the datasets. To solve the problem, the network named Collection-Net is trained on the Pose-dataset to locate the robot and the robot base in the color image to collect the Base-dataset, and it is elaborated in Sect. 4. Compared to hand-eye calibration, this approach eliminates the cumbersome calibration process at the expense of a little precision. Combining the position of the robot base in the image with the depth information from the Kinect sensor, the 3D position of the robot base could be calculated in real time at different viewpoints. During the generation of the Base-dataset, we only focus on the 3D position of the robot base rather than the robot pose. Thus each instance only contains a 1920 × 1080 pixels color image, pixel coordinates and depth information of the robot base. In the end, we created the Base-dataset from 50 viewpoints, and the number of samples per dataset was kept at 25.

The result of the RGB camera calibration was saved with the datasets to rectify the color images to ensure the accuracy of the datasets. For the Base-dataset, the training set and the validation set were divided by ratios of 90% and 10% using a random sampling method. Each dataset in the Pose-dataset was serialized in chronological order, then the top 90% was taken as the training set, and the remaining 10% was taken as the validation set (Table 2).

Table 2. Basic information of datasets

Information	Pose-dataset	Base-dataset
Number of samples per viewpoint	1500	25
Number of viewpoint	8	50
Total number of samples	12000	1250
Ground truth data	Pixel coordinates and cartesian coordinates of the key points, a rough bounding box	Pixel coordinates and depth information of the robot base

4   Method

Our method uses a CNN structure, and the feature extraction network is the extraction module as shown in Fig. 4(b), which is a simplified hourglass module [14] and also combines the multi-dimensional features of the robot in the image. As mentioned above, the output of the detection-based method is heat maps which have some limitations. Thus the integral regression method [16] for the heat maps is introduced to achieve end-to-end training. In this way, the detection problem is actually transformed into a regression problem to avoid the quantization error, and the goal is to reduce the regression loss of the positions of the key points in both 2D and 3D. The integral regression method avoids the problem of massive parameters of fully connected layers and facilitates the implementation of intermediate supervision in different stages by using multiple networks in series.

4.1   The Structure of the System

The Collection-Net aims to collect the Base-dataset for avoiding hand-eye calibration. The structure of the Collection-Net is shown in Fig. 4(a). The input information of the Collection-Net includes the bounding box of the robot in the previous frame and the current color image. The bounding box information is used to crop the current color image, and then the cropped and scaled image with 256 × 256 pixels is fed into the network. The input image is the most likely area for the robot in the current image, and it contains less background information than the entire image. Data augmentation is used in both the input image and the bounding box to improve the generalization capabilities of the Collection-Net. After the input image passes through a series of

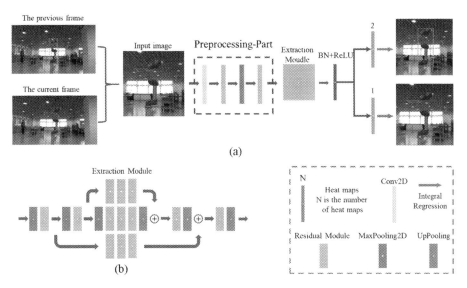

Fig. 4. (a) The structure of the Collection-Net. The Collection-Net aims to locate the robot and the robot base in the image, and it is trained on the Pose-datasets. The bounding box of the robot in the previous frame is used to crop the current color image, and then the cropped image is scaled to 256×256 pixels as the input image. After the input image passes through the Preprocessing-Part, it is input into the extraction module followed by batch normalization and ReLU activation. The two branches aim to regress the bounding box and the position of the robot base in the image. (b) The internal structure of the extraction module.

convolution layers, residual modules [14] and max-pooling layers named Preprocessing-Part, it is input into the extraction module to extract features followed by batch normalization and ReLU activation. Finally, the output is divided into two branches, and the integral regression method is applied to calculate the estimated bounding box and position of the robot base in the image. Noted that the trained Collection-Net will be reused in the pose estimation task.

The architecture of the system for 3D pose estimation of the robot arm is shown in Fig. 5. The system consists of two parts, named Base-Net and Pose-Net, corresponding to the estimation of the 3D position of the robot base and the relative 3D positions of the predefined key points to the robot base respectively. When the current color image input the system, it is processed for different targets. In front of the Pose-Net, the color image is cropped and scaled as the input image the same as the Collection-Net according to the bounding box information of the previous frame, and the fully trained Preprocessing-Part of the Collection-Net is reused. The Pose-Net is a cascade CNN structure. In the front of the Pose-Net, the positions of the key points in the image are estimated firstly to guide the training named intermediate supervision. The Pose-Net should pay more attention to these key points in the image, which provide an additional learning basis. The output of the Pose-Net is divided into two branches. One branch is flattened into a series of vectors to estimate the depth of each key point, and another is used to estimate the positions of the key points in the other two dimensions. It is

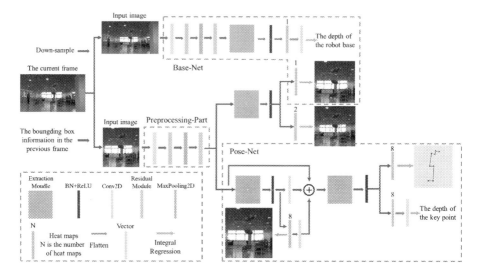

Fig. 5. The architecture of the system for 3D pose estimation of the robot arm. The system includes the Base-Net and Pose-Net. The fully trained Preprocessing-Part and one branch of the Collection-Net are reused in the system. In the Pose-Net, the positions of the key points in the image are first estimated to guide the training. The Base-Net obtains the 3D position of the robot base by estimating the depth and using the position of the robot base in the image estimated by the Collection-Net.

noteworthy that the results of the Pose-Net are the relative 3D positions of the key points to the robot base in the camera coordinate system. As for the Base-Net, the color image is down-sampled as the input image without the cropping operation. The Base-Net is composed of one fully trained branch of the Collection-Net and another part, which aims to estimate the depth of the robot base. After knowing the position of the robot base in the image and the depth, the 3D position of the robot base can be calculated by combining the camera parameters. Combining the outputs of the Pose-Net and Base-Net, the 3D pose of the robot arm in the camera coordinate system is obtained. It is needed to set a reasonable bounding box of the robot before inputting the first image when the system starts working. Noted that the next frame image and the estimated bounding box of the current color image would be used as the new input of the system.

4.2 Loss Functions

After the network structure is built, several loss functions are defined for the system to optimize the network parameters. In the Collection-Net, the loss function is designed to adjust the estimated bounding box and position of the robot base in the image, and it is defined in L2 loss as:

$$\begin{cases} l_{base} = \lambda \cdot l_{box} + l_{locate} \\ l_{box} = \|b^{est} - b^{gt}\|_2 \\ l_{locate} = \|p^{est} - p^{gt}\|_2 \end{cases} \tag{1}$$

where b^{est} and p^{est} are the estimated bounding box and position of the robot base. b^{gt} and p^{gt} are the ground truth data. λ is a coefficient between 0 and 1 to weight the two losses of the bounding box and the position of the robot base in the image. λ is usually set to 0.5. l_{base} is the final loss of the Collection-Net.

In the Pose-Net, l_{locate} in (1) is modified to describe the loss of locating the key points in the image as:

$$l_{position} = \frac{1}{N} \sum_{i=1}^{N} \left\| p_i^{est} - p_i^{gt} \right\|_2 \tag{2}$$

where p_i^{est} is the estimated position of the ith key point in the image. N is the number of the key points and is set to 8 in our case. As for the loss of the 3D positions of the key points, it is defined similarly to $l_{position}$ as in (3), where J_i^{est} is the estimated 3D position of the ith key point and N is set to 8.

$$l_{pose} = \frac{1}{N} \sum_{i=1}^{N} \left\| J_i^{est} - J_i^{gt} \right\|_2 \tag{3}$$

Considering the length of the robot link is known in advance, it can be used as prior knowledge to guide the training, and the loss of the link length is defined as:

$$l_{link} = \frac{1}{L} \sum_{i=1}^{L} \left| t_i^{est} - t_i^{gt} \right| \tag{4}$$

where t_i^{est} is the estimated length of the ith link, calculated according to the estimated 3D positions of the key points and L is the number of links, which is 8 in our case. The final loss function l_{final} is the weighted combination of $l_{position}$, l_{pose} and l_{link} in (5), and these losses are optimized simultaneously during the training process in the pose estimation task. The larger the weight w, the more important the predicted result is. In the Base-Net, the loss is calculated as l_{pose} and N is set to 1.

$$l_{final} = w_{position} \cdot l_{position} + w_{pose} \cdot l_{pose} + w_{link} \cdot l_{link} \tag{5}$$

5   Network Training and Experiment Results

5.1   Training Procedure

The training process is divided into three steps. Firstly, the Collection-Net was trained on the Pose-dataset to collect the Base-dataset. The error between the predicted position of the robot base and the ground truth data was limited within 0.4 pixels in the image, and it ensured the reliability of the Base-dataset. Secondly, as mentioned in Sect. 4, the

Preprocessing-Part in front of the Pose-Net is part of the Collection-Net. Therefore, there is no need to train the Preprocessing-Part again after training the Collection-Net, and only the Pose-Net was trained on the Pose-dataset. The manually selected weight values were $w_{position}$: 0.7, w_{pose} : 1.2 and w_{link} : 0.5. At last, only the network in the Base-Net for estimating the depth of the robot base was trained on the Base-dataset, and the branch of the Collection-Net was directly reused. The size of the input image was down-sampled from 1920×1080 to 480×270 pixels to speed up the training process.

For all the above networks, the pixel intensity values of the input images were normalized in all training process. The learning rate was set to 0.00025 in the beginning and then gradually decreased to 0.00001 after 8000 iterations. It took 12 h, 20 h and 10 h to train the Collection-Net, Pose-Net, and Base-Net respectively, using an NVIDIA GeForce 1080Ti GTX graphics card.

Table 3. The results of two methods.

Our	method	Miseikis et al. [13]
Robot base error (2D)	0.32 pixels	-
Bounding box error	2.45 pixels	-
Key points error (2D)	1.34 pixels	-
Key points error (3D)	1.99 cm	3.16 cm
Robot base error (3D)	2.35 cm	2.74 cm

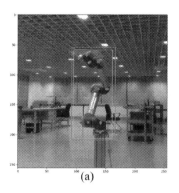 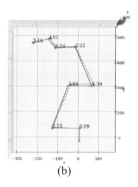

(a)   (b)

Fig. 6. The estimated results (red) and the ground truth data (green) are drawn in the color image and 3D space. (a) The 2D results drawn in the color image consist of the bounding box and the positions of the key points and the robot base. (b) The results drawn in 3D space consist of the relative 3D positions of the key points to the robot base in the camera coordinate system. The blue number is the error of the 3D position of each key point measured in cm. (Color figure online)

5.2 Experiment Results and Analysis

The system including the Collection-Net, Pose-Net and Base-Net were evaluated on the validation set of the Pose-dataset, including 1200 samples. It took 54 ms to inference an input image to estimate the robot pose in the system. Euclidean distance between the estimated results and the ground truth data was calculated as the verification metrics, in both 2D image and 3D space.

In the system, the average error of the bounding box reached 2.45 pixels, and the average 2D position errors of the key points and the robot base reached 1.34 pixels and 0.32 pixels respectively. The average error of the bounding box was larger because the ground truth bounding box was automatically generated according to the 2D positions of the key points in the image while collecting the Pose-dataset. Thus the estimated bounding box is fluctuant compared to the estimated positions of the key points and the robot base in the image.

The average error of the relative 3D positions of the key points to the robot base was 1.99 cm, and the average error of the 3D position of the robot base was 2.35 cm, which is an improvement compared to the errors of 3.16 cm and 2.74 cm in [13]. The results of the two methods are summarized in Table 3. In our method, the model for estimating the 3D position of the robot base was trained in more viewpoints, which enhances the robustness of the model to locating the robot base. When the error of each key point is analyzed, it can be found that the error of the key point near the end-effector is bigger, because the range of motion of the key point is larger. The tendency can be seen in Fig. 6. Besides, the error of each key point in our approach is smaller than [13], except for the key point 8, as seen in Fig. 7.

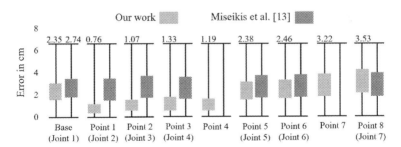

Fig. 7. The errors of the 3D positions of the robot base and each key point obtained in the two methods. There are some key points whose positions are estimated in both our work and [13], and these key points are noted in the figure. The blue number is the average error of the position of each key point (joint) measured in cm. (Color figure online)

6 Conclusion

In this paper, a real-time method is proposed to estimate the 3D pose of the robot arm with a RGB image. The proposed method uses the Pose-Net and the Base-Net to accomplish the task of estimating the positions of the predefined key points and the robot base in the RGB camera coordinate system. Another network named Collection-Net is trained for collecting the Base-dataset and reused in the pose estimation task, which can avoid cumbersome dataset generation procedures including hand-eye calibration. The average errors of the 3D positions of the key points and the robot base are 1.99 cm and 2.35 cm respectively. The experimental results are compared to the multi-objective CNN method [13], which shows improvement in the accuracy of the pose estimation. Our work has multiple possible applications in the scenes where relative motion exists between the camera and the robot and hand-eye calibration is infeasible. For example, when the robot arm is mounted on a mobile platform, the method in this paper can estimate the pose of the robot arm in real time during the motion of the mobile platform and further detect the collision between the robot arm and external environments. In addition, there is no need to fix the camera relative to the robot and perform hand-eye calibration in our method, which increases the flexibility of the system.

Acknowledgment. This research work is partially supported by National Natural Science Foundation of China under Grant No. 51775344.

References

1. Fitzgerald, C.: Developing baxter. In: 2013 IEEE Conference on Technologies for Practical Robot Applications (TePRA), pp. 1–6. IEEE. Greater Boston Area (2013)
2. Halme, R.J., Lanz, M., Kämäräinen, J., Pieters, R., Latokartano, J., Hietanen, A.: Review of vision-based safety systems for human-robot collaboration. Procedia CIRP **72**(1), 111–116 (2018)
3. Miseikis, J., Glette, K., Elle, O.J., Torresen, J.: Automatic calibration of a robot manipulator and multi 3D camera system. In: 2016 IEEE/SICE International Symposium on System Integration (SII), pp. 735–741. IEEE, Sapporo (2016)
4. Stasse, O., Escande, A., Mansard, N., Miossec, S., Evrard, P., Kheddar, A.: Real-time (self)-collision avoidance task on a HRP-2 humanoid robot. In: 2008 IEEE International Conference on Robotics and Automation (ICRA), pp. 3200–3205. IEEE, Pasadena (2008)
5. Besl, P.J., McKay, N.D.: Method for registration of 3-D shapes. In: Sensor Fusion IV: Control Paradigms and Data Structures, vol. 1611, pp. 586–607 (1992)
6. Zeng, A., et al.: Multi-view self-supervised deep learning for 6D pose estimation in the amazon picking challenge. In: 2017 IEEE International Conference on Robotics and Automation (ICRA), pp. 1386–1383. IEEE, Singapore (2017)
7. Tremblay, J., To, T., Sundaralingam, B., Xiang, Y., Fox, D., Birchfield, S.: Deep object pose estimation for semantic robotic grasping of household objects. arXiv preprint arXiv:1809.10790 (2018)
8. Gratal, X., Bohg, J., Björkman, M., Kragic, D.: Scene representation and object grasping using active vision. In: IROS 2010 Workshop on Defining and Solving Realistic Perception Problems in Personal Robotics (2010)
9. Hebert, P., et al.: Combined shape, appearance and silhouette for simultaneous manipulator and object tracking. In: 2012 IEEE International Conference on Robotics and Automation (ICRA), pp. 2405–2412. IEEE, St. Paul (2012)
10. Krainin, M., Henry, P., Ren, X., Fox, D.: Manipulator and object tracking for in-hand 3D object modeling. Int. J. Robot. Res. **30**(11), 1311–1327 (2011)

11. Bohg, J., Romero, J., Herzog, A., Schaal, S.: Robot arm pose estimation through pixel-wise part classification. In: 2014 IEEE International Conference on Robotics and Automation (ICRA), pp. 3143–3150. IEEE, Hong Kong (2014)
12. Widmaier, F., Kappler, D., Schaal, S., Bohg, J.: Robot arm pose estimation by pixel-wise regression of joint angles. In: 2016 IEEE International Conference on Robotics and Automation (ICRA), pp. 616–623. IEEE, Stockholm (2016)
13. Miseikis, J., Brijacak, I., Yahyanejad, S., Glette, K., Elle, O.J., Torresen, J.: Multi-objective convolutional neural networks for robot localisation and 3D position estimation in 2D camera images. In: 2018 15th International Conference on Ubiquitous Robots (UR), pp. 597–603. IEEE, Honolulu (2018)
14. Newell, A., Yang, K., Deng, J.: Stacked hourglass networks for human pose estimation. In: Leibe, B., Matas, J., Sebe, N., Welling, M. (eds.) ECCV 2016. LNCS, vol. 9912, pp. 483–499. Springer, Cham (2016). https://doi.org/10.1007/978-3-319-46484-8_29
15. Mehta, D., et al.: VNect: real-time 3D human pose estimation with a single RGB camera. ACM Trans. Graph. (TOG) 36(4), 44 (2017)
16. Sun, X., Xiao, B., Wei, F., Liang, S., Wei, Y.: Integral human pose regression. In: Ferrari, V., Hebert, M., Sminchisescu, C., Weiss, Y. (eds.) ECCV 2018. LNCS, vol. 11210, pp. 536–553. Springer, Cham (2018). https://doi.org/10.1007/978-3-030-01231-1_33

Straightness Error Assessment Model of the Linear Axis of Machine Tool Based on Data-Driven Method

Yang Hui[1,2], Xuesong Mei[1,2], Gedong Jiang[1,2], and Fei Zhao[1,2(✉)]

[1] State Key Laboratory for Manufacturing Systems Engineering,
Xi'an Jiaotong University, Xi'an 710049, China
ztzhao@mail.xjtu.edu.cn
[2] School of Mechanical Engineering, Xi'an Jiaotong University,
Xi'an 710049, China

Abstract. In batch assembly, fast and accurate assessment of MT-LA straightness error is significant important for controlling of MT-LA assembly quality. In this study, in order to construct MT-LA straightness error assessment model, a data-driven method based on the bootstrap resampling approach improved fast correlation based filter (BR-FCBF) algorithm and genetic algorithm optimized multi-class support vector machine (GA-MSVM) algorithm is proposed. Firstly, the BR-FCBF algorithm is used to select the key assembly parameters that affect the straightness error. Secondly, the GA-MSVM algorithm is applied to construct the straightness error assessment model. Finally, the assembly-related data collected on a MT-LA assembly workshop is used to verify the proposed method. The experimental results show that the constructed straightness error assessment model has shown good performance in straightness error assessment.

Keywords: Linear axis · Straightness error assessment model · Data-driven · BR-FCBF · GA-MSVM

1 Introduction

With the continuous improvement of the linear axis parts machining precision, the manufacturing quality of the linear axis of machine tool (MT-LA) is depends mainly on its assembly quality [1, 2]. Since the straightness error is one of the main indicators to assess MT-LA assembly quality, techniques for realizing straightness error assessment are great significance important to control MT-LA assembly quality.

Over the last few decades, a large amount of studies has been conducted on MT-LA theoretical model to realize straightness error assessment. Du et al. [3] established a MT-LA geometric error model by using the Jacobian-torsor theory method. Based on the 3-2-1 localization theory and considered component deformation caused by gravity, Ma et al. [4] presented an MT-LA assembly error model. By dividing the errors of a linear motion system into four tiers according to the assembly sequence, He et al. [5] proposed a hierarchical error model to estimate the kinematic error of a linear motion bearing table. Rahmani et al. [1] and Majda et al. [6] investigated the influence of the

© Springer Nature Switzerland AG 2019
H. Yu et al. (Eds.): ICIRA 2019, LNAI 11743, pp. 554–563, 2019.
https://doi.org/10.1007/978-3-030-27538-9_47

linear guideway errors on MT-LA kinematic errors by FEM model. Moreover, the stream of variation theory [7] and homogeneous transformation matrices [8] that used to establish geometric error model of multi-axis systems were also provided an idea on constructing MT-LA assembly error model. However, due to the complexity of MT-LA theoretical model, the modeling process must be simplified, and the limited assembly parameters are considered in the model. Therefore, the MT-LA theoretical model is not adapted to the needs of MT-LA straightness error assessment in the actual dynamic assembly process.

Different from the theoretical model method, the core of the data-driven method is obtaining useful information from a large amount of data, and it can effectively solve industrial problems in various operating state [9]. Yin et al. [10] realized the application of data-driven methods in wind turbine fault monitoring. In order to achieve chemical industry products real-time control, Wang et al. [11] constructed a real-time quality prediction model by data-driven method. Tao et al. [12] proposed a data-driven intelligent manufacturing concept, and discussed its application in product quality control. Wang et al. [13] implemented quality related fault detection based on data-driven method by using orthogonal signal correction and modified partial least squares. Hsu et al. [14] developed a novel method based on integrating independent component analysis and support vector machine learning to realize multivariate process monitoring. It can be seen that the data-driven approach provides a new perspective for the quality assessment and improvement. Therefore, in this paper, in order to assess straightness error in MT-LA batch assembly process, a MT-LA straightness error assessment model based on data-driven method by using the bootstrap resampling method improved fast correlation based filter (BR-FCBF) algorithm and genetic algorithm optimized multi-class support vector machine (GA-MSVM) algorithm is constructed.

The rest of paper is organized as follows. In Sect. 2, the BR-FCBF algorithm is introduced. In Sect. 3, the assembly flow of the linear axis is analyzed. In Sect. 4, the MT-LA straightness error assessment model based on data-driven approach is proposed. In Sect. 5, the results and discussions are presented. Finally, the conclusions of this study are laid out in Sect. 6.

2   B-FCBF Algorithm

The fast correlation based filter (FCBF) [15] algorithm is a multi-feature selection method which uses symmetry uncertainty to calculate dependences of features. The FCBF algorithm finds best subset using backward selection technique with sequential search strategy.

Assuming X and Y are random variables, the symmetric uncertainty calculation formula can be expressed as:

$$SU(X, Y) = 2\left[\frac{H(X) - H(X|Y)}{H(X) + H(Y)}\right] \tag{1}$$

Where $H(X)$ is the entropy of X, $H(Y)$ is the entropy of Y, and $H(X|Y)$ is conditional entropy of X over Y.

The mutual information between X and Y can be expressed as:

$$IG(X;Y) = H(X) - H(X|Y) = H(Y) - H(Y|X) \tag{2}$$

So, from Eqs. (1) and (2), the symmetric uncertainty can be rewritten as:

$$SU(X,Y) = 2\left[\frac{IG(X;Y)}{H(X) + H(Y)}\right] \tag{3}$$

From Eq. (3), it can be seen that the symmetric uncertainty is a normalized form of the mutual information. And the mutual information can be expressed as:

$$IG(X;Y) = \sum_{i=1}^{n}\sum_{j=1}^{n} p(x_i, y_j) \log_2^{\frac{p(x_i, y_j)}{p(x_i)p(x_j)}} \tag{4}$$

When X and Y are independent of each other, $p(x_i, y_j) = p(x_i)p(y_j)$, and the mutual information $IG(X;Y) = 0$, which means that there is no correlation between X and Y. On the contrary, if the correlation between X and Y is high, the value of the mutual information $IG(X;Y)$ is large.

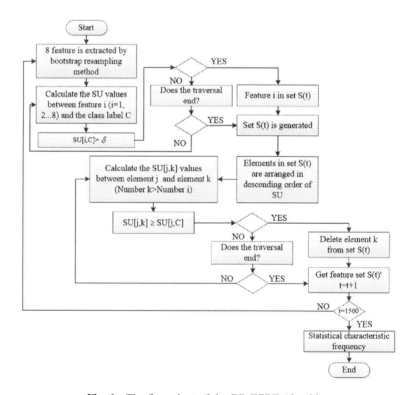

Fig. 1. The flow chart of the BR-FCBF Algorithm

From the paper [16], if inputs data are highly correlated, the FCBF algorithm may eliminate too many features, and we cannot obtain the best subset which has k features. Due to the higher correlation between machine tool assembly parameters. In order to get an appropriate assembly parameters subset that really affect MT-LA straightness error, the bootstrap resampling method is used to improved FCBF, and a bootstrap resampling FCBF (BR-FCBF) algorithm which can reduce the probability of all assembly parameters appearing at the same time is proposed to avoid the highly correlated assembly parameters are deleted. The flow chart of the BR-FCBF algorithm is shown in Fig. 1.

3   Assembly Flow Analysis of MT-LA

In Fig. 2, MT-LA assembly flow is described. It can be seen that MT-LA assembly flow can be divided into four stages, namely bed adjustment stage, guideway assembly stage, ball screw assembly stage, and workbench assembly stage. In bed adjustment stage, to ensure the straightness error of bed guideway installation surface is kept within the assembly tolerance requirements range, the concave-convex error and the distortion error of bed need to be adjusted and controlled. In guideway assembly stage, two guideways are installed on the bed guideway installation surface, so the straightness error of each guideways and the parallelism error between two guideways are need to be adjusted and controlled. In ball screw assembly stage, to ensure the parallelism error between the ball screw and the guideway meets the assembly tolerance requirements, the coaxiality error between the motor seat and the bearing seat must be adjusted before the ball screw is installed. In workbench assembly stage, after the ball screw nut and the nut seat, the worktable and four sliders are connected, the MT-LA assembly is completed. In order to judge whether the final MT-LA assembly quality meets the assembly requirement of machine tool manufacturing enterprise, the MT-LA six motion errors such as positioning error, straightness error in horizontal and vertical planes, pitch error, roll error and yaw error are measured. Obviously, the MT-LA assembly quality is mainly depending on the various assembly parameters, and there are many assembly parameters are existing in the MT-LA assembly process.

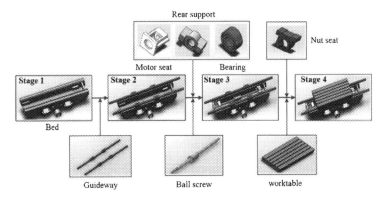

Fig. 2. Assembly flow analysis of MT-LA

Besides, the multiple dimensional chains characteristic in MT-LA assembly process, resulting in the multiple correlations among the assembly parameters.

4   The Modeling Method for MT-LA Straightness Error Assessment Model

In this section, the flow chart of the modeling method for MT-LA straightness error assessment model is illustrated in Fig. 3. Firstly, the assembly-related data including assembly parameters data and straightness error data is obtained in MT-LA batch assembly process. Secondly, in order to solve the class imbalance problem and the data normalization problem, the data preprocessing method such as the SMOTE method [17] and the Max-Min normalization method is used respectively. Thirdly, the BR-FCBF algorithm is used to select the key assembly parameters that affect MT-LA straightness error. Fourthly, based on the selected key assembly parameters, the GA-MSVM algorithm [18] is applied to construct straightness error assessment model. Finally, the corresponding performance evaluation indicators are used to evaluate the performance of the model.

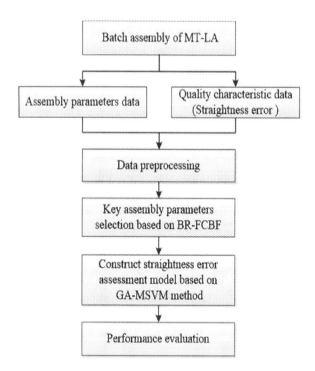

Fig. 3. Flow chart of the proposed modeling method

5 Experimental Results and Analysis

5.1 Data Collection

In this paper, the assembly-related data were collected in X-axis assembly process of a three-axis vertical machining center, and the assembly-related data obtained process were described in Fig. 4. There were 95 groups of the assembly-related data collected and each assembly-related data was consisted of 20 assembly parameters data and one straightness error data. Some of the assembly-related data were shown in Table 1. In Table 1, CCEB represents the concave-convex error of bed, DEB represents the distortion error of bed, SEG-I represents the straightness error of guideway I, SEG-II represents the straightness error of guideway II, PE represents the parallelism error between two guideways in horizontal plane, and Z-SE represents the straightness error of X-axis in Z direction.

Assembly site

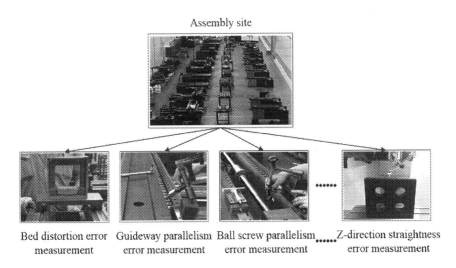

| Bed distortion error measurement | Guideway parallelism error measurement | Ball screw parallelism error measurement | •••••• | Z-direction straightness error measurement |

Fig. 4. Experimental data acquisition in assembly workshop

Table 1. Some obtained assembly-related data in X-axis batch assembly process

Number	CCEB (grid)	DEB (grid)	SEG-I (mm)	SEG-II (mm)	PE (mm)	⋯	Z-SE (mm)
1	8.5	0.5	0.004	0.004	0.01	⋯	0.007
2	8	0.5	0.004	0.005	0.01	⋯	0.007
3	9.5	0.5	0.003	0.006	0.005	⋯	0.006
4	9	1	0.008	0.007	0.01	⋯	0.007
5	9	0.5	0.007	0.007	0.01	⋯	0.01
6	9	0.5	0.006	0.004	0.008	⋯	0.007
7	8	1	0.008	0.008	0.01	⋯	0.008
⋯	⋯	⋯	⋯	⋯	⋯	⋯	⋯

5.2   Key Assembly Parameters Selection by BR-FCBF Algorithm

In order to find the key assembly parameters that affected MT-LA straightness error, the 95 groups of the assembly-related data were analyzed by BR-FCBF algorithm, and the correlation degree between 20 assembly parameters and straightness error was shown in Fig. 5. In the figure, the red curve represented the frequency ratio between occurrence times of 20 assembly parameters and total sampling times in 1500 sampling analysis. The larger of frequency ratio for each assembly parameters, the correlation between each assembly parameter and the straightness error was higher. The green curve represented the decision curve f, and it was used to selected the key assembly parameters that affected MT-LA straightness error. Through comprehensive consideration, the decision curve $f = 0.15$ was taken, and the six key assembly parameters were selected. The detailed description of the six key assembly parameters were shown in Table 2.

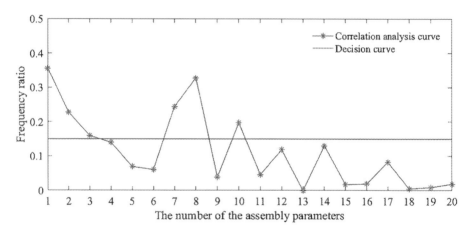

Fig. 5. The correlation degree between 20 assembly parameters and straightness error (Color figure online)

Table 2. The key assembly parameters selection result by BR-FCBF algorithm

Number	The name of the assembly parameters	Frequency ratio
1	The concave-convex error of bed	0.3553
2	The distortion error of bed	0.2273
3	The straightness error of guideway I	0.1593
7	The parallelism error between worktable and Y-axis	0.2440
8	The parallelism error between worktable and X-axis	0.3273
10	The parallelism error between motor seat and guideway I	0.1973

Comparing with the key assembly parameters selection result by BR-FCBF algorithm, only assembly parameter 1 and 8 were selected by FCBF algorithm, as shown in Table 3. It is shows that the BR-FCBF algorithm overcomes the problem of FCBF algorithm, and it can effectively select more assembly parameters that are highly correlated with X-axis straightness error.

Table 3. The key assembly parameters selection results by FCBF algorithm

Number	The name of the assembly parameters
1	The concave-convex error of bed
8	The parallelism error between worktable and X-axis

5.3 Straightness Error Assessment Model Training and Performance Evaluation

It was not possible to obtain the balanced datasets in real assembly process. In order to alleviate the interference of the class imbalance problem on the generalization performance of the MSVM algorithm, after the straightness error data were labeled with corresponding straightness error grades (class label: 0, 1, 2), the obtained assembly-related data were preprocessed by SMOTE method. Then, the Max-Min normalization method was used to standardize and normalize the assembly-related data to the range of [0 1].

In order to realize X-axis straightness error assessment, the X-axis straightness error assessment model must be constructed. Firstly, the processed assembly-related data was divided into an 80% training data set and an 20% testing data set, and the radial basis function (RBF) kernel was used as a kernel function of MSVM. Then, the training data set was input into MSVM algorithm to train the straightness error assessment model, and the GA method was applied to determine the penalty parameter c and the kernel function parameter g of the MSVM algorithm. Finally, after the optimal parameters $c = 6.7322$ and $g = 35.5186$ were determined, the X-axis straightness error assessment model was obtained. Based on this model, the X-axis straightness error assessment results were shown in Fig. 6, it can be seen that the straightness error assessment accuracy was 87.8049%.

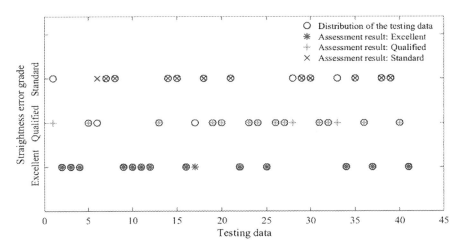

Fig. 6. The X-axis straightness error assessment results for the testing data set

Accuracy rate is not an appropriate performance indicator with imbalanced data-sets, because accuracy rate may lead to erroneous conclusions since the minority class has very little impact on accuracy as compared to the majority classes [19]. In this paper, anther commonly used classification performance evaluation indicators such as *precision, Recall, F*-measure and *G*-mean were adopted here [20]. Based on those performance evaluation indicators, the performance evaluation results of the X-axis straightness error assessment model were listed in Table 4. It can be seen that the constructed X-axis straightness error assessment model had shown a good performance for straightness error assessment, and the model had higher recognition accuracy for class 0. Although the precision evaluation result of class 3 was only 0.79, but the other evaluation results were relatively good. As well as, the overall evaluation result of the model based on *G*-mean was 0.88. Therefore, the constructed straightness error assessment model was promising to be used in MT-LA straightness error assessment.

Table 4. Performance evaluation results of the X-axis straightness error assessment model

Class label	Precision	Recall	F-measure	G-mean
0	1	0.93	0.96	0.88
1	0.86	0.80	0.83	
2	0.79	0.92	0.85	

6   Conclusions

In this study, a new MT-LA straightness error assessment model is proposed, and a data-driven method based on BR-FCBF algorithm and GA-MSVM algorithm is used to realize it. And the following conclusions are obtained: first, comparing with FCBF algorithm, the proposed BR-FCBF algorithm can effectively select more assembly parameters that highly correlated with straightness error. Then, the GA-MSVM algorithm is more suitable for constructing MT-LA straightness error assessment model. Additionally, the data-driven method takes more assembly parameters into consideration in the modeling process.

Acknowledgments. This research is supported by the Key Project of Shaanxi Province (No. 2017ZDCXL-GY-01-02-02) and the National Key Research and Development Project of China (No. 2018YFB1701200).

References

1. Rahmani, M., Bleicher, F.: Experimental and numerical studies of the influence of geometric deviations in the performance of machine tools linear guides. Procedia CIRP **41**, 818–823 (2016)
2. Li, D.Y., Zhang, G.B., Li, M.Q., et al.: The diagnosis of abnormal assembly quality based on fuzzy relation equations. Adv. Mech. Eng. **6**, 437364 (2014)

3. Du, Z., Wu, J., Yang, J.: Geometric error modeling and sensitivity analysis of single-axis assembly in three-axis vertical machine center based on Jacobian-Torsor model. ASCE-ASME J. Risk Uncertainty Eng. Syst. Part B: Mech. Eng. **4**(3), 031004 (2018)
4. Ma, J., Lu, D., Zhao, W.: Assembly errors analysis of linear axis of CNC machine tool considering component deformation. Int. J. Adv. Manuf. Technol. **86**(1–4), 281–289 (2016)
5. He, G., Sun, G., Zhang, H., et al.: Hierarchical error model to estimate motion error of linear motion bearing table. Int. J. Adv. Manuf. Technol. **93**(5–8), 1915–1927 (2017)
6. Majda, P.: Modeling of geometric errors of linear guideway and their influence on joint kinematic error in machine tools. Precis. Eng. **36**(3), 369–378 (2012)
7. Tang, H., Duan, J., Lan, S., et al.: A new geometric error modeling approach for multi-axis system based on stream of variation theory. Int. J. Mach. Tools Manuf. **92**, 41–51 (2015)
8. Lee, R.S., Lin, Y.H.: Applying bidirectional kinematics to assembly error analysis for five-axis machine tools with general orthogonal configuration. Int. J. Adv. Manuf. Technol. **62** (9–12), 1261–1272 (2012)
9. Yin, S., Li, X., Gao, H., et al.: Data-based techniques focused on modern industry: an overview. IEEE Trans. Industr. Electron. **62**(1), 657–667 (2015)
10. Yin, S., Wang, G., Karimi, H.R.: Data-driven design of robust fault detection system for wind turbines. Mechatronics **24**(4), 298–306 (2014)
11. Wang, D.: Robust data-driven modeling approach for real-time final product quality prediction in batch process operation. IEEE Trans. Industr. Inf. **7**(2), 371–377 (2011)
12. Tao, F., Qi, Q., Liu, A., et al.: Data-driven smart manufacturing. J. Manuf. Syst. **48**, 157–169 (2018)
13. Wang, G., Yin, S.: Quality-related fault detection approach based on orthogonal signal correction and modified PLS. IEEE Trans. Industr. Inf. **11**(2), 398–405 (2015)
14. Hsu, C.C., Chen, M.C., Chen, L.S.: Integrating independent component analysis and support vector machine for multivariate process monitoring. Comput. Ind. Eng. **59**(1), 145–156 (2010)
15. Yu, L., Liu, H.: Feature selection for high-dimensional data: a fast correlation-based filter solution. In: Proceedings of the 20th International Conference on Machine Learning (ICML-03), pp. 856–863
16. Şen, B., Peker, M.: Novel approaches for automated epileptic diagnosis using FCBF selection and classification algorithms. Turk. J. Electr. Eng. Comput. Sci. **21**(Suppl. 1), 2092–2109 (2013)
17. Chawla, N.V., Bowyer, K.W., Hall, L.O., et al.: SMOTE: synthetic minority over-sampling technique. J. Artif. Intell. Res. **16**, 321–357 (2002)
18. Zhang, M., Cheng, W.: Recognition of mixture control chart pattern using multiclass support vector machine and genetic algorithm based on statistical and shape features. Math. Probl. Eng. **2015** (2015)
19. López, V., Fernández, A., García, S., et al.: An insight into classification with imbalanced data: empirical results and current trends on using data intrinsic characteristics. Inf. Sci. **250**, 113–141 (2013)
20. Bhagat, R.C., Patil, S.S.: Enhanced SMOTE algorithm for classification of imbalanced big-data using random forest. In: 2015 IEEE International Advance Computing Conference (IACC), pp. 403–408. IEEE (2015)

View Invariant Human Action Recognition Using 3D Geometric Features

Qingsong Zhao[1,2,3], Shijie Sun[1,2,3], Xiaopeng Ji[4], Lei Wang[2,3], and Jun Cheng[2,3(✉)]

[1] Shenzhen College of Advanced Technology,
University of Chinese Academy of Sciences, Beijing, China
[2] Shenzhen Institutes of Advanced Technology,
Chinese Academy of Sciences, Beijing, China
{qs.zhao,sj.sun,lei.wangl,jun.cheng}@siat.ac.cn
[3] The Chinese University of Hong Kong, Hong Kong, China
[4] State Key Lab of CAD&CG, Zhejiang University, Hangzhou, China
xp.ji@cad.zju.edu.cn

Abstract. Action recognition based on 2D information has encountered intrinsic difficulties such as occlusion and view etc. Especially suffering with complicated changes of perspective. In this paper, we present a straightforward and efficient approach for 3D human action recognition based on skeleton sequences. A rough geometric feature, termed planes of 3D joint motions vector (PoJM3D) is extracted from the raw skeleton data to capture the omnidirectional short-term motion cues. A customized 3D convolutional neural network is employed to learn the global long-term representation of spatial appearance and temporal motion information with a scheme called dynamic temporal sparse sampling (DTSS). Extensive experiments on three public benchmark datasets, including UTD-MVAD, UTD-MHAD, and CAS-YNU-MHAD demonstrate the effectiveness of our method compared to the current state-of-the-art in cross-view evaluation, and significant improvement in cross-subjects evaluation. The code of our proposed approach is available at released on GitHub.

Keywords: 3D action recognition · View invariant · 3D ConvNets · Geometric features

1 Introduction

Human action recognition has always been a hot research topic in computer vision area over the past few decades. Depth maps can adapt to changes in lighting conditions through the use of infrared radiation compared to RGB videos. Various methods have been proposed to recognize human actions from depth cameras [1–5]. However, depth maps usually lack texture information and contain more noise compared with the conventional RGB videos. Furthermore, depth maps are more difficult to obtain than RGB videos. These reasons making them difficult to implement for practical application.

© Springer Nature Switzerland AG 2019
H. Yu et al. (Eds.): ICIRA 2019, LNAI 11743, pp. 564–575, 2019.
https://doi.org/10.1007/978-3-030-27538-9_48

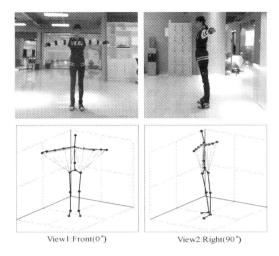

View1:Front(0°)   View2:Right(90°)

Fig. 1. Visualizing the sampled RGB images (top row) and planes of 3D joint motions vector (bottom row).

Fortunately, with the progress and development of human pose estimation, the acquisition of human skeleton data from RGB videos is becoming more and more simple. Yoshiyasu et al. [6] have used SkeletonNet to estimate human 3D skeleton information from a single RGB image. In addition, the skeleton data can be obtained from the depth maps, inertial data etc. Since skeleton data are robust to the variation in perspective and less computation complex than other input data in the task of action recognition. Thus, skeleton-based approaches have become a popular research focus e.g. [9, 10].

The human skeleton model is a relatively high-level expression of human body, which can effectively reflect the semantic information of motion in three-dimensional space [7]. Many approaches have been proposed by designing the discriminative hand-crafted features [8]. Usually, the action categories can be judged by several key joints. However, in practice, many positions of human joints may be completely imprecisely estimated because of serious occlusions occur or the body involves in a complex background. So, these are main challenges need to be solved in the task of action recognition for skeleton-based method. The skeleton-based approaches could collapse when suffering noise and occlusions. Especially, in the case of cross-view action recognition, due to the great changes in perspective, skeleton data has existed various defects, which brings great difficulties to feature learning. In addition, there are still some challenges, such as camera jitters, local noise and so on. These jitters also make the current skeleton-based methods less robust. This requires a representation that can address the above defects even on partial inaccurate and unstable skeleton data.

Aim at this issue, we propose a novel and simple approach to enhance the capability of feature learning for 3D human action recognition from human skeleton sequences. Specifically, we introduce a simple but efficient feature, termed planes of 3D joint motions vector (PoJM3D), to capture the geometric cues of frame-level motion cues from the raw skeleton sequences. The visualization of sampled RGB images and

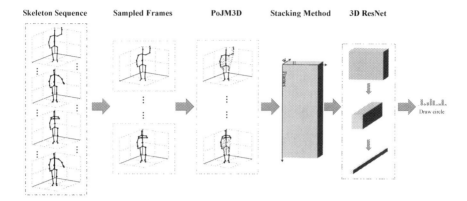

Fig. 2. Pipeline of the proposed method

feature descriptor of PoJM3D is shown Fig. 1. Furthermore, the ingenious stacking method and dynamic temporal sparse sampling scheme with 3D ConvNets is used to aggregate the geometric appearance movement scattered in long durations.

The main contributions of this paper are summarized as follows:

- We develop a view invariant frame-level geometric feature to capture the human appearance and motion in a frame, which is proved as an efficient way to fill the gap between rough skeleton data and feature learning networks.
- We propose a novel and simple framework for modeling the action from skeleton data, by considering the short-term and long-term dependencies of human action representation.
- We demonstrate the significant performance improvements of the proposed approach compared to the state of the art on all three benchmarks.

2   The Proposed Method

The overall framework of our proposed approach for human action recognition is illustrated in Fig. 2. For each input skeleton sequence, we first apply the dynamic temporal sparse sampling scheme to obtain a frame from the sequences. The planes of 3D joint motions vector are extracted from these frames. In order to learn geometric appearance and motion information, the planes of 3D joint motions vector from divided segments is stacked and fed into the 3D ResNet-based network architecture. The action label is assigned with the highest output score.

2.1   Planes of 3D Joint Motions Vector

In Sect. 1, we have analyzed that the partial inaccurate positions of human joints may be completely imprecisely estimated. If these problematic skeleton sequences are directly used for feature learning, higher requirements will be put forward for network structure. According to our knowledge, the position information and distance information are not invariant for the perspective. However, three points in space can determine a triangle plane. Even in different camera coordinates, the three angles of those planes will not change. Those planes contain the short-term motion cues between skeleton joints. It is important that conversion of camera coordinates does not change these planes. Among many spatial geometric features, we choose the angle cosine values of those planes to form our PoJM3D vectors. To prove the validity of this method, we have also tried to describe this triangle with other geometric features, which will be described in detail in the following Sect. 3.

Before extracting features, skeleton data need to be pre-processed. Firstly, referring to the practice of Luvizon [24], the skeleton data of 25 joints are converted to 20 joints. Then the mean and standard deviation of the whole dataset are calculated. We make the processed data be conformed to the standard normal distribution of 0-variance-1 with the operation of decentration. The planes are extracted from 20 joints by permutation and combination. Resulting in $C_{20}^3 = 1140$ possible planes. These planes can be expressed by $C_p = \{P_i, P_j, P_k\}$, where $p \in N^+[1, 1140]$, $i, j, k \in N^+[1, 20]$. We selected three points from these points, three vectors can be obtained, expressed as:

$$V_{i,j} = \left(P_i^x - P_j^x, P_i^y - P_j^y, P_i^z - P_j^z \right) \tag{1}$$

where $i, j \in \{1, 2, 3\}$.

Next, the angle cosine values between those vectors can be obtained as:

$$\cos \alpha = \frac{V_1 \cdot V_2}{|V_1| * |V_2|} \tag{2}$$

where $V_1, V_2 \in \{V_{1,2}, V_{1,3}, V_{2,3}\}$.

Many traditional methods rely on designing some exquisite hand-crafted features, which also brings more computing overhead and poor generalization ability of the model e.g. [9]. On the contrary, we simply deal with the cosine angle obtained from a single frame and arrange these angles into a tensor which constitutes the proposed PoJM3D feature. For instance, the dimensions of PoJM3D feature are C × H × W, where C, H, W represent channel, high, width, respectively.

Nevertheless, the planes of 3D joint motions vector encode the appearance stream of the skeleton sequences into an angle space which is insensitive to the camera coordinate system. In addition, the planes of 3D joint motions vector are still rough feature for frames-level, which considerably allow ConvNets to learn the latent spatio-temporal pattern.

2.2 Spatio-Temporal Feature Learning

We stack the extracted PoJM3D features in time dimension. Considering that there is no spatial correlation between these planes. So, we stack each frame into a vector like C × 1140 × 1.

2.2.1   Dynamic Temporal Sparse Sampling

Inspired by the process of Wang et al. in [12]. We propose a dynamic temporal sparse sampling scheme with 3D ConvNets to model the spatio-temporal feature scattered in the long-range duration, instead of dense sampling strategy. Given a sequence S with L frames, the sequence length is truncated to L′ frames by randomly choosing a ratio from the set of {0.8, 0.9, 1.0.}. The L′ frames are divided into K segments of equal durations. For each segment, a snippet skeleton frame D_m is randomly sampled from the sequence to calculate the planes of 3D joint motions vector V_m, where $1 \leq m \leq K$ is the index of segments.

2.2.2   Network Architecture

Residual learning [13] has been practically introduced to improve the performance of image classification by flexibly stacking the residual blocks to increase the depth of 2D ConvNets. Unlike previous work on extending ResNet [14], the aim of this work is to examine the dynamic temporal sparse sampling with 3D ConvNets is efficient to learn the spatio-temporal representation of the skeleton data. The network architecture is summarized in Table 1.

Our network is built on the basic block of 2D ResNet18. N_c is the category number. The spatial down-sampling stays the same with 2D ResNet18. The **Conv1** is a full connection layer implementation scheme, which is to update the weight of each plane from a PoJM3D vector. Each convolutional layer is followed by batch normalization [15] and ReLU [16] in the step of spatio-temporal feature learning.

Table 1. Our network of extended 3D ResNet18.

Layer name	Output size	3D ResNet18
Conv1	$3 \times K \times H \times W$	$1 \times 1 \times 1$, 64, $S(1, 1, 1)$
Conv2	$64 \times K^1 \times H^1 \times W^1$	$3 \times 3 \times 3$, 64
Block_1	$64 \times K^2 \times H^2 \times W^2$	$\begin{bmatrix} 3 \times 3 \times 3, & 64 \\ 3 \times 3 \times 3, & 64 \end{bmatrix} \times 2$
Block_2	$128 \times K^3 \times H^3 \times W^3$	$\begin{bmatrix} 3 \times 3 \times 3, & 128 \\ 3 \times 3 \times 3, & 128 \end{bmatrix} \times 2$
Block_3	$256 \times K^4 \times H^4 \times W^4$	$\begin{bmatrix} 3 \times 3 \times 3, & 256 \\ 3 \times 3 \times 3, & 256 \end{bmatrix} \times 2$
Block_4	$512 \times K^5 \times H^5 \times W^5$	$\begin{bmatrix} 3 \times 3 \times 3, & 512 \\ 3 \times 3 \times 3, & 512 \end{bmatrix} \times 2$
Fc	$1 \times N_C$	$K^5 \times H^5 \times W^5$ Average Pool $512 \times N_c$ fc

3   Experiments

To investigate the effectiveness of our approach, we conduct experiments on three public multi-model datasets, including UTD MVAD [17], UTD-MHAD [18], and CAS-YNU-MHAD [19] datasets. We employ the Pytorch framework to implement the proposed method, and the code will be released on GitHub in the near future. We introduce the evaluation datasets and implementation details of our approaches. Then, in order to verify the effectiveness of our proposed geometric features, we conducted ablation study. We compared other primary geometric features based on skeleton under the same framework. Finally, we compare the performance of our approaches with the state-of-the-art benchmarks.

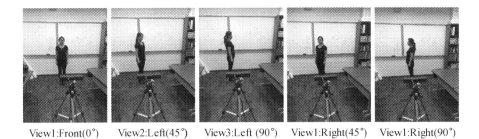

View1:Front(0°)   View2:Left(45°)   View3:Left (90°)   View1:Right(45°)   View1:Right(90°)

Fig. 3. Five different standing positions of a subject with respect to the Kinect depth camera

3.1   Datasets and Setting

The UTD-MVAD was collected for a study of view-invariance action recognition. The dataset was collected by using a Kinect V2, and included the following six actions: "1-catch", "2-draw circle", "3-draw tick", "4-draw triangle", "5-knock and 6-throw". These six actions were chosen from the UTD-MVAD dataset due to their similarities thus making the action recognition problem more challenging. Five subjects were asked to perform each action with five different subject orientations or views as shown in Fig. 3. For each view, a subject repeated an action 6 times. Therefore, in total 900 action samples were generated. We selected subjects 1, 3, 5 as the training set and the others as the test set as a cross-subject evaluation, and selected views 1, 3, 5 as the training set and the others as the test set as a cross-view evaluation.

The UTD-MHAD dataset is a multi-modal action recognition dataset collected using a Kinect V2 and a wearable inertial sensor. The dataset includes 20 joints for each subject in each skeleton sequence and contains 27 actions collected by eight individuals, resulting in 861 action sequences. The provided protocol [17] only provides a cross subject evaluation. We selected subjects 1, 3, 5, 7 as the training set and the others as the test set.

The CAS-YNU-MHAD dataset used two Kinect V2 to capture action data from two different views (front and side) as shown in Fig. 1. All subjects performed about 10 repetitions of each action, yielding about 9903 valid multi-model samples. In cross-subject test, we selected subjects 1, 3, 5, 7, 9 as the train set and the others as the test set. In cross-view evaluation, we selected the front view as the train set and the side view as the test set.

3.2   Implementation Details

For model training, we set the maximum epoch number as 81 with batch size of 64. The learning rate is initialized as 0.01 and decreased to its 0.1 times every 20 epochs. The weight decay of 1×10^{-5} with momentum of 0.9 is specified for regularize the network training. To reduce the effect of over-fitting, we add a dropout layer with ratio 0.5 before the fully connected layer. Specially, due to the total samples of UTD-MVAD and UTD-MHAD datasets are less than 1000. We repeatedly tail list of samples if the number is less than 1000 for the data augmentation. To speed up the training process, we conduct the experiments on four NVIDIA TITAN XP GPU accelerators and apply data parallel operation.

Test set stacking method is consistent with train set, but test set does not adopt DTSS strategy. And the temporal snippets are sampled from the middle position of the corresponding segments at length scale 1.

Table 2. Ablation study on UTD-MVAD with other geometric features.

Geometric features	X-sub %	X-view %	Data
RDS	55.00	74.44	Skeleton
SM	61.94	81.11	Skeleton
DV	67.78	74.44	Skeleton
NVP	58.89	47.22	Skeleton
TPC	60.00	58.89	Skeleton
CAV	61.94	69.44	Skeleton
PoJM3D	**78.06**	**90.56**	Skeleton

Table 3. Ablation study on UTD-MHAD with other geometric features.

Geometric features	X-sub %	Data
RDS	83.72	Skeleton
SM	85.35	Skeleton
DV	90.23	Skeleton
NVP	69.77	Skeleton
TPC	78.37	Skeleton
CAV	48.37	Skeleton
PoJM3D	**92.33**	Skeleton

Table 4. Ablation study on CAS-YNU-MHAD with other geometric features.

Geometric Features	X-sub %	X-view %	Data
RDS	88.74	43.44	Skeleton
SM	88.41	49.43	Skeleton
DV	89.89	47.27	Skeleton
NVP	89.14	35.19	Skeleton
TPC	84.67	56.97	Skeleton
PoJM3D	88.17	**69.57**	Skeleton

Table 5. Performance comparison on UTD-MVAD with other state-of-the-art methods.

Method	X-sub %	X-view %	Data
SNV [22]	57.78	44.16	Depth
DMM [23]	29.17	22.78	Depth
HoJ3D [10]	31.11	21.67	Skeleton
Ours	**78.06**	**90.56**	Skeleton

Table 6. Performance comparison on UTD-MHAD with other state-of-the-art methods.

Method	X-sub %	Data
JTM [20]	85.81	Skeleton
JDM [21]	88.10	Skeleton
SOS [25]	69.20	Skeleton
Ijjina et al. [27]	91.20	Depth + videos
Ours	**92.33**	skeleton

Table 7. Performance comparison on CAS-YNU-MHAD with other state-of-the-art methods.

Method	X-sub %	X-view %	Data
JDM [21]	88.90	55.80	Skeleton
HoJ3D [10]	66.56	20.67	Skeleton
SOS [25]	81.19	31.23	Skeleton
STCP-DMS [26]	87.56	39.19	Depth
Ours	88.17	**69.57**	Skeleton

3.3 Ablation Study

We choose the angle cosine values of the planes to form our PoJM3D vectors. In order to prove its rationality, we use six skeleton-based geometric features to conduct comparative experiments under the same framework.

3.3.1 Other Geometric Features

Row Data Stacking (RDS): The original skeleton data has 20 nodes per frame. Copy 20 copies of the data of the 20 nodes by line. Finally, the skeleton data of each frame constitutes a vector of $3 \times 20 \times 20$. Li et al. [20], who once proposed HCN network, also arranged the skeleton data in this way.

Symmetric Matrix (SM): Taking a frame of data in skeleton sequence, 20 nodes in each direction are taken out named S_i, and converted S_i into column vectors S_i'. A symmetric matrix can be obtained by multiplying the original row vectors S_i and column vectors S_i'. Finally, the skeleton data of each frame constitutes a vector of $3 \times 20 \times 20$.

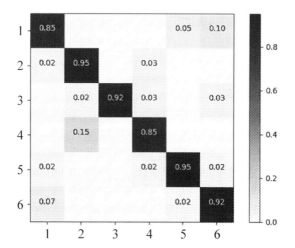

Fig. 4. Confusion matrix of the cross-view test of UTD-MVAD

Displacement Vector (DV): Take a frame of data in the skeleton sequence and take one of the nodes P_i to subtract all nodes from this node, where $i \in N^+[1, 20]$. Finally, the skeleton data of each frame constitutes a vector of $3 \times 20 \times 20$.

Norm Vector of Plane (NVP): The camera coordinate system is transformed into the object coordinate system with the hip center joint as the origin. Then, three nodes are extracted from 20 nodes by permutation and combination. As shown in Eq. 2, there are 1140 possible combinations. The normal vectors of the triangular planes are obtained by cross-multiplication of $V_{1,2}$ and $V_{1,3}$ in Eq. 1, then those vectors need execute L2 normalization. Finally, the skeleton data of each frame constitutes a vector of $3 \times 1140 \times 1$.

Two-Points Cosine (TPC): The coordinate system is converted first. Then, two nodes are extracted from 20 nodes by combination there are $C_{20}^2 = 190$ combinations. Take two points P_1, P_2 from all nodes. Equation 2 is used to calculate the cosine angle with P_1, P_2 and coordinate origin.

Cosine Angular Velocity (CAV): Two consecutive frames of skeleton are selected to extract proposed PoJM3D features P_1, P_2, make a subtraction between P_1 and P_2.

3.3.2   Effectiveness of the Proposed Features

As shown in Table 3, the proposed PoJM3D is far superior to other geometric features. In addition, a detail results of UTD-MVAD is list in Table 2. The comparison experiments on this dataset also shows that the proposed PoJM3D is not only outstanding in the cross-view evaluation, but also has good performance and stability in the cross-subjects evaluation. The confusion matrix of the cross-view evaluation of UTD-MVAD is given in Fig. 4, and we can see that the proposed method has a balanced performance for all action categories. As shown in Table 4, we have achieved the best performance in the cross-view evaluation of CAS-YNU-MHAD, which is far superior to other geometric features, except that the cross-subjects evaluation is slightly higher than the feature of TPC, it is lower than all other features. As far as we know, our approach probably is sensitive to the change of object attributes.

3.4   Comparison to State-of-the-Art Methods

We compare JTM [20], JDM [21], SNV [22] and other state-of-the-art approaches [10, 11, 23, 25, 26] on three datasets. The detailed comparisons on all three datasets are shown in Tables 5, 6 and 7. Using the same evaluation protocol, our framework is **1.13%** higher than the current best results in cross-subjects evaluation of UTD-MHAD. Specially, the method proposed by Ijjina et al. [27] achieved a better performance by fusing multi-modal input data. However, our approach just employs skeleton data to verify that the proposed geometric feature is sufficient to encode the action cues. In the CAS-YNU-MHAD cross-view evaluation, it is **13.77%** higher than the best method at present, as shown in Table 7. In the UTD-MVAD dataset, our method is much higher than the existing methods, both in the evaluations of cross-subjects and cross-view.

4   Conclusion

We propose a novel and simple method using planes of 3D joint motions vector and 3D ResNet-based ConvNets combined with dynamic temporal sparse sampling scheme to model the spatial and temporal structure of human action based on skeleton sequences. Compared to the recent researches in 3D human action recognition, our method is more flexible and efficiency to learn the latent pattern in 3D actions. The experimental results also prove our approach outperform the existing representative methods and achieve the state-of-the-art performance especially in cross-view evaluation on three benchmark datasets. In the future, we will combine this work with temporal proposal network to achieve end-to-end model training of action detection and classification based on continuous skeleton sequences.

Acknowledgement. The study is supported by National Natural Science Foundation of China (61772508, U1713213), Key Research and Development Program of Guangdong Province [grant numbers 2019B090915001], CAS Key Technology Talent Program, Shenzhen Technology Project (JCYJ20170413152535587, JCYJ20180507182610734).

References

1. Xiao, J., Stolkin, R., Gao, Y., Leonardis, A.: Robust fusion of color and depth data for RGB-D target tracking using adaptive range-invariant depth models and spatio-temporal consistency constraints. IEEE Trans. Cybern. **48**, 2485–2499 (2018)
2. Wang, P., Li, W., Gao, Z., Tang, C., Ogunbona, P.O.: Depth pooling based large-scale 3-D action recognition with convolutional neural networks. IEEE Trans. Multimedia **20**, 1051–1061 (2018)

3. Ji, X., Cheng, J., Feng, W.: Spatio-temporal cuboid pyramid for action recognition using depth motion sequences. In: International Conference Advanced Computational Intelligence (ICACI) (2016)
4. Liu, M., Liu, H., Chen, C.: Robust 3D action recognition through sampling local appearances and global distributions. IEEE Trans. Multimedia **20**, 1932–1947 (2018)
5. Ji, X., Cheng, J., Tao, D.: Local mean spatio-temporal feature for depth image-based speed-up action recognition. In: IEEE International Conference on Image Processing (ICIP), pp. 2389–2393 (2015)
6. Yoshiyasu, Y., Sagawa, R., Ayusawa, K., Murai, A.: Skeleton transformer networks: 3D human pose and skinned mesh from single RGB image. arXiv preprint arXiv:1812.11328 (2018)
7. Presti, L.L., La Cascia, M.: 3D skeleton-based human action classification: a survey. Pattern Recogn. **53**, 130–147 (2016)
8. Hu, J.-F., Zheng, W.-S., Lai, J., Zhang, J.: Jointly learning heterogeneous features for RGB-D activity recognition. In: Proceedings of the IEEE Conference on Computer Vision and Pattern Recognition (2015)
9. Zhang, S., Yang, Y., Xiao, J., Liu, X., Yang, Y., Xie, D., et al.: Fusing geometric features for skeleton-based action recognition using multilayer LSTM networks. IEEE Trans. Multimedia **20**, 2330–2343 (2018)
10. Xia, L., Chen, C., Aggarwal, J.K.: View invariant human action recognition using histograms of 3D joints. In: 2012 IEEE Computer Society Conference on Computer Vision and Pattern Recognition Workshops (2012)
11. Ding, R., He, Q., Liu, H., Liu, M.: Combining adaptive hierarchical depth motion maps with skeletal joints for human action recognition. IEEE Access **7**, 5597–5608 (2019)
12. Wang, L., et al.: Temporal segment networks: towards good practices for deep action recognition. In: Leibe, B., Matas, J., Sebe, N., Welling, M. (eds.) ECCV 2016. LNCS, vol. 9912, pp. 20–36. Springer, Cham (2016). https://doi.org/10.1007/978-3-319-46484-8_2
13. He, K., Zhang, X., Ren, S., Sun, J.: Deep residual learning for image recognition. In: Proceedings of the IEEE Conference on Computer Vision and Pattern Recognition (2016)
14. Hara, K., Kataoka, H., Satoh, Y.: Can spatiotemporal 3D CNNs retrace the history of 2D CNNs and ImageNet. In: Proceedings of the IEEE Conference on Computer Vision and Pattern Recognition, Salt Lake City, UT, USA (2018)
15. Ioffe, S., Szegedy, C.: Batch normalization: accelerating deep network training by reducing internal covariate shift. In: International Conference on Machine Learning (2015)
16. Nair, V., Hinton, G.E.: Rectified linear units improve restricted boltzmann machines. In: Proceedings of the 27th International Conference on Machine Learning (ICML-10) (2010)
17. Chen, C., Jafari, R., Kehtarnavaz, N.: UTD Multimodal Human Action Dataset (UTD-MHAD), February 2019. http://www.utdallas.edu/~kehtar/UTD-MHAD.html
18. Chen, C., Jafari, R., Kehtarnavaz, N.: UTD-MHAD: a multimodal dataset for human action recognition utilizing a depth camera and a wearable inertial sensor. In: 2015 IEEE International Conference on Image Processing (ICIP) (2015)
19. Zhao, Q., Cheng, J., Tao, D., Ji, X., Wang, L.: CAS-YNU multi-modal cross-view human action dataset. In: International Conference on Information and Automation (ICIA) (2018)
20. Wang, P., Li, Z., Hou, Y., Li, W.: Action recognition based on joint trajectory maps using convolutional neural networks. In: ACM MM, pp. 102–106 (2018)
21. Li, C., Hou, Y., Wang, P., Li, W.: Joint distance maps based action recognition with convolutional neural networks. IEEE Signal Process. Lett. **24**(5), 624–628 (2017)
22. Yang, X., Tian, Y.: Super normal vector for activity recognition using depth sequences. In: CVPR, pp. 804–811 (2014)

23. Chen, C., Liu, K., Kehtarnavaz, N.: Real-time human action recognition based on depth motion maps. Real-Time Image Process **12**, 155–163 (2016)
24. Luvizon, D.C., Tabia, H., Picard, D.: Learning features combination for human action recognition from skeleton sequences. Pattern Recogn. Lett. **99**, 13–20 (2017)
25. Hou, Y., Li, Z., Wang, P., Li, W.: Skeleton optical spectra based action recognition using convolutional neural networks. IEEE Trans. Circuits Syst. Video Technol. **28**(3), 807–811 (2018)
26. Ji, X., Cheng, J., Tao, D., Wu, X., Feng, W.: The spatial Laplacian and temporal energy pyramid representation for human action recognition using depth sequences. Knowl.-Based Syst. **122**, 64–74 (2017)
27. Ijjina, E.P., Chalavadi, K.M.: Human action recognition in RGB-D videos using motion sequence information and deep learning. Pattern Recogn. **72**, 504–516 (2017)

Non-concentric Circular Texture Removal for Workpiece Defect Detection

Shujia Qin[1,2(✉)], Di Guo[1], Heping Chen[1], and Ning Xi[3]

[1] Shenzhen Academy of Robotics, Shenzhen 518000, People's Republic of China
[2] Shenyang Institute of Automation, CAS,
Shenyang 110000, People's Republic of China
stanqin@gmail.com
[3] The University of Hong Kong, Pok Fu Lam, Hong Kong

Abstract. Since workpiece defect detection is a typical problem in computer vision with small datasets, generally its solutions cannot exploit the advantages of high accuracy, generalization ability, and neural network structures from the deep learning paradigm. Thus, traditional image processing techniques are still widely applied in such requirements. Aiming at three types of defects (crack, pitting and scratch) on a workpiece with non-concentric circular textures that severely interfere in the defect recognition stage, this paper proposes a sliding window filter for the texture detection. Experiments compare the proposed method with the polar coordinate mapping method and the T-smooth texture removal algorithm. Results show that the proposed method reveals the three types of defects better than the other two methods.

Keywords: Defect detection · Non-concentric circle · Small dataset

1 Introduction

With advantages of low cost, simple deployment, objectivity and high efficiency, computer vision based solutions are extensively applied in the field of workpiece defect detection. Generally, workpiece defects can be grouped into cracks, pitting (pinhole and blowhole), scratch, scarfing defects, seam, *etc.*, which are similar to the classification in the steel industry [1,2]. To tackle these defects, traditional and machine learning based image processing methods are widely investigated during the recent decades.

The traditional methods for defect detection are grounded on the abnormal features presented in the morphology, transformed domains, or specific models. These methods typically exploit histogram properties [3,4], co-occurrence matrices [5,6], local binary patterns [7,8], morphological operations [9,10], spatial domain filtering [11–14], frequency domain analyses [15–17], joint spatial-frequency analyses [18–20], fractal models [21], Gaussian mixture entropy models [22], and low-rank matrix models [23]. The well-known disadvantages of traditional image processing include the inflexibility for different scenarios and the over-sensitivity to imaging conditions.

© Springer Nature Switzerland AG 2019
H. Yu et al. (Eds.): ICIRA 2019, LNAI 11743, pp. 576–584, 2019.
https://doi.org/10.1007/978-3-030-27538-9_49

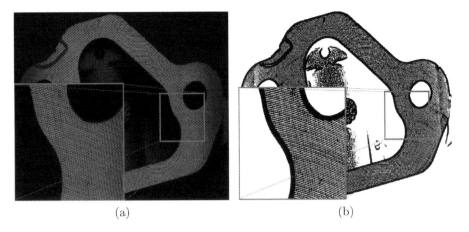

(a)   (b)

Fig. 1. The workpiece (a) and its preprocessing result (b). The zoom-in areas at the bottom left display the non-concentric circular textures.

In contrast, the machine learning based methods for defect detection are data driven—its capability of generalization essentially depends on the scale of training data. Inspired by successful applications in object detection, various convolutional neural network (CNN) based methods are proposed for defect detection, such as a multi-scale pyramidal CNN for steel defects [24], a CNN with a sliding window for product damage localization [25], a Faster R-CNN for surface damages [26], and a fully convolutional network (FCN) for galvanized stamping parts [27]. Unlike traditional methods, the machine learning based methods have a stable performance in complex scenarios without handcrafted feature descriptions, given a suitable dataset is available.

When the situation comes to workpieces with a complex background and a small dataset, specifically, workpieces with a non-concentric circular texture and only a few samples, the dilemma arises: on the one hand, circular textures are commonly produced during workpiece manufacture, as shown in Fig. 1; on the other hand, large labeled datasets are currently unavailable for machine learning solutions in this scenario. Thus, a circular texture removal method deserves a study. General texture removal methods, such as the T-smooth algorithm using the relative total variation [28], do not utilize the morphological information of the texture, so defects could be also wiped off along with the texture. Hough transform based methods require long computation time and enormous storage [29,30], which hinder the method from being a practical solution of this task. A common workaround converts circular textures to parallel lines, and then multiple frequency domain methods, such as those in [31,32], can be applied; however, this solution can only manage concentric circular textures.

Focusing on the non-concentric circular texture removal problem for workpiece defect detection, this paper utilizes traditional image preprocessing methods, and proposes a sliding window filter to mark whether a pixel belongs to a circular texture. Experiments are carried out to compare the proposed method

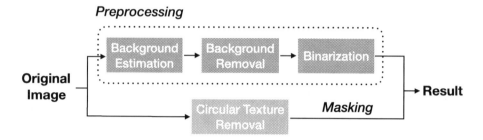

Fig. 2. Schematic diagram of the proposed algorithm

with the polar coordinate mapping method and the T-smooth texture removal algorithm.

2   Methods

The procedure of the proposed method includes the following steps: the background estimation, the background removal, the binarization, the circular texture detection (mask generation), and the final result synthesis, as shown in Fig. 2. The first three steps are a preprocessing treatment for the image; the output is a binarized image. The circular texture detection utilizes a filter to scan the original image; when circular textures are detected, the filter generates a mask. The final result is the masking synthesis output of the binarized image.

2.1   Preprocessing

The **background estimation** blurs the original image by averaging the sliding window areas with an outlier exclusion treatment. Let $I \in \mathbb{R}^{m \times n}$ be the grayscale original image, $I(i,j)$ denote the pixel at the i-th row and the j-th column, W be a $p \times q$ sliding window, and $W_{i,j}$ denote that the upper left cell of the sliding window is superposed on $I(i,j)$. The original image will be padded by zeros if part of the sliding windows falls outside the $m \times n$ pixel area. Let the cells of the sliding window W obtain the same value as the corresponding superposed pixel of I, i.e. we can consider $W_{i,j}$ is a snip cut from $I(i,j)$. Then the background $B \in \mathbb{R}^{m \times n}$ can be expressed as

$$B(i,j) = \frac{1}{|\Omega|} \sum_{x} \{x | x \in \Omega(W_{i,j})\} \tag{1}$$

where $B(i,j)$ denotes the pixel value of the i-th row and the j-th column on the background image, $\Omega(\cdot)$ is a subset consisting of the $W_{i,j}$ values, and $|\Omega|$ denotes the cardinality of Ω. In practice, Ω is obtained by sorting the values of $W_{i,j}$ and picking out the largest k values (the maximum would be excluded for eliminating the outlier effect).

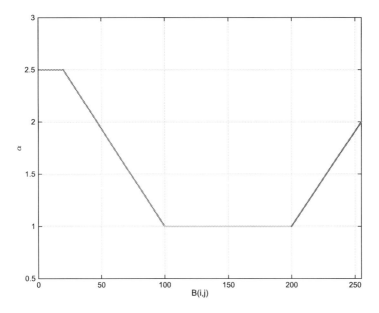

Fig. 3. A typical implementation of the piecewise function α

To balance possible high lighting ratios, the **background removal** involves a threshold method to neutralize the image. Let f be the maximum value of the gray scale (typically, 255 for an 8-bit unsigned integer), then the image after background removal $R \in \mathbb{R}^{m \times n}$ is

$$R(i,j) = \begin{cases} f, & B(i,j) - I(i,j) \leq 0 \\ f - \alpha\left[B(i,j) - I(i,j)\right], & 0 < B(i,j) - I(i,j) \leq \frac{(1-\beta)f}{\alpha} \\ \beta f, & \text{otherwise} \end{cases} \tag{2}$$

where $\beta \in [0,1)$ is a tuning parameter with a typical value of $\frac{3}{4}$, and α is a piecewise function of $B(i,j)$. A typical implementation of α is shown in Fig. 3. Depending on the difference between $B(i,j)$ and $I(i,j)$, the formula of $R(i,j)$ clamps the value within $[\beta f, f]$, and assigns a suitable gain α for $B(i,j)$ at different ranges: when $B(i,j)$ is dark, e.g. with a small value less than 100 in Fig. 3, a larger α can push $R(i,j)$ towards βf; when $B(i,j)$ is too bright, e.g. with a value larger than 200 in Fig. 3, a larger α can restrain $R(i,j)$ from being too bright as $B(i,j)$.

Binarization is the final step for preprocessing. A threshold γ is set for determining whether a pixel should be 0 or 1:

$$P(i,j) = \begin{cases} 1, & R(i,j) \geq \gamma \\ 0, & R(i,j) < \gamma \end{cases} \tag{3}$$

where $P \in \{0,1\}^{m \times n}$ is the final result of the preprocessing stage.

2.2   Non-concentric Circular Texture Removal

The ideal result for circular texture removal is a separation of textures based on the context, which requires knowledge on the background or the foreground. Since morphology based methods expect a set of rules to describe non-concentric circles, to accelerate the processing, the proposed method avoids such complexity by applying a sliding window as a local filter $F : I, i, j, r, s \rightarrow \{0, 1\}$ for the texture detection, where the sliding window covers $r \times s$ pixels at (i, j) as the upper left anchor. The mask $M \in \mathbb{R}^{m \times n}$ is then defined by

$$M(i, j) = F(I, i, j, r, s) \tag{4}$$

In practice, F is generally a convolutional neural network based nonlinear mapping trained by sufficient labeled dataset. However, as the workpiece samples are insufficient (less than 100), the filter F is roughly crafted as

$$M(i,j) = \begin{cases} 0, \sum K \otimes I'(i : i + r - 1, j : j + s - 1) \leq \eta \\ 1, \sum K \otimes I'(i : i + r - 1, j : j + s - 1) > \eta \end{cases} \tag{5}$$

where $I(i : i + r - 1, j : j + s - 1)$ denotes the submatrix consisting of the i-th to $(i + r - 1)$-th rows and the j-th to $(j + s - 1)$-th columns of I, and I' is its linearly normalized counterpart; $K \in \mathbb{R}^{r \times s}$ denotes a constant kernel; $\otimes$ denotes the entry-wise multiplication; $\sum$ denotes a sum of all entries; η is a constant threshold. Later experiments will show that even such an inaccurate implementation of the filter works well for the task.

3   Experiments

A straightforward method to remove circular textures is transforming the original image to the polar coordinate—if the circles are concentric, they will be transformed to a set of parallel lines and then easy to be removed. A simple algorithm for the polar coordinate mapping was applied in our experiments:

1. Detect the center coordinate (x_c, y_c) of one circle, so that the view angle θ_s from the center and the scan radius r_s (the distance between the center and the farthest point) for the original image can be calculated.
2. Set the resolution constants m_p and n_p respectively through the directions of r_s and θ_s, so that the gaps between the sampling points are

$$\Delta r = \frac{\max(r_s) - \min(r_s)}{m_p} \tag{6}$$

$$\Delta \theta = \frac{\max(\theta_s) - \min(\theta_s)}{n_p} \tag{7}$$

3. Initialize a blank image P_o with $m_p \times n_p$ pixels.

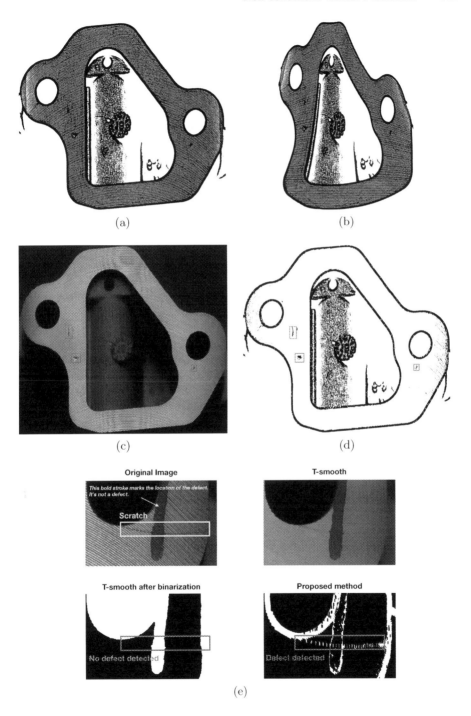

Fig. 4. (a) Original image of a pitting sample; (b) Polar coordinate mapping of the pitting sample; (c) Result after the T-smooth method of the pitting sample; (d) Result after the proposed method of the pitting sample; (e) Comparison between T-smooth and the proposed method on a scratch sample.

4. Loop r_i and θ_i through all the sampling points on r_s and θ_s with Δr and $\Delta\theta$. Thus the coordinates of the corresponding sampling point on the original image are

$$x_i = r_i \cos\theta_i + x_c, \tag{8}$$
$$y_i = r_i \sin\theta_i + y_c. \tag{9}$$

If (x_i, y_i) falls inside the original image $I \in \mathbb{R}^{m \times n}$, then assign the result image

$$P_o(i,j) = I(\lceil m - y_i \rceil, \lceil n - x_i \rceil) \tag{10}$$

A sample with pitting defect after preprocessing is shown in Fig. 4a, and its polar coordinate mapping result is shown in Fig. 4b. Because the circular texture of the workpiece is non-concentric, not all but the bottom selected circles are transformed into straight lines. This result indicates the polar coordinate mapping would be unsuitable for the non-concentric cases.

The processing result by the T-smooth algorithm for Fig. 4a is shown in Fig. 4c as an example. The rectangles mark the locations of the pitting defects, which are sharply distinguishable from the blurred background texture. As a comparison, the circular texture removal result by the proposed method is shown in Fig. 4d. The result shows that the circular background is clearly removed, and the pitting defects can be traced by the stains. These two results indicate that both methods can handle the pitting defect which has a concentrated shape with a relatively large area.

However, the scratch defect is thin and similar to the circular texture. As shown in Fig. 4e, the T-smooth algorithm fails to recognize the scratch and blurs it close to the background texture, so after binarization, the scratch cannot be found on the image. As a comparison, the proposed method filters out the circular background and leaves the scratch discernible as a track.

4   Conclusion

This paper proposes a sliding window filter for the texture detection. Experiment results show that the proposed method reveals the three types of defects better than the polar coordinate mapping and the T-smooth algorithm, especially for minor scratches. The future work of this paper is to combine the advantages of traditional and deep learning methods and study the online learning paradigm which gradually transfers the knowledge from handcrafted features to deep networks by semi-supervision.

Acknowledgements. This work was supported by the Shenzhen Overseas High Level Talent (Peacock Plan) Program KQTD20140630154026047, the Shenzhen Theme-Based Basic Research Program JCYJ20180504170303184, and the National Natural Science Foundation of China (under Grant No. 61703284).

References

1. Stahlinstitut Stahlinstitut VDEh: Fehlerkatalog Grobblech/Catalogue of Heavy Plates Defects, Stahleisen (2015)
2. Neogi, N., Mohanta, D.K., Dutta, P.K.: Review of vision-based steel surface inspection systems. EURASIP J. Image Video Process. **2014**(1), 50 (2014)
3. Liu, W., Yan, Y., Li, J., Zhang, Y., Sun, H.: Automated on-line fast detection for surface defect of steel strip based on multivariate discriminant function. In: 2008 Second International Symposium on Intelligent Information Technology Application, vol. 2, pp. 493–497. IEEE (2008)
4. Ding, S., Liu, Z., Li, C.: AdaBoost learning for fabric defect detection based on hog and SVM. In: 2011 International conference on multimedia technology, pp. 2903–2906. IEEE (2011)
5. Caleb, P., Steuer, M.: Classification of surface defects on hot rolled steel using adaptive learning methods. In: Proceedings of the KES'2000 Fourth International Conference on Knowledge-Based Intelligent Engineering Systems and Allied Technologies, (Cat. No. 00TH8516), vol. 1, pp. 103–108. IEEE (2000)
6. Chondronasios, A., Popov, I., Jordanov, I.: Feature selection for surface defect classification of extruded aluminum profiles. Int. J. Adv. Manuf. Technol. **83**(1–4), 33–41 (2016)
7. Maenpaa, T.: Surface quality assessment with advanced texture analysis techniques. In: Proceedings of the International Surface Inspection Summit, Luxembourg (2006)
8. Song, K., Yan, Y.: A noise robust method based on completed local binary patterns for hot-rolled steel strip surface defects. Appl. Surf. Sci. **285**, 858–864 (2013)
9. Mak, K.-L., Peng, P., Yiu, K.F.C.: Fabric defect detection using morphological filters. Image Vis. Comput. **27**(10), 1585–1592 (2009)
10. Zheng, H., Kong, L.X., Nahavandi, S.: Automatic inspection of metallic surface defects using genetic algorithms. J. Mater. Process. Technol. **125**, 427–433 (2002)
11. Luiz, A.O.M., Flávio, L.C.P., Paulo, E.M.A.: Automatic detection of surface defects on rolled steel using computer vision and artificial neural networks. In: IECON 2010–36th Annual Conference on IEEE Industrial Electronics Society, pp. 1081–1086. IEEE (2010)
12. Bulnes, F.G., Usamentiaga, R., García, D.F., Molleda, J.: Vision-based sensor for early detection of periodical defects in web materials. Sensors **12**(8), 10788–10809 (2012)
13. Yichi, Z., Lv, W., Xuedong, L.: Defects detection of cold-roll steel surface based on MATLAB. In: 2011 Third International Conference on Measuring Technology and Mechatronics Automation, vol. 1, pp. 827–830. IEEE (2011)
14. Li, W., Lu, C., Zhang, J.: A local annular contrast based real-time inspection algorithm for steel bar surface defects. Appl. Surf. Sci. **258**(16), 6080–6086 (2012)
15. Bai, X., Fang, Y., Lin, W., Wang, L., Ju, B.-F.: Saliency-based defect detection in industrial images by using phase spectrum. IEEE Trans. Ind. Inf. **10**(4), 2135–2145 (2014)
16. Borwankar, R., Ludwig, R.: An optical surface inspection and automatic classification technique using the rotated wavelet transform. IEEE Trans. Instr. Meas. **67**(3), 690–697 (2018)
17. Hu, G.-H.: Automated defect detection in textured surfaces using optimal elliptical gabor filters. Optik **126**(14), 1331–1340 (2015)

18. Jeon, Y.-J., Choi, D.-C., Lee, S.J., Yun, J.P., Kim, S.W.: Defect detection for corner cracks in steel billets using a wavelet reconstruction method. JOSA A, **31**(2), 227–237 (2014)
19. Ghorai, S., Mukherjee, A., Gangadaran, M., Dutta, P.K.: Automatic defect detection on hot-rolled flat steel products. IEEE Trans. Instrum. Measur. **62**(3), 612–621 (2012)
20. Choi, D.C., Jeon, Y.J., Yun, J.P., Yun, S.W., Kim, S.W.: An algorithm for detecting seam cracks in steel plates. World Acad. Sci. Eng. Technol. **6**, 1456–1459 (2012)
21. Blackledge, J., Dubovitskiy, D.: A surface inspection machine vision system that includes fractal texture analysis. J. Intell. Syst. **3**(2), 76–89 (2008)
22. Susan, S., Sharma, M.: Automatic texture defect detection using gaussian mixture entropy modeling. Neurocomputing **239**, 232–237 (2017)
23. Cen, Y.-G., Zhao, R.-Z., Cen, L.-H., Cui, L.-H., Miao, Z.-J., Wei, Z.: Defect inspection for TFT-LCD images based on the low-rank matrix reconstruction. Neurocomputing **149**, 1206–1215 (2015)
24. Masci, J., Meier, U., Fricout, G., Schmidhuber, J.: Multi-scale pyramidal pooling network for generic steel defect classification. In: The 2013 International Joint Conference on Neural Networks (IJCNN), pp. 1–8. IEEE (2013)
25. Wang, T., Chen, Y., Qiao, M., Snoussi, H.: A fast and robust convolutional neural network-based defect detection model in product quality control. Int. J. Adv. Manuf. Technol. **94**(9–12), 3465–3471 (2018)
26. Cha, Y.-J., Choi, W., Suh, G., Mahmoudkhani, S., Büyüköztürk, O.: Autonomous structural visual inspection using region-based deep learning for detecting multiple damage types. Comput.-Aided Civ. Infrastruct. Eng. **33**(9), 731–747 (2018)
27. Xiao, Z., Leng, Y., Geng, L., Xi, J.: Defect detection and classification of galvanized stamping parts based on fully convolution neural network. In: Ninth International Conference on Graphic and Image Processing (ICGIP 2017), vol. 10615, pp. 106150K. International Society for Optics and Photonics (2018)
28. Li, X., Yan, Q., Xia, Y., Jia, J.: Structure extraction from texture via relative total variation. ACM Trans. Graph. (TOG) **31**(6), 139 (2012)
29. Hassanein, A.S., Mohammad, S., Sameer, M., Ragab, M.E.: A survey on Hough transform, theory, techniques and applications. arXiv preprint arXiv:1502.02160 (2015)
30. Rahmdel, P.S., Comley, R., Shi, D., McElduff, S.: A review of Hough transform and line segment detection approaches. In: VISAPP, vol. 1, pp. 411–418 (2015)
31. Sur, F., Grediac, M.: Automated removal of quasiperiodic noise using frequency domain statistics. J. Electron. Imaging **24**(1), 013003 (2015)
32. W Chen, S., Pellequer, J.-L.: DeStripe: frequency-based algorithm for removing stripe noises from AFM images. BMC struct. Biol. **11**(1), 7 (2011)

Sound Source Localization Based on PSVM algorithm

Bowen Sheng, Qinyu Jiang, and Faliang Chang[✉]

School of Control Science and Engineering, Shandong University,
No. 17923 Jingshi Road, Jinan 250061, People's Republic of China
flchang@sdu.edu.cn

Abstract. Sound source localization is one of the major audiovisual functions of intelligent robots. With the development of computer technology, high-quality sound signal acquisition technology has been widely used in many fields such as microphone array sound source localization. Support Vector Machine (SVM) is a kind of machine learning based on statistical learning theory and structural risk minimization principle. Many parameters will affect the performance of SVM. By changing parameters, the ability of anti-noise can be improved. However it comes at the expense of computation and speed. Proximal support vector machine (PSVM) is an improvement on classical SVM. It has smaller amount of calculation and faster speed. In this paper, by extracting the characteristics of generalized cross-correlation function of sound source signal and using PSVM to locate the sound source, the sound source localization accuracy is better in the reverberation and noise environment, and it has good robust performance.

Keywords: Sound source localization · Microphone array ·
Generalized cross-correlation function ·
Proximal support vector machine

1 Introduction

With the development of robotics, more and more intelligent robots are used in human life. Robot is the core of human-robot interaction. Sound source localization is an important component of robots. Sound source localization is widely studied in the field of robotics [1]. When the user interacts with the robot, the robot must quickly and accurately locate the user's location. The robot's visual function is affected by light, and the microphone-based array captures sound in all directions without being affected by light [2–4].

In recent years, with the development of artificial intelligence technology, such as human interaction, machine learning and pattern recognition. Signal processing based on microphone array is paied more and more attention. In practice, the signals collected by microphone arrays are easy to disturb by environmental noise. In signal processing based on microphone array, Sound Source Localization is called a research hotspot in the field of signal processing. Localization

© Springer Nature Switzerland AG 2019
H. Yu et al. (Eds.): ICIRA 2019, LNAI 11743, pp. 585–593, 2019.
https://doi.org/10.1007/978-3-030-27538-9_50

systems are based on microphone arrays. The other is small microphone arrays, such as mobile phones, video conferencing and other electronic products.

Sound source locationing algorithms based on microphone array include based on steered response power [5,6], based on time delay estimation [7–9] and based on high resolution spectral estimation [10,11]. Time delay estimation is to characterize the signal parameters by the time difference of the same source signal received by different array elements. Since Knapp and Carter proposed generalized cross-correlation time delay estimation in 1976 [12], least mean square adaptive filtering and cross power spectrum correlation methods have been proposed.

Support vector machine (SVM) is a learning method proposed by Vapnik et al. according to statistical learning theory [13,14]. It is widely used because it supports small sample problems, nonlinear problems and high dimensional space problems. In the field of bearing fault diagnosis, face recognition and other aspects have achieved good achievements [15–17].

The proximal support vector machine (PSVM) proposed by Fung and Mangasarian [18], the main difference from the classical SVM is that the constraints of the optimization problem are different. PSVM directly solves the non-singular linear equations, which has the advantages of simple algorithm and fast operation speed. Therefore, it is particularly suitable for large data volume calculations [19,20].

In this paper, we extract the features of generalized cross-correlation generalized by cross-correlation phase transform function and use PSVM to locate the sound source. Then, the parameters of PSVM are adjusted, and the best localization effect can be achieved.

The organized of this paper are: In Sect. 2, the generalized cross-correlation function is introduced and its features are extracted. The algorithm PSVM is proposed in Sect. 3. Experimental results and performance of sound source localization in Sect. 4. Finally, future work and summary.

2   Feature Extraction

The DARPA TIMIT Acoustic-Phonetic Continuous Speech Corpus (TIMIT) is used in the experiment, which contains 6300 rich speech sentences. Corpus design was a joint effort among the Massachusetts Institute of Technology (MIT), SRI International (SRI) and Texas Instruments, Inc. (TI). The file is 16-bit 16 kHz speech waveform file [21].

The pre-processing of speech signal includes enframe and add window, endpoint detection etc. Decomposition of non-stationary speech signals into a series of short-term stationary signals by framing and add windowing. The frame length is 20 ms, the frame is shifted by 10 ms, and the continuous of each frame signal is 20 ms. The window is processed by the Hanning window. The speech signal of the acquired signal has a relatively large influence on the delay estimation, and the end point detection is performed on the original signal.

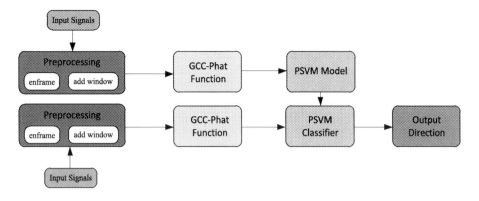

Fig. 1. Source localization using PSVM classifier

Figure 1 shows source localization using PSVM classifier. First, generalized cross-correlation (GCC-Phat) function of the training set is calculated to generate the PSVM model of sound source localization. Second, the GCC-Phat function from the test set is calculated to form a feature vector. Finally, the source location is estimated by PSVM classifier.

The signals received by two microphones in a microphone array are expressed as $x_i(n)$, $i = 1, 2$

$$\begin{cases} x_1(n) = \alpha_1 s(n - \tau_1) + w_1(n) \\ x_2(n) = \alpha_2 s(n - \tau_2) + w_2(n) \end{cases} \tag{1}$$

where $s(n)$ is the source signal, $w_i(n)$ is unrelated Gaussian white noise and is unrelated $s(n)$, τ_i is the time from the sound source to the microphone, α_i is the attenuation coefficient of sound wave, $i = 1, 2$.

The GCC-Phat function between $x_1(n)$ and $x_2(n)$ is calculated in the time-domain:

$$R_{12}(\tau) = E(x_1(n)x_2(n - \tau)) \tag{2}$$

Fourier transform of cross-correlation function transformation of two signals is its power spectral density function.

$$R_{12}(\tau) = \int_{-\infty}^{+\infty} X_1(w)X_2^*(w)e^{-jwt}dw \tag{3}$$

Where $X_1(w)$ is the Fourier transform of $x_1(n)$, $X_2(w)$ is the Fourier transform of $x_2(n)$, $*$ stands for complex conjugate.

In practice, due to the interference of noise and reverberation, the correlation function is often affected by the following factors: the maximum peak is weakened, and the emergence of multiple peaks. GCC-Phat is a weighted processing of the cross-power spectrum of a pair of microphone signals, which makes the correlation function more prominent at the peak position of time delay.

$$R_{12}(\tau) = \int_{-\infty}^{+\infty} \phi_{1,2}X_1(w)X_2^*(w)e^{-jwt}dw \tag{4}$$

$$\phi_{1,2} = \frac{1}{|X_1(w)X_2^*(w)|} \tag{5}$$

Substituting Eq. 5 into Eq. 4, we get

$$R_{12}(\tau) = \int_{-\infty}^{+\infty} \frac{X_1(w)X_2^*(w)}{|X_1(w)X_2^*(w)|} e^{-jwt} dw \tag{6}$$

The signal received by the microphone can also indicate:

$$x_i(n) = h(r_s, n) * s(n) \quad i = 1, 2 \tag{7}$$

Where $s(n)$ is the source signal located at r_s, $h(r_s, n)$ is the room impulse response from the sound source to the ith microphone. Fourier transform of signal $x_i(n)$

$$X_i(w) = H(r_s, w) * S(w) \tag{8}$$

Substituting Eq. 8 into Eq. 6 , we get

$$R_{12}(\tau) = \int_{-\infty}^{+\infty} \frac{H_1(r_s, w)H_2^*(r_s, w)}{|H_1(r_s, w)H_2^*(r_s, w)|} e^{-jwt} dw \tag{9}$$

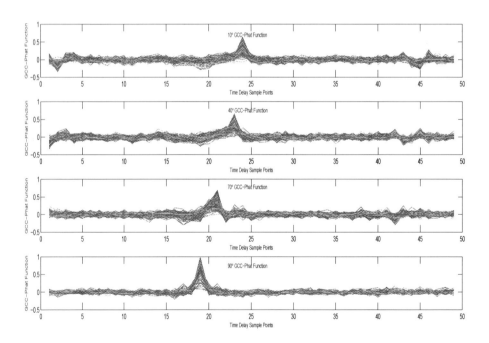

Fig. 2. Comparison of GCC-Phat functions with different azimuths in T60 = 200 ms and SNR = 10 dB environments

In this paper, the sound source is located at a center distance of 2 m on the center of the microphone array. According to the GCC-Phat function symmetry, the sound source in the direction of $10°, 40°, 70°, 90°$ is selected for locationing. Figure 2 shows that the delay sample points are different in these four directions, so the sound source is in different directions and the GCC-Phat function is different. Feature vector z is formed from the GCC-Phat function.

$$z = [R_{12}(-\tau_{max}), R_{12}(-\tau_{max} + 1), ..., R_{12}(\tau_{max} - 1), ..., R_{12}(\tau_{max})]^T \quad (10)$$

Considering the sound speed and the size of microphone array, the value of the GCC-Phat function peak left and right interval lengths of 3 ms is taken. The ITMIT corpus data used in this paper is 16KHz, which corresponds to 49 cross-correlation values between the range ±24 of τ. The feature vector of each frame are GCC-Phat function of length $L = 49$.

3 Classification Algorithm

Proximal support vector machine (PSVM) is a modified version of classical SVM. Comparing with classical SVM, it is faster and more simple Supposing the training data have n sample pairs $\{(x_1, y_1), (x_2, y_2), ..., (x_n, y_n)\}$, where $x_i \in R^m, y_i \in \{-1, 1\}$. Object function in classical SVM algorithm is

$$\min_{(w,\gamma,y)\in R^{n+m+1}} (ve^T y + \frac{1}{2}w^T w) \quad (11)$$

s.t. $D(Aw - e\gamma) + y \geq e, y \geq 0$, where $A \in R^{n\times m}, D \in \{-1, +1\}^{m\times 1}, e = 1^{m\times 1}$. PSVM is an optimization for classical SVM, replacing Eq. 11 with Eq. 12.

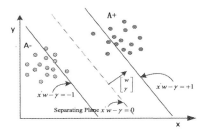

Fig. 3. Proximal support vector classification

$$\min_{(w,\gamma,y)\in R^{n+m+1}} (v \times \frac{1}{2}\|y\|^2 + \frac{1}{2}(w^T w + \gamma)) \quad (12)$$

s.t. $D(Aw - e\gamma) + y = e$

$$D = \begin{cases} 1 & A_i w \geq \gamma - 1 \\ -1 & A_i w < \gamma - 1 \end{cases} \quad (13)$$

After training, all new feature prediction can be expressed by functions of w and γ.

$$f(x) = sign(w^T x - \gamma) \tag{14}$$

Figure 3 shows that if the function value of $f(x)$ is positive, the new set of features belongs to class $A+$, otherwise it belongs to class $A-$. Multi-class classification is accomplished by combining multiple PSVM classifiers. Classifying multiple classes is commonly performed by combining several binary SVM classifiers in a tournament manner, either one-against-all or one-against-one, the latter approach required substantially more computational effort.

In this paper, feature vectors z are extracted from sound sources in different directions. The feature data includes training set and test set. The training set is used to establish PSVM multi-classification model. The test set input classification model is used to estimate the sound source location to obtain test accuracy.

4   Results

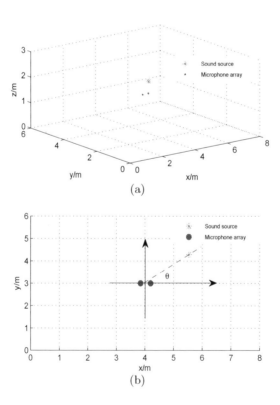

Fig. 4. Simulated room model (a) 3D Stereogram (b) Floor plan

In this paper, the room impulse responses are generated by the image method. We simulate room impulse response using RoomSim tool [22]. Figure 4 shows the model of simulation room, which size is $(8\,\text{m},\ 6\,\text{m},\ 3\,\text{m})$. Supposing two microphones are used to form a microphone array and the microphone position is $(3.85\,\text{m},\ 3\,\text{m},\ 1.5\,\text{m})$, $(4.2\,\text{m},\ 3\,\text{m},\ 1.5\,\text{m})$.

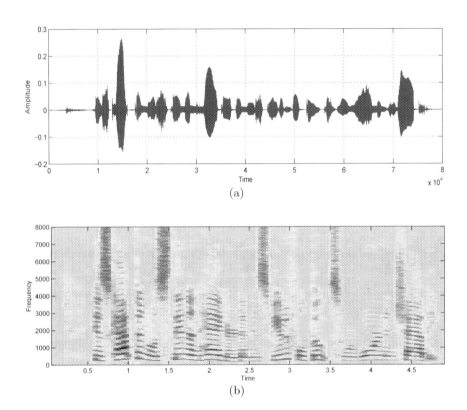

Fig. 5. Speech signal waveform (a) Time domain (b) Spectrogram

Figure 5 shows the time domain and frequency domain waveforms of the speech signal waveform The ITMIT corpus database is used to mix with noise under reverberation $T_{60} = 200\,\text{ms}$ and $T_{60} = 600\,\text{ms}$. The signal-to-noise ratio is clean, 5 mdB, 10 mdB, 15 mdB and 20 mdB.

Figure 6 shows the relationship between reverberation, SNR and positioning accuracy. As the reverberation increases, the positioning accuracy decreases. As the signal to noise ratio increases, the positioning accuracy increases. Experiments show that the reverberation time increases, the signal-to-noise ratio decreases, and the PSVM positioning accuracy is more accurate. When dealing with large amounts of data, PSVM exhibits faster calculations and better robust performance.

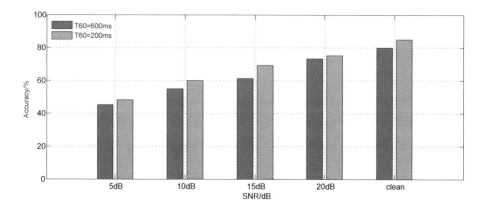

Fig. 6. Accuracy of PSVM classifier at different SNR

5 Summary

In this paper, based on the existing sound source localization algorithm, 49 GCC-Phat function features are extracted for each frame signal, and the sound source is located based on the PSVM algorithm. The algorithm improves the calculation speed and robust performance of sound source localization, and improves the problem of inaccurate sound source localization in harsh environments.

Acknowledgement. This work was supported by the National Key R&D Program of China (2018YFB1305300), and National Nature Science Foundation of China (61673244, 61703240).

References

1. Nakamura, K., Nakadai, K., Ince, G.: Real-time super-resolution sound source localization for robots. In: 2012 IEEE/RSJ International Conference on IEEE, Intelligent Robots and Systems (IROS), pp. 694–699 (2012). https://doi.org/10.1109/IROS.2012.6385494
2. Hu, J.S., Yang, C.H., Wang, C.K.: Sound source localization by microphone array on a mobile robot using eigen-structure based generalized cross correlation. In: 2008 IEEE Workshop on Advanced Robotics and Its Social Impacts IEEE, pp. 1–6 (2008). https://doi.org/10.1109/ARSO.2008.4653625
3. Nakamura, K., et al.: Correlation matrix interpolation in sound source localization for a robot. In: 2011 IEEE International Conference on Acoustics, pp. 4324–4327. IEEE (2011). https://doi.org/10.1109/ICASSP.2011.5947310
4. Grondin, F., Michaud, F.: Time difference of arrival estimation based on binary frequency mask for sound source localization on mobile robots. In: 2015 IEEE/RSJ International Conference on Intelligent Robots & Systems, pp. 6149–6154. IEEE (2015). https://doi.org/10.1109/IROS.2015.7354253
5. Cho, Y., et al.: Sound source localization for robot auditory systems. IEEE Trans. Consum. Electron. **3**(55), 1663–1668 (2009). https://doi.org/10.1109/TCE.2009.5278040

6. Traa, J., et al.: Robust source localization and enhancement with a probabilistic steered response power model. IEEE/ACM Trans. Audio Speech Lang. Process. **3**(24), 493–503 (2016). https://doi.org/10.1109/taslp.2015.2512499

7. Li, X., Liu, H.: Sound source localization for HRI using FOC-based time difference feature and spatial grid matching. IEEE Trans. Cybern. **4**(43), 1199–1212 (2013). https://doi.org/10.1109/TSMCB.2012.2226443

8. Kim, U.H., Nakadai, K., Okuno, H.G.: Improved sound source localization in horizontal plane for binaural robot audition. Appl. Intell. **1**(42), 63–74 (2015). https://doi.org/10.1007/s10489-014-0544-y

9. Wan, X., Wu, Z.: Sound source localization based on discrimination of cross-correlation functions. Appl. Acoust. **1**(74), 28–37 (2013). https://doi.org/10.1016/j.apacoust.2012.06.006

10. Li, X., et al.: Contributed review: source-localization algorithms and applications using time of arrival and time difference of arrival measurements. Rev. Sci. Instrum. **4**(87), 041502 (2016). https://doi.org/10.1063/1.4947001

11. Pavlidi, D., et al.: Real-time multiple sound source localization and counting using a circular microphone array. IEEE Trans. Audio Speech Lang. Process. **10**(21), 2193–2206 (2013). https://doi.org/10.1109/TASL.2013.2272524

12. Knapp, C., Carter, G.: The generalized correlation method for estimation of time delay. IEEE Trans. Acoust. Speech Signal Process. **4**(24), 320–327 (2003). https://doi.org/10.1109/TASSP.1976.1162830

13. Vapnik, V.: The Nature of Statistical Learning Theory. Springer, Heidelberg (1995). https://doi.org/10.1007/978-1-4757-2440-0

14. Vapnik, V.N.: An overview of statistical learning theory. IEEE Trans. Neural Netw. **5**(10), 988–999 (1999). https://doi.org/10.1109/72.788640

15. Salvati, D., Drioli, C., Foresti, G.L.: A weighted MVDR beamformer based on SVM learning for sound source localization. Pattern Recogn. Lett. **84**, 15–21 (2016). https://doi.org/10.1016/j.patrec.2016.07.003

16. Wang, R., Zhou, H.: Application of SVM in fault diagnosis of power electronics rectifier. In: 7th World Congress on Intelligent Control and Automation, pp. 1256–1260. IEEE (2008). https://doi.org/10.1109/WCICA.2008.4593104

17. Gumus, E., et al.: Evaluation of face recognition techniques using PCA, wavelets and SVM. Expert Syst. Appl. **9**(37), 6404–6408 (2010). https://doi.org/10.1016/j.eswa.2010.02.079

18. Fung, G., Mangasarian,O.L.: Proximal support vector machine classifiers. In: Proceedings of the Seventh ACM SIGKDD International Conference on Knowledge Discovery and Data Mining, pp. 77–86. ACM (2001). https://doi.org/10.1145/502512.502527

19. Fung, G.M., Mangasarian, O.L.: Multicategory proximal support vector machine classifiers. Mach. Learn. **1–2**(59), 77–97 (2005). https://doi.org/10.1007/s10994-005-0463-6

20. Sugumaran, V., Ramachandran, K.I.: Effect of number of features on classification of roller bearing faults using SVM and PSVM. Expert Syst. Appl. **4**(38), 4088–4096 (2011). https://doi.org/10.1016/j.eswa.2010.09.072

21. Garofolo, J.S., et al.: TIMIT Acoustic-Phonetic Continuous Speech Corpus LDC93S1 (1993). https://catalog.ldc.upenn.edu/LDC93S1

22. Campbell, D.R., et al.: A MATLAB simulation of "shoebox" room acoustics for use in research and teaching. Comput. Inf. Syst. **9**, 48 (2005)

Multi-scale Densely Connected Dehazing Network

Tong Cui[1,2,3], Zhen Zhang[1,2,3], Yandong Tang[1,2(✉)], and Jiandong Tian[1,2]

[1] State Key Laboratory of Robotics, Shenyang Institute of Automation,
Chinese Academy of Sciences, Shenyang 110016, China
ytang@sia.cn
[2] Institutes for Robotics and Intelligent Manufacturing,
Chinese Academy of Sciences, Shenyang 110016, China
[3] University of Chinese Academy of Sciences, Beijing 100049, China

Abstract. Single image dehazing is a challenging ill-posed problem. The traditional methods mainly focus on estimating the transmission of atmospheric-light medium with some priors or constraints. In this paper, we propose a novel end-to-end convolutional neural network (CNN) for image dehazing, called multi-scale densely connected dehazing network (MDCDN). The proposed network consists of a parallel multi-scale densely connected CNN network and an encoder-decoder U net. The parallel multi-scale dense-net can estimate transmission map accurately. The encoder-decoder U net is used to estimate the atmospheric light intensity. The all-in-one training can jointly learn the transmission map, atmospheric light, and dehazing images all together with jointly MSE error and a discriminator loss. We also create a dataset with indoor and outdoor data based on the LFSD, NLPR, and NYU2 depth datasets to train our network. Extensive experiments demonstrate that, in most cases, the proposed method achieves significant improvements over the state-of-the-art methods.

Keywords: Deep learning image dehazing ·
Multi-scale dense network · One-in-all training · Large-scale dataset

1 Introduction

Haze is a common natural phenomenon which is caused by the absorption and scattering of atmospheric medium, e.g. water vapour, aerosol, and some dry particles. Haze usually results in low visibility for human eyes, degrades the quality of image, and impacts the performances of many high-level computer vision tasks. The image dehazing methods [1,2] aim to estimate the unknown clean image from the low-quality information provided by a hazy image. The image dehazing methods can improve the quality of hazy images, enhance the performances of the high-level computer vision algorithms under the hazy weather, and greatly expands the applicable environment of computer vision algorithm. Hence, the image dehazing method is urgently needed in many application fields

© Springer Nature Switzerland AG 2019
H. Yu et al. (Eds.): ICIRA 2019, LNAI 11743, pp. 594–604, 2019.
https://doi.org/10.1007/978-3-030-27538-9_51

[3–6], such as the outdoor mobile robots, pilotless automobile, unmanned aerial vehicle (UAV), and so on. The image dehazing algorithms can improve the vision systems in locating, detecting, and tracking. Early methods mainly focus on researching on the handcrafted features based on the statistics or the condition methods, such as dark channel prior [1] and boundary constraint [7]. Recently, the works [8–11] on image dehazing automatically learns haze relevant features by convolutional neural networks (CNNs). In the image dehazing area, the imaging process is usually modeled [12] as:

$$I(x) = t(x)J(x) + (1 - t(x))A \tag{1}$$

where x expresses the location of a pixel, I is the observed intensity of hazy image at pixel x, J indicates the clear scene radiance of a haze-free image, which is the final goal of dehazing problem, and A represents the constant atmospheric light intensity. The transmission t describes the proportion of scene radiance that arrives to the lens through the propagation medium.

Many dehazing methods have been proposed in recent years. Most of the researchers in image dehazing area mainly focus on estimating an accurate medium transmission map. However, these transmission approximations are inaccurate, especially in the cases of the scenes where the colors of objects are similar to those of haze noises and atmospheric lights. Note that such an erroneous transmission estimation directly affects the quality of the recovered image, resulting in undesired haze artifacts. With the development of deep learning, some researchers apply convolutional neural networks (CNNs) to learn the transmission directly from the training data without any physical model. However, due to these deep learning methods do not consider the physical mechanism of hazy environment imaging and most of them only use the indoor depth dataset to train their networks, their effects of dehazing are not good enough and the generalizations of these networks are somewhat low.

In order to obtain the accurate haze-free images, we propose a novel image dehazing method called multi-scale densely connected dehazing network (MDCDN). The proposed MDCDN consists of a parallel multi-scale densely network and a encoder-decoder U net. The parallel multi-scale densely network can efficiently estimate the transmission map. The encoder-decoder U net is used to estimate the atmospheric light intensity. Then, we substitute the transmission and atmospheric light into classical atmospheric scattering model. To refine the results of the scattering model which is used to compare with the corresponding ground-truth images and accelerate the training of network, we set a three-levels convolution neural network between the scattering imaging model and the final loss function. We joint MSE error and a discriminator loss to train our network. The all-in-one learning can jointly learn the transmission map, atmospheric light and dehazing images all together. We synthesize a large-scale hazy images dataset from the LFSD, NLPR, and NYU2 datasets as the training and testing data of our network. The depth databases LFSD [13] and NLPR [14] include both indoor and outdoor data, and NYU2 [15] is an indoor depth database. With indoor and outdoor synthetic data, the generalization ability of the proposed network is greatly improved. Extensive experiments demonstrate that the proposed method achieves significant improvements over the state-of-the-art methods.

This paper makes the following contributions:

1. A parallel multi-scale densely network which automatically estimate the transmission is proposed.
2. The proposed a novel encoder-decoder U net can efficiently estimate the atmospheric light intensity.
3. We also create a large-scale dataset based on the LFSD, NLPR, and NYU2 datasets to train our network. The large-scale dataset including both indoor and outdoor data can improve the generalization ability of the proposed network.

2   Related Work

Currently, the mainstream image dehazing methods include the handcrafted prior-based methods and deep learning methods. The handcrafted prior-based methods can be generally split into statistic priors [1,16,17], boundary constraint [7,18], geometrical cluster distribution [19–21].

2.1   Handcrafted Prior-Based Methods

Statistic Priors: He et al. [1] proposed the famous Dark Channel Prior (DCP) based on empirical statistics of experiments on haze-free images, which shows at least one color channel has very low intensity in the haze-free patches. For accelerating transmission optimization, the authors of [22] further proposed an edge-preserving smoothing operator called guided image filter. However, DCP cannot get good dehazing effects in the bright regions. Nishino et al. [16] used a Bayesian statistical prior to jointly estimate the scene radiation intensity and transmission. Zhu et al. [17] proposed the global color-attenuation prior (CAP) to build a linear relationship among scene depth, brightness and saturation of a hazy image.

Boundary Constraint: Meng et al. [7] proposed an effective regularization dehazing method to restore the haze-free image by exploring the inherent boundary constraint based on Radiance Cube. Cui et al. [18] proposed different boundary constraint conditions in bright and non-bright regions respectively. The boundary constraint conditions can efficiently correct the erroneous transmissions estimated by DCP, especially in the bright regions.

Geometrical Cluster Distribution: Fattal [19] proposed a dehazing method based on the color-line prior [23]. The constructed lines shift from the atmosphere were defined as rough transmission. Berman et al. [20] proposed haze-line method, they classified all pixel values into color clusters. In [21] and [24], the transmission values are calculated through color ellipsoid geometry. Both of these two algorithms result in over-saturation due to excessively stretching the hazy vector cluster.

2.2   Deep Learning Methods

Cai et al. [8] built an end-to-end CNN network with a nonlinear activation function BReLU to estimate the transmission. The authors claimed that the features extracted by their convolution kernels correspond to four existing effective priors. Zhu et al. [25] created a linear model for estimating the scene depth of the hazy image under color attenuation prior and learns the parameters of the model with a supervised method. Ren et al. [9] proposed a multi-scale network to dehaze by learning the non-linear relationship between hazy images and the corresponding transmission. Li et al. [10] proposed an all-in-one dehazing network and a linear transformation to encode the transmission map and the atmospheric light into one variable. The three deep learning methods all train the networks in the indoor synthesis database. This training strategy limits the capabilities of these methods in handling the real-world images.

Multi-scale Networks: The multi-scale networks have been proved that can efficiently extract deep features and represent the image context [26,26,28]. Multi-scale feature extraction is also effective to achieve scale invariance. For example, the inception architecture in GoogLeNet [29] uses parallel convolutions with varying filter sizes, and better addresses the issue of objects matching, resulting in state-of-the-art performance in ILSVRC14 [30]. Multi-scale features have been employed to solve various problems such as single image super-resolution [31], depth estimation [32], single image de-raining [33], also in single image dehazing [9].

Densely Connected Convolutional Networks: Densely Connected Convolutional Networks (DCCN) [27] connect each layer to every other layer in the entire architecture. The networks with dense block can maximize the information flow along the features and guarantee better convergence via connecting all layers. They also alleviate the vanishing-gradient problem, strengthen feature propagation, encourage feature reuse, and substantially reduce the number of parameters. Densely Connected Convolutional Networks have been employed in the applications of single image super-resolution pur:man and single image dehazing [11]. But, we propose a different DCCN based dehazing network with [11]. Compared with method [11], our novel dehazing network can effectively recover clearer texture details, more properly improve image contrast.

3   Proposed Networks

Motivated by the methods of multi-scale features extraction for estimating the transmission and densely connected convolutional networks, we propose a novel multi-scale densely connected architecture MDCDN which extracts deep features from multiple parallel dense blocks, where the size of each convolution filter is 3×3, 7×7 and 11×11 respectively. With the indoor and outdoor date synthesised by us, the MDCDN can accurately estimate the transmission. To estimate the atmospheric-light, we propose a 4-block U-net structure. The integral network architecture is illustrated in Fig. 1.

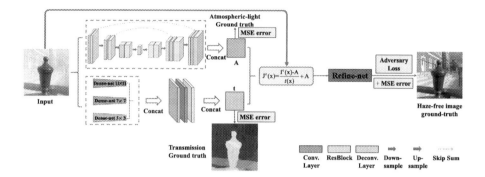

Fig. 1. Multi-scale densely connected dehazing network.

Transmission Estimation. Dehazing is an especially challenging issue due to the global inhomogeneity of haze noise. However, the same object or the neighbouring objects satisfy the local consistency, namely they have the similar transmissions. If we only use one big size convolution kernel to extract the features associated with transmission, the networks may not detect the small size objects. If we only use one convolution kernel with small size, the transmission maps of big size objects obtained by the networks will be split into many smaller patches. The more detail textures and redundant boundaries in transmission map will make the dehazing result look like a canvas painting with many contaminated blocks. We think that the different size convolution kernels can ensure the local consistency of transmission for different size objects. Hence, we combine the features from different scales to get more accurate transmission.

Inspired by the previous methods that use multi-level features for estimating the transmission map, we propose a multiple parallel densely connected structure that makes use of the features from multiple layers of a CNN. We select the dense block because it can maximize the information flow along those features and guarantee better convergence via connecting all layers. Our multi-scale densely connected network consists of three parallel dense-nets with different kernel sizes. These three dense-nets have the same structure that includes two down-sample transition layers, two no-sampling transition layers, two up-sample transition layers. The dense-net structure is illustrated in the Fig. 2. Finally, all the features from each dense block are concatenated together for transmission estimation.

Atmospheric Light Estimation. In the classical atmospheric scattering model, atmospheric light is a global constant. Hence, our ground truth of atmospheric light is a single channel map with the same value. The size of atmospheric light ground truth map is the same as that of the input image. We propose a U-net which consists of three down-sample Conv-Res-Relu blocks and three symmetric Dconv-Res-Relu blocks to estimate the atmospheric light.

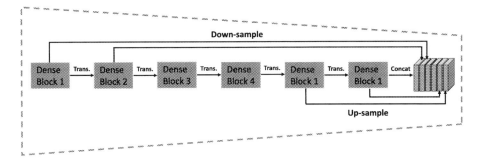

Fig. 2. The dense-net structure.

Loss Function. At the end of the multiple parallel densely connected network and the U-net, we calculate the MSE errors of the transmission and atmospheric-light with their corresponding ground-truth maps. The decreasing MSE errors ensure the accuracy of transmission and atmospheric-light intensity before they are substituted into the atmospheric scattering model.

Finally, the overall MDCDN architecture is trained using the joint loss with MSE errors and discriminator loss. The loss function is as following:

$$L = L^m + \lambda L^d \tag{2}$$

where L^m is the MSE error, L^d represents discriminator loss, and λ is the constant weight of L^d.

The discriminator loss L^d is defined as following:

$$L^d = -log(D(G_t(I))) - log(D(G_g(I))) \tag{3}$$

where G expresses the generator network, D expresses the discriminator network, t is the transmission obtained by the proposed network, and g is the transmission ground-truth.

Radiance Restoration. To further improve the rough dehazed results and make sure better details well preserved, we use a three-layers convolutional network with ReLU to refine the results of the atmospheric scattering model. Then we optimize the entire network with the refined dehazed results and the corresponding ground-truth.

4   Experimental Results

In this section, we compare the proposed method with the following state-of-the-art algorithms [1,8–10]on real-world and synthetic data. Dehazing performance on the synthetic data is evaluated by PSNR and SSIM. Performance on real-world images is evaluated visually since the ground truth images are not available. For fair comparison, we download the codes uploaded by the authors from Github to generate the comparative data. We conduct all the program on a server with one TITAN X graphics card which owns 12 GM video memory.

(a) Input   (b) He et al.[1]   (c) Cai et al.[8]   (d) Ren et al.[9]   (e) Li et al.[10]   (f) Our results   (g) Ground-truth

Fig. 3. The comparison of dehazed results on synthetic data.

Synthetic Dataset. Similar to the existing deep learning-based dehazing methods [8–10], we synthesize the hazy image with the clear haze-free image, the depth information provided by the depth datasets, the random scattering coefficient $\beta \in [0.5, 1.5]$, and three different random atmospheric light intensities within [0.6, 1]. We randomly select 1600 images from the LFSD, NLPR, and NYU2 depth datasets to generate the training set. Hence, there are in total 4800 training images. A test dataset consisting of 800 images from the mentioned above datasets are built. The testing images are all excluded from the training set.

Training Details. The entire network is trained using the Pytorch framework. During training, a 512—512 image is randomly cropped from the input image. We use Adam as our optimization algorithm. The training mini-batch size is set as 4. The learning rate starts from 0.001 and decreases 10 times after each 20 epoch. The maximum number of iterations is 10^7. We set the weight decay as 0.0001, the momentum as 0.9, and $\lambda = 0.25$. All the parameters are chosen via cross-validation.

Comparison Experiments. To demonstrate the effectiveness of the proposed method, we compare the results of our method with four state-of-the-art methods [1,8–10] on both synthetic and real-world data.

Comparison on Synthetic Data. For synthetic data, we compare the performances of the proposed method and each comparison method on the proposed test dataset with indoor and outdoor data. The dehazed image samples of the comparison methods are illustrated in Fig. 3. Since the clear ground-truth images

Table 1. Quantitative PSNR/SSIM results on the synthetic dataset.

Metric	Methods				
	He et al. [1]	Cai et al. [8]	Ren et al. [9]	Li et al. [10]	Our method
PSNR	18.6616	19.2758	23.0602	21.3647	24.5725
SSIM	0.8452	0.8682	0.8238	0.8988	0.9056

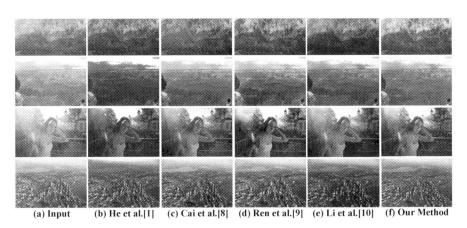

(a) Input   (b) He et al.[1]   (c) Cai et al.[8]   (d) Ren et al.[9]   (e) Li et al.[10]   (f) Our Method

Fig. 4. The comparison of dehazed results on real-world data.

and the ground-truth transmission are available, we qualitatively evaluate the performances of the comparison methods with the reference evaluation metrics PSNR and SSIM. The average qualitative evaluation results for the whole test dataset are displayed in Table 1. From Fig. 3(b), we can observed that the traditional method [1] usually excessively enhances the contrast of dehazed results. The results of method [8] have good color fidelity, but the effect of dehazing is unsatisfactory. The methods [9] and [10] sometimes leave some haze or generate some color distortions in the result. In contrast, the proposed method can generate higher contrast and less color distortion clear haze-free images. The qualitative evaluation results in Table 1 proofs that, in most cases, the proposed method is superior to other comparison methods.

Comparison on Real-World Data. To demonstrate the generalization ability of the proposed method, we compare the dehazed results of the comparison methods on some real-world hazy images downloaded from the Internet. Four samples are shown in Fig. 4. For the real-world images, because we train our network with both indoor and outdoor datesets, our method can obtain higher color fidelity and better dehazing effect than the other three deep learning based methods [8–10] which only use indoor datasets to train networks. The traditional method [1] usually tends to darken the scene.

5 Conclusion

In this paper, we propose a novel image dehazing method called multi-scale densely connected dehazing network (MDCDN). The proposed MDCDN consists of a parallel multi-scale densely network and a encoder-decoder U net. The parallel multi-scale densely network can efficiently estimate the transmission map. The encoder-decoder U net is used to estimate the atmospheric light intensity. We substitute the transmission and atmospheric light into classical atmospheric scattering model. The end-to-end learning is achieved by directly embedding the atmospheric scattering model into the network, thereby ensuring that the proposed method strictly follows the physics-driven scattering model for dehazing. We set a three levels convolution network between the scattering imaging model and the final loss function to refine the results of the scattering model. MSE error and a discriminator loss is jointly employed to train our network. The all-in-one learning can jointly learn the transmission map, atmospheric light and dehazing images all together. Extensive experiments demonstrate that, compared against other comparison state-of-the-art methods, the proposed method can effectively recover clearer texture details, more properly improve image contrast. The colors of our dehazing results are more natural and authentic.

Acknowledgements. The work presented in this paper was supported by the Natural Science Foundation of China under Grant No. 91648118.

References

1. He, K., Sun, J., Tang, X.: Single image haze removal using dark channel prior. IEEE Trans. Pattern Anal. Mach. Intell. **33**(12), 2341–2353 (2011)
2. Kopf, J., et al.: Deep photo: model-based photograph enhancement and viewing, vol. 27, no. 5, p. 116. ACM (2008)
3. Sakaridis, C., Dai, D. Van Gool, L.: Semantic foggy scene understanding with synthetic data. Int. J. Comput. Vis. 1–20 (2018)
4. Song, Y., Bao, L., Yang, Q.: Real-time video decolorization using bilateral filtering. In: IEEE Winter Conference on Applications of Computer Vision, pp. 159–166. IEEE (2014)
5. Yuan, Y., Liang, X., Wang, X., Yeung, D.Y. Gupta, A.: Temporal dynamic graph LSTM for action-driven video object detection. In: Proceedings of the IEEE International Conference on Computer Vision, pp. 1801–1810 (2017)
6. Qing, C., Huang, W., Zhu, S., Xu, X.: Underwater image enhancement with an adaptive dehazing framework. In: 2015 IEEE International Conference on Digital Signal Processing (DSP), pp. 338–342. IEEE (2015)
7. Meng, G., Wang, Y., Duan, J., Xiang, S., Pan, C.: Efficient image dehazing with boundary constraint and contextual regularization. In: Proceedings of the IEEE International Conference on Computer Vision, pp. 617–624 (2013)
8. Cai, B., Xu, X., Jia, K., Qing, C., Tao, D.: Dehazenet: an end-to-end system for single image haze removal. IEEE Trans. Image Process. **25**(11), 5187–5198 (2016)
9. Ren, W., Liu, S., Zhang, H., Pan, J., Cao, X., Yang, M.-H.: Single image dehazing via multi-scale convolutional neural networks. In: Leibe, B., Matas, J., Sebe, N., Welling, M. (eds.) ECCV 2016. LNCS, vol. 9906, pp. 154–169. Springer, Cham (2016). https://doi.org/10.1007/978-3-319-46475-6_10

10. Li, B., Peng, X., Wang, Z., Xu, J., Feng, D.: An all-in-one network for dehazing and beyond. arXiv preprint arXiv:1707.06543 (2017)
11. Zhang, H., Patel, V.M.: Densely connected pyramid dehazing network. In: Proceedings of the IEEE Conference on Computer Vision and Pattern Recognition, pp. 3194–3203 (2018)
12. Nayar, S.K., Narasimhan, S.G.: Vision in bad weather. In: Proceedings of the Seventh IEEE International Conference on Computer Vision, vol. 2, pp. 820–827. IEEE (1999)
13. Li, N., Ye, J., Ji, Y., Ling, H., Yu, J.: Saliency detection on light field. In: Proceedings of the IEEE Conference on Computer Vision and Pattern Recognition, pp. 2806–2813 (2014)
14. Peng, H., Li, B., Xiong, W., Hu, W., Ji, R.: RGBD salient object detection: a benchmark and algorithms. In: Fleet, D., Pajdla, T., Schiele, B., Tuytelaars, T. (eds.) ECCV 2014. LNCS, vol. 8691, pp. 92–109. Springer, Cham (2014). https://doi.org/10.1007/978-3-319-10578-9_7
15. Silberman, N., Hoiem, D., Kohli, P., Fergus, R.: Indoor segmentation and support inference from RGBD images. In: Fitzgibbon, A., Lazebnik, S., Perona, P., Sato, Y., Schmid, C. (eds.) ECCV 2012. LNCS, vol. 7576, pp. 746–760. Springer, Heidelberg (2012). https://doi.org/10.1007/978-3-642-33715-4_54
16. Nishino, K., Kratz, L., Lombardi, S.: Bayesian defogging. Int. J. Comput. Vision **98**(3), 263–278 (2012)
17. Zhu, Q., Mai, J., Shao, L.: Single image dehazing using color attenuation prior. In: BMVC (2014)
18. Cui, T., Tian, J., Wang, E., Tang, Y.: Single image dehazing by latent region-segmentation based transmission estimation and weighted l 1-norm regularisation. IET Image Process. **11**(2), 145–154 (2016)
19. Fattal, R.: Dehazing using color-lines. ACM Trans. Graph. (TOG) **34**(1), 13 (2014)
20. Berman, D., Avidan, S.: Non-local image dehazing. In: Proceedings of the IEEE Conference on Computer Vision and Pattern Recognition, pp. 1674–1682 (2016)
21. Gibson, K.B., Nguyen, T.Q.: An analysis of single image defogging methods using a color ellipsoid framework. EURASIP J. Image Video Process. **2013**(1), 37 (2013)
22. He, K., Sun, J., Tang, X.: Guided image filtering. IEEE Trans. Pattern Anal. Mach. Intell. **35**(6), 1397–1409 (2013)
23. Omer, I., Werman, M.: Color lines: image specific color representation. In: Proceedings of the 2004 IEEE Computer Society Conference on Computer Vision and Pattern Recognition, CVPR 2004, vol. 2, p. II. IEEE (2004)
24. Gibson, K.B., Vo, D.T., Nguyen, T.Q.: An investigation of dehazing effects on image and video coding. IEEE Trans. Image Process. **21**(2), 662–673 (2012)
25. Zhu, Q., Mai, J., Shao, L.: A fast single image haze removal algorithm using color attenuation prior. IEEE Trans. Image Process. **24**(11), 3522–3533 (2015)
26. He, K., Zhang, X., Ren, S., Sun, J.: Spatial pyramid pooling in deep convolutional networks for visual recognition. IEEE Trans. Pattern Anal. Mach. Intell. **37**(9), 1904–1916 (2015)
27. Huang, G., Liu, Z., Van Der Maaten, L., Weinberger, K.Q.: Densely connected convolutional networks. In: Proceedings of the IEEE Conference on Computer Vision and Pattern Recognition, pp. 4700–4708 (2017)
28. Zhao, H., Shi, J., Qi, X., Wang, X., Jia, J.: Pyramid scene parsing network. In: Proceedings of the IEEE Conference on Computer Vision and Pattern Recognition, pp. 2881–2890 (2017)
29. Szegedy, C., et al.: Going deeper with convolutions. In: Proceedings of the IEEE Conference on Computer Vision and Pattern Recognition, pp. 1–9 (2015)

30. Russakovsky, O., et al.: Imagenet large scale visual recognition challenge. Int. J. Comput. Vis. **115**(3), 211–252 (2015)
31. Zhang, Y., Tian, Y., Kong, Y., Zhong, B., Fu, Y.: Residual dense network for image super-resolution. In: Proceedings of the IEEE Conference on Computer Vision and Pattern Recognition, pp. 2472–2481 (2018)
32. Eigen, D., Puhrsch, C., Fergus, R.: Depth map prediction from a single image using a multi-scale deep network. In: Advances in Neural Information Processing Systems, pp. 2366–2374 (2014)
33. Zhang, H., Patel, V.M.: Density-aware single image de-raining using a multi-stream dense network. In: Proceedings of the IEEE Conference on Computer Vision and Pattern Recognition, pp. 695–704 (2018)
34. Purohit, K., Mandal, S., Rajagopalan, A.N.: Scale-recurrent multi-residual dense network for image super-resolution. In: Leal-Taixé, L., Roth, S. (eds.) ECCV 2018. LNCS, vol. 11133, pp. 132–149. Springer, Cham (2019). https://doi.org/10.1007/978-3-030-11021-5_9

Residual Attention Regression for 3D Hand Pose Estimation

Jing Li[1] [ID], Long Zhang[1] [ID], and Zhaojie Ju[2(✉)] [ID]

[1] School of Information Engineering, Nanchang University,
Nanchang 330031, China
[2] School of Computing, University of Portsmouth, Portsmouth PO1 3HE, UK
zhaojie.ju@port.ac.uk

Abstract. 3D hand pose estimation is an important and challenging task for virtual reality and human-computer interaction. In this paper, we propose a simple and effective residual attention regression model for accurate 3D hand pose estimation from a depth image. The model is trained in an end-to-end fashion. Specifically, we stack different attention modules to capture different types of attention-aware features, and then implement physical constraints of the hand by projecting the pose parameters into a lower-dimensional space. In this way, 3D coordinates of hand joints are estimated directly. The experimental results demonstrate that our proposed residual attention network can achieve superior or comparable performance on three main challenging datasets, where the average 3D error is 9.7 mm on the MSRA dataset, 7.8 mm on the ICVL dataset, and 17.6 mm on the NYU dataset.

Keywords: 3D hand pose estimation · Attention mechanism ·
Convolutional neural network · Depth images

1 Introduction

Vision-based articulated hand pose estimation has made steady progress in recent years [1–3], since it is a key technology for human-computer interaction [30] in virtual reality and augmented reality applications. For the diagnosis and therapy of autism spectrum disorder (ASD), hand pose estimation can help diagnose children with autism, because the hand behaviors of ASD children are different from those of typically developing children. Moreover, it can assist ASD children to interact with robots in order to improve their social ability, i.e., robots can better understand ASD children's commands by hand pose estimation and provide appropriate feedback. Although recent progress has been achieved in 3D hand pose estimation with depth cameras [4, 5], there also remains a lot of challenges for efficient and robust estimation due to the high degree of freedom (DOF) of hand pose, severe self-occlusions, viewpoint changes, self-similarity of fingers, large variations in hand pose and background noises.

Existing human hand pose estimation methods can be categorized into two complementary paradigms: (1) learning-based (discriminative); and (2) model-based (generative). The former learns a direct regression function which maps the image appearance to hand pose, and either uses random forests [6, 8, 11] or deep

© Springer Nature Switzerland AG 2019
H. Yu et al. (Eds.): ICIRA 2019, LNAI 11743, pp. 605–614, 2019.
https://doi.org/10.1007/978-3-030-27538-9_52

convolutional neural networks to estimate hand pose. Generally, it is much more efficient to evaluate the regression function than model-based optimization, but the estimation is rough and can serve as initialization for later model-based optimization [9]. Nevertheless, learning-based methods are becoming popular because they are robust and fast. The latter synthesizes images according to hand geometry, and then defines an objective function between the synthesized image and the observed image to quantify the discrepancy, and finally optimizes the objective function to obtain the hand pose.

Recently, deep convolutional neural networks (CNNs) have exhibited great performance across various computer vision tasks such as object classification [20], object detection [7, 21], semantic segmentation [22] and human pose estimation [15] because of the good modeling capacity and end-to-end feature learning. For hand pose estimation, discriminative data-driven approaches leveraging CNNs surpass traditional generative model-driven approaches in terms of accuracy and speed, and most of the recent proposed 3D hand pose estimation methods have achieved drastic performance improvement on large hand pose datasets [10–13]. Thanks to the success of CNNs and the availability of low-cost depth cameras, many research efforts have been devoted to hand pose estimation from depth images, including directly taking 2D depth images as input into CNNs and outputting heat-maps [23], the 3D joint locations or the 3D pose parameters [14] such as joint angles.

Given a single depth image as input, there are two main regression-based approaches. The first approach directly regresses depth images to continuous joint 2D or 3D positions [16, 17] either in 2D or 3D space; the other approach outputs discrete heat-maps [23] for each hand joint as an intermediate result and performs some additional post-processing steps to obtain the final hand pose. However, it is non-trivial to lift 2D heat-maps to 3D joint locations. One straightforward solution is to generate volumetric heat-maps using 3D CNNs, but it is inefficient and requires much computing resources.

In this work, inspired by the attention mechanism used in image classification [19] and human pose estimation [15], we design a novel residual attention regression model based on CNNs to estimate 3D hand pose from single depth images by introducing the attention mechanism that can directly regresses the 3D joint coordinates with end-to-end training. More specifically, our main contributions are summarized as follows:

(1) We propose a novel residual attention regression model to directly regress 3D coordinates of hand joints. Our network architecture is composed of multiple attention modules, generating different attention-aware features from different modules which change adaptively as layers going deeper. Our network is in an end-to-end training fashion without extra post-processing.

(2) We apply a prior layer to learn a prior model from hand pose and integrate it into our network with fewer neurons on the end of the network.

(3) We conduct extensive comparison experiments on three challenging hand pose datasets (e.g., MSRA datasets [12], NYU datasets [11] and ICVL datasets [10]) To evaluate the performance our proposed regression model with other representative hand pose estimation methods. Experimental results show our model is efficient and performs better on the MSRA dataset and the ICVL dataset.

2 Related Works

3D hand pose estimation is an old and long-lasting problem in computer vision research areas. Recently, it has captured much attention due to its widespread applications in augmented reality and the popularity of depth cameras, such as Microsoft Kinect and Intel RealSense. To infer 3D hand pose, Tompson et al. [11] applied CNNs to produce 2D heat-maps which represent the probability distributions of hand joints and used model-based inverse kinematics to recover 3D hand pose from estimated heat-maps. Ge et al. [24] firstly employed 3D CNN to capture spatial features in 3D space by projecting depth images into three different views and estimating 3D hand pose from multi-view heat-maps. Oberweger et al. [16, 17] proposed a framework that directly regresses 3D coordinates of hand joints with multi-stage CNNs and used a linear layer as pose prior. They [29] also introduced a feedback loop which contains a discriminative network for initial pose estimation, a CNN for image synthesis and a CNN for refining hand pose iteratively. Chen et al. [25] designed a pose guided structured region ensemble network to capture the tree-like structure of the hand. Moon et al. [26] cast the 3D hand and human pose estimation problems from a single depth map into a voxel-to-voxel prediction which used a 3D voxelized grid and estimated the per-voxel likelihood for each keypoint of hand. Wan et al. [18] proposed to jointly train a generator for updating with the back-propagated gradient from the discriminator to synthesize realistic depth maps of the articulated hand and a discriminator to estimate the posterior of the latent pose given some depth maps. Ye et al. [27] proposed a hybrid hand pose estimation method and applied the kinematic hierarchy strategy to the input space of the discriminative method by a spatial attention mechanism in order to optimize the generative method by hierarchical Particle Swarm Optimization (PSO). Deng et al. [28] converted the depth images to a 3D volume and used a 3D CNN to predict joint locations; however, 3D networks show a low-computational efficiency.

However, most of the above-mentioned networks focus on training feedforward convolutional neural networks using a "very deep" structure to deal with the hand pose estimation problem. In this paper, we apply a residual attention network which contains a bottom-up and top-down feedforward mask branch that can generate attention-aware features to guide feature learning and regress hand joint coordinates in an end-to-end training fashion.

3 Model Overview

The goal of our model is to estimate J 3D hand joint coordinates $S = \{j_i\}_1^J$ with $j_i = (u_i, v_i, d_i)$ from a single depth image. Like in the previous work [16], firstly we estimate a coarse 3D bounding box containing the hand and segment the foreground based on the assumption that the hand is the closest object to the depth camera. In this way, we extract a fixed-size cube in the center of mass of this object from the depth image. Then, the cube is resized to 128×128 patch of depth values normalized to $[-1, 1]$ as the input for the CNNs. The points for which depth is not available, or the depth values deeper than the back face of the cube, are assigned with a fixed value of

1.0. In order to be invariant to different distances between the hand and the camera for the CNN, the normalization is a key pre-processing step.

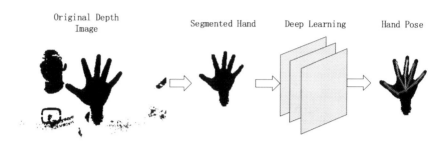

Fig. 1. The pipeline of hand pose estimation

The pipeline of our hand pose estimation framework is given in Fig. 1. Firstly, we segment the hand from the original depth image, and then we feed it into our network as input to generate the coordinates of hand joints which are used to recover the hand pose. The architecture of our proposed residual attention regression model is shown in Fig. 2. It is constructed by stacking three attention modules with a residual unit between two modules. The network accepts a 128×128 depth image as the input. Each attention module consists of two branches: the trunk branch and the mask branch. The trunk branch is for feature extraction and we use residual units as basic units of our residual attention module. Denote the trunk branch output $T(x)$ with input x, the mask branch has the same size as $M(x)$ which uses a bottom-up and top-down structure. The output of the attention module H is:

$$H_{i,c}(x) = \left(1 + M_{i,c}(x)\right) * T_{i,c}(x) \tag{1}$$

where $M_{i,c}(x)$ ranges from [0, 1] for it is after a sigmoid layer, $T_{i,c}(x)$ indicates the features learned by the deep convolutional neural network. The mask branches are the key for attention modules since they have the ability to enhance good features and suppress noises from trunk features as feature selectors.

At the end of the network, instead of directly predicting the 3D joint locations, we predict the pose parameters in a lower-dimensional space. A previous work [16] demonstrated that this can improve the prediction reliability because it enforces constraints of the hand pose. We apply Principal Component Analysis (PCA) to learn a low-dimensional representation of the training data, which implements the physical constraints of the hand. Then, we compute the hand pose parameters by projecting them into the 3·J-dimensional joint space with the last prior layer. In order to show the estimated hand pose in the depth image, we project the predicted real-world 3D coordinates into the image pixel coordinates using the intrinsic parameters of the depth camera, as shown in Eq. 2:

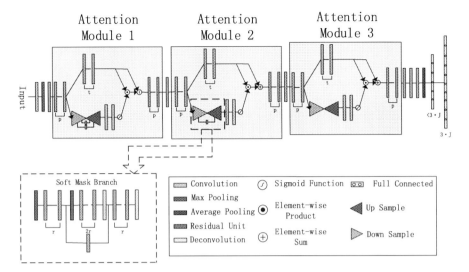

Fig. 2. The architecture of our proposed residual attention regression model. It consists of three different modules and there are three hyper-parameters: p, t, and r. The last fully-connected layer is the prior layer.

$$(P_{x,i}, P_{y,i}, P_{z,i}) = proj(P_{u,i}, P_{v,i}, P_{d,i}) \qquad (2)$$

where $(P_{x,i}, P_{y,i})$ is in pixel coordinate and $P_{z,i}$ is the distance between the depth camera and the object.

4   Experiment

We evaluate our proposed deep convolutional network architecture on three public hand pose datasets: MSRA Hand Pose Dataset [12], ICVL Hand Pose Dataset [10] and NYU Hand Pose Dataset [11].

The MSRA dataset [12] contains over 76k depth frames captured by Intel's Creative Interactive Gesture Camera which uses a time-of-flight. For each frame, it contains 3D locations of 21 annotated hand joints. The dataset contains 9 subjects. For each subject, there are 17 gestures, each of which contains about 500 segmented hand images from depth images. We train our neural network on 8 subjects and evaluate on the remaining one.

The ICVL dataset [10] contains about 330k training samples and 1.6k testing samples and there is a large discrepancy between the training and testing sequences. The dataset was recorded using a time-of-flight Intel Creative Interactive Gesture Camera and the ground truth of each frame contains 16 hand joint locations with (x, y) in pixels and z in mm, and thus we should project the image pixel coordinates into the real-world 3D space by using the intrinsic parameters of the depth camera. Although different artificially in-plane rotations were applied to the collected samples, we only use the original 22k samples.

The NYU dataset [11] contains about 72k depth images for training and 8 k depth images for testing. Each frame was captured using the Primesense Carmine 1.09, which is a structured light-based sensor and the depth maps show missing values are mostly along the occluding boundaries as well as noisy outlines. The ground truth annotation of each depth image contains 3D locations of 36 hand joints, but we just use a subset of 14 hand joints as in previous works [16–18, 28]. The dataset contains very noisy images and has a very wide range of poses, making a challenge to most hand pose estimation methods.

We adopt two different evaluation metrics to evaluate the performance of our proposed hand pose estimation method. The first metric is the per-joint mean error distance between the predicted 3D joint location and the ground truth overall testing frames as well as the overall mean error distance for all joints on all testing frames, as shown in Eq. 3. As given by Eq. 4, the second metric is the percentage of good frames in which the worst joint error is below a given threshold, which is more challenging and strict. We remove the mean error distance of the center joint for it is used for normalization.

$$avg\,error = \frac{\sum_{s=1}^{S} \sum_{j=1}^{J} Err_{(s,j)}}{S * J} \tag{3}$$

where $Err_{(s,j)}$ is the Euclidean Distance between the ground truth and the predicted location of each joint, S is the number of testing frames, and J is the number of joints in each frame.

$$per = \frac{n}{S} \tag{4}$$

where n indicates the number of frames in which the average joint error is within a maximum distance from the ground truth, and S is the number of testing frames.

We train and evaluate our proposed deep neural network model on a computer equipped with an Intel Core I7 CPU, 32 GB of RAM, and two GeForce GTX 1080Ti GPUs. Our deep neural network model is implemented in Python within the TensorFlow framework. We use Adam optimizer with initial learning rate 0.0001, batch size 128, L2 regularization weight delay rate 0.0003, and the learning rate is divided by 10 after 30 epochs. We stop the training process after 70 epochs to avoid overfitting. We do not perform any data augmentation on these datasets.

In Figs. 3, 4 and 5, we give the results of our model on the three datasets mentioned above by adopting two different evaluation metrics. The average 3D errors are 9.7 mm, 7.8 mm, 17.6 mm on MSRA dataset, ICVL dataset and NYU dataset, respectively. And we also compare the 3D average error of our methods with several popular approaches in Table 1. We can see that our approach outperforms Wan et al. [18] and Oberweger et al. [16] with about 20% and 13% absolute improvement on the NYU dataset and ICVL dataset, respectively. Figure 6 shows qualitative hand pose estimation results on three datasets.

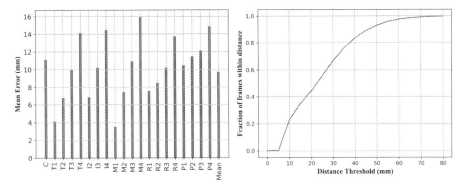

Fig. 3. Distance error (left) and percentage of success frames (right) on the MSRA dataset.

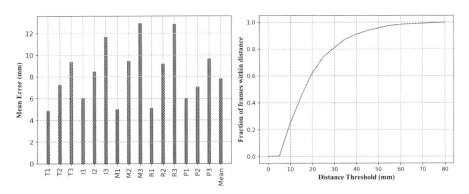

Fig. 4. Distance error (left) and percentage of success frames (right) on the ICVL dataset.

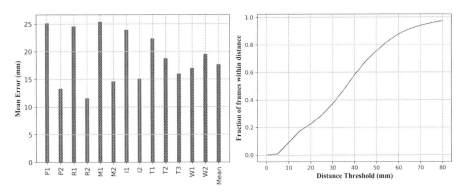

Fig. 5. Distance error (left) and percentage of success frames (right) on the NYU dataset.

Table 1. The 3D average error comparison of different methods on MSRA, ICVL and NYU datasets without augmentation, the "aug" denotes data augmentation.

Method	Dataset		
	MSRA	ICVL	NYU
Oberweger et al. [16]	–	9.0 mm	20.7 mm
Wan et al. [18]	12.2 mm	10.2 mm	**15.5 mm**
Sun et al. [12]	15.2 mm	–	–
Deng et al. [28]	–	10–11 mm (aug)	17.6 mm (aug)
Our	**9.7 mm**	**7.8 mm**	17.6 mm

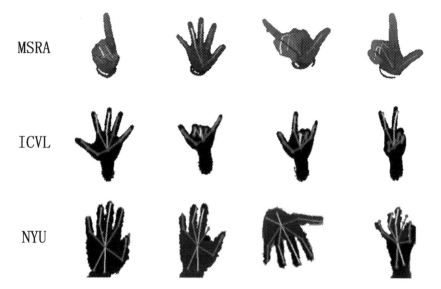

MSRA

ICVL

NYU

Fig. 6. Qualitative hand pose estimation results on three datasets.

5 Conclusions

In this paper, we propose a novel 3D hand pose regression model based on residual attention network from a single depth image. Our method applies different attention modules to capture different types of attention to guide feature learning for 3D hand pose regression and can predict accurate real-world 3D coordinates of hand joints. To avoid the distance influence between the camera and the hand, we crop the hand with a fixed cube according to the center of mass and normalize the depth image and the ground truth. Further, we apply pose prior to add the physical constraints of the hand to estimate accurate hand pose. Experimental results on the three challenging hand pose datasets show that our model achieves superior or comparable performance without data augmentation.

References

1. Hui, L., Yuan, J., Thalmann, D.: Resolving ambiguous hand pose predictions by exploiting part correlations. IEEE Trans. Circuits Syst. Video Technol. **25**(7), 1125–1139 (2015)
2. Oberweger, M., Riegler G., Wohlhart, P., Vincent, L.: Efficiently creating 3D training data for fine hand pose estimation. In: 2016 IEEE Conference on Computer Vision and Pattern Recognition (CVPR), Las Vegas, NV, USA, pp. 4957–4965. IEEE (2016)
3. Oikonomidis, I., Kyriazis, N., Argyros, A.: Efficient model-based 3D tracking of hand articulations using Kinect. In: Proceedings of the 22nd British Machine Vision Conference (BMVC), pp. 101.1–101.11. BMVA Press, University of Dundee, UK (2011)
4. Xu, C., Cheng, L.: Efficient hand pose estimation from a single depth image. In: 2013 IEEE International Conference on Computer Vision (ICCV), Sydney, NSW, Australia, pp. 3456–3462. IEEE (2013)
5. Ge, L., Liang, H., Yuan, J., Thalmann, D.: 3D convolutional neural networks for efficient and robust hand pose estimation from single depth images. In: 2017 IEEE Conference on Computer Vision and Pattern Recognition (CVPR), Honolulu, HI, USA, pp. 5679–5688. IEEE (2017)
6. Tang, D., Yu, T., Kim, T.K.: Real-time articulated hand pose estimation using semi-supervised transductive regression forests. In: 2013 IEEE International Conference on Computer Vision (ICCV), Sydney, NSW, Australia, pp. 3224–3231. IEEE (2013)
7. Liu, W., et al.: SSD: single shot multibox detector. In: Leibe, B., Matas, J., Sebe, N., Welling, M. (eds.) ECCV 2016. LNCS, vol. 9905, pp. 21–37. Springer, Cham (2016). https://doi.org/10.1007/978-3-319-46448-0_2
8. Li, P., Ling, H., Li, X., Liao, C.: 3D hand pose estimation using randomized decision forest with segmentation index points. In: 2015 IEEE International Conference on Computer Vision (ICCV), Santiago, Chile, pp. 819–827. IEEE (2015)
9. Srinath, S., Franziska, M., Antti, O., Christian, T.: Fast and robust hand tracking using detection-guided optimization. In: 2015 IEEE Conference on Computer Vision and Pattern Recognition (CVPR), Boston, MA, USA, pp. 3213–3221. IEEE (2015)
10. Tang, D., Chang, H.J., Tejani, A., Kim, T.K.: Latent regression forest: structured estimation of 3D articulated hand posture. In: 2014 IEEE Conference on Computer Vision and Pattern Recognition (CVPR), Columbus, OH, USA, pp. 3786–3793. IEEE (2014)
11. Tompson, J., Stein, M., Lecun, Y., Perlin, K.: Real-time continuous pose recovery of human hands using convolutional networks. ACM Trans. Graph. **33**(5), 169 (2014)
12. Sun, X., Wei, Y., Liang, S., Tang, X., Sun, J.: Cascaded hand pose regression. In: 2015 IEEE Conference on Computer Vision and Pattern Recognition (CVPR), Boston, MA, USA, pp. 824–832. IEEE (2015)
13. Yuan, S., Ye, Q., Stenger, B., Jain, S., Kim, T.K.: Bighand2.2m benchmark: hand pose dataset and state of the art analysis. In: 2017 IEEE Conference on Computer Vision and Pattern Recognition (CVPR), Honolulu, HI, USA, pp. 2605–2613. IEEE (2017)
14. Zhou, X., Wan, Q., Zhang, W., Xue, X., Wei, Y.: Model based deep hand pose estimation. In: Proceeding of the Twenty-Fifth International Joint Conference on Artificial Intelligence, IJCAI 2016, pp. 2421–2427 (2016)
15. Newell, A., Yang, K., Deng, J.: Stacked hourglass networks for human pose estimation. In: Leibe, B., Matas, J., Sebe, N., Welling, M. (eds.) ECCV 2016. LNCS, vol. 9912, pp. 483–499. Springer, Cham (2016). https://doi.org/10.1007/978-3-319-46484-8_29
16. Oberweger, M., Wohlhart, P., Lepetit, V.: Hands deep in deep learning for hand pose estimation. In: 2015 Computer Vision Winter Workshop (CVWW), pp. 1–10 (2015)

17. Oberweger, M., Lepetit, V.: DeepPrior++: improving fast and accurate 3D hand pose estimation. In: 2017 IEEE International Conference on Computer Vision Workshops (ICCVW) (2017), Venice, Italy, pp. 585–594. IEEE (2017)

18. Wan, C., Thomas P., Van Gool, L., Yao, A.: Crossing nets: combining GANs and VAEs with a shared latent space for hand pose estimation. In: 2017 IEEE Conference on Computer Vision and Pattern Recognition (CVPR), Honolulu, HI, USA, pp. 1196–1205. IEEE (2017)

19. Wang, F., Jiang, M., Qian, C., Yang, S., Li, C., Zhang, H.: Residual attention network for image classification. In: 2017 IEEE Conference on Computer Vision and Pattern Recognition (CVPR), Honolulu, HI, USA, pp. 6450–6458. IEEE (2017)

20. Alex, K., Ilya, S., Hinton, G.E.: ImageNet classification with deep convolutional neural networks. Advances in Neural Information Processing Systems, vol. 25, no. 2, pp. 1097–1105 (2012)

21. Girshick, R., Donahue, J., Darrell, T., Malik, J.: Region-based convolutional networks for accurate object detection and segmentation. IEEE Trans. Pattern Anal. Mach. Intell. **38**(1), 142–158 (2016)

22. Chen, L.-C., Papandreou, G., Kokkinos, I., Murphy, K., Yuille, A.L.: DeepLab: semantic image segmentation with deep convolutional nets, atrous convolution, and fully connected CRFs. arXiv:1606.00915 (2016)

23. Choi, C., Kim, S., Ramani, K.: Learning hand articulations by hallucinating heat distribution. In: 2017 IEEE International Conference on Computer Vision (ICCV 2017), Venice, Italy, pp. 3123–3132. IEEE (2017)

24. Ge, L., Liang, H., Yuan, J., Thalmann, D.: Robust 3D hand pose estimation from single depth images using multi-view CNNs. IEEE Trans. Image Process. **27**(9), 4422–4436 (2018)

25. Chen, X., Wang, G., Guo, H., Zhang, C.: Pose guided structured region ensemble network for cascaded hand pose estimation. arXiv:1708.03416 (2017)

26. Moon, G., Chang, J.Y., Lee, K.M.: V2V-PoseNet: voxel-to-voxel prediction network for accurate 3D hand and human pose estimation from a single depth map. In: 2018 IEEE Conference on Computer Vision and Pattern Recognition (CVPR), Salt Lake City, UT, USA, pp. 5079–5088. IEEE (2018)

27. Ye, Q., Yuan, S., Kim, T.-K.: Spatial attention deep net with partial PSO for hierarchical hybrid hand pose estimation. In: Leibe, B., Matas, J., Sebe, N., Welling, M. (eds.) ECCV 2016. LNCS, vol. 9912, pp. 346–361. Springer, Cham (2016). https://doi.org/10.1007/978-3-319-46484-8_21

28. Deng, X., Yang, S., Zhang, Y., Tan, P., Chang, L., Wang, H.: Hand3D: hand pose estimation using 3D neural network. arXiv:1704.02224 (2017)

29. Oberweger, M., Wohlhart, P., Lepetit, V.: Training a feedback loop for hand pose estimation. In: 2015 IEEE International Conference on Computer Vision (ICCV), Santiago, Chile, pp. 3316–3324. IEEE (2015)

30. Li, J., Wang, J., Ju, Z.: A novel hand gesture recognition based on high-level features. Int. J. Humanoid Rob. **15**(1), 1750022 (2018)

Fixation Based Object Recognition in Autism Clinic Setting

Sheng Sun[1], Shuangmei Li[2], Wenbo Liu[3], Xiaobing Zou[4], and Ming Li[5(✉)]

[1] School of Electronics and Information Technology, Sun Yat-sen University,
Guangzhou, China
[2] PuJiang Institute, Nanjing Tech University, Nanjing, China
[3] Department of Electrical and Computer Engineering, Carnegie Mellon University,
Pittsburgh, USA
[4] The Third Affiliated Hospital of Sun Yat-sen University, Guangzhou, China
[5] Data Science Research Center, Duke Kunshan University, Suzhou, China
ming.li369@duke.edu,
https://scholars.duke.edu/person/MingLi

Abstract. With the increasing popularity of portable eye tracking devices, one can conveniently use them to find fixation points, i.e., the location and region one is attracted by and looking at. However, region of interest alone is not enough to fully support further behavior and psychological analysis since it ignores the abundant information of visual information one perceives. Rather than the raw coordinates, we are interested to know the visual content one is looking at. In this work, we first collect a video dataset using a wearable eye tracker in an autism screening room setting with 14 different commonly used assessment tools. We then propose an improved fixation identification algorithm to select stable and reliable fixation points. The fixation points are used to localize and select object proposals in combination with object proposal generation methods. Moreover, we propose a cropping generation algorithm to determine the optimal bounding boxes of viewing objects based on the input proposals and fixation points. The resulted cropped images form a dataset for the subsequent object recognition task. We adopt the AlexNet based convolutional neural network framework for object recognition. Our evaluation metrics include classification accuracy and intersection-over-union (IoU), and the proposed framework achieves 92.5% and 88.3% recognition accuracy on different testing sessions, respectively.

1 Introduction

Research on human eyes is becoming increasingly attractive in the past few decades [1,2]. Researchers found that the trajectory movements of our eyes often contain some specific patterns [3,4] and can be mainly described by fixations and saccades. When someone stares at a point, the gaze may not be strictly fixed, sometimes jitters within a very small region. On the other hand, saccades are quick movements of our gazes when we read texts or view scenes. Both fixations

© Springer Nature Switzerland AG 2019
H. Yu et al. (Eds.): ICIRA 2019, LNAI 11743, pp. 615–628, 2019.
https://doi.org/10.1007/978-3-030-27538-9_53

and saccades can vary rapidly along the time. It is therefore almost impossible to observe and accurately measure eye movement by naked eyes.

Eye research relies heavily on eye tracking devices which can generate information including front scene and fixation point, i.e., the point of gaze. There are mainly two types of eye tracking devices. The first type is table-mounted ones that contain an illuminator and a camera mounted above or below the computer screen. The second ones are head-mounted devices that typically contain an illuminator, a front view camera that records the scene one is looking at, and one or two cameras that capture the movements of the eyes. Table-mounted ones are suitable for tasks such as texts reading, advertisement viewing, or visual searching on computer screens, while head-mounted wearable ones are more portable so that the viewer can walk around and perform eye tracking experiments in real world environments. These wearable eye tracking devices provide great opportunities for research on psychological behavior analysis, advanced human-computer interaction, Augmented Reality (AR) applications, etc.

Recently, considerable progress on high-level computer vision, especially object recognition has been made with the advancement of deep representation learning. Traditionally, hand-crafted features such as scale-invariant feature transform (SIFT) [4] and histogram of oriented gradients [5] present the main visual representation methods as they are designed to be invariant to scale, orientation, affine distortion, and illumination changes. Later, convolutional Neural Networks (CNNs), which consider deeply layered nonlinear representations with neurons, pushed the boundaries of object recognition to new levels. Some large scale datasets such as ImageNet [6] are widely used to pretrain a network model from scratch, and then researchers can fine tune the model with domain specific data. There are several popular network structures, from the simple Alexnet [7], to GoogLeNet, VGGNet, and ResNet. CNNs require a large amount of training data and computing resources, so the introduction of large scale image databases and the advance of GPU computing pave the way for the rapid improvement in object recognition. Also, the emerging deep learning frameworks such as Caffe [8], Torch, and TensorFlow make it easier to implement the powerful CNNs. Similarly, performance of the object detection method has also been enhanced significantly due to the usage of CNNs. Histogram of Oriented Gradients (HOG) features and Deformable Part Models (DPM) with Support Vector Machine (SVM) have been used to detect objects, however, only moderate recognition accuracy was achieved. Currently, several novel CNN based models such as faster R-CNN and You Only Look Once (YOLO) [9] dramatically improve the accuracy on the PASCAL VOC and COCO dataset.

As these fields develop rapidly, we come up with an idea of combining them and trying to identify what we are looking at instead of simply where. This is of great importance because when we want to analyze a video clip with fixation point included, we first need to label the frame of interest and objects manually, which is a time-consuming task. If we can utilize the computer vision technology to automatically label the object, we would save plenty of time and money for in-depth analysis of the data. What's more, when we want to know the conspicuity of the objects or the histogram of eye fixations on different objects, the proposed method can generate the results more efficiently and objectively.

In our study, eye tracking and object recognition are standard tasks individually, but when combined together, multiple new challenges emerge. Firstly, since there is few related work, the open databases are scarce. Therefore, we have to collect a database to perform experiments. Secondly, the eye tracking devices use fisheye lenses, which produce strong distortion and negatively affect the recognition accuracy when we use the pre-trained models. Thirdly, we seldom look at the center of an object, so the fixation generated by the eye tracking device is usually at the edge or even a few pixels away, making it difficult to determine whether the viewer is actually watching the object or just looking at another place that is close to the object. Fourthly, the resolution of the captured videos is relatively low, making small and far away objects more difficult to be distinguished. Last but not the least, it is both labor and cost expensive to collect sufficient amount of training data for large-scaled network training.

In this paper, we first introduce a fixation based object recognition dataset. The setting is in an Autism Diagnostic Observation Schedule (ADOS) screening room where the subject looks at those assessment tools. Knowing what the children look at and how their eye movements behave when stimuli appear will benefit the diagnosis of Autism and other psychological experiments. In this scenario, we select 14 commonly used ADOS assessment tools, which are shown in Fig. 1. There are two main reasons for this choice. First, these 14 assessment tools are standard and widely used in different ADOS screenings. Second, they are big enough for the eye tracking device to clearly capture.

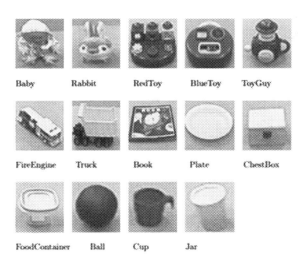

Fig. 1. Sample images of the selected 14 assessment tools and their labels.

After collecting the data, we preprocess images by identifying fixations. During the testing phase, we first determine the region based on the fixation point and the bounding boxes generated by the object detection module, then we predict the class label using our object recognition system.

The remainder of the paper is organized as follows. In Sect. 2, we present the related works. In Sect. 3, we introduce the data collection procedure and in Sect. 4, we describe the methods in details. Experimental results are provided in Sect. 5 followed by the conclusions in Sect. 6.

2   Related Works

With the increasing popularity of eye tracking devices, more and more research on eye-gaze pattern analysis appears. Portable and wearable eye tracking devises are more convenient for real world eye tracking experiments.

German Research Center for Artificial Intelligence (DFKI) has been working on this topic [10–12]. The goal of their research is to develop an AR human computer interaction application, namely, Museum Guide 2.0. It can provide tourists with personal guide in the museum. The tourist wears the eye tracking device while walking around. If he looks at an exhibit item, the application can detect the gaze and present relevant information such as audio descriptions so that the tourist would have a better understating of the exhibition. The original implementation of their method is shown as follows: 1. Creation of exhibits database: take images from different angles with eye tracking device, then extract SIFT features and label them. 2. Object recognition: crop a region with fixed size around the fixation point and extract SIFT features. Compare it with every sample in the database and find the nearest one using Euclidean distance.

Later Shdaifat Mustafa et al. [12] proposed a segmentation-based method to generate dynamic region size instead of the fixed region size method in step 2. They first conduct a series of image pre-processing steps, including Canny edge detection, morphology operations, etc. Then, the proper boundary and bounding box was selected based on the position of the fixation point.

However, the aforementioned methods have certain limitations. First, during testing, the SIFT descriptors of the test image needs to be compared with all the samples in the database, which is not time efficient. Second, SIFT feature is not robust enough to achieve highly accurate recognition performance. Third, the segmentation based bounding box detection method is not robust against fixation deviation and offset. We believe that, using the state-of-the-art YOLO framework with out proposed selection method for bounding box generation and the Alexnet model for object recognition would significantly enhance the overall accuracy and efficiency.

3   Data Collection

3.1   Eye Tracking Device

The eye tracking device used in this study is the UltraFlex headgear designed by Positive Science [13]. The head-mounted eye tracker includes eye/scene cameras,

audio, and infrared illumination. The scene camera faces front and the eye camera capture the right eye. Figure 2 shows the eye tracking device and one sample
frame [14]. The IRLED illuminates the eye, then the device and corresponding
software estimate the gaze location by center of the pupil and corneal reflection
and then project the coordinate onto the video captured by the scene camera.
The device operates at 28 frames per second with a resolution of 640×480 for
the scene view and 320×240 for the eye view.

Fig. 2. The three main components of the DB9-KHG-1 Child Headgear eye tracking
device and the views of the scene camera and the eye camera with detailed information.

3.2   Training Data Collection

In this work, we proposed a new object recognition dataset with a wearable eye
tracking device. This is a close-set datset in which the objects in the testing set
is a subset of the ones in the training set.

In the collection of training data, we collected the images of each object
from different views. The object was put on the table, and the subject wearing
the wearable eye tracking device looks at the object from different angles. If the
object has more than one formats, we treat them as different classes. For instance,
the baby toy can be converted into two different shapes, sitting and lying. We
name them as sitting baby and lying baby separately. Figure 3(a) illustrates these
two classes of baby. After collecting the training data, we extract frames from
the scene video every 10 frames and use the open source tool named LabelImg
to annotate the bounding box of the object of interest. Note that we also create
a special class named "Others", which represents the objects that do not belong
to the pre-defined 14 classes, including the table, the floor, and the wall in the
background, etc. Some examples of class "Others" were shown in Fig. 3(b).

3.3   Testing Data Collection

The testing data was collected in two different sessions with objects in short and
long distances.

In session 1, the objects are laid on the table the same way as the training
data collection. In order to efficiently collect the testing data in a real autism
clinic setting, we group the objects into seven categories, which is shown in

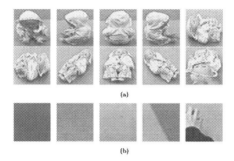

Fig. 3. Sample training images for the class Baby (a) and Others (b).

Table 1. During each round, all objects from one category are put on the table. The participant is asked to look at the objects from random positions and angles. Furthermore, the locations of objects were changed several times during the testing data collection to enhance the generalization. Figure 4 shows the experiment setup for this scenario.

In session 2, the subject sits on the ground with most of the objects surrounding him in a circle as shown in Fig. 5. This setting is different from the one in our training data and session 1. We want to evaluate the robustness of our model against the recording environment changes.

Table 1. The seven categories of the ADOS assessment tools

Category	Assessment tools
1	Baby, Rabbit
2	RedToy, BlueToy, ToyGuy
3	FireEngine, Truck
4	Book, Plate
5	ChestBox, FoodContainer
6	Ball
7	Cup, Jar

Fig. 4. Data collection setup for session 1 testing data.

Fig. 5. Data collection setup for session 2 testing data.

3.4 Fixation Identification

The eye movements include two types: saccade and fixation. Saccades are the type of eye movement used to move rapidly from one point to another, while for fixation, the eye movements are relatively stable in a certain duration. We are more interested in conducting recognition in fixation points because fixation is a natural description of the observed eye movement behaviors.

In order to differentiate the fixations from saccades, we use modified Dispersion-Threshold Identification (I-DT) algorithm similar with the Dispersion-Threshold algorithm (DT) proposed by Salvucci et al. [15].

When there is a fixation, the gaze points tend to cluster together in a specific timing interval. We utilize the sliding window technique to identify the fixation points. Two parameters are important in defining window size: the duration and the dispersion threshold. As mentioned in [16], the duration of a fixation varies from task to task. Specifically, in the scene viewing task, the duration is usually set to be at least 200 ms. In our experiment, the duration is set at 350 ms which is around 10 frames. Dispersion threshold emphasizes the dispersion (i.e.,spread distance) of a fixation point. In terms of the dispersion, we simply compute the dispersion in each window as follows:

$$Dispersion = max(x) - min(x) + max(y) - min(y) \qquad (1)$$

We set the maximum dispersion as 20 pixel, which could generates a reasonable amount of fixations [17].

We ignore the noisy samples in the following two conditions. First, the eye tracking device fails to detect the corneal reflection. Second, the point is beyond the image boundary. We perform window sliding on the time axis, and obtain the fixation points based on both duration and dispersion threshold. The pseudo code for this algorithm is shown in Algorithm 1.

This modified Dispersion-Threshold Identification (I-DT) algorithm is more computational efficient than the original DT algorithm because we directly set the new start to the frame that incurs termination or the frame next to it instead of shifting the window by one frame.

Algorithm 1. Fixation identification algorithm

---

1 **Function** Modified I-DT (duration, dispersion threshold) **Result:** Fixations
2 Initialize the start of the window to the first point **while** *there are still points* **do**
3 | Inspect current point i **if** *the point is invalid* **then**
4 | | **if** $n \geq duration$ **then**
5 | | | n is the number of points in the window The fixation is the middle point of the window
6 | | **else**
7 | | | Abandon the current window
8 | | **end**
9 | | Set the new start to $i + 1$
10 | **else**
11 | | Update the current dispersion with point i **if** $dispersion \geq dispersion threshold$ **then**
12 | | | **if** $n \geq duration$ **then**
13 | | | | The fixation is the middle point of the window
14 | | | **else**
15 | | | | Abandon the current window
16 | | | **end**
17 | | | Set the new start to i
18 | | **else**
19 | | | Add point i to the window
20 | | **end**
21 | | Move to the next point $i + 1$
22 | **end**
23 **end**
24 **if** $n \geq duration$ **then**
25 | The fixation is the middle point of the window
26 **end**
27 return fixation

---

4   Methods

4.1   Data Augmentation

After collecting the training data, we split it into the training set and the validation set. For each object, we first count the number of images and randomly choose 75% of the images as the training set and the remaining 25% images as the validation set.

We first augment the training set by altering the color, contrast, and brightness of the original images [18]. And then, we generate five more crops, namely, top-left, top-right, bottom-left, bottom-right, and central by using two-thirds of the region along each axis. This augmentation strengthens our model because test crops may not be perfect and some of them contain only a portion of the object. With partial images included in our training set, our model can have better generalization.

We added nine times more images to the training set using the aforementioned two augmentation methods, which benefit the training of our CNN models.

4.2   Segmentation and Bounding Box Selection

For each video frame, the first step is to find the optimal bounding box around the fixation point. We adopt two different bounding box generation methods.

The first one is the fixed size method. We use multiple fixed cropping sizes from 64×64, 96×96, to 128×128 around the fixation and group them together for testing.

The second one is the deep learning based object detection method. We use YOLOv2 model pre-trained by the VOC 2007 and VOC 2012 datasets. We feed testing images into the network and generate detected bounding boxes. Every input image has multiple detected bounding boxes. So we need to filter out some nonrelevant detections. First of all, we filter out some severely occluded cropping boxes based on the RGB threshold. For instance, when the subject rotates the object, the captured image is very likely to suffer from occlusion with the subject' hands. Figure 6 illustrates this situation. Secondly, we select the bounding boxes based on their sizes. As YOLOv2 is a general object detection model, the system tends to output some unrelated objects such as table, bed, and person, which are relatively bigger than the objects we are interested in. So we set another size threshold to further filter out bounding boxes with large sizes.

After bounding box selection, there are still multiple bonding boxes on each single image. We need to choose correct box around the fixation point. For each fixation point, we set the fist bounding box contains the fixation as the initial crop. If there is another bounding box also containing the same fixation point, we deploy a special selection process to select the final bounding box. It works as follows: if there is an encompassment relationship of two boxes, we choose the smaller one as the new crop. Otherwise, we calculate the distance from the two centers to the fixation and choose the one with smaller distance. In an extremely rare case when the distance is equal, the two bounding boxes are merged. Figure 7 illustrate the final bounding box generated by the proposed algorithm.

This bounding box selection method is better than the simple union and intersection. As for the union, the cropping box is likely to grow very big and contains many unnecessary objects when multiple detection boxes contain the fixation point. On the contrary side, the intersection of the boxes cannot fully include the object of interest, and the partial image fails to represent the characteristic of the whole object.

Note that there are some special cases when the system fails to detect any object or none of the bounding box contains the fixation; we simply use the default 96×96 region around the fixation. We also consider the case when the fixation slightly deviates from the object, as shown in Fig. 8, so we try a 16-pixels soft boundary in all four directions.

4.3 Object Recognition

After augmentation, we have 9000 cropped images for training and another 297 images for validation. Due to the relatively small scale of our training data, we use the Alexnet structure for CNN modeling. The model is trained from scratch with a batch size of 128, base learning rate of 0.01, momentum of 0.9, and weight decay of 0.005. We adopt the step policy for learning rate decrement, reducing it by a factor of 10 for 1000 iterations. After 2500 iterations, the network is fully trained, which takes 64 min on a desktop with NVIDIA GeForce GTX 745.

Fig. 6. Some example images when the subject's hands occlude with the object of interest.

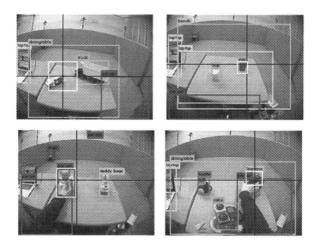

Fig. 7. Four final bounding boxes generated by our algorithm are marked as white rectangles. The rectangles with labels are the raw bounding boxes generated by the YOLOv2 detection system. The blue points are the fixation outputs from the wearable eye tracker. (Color figure online)

Fig. 8. Sample images when the fixation point slightly deviates from the object.

4.4   Evaluation

In the testing step, we first obtain cropped images, then feed them into the network to receive output scores. We use classification accuracy as an evaluation metric for the recognition system and intersection-over-union (IoU) for the detection system. The algorithm works as follows: we go through all the ground truth bounding boxes of an image. If the fixation point is in a bounding box (with some deviation toleration), we first calculate the IoU between the detection output and this bounding box, and then evaluate the classification accuracy. If none of the ground truth bounding boxes contains the fixation point, we believe that the subject is looking at some objects not belong to our pre-defined class. In this case, we need to verify whether the proposed system successfully predicts it as class "Others". Algorithm 2 shows the pseudo code for this algorithm.

Algorithm 2. Test result evaluation algrithm

```
1  Function Evaluation()
2  for all gt ∈ groundtruths(GT) do
3  │    if the bounding box of GT contains fixation then
4  │    │    Calculate IoU
5  │    │    Compare predication class of GT
6  │    end
7  end
8  if None of the GT bounding box tontains fixation then
9  │    Compare prediction with class label "Others"
10 end
```

---

5 Experimental Results

5.1 Cropped Image Generation

In our experiment, we find that using the general YOLOv2 detection system combined with our customized bounding box selection method improves the overall fixation aware object recognition performance by 9% absolutely compared to the fixed size cropping baseline as shown in Table 2.

As for IoU, the proposed approach outperforms the baseline by 2%. Since we only calculate IoU when the final object recognition prediction is correct, the improvement on IoU is not that high compared to the accuracy. The main reason might be that when the prediction is correct, the region covered by the baseline fixed size cropping is very similar to our selected bounding box.

Table 2. Comparison of two bounding box selection methods

Type	Session 1 testing data	Session 2 testing data	IoU
Fixed size bounding box	83.3%	79.9%	56.9%
Our proposed method	92.5%	88.2%	58.3%

5.2 Object Recognition

Table 3 shows the recognition accuracy for each of the selected 14 commonly used assessment tools. Our system achieves 100% recognition accuracy in the flowing classes: Baby, RedToy, Truck, ChestBox, FoodContainer, and Jar. It works fairly well in recognizing Rabbit, BlueToy, FireEngine, Book, Ball, and Others. However, the performance in ToyGuy, Plate, and Cup is not very satisfying. In Fig. 9(a), the system detects the baby and the fixation point is in the region.

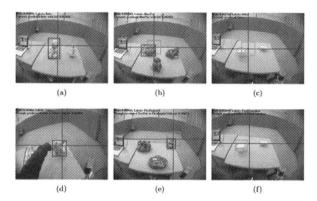

Fig. 9. Sample predictions of our system. (a)–(c) and (f) are the correct samples while (d)–(e) are the misclassified samples. The cyan rectangles are the bounding boxes generated by Sect. 4.2 while the red rectangles are the human annotated ground truths. The blue points are the fixation points. (Color figure online)

Table 3. Performance of our proposed method on the session 1 testing data, including the number of correct predictions, total number of test images, and the recognition accuracy.

Class	Correct	Total	Accuracy
Baby	23	23	100.0%
Rabbit	19	20	95.0%
RedToy	17	17	100.0%
BlueToy	24	25	96.0%
ToyGuy	13	18	72.2%
FireEngine	11	12	91.7%
Truck	10	10	100.0%
Book	8	9	88.9%
Plate	4	5	80.0%
ChestBox	3	3	100.0%
FoodContainer	12	12	100.0%
Ball	18	20	90.0%
Cup	11	13	84.6%
Jar	8	8	100.0%
Others	30	33	90.9%
All	211	228	92.5%

However in Fig. 9(b), the system fails to detect the blue toy, so we use a default region of 96×96 for test. Figure 9(c) is similar to (b), except that there is no ground truth bounding box containing the fixation, so we classify it to class "Others". In Fig. 9(d), the detection system outputs a small part of the rabbit, and coincidently the fixation is also in that region, which leads to the wrong prediction as class "Others". In Fig. 9(e), we use a default region, but since it is quite larger than the toy guy, our system makes a wrong prediction that it is a blue toy. The example shown in Fig. 9(f) is a soft boundary sample. The fixation point is within 16 pixels from the detection bounding box, and the system recognizes it as a food container.

As shown in Table 3, our proposed system achieves 92.5% and 88.2% accuracy for the overall fixation aware object recognition task for testing session 1 and 2, respectively. Because the data collection setup for the training data collection and testing session 1 are the same, so the recognition accuracy on testing session 1 is higher than testing session 2. The performance can be further enhanced if the outputs from the wearable eye tracking devices are more accurate, robust and with high resolution.

6   Conclusions

In this paper, we introduce a new wearable eye tracking video dataset captured in a real autism clinic setting. We try to develop an algorithm that combines the eye tracking and computer vision technologies together to recognize the object tag when one is looking at. With the usage of deep learning object detection and recognition network, the proposed system could enable researchers to easily analyze and label the data. We believe that the proposed method shows great potential to extend our application beyond the computer screen setting to more general indoor settings, such as home, office, hospital, supermarket, etc. We can also consider outdoor activities, such as driving and campus walking. Future works include collecting more data, using more advanced network models and utilizing unsupervised clustering methods for better accuracy and efficiency.

Acknowledgement. This research was funded in part by the National Natural Science Foundation of China (61773413), Natural Science Foundation of Guangzhou City (201707010363), Six talent peaks project in Jiangsu Province (JY-074), and Science and Technology Program of Guangzhou City (201903010040).

References

1. Yarbus, A.L.: Eye Movements and Vision. Springer, US (1967). https://doi.org/10.1007/978-1-4899-5379-7
2. Hayhoe, M., Ballard, D.: Eye movements in natural behavior. Trends Cogn. Sci. **9**(4), 188–194 (2005)
3. Rayner, K.: Eye movements and attention in reading, scene perception, and visual search. Q. J. Exp. Psychol. **62**(8), 1457–1506 (2009)
4. Lowe, D.G.: Distinctive image features from scale-invariant keypoints. Int. J. Comput. Vision **60**(2), 91–110 (2004)
5. Dalal, N., Triggs, B.: Histograms of oriented gradients for human detection. In: IEEE Computer Society Conference on Computer Vision and Pattern Recognition, CVPR 2005, vol. 1, pp. 886–893. IEEE (2005)

6. Deng, J., Dong, W., Socher, R., Li, L.J., Li, K., Li, F.: ImageNet: a large-scale hierarchical image database. In: IEEE Conference on Computer Vision and Pattern Recognition, CVPR 2009, pp. 248–255 (2009)
7. Krizhevsky, A., Sutskever, I., Hinton, G.E.: ImageNet classification with deep convolutional neural networks. In: International Conference on Neural Information Processing Systems, pp. 1097–1105 (2012)
8. Jia, Y., et al.: Caffe: convolutional architecture for fast feature embedding, pp. 675–678 (2014)
9. Redmon, J., Farhadi, A.: YOLO9000: better, faster, stronger, pp. 6517–6525 (2016)
10. Toyama, T.: Object recognition system guided by gaze of the user with a wearable eye tracker. In: Mester, R., Felsberg, M. (eds.) DAGM 2011. LNCS, vol. 6835, pp. 444–449. Springer, Heidelberg (2011). https://doi.org/10.1007/978-3-642-23123-0_46
11. Toyama, T., Kieninger, T., Shafait, F., Dengel, A.: Gaze guided object recognition using a head-mounted eye tracker. In: Biennial Symposium on Eye Tracking Research Applications, ETRA 2012, pp. 91–98 (2012)
12. Shdaifat, M., Bukhari, S.S., Toyama, T., Dengel, A.: Robust object recognition in wearable eye tracking system. In: Pattern Recognition, pp. 650–654 (2016)
13. Positivescience eye tracker. http://positivescience.com
14. Positive Science. Yarbus eye-tracking software user guide (2014)
15. Salvucci, D.D., Goldberg, J.H.: Identifying fixations and saccades in eye-tracking protocols, pp. 71–78 (2000)
16. Rayner K., Castelhano, M.S.: Eye movements during reading, scene perception, visual search, and while looking at print advertisements. Visual Advertising Hillsdale (2008)
17. Blignaut, P.: Fixation identification: the optimum threshold for a dispersion algorithm. Attention Percept. Psychophysics **71**(4), 881 (2009)
18. Howard, A.G.: Some improvements on deep convolutional neural network based image classification. Comput. Sci. (2013)

Towards Deep Learning Based Robot Automatic Choreography System

Ruiqi Wu[1], Wenyao Peng[1], Changle Zhou[1], Fei Chao[1,4(✉)], Longzhi Yang[2], Chih-Min Lin[3], and Changjing Shang[4]

[1] Cognitive Science Department, School of Information Science and Engineering, Xiamen University, Xiamen, China
`fchao@xmu.edu.cn`
[2] Department of Computer and Information Sciences, Northumbria University, Newcastle, UK
[3] Department of Electrical Engineering, Yuan Ze University, Taoyuan City, Taiwan
[4] Department of Computer Science, Institute of Mathematics, Physics and Computer Science, Aberystwyth University, Aberystwyth, UK

Abstract. It is a challenge task to enable a robot to dance according to different types of music. However, two problems have not been well resolved yet: (1) how to assign a dance to a certain type of music, and (2) how to ensure a dancing robot to keep in balance. To tackle these challenges, a robot automatic choreography system based on the deep learning technology is introduced in this paper. First, two deep learning neural network models are built to convert local and global features of music to corresponding features of dance, respectively. Then, an action graph is built based on the collected dance segments; the main function of the action graph is to generate a complete dance sequence based on the dance features generated by the two deep learning models. Finally, the generated dance sequence is performed by a humanoid robot. The experimental results shows that, according to the input music, the proposed model can successfully generate dance sequences that match the input music; also, the robot can maintain its balance while it is dancing. In addition, compared with the dance sequences in the training dataset, the dance sequences generated by the model has reached the level of artificial choreography in both diversity and innovation. Therefore, this method provides a promising solution for robotic choreography automation and design assistance.

Keywords: Robot dance · Motion planning · Gesture relation · Action graph · Deep learning

1 Introduction

As a traditional art representation, dance has an important position in the art field and is also an indispensable part of human's entertainment programs. With the advancement of artificial intelligence technology and robotics technology,

© Springer Nature Switzerland AG 2019
H. Yu et al. (Eds.): ICIRA 2019, LNAI 11743, pp. 629–640, 2019.
https://doi.org/10.1007/978-3-030-27538-9_54

robotic choreography has also become a popular research field [1–3]. Since the robotic automate choreography, as an interdisciplinary research of robotic control, artificial intelligence and artistic creation, owns a unique research significance for robot motion planning and human art cognition and computing [4]. Moreover, the robotic automatic choreography also has an important application potentials in the inheritance of traditional dance, assisting artists in choreography, and expanding the ability of entertainment robots.

Robot automatic choreography is regarded as a robotic motion generation process, in which the robot generates a corresponding sequence of actions based on the given signals with the constraints of dance creation rules and human aesthetic preferences [5]. The given signal can be a piece of music, a series of light changes, or human's emotional changes over a period of time. Many researchers have studied various aspects of the robot dance. For example, Tholley et al. [6] constructed a dance system on a dog-shaped robot in a bottom-up manner, which first combines postures into dance fragments, and then combines the dance fragments into a complete dance according to the conventional theory of dance. With the assistances of the human evaluation, this method improved the quality of robot dance through reinforcement learning. Xia et al. [7] used a machine learning method to study the style and emotional relationships between music fragments and robot action fragments, and then combined the action fragments that satisfy the condition into a complete dance based on an artificially designed action similarity function. Since the structure information of music has an important role in the dance creation, Qin et al. [8] proposed a robot automatic choreography method based on the structure of music. First, the music is segmented according to its structured information, and then the emotions, beats, and other features of each musical fragment are extracted. Finally, according to these extracted music features, a series of dance actions are generated by a hidden Markov model. Although these researchers have studied robotic independent choreography from different perspectives, the process of solving robot choreography of their work is consistent. Thus, the current robot choreography methods can be summarised in three steps: First, dance and music are divided into a series of fragments. Second, a mapping model is built between music fragments and action fragments. Finally, the action fragments are recombined according to the given music. These types of solution can generated dance actions, however, these methods ignored the timing relationship between motion and music. Therefore, it is difficult to embed the global features of music in the generated dance. In addition, the music features selected by human can not always exactly correspond to labels of dance actions.

On the other hand, due to the excellent performance of deep learning technologies in processing sequence data [9,10], many researchers have introduced deep learning technologies into robot dance generation. For example, Crnkovicfriis et al. [11] successfully constructed a Mixture Density Long and Short Time Memory neural network model (Mixture Density LSTM), which generated animated dance postures according to the input music. Such deep learning model assisted artists in their dance creation. Chu et al. [12] built another deep learning model to generate music, and then modified the learning model slightly to enable it to generate animated dance. These deep learning methods use the end-to-end learning strategy to generate dance directly from music. Such dance creation process is similar to the language translation, which converts one sequence data to another sequence data directly [13]. However, due to the flexibility and internal logic of music and dance, it is difficult for the end-to-end learning strategy to learn information that meets people's expectations. In addition, because of the heavy dependence of deep learning models on training data, these deep learning based models required a large number of dance animations as training data. As a result, the selection of the training data constrains the generated dance actions to be represented as an animated form. However, such animated dance ignored the robot's balance problems and joint limitations.

In order to solve the problems encountered by the above two types of automatic choreography strategies, this paper proposes a robot automatic choreography system based on deep learning model and action graph. Unlike the deep learning strategies described above, our approach does not use an end-to-end learning strategy. Conversely, two deep neural networks are used in our model to generate local and global information on the dance based on the input music features, and then the model generates appropriates dance action sequence from a constructed action graph. These two deep neural networks ensure that the music sequence and the generated dance sequence correspond locally and globally. Moreover, the proposed model generates dance action by sampling from an action graph, which ensures the generated dance action to keep the robot's balance, and ensures the generated action to stay with the range of the robot's joints. The proposed model is experimented on a humanoid robot.

The remainder of the rest paper is organized as follows: Sect. 2 introduces some knowledge background of our research work. Section 3 details the proposed model. Section 4 presents and discusses the experimental results. Finally, Sect. 5 concludes the paper and provides directions for future work.

2   Background

2.1   Music Features

In the field of music information retrieval, the music features extracted from music could be divided into two categories: music rule based features and audio signal based features. The music rule based features obey the precise definition of music from the perspective of music theory, such as pitch, beat, tempo, key, and so on. On the contrary, the audio-signal based features define the facts of music from the perspective of signal processing, such as short-time Fourier transform (STFT), Constant Q transform (CQT), Chromagram, and Mel-Frequency Cepstral Coefficients (MFCC). These features are more in line with the principles of human auditory perception.

These two types of features contain both advantages and disadvantages in representing music. The feature based on the music rules is good at presenting the global feature of music, and the audio signal based feature is more focused on the local changes of music. Taking into account the advantages of these two types of features at different perspectives, beat feature and Mel-spectrogram feature of the music are used as the input of the deep learning model in proposed model.

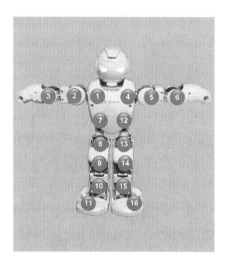

Fig. 1. The hardware system of robot.

2.2   Features of Robotic Dance Sequence

Dance movements are regarded as a continuous transition amongst a set of postures. For robot dance, each posture is represented by the joint value of the whole body. As shown in Fig. 1, a robot posture is represented as $pos = [j_1, j_2, \ldots, j_{15}, j_{16}]$, where j_n represented the value of the n-th joint. More than two postures constitute a dance action, and therefore, a dance is represented as $d = [pos_1, pos_2, \ldots, pos_t]$.

In addition, studies of dance showed that at least three types of posture relations reflect the rules of dance [6]:

(1) Symmetry: The symmetrical joints of the robot move at the same time and the directions of motion are identical. For example, for a dance action with only hand movements, the joints of the robot always satisfy this condition:

$$[j_1, j_2, j_3] = 180 - [j_4, j_5, j_6]. \tag{1}$$

(2) Cannon: When a part of the robot's joints changed, the joints symmetrical with these joints produce successive or oppositive movements. For example: $pos_t([j_1, j_2, j_3]) = pos_{t+1}([j_4, j_5, j_6])$ or $pos_t([j_1, j_2, j_3]) = pos_{t+1}(180 - [j_4, j_5, j_6])$.

$$pos_t([j_1, j_2, j_3]) = \begin{cases} pos_{t+1}([j_4, j_5, j_6]) \\ pos_{t+1}(180 - [j_4, j_5, j_6]). \end{cases} \quad (2)$$

(3) Form: In a dance action, a posture of the robot is cyclicly transformed. For example, in a dance action $[pos_{t-3}, pos_{t-2}, pos_{t-1}, pos_t, pos_{t+1}, pos_{t+2}, pos_{t+3}]$, these postures satisfy the condition that:

$$[pos_{t-3}, pos_{t-2}, pos_{t-1}] = [pos_{t+1}, pos_{t+2}, pos_{t+3}]. \quad (3)$$

Based on these three basic posture relations, the posture relation can be further subdivided by determining whether the last pose of the motion is symmetrical. Therefore, the posture relation is divided as: Symmetrical Form, Symmetry, Asymmetric Form, Asymmetry, Cannon, Pose (retain a pose for a while) and Other.

The transformed sequence of the posture relation in dance describes the global features of the dance. On the other hand, the local features of the dance are represented by the action density, which is the number of actions within one beat. Thus, the action relation and action density are used in the proposed model.

2.3 Robot Hardware and Data Sets

Our work is based on an Alpha1S robot, which produced by the UBtech a China humanoid robotic company. The Alpha1S is shown in Fig. 1, as a home entertainment robot it has 16 joints and can communicate with other devices via Bluetooth. So it is very suitable for the study of robotic automatic choreography.

In order to train our model, we collected 53 dances and corresponding music files from the application provided by UBtech. These 53 dances are generated in two ways: part of which is choreographed by the professionals within the UBtech company, and the remaining part is choreographed by the users of the Application. Furthermore, all of these 53 dances are widely praised by users.

3 Automatic Choreography System

The proposed model consists of four parts: (1) feature extraction module, (2) posture relation generation model, (3) action density prediction model and (4) action graph model. The working process of the proposed model is shown in Fig. 2: First, the beat features and global Mel-spectrogram of music are extracted in the feature extraction module. Then, the global Mel-spectrogram is segmented to a set of local Mel-spectrogram according to the beat information. Second, the local Mel-spectrogram is sent to the relation generation model and action density prediction model, respectively. Thus, a series of posture relation and an action density sequence are calculated by these two models. Finally, the action graph model generates a series of dance actions based on the posture relation sequence and action density sequence.

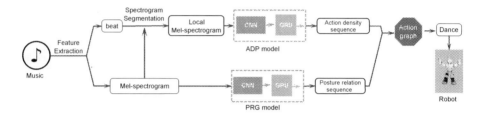

Fig. 2. The flowchart of the proposed automatic choreography model.

3.1 Feature Extraction

The music feature extraction module is to preprocess the music for the relation generation model and action density prediction model. Librosa, an open-source audio processing python library [14] is used to implement this module. The extraction process of music features is: First, the beat points and tempo are extracted using a beat detection algorithm [15]. Second, the Mel-spectrogram of the entire music is obtained from the default algorithm in librosa library. Finally, the Mel-spectrogram of each beat is obtained by segment the entire Mel-spectrogram.

Before the training of the proposed method, the dance features in the dataset also must be extracted. The extraction process of a posture relation feature is: First, the two adjacent actions in the dance action sequence are taken as a basic unit, then the relation type of the unit is determined according to the change pattern of the robot joint in the unit. According to this process, the relations of all the units in the dance are extracted. The determination of relation type is base on the definition of posture relation. On the contrary, the extraction of action density sequence must refer to the beat information of the corresponding music. The extraction is defined by: Fist, the dance action sequence is divided into a series of action segments according to the beat information of the corresponding music. Second, n, the number of action transition in each action segment, is counted. Finally, since the tempo of different music is different, it is necessary to eliminate the influence of tempo in the density calculation. Hence, the action density is calculated by:

$$density = n * \frac{tempo}{100}. \tag{4}$$

3.2 Posture Relation Generation Model

The structure of the posture relation generation model (PRG model) is shown in Fig. 3a, which consists of a Convolutional Neural Network (CNN) and a Gated

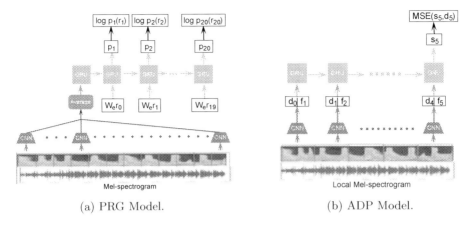

(a) PRG Model.   (b) ADP Model.

Fig. 3. The architecture of two sub models.

Recurrent Unit (GRU) network [16]. In the structural design of the CNN, we refer to the work of Choi et al. [12]. In their work, a convolutional neural network is designed for music style recognition. The GRU network consists of three layers: input layer, GRU and output layer. The input layer is an embedding layer with 5 neurons, and the output layer is a Softmax layer with 7 neurons.

The training data of the PRG model consists of a posture relation sequence (whose length is 20) and a set of Mel-spectrogram extracted from the corresponding music pieces. The posture relation sequence is defined as $R = [r_1, r_2, \ldots, r_{20}]$, and the Mel-spectrogram sequence is defined as $M = [m_1, m_2, \ldots, m_k]$. Then, calculation process of the PRG model is as follows: First, the feature vectors of each Mel-spectrogram are calculated by the CNN network. Second, the average of all these feature vectors is calculated to be the global features of the music pieces. Furthermore, this global features are used as the initial values of the hidden layer of the GRU. Finally, the 20 posture relations are sequentially inputted to the GRU to predict the relation type at the next process. Therefore, the forward propagation process of the relation generation model is expressed as:

$$h_0 = \frac{1}{k} \sum_{i=1}^{k} CNN(m_i); \tag{5}$$

$$x_t = W_e r_t, \quad t \in \{0, \ldots, 19\}; \tag{6}$$

$$p_{t+1} = GRU(x_t, h_t), \quad t \in \{0, \ldots, 19\}, \tag{7}$$

where W_e denotes the embedding matrix; x_t denotes the embedded form of the posture relation; p_t denotes the probability distribution output by the GRU at time t. Noted that the value of r_t is a 7-dimensional on-hot code for the relation type, and the value of the r_0 is a random posture relation type.

Since the output of the GRU is a probability distribution, a cross-entropy function is used as the loss function of PRG model. The loss value is a cross-entropy between the predicted probability distribution and real label for each moment. Then, its loss function is defined as that:

$$L_t(M, R) = log\ p_t(r_t),\qquad(8)$$

where $p_t(r_t)$ denotes the probability value of the real posture relation predicted by the PRG model at t moment.

3.3   Action Density Prediction Model

The structure of the action density prediction model (ADP model) is similar to the PRG model, and is also composed of a CNN network and a GRU network. In fact, the structure of the CNN module is the same as the CNN of the PRG model and their parameters are shared. However, the CNN network is used differently in both models. As shown in Fig. 3b, the feature vectors output of the CNN are not all inputted into the GRU network at one time, but only one at each time. In addition, the GRU network also consists of three layers: input layer, GRU and output layer. The input layer is the combination of the feature vector output from the CNN network and the action density of the previous time, and the output layer is a one-dimensional representation of the action density.

The training data of the ADP model consists of a set of Mel-spectrogram (whose length is 5) and the corresponding action density sequence. Then, the training data are described that: Mel-spectrogram sequence, $M = [m_1, m_2, \ldots, m_5]$ and the action density sequence, $D = [d_1, d_2, \ldots, d_5]$. Furthermore, the forward propagation process of the RGP model can be expressed as:

$$f_t = CNN(m_t),\quad t \in \{1, \ldots, 5\};\qquad(9)$$

$$x'_t = d_t \,|\, f_{t+1},\quad t \in \{0, \ldots, 4\};\qquad(10)$$

$$s_{t+1} = GRU(x'_t),\quad t \in \{0, \ldots, 4\},\qquad(11)$$

where s_t denotes the action density value predicted by the ADP model at t moment. Moreover, The value of the d_0 is also a randomly generated number, and its ranges in $[0, 3]$.

Since the representation of the action density is a continues value, the mean square error (MSE) between the output value of the model and label is selected as the loss function of the ADP model, which is defined as:

$$L(d, M) = (s_5 - d_5)^2\qquad(12)$$

Noted that only the last output of the model is used to update the parameters of the entire model.

3.4   Action Graph

Since the actions generated by our model are performed on a humanoid robot, the balance of the robot must be considered in the action generation. To solve this problem, an action graph model is built in the proposed method [17,18]. First, a number of actions are collected from the dataset, and these actions have been verified that the actions cannot cause the robot to fall. Then, all the collected actions are built into an action graph.

Action Digraph Construction: First, all postures in the data set are built into an action digraph. As long as the two postures are adjacent in the data set, a direct edge is inserted between them. Then, the digraph is optimized by a clustering algorithm. Because the entire data set has more than 3,000 different postures, it is necessary to merge the actions to reduce the complexity of the graph so as to increase the connectivity within the graph. The principle of the merging is merge similar poses into one posture and retain the one with the highest frequency in the data set. After merging, an action digraph containing 2,300 nodes is finally created. Once all actions used to build the action graph have been verified in balance, the action sampled from the action graph can ensure the robot to retain balanced.

Sampling and Planning: After the construction of the action digraph, dance actions can be sampled from the graph based on the posture relation sequence generated by the PRG model. The principle of motion sampling is: (1) When the current posture has a plurality of adjacent postures conforming to the posture relation type, one posture is randomly selected from the adjacent postures; (2) When the current posture does not have an adjacent posture conforming to the posture relation type, the "Symmetry" is used to replace the original relation type; (3) If the posture does not have an adjacent posture conforming to "Symmetry", the initial action is used directly.

After an action sequence is sampled according to the above principles, the number of actions in each beat, n can be determined. According to the action density sequence and Eq. 4, the values of n in each beat are calculated. Then, the duration time of each posture and the conversion time between two adjacent postures are determined according to the duration of the beat and the value of n. Thus, a complete dance is created.

4 Experimentation

4.1 Experiment Result

The proposed model is experimented on an alpha1S robot and the corresponding data set. In addition, the data set must be pre-processed before it is used to train the model. First, the music and dance are converted into corresponding feature data. Then, the pre-processed data set is divided into training set, test set and validation set in a ratio of $7 : 2 : 1$.

Then, the model is trained based on the pre-processed data set, and its loss curve on the training set and the validation set are shown in Fig. 4. After training, the model can successfully generate a complete dance based on the input music. The resulting dance actions are shown in Fig. 5.[1]

---

[1] The complete dance performances can be seen on the website: https://dwz.cn/ ocj9m2eP.

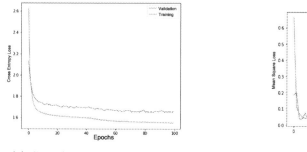
(a) Cost change of PRG Model.

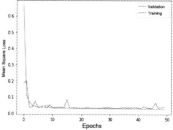
(b) Cost change of ADP Model.

Fig. 4. Cost change of two sub-models during the training process.

4.2   Comparison and Analysis

After the training of the model, the performance of the model is tested on the test data set. In the action density prediction model, the MSE loss on the test set is 0.026, which is very close to the loss of the training and verification sets. Such low loss on the test set indicates that the model has excellent generalization ability. On the other hand, the accuracy of the posture relation generation model on the test set is 0.46. Although the accuracy is less than 0.5, it is about twice as high as the random selection. In the data set, the largest proportion of the posture relation is only 0.21.

Another experiment is designed to test the innovation of the dance generated by the model. In this experiment, 53 dances in the database are compared. Then, the length of the maximum repetitive action sequence between any two dances are calculated. The calculation results show that the average length of the maximum repetitive action sequence is 10.58 in the data set. On the other hand, other 100 dance sequences are generated by the model. Then, the 100 dance sequences are compared to the 53 dances of the data set whose maximum repeating action sequences are calculated. This comparison shows how long the generated dance sequence is copied directly from the data set. The comparison shows that the average length of the maximum repetitive action sequence is 10.53 in the generated dance and the data set. However, the average length of these 100 generated dances is 46.88. In addition, the average length of the maximum repetitive action sequence between these 100 dances is calculated, the value is 10.34. This value represents the internal diversity of the generated dances. Through the above three comparisons, these length values are very close. Therefore, the model has the same level of innovation capability as artificiality choreography.

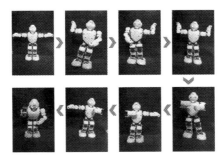

Fig. 5. Part of postures of the generated dance.

5 Conclusion

This paper presented a robot automatic choreography model based on deep learning and graph theory. The proposed model can generate smooth dance based on the global and local features extracted from music. The process of generating dance is that: the proposed model first converts musical features into dance features, and then according to these dance features generates dance. To convert the global and local features of the music, two sub-models are built based on deep learning technology. Moreover, to tackle the balance problem encountered when the dance action is performed on the robot, an action digraph was built to generate the dance based on the dance features. After that, the proposed model was validated on an alpha1S robot. Result of the experiment showed that the dance generated by the proposed model was successfully performed by the robot. Furthermore, the comparison and analysis with the data set proved that the dance generated by the model owned good diversity and innovation.

Although the proposed model is able to automatic choreography for the robot, it still has room for improvement. First, the model only learns automatic choreography based on the correspondence relation between music and dance in the data set, and it does not consider human preference. If the preference of human is added to the model, the generated dance may be closer to human dances. Second, the proposed model ensures the robot remains balance by constructing an action digraph. However, this design limited the variety of generated actions. If a solution allows the model to eliminate the limitation of action digraph and the generated action, it will further enhance the innovation of generated dance.

Acknowledgment. This work was supported by the National Natural Science Foundation of China (No. 61673322, 61673326, and 91746103), the Fundamental Research Funds for the Central Universities (No. 20720190142), Natural Science Foundation of Fujian Province of China (No. 2017J01128 and 2017J01129), and the European Union's Horizon 2020 research and innovation programme under the Marie Sklodowska-Curie grant agreement (No. 663830).

References

1. Eaton, M.: An approach to the synthesis of humanoid robot dance using non-interactive evolutionary techniques. In: 2013 IEEE International Conference on Systems, Man, and Cybernetics, pp. 3305–3309. IEEE (2013)
2. Peng, H., Zhou, C., Hu, H., Chao, F., Li, J.: Robotic dance in social robotics–a taxonomy. IEEE Trans. Hum.-Mach. Syst. **45**(3), 281–293 (2015). https://doi.org/10.1109/THMS.2015.2393558
3. Peng, H., Hu, H., Chao, F., Zhou, C., Li, J.: Autonomous robotic choreography creation via semi-interactive evolutionary computation. Int. J. Soc. Robot. **8**(5), 649–661 (2016)
4. Manfrè, A., Infantino, I., Vella, F., Gaglio, S.: An automatic system for humanoid dance creation. Biol. Inspired Cogn. Architect. **15**, 1–9 (2016)
5. Meng, Q., Tholley, I., Chung, P.W.: Robots learn to dance through interaction with humans. Neural Comput. Appl. **24**(1), 117–124 (2014)
6. Tholley, I.S.: Towards a framework to make robots learn to dance. Ph.D. thesis, Ibrahim S. Tholley (2012)
7. Xia, G., Tay, J., Dannenberg, R., Veloso, M.: Autonomous robot dancing driven by beats and emotions of music. In: Proceedings of the 11th International Conference on Autonomous Agents and Multiagent Systems, vol. 1, pp. 205–212. International Foundation for Autonomous Agents and Multiagent Systems (2012)
8. Qin, R., Zhou, C., Zhu, H., Shi, M., Chao, F., Li, N.: A music-driven dance system of humanoid robots. Int. J. Hum. Robot. **15**(05), 1850023 (2018)
9. Chu, H., Urtasun, R., Fidler, S.: Song from PI: a musically plausible network for pop music generation. CoRR abs/1611.03477 (2016). http://arxiv.org/abs/1611.03477
10. Vinyals, O., Toshev, A., Bengio, S., Erhan, D.: Show and tell: a neural image caption generator. In: The IEEE Conference on Computer Vision and Pattern Recognition (CVPR) (2015)
11. Crnkovic-Friis, L., Crnkovic-Friis, L.: Generative choreography using deep learning. In: Proceedings of the Seventh International Conference on Computational Creativity (2016)
12. Choi, K., Fazekas, G., Cho, K., Sandler, M.B.: A tutorial on deep learning for music information retrieval. CoRR abs/1709.04396 (2017). http://arxiv.org/abs/1709.04396
13. Cho, K., van Merrienboer, B., Gülçehre, Ç., Bougares, F., Schwenk, H., Bengio, Y.: Learning phrase representations using RNN encoder-decoder for statistical machine translation. CoRR abs/1406.1078 (2014). http://arxiv.org/abs/1406.1078
14. McFee, B., et al.: Librosa: audio and music signal analysis in python. In: Proceedings of the 14th Python in Science Conference, pp. 18–25 (2015)
15. Ellis, D.P.: Beat tracking by dynamic programming. J. New Music Res. **36**(1), 51–60 (2007)
16. Mikolov, T., Karafiát, M., Burget, L., Černockỳ, J., Khudanpur, S.: Recurrent neural network based language model. In: Eleventh Annual Conference of the International Speech Communication Association (2010)
17. Zhao, L., Safonova, A.: Achieving good connectivity in motion graphs. Graph. Models **71**(4), 139–152 (2009)
18. Kovar, L., Gleicher, M., Pighin, F.: Motion graphs. In: ACM SIGGRAPH 2008 Classes, p. 51. ACM (2008)

Navigation/Localization

An Underwater Robot Positioning Method Based on EM-ELF Signals

Guan Wang$^{(\boxtimes)}$, Huanyu Ding, Hongwei Xia, and Changhong Wang

Space Control and Inertial Technology Research Center,
Harbin Institute of Technology, Harbin 150001, People's Republic of China
guanwang@hit.edu.cn

Abstract. In view of the limited positioning of underwater robots using GPS and high-frequency radio waves, extremely low frequency electromagnetic (EM-ELF) signals are effective ways to solve the positioning accuracy of underwater robots due to their strong penetrating power, low loss and low interference. Based on the localization method, first proposed by Sheinker et al. [1], and combined with the excellent characteristics of firefly algorithm, this paper proposes an underwater robot positioning method based on ultra-low frequency electromagnetic signals. The method in this paper has the following advantages: (1) It compensates for the problem that the accuracy is reduced in a short time when the electromagnetic signal is used for positioning, and the robustness of the positioning is improved; (2) Under the condition of not using the geophysical reference map, it can realize the autonomous positioning of the underwater robot all day, and improve the accuracy of the positioning system; (3) It has strong anti-interference ability and is suitable for underwater robot navigation under weak illumination and time-varying interference environment. The experimental results also show that the method has small positioning error and can accurately locate the underwater robot.

Keywords: Underwater positioning · Extremely low frequency · EM signal · Firefly algorithm

1 Introduction

In recent years, with the deepening of the marine development process, underwater robots [2] have played an increasingly important role in marine exploration and marine rescue. The autonomous positioning technology of underwater robots is the basis for completing complex practical tasks. At the same time, the high-frequency radio waves in the water are attenuated very fast, and the GPS signals cannot be received underwater. The commonly used navigation and positioning technology performs poorly in key areas such as underwater, offshore, and island reefs. At present, the techniques for underwater robot positioning, such as underwater acoustic positioning system, SLAM-based positioning method, and vision-based positioning method, have some problems affecting tracking and positioning. For example, acoustic positioning has multipath effects, undulation effects and propagation losses, as well as limitations that are difficult to deploy, calibrate, and maintain [3].

© Springer Nature Switzerland AG 2019
H. Yu et al. (Eds.): ICIRA 2019, LNAI 11743, pp. 643–650, 2019.
https://doi.org/10.1007/978-3-030-27538-9_55

EM-ELF signal [4] refers to wireless EM signal with frequency between 3–30 Hz. It can penetrate such things as seawater, rock and even metal media, and is used in resource exploration, earthquake prediction, drilling telemetry, submarine communication and other fields. And it is more suitable for tracking and positioning of underwater robots. Therefore, an underwater robot positioning method for extremely low frequency electromagnetic signals were proposed in this paper. This paper is organized as follows. In Sect. 2, the composition of the positioning system is introduced. In Sect. 3, the algorithm is presented. In Sect. 4, experiment and stimulation results are discussed. Conclusions are summarized in Sect. 5.

2   The Composition of the Positioning System

The underwater robot positioning method studied in this paper is based on the following system:

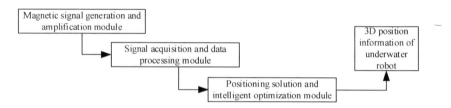

Fig. 1. System framework for positioning methods.

2.1   Magnetic Signal Generation and Amplification

The EM-ELF signal transmitter is installed at the bottom of the ship and mainly includes a low frequency sinusoidal signal generator, a power amplifier and a quadrature magnetic beacon system.

2.2   Signal Detection and Processing

The high-resolution magnetic sensor is mounted on the intelligent robot and its shape should match the shape of the intelligent robot and must not exceed a certain size. The ELF signal generated by the transmitter needs to pass through a medium such as seawater or rock to be received by the receiving device carried by the robot. Compared with the transmitter, the sensor device has the characteristics of low power consumption, so it is more favorable for underwater motion.

After obtaining the ultra-low frequency electromagnetic signal through the high-resolution triaxial magnetometer, the acquired magnetic signal is then processed.

2.3   Construction of Underwater Robot Positioning System

Using the positioning system principle described in Fig. 1, the underwater robot positioning system is built as shown in the following Fig. 2.

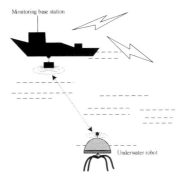

Fig. 2. Schematic diagram of underwater robot positioning system.

3 Algorithm

3.1 An Orthogonal Double Magnetic Beacons Positioning Method

According to [1], the beacons are placed as shown in Fig. 3. And position of the target can be obtained as follows:

$$x = 0.25\left(3\frac{H_{1x}}{H_{1y}} \pm \sqrt{9\left(\frac{H_{1x}}{H_{1y}}\right)^2 + 8}\right)y$$

$$y = \left[\frac{3M}{(H_{1x} - H_{2y})} \cdot \frac{0.0625\left(3\frac{H_{1x}}{H_{1y}} \pm \sqrt{9\left(\frac{H_{1x}}{H_{1y}}\right)^2 + 8}\right)^2 - 1}{\left(0.0625\left(3\frac{H_{1x}}{H_{1y}} \pm \sqrt{9\left(\frac{H_{1x}}{H_{1y}}\right)^2 + 8}\right)^2 + 1\right)^{2.5}}\right]^{\frac{1}{3}} \quad (1)$$

$$z = xH_{2z}/H_{2y}$$

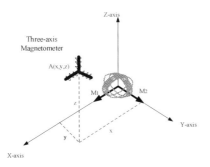

Fig. 3. Model based on magnetic beacon positioning method.

where M is the magnetic moment and H_{1x}, H_{1y}, H_{1z}, H_{2x}, H_{2y}, H_{2z} are the field strength components of the three-axis magnetometer in three directions. The 3D position information of the target can be calculated by (1).

3.2   Quadrature Double-Lock-in Amplifier and Signal Processing

If the frequency of the signal generated by the generator is f, the frequency w_0 of the EM-ELF signal is $2\pi f$, and the corresponding magnetic field strength $H_A(t)$ expression is:

$$H_A(t) = A \cdot \sin(\omega_0 t + \theta) \tag{2}$$

where A is the signal amplitude and θ is the initial phase of the signal.

In the actual detection process, the noise source of the signal is mainly the noise caused by the geomagnetic field and the surrounding environment. Then the input signal $H(t)$ expression is:

$$H(t) = H_A(t) + H_{noise} \tag{3}$$

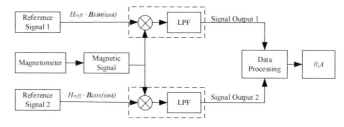

Fig. 4. Orthogonal double-lock-in phase technology schematic.

The principle of orthogonal double-lock-in phase technology [5] is shown in Fig. 4. Here, two reference signals with a phase shift of 90° are selected:

$$\begin{aligned} H_{ref1}(t) &= B \cdot \sin(\omega_0 t) \\ H_{ref2}(t) &= B \cdot \cos(\omega_0 t) \end{aligned} \tag{4}$$

The amplitude and phase of the measured signal can be accurately calculated:

$$\begin{cases} H_{out1} = \frac{1}{2} A \cdot B \cdot \sin\theta, H_{out2} = \frac{1}{2} A \cdot B \cdot \cos\theta \\ \theta = \arctan(H_{out2}/H_{out1}), A = 2\sqrt{H_{out1}^2 + H_{out2}^2}\big/B \end{cases} \tag{5}$$

3.3   EM-ELF Signal Localization Method Based on Firefly Algorithm

By observing Eq. (1), it can be found that there is a defect in the position of the underwater target, especially when $H_{1x}-H_{2y}$ approaches zero. Considering the effects of environmental noise, this method will appear blurred areas.

In order to compensate for the fuzzy area and speed up the search, the firefly algorithm [6] is used to improve the positioning algorithm in 3.1. Figure 5 is the pseudo code of the firefly algorithm, and the Eq. (6) is the objective function.

$$f(x, y, z) = \|\mathbf{H}(x, y, x) - \mathbf{H}(x_i, y_i, z_i)\|_2 \tag{6}$$

Objective function f($\mathbf{x}$), $\mathbf{x}=(x_1,...,x_d)^T$
Generate initial population of fireflies x_i ($i=1,2,...,n$)
Light intensity I_i at x_i is determined by f(x_i)
Define light absorption coefficient γ
while (*t<Max Generation*)
for *i=1:n all n fireflies*
  for *j=1:n all n fireflies (inner loop)*
  if *($I_i>i_j$), move firefly I towards j;* **end if**
    Vary attractiveness with distance r via exp[-γr]
    Evaluate new solutions and update light intensity
  end for *j*
end for *i*
Rank the solutions and find the current best g_*
end while
Postprocess results and visualization

Fig. 5. Pseudo code of the Firefly Algorithm.

The parameters are designed in Table 1, which includes the number of fireflies n, the light absorption intensity coefficient γ, the step factor α, the maximum attraction B_0, and the number of iterations *Max Generation*.

Table 1. Parameters Setting.

Parameter	n	γ	α	B_0	Max generation
Value	20	0.25	0.1	1.0	100

Therefore, when the result of $H_{1x}-H_{2y}$ is within a certain threshold range, the above-mentioned steps are used to supplement the problem that the analytical method reduces the accuracy in the fuzzy region, thereby improving the positioning accuracy of the method.

4   Experiments

4.1   Simulation and Experimental Results

This section further validates the effects of quadrature double-lock-in amplifiers by mathematical simulations in MATLAB. For the double magnetic beacons shown in Fig. 3, a set of 20 Hz and 30 Hz frequency configurations is proposed. The data from one axis measurement of the three-axis magnetometer is then simulated, while white noise is added to the signal and simulated.

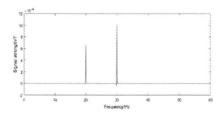

Fig. 6. Magnetic signal processed by quadrature double-lock-in amplifiers.

It can be seen from Fig. 6 that the processing of the quadrature double-lock-in amplifiers can better filter out the noise and restore the characteristics of the specified frequency signal.

4.2   Tracking Trajectory and Error Distribution

Simulation results verify that the method has acceptable accuracy. Then, an underwater experiment was designed to verify the above method (Figs. 7 and 8).

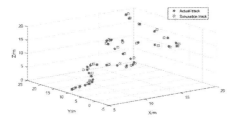

Fig. 7. Actual track and simulation track.

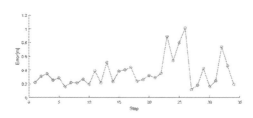

Fig. 8. Positioning error distribution.

4.3 Underwater Experiment

The physical diagram of the experimental measurement system is shown in Fig. 9. It mainly consists of an orthogonal copper coil device (100 turns), a signal generator, two power amplifiers, a three-axis magnetometer and a host computer. We used the experimental setup to perform experiments under water, as shown in Fig. 10.

Fig. 9. Experimental measurement system device.

Fig. 10. Underwater experiment.

Table 2. Experimental Results.

Magnetic moment, A·m^2	Localization error, m			
	Area of 9 m^2		*Area of* 36 m^2	
	Mean	Max	Mean	Max
10	0.402	0.873	1.213	1.746
50	0.154	0.715	0.947	1.502
100	0.076	0.120	0.560	0.936
400	0.023	0.089	0.368	0.681

Through the experimental results in Table 2, the average error and maximum error of the underwater robot positioning method based on EM-ELF signals under different magnetic moments and different measurement ranges are recorded. By comparison, it can be found that the positioning error increases with the increase of the measurement range under the same magnetic moment condition; at the same time, in a certain measurement range, the larger the magnetic moment, the larger the signal-to-noise ratio, and the smaller the positioning error, the higher the accuracy.

5 Conclusions

In this paper, an underwater robot positioning method based on EM-ELF signals is proposed, and its limitations are improved by the superior characteristics of firefly algorithm. Based on simulation experiments and underwater tests, it is proved that this positioning method is feasible in real-time underwater environment. With high positioning accuracy, this positioning method is more robust by combining the data acquired by the sensor with the firefly algorithm using the positioning algorithm.

Due to the complex and varied underwater environment of the robot, not only the sensor itself applied to the robot has errors, but also the noise present in its surrounding environment may cause errors in its output value. Therefore, the analysis of the influence of factors such as magnetic beacon error and sensor alignment error on the positioning accuracy of the system is the problem to be solved in the future research.

References

1. Sheinker, A., Bednarz, L.: Localization in 3-D using beacons of low frequency magnetic field. IEEE Trans. Instrum. Measur. **62**(12), 3194–3201 (2013)
2. Choi, W.S., Hoang, N.M., Jung, J.H., et al.: Navigation system development of the underwater vehicles using the GPS/INS sensor fusion. In: Intelligent Robotics and Applications (2014)
3. Pasku, V., De Angelis, A., De Angelis, G., et al.: Magnetic field based positioning systems. IEEE Commun. Surv. Tutor. **1**(1), 1 (2017)
4. Szarka, L.: Geophysical aspects of man-made electromagnetic noise in the earth—a review. Surv. Geophy. **9**(3–4), 287–318 (1988)
5. Sikora, A., Bednarz, L.: The implementation and the performance analysis of the multi-channel software-based lock-in amplifier for the stiffness mapping with atomic force microscope (AFM). Bull. Pol. Acad. Sci. Tech. Sci. **60**(1), 83–88 (2012)
6. Yang, X.: Firefly algorithm, engineering optimization (2010)

Stereo Visual SLAM Using Bag of Point and Line Word Pairs

Wei Zhao[1,2]([✉]), Kun Qian[1,2], Zhewen Ma[1,2], Xudong Ma[1,2], and Hai Yu[3]

[1] School of Automation, Southeast University, Nanjing 210096, China
{220171525,kqian,220171502,xdma}@seu.edu.cn
[2] Key Laboratory of Measurement and Control of Complex Systems of Engineering, Ministry of Education, Nanjing 210096, China
[3] Global Energy Interconnection Research Institute, Nanjing 210000, China

Abstract. The traditional point-based SLAM algorithm performs poorly due to light changing, low-texture and highly similar scenes, while line segment features can better describe the structural information of the environment. For this problem, a new stereo visual SLAM system based on point and line features is proposed. The Jacobian matrix of the new optimization target combined with point and line features is derived in detail. At the same time, DBoW is extended with line features and the concept of point and line word pairs is proposed. The co-occurrence information and spatial proximity of point and line features are considered in loop closure detection. Experimental results on EuRoC and self-built datasets demonstrate that the proposed method outperforms ORB-SLAM2, which can reduce the localization error in both indoor and outdoor environments and improve the precision and recall of the loop closure detection.

Keywords: Line segment features · Bundle adjustment · Loop closure detection · Word pairs

1 Introduction

With the continuous development of industrial automation and intellectualization, the demands of substation for environment mapping and localization are becoming more and more urgent. Feature-based visual SLAM (simultaneous localization and mapping) algorithm has the advantages of low cost, convenience and reliability, which is a research hotspot at present. However in the long-time and long-distance motion, the traditional point-based SLAM is more susceptible to external factors such as camera jitter, light changing, perspective shift, scene changing, etc., making it difficult to track point features continuously. The

This work is supported by the Science and Technology Program of State Grid Headquarters "Deep-vision-based Intelligent Reconstruction and Recognition of Complex and Dynamic Fieldwork Environment" (SGJSDK00PXJS1800444), and National Natural Science Foundation of China (Grant No. 61573101 and 61573100).

H. Yu et al. (Eds.): ICIRA 2019, LNAI 11743, pp. 651–661, 2019.
https://doi.org/10.1007/978-3-030-27538-9_56

environment map constructed by point features does not favor the scene analysis and environment semantic understanding. The highly similar scene structure can easily cause perceptual aliasing. In artificial structured environments, such as corridors, offices and substations, line segment features are rich while point features are scarce.

ORB-SLAM [1] adopts the framework of PTAM [2] and improves most components in the framework. A complete SLAM system ORB-SLAM2 [3] for monocular, stereo and RGB-D, developed on monocular ORB-SLAM, is superior to similar algorithms. However, ORB-SLAM2 performs poorly in response to light changes and scarcity of point feature. A real-time monocular SLAM using both points and lines to estimate the camera pose is proposed in [4], which provides a new method for monocular initialization. PL-SVO [5] combines point and line features in low-textured and structured environments to work robustly in a wider variety of scenes. Based on PL-SVO, a stereo SLAM named PL-SLAM [6] using point and line features minimizes the re-projection error of point and line features by nonlinear optimization method to estimate the camera motion and improves the closed-loop detection based on points and line segments. In [7], a monocular visual odometer using both points and lines combines the advantages of direct method and feature-based method.

As an important part of SLAM, loop closure detection can eliminate the cumulative error of motion estimation when revisiting the same place. In [8], the Chow-Liu tree is used to express the correlation between words and avoid perceptual aliasing by context. Image is represented as a feature vector composed of words in [9]. Feature vectors are compared to evaluate the similarity between images, and a Bayesian filter is updated iteratively to estimate the loop probability. Improved FAST+BRIEF feature is used to describe features as binary descriptors, and the similarity between images is analyzed by TF-IDF score in [10]. The BoW Pair proposed in [11] employs spatial location information of point features. However, when different scenes contain too many objects with high similarity and low discrimination, place recognition based on point features alone may lead to perceptual aliasing.

In this paper, a new stereo visual SLAM system using both point and line features based on the ORB-SLAM2 framework is proposed. The management of feature tracking and matching in ORB-SLAM2 is applied to both point and line features. The re-projection error combined with both points and lines is defined and the Jacobian matrix of the new optimization target is derived in detail. Another contribution is that we improved the loop closure detection method by extending DBoW (Distributed Bag Of Words) with line features and proposing the concept of point and line word pairs. The co-occurrence information and spatial proximity of point and line features are considered in loop closure detection. The proposed method is fully tested on the EuRoC and self-built datasets. Results demonstrate that the proposed method outperforms ORB-SLAM2, which can reduce the localization error in both indoor and outdoor environments and improve the precision and recall of the loop closure detection.

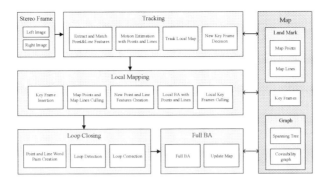

Fig. 1. System overview.

2 SLAM Using Point and Line Features

The proposed method continues the framework of ORB-SLAM2 and improves upon it. As shown in Fig. 1, the system is composed of three parallel threads: tracking, local mapping, and loop closing.

2.1 Bundle Adjustment with Points and Lines

Let $T_{iw} \in SE(3)$ be the pose of the ith key frame, $X_{w,j} \in \mathbb{R}^3$ be the 3D point of the jth point feature observed by the ith key frame, $P_{w,k}, Q_{w,k} \in \mathbb{R}^3$ be the 3D endpoints of the kth line feature observed by the ith key frame and $\tilde{p}_{i,k}, \tilde{q}_{i,k} \in \mathbb{R}^2$ be their projected 2D endpoints in the image plane, where w stands for the world reference. The detection of $X_{w,j}$ in the image plane is $x_{i,j} \in \mathbb{R}^2$; the detections of $P_{w,k}, Q_{w,k}$ in the image plane are $p_{i,k}, q_{i,k} \in \mathbb{R}^2$ whose corresponding homogeneous coordinates are ${}^h p_{i,k}, {}^h q_{i,k} \in \mathbb{R}^3$. The illustration of Line segment feature re-projection error is shown in Fig. 2, where $d_{p_{i,k}}, d_{q_{i,k}}$ are the pixel distance from $p_{i,k}, q_{i,k}$ to the projected line $\overrightarrow{\tilde{p}_{i,k}\tilde{q}_{i,k}}$.

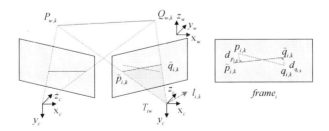

Fig. 2. Left: $P_{w,k}, Q_{w,k} \in \mathbb{R}^3$ is the 3D endpoints of a 3D line in the world coordinate, $\tilde{p}_{i,k}, \tilde{q}_{i,k}$ is the projected 2D endpoints in the image coordinate. Right: $p_{i,k}, q_{i,k}$ is the 2D endpoints of a detected line in the image coordinate, $d_{p_{i,k}}$ and $d_{q_{i,k}}$ is the reprojection error between a detected 2D line and the corresponding projected 3D line.

Let π be the projection model of pinhole camera, and $^h\pi$ be the homogeneous form of π.

$$\pi\left(T_w, P_w\right) = \begin{bmatrix} f_x \frac{g_x}{g_z} + c_x \\ f_y \frac{g_y}{g_z} + c_y \end{bmatrix} \tag{1}$$

where $R_w \in SO(3)$, $t_w \in \mathbb{R}^3$, $t_w \in \mathbb{R}^3$ are respectively the rotation and translation parts of T_{iw}. $P_w \in \mathbb{R}^3$ is a point in the world coordinate, and $\begin{bmatrix} g_x & g_y & g_z \end{bmatrix}^T = R_w P_w + t_w$ is the corresponding point in the camera coordinate. f_x, f_y and c_x, c_y are the focal length and principle point of the camera.

The re-projection error of point features $e_{i,j}^p$ and the re-projection error of line features $e_{i,k}^l$ can be defined respectively as following, where $l_{i,k}$ is the unit normal vector of the plane:

$$e_{i,j}^p = \left[\begin{bmatrix} x_{i,j} \\ y_{i,j} \end{bmatrix} - \pi(T_{iw}, X_{w,j}) \right] \tag{2}$$

$$e_{i,k}^l = \begin{bmatrix} d_{p_{i,k}} \\ d_{q_{i,k}} \end{bmatrix} = \begin{bmatrix} l_{i,k} \cdot \pi^h(T_{iw}, P_{w,k}) \\ l_{i,k} \cdot \pi^h(T_{iw}, Q_{w,k}) \end{bmatrix} \tag{3}$$

Then, the loss function combined with points and lines is:

$$C = \sum_{i \in \mathcal{K}} \left[\sum_{j \in \mathcal{P}} (e_{i,j}^p)^T \Omega_{e_{i,j}^p}^{-1} e_{i,j}^p + \sum_{k \in \mathcal{L}} (e_{i,k}^l)^T \Omega_{e_{i,k}^l}^{-1} e_{i,k}^l \right] \tag{4}$$

where $\Omega_{e_{i,j}^p}, \Omega_{e_{i,k}^l}$ is the information matrix of the re-projection error of points and lines, $\mathcal{K}, \mathcal{P}, \mathcal{L}$ refers to the groups of local key frames, points and lines respectively.

The optimization problem is to solve the camera pose and the position of the points and line segments under the goal of minimizing the loss function C. The key to solving this optimization problem is to derive the Jacobian matrix of the optimization target. Since the Jacobian matrix related to the re-projection error term of point features has been fully deduced in [12], we focuses on deducing the Jacobian matrix related to the re-projection error term of point features with respect to the camera pose $\xi \in \mathfrak{se}(3)$, as shown in Eq. (5):

$$\frac{\partial e_{l_{i,k}}}{\partial \xi} = \begin{bmatrix} \begin{bmatrix} l_0 \\ l_1 \end{bmatrix}^T \frac{\partial \pi(g_p)}{\partial g_p} \frac{\partial g_p}{\partial \xi} \\ \begin{bmatrix} l_0 \\ l_1 \end{bmatrix}^T \frac{\partial \pi(g_q)}{\partial g_q} \frac{\partial g_q}{\partial \xi} \end{bmatrix} = \begin{bmatrix} \begin{bmatrix} l_0 \\ l_1 \end{bmatrix}^T \begin{bmatrix} \frac{f_x}{g_{pz}} & 0 & -\frac{f_x g_{px}}{g_{pz}^2} \\ 0 & \frac{f_y}{g_{pz}} & -\frac{f_y g_{py}}{g_{pz}^2} \end{bmatrix} \begin{bmatrix} I_3 & -[g_p]_\wedge \end{bmatrix} \\ \begin{bmatrix} l_0 \\ l_1 \end{bmatrix}^T \begin{bmatrix} \frac{f_x}{g_{qz}} & 0 & -\frac{f_x g_{qx}}{g_{qz}^2} \\ 0 & \frac{f_y}{g_{qz}} & -\frac{f_y g_{qz}}{g_{qz}^2} \end{bmatrix} \begin{bmatrix} I_3 & -[g_q]_\wedge \end{bmatrix} \end{bmatrix}_{2\times 6}$$

$$= \begin{bmatrix} \frac{f_x}{g_{pz}} l_0 & \frac{f_y}{g_{pz}} l_1 - \frac{f_x g_{px} l_0 + f_y g_{py} l_1}{g_{pz}^2} & -f_x \frac{g_{px} g_{py}}{g_{pz}^2} l_0 - f_y (1 + \frac{g_{py}^2}{g_{pz}^2}) l_1 \\ \frac{f_x}{g_{qz}} l_0 & \frac{f_y}{g_{qz}} l_1 - \frac{f_x g_{qx} l_0 + f_y g_{qy} l_1}{g_{qz}^2} & -f_x \frac{g_{qx} g_{qy}}{g_{qz}^2} l_0 - f_y (1 + \frac{g_{qy}^2}{g_{qz}^2}) l_1 \\ \end{bmatrix}$$

$$\begin{matrix} f_x(1 + \frac{g_{px}^2}{g_{pz}^2}) l_0 + f_y \frac{g_{px} g_{py}}{g_{pz}^2} l_1 & -f_x \frac{g_{py}}{g_{pz}} l_0 + f_y \frac{g_{px}}{g_{pz}} l_1 \\ f_x(1 + \frac{g_{qx}^2}{g_{qz}^2}) l_0 + f_y \frac{g_{qx} g_{qy}}{g_{qz}^2} l_1 & -f_x \frac{g_{qy}}{g_{qz}} l_0 + f_y \frac{g_{qx}}{g_{qz}} l_1 \end{matrix}_{2\times 6} \tag{5}$$

where $\xi \in \mathfrak{se}\,(3)$ is corresponding to the Lie algebra of T_{iw}. $[]_\wedge$ means skew-symmetric matrix operator. g_p and g_q are respectively the corresponding coordinates of $P_{w,k}$ and $Q_{w,k}$ in the camera coordinate system. The components of the three dimensions of g_p and g_q are represented by subscripts x, y, z in Eq. (5).

After deriving the Jacobian matrix, the Levenberg-Marquardt method can be applied to the non-linear optimization problem.

2.2 Loop Closure Detection Based on Bag of Point and Line Word Pairs

In this paper, DBoW (Distributed Bag Of Words) is used to construct the dictionary of point and line features respectively. Since the line segment features represent by 32-bit binary descriptors, the ORB-based DBoW can be easily extended to the DBoW based on point features and line segment features.

Since DBoW only employs the information of whether words appear or not in the image, it does not consider the co-occurrence information and spatial proximity of words in the image. It may cause false loop when the objects in different scenes are similar in the scene. We overcome the problem of perceptual aliasing by generating word pairs of points and lines. The visual words of point features are generated from a 32-bit binary ORB descriptor according to the point feature dictionary. Similarly, the visual words of line features are generated by a 32-bit binary LBD descriptor based on the line feature dictionary. For a point feature, it is composed of the position of the point feature and the scale, forming a circle with the feature scale r as the radius and the feature position p as the centre of the circle; for a line feature, it is composed of the endpoints' position of the line feature. Defining a pair of the point and line as a word pair when the circle of the point feature intersects the line segment of the line feature. For instance, the point p and the line l_1 compose a word pair while the point p and the line l_2 do not compose a word pair, as shown in Fig. 3.

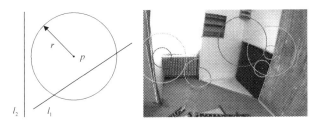

Fig. 3. Left: Understanding relative spatial co-occurrence of words in a pair. Right: Word pairs of Point and Line in a given image.

A K-D tree is employed to search for word pairs of points and lines. The positions of all point features in the image are used to construct the K-D tree. For the midpoint coordinate of the line feature, search the k points closest to the midpoint and verify whether the relative spatial position of the point and the line satisfy the definition of a word pair.

The complete flow of loop closure detection based on word pairs of points and lines is as following:

1. Select the candidate key frames sharing the same words of point and line features, and reject the last 10 frames;
2. Statistics the number of common-view words in the candidate key frame and the current frame, and obtain the maximum number MaxCommonWords of common-view words, and cull the key frames in the candidate key frame whose number of common-view words is lower than $0.8 * \text{MaxCommonWords}$;
3. Statistics the number of the common-view word pairs of points and lines in the candidate key frame and the current frame, get the maximum number MaxCommonWordPairs of the word pairs, and cull the key frames whose number of the word pairs in the candidate key frame is less than $0.8 * \text{MaxCommonWordPairs}$;
4. Calculate the image similarity scores between candidate key frames and the current frame;
5. Calculate the sum of the similarity of the candidate key frames and their adjacent frames with respect to the current frame, and obtain the maximum similarity sum MaxAccScore, and cull the key frames whose sum of the similarity score is less than $0.8*\text{MaxAccScore}$;
6. Perform space consistency verification on the selected candidate key frames.

3   Experimental Results and Analysis

The wearable auxiliary system adopted in this paper follows the hardware structure of the previous work [13], which consists of ZED stereo camera, BT300 smart glasses, a helmet and a portable notebook, as shown in Fig. 4. The configuration of portable notebook is Intel Xeon CPU E3-1505M@2.80 GHz, 16 GB RAM. In order to verify the effectiveness of the proposed method, the system is fully tested on EuRoC and self-built datasets.

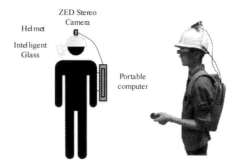

Fig. 4. Left: The architecture of wearable assistive system. Right: Worker wearing the assistive system.

Table 1. Translation and rotation of absolute pose error of ORB-SLAM2 and the proposed method in EuRoC w.r.t ground truth.

Seq.	ORB-SLAM		Proposed method	
	Trans. (m)	Rot. (deg)	Trans. (m)	Rot. (deg)
MH01	0.036799	0.755803	**0.036413**	**0.624045**
MH02	0.046799	0.637756	**0.041685**	**0.378070**
MH03	**0.037546**	**0.665111**	0.041405	2.280268
MH04	0.123971	0.376991	**0.049767**	**0.276506**
MH05	0.064242	2.889234	**0.051842**	**2.001996**
V101	0.087577	0.947981	**0.087448**	**0.926808**
V102	0.065954	0.456998	**0.064069**	**0.473040**
V103	0.094298	2.295838	**0.067585**	**0.657838**

3.1 Experiment on EuRoC Datasets

EuRoC datasets [14] contain real image data collected from indoor structured scenes, which provide rich line segment features, as shown in Fig. 5.

The results on EuRoC datasets with ground truth are shown in Table 1. Evo evaluation tool[1] is employed to compare the proposed method with ORB-SLAM2. The RMSEs (root mean square error) of the absolute translation error and the absolute rotation error on each data set are calculated. In order to objectively compare the trajectories, Umeyama Alignment [15] is used to compare the trajectories with the real trajectories.

Note that the performance of this method on EuRoC is generally superior to ORB-SLAM2. Taking MH_04_difficult and V1_03_difficult as an illustrative example, it can be seen from the upper right figure of Fig. 6 that the trajectory of the method fits real trajectory better, whereas the trajectory of ORB-SLAM2 deviates a lot; in the lower right figure of Fig. 6, due to the violent light changing in the environment and the rapid movement of the camera, the trajectory of the ORB-SLAM2 fluctuates obviously, which is not consistent with the actual

Fig. 5. Left: Point and line features extracted in a given image. Right: 3D map structed with lines.

---

[1] github.com/MichaelGrupp/evo.

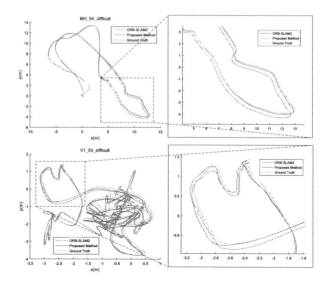

Fig. 6. Top: Trajectory on MH_04_difficult. Bottom: Trajectory on V1_03_difficult.

trajectory, and the proposed method greatly reduces the impact of environmental changes on the accuracy.

3.2 Experiment on Self-built Datasets

In order to verify the effectiveness of the proposed stereo SLAM in the actual environment, we collect datasets and test the system in Jiangsu Electric Power Company Research Institute. The dataset image was captured by Zed Stereo Camera with a frequency of 30 Hz. Each image's resolution is 672 * 376.

The method is compared with ORB-SLAM2, and the results are shown in Fig. 7. Although the self-built dataset lacks ground truth, it can be seen from Fig. 7 that the proposed method conforms with the real walking trajectory better. ORB-SLAM2 based on point features is severely invalid, and cannot track point features and estimate motion accurately, which ultimately leads to an abnormal trajectory after global optimization. At this time, the proposed method is relatively less affected by the exposure instability caused by the direct sunlight, and shows better performance in the substation environment.

3.3 Loop Closure Detection Experiments

In order to verify the validity of the loop closure detection based on word pairs of point and line features, we test it on the self-built datasets. Due to the large number of similar scenes in the substation environment, as shown in Fig. 8, the two image frames contain similar power distribution cabinets, transformers and so on. But they are actually not in the same location. The particularity of the substation environment brings greater challenges for loop closure detection.

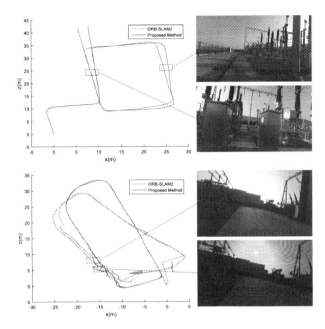

Fig. 7. Top: Comparison of trajectories on No. 1 substation dataset. Bottom: Comparison of trajectories on No. 2 substation dataset.

Fig. 8. Similar scenes in substation.

Similarity matrix S is employed in order to evaluate the results of loop closure detection more intuitively. The value of the ith row and the jth column of the similar matrix S is the similarity between the ith image and the jth image (normalized to 0–1, 0 is the most dissimilar, 1 is the most similar).

For the 2rd substation dataset in Fig. 7, the heat map drawn according to the similarity matrix S is shown in the left figure of Fig. 9. The horizontal and vertical coordinates of the image are the sequence of images, and the area where the image is highlighted represents the occurrence of closed loops. It can be seen that the second half of the sequence of images loop with the first half of the sequence of images, which is consistent with the closed loop result on the 2rd substation dataset. Let TP be the number of the correct loops which are detected, TP+FP be the number of total loops which are detected, and TP+FN be the number of total loops in the datasets. The precision and recall rate of loop closure detection is defined as $precision = \frac{TP}{TP+FP}, recall = \frac{TP}{TP+FN}$

respectively. The PR curves of two loop closure detection methods are shown in the right figure of Fig. 9. Note that the proposed method avoids perceptual aliasing caused by similar words in different scenes, and improves the precision and recall rate of loop closure detection in substation environment.

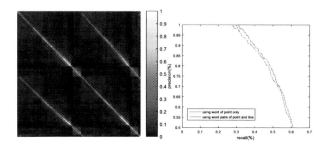

Fig. 9. Left: Similarity matrix in substation. Right: Comparison of P-R curve between using word of point only and using word pairs of point and line in substation.

4   Conclusion

A new stereo visual SLAM system based on point and line features is proposed in this paper, which apply the management of feature tracking and matching in ORB-SLAM2 to both point and line features. The Jacobian matrix of the new optimization target under point and line features is derived in detail. We improve the loop closure detection method based on point and line features. DBoW is extended with line features, and the concept of point and line word pairs is proposed. We incorporate the co-occurrence information of point and line features and spatial proximity into loop closure detection. The proposed method has been fully tested on EuRoC and the self-built datasets, and compared with ORB-SLAM2. The results demonstrate that the proposed method has higher localization accuracy and stronger robustness in indoor and outdoor environments, especially in substation environments. It proves that the employment of line features improves the accuracy of the system in low texture and structured environments, and the bag of point and line word pairs improves the precision and recall rate of loop closure detection as well.

References

1. Mur-Artal, R., Montiel, J.M.M., Tardos, J.D.: ORB-SLAM: a versatile and accurate monocular SLAM system. IEEE Trans. Robot. **31**(5), 1147–1163 (2015)
2. Klein, G., Murray, D.: Parallel tracking and mapping for small AR workspaces. In: 6th IEEE and ACM International Symposium on Mixed and Augmented Reality, ISMAR 2007, pp. 225–234. IEEE (2007)

3. Mur-Artal, R., Tardós, J.D.: ORB-SLAM2: an open-source SLAM system for monocular, stereo, and RGB-D cameras. IEEE Trans. Robot. **33**(5), 1255–1262 (2017)

4. Pumarola, A., Vakhitov, A., Agudo, A., Sanfeliu, A., Moreno-Noguer, F.: PL-SLAM: real-time monocular visual slam with points and lines. In: 2017 IEEE International Conference on Robotics and Automation (ICRA), pp. 4503–4508. IEEE (2017)

5. Gomez-Ojeda, R., Briales, J., Gonzalez-Jimenez, J.: PL-SVO: semi-direct monocular visual odometry by combining points and line segments. In: 2016 IEEE/RSJ International Conference on Intelligent Robots and Systems (IROS), pp. 4211–4216. IEEE (2016)

6. Gomez-Ojeda, R., Zuñiga-Noël, D., Moreno, F.A., Scaramuzza, D., Gonzalez-Jimenez, J.: PL-SLAM: a stereo slam system through the combination of points and line segments. arXiv preprint arXiv:1705.09479 (2017)

7. Yang, S., Scherer, S.: Direct monocular odometry using points and lines. arXiv preprint arXiv:1703.06380 (2017)

8. Cummins, M., Newman, P.: Probabilistic appearance based navigation and loop closing. In: 2007 IEEE International Conference on Robotics and Automation, pp. 2042–2048. IEEE (2007)

9. Angeli, A., Filliat, D., Doncieux, S., Meyer, J.A.: Fast and incremental method for loop-closure detection using bags of visual words. IEEE Trans. Robot. **24**(5), 1027–1037 (2008)

10. Gálvez-López, D., Tardos, J.D.: Bags of binary words for fast place recognition in image sequences. IEEE Trans. Robot. **28**(5), 1188–1197 (2012)

11. Kejriwal, N., Kumar, S., Shibata, T.: High performance loop closure detection using bag of word pairs. Robot. Auton. Syst. **77**, 55–65 (2016)

12. Blanco, J.L.: A tutorial on SE(3) transformation parameterizations and on-manifold optimization. Technical report 3, University of Malaga (2010)

13. Qian, K., Zhao, W., Ma, Z., Ma, J., Ma, X., Yu, H.: Wearable-assisted localization and inspection guidance system using egocentric stereo cameras. IEEE Sens. J. **18**(2), 809–821 (2017)

14. Burri, M., et al.: The EuRoC micro aerial vehicle datasets. Int. J. Robot. Res. (2016). https://doi.org/10.1177/0278364915620033. http://ijr.sagepub.com/content/early/2016/01/21/0278364915620033.abstract

15. Umeyama, S.: Least-squares estimation of transformation parameters between two point patterns. IEEE Trans. Pattern Anal. Mach. Intell. **4**, 376–380 (1991)

Design and Recognition of Two-Dimensional Code for Mobile Robot Positioning

Wei Huang[1(⊠)], Asihaer Maomin[2], and Zhenguo Sun[1,3]

[1] Department of Mechanical Engineering, Tsinghua University,
Beijing 100084, China
649930928@qq.com
[2] Special Equipment Inspection and Research Institute,
Urumqi Xinjiang Uygur Autonomous Region 830013, China
[3] Yangtze Delta Region Institute of Tsinghua University, Jiaxing 314006, China

Abstract. In view of the lack of characteristics for mobile robot positioning which limits the usage of common two-dimensional codes (2-D codes for short), a new 2-D code for positioning is designed. In the new code, its square characteristics for positioning was improved, and the coding method based on Hamming code was used. The recognition algorithm for the new 2-D code under complex backgrounds was studied, which consists of binarization preprocessing, region extraction based on square characteristics and accurate calculation of positioning information. Tests indicate that the 2-D code for positioning greatly improves the positioning accuracy under the premise that its algorithm time consumption is similar to that of DataMatrix. Under the same interference, error of the new code for positioning is much less than DataMatrix in terms of the center position and the rotation angle. Meanwhile, it is able to detect and correct code value information errors, fully adapting to the task of being the basis of mobile robot positioning.

Keywords: Robot positioning · Two-dimensional code · Image recognition

1 Introduction

The mobile robot positioning and navigation technology based on the 2-D code image recognition has been widely used and studied in recent years. For example, Liu Zhi tried to use the concept of convex hull in computational geometry to locate 2-D code in an image, in order to provide navigation information for robots [1]. This kind of technology has the advantages such as simple and rapid algorithm and high positioning accuracy compared with the traditional positioning and navigation technology based on the laser range finder, inertial sensor, motor encoder and other equipment [2], and may effectively eliminate the cumulative drift error during positioning in combination with other positioning technology.

At present, the commonly used QR code [3], Data Matrix [4] and other 2-D codes are based on the background of application of the Internet and industrial production, and more emphasize the data capacity and strong error correction capability of the 2-D codes while the information for determining the position is not abundant enough. As a

© Springer Nature Switzerland AG 2019
H. Yu et al. (Eds.): ICIRA 2019, LNAI 11743, pp. 662–672, 2019.
https://doi.org/10.1007/978-3-030-27538-9_57

consequence, the precision during guiding for positioning with the common codes is relatively low. Besides, a large number of data regions are used for error correction, causing more waste for the information capacity of the 2-D code when applied to the robot assisted positioning and other circumstances not requiring better error correction capability.

Therefore, it is necessary to design a special 2-D code applied to the robot positioning and navigation, which appropriately reduces the data length used for error correction, and increases the image characteristic information for positioning to improve the positioning accuracy under the premise of ensuring certain verification and error correction capability.

2 Design Scheme for New 2-D Codes for Positioning

A new type of overall design scheme for positioning 2-D code is shown in Fig. 1. The 2-D code is composed of 10×10 black-white pixel modules, which can be divided into the characteristic region and code value region for analysis.

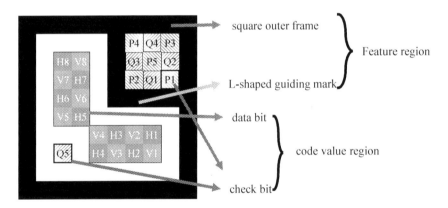

Fig. 1. Overall design scheme for new 2-D codes for positioning

2.1 Feature Region Design for Enhanced Positioning Features

The characteristic region mainly includes all black modules and their internal and external white modules, and provides the basis reference for image recognition through the obvious boundary line between the black and white modules. The black module width of the entire characteristic region is one module, including a complete square outer frame and its internal L-shaped guiding mark, of which the outer vertex is the center point of the 2-D code.

The complete square outer frame makes the 2-D code image have the square external boundary during subsequent processing, to quickly screen all boundaries in the image according to the shape features of the square, greatly improving the image processing efficiency and accuracy.

The L-shaped guiding mark inside the outer frame is used to specify the positive direction of the 2-D code. The square outer frame can be used to determine that the rotation angle of the 2-D code in the image is [0°, 90°); however, after the positive direction is determined by the L-shaped guiding mark, the recognition interval can be expanded to [0°, 360°).

In addition, the relatively long boundary line (including external and internal ones) of the new 2-D code for positioning further improves the positioning accuracy, while the number of usable angular points increases from 3 to 10 compared to DataMatrix, which also effectively improves the reliability of the calculation result for the central position of the 2-D code.

2.2   Design of Code Value Region Based on Hamming Code

The 2-D codes are arranged at uniform intervals on the ground in horizontal and vertical directions, respectively, to form the 2-D code grid. Each 2-D code shall have a corresponding grid coordinate in the grid. Therefore, the 2-D code for positioning shall contain two kinds of information, i.e., the grid abscissa m and grid ordinate n.

The orange solid pixel module (H1–H8) has 8 bits in total, representing the abscissa information m with the value range of 0–255, and the orange slash pixel module (P1–P5) has 5 bits in total, which are the check bits of 8-bit horizontal coordinate information m; the blue solid pixel module (V1–V8) and the slash module (Q1–Q5) respectively represent the data bits and check bits of the vertical coordinate information n, which has the same data capacity as that of the horizontal coordinate.

The coding rule for the horizontal and vertical coordinate information is Hamming code [5], which not only can detect whether the data is wrong, but also provides 1 bit error correction capability. In Fig. 1, the coding mode in which the horizontal and vertical coordinate data are interleaved is adopted, so distance of two contiguous data bits in the same data group is elongated, which reduces the probability of error.

3   Recognition Algorithm of the 2-D Code for Positioning

It is assumed that the size of the captured image is 200 mm × 150 mm, and the image resolution is 640 × 480. The used 2-D code for positioning has a side length of 25 mm, with a 7.5 mm wide reserved contrast region outside, and the overall square side length formed is 40 mm. The region excluding the 2-D code has a messy and irregular environment.

3.1   Image Binarization Preprocessing

The original image, with the resolution of up to 640 × 480, contains a lot of detailed information; however, such information is useless for the 2-D code in the preliminary positioning image at the initial stage of image processing, and the bit operation of a large number of pixels greatly increases the time consumption of the algorithm. Therefore, it is necessary to appropriately reduce the resolution of the image in the initial pre-processing stage under the premise of retaining the necessary characteristic information. Gaussian pyramid [6] is a common downsampling algorithm, which can effectively reduce Gaussian noise in the 2-D code image at the same time.

A reasonable threshold for image binarization can greatly reduce the redundant information and enhance the contrast. For the image stream obtained by the camera carried by the robot, the characteristics such as brightness, darkness and texture may change at any time; therefore, it is necessary to automatically select the threshold for segmentation according to the characteristics of the images to ensure the robustness of the algorithm. In the image to be detected, the pixels included in the 2-D code region only accounts for 5% of the total, which means the threshold calculated by common threshold segmentation methods such as Otsu method [7] and iterative method [8] will not be affected by the 2-D code region. However, the maximum entropy method [9], which segments the threshold value that maximizes the amount of information contained in the binary image, can achieve the best effect for the situation in this paper.

The effect with Gaussian pyramid and the maximum entropy method is shown in Fig. 2.

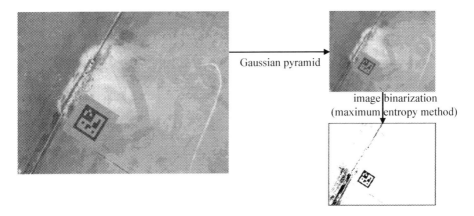

Fig. 2. Effect diagram of Gaussian pyramid and threshold segmentation with maximum entropy method

3.2 Extraction of 2-D Code Region Based on Square Characteristics

If the binarized image to be detected contains the 2-D code for positioning, then the image necessarily includes a square connected region, and the external boundary of the connected region conforms to the shape characteristics of the square; however, for the interference characteristics in other backgrounds, the boundary generally does not conform to the laws of man-made characteristics. Therefore, the exhaustion testing may be conducted on all the boundaries in the binarized image to eliminate the connected regions that do not conform to the square characteristics, and the 2-D code region can be extracted simply and quickly.

First, the four vertices S_1–S_4 of the connected region in the coordinate axis direction are extracted, with the horizontal and vertical coordinates respectively expressed as (x_1, y_1), ..., (x_4, y_4), then the two points of the diagonal are respectively connected, and the obtained intersection point is (x_o, y_o), as shown in Fig. 3.

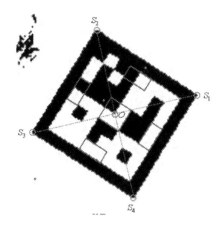

Fig. 3. Characteristics for judgment and extraction of 2-D codes

Then for a square boundary, all parameters shall satisfy the equations as follows:

$$x_1 - x_o = x_o - x_3 = y_2 - y_o = y_o - y_4 \tag{1}$$

$$y_1 - y_o = y_o - y_3 = x_2 - x_o = x_o - x_4 \tag{2}$$

During the actual image processing, considering the errors in many aspects, the definition of the two equal equations can be appropriately relaxed during judgment, and the tolerance is generally 1–2 pixels (for the downsampled image with the resolution of 320×240, 2 pixels are half of the side length of the 2-D code module). After this judgment, most of the interference information in the binary image can be eliminated by screening.

Further judgment is made on the internal situation of the remaining connected regions. A quadrilateral is made with S_1–S_4 as vertices, and the 10×10 grid division of the quadrilateral is carried out with the vertices as the reference. Boolean values are extracted for the 12 modules circled by the red boxes in Fig. 3. Characteristics for judgment and extraction of 2-D codes, and each vertex corresponds to the three modules closest to it. If the Boolean values of the three modules corresponding to a vertex are 1, while the Boolean values of the modules corresponding to other vertices are 0, then such vertex is the upper right corner of the 2-D code; otherwise, the connected region does not belong to the target two- dimensional code, or the two - dimensional code region is damaged and cannot be read.

3.3   Accurate Calculation of 2-D Code Positioning Information

According to the preliminary positioning information of the region where the 2-D code is located in the binarized image subject to the Gaussian pyramid downsampling, the 2-D code region is set as the region of interest (ROI) in the original image, and the subsequent algorithm is performed on the basis of ROI, which can fully utilize the advantages of the high resolution of the original image and improve the accuracy of the calculation of the positioning information of the 2-D code. For ROI extracted from the original image, the binarization operation shall be first performed again.

In the high-resolution binary image of the 2-D code, the external square boundary and internal L-shaped boundary with higher precision of the 2-D code can be extracted, as shown in Fig. 4.

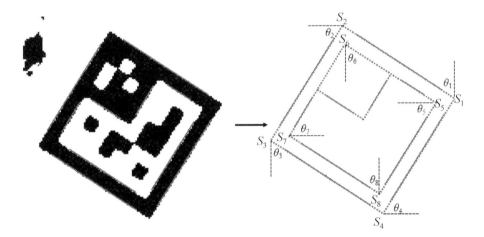

Fig. 4. Accurate estimation of 2-D code positioning parameters with least square law

In the practical application background, the sharp corners of the boundary are easily polluted and damaged, and are not suitable for being the basis of accurate positioning of the 2-D code. Therefore, the pixel points near the angular points are eliminated, and the least squares fitting shall be carried out on a large number of pixel points between the diagonal points, to obtain the fitting straight-line equation.

The slopes obtained of all fitting straight lines are converted into the relative rotation angles θ_i, and the weighted average is taken according to the number of pixels; the intersection point of all fitting straight lines is recorded as the corrected new angular point S_i, and the weighted average of the new angular point is taken as the coordinate of the center point of the 2-D code and shall be the optimal estimates of the accurate positioning information of the 2-D code.

4   Testing of Recognition Effect of the 2-D Code for Positioning

4.1   Recognition Algorithm Robustness Test

In order to verify the robustness of recognition algorithm of the new 2-D code for positioning, the algorithm is used to recognize the 2-D codes with different environmental backgrounds, rotation angles and center positions. The size of the background portion in the Figure is 200 mm × 150 mm, the size of the 2-D code chip is 40 mm × 40 mm, and the boundary size of the 2-D code is 25 mm × 25 mm. The recognition algorithm will return whether the 2-D code is recognized in the Figure. If the 2-D code is recognized, the positioning information such as the center coordinate of the 2-D code, the rotation inclination angle, and the horizontal and vertical coordinates represented by the code value will be returned.

The recognition result is shown in Fig. 5. It can be seen that in the case of different complicated backgrounds and multiple interferences, the algorithm can well recognize the 2-D code contained in the image and can calculate all the positioning information included in the image, which can be used to assist the detection robot in performing its own positioning guidance and to eliminate the accumulated drift error in the positioning information of the integral sensor.

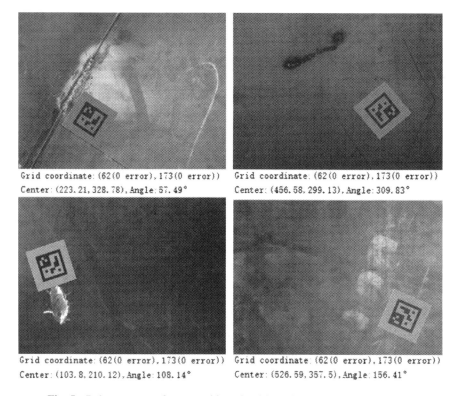

Fig. 5. Robustness test for recognition algorithm of 2-D code for positioning

4.2   Image Recognition Time Compared with DataMatrix

In order to verify the difference in processing efficiency between the new 2-D code for positioning and the traditional 2-D code, the new 2-D code for positioning in Fig. 6(a) is replaced with the DataMatrix in Fig. 6(b). Under the premise that the environment background and the positioning information of both are basically the same, the time consumed by each algorithm flow in the two recognition algorithms are analyzed and compared, and the results are shown in Table 1.

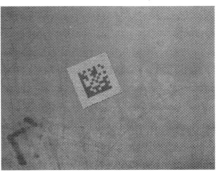

(a) 2-D Code for Positioning   (b) DataMatrix

Fig. 6. 2-D code for positioning and DataMatrix in the same background

Table 1. Comparison of time consumption of 2-D code recognition algorithms

Algorithm time consumption/ms	2-D code for positioning	DataMatrix
Gaussian pyramid	9.3	9.5
Threshold segmentation	31.2	31.9
Region extraction	5.7	11.9
Re-segmentation	2.8	2.8
Accurate positioning	12.8	8.1
Total	61.8	64.2

It can be seen that both have almost the same overall processing time, but have different emphases in processing time. In the region extraction phase, DataMatrix's time consumption is 6.2 ms longer than that of the 2-D code for positioning because DataMatrix does not have the external boundary of a square and needs to extract the square characteristics of the DataMatrix by means of morphological opening operations such as corrosion and expansion. However, the morphological opening operation is an algorithm that convolves with the entire image, consuming more time. In the precise positioning stage, the time consumed by the 2-D code for positioning is 4.7 ms longer than that of DataMatrix because the calculation is required for more boundary points to improve the positioning accuracy.

4.3   Comparison with the Impact of Error on DataMatrix Images

Compared with DataMatrix, the recognition algorithm of the 2-D code for positioning uses more boundary points to calculate its positioning information. In order to verify the effect of this algorithm, multiple types of pollution interferences are added to the external boundary of the 2-D code for positioning and DataMatrix with the same background as shown in Fig. 6. The interference types are shown in Fig. 7. The degree of deviation are compared of the positioning information of the 2-D code for positioning and DataMatrix in the case of being interfered, whose results are shown in Table 2.

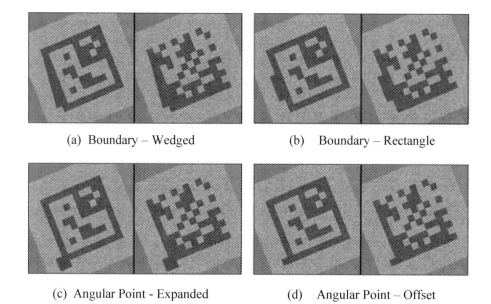

(a) Boundary – Wedged   (b)   Boundary – Rectangle

(c) Angular Point - Expanded   (d)   Angular Point – Offset

Fig. 7. Multiple interferences for recognition characteristics

Table 2. Comparison of positioning deviation of 2-D codes subject to interference

	2-D code for positioning		DataMatrix	
	Center offset/px	Inclination deviation/°	Center offset/px	Inclination deviation/°
Boundary – wedged	2.55	0.98	4.86	2.82
Boundary – rectangle	2.28	0.73	4.13	1.97
Angular point - expanded	1.53	0.35	4.46	0.97
Angular point – offset	0.44	0.20	0.82	0.75
Average value	1.70	0.57	3.57	1.63

It can be seen that when the 2-D code for positioning is subjected to accidental interference in terms of positioning characteristics (boundary, angular point, etc.), compared to the non-interference case, the average deviation of the recognized center position is 1.7 pixels, which is only 47.6% of that of DataMatrix, and the average deviation of the recognized rotation angle is 0.57°, which is only 35.0% of that of DataMatrix, which fully proves that the 2-D code for positioning has advantages in positioning accuracy and has better adaptability than the traditional and commonly used 2-D codes in assisting the detection robot in self-positioning, guiding and other application fields.

4.4   Contamination Resistance Check and Error Correction Ability Test

In order to verify the reliability of the coding method based on Hamming code for the 2-D code for positioning, different degrees of contamination are applied to the code value region, with the correction results shown in Fig. 8.

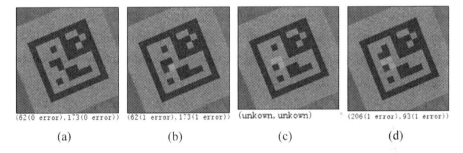

| (a) | (b) | (c) | (d) |

Fig. 8. Reading results of code value subject to different degrees of contamination

It can be seen that when only one bit of data is contaminated respectively in the horizontal and vertical coordinates in the code value region, the error location can be detected and the inverse correction can be carried out, to finally output the correct horizontal and vertical coordinate information values, as shown in Fig. 8(b); when it is wrong due to contamination of 2 bits of the data, it can indicate that there is an error, but it cannot be corrected, as shown in Fig. 8(c); when there are errors in 3 bits or more, the errors cannot be detected correctly and the wrong coordinate values may be output, as shown in Fig. 8(d). Therefore, the 2-D code for positioning based on Hamming code has certain error detection and error correction capability and certain anti-interference ability in the face of possible contamination in the working environment, and can well perform the assisted positioning work.

5   Conclusion

For the mobile robot assisted positioning technology based on 2-D code recognition, a 2-D code specially for mobile robot assisted positioning is designed to improve its square characteristics for positioning, and the coding method based on Hamming code is used. Aiming at the recognition algorithm of this new 2-D code for positioning in complicated background, the algorithm flow is studied from the aspects of binarization preprocessing, region extraction based on square characteristics and accurate calculation of positioning information. The recognition ability and positioning accuracy of the algorithm are tested. The experimental results show that, under the premise that its algorithm time consumption is similar to that of DataMatrix, the 2-D code for positioning greatly improves the positioning accuracy, with the deviation equal to 47.6% of DataMatrix's in terms of the center position and 35.0% of DataMatrix's in terms of the rotation angle under the same interference, and meanwhile has the ability to detect and correct code value information errors, fully adapting to the task of being the basis of mobile robot assisted positioning.

References

1. Liu, Z., Zheng, H., Cai, W.: Research on two-dimensional bar code positioning approach based on convex hull algorithm. In: International Conference on Digital Image Processing, Bangkok, pp. 177–180 (2009)
2. Aggarwal, S., Sharma, K., Priyadarshini, M.: Robot navigation: review of techniques and research challenges. In: 2016 3rd International Conference on Computing for Sustainable Global Development (INDIACom), New Delhi, pp. 3660–3665 (2016)
3. Liu, Y., Yang, J., Liu, M.: Recognition of QR code with mobile phones. In: 2008 Chinese Control and Decision Conference, Yantai, Shandong, pp. 203–206 (2008)
4. Dita, I., Otesteanu, M., Quint F.: Data matrix code—a reliable optical identification of microelectronic components. In: 2011 IEEE 17th International Symposium for Design and Technology in Electronic Packaging (SIITME), Timisoara, pp. 39–44 (2011)
5. Nguyen, G.D.: Error-detection codes: algorithms and fast implementation. IEEE Trans. Comput. **54**(1), 1–11 (2005)
6. Gil, D.C., Langlois, J.M.P., Savaria, Y.: Accelerating a modified Gaussian pyramid with a customized processor. In: 2013 Conference on Design and Architectures for Signal and Image Processing, Cagliari, pp. 259–264 (2013)
7. Otsu, N.: A threshold selection method from gray-level histograms. IEEE Trans. Syst. Man Cybern. **9**(1), 62–66 (1979)
8. Wang, J., Cohen, M.F.: An iterative optimization approach for unified image segmentation and matting. In: Tenth IEEE International Conference on Computer Vision (ICCV 2005), Beijing, vol. 1, pp. 936–943 (2005)
9. Yan, H., Liu, J., Wang, P.: An improved algorithm of the maximum entropy image segmentation. In: 2014 Fifth International Conference on Intelligent Systems Design and Engineering Applications, Hunan, pp. 157–160 (2014)

A Separate Data Structure for Online Multi-hypothesis Topological Mapping

Changyang Gong, Gang Chen, Wei Dong, Xinjun Sheng[✉],
and Xiangyang Zhu

State Key Laboratory of Mechanical System and Vibration,
Shanghai Jiao Tong University, Shanghai, China
xjsheng@sjtu.edu.cn

Abstract. This paper proposes an algorithm for topological simultaneous localization and mapping (SLAM) using multi-hypothesis method. This algorithm focuses on improving on-board computational efficiency and capability of finding out the correct hypothesis as early as possible. In the algorithm, an innovative data structure is applied, in which the edges and vertexes of the topological graph are stored separately. So that detailed information of the vertexes has only one copy in the storage, which also benefits saving communication bandwidth. Then, lots of repetitive loop-closing tests in similar hypothesizes are simplified to one single test that only uses vertexes storage. Lastly, incorporating with the data structure, loop closure situations can be evaluated as soon as it happens. In a word, the algorithm is highly efficient to cope with the hyper-exponential growth disaster caused by perceptual aliasing. The work is evaluated by simulations and demonstrated on a maze-like scenario with a Micro-Aerial Vehicle (MAV) equipped a computational resources restricted computer.

Keywords: Topology map · SLAM · Multi-hypothesis · Unmanned system

1 Introduction and Related Works

Simultaneous localization and mapping (SLAM), which constructs a map of an unknown environment and localize the agent within the map at the same time, is a critical technology in unmanned systems nowadays. In general, the maps generated from SLAM can be divided into two rough types: metric maps and topological maps.

In metric maps, size information is essential, which brings convenience for localization and path planning. [1,2] However, the amount of data is enormous, and the computational cost is expensive, especially for current famous vision-based methods. Also, the robustness of this kind of map is usually fragile because of the noises from sensors, which may cause fatal consequences when facing 'loop-closing' problems in a large scale environment. For an unmanned system with

© Springer Nature Switzerland AG 2019
H. Yu et al. (Eds.): ICIRA 2019, LNAI 11743, pp. 673–685, 2019.
https://doi.org/10.1007/978-3-030-27538-9_58

limited computational resources, for example, MAV. In general, metric maps based SLAM is hard to apply in a large indoor environment with multiple loops and similar intersections.

In topological maps, as focused by this paper, the environment is represented by a graph including a set of vertexes and edges. In our approach, each vertex represents a "special" place in the environment, which can be an intersection, a door or a landmark. Moreover, the edges represent the connectivity between the vertexes. In this paper, topological map is not only a data structure to manage the sensor data, but also a semantic abstraction of the environment. So, the map can be quickly and easily understood by human beings. As people perceiving the geometry environment in a topological way [3], topological map is born for human-computer interaction.

Comparing with metric maps, the data amount of topological maps is quite small. However, the lack of detailed information brings another problem, perception aliasing [4]. It is related to the loop-closing problem, which occurs when the agent moves to a vertex which is similar to a previous visited one. In this situation, false positive matches (regard a new vertex as an old vertex) and false negative matches (regard an old vertex as brand new vertex) can happen. If any error happens in the mapping process, the map building process would never recover to the correct result.

Multi-hypothesis method is widely used to deal with this problem. In this method, multiple topological hypothesizes will be retained as long as they are according with the sensor measurement. In other words, when serveral explanations meet current measurements, all the explanations would be retained. With further exploration, finally, the wrong hypothesis will have contradictions with the observation and be purged. So the correct hypothesis will survive and be proved to be the right one. However, unfortunately, in the worst situation of perception aliasing, the growth of the hypothesis could be hyper-exponential [5].

To cope with the hyper-exponential growth problem, there are several approaches.

First of all, as Marinakis *et al.*'s work [6] shows, improving the correctness of the sensor measurements or getting more useful information is always the first solution to ease the perception aliasing. Though distinguishable features like consist vision features are hard to achieve from the environment. Nevertheless, some useful simple features and information can be easily extracted. For example, the angles between paths and rough distance between different vertexes can be used to construct a labeled graph, which is also how people learn from the environment according to the work of Chrastil *et al.* [7]. Also, magnetometer information is beneficial in an orientation fixed environment, like buildings or underground facilities, which are the most common applications for unmanned systems.

Secondly, purge the hypothesis with logical mistakes. Degree test [8] is one of the basic methods. Each hypothesis will be tested if the degree of the arriving vertex is equal to the one in the hypothesis. Also, Savelli *et al.* [9] uses the planarity assumption to purge the hypothesis in which two edges across each other without detecting a vertex. This method is efficient and can purge many hypothesizes without risk pruning a correct hypothesis. However, it is only useable in a planar environment, not in a multi-story building. Because there exists shortcuts between floors that are feasible for agile unmanned systems like MAVs. The planarity assumption could be overturned even on a single floor.

Thirdly, keep only an appropriate amount of hypothesizes. The key idea of this approach is the sort algorithm to determine which hypothesis is more likely to be the correct one. Marinakis *et al.* [6] applies the principle of Occams Razor, where hypothesizes are sorted according to the simplicity of the graph. The graph with fewer vertexes and pending gateways (an edge leaving a vertex to an unexplored vertex) are ranked higher. However, this approach is not capable in some complex environments. Probabilistic techniques [10–12] are applied to this question widely.

Tully *et al.* [10] uses Bayes Law and appropriate model to calculate the possibility of each map hypothesis incrementally. So, the possibility of each map can be inferred efficiently whenever the agent moves to another vertex, which is used to purge the maps that fit poorly to the sensor data. In this progress, they use odometry data on the edges the agent moved on to do the calculation. However, the correct hypothesis cannot emerge from a large number of maps at the early steps, because the critical issue of loop-closing cannot be evaluated as soon as the loop closure happened. Finally, there is still a chance for the system to purge the correct hypothesis.

In Johnson's work [12], the hypothesizes with low possibility are not purged but just stop updating. This approach eliminates the last possibility of ruling out the correct hypothesis. These abandoned models are taken back into consideration when the survived hypothesizes turn out to be a low possibility.

At last, Marinakis *et al.*'s work [6] also takes the exploration strategy into account to slow the growing speed of the number of map hypothesizes. They proposed a new strategy named Loop-Based Exploration, in which the robot tries to go back to places where it has been to, via a different way, to find out and verify the loop structure of the environment. Accordingly, finding closed loop structures does good to the exploration of the environment.

In our algorithm, multi-hypothesis approach is used, and the hypothesizes are sorted according to the posterior possibility inferred from Bayesian Law. Different from existed approaches, we use distinctive strategy of dealing with sensor data. First of all, in our approach, magnetometer data is vital, since it is easy to achieve in unmanned systems and is of great help to reduce perception aliasing between vertexes. Secondly, the odometry data of the whole process is recorded too. Considering the lack of computational resources, global optimization like the work by Ranganathan *et al.* [5] is avoided. Global odometry data is only used when a new loop closure is created, and the odometry data only accumulates along the agent moved path to calculate the error and possibility correction of the map hypothesis.

The main contributions of this work are the separate data structure and the related efficient matching algorithm. First of all, with the innovative way of data management, not only the storage space but also the communication bandwidth is saved. Secondly, the algorithm is highly efficient, so that the whole computation processing is able to occur online on a computational resources restricted computer. Finally, the algorithm can give a possibility correction as soon as a possible loop closure occurs. As a result, the correct map hypothesis could emerge from the massive map hypothesizes at the early stage to get better mapping results at the beginning.

2   Separate Data Structure and Construction Algorithm

2.1   Labeled Topological Graph

Like standard graphs, labeled graphs consist of vertexes V_k^h and edges E_k^h. Each vertex includes a list L_v^h recording the edges connected to the vertex in counterclockwise. For example, $L_v^h(j)$ represents the edge on the j-th exit, and for convenient, $L_v^h[j]$ represents the neighboring vertex of v along the j-th edge. In most cases, the map is partially explored, so some edge is marked as *unexplored*. The upscript h represents the related map hypothesis.

What differs from the standard graph is that labeled graphs incorporate local metric information. Each vertex v has extra information like relative positions between gates (the start point of an edge in a vertex) P_v^h, and the outgoing directions of each edge A_v^h. And in each edge e, odometry data O_e^h are also recorded. With the help of magnetometers, the direction of these informations can remain almost unchanged when the agent arrives a same vertex at different times (Fig. 1).

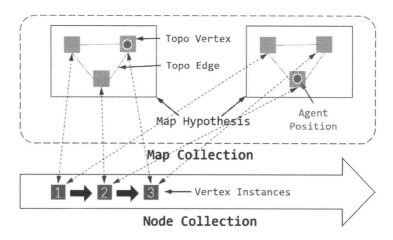

Fig. 1. The separate data structure. The big boxes surrounded by the upper dotted line fillet rectangle represents the hypothesizes of the current environment, including vertexes, edges and the agent position. However the detailed informations of the vertexes are stored as vertex instances in the downer big arrow-shaped container. And for loop closure detection, the vertex usages of the instance are stored in the instance. too So there are links (double-sided dotted line arrow) between the vertex in hypothesis and the instance

2.2   Separate Data Structure

A separate data structure is adopted in the multi-hypothesis approach. In the structure, the vertex instances extracted from the environment i_k and the map hypothesizes h are stored in two different sets. We call them Node Collection N and Map Collection M.

Each hypothesis h stores a topological graph, $G_k^h = (V_k^h, E_k^h)$, and the agent position in the graph, X_k^h. The position includes the vertex currently located (or departed from), x_v^h, and the edge moving (or just moved along), x_e^h, thus $X_k^h = (x_v^h, x_e^h)$. The subscript k represents the time step in the mapping progress.

In each vertex instance, a usage list U_i is stored to record which vertex in which hypothesis is using the vertex instance. On the other hand, every vertex v stores a list of corresponding instances C_v^h.

The connotation of the data structure is that the detailed information of the environment is stored in the Node Collection N, as vertex instances i_k. Moreover, the connectivity information represented by vertexes V_k^h and edges E_k^h are stored in the graph G_k^h of each hypothesis h in Map Collection M.

2.3   Incremental Construction of Hypothesizes

In order to build the map efficiently and space economically, we use a separate data structure. As a result, a new construction policy to maintain the structure is required, which is different from that in Ref. [13].

In the beginning, we assume the agent starts mapping at a vertex, so the structure is initialized with only the current vertex instance stored in Node Collection and Map Collection only has one hypothesis, which only has a vertex. Then, at each time step k, the agent chooses a motion u_k, departing along the j-th exit of last vertex, and arrive at the next vertex at a-th exit. The arrival vertex i_k, the motion $u_k = [j, a]$ and odometry data o_k are the input of the construction algorithm.

The main problem of topological SLAM is loop-closure, and the main difference between separate data structure and others is how we detect loop-closure.

When the agent arrives at a vertex, at first, each map hypothesis in the Map Collection deduces according to the new arrival vertex's information detected from the environment. For the hypothesis whose agent's position is at an edge that has been explored, a contradiction may happen. More concretely, the contradiction is that the real arrival vertex is quite different from the vertex that should be arrived at according to the hypothesis. In this case, the hypothesis with contradiction will be purged. For the hypothesis whose agent is moving on a new edge that has not yet traversed, at this deduction step, the new vertex is considered as a brand new vertex.

The next step is detecting the loop-closure. Every vertex instance in the Node Collection that is similar to the new arrival vertex will be checked. Each hypothesis usage of the checked vertex instance will be evaluated if the loop-closure is feasible. If the loop-closure is feasible, a confidence correction would be calculated, which is explained in the next section.

Algorithm 1. Construction progress

Input: The newly arrived vertex i_k; The agent motion $u_k = [j, a]$; Odometry data o_k;

1: **for** each $h \in M$ **do**
2:     **if** $L_{xv}^h(j) = unexplored$ **then**
3:         $C_{vk}^h = i_k$; $V_k^h = V_{k-1}^h \cup v_k^h$; $x_v^h = v_k^h$;
4:         $O_{ek}^h = o_k$; $E_k^h = E_{k-1}^h \cup e_k^h$; $x_e^h = e_k^h$;
5:         $L_{vk}^h(a) = e_k^h$; $L_{v(k-1)}^h(j) = e_k^h$;
6:     **else**
7:         $x_v^h = L_{xv}^h[j]$; $x_e^h = L_{xv}^h(j)$;
8:         **if** $notSimilar(C_{xv}^h, i_k)$ **then**
9:             $M.purge(h)$;
10:        **end if**
11:    **end if**
12: **end for**
13: **for all** i such that $i \in N \wedge isSimilar(i, i_k)$ **do**
14:     **for all** v_s, h such that $(v_s, h) \in U_i \wedge L_{vs}^h(a) = unexplored \wedge C_{xv}^h = i_k$ **do**
15:         $h' \leftarrow cloneHypothesis(h)$;
16:         $x_e^{h'}.changeExit(x_v^{h'}, v_s)$;
17:         $V_k^{h'}.purge(x_v^{h'})$; $x_v^{h'} = v_s$;
18:         $M = M \cup h'$;
19:     **end for**
20: **end for**
21: $N = N \cup i_k$

In Algorithm 1 Some processing details are omitted for concise. For example, when a map hypothesis is purged from the Map Collection or cloned from another hypothesis, not only the hypothesis itself is changed, but also the usages in vertex instances are modified. Also, for on-board efficiency, the vertex instances are stored by basic classification besides the normal sequence storage according to time.

3   Hypothesizes Sort Based on Bayes Law

After the construction of hypothesizes, we must determine which map hypothesis is more likely to be the correct one. To do this, we consult Tully *et al.*'s work [11]. Given a sequence of sensor measurements, the posterior probability of each hypothesis is calculated. The hypothesis with a better fit to the sensor data will produce higher posterior probability.

3.1   Posterior Probability

At time step k, the agent collects the odometry data $o_{1:k}$ and vertex instances $i_{0:k}$ from the beginning, with the motion at every step $u_{1:k}$. The posterior probability of a hypothesis is as follows:

$$p(X_k^h, G_k^h | o_{1:k}, i_{0:k}, u_{1:k}) \tag{1}$$

and according to the Bayes law, the posterior probability can be computed:

$$
\begin{aligned}
p(X_k^h, & G_k^h | o_{1:k}, i_{0:k}, u_{1:k}) \\
&= \lambda\, p(o_{1:k}, i_{1:k} | X_k^h, G_k^h, u_{1:k})\, p(X_k^h, G_k^h | u_{1:k}) \\
&= \lambda\, p(o_{1:k}, i_{1:k} | X_k^h, G_k^h, u_{1:k})\, p(X_k^h | G_k^h, u_{1:k})\, p(G_k^h | u_{1:k}) \\
&= \lambda\, p(o_{1:k}, i_{1:k} | X_k^h, G_k^h, u_{1:k})\, p(G_k^h | u_{1:k})
\end{aligned}
\tag{2}
$$

where $p(o_{1:k}, u_{1:k} | X_k^h, G_k^h, u_{1:k})$ is the measurement likeihood function. As we assume the agent always follows the motion inputs and performs correctly, $p(X_k^h | G_k^h, u_{1:k})$ equals to one and the prior on hypothesis $p(X_k^h, G_k^h | u_{1:k})$ is reduced to $p(G_k^h | u_{1:k})$. The scalar value λ in Eq. (2) is used to normalize the possibilities to meet

$$
\sum_{h \in M} p(X_k^h, G_k^h | o_{1:k}, i_{0:k}, u_{1:k}) = 1
\tag{3}
$$

which is valid because there must be a hypothesis in the Map Collection that represents the real environment.

3.2   Likelihood Function and Prior Distribution

One of the main contributions of this paper is the practical way to calculate the likelihood function, which can figure out a better posterior probability of a map hypothesis as soon as the loop closure happens.

First of all, the likelihood term of a hypothesis h' can be computed recursively given the likelihood of the parent hypothesis h:

$$
\begin{aligned}
p(o_{1:k}, & i_{1:k} | X_k^h, G_k^h, u_{1:k}) \\
&= p(o_k, i_k | o_{1:k-1}, i_{0:k-1}, X_k^{h'}, G_k^{h'}, u_{1:k}) p(o_{1:k-1}, i_{0:k-1} | X_k^h, G_k^h, u_{1:k-1})
\end{aligned}
\tag{4}
$$

The first term of the function is the update at every time step k as:

$$
\begin{aligned}
p(o_k, i_k | o_{1:k}, & i_{0:k}, X_k^{h'}, G_k^{h'}, u_{1:k}) \propto \\
& \exp\left(-\frac{1}{2}\left(o_k - \mu_{k-1}^h(O_{xe}^h)\right)^T C_k^{e-1}\left(o_k - \mu_{k-1}^h(O_{xe}^h)\right) \right) \\
& \times \exp\left(-\frac{1}{2}\left(o_{k':k}\right)^T C_{k:k'}^{o}{}^{-1}\left(o_{k':k}\right) \right)
\end{aligned}
\tag{5}
$$

and the matrices used in Eq. (5) are as follows:

$$
C_k^e = \left(1 + \frac{1}{size(O_{xe}^h)} \right) R_o \|\mu_{k-1}^h(O_{xe}^h)\|^2 \qquad C_{k:k'}^o = R_o \left(\sum_{n=k'}^{k} \|o_n^h\| \right)^2
\tag{6}
$$

In the first part of the update in Eq. (5), the newly received odometry data o_k is compared with the odometry mean $\mu_{k-1}^h(O_{xe}^h)$ stored in every edge. The odometry is assumed to have zero mean white Gaussian noise with covariance R_o in unit length.

However, The first part of the update lacks the ability to verify the correctness of the loop-closing at first place, because the wrong closed loop can only be detected as the agent moves in the loop again. As consequences, some hypothesizes with obvious wrong closed loops can't be purged as soon as the agent has not moved to the wrong loop again. Nevertheless, some of the wrong closed loops could be ruled out at first place using odometry data. For example, if the agent keeps moving towards the west and never turns back, then a vertex instance being similar to the first vertex appears. The new hypothesis assuming the new vertex as the first vertex can be ruled out almost immediately, even if the odometry data is noisy.

The second part of the update is proposed to implement this idea, which is only computed when a new loop closed. In this part of correction, the accumulated odometry error $o_{k':k}$ is verified according to the distance that agent has moved since the time step k' which is the last time when the agent leaves the similar vertex instance.

When verifying the correctness of the closed loop, the most accurate way to use odometry data is to find the smallest loop that includes the newly made edge, instead of accumulating along the agent path. However, to achieve this, a breadth-first search is needed in every single hypothesis, whose cost is quite huge for an realtime system. In our method, As the path follows the vertex instances' order in Node Collection, the second part of correction could be quickly computed in loop searching step, without information of hypothesizes stored in Map Collection.

This method is also different from Ranganathan *et al.*'s work [14]. Since the optimization of the global position from odometry data measurements is expensive for an on-board computer and the odometry data is usually noisy.

The prior distribution we used in Eq. (2) is the same as Tully *et al.*'s work [10] as follows:

$$p(G_k^h | u_{1:k}) \propto \exp\left(-size(V_k^h) \log k\right) \tag{7}$$

which means that smaller hypothesizes is prefered when serval hypothesis meets the sensors measurements up to now.

3.3   Hypothesizes Purge

As proved in Ref. [5], the number of hypothesizes grows hyper exponentially. In order to maintain the problem computationally feasibly, some tests are applied to purge the hypothesizes that are less likely to be correct.

The first test is the degree test, which is the basic idea derived from multi-hypothesizes method. As shown in Alg.1, if the newly arrived vertex instance does not agree with the should-be vertex in the hypothesis, the hypothesis would be purged immediately. The conflict may be caused by different degrees or different intersection aiming, where the magnetometer data helps a lot.

The second is the test in likelihood update. If a single measurement exceeds a 4-sigma error bound (Eq. (5)), the hypothesis would be purged too. This situation implies that the measurement does not accord with the measurement history and incorrect loop closures in the hypothesis.

At last, any hypothesis with posterior probability (Eq. (1)) below a threshold ε is purged. As the hypothesis has a poor fit to the sensor data or there is a hypothesis consisting with the measurements with a much smaller size.

The planarity test in [9,15] is not applied in our method, because for agile unmanned systems like MAVs, shortcuts between floors may break the planar assumption.

4   Experiments and Results

For convenient communication and extensibility in the future, the algorithm is implemented by C++ in ROS (Robot Operating System) Framework.[1] Both simulation and real-time experiments are conducted to evaluate our mapping algorithm. The movements of the agent in experiments are all sent by a human, to focus on the performance when the loop closes. The simulation aims to evaluate the correctness of our algorithm. In the real-time experiment, the algorithm is deployed on a MAV equipped with 2.1 GHz embedded computer real time to test the high efficiency.

4.1   Simulations

A simulation interface is made for the experiment. We can simulate an agent moving in any fictitious map we assigned, providing the algorithm with artificial

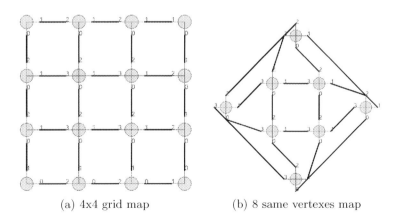

(a) 4x4 grid map   (b) 8 same vertexes map

Fig. 2. The fictitious maps built for simulation

---

[1] All source code in this paper can be found here:
https://github.com/StumboEugen/topology_map.

noisy odometry data and detailed information of the arrived vertex. The interface can also visualize the map hypothesizes fetched from the algorithm. The standard deviation of the artificial odometry noise per meter is 0.1 m for default.

Using magnetometer data, the 3×3 grid map used in [8] would be too easy, because all nine vertexes are unique. So the first fictitious map built for simulations is a 4×4 grid map (Fig. 2(a)), which is the same as the one in the real-time experiment.

As shown in Fig. 3(a), the correct hypothesis's posterior possibility shakes in the early stage of the mapping process. Nevertheless, the correct one still dominates the incorrect ones quickly, because we can evaluate the map as soon as the loop closed. However, there are still serval unique vertexes in the 4×4 grid, which makes the process easy.

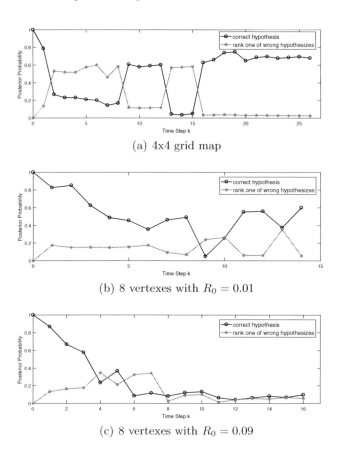

(a) 4x4 grid map

(b) 8 vertexes with $R_0 = 0.01$

(c) 8 vertexes with $R_0 = 0.09$

Fig. 3. The posterior probabilities of the correct hypothesis and the most possibile hypothesis in incorrect ones durning the simulation

To fully test the algorithm, we build a map consisting of eight vertexes that are all the same (Fig. 2(b)), where two simulations are conducted. The only difference between them is the standard deviation (R_0 in Eq. (6)). In the first simulation, standard deviation per meter is 0.1 m ($R_0 = 0.01$), and the standard deviation per meter is 0.3 m ($R_0 = 0.09$) in the other simulation.

As Fig. 3 shows, the correct hypothesis has the highest posterior possibility at the end of both two simulations. But in the simulation with $R_0 = 0.09$, the correct hypothesis doesn't have overwhelming advantages of incorrect ones(Fig. 3(c)). Also, the type of hypothesizes that falls behind is different. In the first simulation (Fig. 4(a)), the leaders of the incorrect ones have almost the same graph as the correct one. The only difference is that one vertex is considered as two different vertexes, which is false negative matches. On the other hand, in the simulation where $R_0 = 0.09$ (Fig. 4(b)), the topological structure is full of strange and weird loop closures, which is false positive matches.

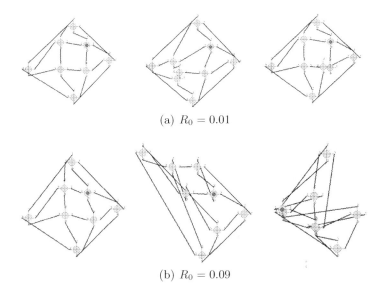

(a) $R_0 = 0.01$

(b) $R_0 = 0.09$

Fig. 4. The result maps at the last time step. The posterior probability of the hypothesis decreases from left to right, in each group.

The phenomenon is not hard to understand. A higher standard deviation in posterior possibility computation means that we accept larger odometry drift. Therefore the hypothesis with wrong loop closures that violates odometry data is not penalized and has a higher posterior possibility. Also, the correct hypothesis is also affected, because better odometry data does not have advantages when R_0 is large. As a result, the posterior possibilities of hypothesizes are all small and roughly the same. So using odometry data can make the correct hypothesis taking the lead more quickly as soon as the loop closed.

4.2   Real-Time Experiment

In order to test the real-time on-board performance, a simple scaled down scenario is made. In the scenario, the world is a 4×4 grid, and the size of the grid is about 1×1 m (Fig. 2(a)). The MAV takes off at one of the vertexes and performs line-tracking as the movement in the topological world. The line-tracking, local position control and the extraction of vertexes information is implemented by a downward camera and simple computer vision methods. Via the interface mentioned in the last subsection, the whole mapping process can be monitored and controlled remotely.[2]

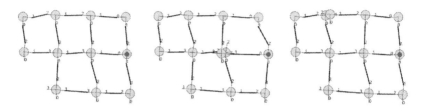

Fig. 5. The result of the real-time experiment. Three hypothesizes that has highest posterior possibility: 0.65186 0.03948 0.03939

Influenced by dynamics and battery capacity, the MAV did not complete the whole mapping process. The standard deviation in the real-time experiment is 0.1 m too. The result is shown in Fig. 5, which is similar with the result in the first simulation in the 8 vertexes map (Fig. 4(a)).

In the experiment, though the MAV position control is not very stable caused by sensitive dynamics parameters, the mapping algorithm always responds within half a second.

5   Conclusion

By separating detailed information and topological connectivity into two different storage set, the topological mapping based on multi-hypothesis method is of high computational and bandwidth efficiency. In order to find out the correct map hypothesis, we calculate the posterior probability of every hypothesis. Incorporating with the structure, a fast evaluation using odometry is conducted, which can give a likelihood update as soon as the loop closure happens.

In this paper, we just focus on the mapping problem itself. In the future, we may consider extracting the vertex information from the real environment and dealing with the robot motion and sensor problem raised from it. For example, the agent may have an incorrect extraction of the vertex or even miss a vertex, which is fatal and irretrievable.

---

[2] The experiment video can be found here:
https://jbox.sjtu.edu.cn/l/uoaCIv.

Acknowledgement. This work was partially supported by National Science and Technology Major Project (2017ZX01041101-003) and National Natural Science Foundation of China (Grant No. 51605282).

References

1. Mur-Artal, R., Montiel, J.M.M., Tardos, J.D.: ORB-SLAM: a versatile and accurate monocular slam system. IEEE Trans. Robot. **31**(5), 1147–1163 (2015)
2. Hornung, A., Wurm, K.M., Bennewitz, M., Stachniss, C., Burgard, W.: OctoMap: an efficient probabilistic 3D mapping framework based on octrees. Auton. Robot. **34**(3), 189–206 (2013)
3. Chrastil, E.R., Warren, W.H.: Active and passive spatial learning in human navigation: acquisition of graph knowledge. J. Exp. Psychol. Learn. Mem. Cogn. **39**(5), 1520–1537 (2013)
4. Kuipers, B., Browning, R., Gribble, B., Hewett, M., Remolina, E.: The spatial semantic hierarchy. Artif. Intell. **119**(1–2), 191–233 (2000)
5. Ranganathan, A., Dellaert, F.: Inference in the space of topological maps: an MCMC-based approach. In: IEEE/RSJ International Conference on Intelligent Robots & Systems (2008)
6. Marinakis, D., Dudek, G.: Pure topological mapping in mobile robotics. IEEE Trans. Robot. **26**(6), 1051–1064 (2010)
7. Chrastil, E.R., Warren, W.H.: From cognitive maps to cognitive graphs. PLoS ONE **9**(11), e112544 (2014)
8. Kuipers, B., Modayil, J., Beeson, P., Macmahon, M., Savelli, F.: Local metrical and global topological maps in the hybrid spatial semantic hierarchy. In: IEEE International Conference on Robotics & Automation (2004)
9. Savelli, F., Kuipers, B.: Loop-closing and planarity in topological map-building. In: IEEE/RSJ International Conference on Intelligent Robots & Systems (2004)
10. Tully, S., Kantor, G., Choset, H., Werner, F.: Multi-hypothesis topological slam approach for loop closing on edge-ordered graphs. In: IEEE/RSJ International Conference on Intelligent Robots & Systems (2009)
11. Tully, S., Kantor, G., Choset, H.: A unified Bayesian framework for global localization and SLAM in hybrid metric/topological maps (2012)
12. Johnson, C., Kuipers, B.: Efficient search for correct and useful topological maps. In: IEEE/RSJ International Conference on Intelligent Robots & Systems (2012)
13. Remolina, E., Kuipers, B.: Towards a general theory of topological maps. Artif. Intell. **152**(1), 47–104 (2004)
14. Ranganathan, A., Dellaert, F.: Online probabilistic topological mapping. Int. J. Robot. Res. **30**(6), 755–771 (2011)
15. Vijayan, G., Wigderson, A.: Planarity of edge ordered graphs. Technical report 307, Depart (1982)

Indoor Navigation System Using the Fetch Robot

Huishen Zhu[1], Brenton Leighton[2], Yongbo Chen[2(✉)], Xijun Ke[1], Songtao Liu[1], and Liang Zhao[2]

[1] Shanghai Institute of Micro Motor (The 21st Research Institute of China Electronics Technology Group Corporation), SIMM (CETC21), Shanghai, China
[2] Centre for Autonomous Systems, University of Technology Sydney, Sydney, NSW 2007, Australia
Yongbo.Chen@student.uts.edu.au

Abstract. In this paper, we present a navigation system, including off-line mapping and on-line localization, for the Fetch robot in an indoor environment using Cartographer. This framework aims to build a practical, robust, and accurate Robot Operating System (ROS) package for the Fetch robot. Firstly, using Cartographer and the fusion of data from a laser scan and RGB-D camera, a two-dimensional (2D) off-line map is built. Then, the Adaptive Monte Carlo Localization (AMCL) ROS package is used to perform on-line localization. We use a simulation to validate this method of mapping and localization, then demonstrate our method live on the Fetch robot. A video about the simulation and experiment is shown in https://youtu.be/oOvxTOowe34.

Keywords: Data fusion · ROS framework · Fetch robot · Mapping · Localization

1 Introduction

The aim of indoor navigation is to provide a robot its location with respect to a map of an indoor environment. Simultaneous Localization and Mapping (SLAM) is commonly used to generate the map on an unknown environment [1]. Broadly speaking, the process of solving the SLAM problem can be divided into two parts; the front-end and the back-end. The front-end involves processing input sensor data, while the back-end is an optimization process to create a consistent map. The design of the front-end varies based on the sensor type, for example laser scan [2] or vision [3]. For laser scan based SLAM, the system may create an occupancy grid [4] or a point cloud using Iterative closest point (ICP) [5]. This paper aims to obtain the occupancy grid map.

This paper focuses on the navigation system of Fetch robot based on the fusion of the 2D laser sensor and the RGB-D camera sensor. This work provides

Supported by Shanghai Institute of Micro Motor (SIMM) project: "Develop the SLAM Algorithm for Fetch Robot in the Indoor Office and Corridor Environment".

H. Yu et al. (Eds.): ICIRA 2019, LNAI 11743, pp. 686–696, 2019.
https://doi.org/10.1007/978-3-030-27538-9_59

mapping and localization for path planning and following, which is the basis of a larger application involving the Fetch robot. The basic algorithms of this paper are the Cartographer [2] SLAM system and the Adaptive Monte Carlo Localization (AMCL) Robot Operating System (ROS) package. Cartographer is a system that provides real-time SLAM in 2D and 3D across multiple platforms and sensor configurations. It is the state of the art technology in the field of laser scan based SLAM, and performs well in some challenging environments. AMCL is a 2D probabilistic localization system for a mobile robot, which implements the KLD-sampling Monte Carlo localization approach. A fused laser scan, generated from laser scan and point cloud data, is provided to Cartographer to create the occupancy grid map, which AMCL uses for localization of the Fetch robot.

The main structure of this paper is shown as follows: In Sect. 3 we describe the problem and offer a practical solution framework. In Sect. 4 we describe the implementation, including data collection, data pre-processing, off-line mapping and on-line localization. In Sect. 5 we describe the simulations and experiments performed to verify the correctness and practicality of the proposed method. Finally, in Sect. 6, we make a brief conclusion of this paper.

2   Related Work

Early SLAM techniques primarily focused on the filter-based method, including Extended Kalman Filter (EKF) [6], Particle filter (PF) [7], and so on. In [8], Christopher Weyers and Gilbert Peterson presents a SLAM solution combining stereo cameras, inertial measurements, and vehicle odometry into a Multiple Integrated Navigation Sensor (MINS) path based on the Kalman Filter (KF) and FastSLAM algorithm, which operates a Rao-Blackwellized Particle Filter (RBPF). Zhang, Ou et al. apply the RBPF method in the SLAM task of a restaurant service robot using a depth camera and a move base with odometry and gyro [9].

It is well-known that SLAM technology develops from the filter-based method to the optimization-based method. Because of the better consistency and efficiency, the optimization-based method, especially for the pose-graph SLAM framework [10], is widely used in the indoor navigation method of the robot system. Lee and Park present a mobile mapping system (MMS) whose front-end is the map-based scan matching and back-end is the graph-based optimization [11]. The pose-graph optimization method is a very general and efficient method. Cartographer is a popular system for 2D laser scan SLAM, and is also based on this technique.

It is easy to know that a single sensor can not offer the platform a accurate and robust solution. So the fusion between laser and camera is one of the popular solutions. Su, Zhou et al. propose a reliable global localization approach with the capability of addressing the kidnapped robot problem, where both laser and camera sensors are used based on the pose graph optimization [12]. Based on the ICP and pose-graph optimization, Adrian Ratter and Claude Sammut present a novel algorithm for fusing Laser Rangefinder and RGB-D data to accurately track the position of a robot and generate large 3D maps [13].

3   Problem Description and Solution Framework

Assume that the robot is performing some tasks in an unknown environment
such as coverage, exploration or search. Our navigation framework is used to
build a highly accurate and practical 2D map for the surrounding environment,
for the purpose of localization. This navigation framework will offer the real-
time robot poses for the Fetch robot [14] and help it to finish tasks such as path
planning and control.

The solution framework can be divided into two main parts: the off-line part
and the on-line part. In the on-line part, we capture data and fuse the laser scan
with the point cloud from the RGB-D camera. In the off-line part we use the
generated data to create a map of the environment. Once the map is generated
we can then localize on-line. The basic solution framework is summarized and
presented in Fig. 1. This framework is written as a ROS package [15] and applied
in the real robot system.

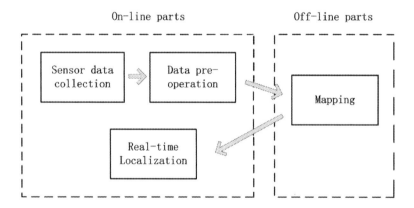

Fig. 1. Solution framework

4   Implementation

In this section we present the methodology and the implementation details of
the system.

4.1   Sensors and Data Collection

Our ROS package is built for the Fetch robot. There are multiple kinds of sensors
in Fetch robot, including a SICK TIM571 laser, a 6-axis inertial measurement
unit (IMU), a Primesense Carmine 1.09 short-range RGBD sensor and gripper
sensors (Fig. 2) [14]. For our application, the laser scanner and head camera
are the most useful data sources on the Fetch robot. These sensors publish to
the ROS topics 'head_camera/depth_ downsampled/points' and 'base_scan'. The
Fetch robot publishes many useful ROS topics and we can easily subscribe them.

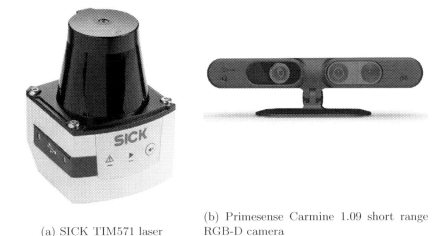

(a) SICK TIM571 laser

(b) Primesense Carmine 1.09 short range RGB-D camera

Fig. 2. Important sensors on Fetch robot

4.2 Laser Scan and RGB-D Point Cloud Data Fusion

Prior to the mapping process, it is necessary to fuse the laser scan data and RGB-D camera point cloud data to create the map. Our pre-processing involves transforming the point cloud from the RGB-D camera into the frame of the laser scanner, removing points that belong to the floor, converting the point cloud into a laser scan, then combing the generated laser scan with the actual laser scan.

The ROS topic 'head_camera/depth_downsampled/points' is a 3D point cloud, and may include points belonging to the floor. In order to avoid the effect of these floor points we remove any points lower than the level of the laser scanner. This is achieved by transforming the points into the laser scanner frame using the ROS tf2 package, filtering any points with a Z axis values less than zero using Point Cloud Library (PCL), then transforming the point cloud back into the RGB-D camera frame for publishing.

With the floor removed from the point cloud, the data is flattened into a pseudo laser scan, so that is can be combined with the real laser scan. The pseudo laser scan is created with the same field of view and step angle as the real laser scan, and the two are combined by iterating through both and saving the shorter range value into the combined laser scan data. Figures 3 and 4 show this process. The fused data is published as the ROS topic 'base_scan_combined', and is used by Cartographer for creating a map.

4.3 Mapping Using Cartographer

We save a ROS bag of the fused data and apply Cartographer off-line to create the occupancy grid map. Cartographer's mapping node outputs a protocol buffer stream file, which can be used in various ways.

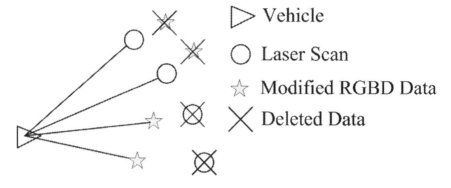

Fig. 3. Data fusion

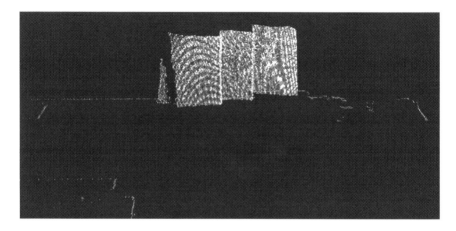

Fig. 4. Data fusion in real dataset (White wall points are the camera data, colourful points are laser data and the white horizon points are fused data) (Color figure online)

Using the fused laser scan presents an issue for mapping, because the ranges and fields of view of the two sensors are significantly different The RGB-D camera has a maximum range of 3 m and horizontal field of view of 54°, while the laser scanner has a range of up to 25 m and a field of view of 220°. During the mapping process, obstacles that appear only in the point cloud are quickly erased once they are out of range of the RGB-D camera. To keep the point cloud obstacles we set the "insert_free_space" to false when generating the obstacle grid from the protocol buffer stream file. This results in a map containing all obstacles but no unoccupied cells, which are needed for localization and path planning. To solve this problem we generate another map with "insert_free_space" set to true, and combine the two maps with MATLAB, to produce a map that contains both free space and all obstacles.

4.4 On-Line Localization Using AMCL

As the final step in our method, localization is performed on-line using the AMCL [16] package. It is noted that, because our map is generated from the fused data of the laser scanner and RGB-D camera, our AMCL node needs to subscribe the 'base_scan_combined' topic instead of the laser scan only topic.

5 Simulations and Experiments

In order to verify the correctness and practicality of our proposed method, we present some simulations and experiments.

5.1 Simulations

In this part, we build two simulations in the ROS Gazebo simulation environment and perform the mapping and localization process based on these two environments.

Simulation 1. This environment is an indoor office environment with some tables and chairs. The simulated Fetch moves around this office, collecting sufficient laser and point cloud data to build a complete map. The simulated Fetch robot and surrounding environment are shown in Figs. 5 and 6.

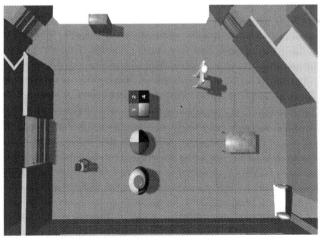

Fig. 5. Simulation environment 1

Fig. 6. Fetch robot simulator

The results including the built map and localization are presented in Fig. 7. The relative coordinate errors are presented in Fig. 8.

In Fig. 8, it is easy to find that localization errors are small, which verifies the accuracy of our proposed method.

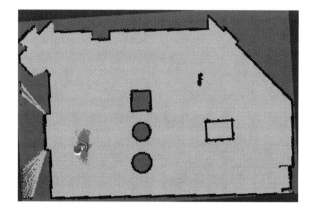

Fig. 7. Mapping and localization results of Simulation 1

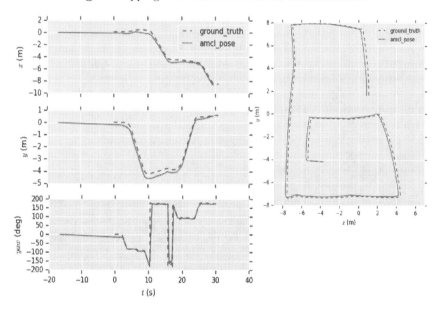

Fig. 8. Relative errors between the coordinates (Left) and trajectories (Right) of ground truth and AMCL result of Simulation 1

Simulation 2. Similar to the previous simulation, we perform our method in an indoor office environment with some tables and produce the map and localization result in Fig. 9. We also output the relative error of the localization coordinate and trajectory, shown in Fig. 10.

5.2 Experimental Results in an Indoor Environment

For the on-line experiment, we use the real Fetch robot to perform the complete process.

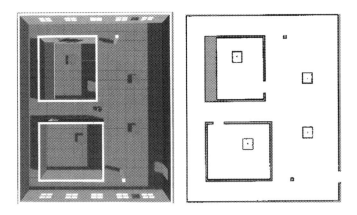

Fig. 9. Simulation environment 2 and built map

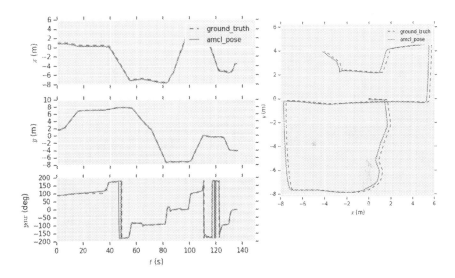

Fig. 10. Relative errors between the coordinates (Left) and trajectories (Right) of ground truth and AMCL result of Simulation 2

Scenario 1. The first on-line scenario is a corridor environment of UTS Tech Lab. We combine two maps obtained by cartographer and get the final map with some obstacles, like chairs and tables, shown in Fig. 11. The surrounding environment from on-board camera, built map and localization results are shown in Fig. 12.

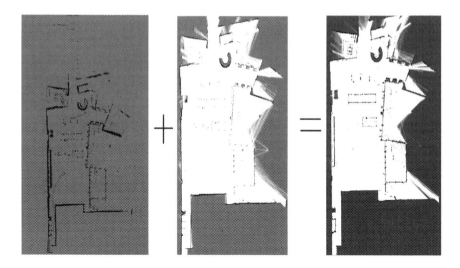

Fig. 11. Built maps

Fig. 12. Built map, localization results and corresponding camera image of the on-line experiment 1

Scenario 2. The second scenario is in an experimental room of UTS Tech Lab. Using a similar technique, we can get the following map and localization result and the corresponding camera image from Fetch robot, shown in Fig. 13.

Based on these results, we can find that our method can be successfully used in the practical environment.

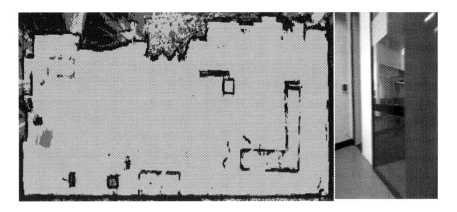

Fig. 13. Built map, localization results and corresponding camera image of the on-line experiment 2

6   Conclusion and Future Work

This paper presents a practical ROS system for mapping and localization on the Fetch robot. We first collect the laser scan and point cloud data, and fuse them using them into a combined laser scan. Based on the fused data and Cartographer, two maps are created that are combined and used for on-line localization with AMCL. The majority of this process is written by C++ and tested both in the Gazebo simulation and on the real Fetch robot. The simulation and experiment results prove that our solution framework is efficient and practical.

This is just the first step of our research on the navigation system of the Fetch robot. In the future work we will introduce the machine learning based computer vision technology and the sub-map localization method into this navigation system.

References

1. Cadena, C., et al.: Past, present, and future of simultaneous localization and mapping: towards the robust-perception age. IEEE Trans. Robot. **32**(6), 1309–1332 (2016)
2. Hess, W., Damon, K., Holger, R., Daniel, A.: Real-time loop closure in 2D LIDAR SLAM. In: 2016 IEEE International Conference on Robotics and Automation (ICRA), pp. 1271–1278. IEEE (2016)
3. Mur-Artal, R., Tardós, J.D.: ORB-SLAM2: an open-source slam system for monocular, stereo, and RGB-D cameras. IEEE Trans. Robot. **33**(5), 1255–1262 (2017)
4. Strom, J., Edwin, O.: Occupancy grid rasterization in large environments for teams of robots. In: 2011 IEEE/RSJ International Conference on Intelligent Robots and Systems, pp. 4271–4276. IEEE (2011)
5. A real-time 2D and 3D ICP-based SLAM system. http://wiki.ros.org/ethzasl_icp_mapping

6. Dissanayake, M.G., Newman, P., Clark, S., Durrant-Whyte, H.F., Csorba, M.: A solution to the simultaneous localization and map building (SLAM) problem. IEEE Trans. Robot. Autom. **17**(3), 229–241 (2001)
7. Thrun, S., Fox, D., Burgard, W., Dellaert, F.: Robust monte carlo localization for mobile robots. Artif. Intell. **128**(1–2), 99–141 (2001)
8. Weyers, C., Peterson, G.: Improving occupancy grid FastSLAM by integrating navigation sensors. In: IEEE/RSJ International Conference on Intelligent Robots and Systems, pp. 859–864 (2011)
9. Zhang, J., Ou, Y., Jiang, G., Zhou, Y.: An approach to restaurant service robot SLAM. In: Proceedings of the IEEE International Conference on Robotics and Biomimetics, pp. 2122–2127 (2016)
10. Hu, G., Huang, S., Dissanayake, G.: Evaluation of pose only SLAM. In: IEEE/RSJ International Conference on Intelligent Robots and Systems, pp. 3732–3738 (2010)
11. Lee, Y.C., Park, S.H.: 3D map building method with mobile mapping system in indoor environments. In: 2013 16th International Conference on Advanced Robotics (ICAR), pp. 1–7. IEEE (2013)
12. Su, Z., Zhou, X., Cheng, T., Zhang, H., Xu, B., Chen, W.: Global localization of a mobile robot using Lidar and visual features. In: Proceedings of the IEEE International Conference on Robotics and Biomimetics, pp. 2377–2383 (2017)
13. Ratter, A., Sammut, C.: Fused 2D/3D position tracking for robust SLAM on mobile robots. In: IEEE/RSJ International Conference on Intelligent Robots and Systems (IROS), pp. 1962–1969 (2015)
14. Fetch Robotics. https://docs.fetchrobotics.com/
15. Robot Operating System (ROS). https://docs.fetchrobotics.com/
16. Thrun, S., Burgard, W., Fox, D.: Probabilistic Robotics. MIT Press, Cambridge (2005)

Keyframe-Based Dynamic Elimination SLAM System Using YOLO Detection

Gumin Jin[1(✉)], Xingjun Zhong[2], Shaoqing Fang[1], Xiangyu Deng[1],
and Jianxun Li[1]

[1] Department of Automation, Shanghai Jiao Tong University,
Shanghai 201100, China
jingumin@sjtu.edu.cn
[2] Student Innovation Center, Shanghai Jiao Tong University, Shanghai 201100, China

Abstract. The assumption of static scene is typical in SLAM algorithms, which limits the use of visual SLAM systems in real-world dynamic environments. Dynamic elimination, detecting or segmenting the static and dynamic region in the image and regarding the features in dynamic parts as outliers, is proved to an effective solution to solve the dynamic SLAM problem. However, traditional dynamic elimination methods processing each frame are very time consuming. In this paper, dynamic elimination is implemented only on keyframes utilizing YOLO as the fast dynamic detection network. This keyframe-based improvement ensures localization accuracy by ensuring map accuracy, and at the same time increases the speed of the SLAM system with dynamic elimination greatly. Experiments are conducted both in real-world environment and on the public TUM datasets. The results demonstrate the effectiveness as well as efficiency of our method.

Keywords: Dynamic elimination · YOLO detection ·
Keyframe processing · SLAM

1 Introduction

Simultaneous Localization and Mapping (SLAM), concurrently estimating the sensor pose and reconstructing environment models from sensor measurements, have gained significant interest from both the computer vision and robotic communities, which has made an impact on robot navigation [1] autonomous driving [2] and augmented reality [3].

Despite the remarkable results in visual SLAM, most approaches work based on the assumption that the observed environments are static. The data associations in the SLAM front end can be hindered by moving object. With wrong data associations fed into the SLAM back end, the graph optimization process could be severely jeopardized, which finally leads to a catastrophic failure for the localization and mapping process.

© Springer Nature Switzerland AG 2019
H. Yu et al. (Eds.): ICIRA 2019, LNAI 11743, pp. 697–705, 2019.
https://doi.org/10.1007/978-3-030-27538-9_60

Dynamic elimination or motion segmentation and removal, cascaded before standard SLAM system is proved to be an effective solution to solve the dynamic problem [4]. Robustness is achieved by segmenting the dynamic region in the image and then computing pose estimation based on the static parts only. With the development of deep learning, detection networks have achieved good performance in semantic segmentation. Therefore, combining detection networks with SLAM may improve system robustness and the perception level of robots.

The existing elimination methods [4–6] based on each frame are very time consuming, which is actually designed for visual odometry but not for SLAM system. Different from visual odometry, SLAM system finds more matches by local map after frame-to-frame tracking stage and then perform the BA optimization. As the map is constructed by keyframes, in this paper, we propose a method of dynamic elimination only processing keyframes. By constructing an accurate map from keyframes, the mismatch between the frame and map can be avoid, which ensures the localization accuracy. As keyframes are a part of all frames, so the computing time can be effectively saved.

The main contributions of this paper include:

1. YOLO is introduced as a dynamic detection module into SLAM system, and the accuracy of localization is improved greatly.
2. Dynamic elimination is only performed on keyframes instead of all frames to balance the precision and speed.
3. Effectiveness as well as efficiency of our method are verified through self-built and public datasets.

In the rest of this paper, the structure is as follows, Sect. 2 provides a overview of accomplishments about dynamic elimination and semantic networks in SLAM. Then Sect. 3 introduce the whole system in detail, Sect. 4 provide experimental results of our method both in a real-world environment and public datasets. A brief conclusion is given in the Sect. 5.

2   Related Work

2.1   Dynamic Elimination in SLAM

In dynamic environments, wrong data associations are mainly caused by the moving objects. Removing moving objects helps to prevent the mismatch, reducing the influence on the localization and mapping optimizer. Sun et al. [4] propose an RGB-D data-based motion removal approach and integrate it into the front end of the DVO SLAM algorithm. Next year, they improve their method to require no pri6or-known moving-object information [5]. Fan et al. [6] locate the region where the dynamic objects existed by the two proposed constraints which are determined by the camera motion.

2.2   Semantic Network in SLAM

Since traditional SLAM maps could not provide conceptual knowledge of the surroundings to facilitate complex tasks, associating semantic concepts, such as detection or segmentation networks, with geometry entities in the environment has become a popular research domain recently. Bescos et al. [7] use Mask R-CNN detecting dynamic objects to obtains a pixel-wise semantic segmentation of the images. Similarly, Yu et al. [8] adopt SegNet to provide semantic segmentation based on caffe for removal. Qi et al. [9] present a method to build a dense semantic map, which utilizes both two-dimensional (2D) detection labels and 3D geometric information.

Although detection-based method has be introduced to SLAM, we do dynamic detection and removal only on keyframes to ensure the robustness and rapidity of SLAM system in dynamic environment, which will be presented in detail in the next section.

3 System Introduction

3.1 Framework of System

In our system, we adopt ORB-SLAM2 [10] to provide a global feature-based SLAM solution that enables us to estimate the camera pose and construct the map in dynamic environment, the overview of our proposed method is shown in Fig. 1. The dotted line indicates the data processing direction, and the blue box indicates the parallel threads in the system. The RGB and depth frames are first fed to the tracking thread, where Yolo detection and dynamic segmentation are only performed after initialization decision and keyframe decision to guarantee the tracking speed and build an accurate local map. Then keyframes are sent to the other three threads.

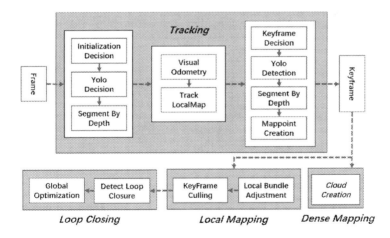

Fig. 1. The framework of our method consists of four threads. Local mapping and loop closing are the same as ORB-SLAM2. YOLO detection and dynamic segmentation are only performed after initialization decision and keyframe decision in tracking. A static map is constructed by cloud creation module.

3.2   Integrated System

In ORB-SLAM2 system, localization is implemented in the tracking module. After feature extraction, visual odometry is used to get initial pose estimation from previous frame, then the map is projected into the current frame to search more correspondences. The camera pose is finally optimized with all the map-points. The local mapping thread focuses on building the local 3D sparse map. It optimizes both local map and the keyframe poses by performing local bundle adjustment (BA). The loop closing thread detects loops and then corrects the accumulated drifts by pose graph optimization. Different from original system, we add a dense mapping module to generate the dense cloud of static parts, which could be useful for high-level tasks.

3.3   Dynamic Detection Using YOLO

We propose to use a CNN to obtains the dynamic region of the images in SLAM system. Object detection algorithms based on CNN are basically divided into 2 two categories: one-stage methods (R-CNN [11], Fast R-CNN [12] and Faster R-CNN [13]) and two-stage methods (YOLO [14] and SSD [15]). The former focuses on speed while the latter focuses on accuracy. SLAM tries to concurrently estimates poses and reconstructs the map in real time, so we choose YOLO to be our detection network, which detects every frame for about 36 ms in our CPU-only laptop.

The input of YOLO net is raw RGB images, and the output consists of a detected class, a score quantifying the detection confidence and a bounding box. Considering people are most likely to be dynamic objects in real applications, we only use the bounding box detection results when the class is person and the corresponding score is higher than 0.8.

When person expands the body or approaches the camera, the rectangle bounding box actually contain many static parts. For RGBD input, we offer an optional method based on depth image to get a better region from box-wise detection to a pixel-wise segmentation of the image. Figure 2 show the detection and segmentation results and feature keypoints filtered after corresponding mask. But pixel-wise segmentation consumes more computing resource, which will influence the real-time performance of SLAM.

3.4   Dynamic Removal Based on Keyframes

So far, we get the dynamic region, in which feature points located are most likely to be outliers. Different from general dynamic removal methods in SLAM which process each frame, considering that the RANSAC-used visual odometry can provide a initial pose estimation, camera pose is finally optimized with local map, which is constructed by keyframes. We only do the time-consuming dynamic detection and removal when the frame is decided to be a keyframe. We create a keyframe mask as the same size as the original image. The region of dynamic objects is set to 0 in mask, the other is 1. We use this mask to form a new

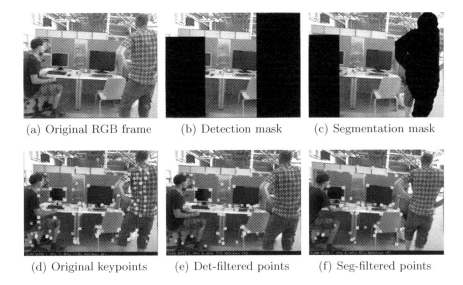

(a) Original RGB frame   (b) Detection mask   (c) Segmentation mask

(d) Original keypoints   (e) Det-filtered points   (f) Seg-filtered points

Fig. 2. Detection and segmentation mask (up) and feature keypoints filtered after corresponding mask (bottom).

keyframe before it creates new mappoints. Because keyframes are a part of all frames and an accurate static map is established, accuracy can be achieved almost to the same level as every-frame elimination method, but the computing time is greatly saved.

4   Experimental Results

In the section, experimental results would be presented to demonstrate the effectiveness and efficiency of our improved SLAM system. We evaluate the accuracy performance and test the time for our system in dynamic environment through both self-generated and public RGB-D datasets.

Metrics Absolute Trajectory Error (ATE) and Relative Pose Error (RPE) are used for quantitative accuracy evaluation. Metric ATE stands for global consistency of trajectory, while metric RPE measures the translational drift. We present the values of RMSE, Mean Error, Median Error and the Standard Deviation (S.D.). Among these, RMSE can better indicate the robustness and S.D. encodes the stability of the system.

All the experiments are performed on our desktop computer with Intel i5 CPU, GeForce 940MX GPU, and 8 GB memory. Note that our computing configuration is very low (Fig. 3).

(a) Motion capture system   (b) Drone with ZR300 sensor

Fig. 3. We present a real flying dataset collected by Intel ZR300 RGBD camera and record groundtruth by Optitrack motion capture system.

4.1 Evaluation Using Self-generated Dataset Compared with Integrated System

We generate an RGB-D dataset (320×240 resolution, 613 frames toally) with moving person in the scene using a quadrotor-hold zr300 RGB-D camera, and at the same time use an indoor motion capture system to track the camera pose for evaluation, we will online the experiment procedures as well as the dataset.

Table 1. Accuracy performance of self-generate dataset.

Method	RMSE	Mean	Median	S.D
ORB-SLAM2	0.566	0.478	0.369	0.301
Yolo-KEY	0.033	0.028	0.023	0.018

As we can see from Table 1, YOLO detecting-every keyframe system (YOLO-KEY) rejects the bad association by dynamic detection, thus the RMSE, mean, median and S.D. improvement values can reach up to 94.0%, 94.0%, 93.6% and 97.1% respectively.

Figure 4 show ATE plots from original ORB-SLAM2 and improved YOLO-SLAM in our sequence respectively. As we can see, the errors are significantly reduced in our method.

For practical applications, real-time performance is a crucial indicator to evaluate SLAM system, we test the time required for some major modules to process. The results are shown in Table 2. The average tracking time to process each frame is 46.41 ms, including feature extraction, visual odometry, map tracking and YOLO detection, and among totally 613 frames, 33 frames are chosen to be keyframe. On the same device, compared with previous every-frame methods to filter out dynamic objects, such as [7,8], our keyframe method is more satisfied with the needs of the real time.

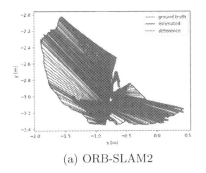

(a) ORB-SLAM2

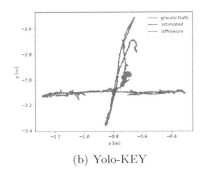

(b) Yolo-KEY

Fig. 4. ATE plot of our self-generated dataset.

Table 2. Time evaluation of self-generate dataset.

Module	Feature extraction	Visual odometry	Map tracking	Yolo detection	Average tracking
Time (ms)	9.17	6.17	9.91	36	46.41

4.2 Evaluation Using Public Tum Dataset Compared with Different Removal Systems

In TUM datasets, the Dynamic Object sequences are designed to evaluate SLAM algorithms in dynamic environments. Among the sequences, the siting sequences depict low-dynamic scenarios, while the walking sequences depict high dynamic scenarios. As the former are well solved by original ORB-SLAM2, we only use the challenging high-dynamic sequences (half, rpy, static, xyz) here to evaluate.

As in Table 3, compared with original ORB-SLAM2, in the dynamic environment, the accuracy of the three dynamic elimination systems, YOLO detecting every-frame system (YOLO-ALL), YOLO detecting every-keyframe system (YOLO-KEY), and YOLO detecting/segmenting every-keyframe system (Yolo-KEY-SEG), have all been significantly improved. The accuracy of the key-frame elimination method is lower than that of the YOLO-ALL method, but the

Table 3. Accuracy performance of public TUM dataset.

SEQ	ATE		RPE(T)		RPE(R)		ATE		RPE(T)		RPE(R)	
	ORB-SLAM2						YOLO-ALL					
Half	0.66	0.0	1.01	0.0	22.79	0.0	0.04	+94.4%	0.05	+94.7%	0.95	+95.8%
rpy	0.79	0.0	1.19	0.0	21.87	0.0	NOT INITIALIZATION					
Static	0.66	0.0	1.01	0.0	22.79	0.0	0.04	+94.4%	0.05	+94.7%	0.95	+95.8%
xyz	0.66	0.0	1.01	0.0	22.79	0.0	0.04	+94.4%	0.05	+94.7%	0.95	+95.8%
	Yolo-KEY						Yolo-KEY-SEG					
Half	0.04	+93.7%	0.06	+94.1%	1.28	+94.4%	0.04	+94.4%	0.05	+94.7%	0.95	+95.8%
rpy	0.18	+77.3%	0.26	+78.6%	4.90	+77.6%	0.04	+94.4%	0.05	+94.7%	0.95	+95.8%
Static	0.01	+96.7%	0.01	+96.4%	0.37	+94.6%	0.04	+94.4%	0.05	+94.7%	0.95	+95.8%
xyz	0.02	+98.1%	0.02	+98.1%	0.62	+97.2%	0.04	+94.4%	0.05	+94.7%	0.95	+95.8%

decrease is very small, and with more static feature points used, the refined segmentation also improves the localization accuracy to some extent. When the dynamic region represented by detection bounding boxes takes up most of the image, few region is left for SLAM to match the feature points, which contribute to initialization failure in the rpy sequence.

(a) Without elimination

(b) With elimination

Fig. 5. The point cloud map after without and with elimination.

Figure 5 shows the point cloud map without and with elimination. In the left picture, we can clearly see the overlapping of dynamic characters, while in the right picture we get the ideal static point cloud image.

In the case that the accuracy remains basically the same, compared to every-frame method, in the half ryp and xyz sequences, the speed of key-frame method has increased by 77.6%, 7.2%, 84.6%, as in Table 4. For the static sequence, nearly half of the frames are created as keyframes, so the time of Yolo-KEY are nearly the same as YOLO-ALL. Note that the segmentation takes more time. Although the system speeds up, on the low-cost platform of our experiment, the real-time still cannot be achieve. One of the main reasons is the detection of keyframes and mappoints creation module are still in the tracking thread. It is more reasonable that a separate thread should be created for dynamic elimination, which will be conducted in our following research.

Table 4. Time evaluation of public TUM dataset.

Seq	ORB-SLAM2	YOLO-ALL		Yolo-KEY		Yolo-KEY-SEG	
Half	0.038	0.389	77.6%	0.219	0.0%	0.638	+191.2%
rpy	0.032	NOT INITIALIZATION		0.275	0.0%	0.776	182.8%
Static	0.030	0.414	−7.2%	0.386	0.0%	1.046	+170.9%
xyz	0.039	0.397	−84.6%	0.215	0.0%	0.631	+192.1%

5   Conclusion

In this paper, a keyframe-based dynamic elimination method using YOLO detection is proposed for SLAM system in dynamic environment. Dynamic detection and removal of keyframes ensure the accuracy by establishing a accurate map and at the same time speed up the system greatly. The method integrated in ORB-SLAM2 system is proved to be effective and efficient by evaluating in the self-generated dataset and the public TUM datasets.

References

1. Sirmaçek, B., Botteghi, N., Khaled, M.: Reinforcement learning and slam based approach for mobile robot navigation in unknown environments. In: ISPRS Workshop Indoor 3D 2019 (2019)
2. Marques, F., Costa, P., Castro, F., Parente, M., et al.: Self-supervised subsea slam for autonomous operations. In: Offshore Technology Conference. Offshore Technology Conference (2019)
3. Liu, R., Zhang, J., Yin, K., Wu, J., Lin, R., Chen, S.: Instant slam initialization for outdoor omnidirectional augmented reality. In: Proceedings of the 31st International Conference on Computer Animation and Social Agents, pp. 66–70. ACM (2018)
4. Sun, Y., Liu, M., Meng, M.Q.H.: Improving RGB-D SLAM in dynamic environments: a motion removal approach. Robot. Auton. Syst. **89**, 110–122 (2017)
5. Sun, Y., Liu, M., Meng, M.Q.H.: Motion removal for reliable RGB-D SLAM in dynamic environments. Robot. Auton. Syst. **108**, 115–128 (2018)
6. Fan, Y., Han, H., Tang, Y., Zhi, T.: Dynamic objects elimination in slam based on image fusion. Pattern Recogn. Lett. (2018)
7. Bescos, B., Fácil, J.M., Civera, J., Neira, J.: DynaSLAM: tracking, mapping, and inpainting in dynamic scenes. IEEE Robot. Autom. Lett. **3**(4), 4076–4083 (2018)
8. Yu, C., et al.: DS-SLAM: a semantic visual slam towards dynamic environments. In: 2018 IEEE/RSJ International Conference on Intelligent Robots and Systems (IROS), pp. 1168–1174. IEEE (2018)
9. Qi, X., Yang, S., Yan, Y.: Deep learning based semantic labelling of 3D point cloud in visual slam. In: IOP Conference Series: Materials Science and Engineering, vol. 428, p. 012023. IOP Publishing (2018)
10. Mur-Artal, R., Tardós, J.D.: ORB-SLAM2: an open-source slam system for monocular, stereo, and RGB-D cameras. IEEE Trans. Rob. **33**(5), 1255–1262 (2017)
11. Girshick, R., Donahue, J., Darrell, T., Malik, J.: Rich feature hierarchies for accurate object detection and semantic segmentation. In: Proceedings of the IEEE Conference on Computer Vision and Pattern Recognition, pp. 580–587 (2014)
12. Girshick, R.: Fast R-CNN. In: Proceedings of the IEEE International Conference on Computer Vision, pp. 1440–1448 (2015)
13. Ren, S., He, K., Girshick, R., Sun, J.: Faster R-CNN: towards real-time object detection with region proposal networks. In: Advances in Neural Information Processing Systems, pp. 91–99 (2015)
14. Redmon, J., Divvala, S., Girshick, R., Farhadi, A.: You only look once: unified, real-time object detection. In: Proceedings of the IEEE Conference on Computer Vision and Pattern Recognition, pp. 779–788 (2016)
15. Liu, W., et al.: SSD: single shot MultiBox detector. In: Leibe, B., Matas, J., Sebe, N., Welling, M. (eds.) ECCV 2016. LNCS, vol. 9905, pp. 21–37. Springer, Cham (2016). https://doi.org/10.1007/978-3-319-46448-0_2

Monocular Visual-Inertial SLAM with Camera-IMU Extrinsic Automatic Calibration and Online Estimation

Linhao Pan$^{(\boxtimes)}$, Fuqing Tian, Wenjian Ying, and Bo She

Department of Weapon, Naval University of Engineering,
Wuhan 430033, Hubei, China
jaypancool@gmail.com

Abstract. An approach of automatic calibration and online estimation for camera-IMU extrinsic parameters in monocular visual-inertial SLAM (Simultaneous Localization and Mapping) is proposed in this paper. Firstly, the camera-IMU extrinsic rotation is estimated with the hand-eye calibration as well as the gyroscope bias. Secondly, the scale factor, gravity and camera-IMU extrinsic translation are approximated without considering the accelerometer bias. All these parameters are refined with the gravitational magnitude and accelerometer bias taken into account at last. Furthermore, the camera-IMU extrinsic parameters are put into state vectors for online estimation. Experiment result with the EuRoC dataset shows that the algorithm automatically calibrates and estimates the camera-IMU extrinsic parameter with the extrinsic orientation and translation's error within 0.5° and 0.02 m separately, which contributes to the rapid use and accuracy of the VI-SLAM system.

Keywords: VI-SLAM · Sensor fusion · Initialization · Extrinsic calibration · State estimation

1 Introduction

VI-SLAM (Visual-Inertial Simultaneous Localization and Mapping) plays an important role in giving autonomous robots the ability to build the map of surroundings as well as estimate their states. Visual camera and inertial measurement unit (IMU) are ideal choice for SLAM since they could complement each other. On the one hand, the rich representation of environments projected by a camera helps to build a map and to estimate the trajectory of the robot up-to-scale. On the other hand, gyroscope and accelerometer of an IMU can obtain the angular velocity and linear acceleration of the sensor suite, which helps to recover the absolute scale information as well as make the gravity and the pitch and roll angle of the robot observable; however, the collected data will be affected by the measurement noise and drift with time [1]. Their superior size, weight and energy consumption make them widely used in the fields of robot navigation [2], UAVs [3] etc.

Recent years, several visual-inertial techniques have been presented in the field, such as the EKF based VI-SLAM [4, 5] algorithm and the nonlinear optimization

© Springer Nature Switzerland AG 2019
H. Yu et al. (Eds.): ICIRA 2019, LNAI 11743, pp. 706–721, 2019.
https://doi.org/10.1007/978-3-030-27538-9_61

methods [6, 7]. However, all the VI-SLAM algorithms depend heavily on accurate system initialization and prior precise extrinsic calibration of the 6DoF (Degree-of-Freedom) transformation between the camera and the IMU. Extrinsic parameters play a bridge role in the state transformation between camera reference frame and IMU reference frame.

At present, there are two main calibration methods for monocular camera-IMU extrinsic parameters: offline method and automatic calibration in system initialization. Offline calibration method requires technicians to carefully move the calibration checkboard in front of the sensor suite [8], which is complex and time-consuming. Automatic calibration in system initialization jointly estimate initial values and extrinsic parameters. Li [9], incorporating the camera-IMU transformation into the state vector, uses the extended Kalman filter (EKF) to estimate them. The convergence of the algorithm depends on the accuracy of the state estimation in initialization, and there is no systematic analysis of the results in the literature. Dong-Si proposed a geometric method to calibrate the camera-IMU extrinsic parameters in [10]. However, this method does not consider the noise of the sensor and tracking accuracy of the system will be affected by the accumulation of IMU bias. Yang and Shen [11], based on Lupton [12] and Martineli [13], calibrate the parameters (except for IMU bias) with an optimization-based linear estimator. The IMU bias is estimated as a state variable in the sliding window nonlinear estimator in their subsequent work of VI-SLAM system [14]. In the work of Huang [15], based on the work of Mur-Artal [16], a linear equation system is established to estimate the camera-IMU extrinsic parameters and other initialization parameters. This method has high initialization accuracy, but the camera-IMU extrinsic parameters become fixed after initialization without online estimation.

In this paper, we realize a VI-SLAM algorithm with monocular camera-IMU extrinsic automatic calibration and online estimation. Without knowing the mechanical configuration of the sensor suite, the scale factor, gravity, IMU biases and extrinsic parameters are jointly estimated in the initialization, as well as online estimation of camera-IMU extrinsic parameters during motion.

The rest of this paper is organized as follows. Section 2 describes the preliminaries of this algorithm. Then the initialization process with camera-IMU extrinsic automatic calibration is proposed in Sect. 3. Section 4 describes online estimation algorithm of camera-IMU extrinsic parameters. Experimental results are shown in Sect. 5. Finally, conclusions are given in Sect. 6.

2 Preliminaries

This section provides the necessary explanations for the notation and geometric concepts involved in this article. In addition, the relationship between reference frames and the IMU preintegration model on manifold are also described.

2.1 Notation

The matrices and vectors used here are indicated in bold uppercase and lowercase respectively. The letter in the upper right corner of the vector indicates the reference frames of the vector, e.g. v^W for the vector v expressed in frame W. Incorporating geometric meaning, p_B^C and v_B^W represent the point p_B and velocity vector v_B in the reference frames C and W respectively. In the frame C, the rotation matrix and translation matrix of the frame B are represented by R_{CB} and T_{CB} respectively.

2.2   Reference Frames

The VI-SLAM system mainly involves four frames: camera frame C, IMU body frame B, world frame W and inertial frame E. As shown in Fig. 1,

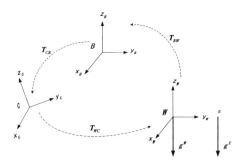

Fig. 1. The Reference frame transformation.

The monocular camera and the IMU are fixed by external devices, and the transformation matrix $T_{CB} = \{R_{CB}|p_B^C\}$ between them needs to be calibrated. Since the VI-SLAM system measures the relative motion, the absolute attitude in the earth's inertial frame E cannot be determined. Therefore, the coordinate system of the first keyframe determined by the VI-SLAM system generally coincides with the world frame W. The goal is to calibrate the rotation matrix $R_{CB} \in SO(3)$ and translation vector $p_B^C \in \mathbb{R}^3$ between camera frame C and IMU body frame B and estimate the gravitational acceleration in the world frame W. By aligning the gravity in the system's world frame g^W with the gravity in the earth's inertial frame g^E, the absolute pose of the system in the inertial frame is determined. Considering the scale factor s, the transformation between camera frame C and IMU body B frame is

$$R_{WB} = R_{WC} \cdot R_{CB} \tag{1}$$

$$p_B^W = s \cdot p_C^W + R_{WC} \cdot p_B^C \tag{2}$$

2.3   Preintegration

The IMU sensor acquires angular velocity and acceleration of the sensor w.r.t. the IMU body frame B at a certain frequency. However, the gyroscope and accelerometer are subject to white sensor noises η_a and η_g, as well as low-frequency drift biases b_a and

b_g. In the case where the initial state of the system is known, the state estimation of the system can be propagated by integrating the IMU measurements. However, this method is based on the initial state. When the nonlinear optimization adjusts system initial state, the integration process needs to be repeated.

To avoid repeated integration, the concept of preintegraed IMU measurement on the manifold space was proposed by Forster et al [17]. Assuming two consecutive keyframes at time i and j, and the IMU measurement value is constant during the sampling interval. So the pose and velocity relationship can be computed by numerical integration of all measurements within this period

$$R_{WB_j} = R_{WB_i} \prod_{k=i}^{j-1} Exp\left(\left(\omega^{B_k} - b_g^k - \eta_g^k\right)\Delta t\right)$$

$$v_{B_j}^W = v_{B_i}^W + g^W \Delta t_{ij} + \sum_{k=i}^{j-1} R_{WB_k}\left(a^{B_k} - b_a^k - \eta_a^k\right)\Delta t \tag{3}$$

$$p_{B_j}^W = p_{B_i}^W + \sum_{k=i}^{j-1}\left(v_{B_k}^W \Delta t + \frac{1}{2}g^W \Delta t^2 + \frac{1}{2}R_{WB_k}\left(a^{B_k} - b_a^k - \eta_a^k\right)\Delta t^2\right)$$

Where Δt denotes the IMU sampling interval, $\Delta t_{ij} = \sum_{i}^{j-1}\Delta t$ represents time interval between two consecutive frames. According to the definition in [17], $Exp(\cdot)$ maps Lie algebra $so(3)$ to Lie group $SO(3)$. When the bias is assumed to remain constant between two image acquisition moments, a small bias correction w.r.t. previously estimated $\bar{b}_{(\cdot)}^i$ could be $\delta b_{(\cdot)}^i$. The Eq. (8) can be rewritten as

$$R_{WB_j} = R_{WB_i} \Delta \bar{R}_{B_iB_j} Exp\left(J_{\Delta \bar{R}_{B_iB_j}}^g \cdot \delta b_g^i\right)$$

$$v_{B_j}^W = v_{B_i}^W + g^W \Delta t_{ij} + R_{WB_i}\left(\Delta \bar{v}_{B_j}^{B_i} + J_{\Delta \bar{v}_{B_j}^{B_i}}^g \cdot \delta b_g^i + J_{\Delta \bar{v}_{B_j}^{B_i}}^a \cdot \delta b_a^i\right) \tag{4}$$

$$p_{B_j}^W = p_{B_i}^W + v_{B_i}^W \Delta t_{ij} + \frac{1}{2}g^W \Delta t_{ij}^2 + R_{WB_i}\left(\Delta \bar{p}_{B_j}^{B_i} + J_{\Delta \bar{p}_{B_j}^{B_i}}^g \cdot \delta b_g^i + J_{\Delta \bar{p}_{B_j}^{B_i}}^a \cdot \delta b_a^i\right)$$

$J_{(\cdot)}^g$ and $J_{(\cdot)}^a$ are Jacobian matrix of preintegration measurements relative to bias estimation, which is deduced in the appendix of paper [17]. $\Delta \bar{R}_{B_iB_j}$, $\Delta \bar{v}_{B_j}^{B_i}$ and $\Delta \bar{p}_{B_j}^{B_i}$ are the terms of preintegration which are independent of the states at time i and the gravity, used to describe the relative motion of two frames

$$\Delta \bar{R}_{B_i B_j} = \prod_{k=i}^{j-1} Exp\left(\left(\omega^{B_k} - \bar{b}_g^i\right)\Delta t\right)$$

$$\Delta \bar{v}_{B_j}^{B_i} = \sum_{k=i}^{j-1} \Delta \bar{R}_{B_i B_k}\left(a^{B_k} - \bar{b}_a^i\right)\Delta t \tag{5}$$

$$\Delta \bar{p}_{B_j}^{B_i} = \sum_{k=i}^{j-1}\left(\Delta \bar{v}_{B_k}^{B_i}\Delta t + \frac{1}{2}\Delta \bar{R}_{B_i B_k}\left(a^{B_k} - \bar{b}_a^i\right)\Delta t^2\right)$$

3 Initialization with Camera-IMU Extrinsic Automatic Calibration

This section elaborates on the initialization method with camera-IMU extrinsic automatic calibration. This method jointly calibrates the camera-IMU extrinsic parameters T_{CB}, as well as estimates factor scale s, gravity acceleration in the world frame g^W, biases of gyroscope and accelerometer b_a and b_g.

3.1 Camera-IMU Extrinsic Orientation Calibration

The extrinsic rotation between the monocular camera and the IMU is very important for the robustness of the VI-SLAM system. Excessive deviation can cause the system initialization to collapse. The hand-eye calibration method is used to align the rotations of the camera with the integrated IMU rotations. Because the monocular camera can track the pose of the system, to detect the relative rotation $R_{C_i C_{i+1}}$ between consecutive frames. In addition, the angular velocity measured by the gyroscope can be integrated to obtain relative rotation $R_{B_i B_{i+1}}$ in the IMU body frame. So it leads to

$$R_{B_i B_{i+1}} \cdot R_{BC} = R_{BC} \cdot R_{C_i C_{i+1}} \tag{6}$$

With the quaternion representation, (6) can be described as

$$q_{B_i B_{i+1}} \otimes q_{BC} = q_{BC} \otimes q_{C_i C_{i+1}}$$
$$\Rightarrow \left[\left[q_{B_i B_{i+1}}\right]_L - \left[q_{C_i C_{i+1}}\right]_R\right] q_{BC} = Q_{i,i+1} \cdot q_{BC} = 0_{4\times 1} \tag{7}$$

Linear over-determined equation can be established for temporally continuous frames

$$
\begin{bmatrix}
\alpha_{0,1} \cdot \boldsymbol{Q}_{0,1} \\
\alpha_{1,2} \cdot \boldsymbol{Q}_{1,2} \\
\vdots \\
\alpha_{N-1,N} \cdot \boldsymbol{Q}_{N-1,N}
\end{bmatrix}
\boldsymbol{q}_{BC} = \boldsymbol{Q}_N \cdot \boldsymbol{q}_{BC} = \boldsymbol{0}
\tag{8}
$$

N indicates the number of frames used when extrinsic rotation converges; $\alpha_{N-1,N}$ is a weight for outlier handling. As the extrinsic rotation calibration runs with incoming measurements, the previously estimated result $\widehat{\boldsymbol{R}}_{BC}$ can be used as the initial value to weight the residual

$$
r_{i,i+1} = \arccos\left(\left(tr\left(\widehat{\boldsymbol{R}}_{BC}^{-1} \boldsymbol{R}_{B_i B_{i+1}}^{-1} \widehat{\boldsymbol{R}}_{BC} \boldsymbol{R}_{C_i C_{i+1}} \right) - 1 \right)/2 \right)
\tag{9}
$$

The weight is a function of the residual

$$
\alpha_{i,i+1} =
\begin{cases}
1, & r_{i,i+1} < t_0 \\
\frac{t_0}{r_{i,i+1}}, & otherwise
\end{cases}
\tag{10}
$$

t_0 is the threshold. The solution to (8) can be found as the right unit singular vector corresponding to the smallest singular value of $\boldsymbol{Q}_N$.

3.2 Gyroscope Bias Estimation

The gyroscope bias can be estimated by the rotation relationship of consecutive keyframes. This paper assumes that the gyroscope bias remains constant in the initialization stage, and the initial gyroscope bias $\overline{b}_g$ is 0.

Substituting the extrinsic rotation matrix $\widehat{\boldsymbol{R}}_{BC}$ estimated in Sect. 3.1 into (4)

$$
\left(\boldsymbol{R}_{WC_i} \cdot \widehat{\boldsymbol{R}}_{CB} \right)^T \left(\boldsymbol{R}_{WC_{i+1}} \cdot \widehat{\boldsymbol{R}}_{CB} \right) = \Delta \overline{\boldsymbol{R}}_{B_i B_{i+1}} Exp\left(\boldsymbol{J}^g_{\Delta \overline{\boldsymbol{R}}_{B_i B_{i+1}}} \cdot \delta b_g \right)
\tag{11}
$$

For all keyframes during initialization, we use the minimum function for bias estimation,

$$
\delta b_g^* = \arg\min_{\delta b_g} \sum_{i=1}^{N-1} \left\| Log\left(\left(\Delta \overline{\boldsymbol{R}}_{B_i B_{i+1}} Exp\left(\boldsymbol{J}^g_{\Delta \overline{\boldsymbol{R}}_{B_i B_{i+1}}} \cdot \delta b_g \right) \right)^T \widehat{\boldsymbol{R}}_{BC} \boldsymbol{R}_{C_i W} \boldsymbol{R}_{WC_{i+1}} \widehat{\boldsymbol{R}}_{CB} \right) \right\|^2
\tag{12}
$$

where $\|\cdot\|$ is the L2-norm, $Log(\cdot)$ is the inverse of $Exp(\cdot)$. $\boldsymbol{R}_{WC_i}$ and $\Delta \overline{\boldsymbol{R}}_{B_i B_{i+1}}$ are known to be obtained by monocular camera pose tracking and preintegration of gyroscope measurements respectively. This equation can be solved with Gauss-Newton algorithm. The final estimated gyroscope bias is $b_g = \overline{b}_g + \delta b_g^* = \delta b_g^*$.

3.3   Scale, Gravity and Translation Approximation Without Accelerometer Bias

Once the gyroscope bias has been estimated, the preintegrations can be rectified by Eq. (5). And continue to estimate the scale factor s, gravity g^W and extrinsic translation p_B^C approximately. Since the gravity and accelerometer bias are hard to be distinguished, accelerometer bias is not considered in this stage. So the $J^a_{\Delta \bar{v}_{B_j}^{B_i}}$ and $J^a_{\Delta \bar{p}_{B_j}^{B_i}}$ can be set to zero. Substituting Eq. (2) into the third equation of Eq. (4), the relationship of two consecutive keyframes can be obtained,

$$
\begin{aligned}
s \cdot p_{C_{i+1}}^W &= s \cdot p_{C_i}^W + v_{B_i}^W \cdot \Delta t_{i,i+1} + \frac{1}{2} g^W \cdot \Delta t_{i,i+1}^2 \\
&\quad + R_{WC_i} \cdot \widehat{R}_{CB} \cdot \Delta \bar{p}_{B_{i+1}}^{B_i} + \left(R_{WC_i} - R_{WC_{i+1}} \right) p_B^C
\end{aligned}
\tag{13}
$$

The goal is to estimate s, g^W and p_B^C. Using two relations between three consecutive keyframes to eliminate velocities $v_{B_i}^W$, which leads to the following expression:

$$
\begin{bmatrix} \lambda(i) & \beta(i) & \varphi(i) \end{bmatrix}
\begin{bmatrix} s \\ g^W \\ p_B^C \end{bmatrix} = \gamma(i)
\tag{14}
$$

Writing the subscript i, $i+1$, $i+2$ as 1, 2, 3, we have:

$$
\lambda(i) = \left(p_{C_3}^W - p_{C_2}^W \right) \Delta t_{12} + \left(p_{C_1}^W - p_{C_2}^W \right) \Delta t_{23}
$$

$$
\beta(i) = -\frac{1}{2} \left(\Delta t_{12}^2 \Delta t_{23} + \Delta t_{23}^2 \Delta t_{12} \right) \mathbf{I}_{3 \times 3}
$$

$$
\varphi(i) = \left(R_{WC_3} - R_{WC_2} \right) \Delta t_{12} + \left(R_{WC_1} - R_{WC_2} \right) \Delta t_{23}
$$

$$
\begin{aligned}
\gamma(i) &= R_{WC_1} \cdot \widehat{R}_{CB} \cdot \Delta \bar{v}_{B_2}^{B_1} \Delta t_{12} \Delta t_{23} + R_{WC_2} \cdot \widehat{R}_{CB} \cdot \Delta \bar{p}_{B_3}^{B_2} \Delta t_{12} \\
&\quad - R_{WC_1} \cdot \widehat{R}_{CB} \cdot \Delta \bar{p}_{B_2}^{B_1} \Delta t_{23}
\end{aligned}
\tag{15}
$$

For N consecutive keyframes, a linear over-determined equation $A_{3(N-2) \times 7} \cdot x_{7 \times 1} = B_{3(N-2) \times 1}$ can be stacked. $\hat{s}$, $\hat{g}^W$, $\hat{p}_B^C$ can be solved by SVD decomposition. Note that there are $3(N-2)$ linear constraints and 7 unknowns, so at least 5 keyframes is required to solve the equation.

3.4   Accelerometer Bias Estimation, and Scale, Gravity and Translation Refinement

Assuming the gravity g^E in the inertial frame E is known, and $G = 9.8$ represents the magnitude of the gravitational acceleration as well as $\bar{g}^E = (0, 0, -1)$ represents its direction. It is stipulated that the earth's inertial frame E coincides with the origin of the world frame W, the rotation R_{WE} between them can be computed as follows, shown in Fig. 2:

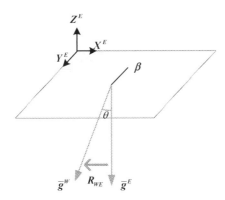

Fig. 2. Diagram of gravity acceleration direction angle.

$$R_{WE} = Exp(\theta\boldsymbol{\beta})$$

$$\boldsymbol{\beta} = \frac{\bar{g}^E \times \bar{g}^W}{\|\bar{g}^E \times \bar{g}^W\|}, \theta = \operatorname{atan2}\left(\|\bar{g}^E \times \bar{g}^W\|, \bar{g}^E \cdot \bar{g}^W\right) \tag{16}$$

As $\bar{g}^W = \hat{g}^W / \|\hat{g}^W\|$ represents the gravity direction in the world frame W estimated in Sect. 3.3. This rotation can be optimized by appending perturbation $\delta\boldsymbol{\theta} \in \mathbb{R}^{3 \times 1}$:

$$\boldsymbol{g}^W = R_{WE} \cdot Exp(\delta\boldsymbol{\theta})\boldsymbol{g}^E \approx R_{WE} \cdot \boldsymbol{g}^E - R_{WE}(\boldsymbol{g}^E)^\wedge \delta\boldsymbol{\theta}$$

$$\delta\boldsymbol{\theta} = \left[\delta\boldsymbol{\theta}_{xy}^T, 0\right]^T, \delta\boldsymbol{\theta}_{xy} = \left[\delta\boldsymbol{\theta}_x, \delta\boldsymbol{\theta}_y\right]^T \tag{17}$$

Substituting Eq. (17) into Eq. (13) and including the effect of accelerometer bias, we have:

$$
\begin{aligned}
s \cdot \boldsymbol{p}_{C_{i+1}}^W =\ & s \cdot \boldsymbol{p}_{C_i}^W + \boldsymbol{v}_{B_i}^W \Delta t_{i,i+1} - \frac{1}{2} R_{WE}(\boldsymbol{g}^E)^\wedge \delta\boldsymbol{\theta} \cdot \Delta t_{i,i+1}^2 \\
& + R_{WC_i} \cdot \widehat{R}_{CB}\left(\Delta \bar{\boldsymbol{p}}_{B_{i+1}}^{B_i} + J_{\Delta \bar{\boldsymbol{p}}_{B_{i+1}}^{B_i}}^a \cdot \delta b_a\right) + \left(R_{WC_i} - R_{WC_{i+1}}\right)\boldsymbol{p}_B^C \\
& + \frac{1}{2} R_{WE} \cdot \boldsymbol{g}^E \cdot \Delta t_{i,i+1}^2
\end{aligned}
\tag{18}
$$

Considering the constraints between three consecutive keyframes as well, we can construct the following linear equations:

$$
\begin{bmatrix} \lambda(i) & \alpha(i) & \phi(i) & \varphi(i) \end{bmatrix}
\begin{bmatrix} s \\ \delta\theta_{xy} \\ \delta b_a \\ p_B^C \end{bmatrix} = \chi(i)
\tag{19}
$$

Where $\lambda(i), \varphi(i)$ remains the same as Eq. (15), $\alpha(i), \phi(i), \chi(i)$ are computed as follow:

$$
\alpha(i) = \left[\frac{1}{2} R_{WE} (g^E)^\wedge \left(\Delta t_{12}^2 \Delta t_{23} + \Delta t_{23}^2 \Delta t_{12} \right) \right]_{(:,1:2)}
$$

$$
\phi(i) = R_{WC_1} \cdot \widehat{R}_{CB} \cdot J^a_{\Delta \bar{p}_{B_2}^{B_1}} \Delta t_{23} - R_{WC_2} \cdot \widehat{R}_{CB} \cdot J^a_{\Delta \bar{p}_{B_3}^{B_2}} \Delta t_{12}
$$

$$
\quad - R_{WC_1} \cdot \widehat{R}_{CB} \cdot J^a_{\Delta \bar{v}_{B_2}^{B_1}} \Delta t_{12} \Delta t_{23}
$$

$$
\chi(i) = R_{WC_2} \cdot \widehat{R}_{CB} \cdot \Delta \bar{p}_{B_3}^{B_2} \Delta t_{12} + R_{WC_1} \cdot \widehat{R}_{CB} \cdot \Delta \bar{v}_{B_2}^{B_1} \Delta t_{12} \Delta t_{23}
$$

$$
\quad + \frac{1}{2} R_{WE} \cdot g^E \left(\Delta t_{12}^2 \Delta t_{23} + \Delta t_{12} \Delta t_{23}^2 \right) - R_{WC_1} \cdot \widehat{R}_{CB} \cdot \Delta \bar{p}_{B_2}^{B_1} \Delta t_{23}
\tag{20}
$$

$[\cdot]_{(:,1:2)}$ in the $\alpha(i)$ means the first two columns of the matrix.

Similar to above, a linear over-determined equation $A_{3(N-2)\times 9} \cdot x_{9\times 1} = B_{3(N-2)\times 1}$ can be constructed to calculate the δb_a^*, s^*, $\delta\theta_{xy}^*$ and p_B^{C*}. Since the initial accelerometer bias is also set to zero, the final estimated accelerometer bias is $\hat{b}_a = \overline{b}_a + \delta b_a^* = \delta b_a^*$. What's more, the gravity in the world frame is adjusted by incorporating perturbation, i.e. $g^{W*} = R_{WE} \cdot Exp(\delta\theta^*)g^E$.

4   Camera-IMU Extrinsic Online Estimation

Through the initialization process with camera-IMU extrinsic calibration, an accurate extrinsic parameter could be estimated. However, during the movement of system, the mechanical configuration of the sensor suite changes slightly. Fixed camera-IMU extrinsic parameters can hardly track this change, which leads to system error affecting the tracking accuracy and robustness of the system. With regards to this, we put the camera-IMU extrinsic parameters into the state vectors for online estimation.

4.1   States and Factor Graph Representation

During the motion of the VI-SLAM system, the states to be estimated in each frame include pose, velocity and IMU biases of the sensor suite. On this basis, the camera-IMU extrinsic parameters are also put into the state vector for online estimation. Defining the IMU body frame as the frame to be estimated, the states to be estimated in each image frame is $\left\{ p_{B_i}^W, R_{WB_i}, v_{B_i}^W, b_g^i, b_a^i, R_{CB}, p_B^C \right\}$. In addition to these, the location of the k th landmark point $l_k^W \in \mathbb{R}^3$ is also included in the states. Using factor graph to describe the constraint relationship between these states, the representation of the VI-SLAM system with the camera-IMU extrinsic parameters online estimation is:

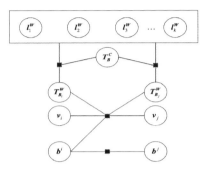

Fig. 3. Factor graph of VI-SLAM system.

As shown in the Fig. 3, the circles represent the variables to be estimated, and squares are the factors. So there are three kinds of constraint in the VI-SLAM system:

(1) Each image pose, camera-IMU extrinsic parameters and landmark point have graph feature position observation constraint;
(2) Poses, velocities and IMU biases of consecutive frames have preintegration constraint of IMU measurements;
(3) IMU biases of consecutive frames have IMU bias random walk constraint.

Therefore, the camera-IMU extrinsic parameters are limited by the graph feature position observation constraint. To estimate it online, it's necessary to construct a nonlinear estimation function of the graph feature position observation constrain.

4.2   Graph Feature Constraint and Its Jacobian

Assuming the states of the frame i is $\left\{ p_{B_i}^W, R_{WB_i}, v_{B_i}^W, b_g^i, b_a^i, R_{CB}, p_B^C \right\}$, and the landmark point k's position in the world frame is l_k^W. The feature position observed on the frame i of the landmark point k is $\hat{p}_{i,k}$ with the uncertainty of one pixel. Pinhole projection model projects the landmark point l_k^W as the pixel $p_{i,k}$.

So the reprojection error $e_{i,k}$ of the graph feature position constraint is:

$$
\begin{aligned}
e_{i,k} &= \hat{p}_{i,k} - \frac{1}{z_C} K[I_3 \; 0_{3\times 1}] \begin{bmatrix} l_k^C \\ 1 \end{bmatrix} \\
&= \hat{p}_{i,k} - \frac{1}{z_C} K[I_3 \; 0_{3\times 1}] T_{CB} \begin{bmatrix} R_{WB_i} & p_{B_i}^W \\ 0 & 1 \end{bmatrix}^{-1} \begin{bmatrix} l_k^W \\ 1 \end{bmatrix}
\end{aligned}
\tag{21}
$$

$K^{2\times3}$ is the camera intrinsic matrix; the three components of l_k^C (landmark k's position in the camera frame C) is x_C, y_C, z_C; l_k^C can be calculated:

$$l_k^C = R_{CB}R_{WB_i}^{-1}\left(l_k^W - p_{B_i}^W\right) + p_B^C \tag{22}$$

According to Eq. (21), the reprojection error $e_{i,k}$'s Jacobian w.r.t. l_k^C is:

$$\frac{\partial e_{i,k}}{\partial l_k^C} = - \begin{bmatrix} \frac{f_x}{z_C} & 0 & -\frac{f_x x_C}{z_C^2} \\ 0 & \frac{f_y}{z_C} & -\frac{f_y y_C}{z_C^2} \end{bmatrix} \tag{23}$$

f_x, f_y, c_x, c_y are parameters of intrinsic matrix K.

In this way, the rejection error $e_{i,k}$ w.r.t. camera-IMU extrinsic translation is:

$$\begin{aligned}
\frac{\partial e_{i,k}}{\partial \delta p} &= \frac{\partial e_{i,k}}{\partial l_k^C} \cdot \frac{\partial l_k^C}{\partial \delta p} \\
&= - \begin{bmatrix} \frac{f_x}{z_C} & 0 & -\frac{f_x x_C}{z_C^2} \\ 0 & \frac{f_y}{z_C} & -\frac{f_y y_C}{z_C^2} \end{bmatrix} R_{CB}
\end{aligned} \tag{24}$$

Similarly, rejection error $e_{i,k}$ w.r.t. camera-IMU extrinsic rotation is:

$$\begin{aligned}
\frac{\partial e_{i,k}}{\partial \delta \theta} &= \frac{\partial e_{i,k}}{\partial l_k^C} \cdot \frac{\partial l_k^C}{\partial \delta \theta} \\
&= \begin{bmatrix} \frac{f_x}{z_C} & 0 & -\frac{f_x x_C}{z_C^2} \\ 0 & \frac{f_y}{z_C} & -\frac{f_y y_C}{z_C^2} \end{bmatrix} \left[R_{CB}R_{WB_i}^{-1}\left(l_k^W - p_{B_i}^W\right)\right]^{\wedge} R_{CB}
\end{aligned} \tag{25}$$

At this point, the camera-IMU extrinsic parameters can be estimated online based on the residual constraint and the Jacobian.

5   Experimental Evaluation

In this section, performances of our VI-SLAM algorithm with camera-IMU extrinsic calibration and online estimation are estimated on the EuRoC dataset which provides accurate position ground-truth and camera-IMU extrinsic parameters. Eleven sequence, recorded with a Micro Aerial Vehicle (MAV), are divided into three levels: simple, medium and difficult according to different speeds of the aircrafts, illumination, image blur and environment texture. All the experiments are carried out with an Intel CPU i7-5500U (3.0 GHz) laptop computer with 4 GB RAM.

5.1   Implementation Details

The extrinsic rotation calibration is placed in the Tracking thread of the ORB-SLAM, because it's easily excited. The rest the initialization method is implemented in the Local Mapping thread, between the Local BA module and the Local Keyframes Culling module. Considering there are not enough observations to limit the camera-IMU extrinsic parameters in the tracking thread, the camera-IMU extrinsic online estimation is executed in the Local BA module. Since the convergence judgment condition is set only for the extrinsic rotation calibration, the time of the remaining initialization method is set to 23 s.

5.2   Initialization Results

Under the experimental condition of this paper, the initialization and camera-IMU extrinsic estimation results are evaluated using the V2_01_easy sequence of the EuRoC dataset. Figures 4 and 5 show the process of camera-IMU extrinsic rotation calibration. The singular values to Eq. (8) become larger as time goes by (Fig. 4). When the second smallest singular value σ_2 reaches the set threshold $\sigma_{thr} = 0.25$, the process is achieved. A convergence plot of the yaw, pitch and roll can be found in Fig. 5 to their benchmark $[89.147953°, 1.476930°, 0.215286°]$.

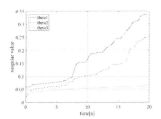

Fig. 4. Time varied singular value.

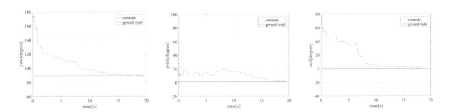

Fig. 5. Process of extrinsic rotation calibration.

The process of camera-IMU extrinsic translation, gyroscope bias, accelerometer bias, scale factor and gravity in world frame is shown in Figs. 6, 7 and 8. Each state quantity begins to converge between 5 s and 10 s after running. The extrinsic translation calibrated will have a few centimeters of error in each axis to its standard $[-0.021, -0.064, 0.009]$m.

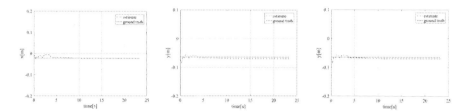

Fig. 6. Process of extrinsic translation calibration.

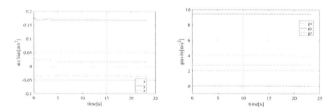

Fig. 7. Process of gyroscope bias and accelerometer bias calibration.

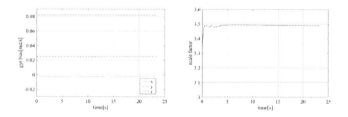

Fig. 8. Process of gravity and scale factor calibration.

5.3   Extrinsic Estimation Results

Figures 9 and 10 illustrate the online estimation process of the camera-IMU extrinsic parameters. During the online estimation process, the deviation of the extrinsic rotation in three axial directions fluctuates within $0.5°$ and the deviation of the extrinsic translation in three axial directions fluctuates within 0.02 m.

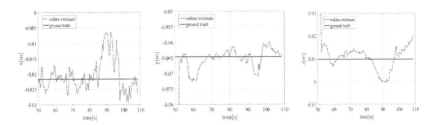

Fig. 9. Process of extrinsic rotation online estimation.

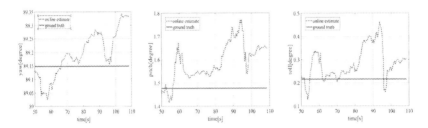

Fig. 10. Process of extrinsic rotation calibration.

Using the V2_01_easy dataset, ten trials for our method, linear and nonlinear processes of VINS-Mono are conducted in Fig. 11. It is observed that the extrinsic rotation calibrated from our method and VINS-Mono' linear process deviates from the benchmark greatly, because we both do not take the gyroscope bias into account. However, our calibrated extrinsic translation is more consistent and accurate than VINS-Mono's linear estimation as we considering the influence of IMU bias. After our online estimation of the extrinsic parameters and VINS-Mono's nonlinear optimization, both camera-IMU extrinsic rotation and translation achieve high precision and consistency. The estimated error of the camera-IMU extrinsic rotation and translation obtained by the method proposed by use, is within 0.5° and 0.02 m separately.

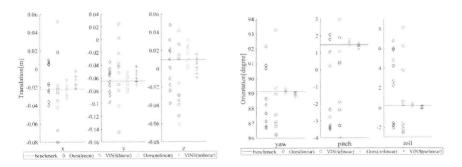

Fig. 11. Process of extrinsic rotation calibration.

6 Conclusion

In this paper, we propose a VI-SLAM algorithm with camera-IMU extrinsic automatic calibration and online estimation without knowing the mechanical configuration of the sensor suite. Compare to VIORB which need prior precise extrinsic calibration, our method is a plug-and-play solution for mobile robots. Through the experiment of EuRoC dataset, the performance of the proposed algorithm in camera-IMU extrinsic calibration and online estimation is verified. The error of the estimated extrinsic rotation and translation is within $0.5°$ and 0.02 m separately. Compare to VINS-Mono, our method achieves comparable or higher precision and consistency. A limitation of our method is the long time (about 35 s) for the convergence of the extrinsic calibration. To overcome this, we plan to set judgment of convergence in our future work.

References

1. Martinelli, A.: Vision and IMU data fusion: closed-form solutions for attitude, speed, absolute scale and bias determination. IEEE Trans. Robot. **28**(1), 44–60 (2012)
2. Liu, H., Wang, Z., Chen, P.: Feature points selection with flocks of features constraint for visual simultaneous localization and mapping. Int. J. Adv. Robot. Syst. **14**(1), 1–11 (2016)
3. Lin, Y., Gao, F., Qin, T., et al.: Autonomous aerial navigation using monocular visual-inertial fusion. J. Field Robot. **35**(1), 23–51 (2017)
4. Li, M., Mourikis, A.: Improving the accuracy of EKF-based visual-inertial odometry. In: 2012 IEEE International Conference on Robotics and Automation, pp. 828–835. IEEE (2012)
5. Tanskanen, P., Naegeli, T., Pollefeys, M., et al.: Semi-direct EKF-based monocular visual-inertial odometry. In: 2015 IEEE/RSJ International Conference on Intelligent Robots and Systems, pp. 6073–6075. IEEE (2015)
6. Leutenegger, S., Lynen, S., Bosse, M., et al.: Keyframe-based visual-inertial odometry using nonlinear optimization. Int. J. Robot. Res. **34**(3), 314–334 (2015)
7. Lin, H., Lv, Q., Wang, G., et al.: Robust stereo visual-inertial SLAM using nonlinear optimization. Robot **40**(6), 911–920 (2018)
8. Rehder, J., Siegwart, R.: Camera/IMU calibration revisited. IEEE Sens. J. **17**(11), 3257–3268 (2017)
9. Li, M., Mourikis, A.: High-precision, consistent EKF-based visual-inertial odometry. Int. J. Robot. Res. **32**(6), 690–711 (2013)
10. Dong-Si, T.C., Mourikis, A.I.: Estimator initialization in vision-aided inertial navigation with unknown camera-IMU calibration. In: 2012 IEEE/RSJ International Conference on Intelligent Robots and Systems, pp. 1064–1071. IEEE, Algarve (2012)
11. Yang, S.: Monocular visual-inertial state estimation with online initialization and camera-IMU extrinsic calibration. IEEE Trans. Autom. Sci. Eng. **14**(1), 39–51 (2017)
12. Lupton, S.: Visual-inertial-aided navigation for high-dynamic motion in built environments without initial conditions. IEEE Trans. Robot. **28**(1), 61–76 (2012)
13. Martinelli, A.: Closed-form solution of visual-inertial structure from motion. Int. J. Comput. Vis. **106**(2), 138–152 (2014)
14. Qin, T., Li, P., Shen, S.: VINS-mono: a robust and versatile monocular visual-inertial state estimator. IEEE Trans. Robot. **34**, 1–17 (2018)

15. Huang, W., Liu, H.: Online initialization and automatic camera-IMU extrinsic calibration for monocular visual-inertial SLAM. In: 2018 IEEE International Conference on Robotics and Automation, pp. 5182–5189. IEEE, Brisbane (2018)
16. Mur-Artal, T.: Visual-inertial monocular SLAM with map reuse. IEEE Robot. Autom. Lett. **2**(2), 796–803 (2016)
17. Forster, C., Carlone, L., Dellaert, F., et al.: On-manifold preintegration for real-time visual-inertial odometry. IEEE Trans. Robot. **33**(1), 1–21 (2015)

An Online Motion Planning Approach of Mobile Robots in Distinctive Homotopic Classes by a Sparse Roadmap

Xiaoyuan Zhang, Biao Zhang, Chenkun Qi[(✉)], Zhousu Li, and Huayang Li

School of Mechanical Engineering, Shanghai Jiao Tong University, Shanghai 200240, China
xiaoyuanzh@163.com,
{biaozhang,chenkqi,zhousuli,huayangli}@sjtu.edu.cn

Abstract. This paper presents a novel approach for online motion planning of mobile robots in distinctive homotopic classes. The approach contains two parts. Firstly, a local planner called TC-SQP (timed control and sequential quadratic programming) is proposed. An optimal trajectory is deformed from an initial path from a global planner, considering collision avoidance, time optimality and kino-dynamic constraints. Our approach takes the control variables rather than position variables as optimization variables in a time horizon. Hence, TC-SQP requires fewer optimization variables (3/4 comparing to the state-of-art method) and parameters. And the transition time is reduced by 14% from the global path. Then, to overcome the issue that there exist several trajectories of local minimum cost, a candidate of global paths of different homotopic classes is maintained by using a sparse graph spanner. These global paths are optimized in parallel, and the lowest cost trajectory is selected as the final trajectory. Our method can generate enough homotopic candidates, and it needs much fewer queries comparing with a Probability Road Map. Besides the simulations, some results are also proved theoretically.

Keywords: Online motion planning · Homotopic classes · Sparse graph · Mobile robots

1 Introduction

In the field of service robotics, rescue robotics and autonomous transport systems, mobile robots are required to navigate autonomously in an unstructured and dynamic environment. So, it is necessary to design a navigation framework for the mobile robots. Nowadays, this navigation problem is usually divided into two layers. A global planner like A^* is used to generate a rough path and give a local goal for the local planning layer. Then an online local planner generates a collision free and kino-dynamic feasible trajectory towards this local goal. An online local planner is preferred because it can response immediately to dynamic changes of the environment, relocate the robot when a perturbation occurs and generate kino-dynamic feasible controls. The Dynamic Window Approach (DWA) [1] approach, as an early local planner, can

© Springer Nature Switzerland AG 2019
H. Yu et al. (Eds.): ICIRA 2019, LNAI 11743, pp. 722–734, 2019.
https://doi.org/10.1007/978-3-030-27538-9_62

generate a sequence of control samples depending on the robot current position and velocity. The simulated trajectories are often evaluated by a human-designed criterion, considering the time-optimality and deviations from the global path. However, the DWA approach is hard to by-pass an unexpected obstacle since it is rather short-sighted. Its total sampling number grows exponentially with the sampling horizon.

The famous Elastic Band (EB) [2], as a gradient descent method, deforms the global path online. Repulsive forces make the path deviate from obstacles and internal forces contract the path. Kurniawati et al. [3] extended the EB approach by incorporating EB with temporal information to deal with kino-dynamic constraints. Rösmann et al. [4, 5] proposed a method called Timed-Elastic-Band (TEB) by further extending EB. The TEB method can optimize the robot trajectory with kino-dynamic constraints and non-holonomic constraints, while the temporal information is used to achieve a time-optimal trajectory. Gu et al. [6], Lau et al. [7] and Shrunk et al. [8] optimized the trajectory using splines model considering kino-dynamic constraints.

In this paper, a novel approach is proposed. The main feature is that the control variables rather than trajectories are used as optimized variables. A vector called augmented controls is defined, and this vector is optimized in order to get a time-optimal trajectory which keeps a given distance from obstacles. However, the TEB method takes trajectories as optimized variables, which is solved by exploiting the sparse structure of its underlying problem. However, this sparse structure (i.e. approximated Hessian matrix) is formed by using extra optimized variables (4N). In contrast, our method only needs 3N optimized variables and most of constraints are linear constraints.

In practice, all of the optimization problems in the above methods including EB [2], TEB [4] and the proposed method in this paper are solved by local optimization methods. In an environment with a lot of obstacles, the optimal trajectory is significantly affected by an initial path of distinctive homotopic class.

Kuderer et al. [9] and Rösmann [10] proposed a two-stage method by first exploring distinctive homotopic classes in a *Voronoi Graph*, then filtering only one path in each homotopic class. However, the size of a *Voronoi Graph* grows exponentially w.r.t the number of obstacles. Hence, it is impossible to explore a *Voronoi Graph* in real-time when the environment is occupied with many obstacles.

Schmitzberger et al. [11] and Jaillet et al. [12] proposed an off-line exploration method by using a Probability Road Map (PRM) [13]. Rösmann in [10] used an additional criteria to the PRM in order to make the PRM smaller. Hence, a real-time query is possible. But the processed PRM is still very large, and the criteria to process a PRM is pretty human-designed.

To distinguish a homotopic class, Bhattacharya et al. [14] proposed a method to classify homotopic equivalent relationships by $\mathcal{H}$-Signature from complexity analysis. Pokorny et al. [15] proposed a method which doesn't require an explicit expression of the robot configuration space by simplicial complexes. Since we have an explicit expression of the robot configuration space, $\mathcal{H}$-Signature is used in this paper.

Our method exploring homotopic classes also depends on a PRM. The difference is that we search homotopic classes by using a sparse roadmap. A sparse roadmap only has around 1/4 edges comparing with the original PRM. But it can guarantee a near-optimal path. A sparse roadmap is first proposed in [16] to prevent the PRM growing too large for single path query problems. In this paper, we use a sparse roadmap to generate paths of distinctive homotopic classes.

This paper is organized as follows. In Sect. 2.1, we propose our method called TC-SQP from a given initial path. In Sect. 2.2 and Sect. 2.3, we explore distinctive homotopic classes by a sparse graph. In Sect. 2.4, we integrate TC-SQP method with homotopic awareness. This integrated method is called TC-SQP-HC in this paper. Simulation results are illustrated in Sect. 3. Section 4 summarizes the results.

2 Online Trajectory Planning

2.1 TC-SQP Local Trajectory Planning

The local trajectory planning problem is dealt as an optimization problem by taking control variables U and control time T as optimization variables. And this problem will be solved by SQP method. Hence, our proposed planner is called Timed-Control-Sequential-Quadratic-Planning (TC-SQP) in this paper. U is defined as a vector composed with the translation and angular velocity $u_i = [v_i, \omega_i]$ in a time horizon of length N

$$U = [v_1, \omega_1, , \ldots, v_N, \omega_N]^T$$

and $\mathcal{T}$ is defined as a vector of control time ΔT_i the control u_i takes.

$$\mathcal{T} = [\Delta T_1, \Delta T_2 \ldots \Delta T_N]^T$$

We denote the timed control $\mathfrak{A}$ as an augmented vector combined with U and $\mathcal{T}$, that is $\mathfrak{A} = [U\mathcal{T}]$.

Given a start position of the robot $s_{start} = [x_1, y_1, \theta_1]^T$, the trajectory of the robot can be simulated by the following difference equation

$$\begin{cases} x_{k+1} = x_k + v_k cos(\theta_k)\Delta T_k \\ y_{k+1} = y_k + v_k sin(\theta_k)\Delta T_k \\ \theta_{k+1} = \theta_k + \omega_k \Delta T_k \end{cases} \tag{1}$$

Let Γ denote the trajectory of the robot

$$\Gamma = [x_1, y_1, \theta_1, \ldots, x_{N+1}, y_{N+1}, \theta_{N+1}] \tag{2}$$

and let Traj$(.,.)$ denote a function such that $\Gamma = $ Traj$(s_{start}, \mathfrak{A})$ and Ctrl$(.,.)$ be the inverse function of Traj$(.,.)$, such that $\mathfrak{A} = $ Ctrl(s_{start}, Γ).

Formally, the local trajectory planning is defined as Problem A, which minimizes an objective function with some constraints.

Problem A

$$U^* = \operatorname*{argmin}_{U} J(\mathfrak{A})$$

$$s.t. \begin{cases} U_{lb} \leq U \leq U_{ub} \\ T_{lb} \leq T \leq T_{ub} \\ U_{acc_{lb}} \leq D_1 U \leq U_{acc_{ub}} \\ c(\mathfrak{A}) = 0_{2\times 1} \end{cases} \tag{3}$$

The objective function $J(\mathfrak{A})$ denotes a cost function containing two parts: (1) the collision avoidance term $J_{obst}(\mathfrak{A})$ to punish the minimal distance from obstacles to the trajectory Γ of the robot; (2) the optimal time term $J_{time}(\mathfrak{A}) = \sum \Delta T_i^2$ (Fig. 1).

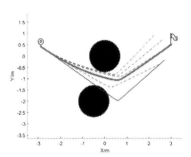

Fig. 1. Illustration of Problem A. The dashed lines show the process of the iterations. Even the goal of the initial trajectory is far from a desired trajectory.

U_{ub} denotes the vector of maximal control, U_{acc_ub} denotes the maximal variation of control, and D_1 denotes the first-order difference matrix as in [17]. All the linear constraints together are denoted as $A(\mathfrak{A}_i + d_i) \leq 0$. A non-linear constraint $c(\mathfrak{A})$ is used to make the robot arrive at a given goal.

Both terms contain a cost weight. Our cost weight scheduling strategy is similar to that used in [17]. In the early stage, most of weight is given to the collision avoidance term.

It is noticed that, the optimal time term is a quadratic function w.r.t the optimization variable $\mathfrak{A}$ and most constraints (10N) are just linear constraints. Hence the Sequential Quadratic Programming (SQP) method can be used to solve Problem A.

Formally, we introduce the Lagrange function of Problem A

$$\mathcal{L}\mathfrak{A}, \mu, \lambda = J(\mathfrak{A}) - \mu c(\mathfrak{A}) - \lambda(A\mathfrak{A} - b) \tag{4}$$

and Lagrange multipliers μ and λ. In each iteration, a local quadratic programming is solved as follows

$$\min_{d_i} \frac{1}{2} d_i^T \nabla^2 H_i d_i + \nabla J_i^T d_i$$

$$s.t. \begin{cases} \nabla c(\mathfrak{A}_i)^T d_i + c(\mathfrak{A}_i) = 0 \\ A(\mathfrak{A}_i + d_i) \le 0 \end{cases} \tag{5}$$

until $|\mathfrak{A}_{i+1} - \mathfrak{A}_i| < \varepsilon$. The Lagrange Hessian matrix $\nabla^2 H_i$ is updated by the BFGS formula. The initial value $\mathfrak{A}_0$ for Problem A is from the initial path Γ_0

$$\mathfrak{A}_0 = \mathrm{Ctrl}(s_{start}, \Gamma_0).$$

2.2   Homotopic Classes

The following sections solve the problem of finding the global optimal trajectory defined in Sect. 2.1. Our method needs some definitions from Algebraic Topology.

Definition 1 (Homotopic Trajectories)
Let Γ_1 and Γ_2 be two trajectories connecting the same start position s_{strat} and goal position s_{end}. Γ_1 and Γ_2 belong to the same homotopic class iff they can be deformed to each other without touching any obstacles. Γ_1 and Γ_2 are called *homotopic equivalent* if they belong to the same homotopic class. The set of all homotopic class is defined all collision free trajectories quotient such equivalent relationship (Fig. 2).

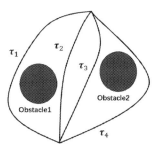

Fig. 2. Homotopic trajectories. τ_2 and τ_3 are of the same homotopic class. τ_1, τ_2, τ_4 are of the different homotopic classes.

With such definition, we can prove that the optimal trajectory solved in Sect. 2.1 is at most a sub-optimal trajectory.

Theorem 1 (Sub-Optimality in One Homotopic Class)
After solving Problem A in Sect. 2.1. The optimal trajectory $\Gamma^* = Traj(s_{start}, \mathfrak{A}^*)$ and $\Gamma_0 = \mathrm{Traj}(s_{start}, \mathfrak{A}_0)$ will belong to the same homotopic class.

Assumption 1
If the distance between the trajectory to the obstacles is less than a threshold ϵ, $J(\mathfrak{A}) \approx J_{obst}(\mathfrak{A})$. This assumption is quite reasonable, because the principal requirement for the trajectory is that it should be collision free. If the distance between the trajectory to the obstacle is far enough, then more cost weights are given to other terms in the cost function $J(\mathfrak{A})$.

Assumption 2
The norm maximal update step is less than ϵ, that is

$$|\mathfrak{A}_{i+1} - \mathfrak{A}_i| < \epsilon.$$

Proof
With the Assumption 2, before the trajectory is to pass through an obstacle, there exists a step such that the distance to the obstacles is less than ϵ. In that time, we have $\nabla J \approx \nabla J_{obst}$. At the same time, with the BFGS formulation, $\nabla^2 H_i$ is always a positive definite matrix. Hence, $\nabla \mathcal{F} d_i < 0$, which means that the trajectory always deviates from the closest obstacle if the distance to the obstacles is small.

In the 2D plane, a homotopic invariant $\mathcal{H}$-Signature can indicate that those trajectories belong to the same homotopic class. More discussions are presented in [14]. A trajectory

$$\Gamma = [s_1, s_2, \ldots s_k, \ldots s_{N+1}]$$

can be represented by a series of points

$$\tilde{\Gamma} = [z_1, z_2, \ldots z_k, \ldots z_{N+1}]$$

on the complex plane, where

$$z_k = x_k + iy_k \in \mathbb{C}$$

The homotopic invariant $\mathcal{H}(\tilde{\Gamma})$ is defined by

$$\mathcal{H}(\tilde{\Gamma}) = \int_{z_1}^{N+1} F(z)dz \tag{7}$$

where

$$F(z) = \frac{1}{\prod_j (z - \zeta_j)} \tag{8}$$

and ζ_i denotes the position of the i-th obstacle on the complex plane. By the Cauthy Residual Theorem

$$\mathcal{H}(\tilde{\Gamma}_1) - \mathcal{H}(\tilde{\Gamma}_2) = 2\pi i \sum_j Res(F, \zeta_j) \tag{9}$$

it indicates that the $\mathcal{H}$-Signature of two trajectories are same iff they belong to the same homotopic class. In our method, the trajectory is discretized by $N+1$ points. We use an approximation value of Eq. (7)

$$\mathcal{H}(\tilde{\Gamma}) \approx \sum_{l=1}^{N+1} \mathcal{H}_{dis}(z_l, z_{l+1}) \tag{10}$$

The following equation is to compute the $\mathcal{H}$-Signature of a line segment from z_l to z_{l+1}

$$\mathcal{H}_{dis}(z_l, z_{l+1}) = \sum_k \frac{[\ln(z_{l+1} - \zeta_k) - \ln(z_l - \zeta_k)]}{\prod_{j \neq k}(\zeta_k - \zeta_j)} \tag{11}$$

2.3 Exploration of Distinctive Homotopic Classes by a Sparse Roadmap

An algorithm to explore all the homotopic classes is developed in this section. There are two steps to explore all distinctive homotopic classes. Firstly, the proposed algorithm generates collision free trajectories in the configure space C_f of the robot. Then only one trajectory in the same homotopic class is kept.

The references [9, 10] proposed a complete exploration of all trajectories of distinctive homotopic classes from a Voronoi graph. However, it is impossible to generate all candidate trajectories in real-time. Since the number of collision free trajectories in a Voronoi graph grow exponentially with respect to the number of obstacles. In order to explore as much as possible homotopic classes in real-time, a sparse graph is used to generate the classes in this paper.

The robot current position z_{start}, the goal z_{goal} and the positions of all obstacles $\mathcal{O} = \{\zeta_1 \ldots \zeta_M\}$ are given. Firstly, a probabilistic roadmap (PRM) $\mathcal{G} = \{\mathcal{V}, \mathcal{E}\}$ [13] is generated by sampling vertexes $\mathcal{V} = \{v_1, v_2, \ldots v_R\}$ uniformly in the configure space C_f of the robot. The reference [10] has made a conclusion that, with 15–20 vertexes, it is adequate to generate enough initial candidates of different homotopic class. However, even with only 20 vertices, the number of edges is up to 200, which is inefficient for online query.

We propose a method to generate as many homotopic classes as possible by using a sparse roadmap. A sparse roadmap is near-optimal graph $\mathcal{G}_s = \{\mathcal{V}, \mathcal{E}_s\}$. Near-optimality means that the length optimal path in $\mathcal{G}_s$ is at worst tc^* in $\mathcal{G}_s$, where t is the stretching factor and c^* is the optimal length in $\mathcal{G}$. However, a sparse roadmap needs much less edges (Fig. 3).

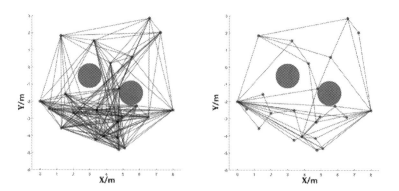

Fig. 3. Comparison of the original PRM $\mathcal{G}$ (left) and sparse roadmap $\mathcal{G}_s$ (right). Stretching factor = 3. It is impossible to search the original graph in real time. $|\mathcal{E}_s| = 49$. $|\mathcal{E}| = 187$.

The reason why a sparse roadmap will work for our local planner TC-SQP can be explained from three aspects:

(1) Our local planner only depends on a rather mild initial path and a near-optimal initial path in $\mathcal{G}_s$ which is enough for TC-SQP. So, it is unnecessary to generate the optimal initial path in $\mathcal{G}$.

(2) A $\mathcal{G}_s$ is enough to generate enough homotopic classes. We prove that under such circumstances, in each homotopic class, there exists a near-optimal path in $\mathcal{G}_s$.

(3) The edges in $\mathcal{G}_s$ are roughly 1/4 in $\mathcal{G}$ [18].

To generate a sparse graph, Algorithm 1 is given as follows [16].

Algorithm 1

$\mathcal{V} = \emptyset \ \mathcal{E}_s = \emptyset$
While number of vertexes $< N_{required}$
$v = sampleFree()$.
$U = Near(v, \delta_{near})$.
Sort U by non-decreasing distance from v
For all $u \in U$ do
If shortestPath$(\mathcal{V}, \mathcal{E}, u, v) > t * Weight(u, v)$ then
If collisionFree(u, v) then
$\mathcal{E}_s = \mathcal{E}_s \cup \{u, v\}$.
$\mathcal{V} = \mathcal{V} \cup \{v\}$.
End

Alg. 1 Building a sparse road map, in which $Weight(u, v)$ is the norm between vertex u and vertex v. Function $Near(v, \delta_{near})$ returns the set of vertexes which are in $\delta_{near} - vicinity$ of . Since not all edges are added to the graph, the edge $\mathcal{E}_s$ is much less than the edge in the original $\mathcal{E}$.

Theorem 2 [16]
The graph generated by Algorithm 1 is near-optimal.

Proof
For each rejected edge (u, v) in $\mathcal{G}_s$, there exists another path in $\mathcal{G}_s$ such that $c(u, v) < t * w(u, v)$. Therefore, there exist a path $\sigma(a, b)$ in $\mathcal{G}_s$, $\sum_{(u,v)} c(u, v) < tc^*$.

In some circumstances, we want to generate two initial paths of distinctive homotopic classes which are far from each other to make the homotopic candidates diverse.

Theorem 3
If there exist two optimal paths σ_1 and σ_2 in $\mathcal{G}$, $\exists v_1 \in \sigma_1$, $\exists v_2 \in \sigma_2$, $\exists o_i \in \mathcal{O}$, s.t $|v_1 - v_2| > 2\delta_{near}$, $|v_2 - o_i| > 2\delta_{near}$ and $|v_2 - o_i| > \delta_{near}$, in which o_i denotes a obstacle. Then there exist two near-optimal paths σ_1' and σ_2' belong to distinctive homotopic classes.

Proof

According to Line 4 of Algorithm 1, the distance of a near-optimal path is at most δ_{near} from the optimal path. Since we know that $\exists o_i \in \mathcal{O}$ s.t $|v_2 - o_i| > 2\delta_{near}$ and $|v_2 - o_i| > \delta_{near}$, σ_1' and σ_2' are of different sides of o_i, so σ_1' and σ_2' are of distinctive homotopic class.

Based on the generated graph $\mathcal{G}_s$, all the acyclic trajectories from z_{start} to z_{goal} are detected by a deep-first search algorithm. The $\mathcal{H}$-Signature of each trajectory is calculated by Eqs. (10) and (11). Trajectories of duplicate $\mathcal{H}$-Signature are discarded.

2.4   Close-Loop Control

This section describes the integration of our proposed algorithm in the previous sections. The robot is equipped with an odometry and a 2D Hokuyo laser. The 2D laser is first to make a local cost map using the method proposed in [19] and obstacles are modeled as polygons by the method proposed in [20]. Then, we explore distinctive homotopic classes by the method we proposed in Sects. 2.2 and II.C. Up to N trajectories of distinctive homotopic classes are chosen as the initial trajectory for TC-SQP planners, which run in parallel. We pick the best trajectory (controls) as the output trajectory (controls). Such planner is called TC-SQP-HC in this paper.

TC-SQP-HC runs at a frequency faster than the control period (10 Hz in the following section). After one execution, the first step (v, ω) of the optimal control $\mathfrak{A}^*$

$$\begin{cases} v = \mathfrak{A}^*(1) \\ \omega = \mathfrak{A}^*(2) \end{cases}$$

are sent to the robot actuators. Considering the control noises, we relocate our robot by a particle filter, fusing the odometry data and laser data (Fig. 4).

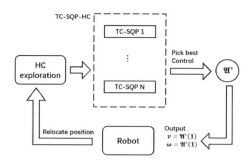

Fig. 4. Closed loop control flow

3   Simulation and Analysis

The proposed distinctive homotopic class generation algorithm in Sect. 2.3 and the proposed local planner in Sect. 2.1 are implemented as a local planner in the ROS navigation stack. The simulations are made in Stage. Algorithms run on a PC with a 2.7

GHZ Intel i7-7500U CPU. Figures 5, 6, 7 and 8 show one procedure of TC-SQP-HC planner.

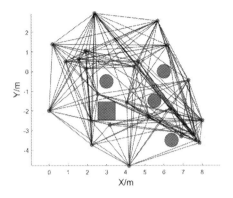

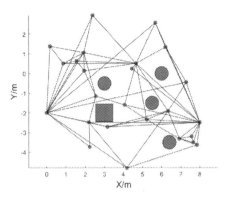

Fig. 5. The red vertexes are generated by sampling, and then a full PRM $\mathcal{G}$ is generated. (Color figure online)

Fig. 6. A more compact graph $\mathcal{G}_s$ is generated by Algorithm 1.

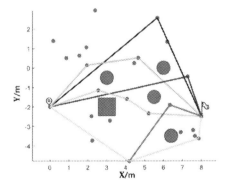

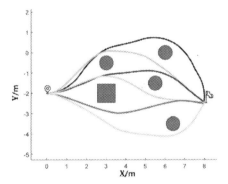

Fig. 7. Filter duplicates homotopic class by $\mathcal{H}$-Signature. The path of different color stands a distinctive homotopic class.

Fig. 8. After TC-SQP optimization in each homotopic class, considering time optimality and the distance to obstacle

We verify that a (near) time-optimal trajectory can be generated from two aspects.

First, all trajectories coverage after 13 iterations in 0.1 s. Second, we compare our trajectories with an A^* planner. Comparison results are shown in Table 1. An A^* planner can find the optimal path in the existence of obstacles [13]. But, for mobile robots, the shortest path is not the time-optimal trajectory. The reason is that, the shortest path usually contains serval line segments, and the robot has to re-orient itself in place at the intersection of two-line segments, which is time consuming. For comparison, DV-SQP-HC is able to re-orient itself in advance, hence the time for re-orientation is saved. The average saved time of DV-SQP-HC is 14%.

Table 1. Travel time comparison

	Traj. 1	Traj. 2	Traj. 3	Traj. 4	Traj. 5	Traj. 6	Aver.
A* global planner (unit: s)	29.7	24.9	21.3	20.4	28.8	25.5	25.1
TC-SQP-HC Before Opt (unit: s)	22.5	21	17.2	19	15.8	19.4	19.15
TC-SQP-HC After Opt (unit: s)	19.99	16.86	15.8	14.83	14.2	16.88	16.43
Time Reduced from A* (unit: %)	11.16	19.71	8.14	21.95	10.13	12.99	14.01

The following simulation validates an application of the proposed DV-SQP-HC algorithm. This experiment is also used in [21] to illustrate that a local planner without homotopic exploring is not enough for navigation in dynamic environments.

The proposed algorithm TC-SQP-HC is compared with the state-of-art local planning algorithm DWA and TC-SQP without homotopic class exploration.

We consider a differential robot with a maximal translate acceleration and $v = 0.6\,\mathrm{m/s}$, $\omega = 0.3\,\mathrm{rad/s}$, a maximal acceleration $acc\_v = 0.6\mathrm{m/s}^2$, $acc\_\omega = 0.4\mathrm{rad/s}^2$. The minimal distance toward obstacles is designed to be $0.2\,\mathrm{m}$. TC-SQP and TC-SQP-HC are both implemented as a local planner plugin in the ROS navigation stack and DWA [1] is already available in ROS. The three local planners pursuit a local goal from a global planner. The global planner in this experiment is A^* global planner.

At early stage of this experiment, there is only one homotopic class. All the planners find the fastest trajectory. However, when a man goes through the global trajectory DWA tries to switch to another side. But a collision can't be avoided. The reason is that, the global planner can only be executed at a frequency much lower than the local planner. Hence, DWA is unable to find the correct global homotopic class in advance.

The same phenomenon occurs for TC-SQP without HC exploring. TC-SQP performs better than DWA. The reason is that, DWA uses a sampling strategy to generate the best current control and this strategy results in a short-sight easily. So, TC-SQP is able to continue a bit further than DWA. However, when the distance between the human and the wall is too narrow, a collision finally occurs at the 6th second. Trajectories, translation and angular velocity profiles are shown in Figs. 9 and 10.

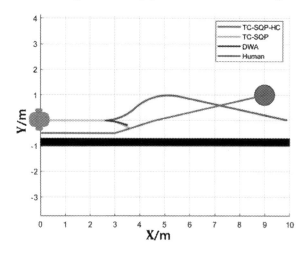

Fig. 9. Trajectories comparison. One grid is 1 m.

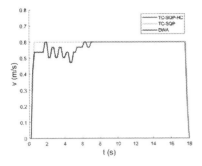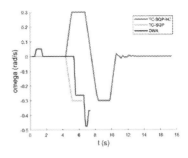

Fig. 10. Velocity and angular velocity profile of three planners.

4 Conclusion

In this paper, a novel local planner called TC-SQP-HC is proposed. TC-SQP-HC has the ability to guide a robot to a goal under the robot kino-dynamic and non-holonomic constraints. TC-SQP-HC also has the ability to navigation in several homotopic classes, by maintaining a sparse roadmap. Future works will focus on extending TC-SQP-HC for multi-robot systems.

Acknowledgement. This work was funded by the National Key Research and Development Plan of China (2017YFE0112200) and National Science and Technology Major Project of China (2017ZX04005001-004).

References

1. Fox, D., Burgard, W., Thrun, S.: The dynamic window approach to collision avoidance. IEEE Robot. Autom. Mag. **4**(1), 23–33 (1997)
2. Quinlan, S.: Real-time Modification of Collision-Free Paths. Stanford University, Stanford (1995)
3. Kurniawati, H., Fraichard, T.: From path to trajectory deformation. In: IEEE-RSJ International Conference on Intelligent Robots and Systems, San Diego, états-Unis (2007)
4. Rösmann, C., et al.: Trajectory modification considering dynamic constraints of autonomous robots. In: Robotics; Proceedings of ROBOTIK 2012; 7th German Conference on VDE (2012)
5. Rösmann, C., Hoffmann, F., Bertram, T.: Kinodynamic trajectory optimization and control for car-like robots. In: IEEE/RSJ International Conference on Intelligent Robots and Systems (IROS), Vancouver, BC, Canada (2017)
6. Gu, T., Atwood, J., Dong, C., Dolan, J.M., Lee, J.-W.: Tunable and stable real-time trajectory planning for urban autonomous driving. In: IEEE International Conference on Intelligent Robots and Systems, pp. 250–256 (2015)
7. Lau, B., Sprunk, C., Burgard, W.: Kinodynamic motion planning for mobile robots using splines. In: Proceedings of the IEEE/RSJ International Conference on Intelligent Robots and Systems (IROS), St. Louis, MO, USA, pp. 2427–2433 (2009)

8. Sprunk, C., Lau, B., Pfaff, P., Burgard, W.: Online generation of kinodynamic trajectories for non-circular omnidirectional robots. In: Proceedings of the IEEE International Conference on Robotics and Automation (ICRA), Shanghai, China, pp. 72–77 (2011)
9. Kuderer, M., Sprunk, C., Kretzschmar, H., Burgard, W.: Online generation of homotopically distinct navigation paths. In: IEEE International Conference on Robotics and Automation, Hong Kong, China, pp. 6462–6467 (2014)
10. Rösmann, C., Hoffmann, F., Bertram, T.: Integrated online trajectory planning and optimization in distinctive topologies. Robot. Auton. Syst. **88**, 142–153 (2016)
11. Schmitzberger, E., Bouchet, J., Dufaut, M., Wolf, D., Husson, R.: Capture of homotopy classes with probabilistic road map. In: IEEE/RSJ International Conference on Intelligent Robots and Systems, vol. 3, pp. 2317–2322 (2002)
12. Jaillet, L., Simeon, T.: Path deformation roadmaps: compact graphs with useful cycles for motion planning. Int. J. Robot. Res. **27**(11–12), 1175–1188 (2008)
13. LaValle, S.M.: Planning Algorithms. Cambridge University Press, Cambridge (2006)
14. Bhattacharya, S., Kumar, V., Likhachev, M.: Search-based path planning with homotopy class constraints. In: Proceedings of National Conference on Artificial Intelligence (2010)
15. Pokorny, F.T., Hawasly, M., Ramamoorthy, S.: Multiscale topological trajectory classification with persistent homology. In: Proceedings of Robotics: Science and Systems, Berkeley, USA (2014)
16. Marble, J.D., Bekris, K.E.: Asymptotically near-optimal is good enough for motion planning. In: Christensen, H., Khatib, O. (eds.) Robotics Research. Springer, Cham (2017). https://doi.org/10.1007/978-3-319-29363-9_24
17. Zucker, M., et al.: CHOMP: covariant Hamiltonian optimization for motion planning. Int. J. Robot. Res. **32**(9-10), 1164–1193 (2013)
18. Dobson, A., Krontiris, A., Bekris, K.E.: Sparse roadmap spanners. In: Frazzoli, E., Lozano-Perez, T., Roy, N., Rus, D. (eds.) Algorithmic Foundations of Robotics X, vol. 86. Springer, Heidelberg (2013). https://doi.org/10.1007/978-3-642-36279-8_17
19. Lu, D.V., Hershberger, D.: Smart, W.D.: Layered costmaps for context-sensitive navigation. In: IEEE/RSJ International Conference on Intelligent Robots & Systems (2014)
20. Park, J.-S., et al.: A new concave hull algorithm and concaveness measure for n-dimensional datasets. J. Inf. Sci. Eng. **28**, 587–600 (2012)
21. Rösmann, C., Hoffmann, F., Bertram, T.: Planning of multiple robot trajectories in distinctive topologies. In: IEEE 2015 European Conference on Mobile Robots (ECMR) - Lincoln, United Kingdom, 2–4 September 2015, pp. 1–6. European Conference on Mobile Robots IEEE (2015)

Author Index

Printed in the United States
By Bookmasters